Canadian
LAW
Dictionary

John A. Yogis, Q.C.

Associate Dean and Professor of Law, Dalhousie University

LL.B., LL.M. (Dalhousie University); LL.M. (University of Michigan)

THIRD EDITION

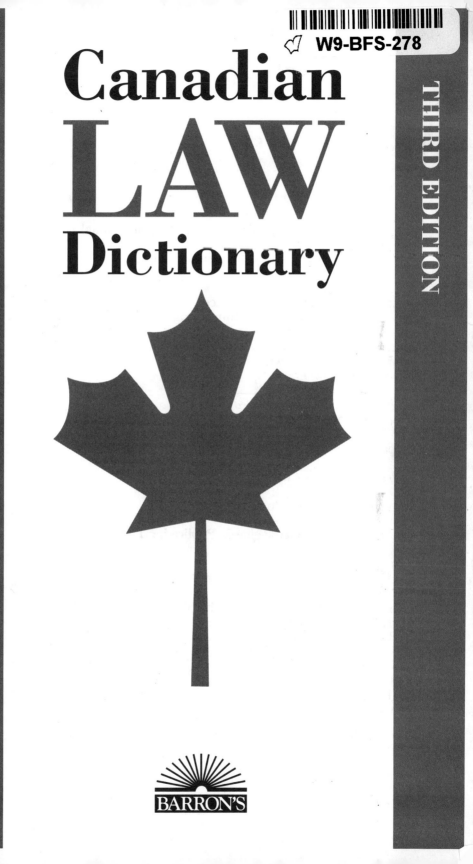

BARRON'S

All inquiries should be addressed to:
Barron's Educational Series, Inc.
250 Wireless Boulevard
Hauppauge, New York 11788

Library of Congress Catalog Card No. 94-35589

International Standard Book No. 0-8120-1887-7

Library of Congress Cataloging-in-Publication Data

Yogis, John.
    Canadian law dictionary / by John A. Yogis.—3rd ed.
       p.   cm.
    "Adapted from Law dictionary, by Steven H. Gifis"—T.p. verso.
    Includes bibliographical references.
    ISBN 0-8120-1887-7
    1. Law—Canada—Dictionaries.   I. Gifis, Steven H. Law diction-
ary.   II. Title.
KE183.Y63 1995
349.71'03—dc20   94-35589
[347.1003]   CIP

PRINTED IN THE UNITED STATES OF AMERICA

678 8800 9876543

Contents

Preface
to the Third Edition

This edition continues the attempt to provide a concise dictionary of legal terms with citations specific to the Anglo-Canadian tradition. The continuing impact of constitutional law, and especially the *Canadian Charter of Rights and Freedoms,* is more evident than in previous editions. The growth in the law with respect to individual and group rights is a phenomenon deserving of increased attention. This edition attempts through new and revised entries and new appendices to provide a more complete picture of this area of Canadian law.

In addition to new and revised entries, substantial updates have been made to statutes, case law, and authoritative texts. To facilitate the lay reader, a brief guide to reading case and statute citations has been provided.

John A. Yogis, Q.C.

Halifax, Nova Scotia
July 1994

Acknowledgements
to the Third Edition

I wish to acknowledge with appreciation the special assistance given to me by Ms. Allison Howard, a second-year student at Dalhousie Law School, with regard to the preparation of the manuscript for this third edition. She carried out her responsibilities with diligence, patience, and keen insight. This edition is greatly improved as a result of her efforts.

I also wish to thank my secretary, Ms. Darlene Cluett, the Dalhousie Law Library, and the faculty and staff of Dalhousie Law School who assisted and encouraged the research and writing of this third edition.

John A. Yogis, Q.C.

Halifax, Nova Scotia
July 1994

Preface
to the Second Edition

Since the first appearance of the *Canadian Law Dictionary* in 1983 a revolution has been occurring in Canadian legal and political circles. The enactment of the *Constitution Act, 1982,* including its most important provision, the *Canadian Charter of Rights and Freedoms,* has added a new dimension to Canadian law and its vocabulary. The courts quickly assumed the task of applying the *Charter* to a vast array of issues encompassing concepts such as "legal rights," "equality rights," and "fundamental freedoms." Changes incorporated in the second edition of this book have attempted to reflect continuing constitutional developments, particularly with reference to the *Charter.* No attempt has been made to examine in detail substantive changes in the law. The emphasis has been to take particular note of the new terminology and of major court decisions that have played interpretive roles.

In this edition I have also attempted to incorporate revisions and additions suggested by commentators on the first edition. Other entries have been updated to acknowledge legislative changes that have occurred, primarily with respect to the federal statutes.

Halifax, Nova Scotia   John A. Yogis, Q.C.

Acknowledgements
to the Second Edition

Special acknowledgement for this second edition must be given to my research assistant, Ms. Suellen Murray (Dalhousie, LL.B., 1990). Ms. Murray devised a "key" that greatly facilitated the revision of existing entries and the addition and deletion of entries, as well as cross-referencing. More important, her enthusiasm, meticulous attention to detail, and ability to work with little supervision were sources of enormous personal satisfaction and assistance.

In addition to basic research, Ms. Murray undertook the task of drafting many of the new entries required for this edition.

Many of my colleagues were again willing to give of their time and expertise during the preparation of the text. In this regard I would like to single out Professor Alastair Bissett-Johnson, Professor Wayne MacKay, and the staff of the Dalhousie Law School Library.

Finally, in the summer of 1990, a third-year law student at Dalhousie, Ms. Susan MacKay, assisted in the painstaking task of proofreading the rough draft of the manuscript.

To those mentioned, and to all others who assisted by way of advice and encouragement, I am truly grateful.

Halifax, Nova Scotia   John A. Yogis, Q.C.

Preface
to the First Edition

In the summer of 1978 I was approached by Barron's Educational Series Inc., to adapt for a Canadian audience the *Law Dictionary* prepared in 1975 by Professor Steven H. Gifis of Rutgers, School of Law, Newark, New Jersey. The aim of the work, as stated in the preface to the American edition, was to provide a portable reference guide for the beginning law student, or the layperson, unfamiliar with basic legal terminology. I agreed to undertake the project because of my general interest in the area of legal research and writing, and because at the time no Canadian legal dictionary was available.

The initial proposal contemplated adding Canadian citations where appropriate, as well as some revision of the terms themselves. Work on the project commenced in the summer of 1979. The task proved to be far lengthier and more complex than originally contemplated. It readily became apparent that many terms would have to be substantially amended or rewritten to reflect Canadian usage. Many terms in Gifis did not apply to the Canadian experience and had to be deleted. In addition, terms peculiar to the Anglo-Canadian legal tradition had to be supplied. Just as the project appeared to be in the homestretch the Parliament of Canada passed the resolution approving the patriation of the Canadian Constitution which included the new *Canadian Charter of Rights and Freedoms*. Further revision became necessary to take account of this significant change in Canadian law.

In spite of the modifications required, an attempt has been made throughout to retain the objectives of the original work. Professor Gifis gave me a free hand in recasting his book. Any merits of the present work must still be attributed to Professor Gifis' concept. However, I take full responsibility for errors and other deficiencies that may have found their way into the book in the process of adaptation.

A book such as this with a specific, but limited, focus is clearly not designed as a Canadian answer to a major work such as *Black's Law Dictionary*. At the time of writing it is my understanding that other dictionary projects are underway in Canada in both the English and the French languages, and one work is already available for the mass market. This is greatly encouraging. My hope is that this book will both serve the purposes for which it was designed and be some encouragement to those who recognize the scope and necessity for further work in this important area.

John A. Yogis, Q.C.

Halifax, Nova Scotia

Acknowledgements
for the First Edition

The preparation of this work involved many individuals and sources to whom the author is greatly indebted. From the beginning of the project, I was assisted in basic research by a group of hard-working second- and third-year law students at Dalhousie Law School, most of whom are now active in the practice of law throughout Canada. My first assistants in the summer of 1979, E. Anne Bastedo and Anu M. Rautaharju, were largely instrumental in developing a research technique that proved to be efficient and of great value to those who followed in their steps. The following were my principal assistants in the period 1980–1983: Calvert C. Miller, Michael A. Power and Gregg A. Yeadon. All of them devoted countless hours and dedicated labour to what often seemed an unrewarding and never-ending project. To the following, who worked for lesser periods of time but with as much dedication, I am equally appreciative: Stephen G. Coughlan, Sherry A. Griffith, Catherine A. Le Blanc, Jan E. McKenzie, Susan E. Mitchell, Jai Pachai, Sheila Ray, Wayne Snider, Christina Tari, Bruce M. Thomson, W. Gary Wharton and Judith D. Wouk. Special assistance was provided by Maria del Mar de Arcos, a librarian, who had worked on the preparation of a legal dictionary in French at the Université de Moncton.

I was particularly fortunate at various stages of the project to have the services of Michael J. Iosipescu, a lawyer with special skills in computerized information retrieval. His work in searching various data bases for terms proved to be of much value in providing information that would not be readily accessible by standard manual methods of research.

This project was partially supported by a research grant from the Law Foundation of Nova Scotia. I express my sincere appreciation to the Foundation and to its Executive Director, Mrs. Mary Burbidge Helleiner, for their cooperation and encouragement.

I am grateful to Dalhousie Law School for making additional funds available for research purposes. I also owe much gratitude to my colleagues at the Law School who were unfailing in their support and who generously gave of their time by means of suggestions, criticism and advice based on their particular areas of expertise.

Two members of the legal profession provided particular assistance on both the personal and the professional level. Randall R. Duplak devoted many days at a critical stage in the project, proofreading portions of the manuscript and checking citations, and assisting in writing many of the Canadian definitions necessary for this work. Susan C. Potts also contributed generously of her time proofreading and assisting in the preparation of the bibliography.

No legal research project can achieve a modicum of success without the support and assistance of the law librarians. I owe an enormous debt of gratitude to the staff of the Dalhousie Law Library. To Professor C. L. Wiktor, Heather Creech, Dorothy Long and Thomas Weeks I extend special thanks.

The typing of the manuscript was principally the work of Catherine Neeson and Monique Dancause. My overworked secretary, Mary Bartlett, assisted with additional typing when required and performed many invaluable administrative tasks. To each of them I express my appreciation for hundreds of hours of work without complaint.

I am also indebted for the generous permission granted by the following publishers to quote portions of their publications throughout this work:

Butterworths
Canada Law Book Limited
Carswell Legal Publications
Richard De Boo Publishers

I would like also to express my thanks to Professor G. H. L. Fridman for permission to quote from his works:

The Law of Contract in Canada (Toronto: The Carswell Company Limited, 1976).

Sale of Goods in Canada (Toronto: The Carswell Company Limited, 1979).

Pronunciation Guide

The decision as to which Latin words, maxims and expressions should be included in this dictionary, in view of the thousands that the user might encounter, was necessarily a somewhat arbitrary one; but an earnest effort has been made to translate and, where appropriate, to illuminate those terms and phrases considered likely to be crucial to a full understanding of important legal concepts. It is hoped that there are no significant omissions and that we have erred only on the side of overinclusiveness.

Each of the Latin and French words and phrases—at least those that continue to be recognised as such and have not become, functionally, a part of the English language—includes a phonetic spelling designed to assist the user in the pronunciation of terms probably unfamiliar to her or him. The purpose in providing this pronunciation guide however, emphatically has not been to indicate the "correct" mode of pronouncing the terms; rather, the goal has been to afford the user a guide to an acceptable pronunciation of them. In the case of Latin words, therefore, neither the classic nor the ecclesiastical pronunciation has been strictly followed; instead, the phonetic spellings provided reflect the often considerable extent to which pronunciation has been Anglicized and/or Americanized, partly through widespread legal usage.

Of course, such a system is anything but uniform, and adoption of it is clearly hazardous from the standpoint of general acceptance as well as that of scholarship. Many, if not most, of these terms have alternative pronunciations in common usage throughout the English-speaking legal world, and there has been some deference to classical or ecclesiastical pronunciation and, hopefully, to consistency. Thus, the choices made here, while in most cases meant to reflect the most commonly accepted pronunciation, inevitably have been the product of the author's personal preferences.

The phonetic symbols employed herein were drawn from what the author perceives as a commonly recognised and understood "system." The following guide should be of some assistance in interpreting them

Vowels

ă as in at

ā as in ape

â as in fare

ä as in army

ȧ as in arrive

aủ as in out

ĕ as in egg

ē as in evil

ê as in earn

ĭ as in ill

ī as in ice

ŏ as in ox

ō as in open

ó as in orgy

ŭ as in up

ū as in rude

û as in urge

Consonants

g as in gas

j as in jump

Key to Effective Use
of This Dictionary

Alphabetization: The reader should note carefully that all entries have been alphabetized letter by letter rather than word by word. Thus *ab initio,* for example, is located between *abeyance* and *aboriginal rights,* rather than at the beginning of the listings. In the same manner, *actionable* appears before, not after, *action ex delicto.*

Brackets: Material in brackets [thus] represents an alternate expression for (or another form of) the preceding word or phrase. For example, "**HABITUAL CRIMINAL [DANGEROUS OFFENDER]**" indicates that dangerous offender is another way of expressing the entry for habitual criminal, while "**ABROGATE [ABROGATION]**" includes a form the reader is likely to encounter.

When the reader is referred to a different main entry for the definition of a particular word or phrase, brackets are also used to indicate that the word or phrase sought is defined under a different subentry of the main word to which the reader is referred. Thus, "**DISPUTABLE PRESUMPTION** See **presumption** [REBUTTABLE PRESUMPTION]" indicates that the definition of disputable presumption appears under the subentry rebuttable presumption, which in turn is found under the heading **PRESUMPTION.** If the word or phrase sought appears itself as a subentry, the reader is just referred to the main entry: "**NOMINAL DAMAGES** See **damages.**"

Cross References: **Boldface type** has been used within the text of the definitions and at the end of them, to call attention to terms that are defined in the dictionary as separate entries and that should be understood and, if necessary, referred to specifically, in order to assure the fullest possible comprehension of the word whose definition has been sought in the first instance.

Terms emphasized in this manner include many that appear in the dictionary only in a different form or as a different part of speech. For example, although the term "alienate" may appear in boldface in the text of a definition, it will not be found as a separate entry, since it is expected that the reader can readily draw the meaning of that term from the definition given for the word "alienation"; likewise, the reader coming across the word "estop" printed in boldface should not despair upon discovering that it is not in fact an entry here, but should instead refer to the term "estoppel."

Also, the reader must not assume that the appearance of a word in regular type precludes the possibility of its having been included as a separate entry, for by no means has every such word been printed in boldface in every definition. Terms emphasized in this manner include primarily those an understanding of which was thought to be essential or very helpful in the reader's quest for adequate comprehension. Many terms that represent very basic and frequently used concepts, such as "property," "possession" and "crime," are often printed in regular type. Furthermore, boldface is used to emphasize a word only the first time that word appears in a particular definition.

Gender: Where masculine nouns and pronouns have been used, they are intended to refer to both men and women and should be so read.

Subentries: Words printed in SMALL CAPITALS include:

(1) those whose significance as legal concepts was not deemed sufficiently substantial to warrant their inclusion in the dictionary as separate entries, though some explanation or illumination was thought desirable, and

(2) those which, though important, are most logically and coherently defined in the context of related or broader terms.

Words emphasized in this manner either have been separately and individually defined in the manner of "subcategories" or have been defined or illustrated, implicitly or explicitly, within the text of the definition of the main entry.

Citations: Abbreviations have been used in citing case names, jurisdictions, statutes, and reports. Sample examples of a statute citation and a case citation are as follows:

(1) Statute Citation

Public Highways Act, R.S.N.S. 1989, c.371, as am. S.N.S. 1990, c.44.

Amendment in annual vol.

Chapter in revision

Year of revision

Jurisdiction—Nova Scotia

Abbreviation for "Revised Statutes"

Title of the act

(2) Case Citation

R. v. *Hogan* (1979), 11 C.R. (3d) 328 (N.S.S.C., A.D.).

Jurisdiction and Court (Nova Scotia Supreme Court, Appeal Division)

Page no. in the report series

Abbreviation for the report series (i.e., Criminal Reports, Third Series)

Volume of the report series

Date of the case

Name of the case

NOTE:
(i) A date in square brackets refers to the year printed on the spine of the volume when it is necessary to know the year of the volume in order to find the correct volume on the shelf. Example: [1932] K.B. 22.
(ii) A date in round brackets is the date of the case itself.
(iii) The year on the volume may or may not be the same as the date of the case.

A complete list of abbreviations used in the citations appears at the back of the book. Citations to books are given with the first initial and last name of the author, title, page(s), edition, year. Citations to periodicals include the last name of the author, title of article, volume number and name of journal, page(s), year.

For further information on legal citation refer to:

M. Iosipescu, J. Yogis and I. Christie: *Legal Writing and Research Manual* (4th ed. 1994).

C.S. Tang, *Guide to Legal Citation and Sources of Citation Aid* (2d ed. 1988).

A

ABANDONMENT The surrender of interests, rights or property by one person to another. It includes both the intention to abandon and the actual physical act of relinquishment. One abandons a **contract** when one knows or believes the contract to be incomplete and fails to complete it—e.g., where the owner abandons a construction contract by repudiating it and the contractor accepts the **repudiation,** thereby terminating the contract. *Taylor* v. *Foran and Ontario Loan and Debenture Co.* (1931), 44 B.C.L.R. 529 (Co.Ct.). The fact that no work has been done on a project does not necessarily mean that there has been abandonment. Cessation of work is not necessarily abandonment of work. *Dieleman Planer Co. Ltd.* v. *Elizabeth Townhouses Ltd.,* [1972] 4 W.W.R. 236 (B.C.Co.Ct.).

One can abandon or desert a child *Criminal Code*, R.S.C. 1985, c. C–46, s. 218. *R.* v. *Hudon*, [1965] R.L. 203 (Que.S.C.).

A defence of abandonment may be used to disprove common intent in s. 21(2) of the *Criminal Code*. To be effective, the intention to abandon must be communicated in such a manner that it "…will serve unequivocal notice upon the other party to the common unlawful cause that if he proceeds upon it he does so without the further aid and assistance of those who withdraw." *R.* v. *Whitehouse*, [1941] 1 W.W.R. 112 (B.C.C.A.).

ABATABLE NUISANCE A **nuisance** that can be removed or rendered harmless, and whose continuation is not authorized under law.

ABATEMENT A reduction or rebate. For example, in **real property**, the purchase price of a plot of land may be abated because of a defect in **title.** An ABATEMENT OF TAXES is a tax rebate or decrease. An ABATEMENT OF A LEGACY is the reduction or extinction of a **legacy** to a **beneficiary** by payment of debts owed by the **decedent's estate.** Also when as-

sets do not satisfy a debt, a proportionate deduction of the balance due may be made. The ABATEMENT OF AN ACTION signifies its death.

ABDUCTION The **criminal** or **tortious** act of taking another person by **fraud,** persuasion or violence. The taking need not be by force, either actual or constructive, and consent obtained by persuasiveness is no defence. *R.* v. *Leboe* (1965), 51 W.W.R. 757 (B.C.Co.Ct.). Under the *Criminal Code*, R.S.C. 1985, c. C–46, the following are all **indictable offences:** s. 280, abduction of a female under sixteen; s. 281, abduction of a child under fourteen. Compare **kidnap.**

ABET To encourage another in the commission of an offence. By s. 21(1)(*c*) of the *Criminal Code*, R.S.C. 1985, c. C–46, a person who abets another in the commission of an offence is a party to that offence. "Evidence of passive acquiescence or mere presence does not constitute aiding and abetting in the commission of a criminal offence, but the circumstances of each case must be considered to see if there was more than 'mere presence' at the scene of the offence." *R.* v. *Clow* (1975), 8 Nfld. & P.E.I.R. 96 at 101 (P.E.I.S.C.). See also **aid and abet.**

ABEYANCE Generally denotes an undetermined or incomplete state of affairs. In British law, an inheritance that has no present owner is in abeyance. In property, when a **freehold estate** is not vested in a presently existing person, it is in abeyance. Common law holds that there must always be a **tenant** of the freehold.

AB INITIO *(ăb ĭn-ĭ′-shē-ō)* Lat.: from the beginning. Most commonly used in referring to the time when a **contract, statute,** marriage, or **deed** becomes legally valid; e.g., an unlawful marriage is void ab initio, from the outset.

ABORIGINAL PEOPLES [OF CANADA] Includes the Indian, Inuit and Métis peoples of Canada. *Constitution Act, 1982*, Part II, Rights of the Aboriginal Peoples of Canada, s. 35(2). See **aboriginal rights.**

ABORIGINAL RIGHTS "[R]efers to a range of rights held by native peoples, not by virtue of **Crown** grant, agreement, or legislation, but by reason of the fact that **aboriginal peoples** were once independent, self-governing entities, in possession of most of the lands now making up Canada." Slattery, *The Constitutional Guarantee of Aboriginal and Treaty Rights*, 8 Queen's L.J. 232 (1982–83). Such rights include aboriginal land title and the right to hunt and fish. See *R.* v. *Guerin* (1984), 13 D.L.R. (4th) 321 (S.C.C.); *Simon* v. *The Queen*, [1985] 2 S.C.R. 387; *R.* v. *Isaac* (1975), 13 N.S.R. (2d) 460 (S.C.A.D.).

Aboriginal rights and freedoms are constitutionally protected in s. 25 of the **Canadian Charter of Rights and Freedoms.** Section 35(1) of the *Constitution Act, 1982* recognises and affirms the existing aboriginal and treaty rights of aboriginal peoples. See *R.* v. *Sparrow* (1990), 70 D.L.R. (4th) 385. See **extinguishment.**

ABORTION Until 1988, abortion, or procuring a miscarriage of a female, was an indictable offence under s. 287 of the *Criminal Code*, R.S.C. 1985, c. C–46. The Supreme Court ruled in *Morgentaler, Smoling, and Scott* v. *The Queen* (1988), 37 C.C.C. (3d) 449 that this provision violated a woman's right to life, liberty, and security of the person, as guaranteed by s. 7 of the **Canadian Charter of Rights and Freedoms.**

See also s. 288 (supplying noxious things with knowledge of the intention to use them for procuring a miscarriage).

ABRIDGMENT A condensation or digest—e.g., the *Canadian Abridgment,* which, **inter alia,** contains digests of reported decisions of the Supreme Court of Canada, the Federal Court, and the courts of the common-law provinces and of Quebec.

ABROGATE [ABROGATION] To annul, revoke or repeal. In law, abrogation is the annulment of a former law by legislative power, by constitutional authority or by usage. Section 2 of the **Canadian Bill of Rights,** R.S.C. 1985, Appendix III, states that unless expressly declared otherwise, Acts of the Canadian Parliament will be construed so as not to abrogate the provisions of the *Bill.* See *R.* v. *Drybones,* [1970] S.C.R. 282; but compare *Attorney-General of Canada* v. *Lavell & Bedard,* [1974] S.C.R. 1349. See also the **Canadian Charter of Rights and Freedoms,** ss. 21, 22, 25, 29, contained in the *Constitution Act, 1982.*

ABSCOND To travel secretly out of the **jurisdiction** of the courts, or to hide in order to avoid a legal process. One must intend to be willfully and permanently absent rather than temporarily absent with intention of returning. *Williams* v. *Sanford* (1911), 10 E.L.R. 151 (N.S.Co.Ct.). Some jurisdictions do not require clandestine departure. An AB-SCONDING DEBTOR is one who remains out of the jurisdiction with the intent to defeat or delay his creditors. Various jurisdictions have defined the absconding debtor by statute, e.g., the *Absconding Debtors Act,* R.S.N.B. 1973, c. A-2. In criminal law, abscond means "voluntarily being absent from trial in order to prevent its continuation." *Grandchamps* v. *Sirois* (1978), 5 C.R. (3d) 376 (Que.S.C.), dealing with s. 475 of the *Criminal Code,* R.S.C. 1985, c. C–46.

ABSOLUTE PRIVILEGE See **libel; privilege.**

ABSQUE HOC *(äb'-skwā hŏk)* Lat.: without this; if it had not been for this. A technical phrase used in pleading at common law by way of special **traverse.** It presents the negative portion of a plea.

ABSTRACT OF TITLE A chronological summary of all recorded instruments and events that entitle a person to **property. It** is a history of the **title** containing reference to conveyances, **grants, wills,** and **transfers,** including all the **encumbrances** to which the property is subject **(liens, judgments, restrictive covenants,** rights of way), and whether the latter have been released. It is designed to allow the purchaser to determine whether he is buying clear and good title. See **chain of title.**

ABUSE OF DISCRETION A legal appellate technique for reviewing the exercise of **discretion** by lower courts and **administrative tribunals;** a rationale to overturn determinations that are unreasonable, arbitrary, or inconsistent with the facts and circumstances before a court.

The "abuse of discretion" standard of review is also used in administrative settings. Thus, where a board has misused discretionary power, the misuse may be corrected by a reviewing court.

The Crown **Prosecutor** has broad discretion whether to prosecute, but it is very difficult to prove abuse of discretion.

ABUSE OF PROCESS A use of the criminal or civil **process** other than one intended by law. Actions that are frivolous, vexatious or in bad faith could be stayed as an abuse of process of the court. It is an abuse of process to set a case for **hearing** that has already been decided by a court of competent **jurisdiction.** *R.* v. *Heric,* [1975] 4 W.W.R. 422 (B.C.Prov.Ct.), held that the accused having been dismissed after being charged under *Criminal Code*, R.S.C. 1985, c. C–46, s. 250, because of the Crown's failure to appear, could not be charged under s. 252 based on the same facts; such activity on the part of the Crown was an abuse of process. The WRIT OF PROHIBITION (see **writ**) is available to prevent abuse of process *(Re Regina and Holst* (1972), 5 C.C.C. (2d) 539 (Alta. S.C.)), and there is residual discretion in the trial court judge to stay proceedings in the clearest of cases of abuse of process. *R.* v. *Mack,* [1988] 2 S.C.R. 903.

In *Guilford Industries Ltd.* v. *Hankinson Management Services Ltd.* (1973), 40 D.L.R. (3d) 398 (B.C.S.C.), the essential elements of the **tort** of abuse of process are outlined: There must be (1) a collateral and improper purpose and (2) a definite act or threat in furtherance of a purpose not legitimate in the use of the process. In the case, a **lien** action devoid of legal foundation, with legal blackmail used to obtain a settlement, was held to be an abuse of process.

ABUT [ABUTTING] To adjoin; to cease at point of contact; to empty onto. *Catkey Construction (Toronto) Ltd.* v. *Bankes,* [1971] 1 O.R. 205 at 206 (C.A.) defined an abutting owner as "an owner, the front, rear or side of whose property is contiguous to *a side of* a highway [in this case] which is stopped up, but does not mean or include an owner whose property is contiguous to either terminus of such a highway."

In its primary meaning, abutting implies a closer proximity than does the term *adjacent,* and whether adjacent is to

be interpreted as lying near to or actually adjoining depends on the facts of each situation.

Abutting **property** is **real property** that borders on another property.

ACCELERATION The hastening of the time for the vesting and enjoyment of an **estate** or other property right that would otherwise have occurred at a later time. This term applies to **personalty** as well as **realty.** It is associated with gifts devised by **will,** to the vesting of a **remainder** due to the premature termination of a **preceding estate,** and with clauses commonly found in **mortgage** agreements (see **acceleration clause**), stipulating that an entire debt may be deemed due upon the default of a single instalment, or other duty of the borrower.

ACCELERATION CLAUSE A provision in a **contract** or document that, upon the occurrence of a certain event, a party's expected interest in the subject **property** will become prematurely **vested.** Such a clause is often found in instalment contracts and can cause an entire debt to become due upon failure to pay an instalment as agreed.

Such clauses are common and are generally enforceable, subject to statutory exceptions such as the *Residential Tenancy Act,* S.B.C. 1984, c. 15, s. 5, which renders acceleration clauses void and unenforceable.

ACCEPTANCE 1. In contracts, acceptance to create a binding **contract** is the assent to an **offer** by words or conduct on the part of the person to whom the offer is made. Whether there has been an acceptance depends upon whether the offeree has conducted himself so that a **reasonable man** would believe that he has accepted. *Con-Force Products Ltd.* v. *Rosen* (1967), 64 D.L.R. (2d) 63 at 75 (Sask.Q.B.). Acceptance may also be governed by **statutes,** as, e.g., the *Sale of Goods Act,* R.S.O. 1990, c. S. 1, s. 34.

2. In property law, it is an element essential to completion of a gift **inter vivos** and a donatio **mortis causa.** The property must be accepted by the recipient as a gift; however, a valid gift may be made without the **donee's** knowledge, subject to his right to repudiate it upon learning of the transfer. *Horne* v. *Huston* (1919), 16 O.W.N. 173 (H.C.). There is a presumption of acceptance of a gift subject to the donee's right of refusal. *Wilson* v. *Hicks* (1911), 23 O.L.R. 496 (C.A.).

3. Acceptance by a bank of a cheque or other **negotiable instrument** is a formal procedure whereby the bank promises to pay the payee named on the **cheque.** Acceptance is the drawee's [bank's] signed engagement to honour the **draft** [negotiable instrument] as presented. It must be written on the draft and may consist of the **drawee's** signature alone. It becomes operative when completed by **delivery** or notification. *Bills of Exchange Act* R.S.C. 1985, c. B–4, s. 2.

4. A **solicitor** may choose to accept service of a **pleading** or court document on behalf of a client.

ACCESSORY *Particeps criminis quasi accedens ad culpam* [as though assenting to the offence]. An accessory performs acts that facilitate others in the commission or attempted commission of a criminal offence or in avoiding apprehension for crime. Compare **accomplice; aid and abet; conspirator.**

ACCESSORY AFTER THE FACT As defined by s. 23(1) of the *Criminal Code*, R.S.C. 1985, c. C–46, "one who, knowing that a person has been a party to the offence, receives, comforts or assists that person for the purpose of enabling that person to escape." Section 23(2) exempts a married person whose spouse has been a party to the offence.

An accessory after the fact may not be tried or enter a valid plea of guilty until the **principal** is convicted. *R.* v. *Vinette*, [1975] 2 S.C.R. 222.

Section 592 of the Code allows an accessory after the fact to be indicted whether or not the principal is indicted, convicted or brought before the law. *R.* v. *Vinette,* supra. The principal may testify against the accessory, and the former's plea of guilty and his conviction are admissible against the latter. See also ss. 240, 463, 469, 593 of the *Criminal Code*.

ACCESSORY BEFORE THE FACT One who counsels, procures, or commands another to commit a crime, but who is not present actively or constructively at such perpetration.

Sections 21 and 22 of the *Criminal Code* are the general sections dealing with accessories before the fact under

the guise of "parties to offence" and "person counselling offence." Section 21(1)(*b*) broadens the definition by defining a party to the offence as anyone who "does or omits to do anything for the purpose of aiding any person to commit it [crime]." See also s. 464, which establishes that an accessory before the fact is guilty of an offence even if the offence he counselled or procured is not committed.

Generally, accessories are punishable on the same basis and to the same extent as the principals to the criminal offence.

ACCOMMODATION ENDORSEMENT
The co-signing of an instrument without **consideration,** solely for the benefit of the holder, creating a liability on the cosigner should the other (accommodated) party fail to pay. In England, this is an ACCOMMODATION BILL. See **endorsement.**

ACCOMMODATION PARTY The *Bills of Exchange Act*, R.S.C. 1985, c. B–4, s. 54(1), defines an accommodation party to a bill as a person "who has signed a bill as **drawer,** acceptor or endorser, without receiving value therefore and for the purpose of lending his name to some other party." The party is gratuitously obligating himself to guarantee the debt of the accommodated party. The accommodation party has a right of recourse against the principal. *Dartmouth Community Credit Union Ltd.* v. *Smith & Hefler* (1977), 24 N.S.R. (2d) 541 (S.C.).

"A name is lent for the purpose of this concept if it is used to support or aid the obtaining of credit by the person to whom it is 'lent.' This necessarily implies that the latter person is himself obligated to the principal creditor in respect of the debt in question. It then follows that the accommodation party will in such circumstances become the **surety** for or guarantor of the person accommodated." *Bank of Montreal* v. *Kilpatrick* (1976), 18 N.S.R. (2d) 173 at 177 (S.C.A.D.).

ACCOMPLICE "An accomplice is one who is concerned with another or others in committing or attempting to commit a criminal offence." *R.* v. *Morrison* (1917), 51 N.S.R. 253 at 270 (S.C.). One who participates in a crime but not necessarily in its actual commission.

An accomplice is liable for the identical offence charged against the accused. See *Criminal Code*, R.S.C. 1985, c. C–46, s. 21 and sections referring to the specific offences. One who knowingly, voluntarily, or purposely and with common intent with the accused unites in the commission or attempted commission of a criminal offence. Mere presence does not make one an accomplice. *R.* v. *Black*, [1970] 4 C.C.C. 251 (B.C.C.A.).

Section 21(2) states that essential to accomplice liability is a common intention to carry out an unlawful purpose and to assist each other therein. The party must know or ought to know that the commission of the offence would be a probable consequence of carrying out the common purpose.

An accused acting under **duress** cannot be a party to an offence if because of threats he was unable to form a genuine common intention to execute the common purpose. *R.* v. *Paquette* (1976), 30 C.C.C. (2d) 417; 70 D.L.R. (3d) 129 (S.C.C.). For a discussion of uncorroborated accomplice evidence see *Horsburgh* v. *The Queen*, [1967] S.C.R. 746; *Sellars* v. *The Queen* (1980), 52 C.C.C. (2d) 345 (S.C.C.).

Compare **accessory; aid and abet; conspirator.**

ACCORD An agreement whereby one party agrees to accept a **consideration** to extinguish another's liability, usually less than what could be claimable under the contractual or other liability of such other party. **Satisfaction** is the execution of such an agreement. *Glascott* v. *Cameron* (1905), 10 O.L.R. 399 (Div.Ct.).

An agreement whereby an earlier obligation is discharged; satisfaction is the consideration that makes the agreement operative. *Williams* v. *Enskat*, [1952] O.W.N. 628 (C.A.)

See **accord and satisfaction; novation; settlement.**

ACCORD AND SATISFACTION "Accord and satisfaction is the purchase of a release from an obligation arising under **contract** or **tort** by means of any valuable **consideration,** not being the actual performance of the obligation itself. The accord is the agreement by which the obligation is discharged. The satisfaction is

the consideration which makes the agreement operative." *British Russian Gazette & Trade Outlook Ltd.* v. *Associated Newspapers*, [1933] 2 K.B. 616 at 643–44; followed in *Dubord* v. *Girard*, [1945] 1 W.W.R. 641 (Alta.S.C.).

See also *Somers* v. *Liberty School District*, [1928] 2 D.L.R. 334 (Alta.Dist.Ct.); *Re Cohen & Sweigman, ex parte Gelman*, [1925] 4 D.L.R. 359 (Ont.S.C.).

ACCOUNT 1. A registry of debts, credits and charges or a detailed statement of a series of receipts, credits and disbursements of money that has taken place between two or more persons. **2.** Any account with a bank, including a checking, interest or savings account.

In **equity,** the principal tool for awarding money is the ACTION OF ACCOUNT, as in an action for **breach of trust,** where the **trustee** has lost the **trust funds.** The action originally lay against certain persons who had received money or **property** belonging to another under circumstances that made them liable to give the owner an accounting, such as **guardians** and **bailiffs.** Their obligation was not to restore the exact thing received, but to make an accounting for its equivalent, or the profit derived from it.

In property law, where one TENANT IN COMMON (see **tenancy**) receives all the profits, he shall account for this in proportionate share to the other co-tenants. See *Sproule* v. *Clements*, [1927] 2 W.W.R. 825 at 833–34 (B.C.C.A.).

ACCRETION The adding on or adhering of something to **property;** a means by which a property owner gains ownership of something additional. **1.** It usually refers to a gradual addition of sediment to the shore by the action of water; it is created by operation of natural causes. It is gradual and imperceptible, whereas **avulsion** is the sudden and perceptible loss or addition to land by the action of water. See, e.g., *Chuckry* v. *The Queen*, [1973] S.C.R. 694.

2. In the law of **succession,** accretion is said to take place when a **co-heir** or colegatee dies before the property **vests,** or when he rejects the **inheritance** or **legacy,** or when he omits to comply with a **condition,** or when he becomes incapable of taking. The result is that the other heirs or legatees can share in his part. Where no contrary intention is shown by **will,** property that falls into the hands of the **executor** after the death of the **testator** is not distributable under the will unless such property is an accretion to the property disposed of by the will. *Re Jardine; Re Carey; Royal Trust Co.* v. *Jardine* (1955), 17 W.W.R. 197 (Alta. S.C.A.D.); *Royal Trust Co. & McMurray* v. *Crawford* (1956), 1 D.L.R. (2nd) 225 (S.C.C.).

3. In situations involving a **trust,** the term refers to any addition to the principal or to income that results from an extraordinary occurrence, that is, an occurrence that is forseeable but that rarely happens.

See **alluvion; avulsion; reliction.**

ACCRUE To accumulate; to come into existence as an enforceable claim. The time that a **cause of action** accrues determines how long a plaintiff may wait to initiate an **action** under the appropriate **statute of limitations.**

ACCUMULATION An increase by repeated additions; profit accruing on the sale of principal **assets,** or the increase derived from their investment, or both. The adding of interest or income of a fund to **principal** pursuant to provisions of a **will** or **deed.** The practice of the **executor** or **trustee** of amassing rents, dividends, and other incomes and treating them as **capital,** investing it and making new capital so that he is said to accumulate the fund; the capital and procured income constitute accumulations.

ACCUSATION A **charge** against a person or corporation. In its broadest sense it includes **indictment,** information, and any other form in which a charge of an offence can be made against an individual. It is a formal charge of having committed a criminal offence, made against a person in accordance with established legal procedure and laid before a magistrate.

It is a criminal offence [public mischief] to mislead a peace officer into accusing a person of an offence. *Criminal Code*, R.S.C. 1985, c. C–46, s. 140.

It is a criminal offence to conspire to falsely accuse someone of an offence that person did not commit. (*Id.*, s. 465(1)(*b*)).

ACCUSE To directly and formally institute legal **proceedings** against a person, charging that he has committed an offence recognized by law, i.e., to **prosecute;** "threaten to accuse" means "threaten to prosecute." *R.* v. *Maloney* (1934), 40 R. de Jur. 351 (Que.Sess.Ct.).

ACCUSED A person against whom a criminal **proceeding** is initiated; the one who in a legal manner is held to answer for an offence at any stage of the proceedings, or against whom a complaint in any lawful manner is made, charging an offence, including all proceedings from the order of **arrest** to final execution. Generally, the person against whom a criminal proceeding is initiated is called the accused if one proceeds by **indictment. If** one proceeds by **summary conviction,** that person is referred to as the **defendant.** This reflects the **felony/misdemeanour** dichotomy in England.

ACKNOWLEDGEMENT An admission, declaration, affirmation, or confession. It may refer to a formal declaration made before an authorized official, by a person who executed an instrument, that it is his free act and deed.

A written promise recognising a debt and an obligation to pay that entitles the creditor to bring an action within the limitation period from the date of the acknowledgement. See, e.g., *The Statute of Limitations,* R.S.N.S. 1989, c. 258, ss. 6, 8, 17.

A COELO USQUE AD CENTRUM *(ä kwā'- lō ūs'-kwā äd sĕn'-trūm)* Lat.: from the sky to the centre of the earth. This outdated **property** maxim that marked the boundaries of land ownership has been modified by the acknowledged rights of airplane flight patterns over land and of the erection of telephone posts and wires, etc., on private property. *LaCroix* v. *The Queen,* [1954] Ex.C.R. 69; *Atlantic Aviation* v. *N.S. Light & Power Co. Ltd.* (1965), 55 D.L.R. (2d) 554 (N.S.S.C.).

ACQUIESCENCE An assent to an **infringement** of rights, by express or implied conduct, by which the right to equitable **relief** is usually lost. It takes place when a person, with full knowledge of his own rights and of acts that infringe them, has, by his conduct, led the persons responsible for the infringement to believe that he has waived or abandoned his rights.

To acquiesce connotes an element of knowledge on the part of the principal. There must be concurrence of the principal's will to act or a tacit concurrence. See *Udell* v. *M.N.R.*, [1969] C.T.C. 704 at 713 (Ex.Ct.).

ACQUIT To set free or judicially discharge from an **accusation** of suspicion of guilt. An individual is acquitted either when a **verdict** of not guilty has been rendered at the close of **trial** or when an appellate court decision has absolved him of the charges that were the bases of the **action.**

ACQUITTAL 1. Broadly, the release or discharge of an acquitted individual, without further prosecution for the same act or transaction. See **double jeopardy.**

2. In **contract,** the release from an obligation, liability, or engagement.

ACT A decree proclaiming the law in an area, passed by a competent legislative body, that may proclaim new law, alter or modify existing law, or repeal previously existing law. See **statute.**

ACTIO *(äk'-tē-ō)* Lat.: performance, activity; also, **proceedings,** lawsuit, **process, action,** permission for a **suit.**

ACTIO NON *(äk'-tē-ō nŏn)* Lat.: not an action. In **pleading,** a **nonfeasance.** See **nonsuit.**

ACTION [AT LAW] A judicial **proceeding** whereby one party (the **plaintiff** or the Crown) **prosecutes** another for a wrong or injury done, for damage caused, or for protection of a right or prevention of a wrong. A proceeding by which one party seeks in a court of justice to enforce some right or to restrain the commission of some wrong by another party. It includes both civil and criminal proceedings. *Dorosh* v. *Bentwood Chair & Table Mfg. Co.,* [1939] 3 D.L.R. 344 (Man.C.A.).

An action is the **common law** mode of obtaining redress for a wrong done or a duty not performed. *Frontenac County* v. *Kingston* (1871), 30 U.C.Q.B. 584 (Ont.Q.B.).

An action or suit does not come to a conclusion when a trial judge renders his decision; as long as a right of appeal exists, the matter has not been finally determined. *Hampton Lumber Mills Ltd.* v. *Joy Logging Ltd.,* [1977] 2 W.W.R. 289 (B.C.S.C.).

ACTIONABLE Giving rise to a **cause of action;** thus, it refers to wrongful conduct that may form the basis of a civil **action,** as in ACTIONABLE NEGLIGENCE, which is the **breach** or non-performance of a **legal duty** through neglect or carelessness, resulting in damage to another. Describes an action that is afforded a **remedy** by law or **equity.**

ACTION EX DELICTO *(ĕks dĕ-lĭk'-tō)* Lat.: arising out of wrongs. A **cause of action** that arises out of fault, misconduct or **misfeance,** and through violation of a **duty.** It is essentially a **tort** action.

ACTION IN PERSONAM An action in which the plaintiff claims that the defendant ought to give or do or make something good for the plaintiff.

An action **in personam** is brought "for the specific recovery of goods and **chattels,** or for damages or other redress for **breach of contract,** or other injuries, of whatever description, the specific recovery of lands, tenements, and hereditaments only excepted...." *McConnell* v. *McGee* (1917), 37 D.L.R. 486 at 489 (Ont.S.C.A.D.). See **jurisdiction.**

ACTION IN REM An action in which the plaintiff claims that the thing in dispute is his against all other persons.

An action **in rem** is "brought for the *specific* recovery of lands, tenements and hereditaments." *McConnell* v. *McGee* (1917), 37 D.L.R. 486 at 489 (Ont.S.C.A.D.).

It is a proceeding to determine the status of the thing itself. *Fry* v. *Botsford & McQuillan* (1902), 9 B.C.R. 234 (C.A.).

An action in rem is a proceeding to determine the disposition of an item under the court's control. Consequently, a judgment in rem exists where the court adjudicates upon the **title** or the right to **possession** of the **property** within its control. See *Warehouse Security Finance Co. Ltd.* v. *Oscar Niemi Ltd.,* [1944] 3 D.L.R. 568 (B.C.C.A.). See **jurisdiction.**

ACTION ON THE CASE An action started by a **writ** permitted as a result of the *Statute of Westminster II, 1285.* The statute contained a provision that a new kind of writ might be granted to a plaintiff in every case where his claim, though not exactly covered by an existing writ, was based upon circumstances like those that would have entitled him to a writ. An action started by one of these new writs was called an action on the case; the commonest type came to be the action of TRESPASS ON THE CASE (see **trespass**), where a plaintiff was unable to prove direct injury (or **trespass**) by the defendant but could show that harm resulted to him indirectly by some act that was like a trespass, e.g., the defendant's **negligence.**

ACTIONS [ACTIO] MIXTA "[A] mixed action is one partaking of the nature of real and personal actions, that is, one in which some **real property** is demanded, as well as personal **damages** for a wrong sustained." *McConnell* v. *McGee* (1917), 37 D.L.R. 486 at 489 (Ont.S.C.A.D.).

ACT OF GOD A manifestation of the forces of nature that are unpredictable and impossible to foresee; a result of the direct, immediate and exclusive operation of the forces of nature, uncontrolled or uninfluenced by the power of man and without human intervention, of such a character that it could not have been prevented or avoided by prudence or foresight. Examples are tempests, lightning, earthquakes and a sudden illness or death of a person. See *Nichols* v. *Marsland* (1876), 2 Ex. D. 1 (C.A.).

ACTUAL DAMAGES See **damages.**

ACTUAL NOTICE See **notice.**

ACTUAL POSSESSION See **possession.**

ACTUAL VALUE See **market value.**

ACTUARY One who computes various insurance and property costs; especially, one who calculates the cost of life insurance risks and insurance premiums.

ACTUS REUS *(ăk'-tŭs rā'-ŭs)* Lat.: loosely, the criminal act; more properly, the guilty act or deed of crime. Every criminal offence has two elements, the physical actus reus and the mental **mens rea.** The actus reus is the actual conduct of the accused that falls within the defini-

tion of the act proscribed. In Canada, all criminal offences are statutory (see Criminal Code, R.S.C. 1985, c. C–46, s. 9), and the statutory definition of the proscribed act or conduct, as construed by the courts, defines the actus reus. In order to constitute a criminal offence, the required mens rea, or intent to commit the offence, must be presented concurrently. (For example, the actus reus of **murder** is **homicide;** the mens rea is the intent—either willful or reckless—that the person die as a consequence of the act.)

Although mens rea is generally required, there are offences of strict and absolute liability for which one may be convicted on the strength of the actus reus alone. For offences of **strict liability,** the doing of the prohibited act **prima facie** imports the offence, leaving the burden on the accused to prove the defence of reasonable care. As for absolute **liability,** there is no defence open to the accused. See *R.* v. *City of Sault Ste. Marie* (1978), 21 N.R. 295 (S.C.C.), where the city was held liable for polluting a river when unknown to the municipality a contractor disposed of collected waste into the water supply.

ADDITUR See **remittitur.**

ADEMPTION Removal or extinction. One of the ways in which a **devise or bequest** lapses is the extinction or withdrawal of the disposition by some subsequent act of the **testator** clearly indicating an intent to revoke such. Ademption may be effected by the testator's **inter vivos** gift of the property devised or bequeathed and/or the existence of attendant circumstances that render it impossible to effect the transfer or payment as directed by the **will.** See, e.g., *Diocesan Synod of Fredericton* v. *Perrett & New Brunswick Protestant Orphans Home,* [1955] S.C.R. 498.

ADHESION CONTRACT Usually a contract in standard form prepared by one party and submitted to the other on a take-it-or-leave-it basis. It implies a grave inequality in bargaining power, resulting in the strict construction of such contracts by the courts.

AD HOC *(ăd hŏk)* Lat.: for this; for this particular purpose. An ad hoc committee is one commissioned for a special purpose.

ADJECTIVE LAW See substantive law.

ADJOINING Neighbouring, near, and sometimes adjacent. See *Dann* v. *Pitt* (1849), 6 N.B.R. 385 (S.C.). Adjoining, as applied to parcels of land, does not necessarily imply that the parcels are to be in physical contact with each other; houses in a row, with a house between two others, are all said to be adjoining. See *McKenzie* v. *Miniota Municipal School District*, [1931] 2 W.W.R. 105 (Man.K.B.). The word *adjoining* has been given a wide, liberal construction in the determination of whether land is adjoining another property. See *Huson* v. *The Township of South Norwich* (1892), 21 S.C.R. 669. Every owner of land is entitled to receive from the adjoining land such support [lateral physical pressure] for his land as is sufficient while it is in its natural state. See *Lotus Ltd.* v. *British Soda Co. Ltd.*, [1972] Ch. 123.

ADJOURN [ADJOURNMENT] To put off or delay to another time or place. Parliament and the provincial legislatures may be adjourned; or, in the discretion of the judge, a court may be adjourned. The term is also used in connection with public and company meetings. An adjournment may be a mere suspension of the original meeting or sitting. If the adjournment is final, it is said to be **sine die.**

ADJUDICATION "A deliberated judicial decision [which] has been come to after a hearing at which both sides ... at least had an opportunity of being heard." *Stewart* v. *Braun & Patterson*, [1924] 2 W.W.R. 1103 at 1107 (Man.K.B.). The determination of a **controversy** and pronouncement of **judgment** based on **evidence** presented; implies a final judgment of the court or other body deciding the matter. Compare **disposition.**

ADJUSTER One who makes a determination of the amount of an insurance claim and then makes an agreement with the insured as to a settlement.

ADMINISTRATIVE LAW Those rules of law that concern the exercise of the powers and privileges of the **executive** branch of government. More specifically, administrative law is concerned with the actions and decisions pursuant to the powers given to the executive by Parliament or the provincial legislatures. Nearly every modern statute delegates to the Governor-in-Council (or the Lieutenant-Governor-in-Council of a province) or to a minister of the Crown the power to make **regulations** to secure desired legislative ends. In addition, numerous statutory bodies or **tribunals** have been set up to administrate various legislative schemes and to make decisions outside the framework of the ordinary courts. Administrative law is particularly concerned with the rules that exist to control **administrative tribunals** and administrative action in its broadest sense.

ADMINISTRATIVE TRIBUNALS A large number of special courts or bodies outside the ordinary judicial framework, generally set up under federal or provincial **statutes** to decide matters that may arise in the administration of some particular area of government: e.g., boards dealing with labour relations, workmen's compensation, public utilities, liquor control, rent review, etc. The required procedures for such tribunals vary greatly. The tribunals are sometimes said to perform a QUASI-JUDICIAL function (see **quasi**). There may or may not be statutory provision for appeal from the decisions of these bodies. However, the tribunals may be subject to the control of the **superior courts** if there has been a serious irregularity in their **proceedings** or failure to abide by the principles of **natural justice.** Some jurisdictions—for example, Ontario—have specific enactments to control the exercise of power by such bodies. See *Statutory Powers Procedure Act*, R.S.O. 1990, c. S. 22.

ADMINISTRATOR One who is appointed to handle the affairs of a person who has died **intestate;** one who manages the **estate** of a person who has left no **executor.** The administrator derives his authority from the **Surrogate Court** (or, in some jurisdictions, the **Probate** Court).

An administrator is empowered to carry out his duties and functions by documents known as LETTERS OF ADMINISTRATION, which are conclusive evidence of the intestacy of the deceased; the person in whose na.ne they are granted has the incontestable right to the administration of the estate. See *Doyle* v. *Diamond Flint Glass Co.* (1904), 8 O.L.R. 499 (Div.Ct.).

**ADMIRALTY AND MARITIME JURISDIC-
TION** Expansive **jurisdiction** over all actions related to events occurring at sea; extends to all transactions relating to sea commerce and navigation, to damages and injuries upon the sea and all maritime contracts, and torts. See *Federal Court Act*, R.S.C. 1985, c. F–7, s. 22.

Admiralty and maritime jurisdiction is the "jurisdiction to hear an action under any statute of the Parliament of Canada in relation to 'any matter coming within the class of subject of navigation and shipping.' *Robert Simpson Montreal Ltd.* **v.** *Hamburg-Amerika Linie Norddeutscher,* [1973] F.C. 1356 at 1361–62 **(C.A.).**

ADMISSIBLE EVIDENCE **Evidence** that may be received by a trial court to aid the **fact finder** (judge or jury) in deciding the merits of the **controversy.** Each jurisdiction has established rules of evidence to determine questions of admissibility. Admissibility signifies compliance with all the exclusionary rules, including the rule prohibiting the receipt of irrelevant evidence. But nowadays, relevance, not competency, is the main consideration, and "generally speaking, all evidence that is relevant to an issue is admissible, while all that is irrelevant is excluded." *Hollington* v. *Hewthorn & Co. Ltd.,* [1943] K.B. 587 at 594; applied in *Re Maritime Asphalt Products Ltd.* (1965), 52 D.L.R. (2d) 8 (P.E.I.S.C.).

Under s. 24(2) of the **Canadian Charter of Rights and Freedoms** when the admissability of evidence is challenged on constitutional grounds, a trial judge may determine whether evidence should be excluded or admitted as a matter of law. "The test to be applied is whether the evidence 'could' bring the administration of justice into disrepute in the eyes of a reasonable person, dispassionate and fully appraised of the circumstances of the case. Thus if the admission of the evidence in some way affects the fairness of the trial then the admission of the evidence would tend to bring the administration of justice into disrepute, and subject to considerations of other factors, the evidence should be excluded. . . . [T]he court must consider whether the judicial system's repute will be better served by the admission or exclusion of the evidence." E. Greenspan, *Martin's Annual*

Criminal Code, 1994 52 (1993). *Collins* v. *The Queen* (1987), 33 C.C.C. (3d) 1 (S.C.C.).

ADMISSIONS 1. In criminal law, the voluntary acknowledgement that certain facts do exist; but of themselves admissions are insufficient to be considered a **confession** of guilt. An admission is a statement by the **accused** that tends to support the **charge** but is not sufficient to determine guilt. **2.** In civil procedure, a pretrial **discovery** device by which one party asks another for a positive affirmation or denial of a **material** fact or **allegation** at issue. Also, a party may request another to admit the truth of any relevant fact or the authenticity of any relevant document.

ADOPTION 1. By court order, a person of the **age of majority** may adopt a child born of another so that the child becomes the child of the adopting parent and the adopting parent becomes the parent of the adopted child. See *Children and Family Services Act*, S.N.S. 1990, c. 5, ss. 65–87; *Child and Family Services Act*, R.S.O. 1990, c. C.11, ss. 136–177.

2. In **contract,** the term is used to suggest the continued acceptance of a contract as binding on both parties, although the circumstances might entitle the injured party to repudiate it.

3. The formal acceptance and making effective of a proposal, finding, resolution or amendment.

ADOPTION BY REFERENCE The adoption of either rules of **substantive law** or rules of **procedure** in force in another jurisdiction; a technique used by legislative bodies, where it is desired to enact the same laws as in another jurisdiction. See *Attorney-General for Ontario* **v.** *Scott,* [1956] S.C.R. 137. There can be no enlargement of the legislative authority of the adopting body, only a borrowing of provisions that are within its legislative competence and were enacted for its own purposes. But neither Parliament nor a provincial legislature is capable of delegating to the other or of receiving from the other any of the powers to make laws conferred upon it by the *Constitution Act, 1867.* See *Coughlin* v. *Ontario Highway Transport Board,* [1968] S.C.R. 569.

AD TESTIFICANDUM *(äd těs-tĭ-fĭ-căn′-dūm)* Lat.: for testifying. A person sought ad testificandum is sought to appear as a **witness.** See **subpoena** [SUBPOENA AD TESTIFICANDUM].

ADULTERATION The human action of including filthy, putrid substances or prohibited additives in the manufacture of a food or drug for sale. See *Food & Drugs Act,* R.S.C. 1985, c. F–27, s. 4.

ADULTERY Voluntary sexual intercourse between persons of the opposite sex, one of whom is married to a third party. *Orford* v. *Orford* (1921), 49 O.L.R. 15 (S.C.C.). Under the *Divorce Act,* R.S.C. 1985 (2nd Supp.). c. 3, s. 8(2)(b)(i), adultery is proof of the only ground for divorce under the Act, which is "breakdown of the marriage." See also *Bezanger* v. *Bezanger* (1969), 1 N.S.R. (2d) 412 (proof of adultery).

AD VALOREM *(ăd và-lô'-rĕm)* Lat.: according to value. Designates an assessment of taxes against **property** at a certain rate upon its value.

AD VALOREM TAX See **tax.**

ADVANCE To move forward in position, time or place. (1) To pay money before it is due. See *Williams Manufacturing Co.* v. *Michener* (1908), 13 O.W.R. 46 (S.C.). (2) To furnish credit, to loan **capital** in aid of a projected enterprise, payment beforehand or in anticipation of payment or security of future reimbursement—hence a loan. See *Diebel* v. *Stratford Improvement Co.* (1916), 37 O.L.R. 492 (S.C.).

ADVANCEMENT "[A] bestowment of **property** by a parent on a child on condition that if the **donee** claims to share in the **intestate** estate of the donor he shall bring in this property for the purpose of equal distribution." *Re Hall* (1887), 14 O.R. 557 at 559 (Ch.D.). A PRESUMPTION OF ADVANCEMENT occurs if the person to whom the money is paid or on whom the property is bestowed is the wife or child of the donor, or someone to whom he stands **in loco parentis.** It is a rebuttable **presumption,** e.g., by evidence that the donor intended to keep the **beneficial interest** for himself. See *Goodfriend* v. *Goodfriend,* [1972] S.C.R. 640. The common-law presumption of advance-ment may be modified by statute placing the onus of proving the advancement upon the person making the assertion, or requiring evidence of the advancement in writing by the intestate or the child. See *Intestate Succession Act,* R.S.N. 1989, c. 236, s. 13(3); *Estates Administration Act,* R.S.O. 1990, c. E.22, s. 25.

ADVERSARY The opponent or **litigant** in a legal controversy or litigation. See **adverse party; adversary proceeding.**

ADVERSARY PROCEEDING A **proceeding** involving a real **controversy** contested by two opposing **parties.** In Canada, the judicial process is based on the adversarial system, as compared to Europe's process, which for the most part is based on the inquisitorial system. In the former, the judge's role is one of an impartial arbiter weighing the **evidence** presented by the opposing parties and determining the applicable decision. The lawyers each present full proof and argument. In the latter process, the judge plays a much greater role in the selection and questioning of witnesses and in the assembling of evidence. Contrast **ex parte.** See also **case.**

ADVERSE INTEREST An interest contrary to and inconsistent with that of some other person.

ADVERSE POSSESSION A method of acquiring complete **title** to land as against all others, including the owner who holds the registered title (see **registry acts**) through certain acts over an uninterrupted period of time, as prescribed by statute. See, e.g., *The Statute of Limitations,* R.S.N. 1989, c. 258, ss. 10–31. The occupation must be "open, actual, exclusive, continuous and notorious ... to give possessory title." Consequently, "isolated acts of **trespass** committed from time to time" do not constitute adverse possession. *Re Colling* (1975), 11 N.B.R. (2d) 516 (S.C.). The purpose of the requirements is to give notice that HOSTILE [adverse] possession had begun. *Sherren* v. *Pearson* (1887), 14 S.C.R. 581. See **notorious possession.**

ADVISORY OPINION A formal opinion by a judge, court, or law officer upon a **question of law** submitted by a legislative body or a government official, but not actually presented in a concrete case at law. Such opinion, while of considerable persuasive value, has no binding force as law. Compare **declaratory judgment.**

ADVOCATE A person professionally conducting and presenting a case in court; in Canada, a **barrister** and **solicitor;** a lawyer.

ADVOCACY 1. The art of persuasion. **2.** In practice, the active espousal of a legal cause and the pleading of the legal rights (or cause) of another in court. "When acting as an advocate, the lawyer must treat the tribunal with courtesy and respect and must represent the client resolutely, honourably and within the limits of the law." C.B.A. *Code of Professional Conduct* (1988).

AFFIDAVIT A written statement in the name of a person known as the **deponent** who signs and swears to its veracity; a written statement made or taken under oath before an officer of the court or a **notary public** or other person who has been duly authorized to certify the statement.

AFFILIATION The act of being allied with another person or group; an association that is less than membership in a certain group.

In family law, affiliation refers to a procedure where a woman issues a complaint against a man who may be the father of a child born out of wedlock. The complaint is based on the fact that the child has been left without support. The mother must be able to produce corroborative evidence to prove the alleged paternity, such as evidence of continuous sexual liaisons between the parties; e.g., *Barath* v. *Bacsek* (1975), 25 R.F.L. 218 (Ont.Div.Ct.). See *McLeod* v. *Hill* (1975), 23 R.F.L. 309 (Sask.Prov.Ct.), concerning facial resemblance between child and alleged father.

An AFFILIATION ORDER may be a declaration of paternity or a maintenance order or both; it varies from jurisdiction to jurisdiction in Canada. *Works* v. *Holt* (1976), 22 R.F.L. 1 (Ont.Prov.Ct.).

AFFINITY A relationship created by marriage. The doctrine of affinity grew out of the idea that marriage makes husband and wife one. The husband has the same relation, by affinity to the wife's blood relations, as she has to them by consanguinity, and vice versa. Affinity is a bar to marriage within prohibited degrees. *Re Schepull and Bekeschus and Provincial Secretary,* [1954] 2 D.L.R. 5 (Ont.H.C.). SECONDARY AFFINITIES are the relationships that subsist between the husband's and the wife's relations. COLLATERAL AFFINITY is the relationship between the husband and the relations of his wife's relations. See **consanguinity.**

AFFIRM 1. To approve, confirm, ratify; refers to the assertion of an **appellate court** that the **judgment** of the court below is correct and should stand. Compare **reversal.**
2. To attest to, as in an affirmation of faith or fidelity.

AFFIRMATIVE ACTION The use of laws, programs, or activities to remedy the negative consequences caused by **discrimination** (e.g., based on sex, race, etc.) against disadvantaged groups or individuals. Although most commonly applied to employment (see, e.g., *Employment Equity Act*, R.S.C. 1985 (2nd Supp.), c. 23.), the term may be applied to any positive measure whose purpose is to reduce discrimination (e.g., paternity support legislation *(Shewchuck* v. *Ricard* (1986), 20 C.R.R. 364 (B.C.S.C.)).

Affirmative action policies are protected by the **Canadian Charter of Rights and Freedoms,** s. 15(2), under the equality rights provision, and by the *Canadian Human Rights Act,* R.S.C. 1985, c. H–6, s. 16, as well as several provincial human rights Codes. See *Action Travail des Femmes* v. *Canadian National Railway Co.,* [1987] 1 S.C.R. 1114; *Human Rights Act,* R.S.N.S. 1989, c. 214, s. 6(i).

AFFIRMATIVE DEFENCE In a statement of **defence,** a plea, which the defendant has the burden of establishing at trial, by which he admits the truth of material facts stated in the plaintiff's statement of claim, but destroys the legal effect of these admissions by pleading "further facts which, if true, avoid the legal consequences argued for by the plaintiff . . ." G. Watson, *Canadian Civil Procedure* 369 (3d ed. 1988). See **burden of proof.**

AFFIX To attach to or add to; to annex, as to affix a **chattel** to **realty;** e.g., to attach a chandelier to the ceiling is to affix it to the **real property.** A tree is affixed to the land.

A FORTIORI *(ä fôr-shē-ô'-rē)* Lat.: from stronger reasoning. Refers to a logical inference that, because a certain conclusion or fact is true, a second included conclusion must also be true. For example, A is not guilty of theft; then, a fortiori, he is not guilty of robbery.

AGAINST THE [MANIFEST] [WEIGHT OF THE] EVIDENCE An evidentiary standard permitting the **trial court,** after **verdict,** to order a new trial, where the verdict, though based on legally sufficient evidence, appears in the view of the trial court judge to be unsupported by the substantial, credible evidence. It is a PERVERSE FINDING by a jury in favour of one party when the evidence at trial would appear to strongly support the case of the other. Compare **directed verdict; judgment n.o.v.**

AGE OF MAJORITY Full legal age; adulthood; the age when a child acquires the right to vote and to bind himself to contracts, and the age when support payment may be terminated by parents. Historically, the age of majority was twenty-one, and this common-law notion was adopted by many Canadian provinces. In Canada, since 1970, the age of majority has been reduced to eighteen years in five jurisdictions and to nineteen in six jurisdictions. For example, *Age of Majority Act,* R.S.N.S. 1989, c. 4.

AGENCY The relationship that exists between two persons when one, called the **agent,** is considered in law to represent the other, called the **principal,** in such a way as to be able to affect the principal's legal position, in respect of strangers to the relationship, by the making of contracts and the disposition of property. Agency is a consensual and **fiduciary** relationship between the parties. See *Bruton* v. *Regina City Policeman's Association, Local 155,* [1945] 2 W.W.R. 273 (Sask.C.A.). See also **apparent authority; respondeat superior; scope of employment.** Compare **partnership.**

AGENT One who, by mutual consent, acts for the benefit of another; one authorized by a party to act on that party's

behalf. Compare **servant; contractor** [INDEPENDENT CONTRACTOR].

AGGRAVATED ASSAULT A form of **assault** that is more heinous than common assault and that provides for a more severe penalty upon conviction. Sections 266 and 270 of the *Criminal Code*, R.S.C. 1985, c. C–46, deal with aggravated assault. See *R.* v. *Stenning,* [1970] S.C.R. 631. In *R.* v. *MacTavish* (1972), 8 C.C.C. (2d) 206 (N.B.S.C.A.D.), a fight between two schoolboys was held to be aggravated assault where one participant used excessive force such as kicks in the head. Common assault is an included offence where the specific intent to inflict injury is not proven. *R.* v. *Wilson,* [1955] 1 All E.R. 744 (C.C.A.).

AGGRIEVED PARTY/PERSONS [or PERSONS AGGRIEVED] 1. One who has been injured or has suffered a loss; **2.** the statutory meaning when discussing the right of the aggrieved party to appeal an **order, conviction, judgment** or determination. "[T]he words 'person aggrieved' do not really mean a man who is disappointed of a benefit which he might have received if some other order had been made. A 'person aggrieved' must be a man who has suffered a legal grievance, a man against whom a decision has been pronounced which has wrongfully deprived him of something, or wrongfully refused him something, or wrongfully affected his title to something." *Ex parte Sidebotham* (1880), 14 Ch.D. 458 at 465, cited and followed in *Re Workmen's Compensation Bd.* (1976), 14 N.S.R. (2d) 693 at 700 (S.C.A.D.); *Halifax Atlantic Invest. Ltd.* v. *City of Halifax* (1978), 28 N.S.R. (2d) 193 at 214 (S.C.A.D.).

AGREEMENT See **contract.**

AID AND ABET To actively or intentionally assist another individual in the commission or attempted commission of a crime. To abet is to encourage or instigate a crime to be committed, whereas to aid means to assist without necessarily encouraging the actor or **principal.** The distinction can be important where the words are used separately, since there are defences available to one charge, but not the other and vice versa. *R.* v. *Rhyno* (1944), 83 C.C.C. 186 (N.S.S.C.). See

A. Mewett & M. Manning, *Criminal Law,* 45–51 (2d ed. 1985). See *Criminal Code,* R.S.C. 1985, c. C–46, ss. 21–22, 463–466. See also **attempt, abet.** Compare **accessory; accomplice; conspirator.**

ALEATORY Uncertain; risky, involving an element of chance.

ALEATORY CONTRACT An agreement, the performance of which by one party depends upon the occurrence of a **contingent** event. An ALEATORY PROMISE is one, the performance of which is by its own terms subject to the happening of an uncertain and fortuitous event or upon some fact the existence or part occurrence of which is also uncertain and undetermined. Examples of such contracts include life and fire insurance contracts. Such agreements are enforceable notwithstanding an uncertainty of terms at the time of the making so long as the risk undertaken clearly appears. A contract where performance is contingent upon the outcome of a bet, however, is a gambling contract and is generally unenforceable by statute or as a matter of public policy.

ALIAS 1. Otherwise known as. **2.** A fictitious name used to disguise one's true identity.

ALIBI A provable account of an individual's whereabouts at the time of the commission of a crime, which would make it impossible or impracticable to place him at the scene of the crime. An alibi therefore negates the physical possibility that the suspected individual could have committed the crime. See, e.g., *R.* v. *O'Neill & Cameron* (1973), 22 C.R.N.S. 359 (N.B.S.C.A.D.).

ALIEN A person born in a foreign country, who owes his allegiance to that country; one not a citizen of the country in which he is living. In Canada, see, e.g., *Citizenship Act,* R.S.C. 1985, c. C–29, ss. 32–39 (status of persons in Canada) and *Immigration Act,* R.S.C. 1985, c. I–2. The term *alien* was dropped from statutory use when these statutes repealed the earlier *Canadian Citizenship Act* and the *Alien Labour Act.*

ALIENABLE Capable of being transferred. See **alienation.**

ALIENATION In the law of **real property,** the voluntary and absolute transfer of **title** and **possession** of real property from one person to another. The law recognizes the power to alienate property as one of the essential ingredients of **fee simple** ownership, and therefore unreasonable restraints on alienation are generally prohibited as contrary to public policy. See, e.g., **Rule Against Perpetuities.**

ALIENATION OF AFFECTION A **tort** that establishes a cause of action for one spouse to sue a third party for **damages** for misconduct that enticed away the marital partner and in that way alienated the affections of the one spouse for the other.

The interference or **enticement** may be (but not necessarily) **adultery** (a tort called **criminal conversation**). *Kungl* v. *Schiefer,* [1962] S.C.R. 443, held that no separate action lay in Ontario for alienation of affection, but alienation was merely in support of the claim for **damages** in an enticement action.

ALIMONY "[T]he word alimony is properly and usually used in reference to financial support payments where the marriage tie still subsists as in the case of judicial separation or in reference to payments for the wife's support pending the hearing of a divorce petition. The word maintenance is the proper term to be used in reference to payments subsequent to the divorce decree." *Black* v. *Hubenet* (1951), 2 W.W.R. (N.S.) 694 at 695 (B.C.S.C.).

Actions for alimony separate from another action are unknown at common law; the right to take action for alimony alone is derived from provincial legislation, e.g., *Alimony Act,* R.S.N.S. 1989, c. 10; *Family Law Act,* R.S.O. 1990, c. F. 3.

ALIQUOT *(ä'-lē-kwō)* Lat.: some; so many. An even part of the whole; one part contained in a whole that is evenly divisible without leaving a **remainder,** as in **real property.** See, e.g., *Re Pinewood Aggregates Ltd. & Director of Titles,* [1964] 1 O.R. 83 at 85–87 (H.C.).

ALIUNDE *(äl-ē-ŭn'-dē)* Lat.: from another source. EVIDENCE ALIUNDE refers to evidence from an outside source.

ALL AND SINGULAR All without exception. A comprehensive term often employed in conveyances, **wills,** and the like that includes the whole and also each of the separate items.

ALLEGATION In **pleading,** an assertion of fact; a statement of the issue that the contributing party is prepared to prove.

ALLOCUTION The requirement at **common law** that, upon the **verdict** of conviction, the trial judge address the **accused** asking him to show legal cause why the sentence of conviction should not be pronounced. Modern appellate procedures have eliminated the original purposes for this formal address. The modern allocution does not ask the **accused** why **sentence** ought not be imposed but rather asks for any statement that he would like to make on his own behalf in mitigation of punishment. See **mitigating circumstances.**

ALLODIAL Owned freely without obligation to one with superior right; not subject to the restriction on **alienation** that existed with feudal **tenures;** free of any superior rights vested in another, such as a lord. No person can now have such an absolute property, since the highest estate is in **fee simple.**

ALLOTMENT The act of assigning a share. In corporate law, "the acceptance by resolution of the board of directors of the application for shares (in a company)." D. Horsley, H. Sutherland, and J. Edmiston, *Fraser's Handbook on Canadian Company Law* 108 (7th ed. 1985). "Allotment is generally neither more nor less than the acceptance by the company of the offer to take shares." *Imperial Bank of Canada* v. *Dennis* (1926), 59 O.L.R. 20 at 23 (S.C.A.D.).

ALLUREMENT [DOCTRINE OF] "[T]he presence, in a frequented place, of some object of attraction, tempting [a child] to meddle where he ought to abstain [constitutes] a trap, and in the case of a child too young to be capable of contributory negligence, it may impose full liability on the owner or occupier, if he ought, as a reasonable man, have anticipated the presence of the child and the attractiveness and peril of the object." *Latham* v. *R. Johnson & Nephew Ltd.,* [1913] 1 K.B. 398 (C.A.), cited and applied in *Daneau* v. *Trynor Construction Co. Ltd.* (1972),

24 D.L.R. (3d) 434 at 442 (N.S.S.C.). (A deep trench with a sandpile on its bank was considered an allurement.) See also *Leadbetter* v. *The Queen* (1970), 12 D.L.R. (3d) 738 (Ex.Ct.) (mailboxes as allurement to young children).

ALLUVION Deposits of sedimentary material (earth, sand, gravel, etc.) that have accumulated gradually and imperceptibly along the bank of a river, lake, or sea. Alluvion is the result of **accretion** and becomes part of the property on which it settles or becomes attached, if it is "gradual and imperceptible in its progress." *Standly* v. *Perry* (1879). 3 S.C.R. 356. See also **Avulsion; reliction.**

ALTERNATIVE DISPUTE RESOLUTION Processes that deal with legal disputes and problems outside of the civil court system. The aim of alternative dispute resolution is to achieve efficient and effective resolutions with a process that is less expensive than the traditional **civil action** route. The processes include mediation, negotiation, and arbitration.

ALTERNATIVE PLEADING Or "pleading in the alternative" as, e.g., in a **statement of defence.** In raising an **affirmative defence,** the defendant will "admit the relevant allegation made by the plaintiff, but then set forth further facts which, if true, avoid the legal consequences argued for by the plaintiff." This plea can be combined with a **traverse** where the defendant denies the plaintiff's allegations placing "the facts denied in issue and the plaintiff then has the burden of proving those facts to the satisfaction of the court at trial." G. Watson, *Canadian Civil Procedure* 369 (3d ed. 1988). For example "a defendant may first deny that a contract was made and then go on to plead in the alternative that if there was a contract as alleged, it was subsequently terminated by further agreement." *Id.* at 370.

AMALGAMATION See **merger.**

AMBIGUITY A double or doubtful meaning. In the case of a written instrument, such as a **will,** a PATENT AMBIGUITY is one that is apparent on the face of the document and a LATENT AMBIGUITY is one that becomes apparent only in the light of surrounding circumstances. See, e.g., *In re Smalley,* [1929] 2 Ch. 112 (C.A.).

AMEND To change, to improve upon. A legislature amends an established law by passing a **statute** (AMENDMENT) that continues the law in changed form. One amends an already existing **pleading** by an addition or a subtraction.

AMICUS CURIAE *(ä-mē'-kŭs kyŭ'-rē-ī)* Lat.: friend of the court. One who gives information to the court on some matter of law that is in doubt. "Also the term is used of persons who have no right to appear in a suit but are allowed to protect their own interest, and finally, of a stranger who, being in Court, calls the Court's attention to some error in the proceedings." *In re Alfred Pehlke* (1939), 20 C.B.R. 415 at 421 (Ont.S.C.).

AMNESTY An act of oblivion for past acts, granted by a government to persons accused of crimes generally of a political nature, e.g., **treason, sedition,** desertion. Legally, amnesty differs from **pardon** in that pardon implies guilt, whereas amnesty does not. Amnesty is the abolition and forgetfulness of the offence.

AMORTIZATION The gradual **extinguishment** of a debt; "the system of repayment of a debt by instalments of principal and interest at the same time, in order to extinguish the debt within a fixed period....The payments are equal in amount and are applied in payment of the accrued interest and a portion of the principal." *Price* v. *Green,* [1951] 4 D.L.R. 596 at 599–600 (Man.C.A.).

ANCIENT LIGHTS The right to light; windows through which the access of light has been enjoyed otherwise than by consent or permission for twenty years and upwards. The right to light has been abolished by statute in some Canadian provinces. See *The Statute of Limitations,* R.S.N.S. 1989, c. 258, s. 33.

ANCILLARY RELIEF Incidental relief, such as an **injunction** where **damages** are the main remedy asked for.

ANIMALS See **ferae naturae.**

ANIMO *(än'-ī-mō)* Lat.: with the intention; purposefully.

ANIMO REVERTENDI The intention to return.

ANIMO REVOCANDI The intention to re**voke.**

ANIMO TESTANDI The intention to make a **will.**

ANNUITANT One who receives the benefits of an **annuity.**

ANNUITY A fixed sum payable periodically, subject to the limitations imposed by the **grantor.** "Ordinarily an annuity is thought of as a series of annual payments which a person has purchased or arranged for with a sum of money or other assets of a capital nature." *W. M. O'Connor* v. *Minister of National Revenue,* [1943] 4 D.L.R. 160 at 167 (Ex.Ct.).

ANNUL To make void; to dissolve what once existed, as to annul the bonds of matrimony. A marriage that is annulled by an **ACTION FOR ANNULMENT** [to have the marriage declared NULL AND VOID— a "declaration of **nullity**"] is void **ab initio,** as compared to a marriage that is dissolved by a decree of **divorce;** divorce only terminates the marriage from that point forward and does not affect the former validity of the marriage. See, e.g., *R.* v. *R.* (1976), 18 N.S.R. (2d) 662 (S.C.A.D.).

ANSWER In pleading, a **defence** on the facts (presented in a **proceeding**). The term also applies more broadly to the **statement of defence,** in which the **accused** or **defendant** "can invoke every means in fact and law to meet the **charge** [or defeat the action]." *R.* v. *Romer* (1914), 23 C.C.C. 235 (Police Ct., Montreal).

ANTICIPATORY BREACH [OF CONTRACT] A **breach** committed before the actual time of required **performance.** It occurs when one party by words or conduct refuses to perform or disables himself from so doing. The terms **renunciation** and repudiation are also used when a party who has partly performed the **contract** refuses by words or conduct to further perform it. See *Hochester* v. *de la Tour* (1853), 2 El. & Bl. 678; 118 E.R. 922. When there has been an anticipatory breach, the **aggrieved party** may (1) treat the contract as at an end for all purposes except that of bringing an action on it for the breach committed by the other in renouncing, or (2) treat it as at an end and sue on a **quantum meruit** for a reasonable reward for service by the aggrieved party under the contract, or (3) treat the contract as still operative, wait for the time of performance, and then hold the other party responsible for all the consequences of non-performance. See *Frost* v. *Knight* (1872), L.R. 7 Ex. 111 at 112.

ANTITRUST LAWS See **combines legislation.**

A POSTERIORI *(ä pŏs-tĕr-ē-ô'-rē)* Lat.: from the latter. From the most recent point of view. Relates to factual knowledge that can be known only from experience. The term relates to the means by which a concept or proposition is known or validated. It is distinguished from **a priori** reasoning, in which a proposition is known or validated solely through logical necessity, rather than actual experience or observation.

APPLICATION FOR PARTICULARS See **bill of particulars.**

APPARENT AUTHORITY Ostensible authority; a doctrine involving the accountability of a **principal** for the acts of his **agent:** "Where a person, by words or conduct, represents or permits it to be represented that another person has authority to act on his behalf, he is bound by the acts of such other person with respect to anyone dealing with him as an agent on the faith of any such representation, to the same extent as if such other person had the authority that he was represented to have, even though he had no actual authority." F. Reynolds & B. Davenport, *Bowstead on Agency* (13th ed. 1968), cited and followed in *Cowe and Ritzhaupt* v. *United Contractors Ltd. and United Contractors (Moncton) Ltd.* (1975), 13 N.B.R. (2d) 573 at 577 (S.C.). See also *Clermont* v. *Mid-West Steel Products Ltd.* (1965), 51 D.L.R. (2d) 340 (Sask. Q.B.).

APPEAL An application for judicial review by a superior court of an inferior court's decision. The judicial system in all Canadian **jurisdictions** provides for a right of appeal in almost all cases. See *Clark* v. *Chutorian; Clark* v. *Orloff,* [1955] 2 D.L.R. 472 (Man.C.A.). In the provinces the appeal from the trial decision will be to the Court of Appeal.

Most appeals deal with errors of law, such as incorrect instruction by the trial judge to the jury, misapplication of the law to the facts, or admitting of **evidence** that is challenged as inadmissible on appeal.

Appeals are argued on the basis of trial transcripts, which form the basis of the APPEAL BOOK, containing the written record of evidence given by witnesses at trial, **affidavits,** the decision and any other pertinent documents or exhibits. The **appellant,** or party who initiates the appeal, files a **factum** containing a statement of facts and an outline of the legal points on which he bases his case. The **respondent** files a similar document. The time period allowed before the right to appeal is lost is set out in the various procedure rules in the provinces.

Further appeals from the provincial courts are to the **Supreme Court of Canada,** the court of final appeal for both civil and criminal matters. Appeals to the Supreme Court are heard where permission has been granted by the provincial appeal court. Also there are automatic rights to appeal (1) in criminal cases where an acquittal has been set aside and there has been a dissenting judgment on a point of law and (2) (prior to abolition) in capital murder convictions. In civil cases, appeals are heard only if leave is given on a matter of public importance, or on an important issue of law or mixed fact and law. See *Supreme Court Act*, R.S.C. 1985, c. S–26, ss. 35–43. See also **appellate court.**

APPEAL, COURT OF See **appellate court.**

APPEARANCE 1. The coming into court by a **party summoned** in an **action,** either by himself or through his lawyer. **2.** The voluntary submitting of oneself to the **jurisdiction** of the court. To enter an appearance, the defendant, in answer to the originating notice or summons would lodge a memorandum of appearance in the office of the court and by having so appeared, the defendant submitted to the jurisdiction of the court. "This procedure has itself now been replaced [in some jurisdictions] by the new procedure entitled 'Acknowledgement of Service.' Under the new provisions ... a defendant who wishes to defend the action [would] complete the Acknowledgement of Service, which accompanies the writ served on him, and return it within the prescribed time [usually fourteen days] to the court office out of which the writ was issued." D. Casson & I. Dennis, *Odgers' Principles of Pleading and Practice* 14 (22d ed. 1981). (For each Canadian jurisdiction, see the provincial *Civil Procedure Rules*.)

APPEARANCE GRATIS An appearance entered before service of summons. A defendant, being aware that **proceedings** have been instituted, can enter such an appearance. This is a substantive right of the defendant to expedite proceedings, since the service of summons is for the benefit of the defendant, and he can waive that right. *Otto* v. *Massel* (1973), 2 O.R. (2d) 706 (H.C.).

APPEARANCE "UNDER PROTEST" See, e.g., *Nelson* v. *Payne* (1968), 64 W.W.R. 175 (B.C.S.C.). An appearance of specific application: "a person served as a partner in a firm, who denies that he was a partner or liable as such, may enter an appearance under protest." *Id.*

COMPULSORY APPEARANCE An appearance in court by one who has been validly served process and so is compelled to appear.

CONDITIONAL APPEARANCE "Where a defendant desires to dispute the jurisdiction of the court to hear the action, by contending that the order permitting service EX JURIS [outside of the jurisdiction] should not properly have been made, he may enter a conditional appearance by leave." W. Williston & R. Rolls, *The Law of Civil Procedure* 358 (1970). Distinguished from UNCONDITIONAL APPEARANCE, whereby the defendant "attorns to the territorial jurisdiction of the court" and "waives the right to subsequently contest the jurisdiction." *Id.* See, e.g., *Proteau* v. *Levesque* (1976), 13 N.B.R. (2d) 323 (S.C.); *Berry & Berry* v. *Banavage* (1969), 70 W.W.R. 702 (B.C.S.C.).

APPEARANCE NOTICE According to the *Criminal Code*, R.S.C. 1985, c. C–46, ss. 493–529, a peace officer can compel the appearance of an **accused** before a justice to answer a **charge** (if the officer does not arrest him immediately)

by serving the accused with an appearance notice. See especially ss. 496 and 501 (contents of an appearance notice). See, e.g., *R.* v. *Burton* (1977), 35 C.C.C. (2d) 292 (B.C.Prov.Ct.). The notice sets out the name of the accused, the substance of the charge, and the time and place the accused must attend court to answer the charge.

APPELLANT The party who appeals a decision; the party who brings the proceeding to a reviewing or **appellate court.** Compare **respondent.**

APPELLATE COURT [COURT OF APPEAL] A court having **jurisdiction** to review the law as applied to a prior determination of the same case. In most instances a **trial court** first decides a lawsuit, with review then available in one or more appellate courts. In Canada, appeals may be heard by the supreme courts, the provincial courts of appeal, and the **Supreme Court of Canada.**

The powers of the appellate court are very broad, ranging from the right to **affirm,** vary, or **reverse** a decision of a lower court. The most important limitation regards the findings of fact by the trial court, which cannot be the basis of an appeal, notwithstanding that the appeal court would have come to a different finding. See also **appeal.**

APPELLATE JURISDICTION See **appeal; appellate court.**

APPLICATION FOR PARTICULARS See **particulars, bill of.**

APPOINTED DAY A day fixed for the coming into force of a statute.

APPOINTMENT, POWER OF See **power of appointment.**

APPORTION To divide fairly or according to the parties' respective interests—proportionately, but not necessarily equally (as in apportionment legislation respecting **joint tortfeasors,** e.g., *Tortfeasors Act,* R.S.N.S. 1989, c. 471).

APPRAISE To estimate the value; to put in writing the worth of property.

APPRECIATE 1. To incrementally increase in value. Compare **depreciation. 2.** To be aware of the value or worth of a thing or person. **3.** In criminal law, as part of the mental disorder test, the word is used to signify the **accused**'s subjective understanding of the wrongfulness of his conduct: Appreciate "involves more than mere knowledge of the physical nature of the act being committed. There must be an appreciation of the factors involved in that act and a capacity to measure and foresee the consequences of the act. ... Appreciate is not synonymous with 'know.' " *R.* v. *Baltzer* (1974), 27 C.C.C. (2d) 118 at 136 (N.S.S.C.A.D.); followed in *R.* v. *Barnier* (1977), 37 C.C.C. (2d) 508 (B.C.C.A.). See *Criminal Code*, R.S.C. 1985, c. C–46, s. 16.

APPREHEND To arrest or seize a person; " 'apprehension' means the seizure or taking hold of a man....It means the taking hold of him and detaining him with a view to his ultimate surrender." *R.* v. *Commercial Brokerage Co. Ltd.*, [1922] 3 W.W.R. 508 (Alta.S.C.).

APPROPRIATE "[T]o exercise dominion over **property** to the extent and for the purpose of making it subserve to one's own proper use and pleasure." *Re Levy* (1924), 26 O.W.N. 300 at 301 (Wk.Ct.).
"To set apart for or assign to a particular purpose, person, or use, to the exclusion of others." *Re Somerville* (1926), 31 O.W.N. 289 at 290 (H.C.).
Compare **conversion; misapplication of property.**

APPROVAL, SALE ON Sale of a **chattel** with the buyer's reserved right to return the goods if not satisfied with them. If he does not return them within a reasonable period, he will be deemed to have accepted them. The **property** in the goods does not pass until the buyer has accepted or has been deemed to accept the goods. *Sale of Goods Act,* R.S.O. 1990, c. S–1, s. 19, r. 4.
The acceptance may be by words or conduct or "any act which is consistent only with his being purchaser." See *Kirkham* v. *Attenborough*, [1897] 1 Q.B. 201. Or the acceptance may be by keeping the goods beyond a reasonable time. *Massh* v. *Hughes-Hallett* (1900), 16 T.L.R. 376 (Q.B.).

APPURTENANT Attached to something else; annexed to, or inseparably connected with. See *R.* v. *Bear* (1968), 63 W.W.R. 754 at 757 (Sask.Dist.Ct.).
In the law of **real property,** the term refers especially to a burden (e.g., an

easement or **covenant**) that is attached to a piece of land and benefits or restricts the owner of such land in his use and enjoyment thereof.

À PRENDRE *(ä prän'-dr')* Fr.: to take, seize. In property law, a PROFIT À PRENDRE is the right to enter on the land of another to take some profit of the soil that is capable of ownership, such as minerals, soil, or trees, for the use of the owner of the right. It is an **incorporeal hereditament** and may be held as a **right in gross.** See *Cherry* v. *Petch,* [1948] O.W.N. 378 (H.C.).
A profit à prendre may be created by **statute, grant,** reservation, or **prescription,** and is to be distinguished from an **easement.**

A PRIORI *(ä prē-ô'-rē)* Lat.: from the preceding; from the first. To reason a priori is to reason with the historical knowledge of certain proven facts, so that certain factual situations that follow in time must follow the reasoning of those truths; e.g., if X is true, then it may be deduced that certain subsequent facts will necessarily follow.

ARBITER A referee, umpire; one appointed informally to decide a controversy, according to the law, although the decision maker is not a judicial officer.

ARBITRATION The settling of a dispute by an **arbitrator;** where arbitrators cannot agree they may appoint an umpire. The decision of an arbitrator is known as an AWARD. See **collective bargaining.**

ARBITRATOR An impartial person, chosen by the parties to resolve a dispute between them, who is vested with the power to make a final determination concerning the issue(s) in controversy. Historically, an arbitrator was said to be bound only by his own discretion, and not restricted by the rules of law or equity. This distinction between an **arbiter** and an arbitrator appears not to be used in the modern context, and the powers and duties of an arbitrator may be just as regulated by law. In Canadian law, the term appears to be used more often in the formal, legal context. It is often synonymous with *umpire* or **referee.** Provision for **arbitration** is made in many provincial statutes. See, e.g., *Arbitration Act,* 1991, S.O. 1991, c. 17. See also *Labour Relations Act,* R.S.O. 1990, c. L. 2, s. 45.

ARGUENDO *(är-gyū-ĕn'-dō)* Lat.: in the course of his argument; for the sake of argument. For example, "Let us assume arguendo that *X* is true." A person arguing in this fashion is not being inconsistent if he later argues that *X* is not true.

ARGUMENT Persuasion by giving reasons; a connected series of statements intended to establish or subvert a position and to induce belief. Often refers specially to an oral argument in appellate **advocacy.**

ARM'S LENGTH, AT A phrase to describe a relationship between two parties who are unrelated or strangers; thus each owes no special obligation to the other party. The term is commonly applied in areas of taxation, corporate law, and **contracts,** describing parties who carry out a particular transaction, each acting in self-interest.

ARRAIGN To call a person in custody to answer the **charge** under which an **indictment** has been handed down. See **arraignment.**

ARRAIGNMENT In criminal procedure, "the calling of the **accused** to the **bar** of that court to plead to a charge made against him ... the clerk of the court will call the accused by name to appear before the presiding judge. He will then read the charges set out in the indictment or information to the accused and ask him to plead to each count." R. Salhany, *Canadian Criminal Procedure* c. 6 at 49–50 (6th ed. 1994). The accused is also put to his election, to have a trial by judge alone or by jury, where the choice is open to him. See *Criminal Code,* R.S.C. 1985, c. C–46, ss. 562, 606, and especially 801. See also *R.* v. *Fraser & Louie* (1971). 17 C.R.N.S. 164 (B.C.C.A.); *R* v. *Smith* (1972), 7 C.C.C. (2d) 174 (Ont.C.A.).

ARRANGEMENT A contract between a creditor and a debtor that becomes binding on the parties by statute; a contemplation of some arrangement between a debtor and a creditor whereby the debtor's assets will be rested or controlled by the trustee in bankruptcy while the arrangement is being carried out. The arrangement is a plan for a settlement, a satisfaction, or an extension of the time of payment of debts. See generally *Bankruptcy and Insolvency Act,* R.S.C. 1985.

c. B–3, ss. 50–66, as amended by S.C. 1992, c. 27, s. 32.

ARREARS That which is unpaid, though due to be paid. A person IN ARREARS is behind in payment. "[S]omething which is behind in payment, or which remains unpaid, as, for instance, arrears of rent, meaning rent not paid at the time agreed upon by the tenant. It means a duty and a default." *Corbett* v. *Taylor* (1864), 23 U.C.Q.B. 454 at 455.

ARREST To deprive an alleged or suspected offender of his liberty by legal authority, by "the actual seizure or touching of [the] person's body with a view to his detention. The mere pronouncing of words of arrest is not an arrest, unless the person sought to be arrested submits to the process and goes with the arresting officer. Arrest may be made either with or without a **warrant.**" 10 *Halsbury's Laws of England* 342 (3d ed.), cited and followed in *R.* v. *Whitfield* (1970), 9 C.R.N.S. 59 at 60 (S.C.C.). See also *Criminal Code,* R.S.C. 1985, c. C–46, ss. 494–495.

Section 10 of the **Canadian Charter of Rights and Freedoms** provides for rights on arrest or **detention** including the right to counsel (see *R.* v. *Brydges* (1990), 74 C.R. (3d) 129 (S.C.C.)) and the right to be informed without reasonable delay of the charge. See **Canadian Charter of Rights and Freedoms—Legal rights.**

ARREST OF JUDGMENT The court's withholding of **judgment** because of some technical error apparent from the face of the **record.**

ARSON An **indictable offence** of willfully setting fire to personal (see **personalty**) or **real property.** See *Criminal Code,* R.S.C. 1985, c. C–46, ss. 433–436; *R.* v. *Jorgenson* (1954), 111 C.C.C. 30 (B.C.C.A.).

ARTICLES OF CLERKSHIP [ARTICLING] Serving a period of apprenticeship (articling) prior to admission to the practice of law. The bar societies in the common law provinces of Canada require a period (normally eight to twelve months, depending upon the jurisdiction) in which the ARTICLED CLERK works in a law office under the supervision of a qualified practitioner with a certain number of years of experience at the bar. In recent years, all or part of the articling period may be served other than with a private law firm, e.g., by working in certain federal or provincial government departments, or by working as a clerk to a judge of the Supreme Court of Canada or to a Supreme Court judge in certain provincial courts.

ARTICLES OF INCORPORATION In Canada, a memorandum of association. See **association, memorandum of.**

ARTIFICE A fraud or a cunning device used to accomplish some evil; usually implies craftiness or deceitfulness. See *R.* v. *Leger* (1975), 28 C.C.C. (2d) 480 (Ont.Co.Ct.).

ARTIFICIAL PERSON A legal entity, not a human being, recognized as a person in law to whom legal rights and duties may attach—e.g., a body corporate. *The Interpretation Act,* R.S.O. 1990, c. I. 11, s. 29(1), states that "person" includes a corporation and the heirs, executors, administrators, or other legal representatives of a person to whom the context can apply according to law. See **corporation.**

ASSAULT In criminal law, the intentional application of force to the person of another without his consent, or the attempt or threat by act or gesture to apply force to another, if the other believes one has the apparent, present ability to do so. See *Criminal Code*, R.S.C. 1985, c. C–46, ss. 265–278. "There must be a threatening act or gesture and no mere words can amount to an assault." *R.* v. *Byrne* (1968), 63 W.W.R. 385 at 387 (B.C.C.A.).

As one of the intentional **torts,** assault "is the intentional creation of the apprehension of imminent harmful or offensive contact." A. Linden, *Canadian Tort Law,* 42 (5th ed. 1993).

Because an assault need not result in a touching so as to constitute a **battery,** no physical injury need be proved to establish an assault. An assault being both a personal tort and a criminal offence, it may be the basis for a civil **action** and/or a criminal **prosecution.**

AGGRAVATED ASSAULT   Any of a variety of serious assaults or particularly reprehensible behaviour calling for a more severe punishment. The *Criminal Code*, R.S.C. 1985, c. C–46, ss. 267, 268, makes a distinction between common assault and assault causing bodily harm, with the latter being one example of aggravated assault. Common assault is an offence punishable on **summary conviction,** whereas assault causing bodily harm is an **indictable** offence carrying a maximum five-year imprisonment. See **sexual assault.**

ASSEMBLY, FREEDOM OF [ASSEMBLY, FREEDOM OF PEACEFUL] The right of the people to meet for any purpose connected with the government; it encompasses meeting to protest government policies and action and the promotion of ideas. See *Dupond* v. *City of Montreal* (1978), 19 N.R. 478 (S.C.C.).

Section 2(c) of the **Canadian Charter of Rights and Freedoms** guarantees freedom of peaceful assembly as a fundamental freedom. See *Re Fraser et al and Attorney-General of Nova Scotia* (1986), 30 D.L.R. (4th) 340 (N.S.S.C.).

ASSEMBLY, UNLAWFUL See **unlawful assembly.**

ASSENT Consent; agreement. See **royal assent.**

ASSESS To determine the value of something; to fix the value of **property** upon which a tax will be imposed.

ASSETS Anything of value; any interest in **real property** or **personal property** that can be **appropriated** for the payment of **debts.**

ASSIGN To transfer one's interest in **property, contract,** or other rights to another. See **assignment of a contract.**

ASSIGNMENT The act whereby one transfers to another his **interest** in a right or **property.**

ASSIGNMENT OF A CONTRACT Generally, the **common law** did not recognize assignments of debts or other contractual rights, although the **Courts of Equity** did assist the assignee by compelling the assignor to bring an **action** or to allow his name to be used as nominal **plaintiff** in an action brought by the assignee. With passage of the English *Supreme Court of Judicature Act, 1873,* specific provision was made for assignment, subject to certain formalities such as writing and notice. Some Canadian jurisdictions have adopted the English provisions. See, e.g., *Conveyancing and Law of Property Act,* R.S.O.

1990, c. C. 34, s. 53(1); *Judicature Act,* R.S.N.S. 1989, c. 240, s. 43(5).

For more detailed treatment see, e.g., G. Fridman, *The Law of Contract in Canada* 619 (2d ed., 1986).

ASSIGNMENT FOR BENEFIT OF CREDITORS A transfer by a **debtor** of his property to an assignee in **trust** to apply that which is transferred to the debts of the ASSIGNOR (debtor). See *Bankruptcy and Insolvency Act,* R.S.C. 1985, c. B–3, ss. 42, 49.

ASSIGNMENT OF A LEASE A transfer of the **lessee's** entire interest in the **lease.** When there exists an express **covenant** in the original lease to pay rent, the assignor (the original **tenant**) remains secondarily liable to the **landlord** after an assignment. Compare **sublease; subtenant.**

ASSIGNS All those who take from or under the ASSIGNOR, whether by **conveyance, devise, descent,** or **operation of law.**

ASSISTANCE, WRIT OF An obsolete writ used by the English Court of Chancery to enforce an order for possession of land. In Canada, "after a number of constitutional challenges, writs of assistance were abolished." R. Salhany, *Canadian Criminal Procedure* c. 3 at 68 (6th ed. 1994). See e.g., *R.* v. *Noble* (1984), 14 D.L.R. (4th) 216 (Ont. C.A.), where provisions for searches under the *Narcotic Control Act,* R.S.C. 1985, c. N-1, and the *Food and Drugs Act,* R.S.C. 1985, c. F-27, authorized by writs of assistance were found to violate s. 8 of the **Charter of Rights and Freedoms** and be of **no force and effect.**

ASSIZE [or ASSISE] **1.** An ancient **writ** issued from a court of assize to the **sheriff** for the recovery of property; **2.** the actions of the special court that issued the writ. See **Court of Assize and Nisi Prius. 3.** Assizes may also refer to the sittings of a court, e.g., the sittings of judges on circuit to the major cities or towns of a province.

ASSOCIATION, ARTICLES OF Regulations, prescribed by statute, concerning the internal management of a company. See, e.g., *Companies Act,* R.S.N.S. 1989, c. 81, ss. 20–23 and Sched. 1, Table C.

ASSOCIATION, MEMORANDUM OF The document, prescribed by statute, regulating the **incorporation** of a company. Generally, the memorandum must state the name of the company, its objectives and the number of shares the company proposes to issue. See, e.g., *Companies Act,* R.S.N.S. 1989, c. 81, ss. 9–19.

ASSUMPSIT *(à-sŭmp'-sĭt)* Lat.: he promised; he undertook. In the old **forms of action,** an ACTION OF ASSUMPSIT lay whenever the defendant had promised to do something or not to do something, and then breached his undertaking. It was a method for the enforcement of contracts not under **seal** and came to cover the whole sphere of simple contracts. In the historical sense, assumpsit is the foundation of our modern law of simple contract. Compare **trespass** [TRESPASS ON THE CASE].

ASSUMPTION OF THE RISK In the law of **torts,** an **affirmative defence** used by the **defendant** to a **negligence** suit in which it is claimed that **plaintiff** had knowledge of a situation obviously dangerous to himself and yet, impliedly or expressly, assented voluntarily to expose himself to the hazard created by the defendant, who is thereby relieved of legal responsibility for resulting injury. "If people consent to run the risk of injury ... they are 'co-authors' of the harm inflicted upon themselves." A. Linden, *Canadian Tort Law* 456 (5th ed., 1993).

Assumption of risk is based fundamentally on consent, whereas CONTRIBUTORY NEGLIGENCE (see **negligence**) arises when the plaintiff fails to exercise **due care.** See *Lagasse* v. *Rural Municipality of Richot,* [1973] 4 W.W.R. 181 (Man.Q.B.).

ASSURED See **insured.**

ASYLUM 1. A shelter for the unfortunate or afflicted, e.g., for the insane, the crippled, the poor, etc. **2.** A POLITICAL ASYLUM is a state that accepts a citizen of another state as a shelter from prosecution by that other state.

ATTACHMENT A **proceeding** in law by which a defendant's **property** is seized and held in legal custody on application by the plaintiff, to be applied against a claim on which the plaintiff seeks a **judgment** against the defendant, e.g., in an action for a debt. See, e.g., *Creditors' Relief Act*, R.S.O. 1990, c. C. 45. See also **garnishment; replevin.**

ATTAINDER See **bill of attainder.**

ATTEMPT An overt act, beyond mere preparation, moving directly toward the actual commission of a criminal offence. "When the preparation to commit a crime is in fact fully complete and ended, the next step done by the **accused** for the purpose and with the intention of committing a specific crime constitutes an **actus reus** sufficient in law to establish a criminal attempt to commit that crime." *R. v. Cline* (1956), 115 C.C.C. 18 at 29 (Ont.C.A.). See *Criminal Code*, R.S.C. 1985, c. C–46, s. 24, which establishes attempt as a separate and complete offence in itself. See also *R. v. Godfrey*, [1974] 4 W.W.R. 677 (Alta. S.C.A.D.). The *Criminal Code* also establishes sanctions for attempts of specific crimes: see, e.g., s. 239 [attempted murder]; s. 322(2) [attempted theft].

ATTEST To affirm as true; to sign one's name as a **witness** to the **execution** of a document; to bear witness to. See *Ridley v. McGregor & Canadian Bank of Commerce*, [1934] 2 D.L.R. 399 (Ont.C.A.).

ATTORNEY, POWER OF See **power of attorney.**

ATTORNEY-GENERAL [OF CANADA OR OF A PROVINCE] The chief law officer of the Crown; the minister in the **Cabinet** responsible for the public prosecution of criminal offenders and for advising the government with respect to legal matters. The Attorney-General is a member of Parliament or of a provincial legislature, appointed to the position by the Crown on the advice of the Prime Minister or the Premier of a province.

ATTRACTIVE NUISANCE See **allurement [doctrine of].**

AUDITOR 1. A public officer charged by law with the duty of examining and approving the payment of public funds; 2. An accountant who performs a similar function for private parties.

AUTREFOIS ACQUIT/CONVICT (ō'-tr' fwä ä'-kē/kōn-vīk') Fr.: formerly acquitted or convicted. See **double jeopardy.**

AVERMENT A positive statement or **allegation** of facts in a pleading as opposed to an argumentative one or one based on inference.

AVULSION An abrupt change in the course of a river or stream, resulting in the sudden loss of part of the land from one **riparian** landowner to another. The sudden and perceptible nature of this change distinguishes avulsion from **accretion.** This distinction is important, for when the change is abrupt, the property in the part separated remains in the original owner, instead of becoming part of the other owner's land, which occurs with gradual accretion. Compare **reliction.** See also **alluvion.**

B

BAD DEBT An uncollectable **debt** that may be written off as a business expense. Such classification is important in tax law. *Associated Investors of Canada Ltd.* v. *M.N.R.*, [1967] 2 Ex.C.R. 96.

BAD FAITH An act undertaken to mislead another party or to neglect the fulfillment of some obligation, not through an honest mistake. Bad faith, or MALA FIDE, is generally used in relation to **fraud.**

BAD TITLE Title that is legally insufficient to **convey** property to the purchaser; title that is not **marketable;** one that a purchaser is not compelled to accept; a radically defective title. A defect in title as opposed to a defect in quality. *Scott* v. *Alvarez*, [1895] 2 Ch. 603 (C.A.).

BAIL Monetary or other security given to insure the **appearance** of the **accused** at every stage of the **proceedings.** Those posting bail are **sureties** or **guarantors,** and the money is the security for the accused's appearance. POSTING BAIL serves two purposes: (1) it relieves the accused of imprisonment and (2) it secures the appearance of the accused at **trial** without burdening the state with the cost and bother of keeping the accused pending trial. Compare **recognizance.**

Absconding while on bail is a criminal offence subject to a penalty. It is an **indictable offence** carrying a two-year term of imprisonment. *Criminal Code,* R.S.C. 1985, c. C–46, s. 145.

The accused is released from the custody of the police and entrusted to his sureties, who are bound to produce him at a specified time and place. Failure to do so results in the forfeiture of the security placed as bail.

Commonly, bail is referred to as JUDICIAL INTERIM RELEASE or PRE-TRIAL RELEASE. See generally *id.*, ss. 493–529.

Section 11(e) of the **Canadian Charter of Rights and Freedoms** provides that "any person charged with an offence has the right not to be denied reasonable bail without just cause."

Bail is in effect a **contract,** but a contract by the person bailed or a third party to indemnify a surety is void as contrary to public policy. *R.* v. *Sanguigni*, [1972] 1 O.R. 826 (Co.Ct.); *R.* v. *Bowman* (1972), 19 C.R.N.S. 4 (Ont.Co.Ct.).

BAIL BOND The document executed to secure the pre-trial release of an individual in **custody** of the law. The **surety's** obligation is satisfied upon the **appearance** of the **accused** at the specified place and time.

BAILEE One to whom the **property** involved in a **bailment** is delivered; the party who holds the goods of another for a specific purpose pursuant to an agreement between the parties; the person to whom possession of goods is entrusted by the owner, but with no intention of transferring ownership.

A bailee acquires a special interest or property in the goods. He is bound to take care of the goods bailed and is liable for **negligence** to an extent that varies with the specifics of negligence. *West* v. *Palmer*, [1943] 3 D.L.R. 400 (N.S.S.C.); *Barbour & Proude* v. *Doucette*, [1942] 2 D.L.R. 624 (P.E.I.S.C.A.D.); *Rutherford & McDonald's Orpheum Garage* v. *Stewart-Warner Sales Co. Ltd.*, [1935] 3 W.W.R. 472 (B.C.Co.Ct.).

BAILIFF A court attendant; a person to whom some authority, **guardianship** or **jurisdiction** is entrusted. A person employed by the **sheriff** to serve **writs** and to make arrests and executions of court orders. The bailiff is bound annually to the sheriff by a bond with **sureties** for the proper execution of his office and is therefore called a BOUND BAILIFF.

BAILMENT The delivery of **personal property** or **chattels** from the **bailor** (he who delivers goods) to the **bailee** (he who receives goods) in **trust,** with a special purpose, to benefit either or both of the parties. The purpose of the trust conforms to an express or implied **contract.** The elements of lawful **possession** and the duty to account for the article as the property of another are important aspects of bailment. *Lessor* v. *Jones* (1920), 47 N.B.R. 318 (S.C.A.D.); *Neil's Tractor & Equipment Ltd.* v. *Butler, Maveety & Meldrum Ltd. and Maryland Casualty Company* (1977), 2 Alta.L.R. (2d) 187 (S.C.).

ACTUAL BAILMENT One established by an actual or constructive delivery of the **property** to the **bailee** or his **agents.**

CONSTRUCTIVE BAILMENT One that arises when the person having **possession** holds it under such circumstances that the law imposes an obligation to deliver to another, even where such person did not come into **possession** voluntarily, and thus no bailment was voluntarily established. *Munn* v. *Wakelin* (1944), 17 M.P.R. 447 (P.E.I.S.C.). A primary example is that of the finder who, although possessing goods without the knowledge or consent of the owner, is deemed to owe him a duty of reasonable care and a duty not to convert the **chattel.**

GRATUITOUS BAILMENT One in which the care and custody of **bailor's** property is accepted without **consideration** by the **bailee.** In this type of bailment, the bailee is liable for the loss of the bailed property only if the loss results from the bailee's gross **negligence.** *King* v. *The Sisters of St. Joseph of the Diocese of Hamilton*, [1952] O.W.N. 345 (H.C.): *Degrace* v. *Central Garage Sales & Service Ltd.* (1979), 24 N.B.R. (2d) 557 (S.C.A.D.).

INVOLUNTARY BAILMENT One that arises whenever the goods of one person have by accident become lodged on another's land or person. If the person upon whose land the **personal property** is located should refuse to deliver the goods to their owner upon demand or to permit him to remove them, he might be liable for **conversion** of said property. *McCutcheon* v. *Lightfoot*, [1929] 1 W.W.R. 694 (Man.C.A.), affirmed [1930] S.C.R. 108.

BAILOR The party who bails or delivers goods, **chattels,** or **personal property** to another in a contract or **bailment.** The bailor need not be the owner of the property involved. *Reichardt* v. *Shard* (1914), 31 T.L.R. 24 (C.A.).

BAIT To set one animal against another that is confined in such a manner that it cannot get away. Anyone encouraging, or assisting at the fighting or baiting of animals is guilty of an offence punishable on **summary conviction.** *Criminal Code*, R.S.C. 1985, c. C–46, ss. 446(1), (2); *Pitts* v. *Millar* (1874), L.R. 9 Q.B. 380; *Rex* v. *Hayes*, [1943] O.W.N. 299 (H.C.).

BAIT AND SWITCH The practice of using articles supplied as loss leaders, for the purpose of advertising to attract customers in the hope of selling them other articles and not for the purpose of making a profit. See *Competition Act*, R.S.C. 1985, c. C–34, s. 61(5).

BANC [EN] See **en banc.**

BANCO [IN] Lat.: literally, a seat or bench. See **en banc.**

BANKRUPTCY Insolvency, i.e., the inability of a **debtor** to pay his **debts** as they become due; the legal process by which assets of the debtor are liquidated to pay off **creditors.** Historically, bankruptcy proceedings could only be brought against traders and were directed solely to preventing fraudulent traders from escaping their creditors. Currently, a bankrupt as defined under the *Bankruptcy and Insolvency Act*, R.S.C. 1985, c. B–3, s. 2, includes anyone who has made an **assignment** or against whom a receiving order has been made—in other words, a person who has the legal status of being bankrupt and has consequently been declared unable to meet his debts and **liabilities.** Bankruptcy proceedings are judicial or quasi-judicial and are for the purpose of distributing the bankrupt's property among his creditors and relieving him of the unpaid balance of his liabilities. A bankrupt may decide alternatively to make voluntary arrangements with his creditors. *Johnson* v. *Harris* (1878), 1 B.C.L.R. (Part I) 93 (S.C.); *Re Colonial Investment Co. of Winnipeg* (1913), 5 W.W.R. 822 (Man.C. A.); *Beiswanger* v. *Swift Current*, [1931] 1 D.L.R. 407 (Sask.C.A.).

BAR 1. A previous **judgment** is a bar to another action by the same parties on the same set of facts. When a judgment becomes absolute, it can no longer be questioned, and hence no further action may be taken between the same parties regarding the same matter. This may also be termed ESTOPPEL BY DEED (see **estoppel**). *Tencer* v. *Rockroy Construction (Hamilton) Ltd.* (1976), 15 O.R. (2d) 526 (Co.Ct.). See also **res judicata; double jeopardy.**

2. If an **action** is not brought within the time set out by **statute,** it is barred by the *Statute of Limitations* (or a similar act, depending on the **jurisdiction**), which is to say that the action can no longer be brought. This is sometimes termed an AB-

SOLUTE BAR; there may also be a PRE-SUMPTIVE BAR that arises from a lapse of time otherwise than under statute. *O'Dell* v. *Hastie* (1968), 63 W.W.R. 632 (Sask.Q.B.).

3. Technically, the bar is the barrier that separates the general public from the space occupied by the judges, the counsel and the parties to the case. In England, outer-barristers stand behind the bar with the public while the other persons dealing with the case stand within the bar, including the solicitors. Thus, counsel appear AT THE BAR to argue a case, and the CASE AT BAR is the case now before the court.

4. The members of the legal profession, the lawyers, are collectively known as MEMBERS OF THE BAR and are CALLED TO THE BAR when they have been accepted into the profession.

5. All persons who are not members of a legislative body and who wish to address the members of that body or who are summoned to it appear AT THE BAR (the outer boundary of the House) for that purpose.

6. Formerly, a PLEA AT BAR was a type of plea that showed a substantial defence to the action.

BARGAIN An **agreement** between two or more persons, intended to be enforceable at law. Bargain and **contract** express the same legal concept. The term also suggests negotiation over the terms of an agreement. *Crossman* v. *The Queen* (1886), 18 Q.B.D. 256; *Ben Ginter Construction Co. Ltd.* v. *Primary Construction Co. Ltd.* (1969), 68 W.W.R. 89 (Y.Ter.Ct.).

BARGAINING AGENT A trade union (or council of trade unions as in Newfoundland) that acts on behalf of employees (1) in **collective bargaining** or (2) as a party to a collective agreement with an employer.

BARGAIN AND SALE Generally applies to land and refers to a **contract** for the sale of any estate or interest in **real property** or **chattels** followed by payment of the agreed purchase price. The phrase is also applied to transfers of **personalty** where there is an **executory** agreement of sale followed by a completed sale. Formerly, the Court of Chancery held that after a bargain and sale the **vendor** held the land to the use of, or for the benefit of, the purchaser. In 1536 the **Statute of Uses** executed the use in favour of the purchaser, thus giving him the same interest in the land as the vendor had. However, bargain and sale as a method of **conveyancing** has now become obsolete. Compare **quitclaim deed; warranty deed.**

BARRISTER AND SOLICITOR A lawyer; a person called to the **bar** by the law society of a particular province. In Canada, a lawyer is both barrister and solicitor, whereas in England, there is a distinction: The barrister does the actual court work, presenting and arguing the case in court, but does not prepare the case from the start; the solicitor's function is to assemble the legal materials, do the research and compile the legal precedents. A solicitor also is employed to perform a wide variety of legal work, such as the preparation of documents like **wills** and **mortgages, conveyancing,** company work and advising on tax matters.

BASTARD An illegitimate child; a child born out of lawful wedlock. The common-law rules relating to illegitimacy have been modified by **statute** in Canada, but the **legislation** is not uniform. In Ontario, the status of a child as a bastard has been abolished, and a child's status is independent of whether the child is born within or outside marriage. *Children's Law Reform Act,* R.S.O. 1990, c. C. 12, s. 1

BATTERY "The least touching of another in anger." *Cole* v. *Turner* (1704), 6 Mod. 149; 87 E.R. 907 (Q.B.). In **tort** law, in order for there to be a battery, there must be actual, unconsented-to physical contact, although there need not be any injury done. If the contact is offensive, even though harmless, it entitles the plaintiff to an award of NOMINAL DAMAGES (see **damages**).

There is no crime of battery in Canada per se. However, the statutory definition of **assault** in the *Criminal Code* recognizes, but obviates, the common-law distinction between assault and battery. *Criminal Code*, R.S.C. 1985, c. C–46, s. 265.

A battery may thus, in effect, result in both tortious and **criminal** liability. See **assault.**

BEARER INSTRUMENT A cheque, note, or draft made payable to the bearer so that anyone who presents the instrument is paid the amount shown on its face. *Day v. Longhurst* (1893), 68 L.T. 17 (Ch.D.).

The *Bills of Exchange Act*, R.S.C. 1985, c. B–4, s. 2, defines the bearer as the person in possession of a bill or note that is payable to the bearer.

BENCH 1. The court; the judges composing the court collectively. **2.** The place where the judge sits (as in APPROACH THE BENCH).

BENCHER A member of the governing body of certain provincial law societies (e.g., the Benchers of the Law Society of Upper Canada), either elected or appointed, **ex officio.** They are responsible for regulation of the profession, including admission to the bar, discipline, and disbarring. See, e.g., the *Law Society Act*, R.S.O. 1990, c. L. 8, ss. 10–25.

BENCH WARRANT A court order empowering the proper legal authorities to arrest a person: most commonly used to compel one's attendance before the court to **answer** a **charge** of **contempt** when, for example, one has failed to answer to a **summons,** to appear as a **witness** after being subpoenaed or to appear for trial after being released on bail. See *Criminal Code*. R.S.C. 1985, c. C–46, ss. 704, 705.

BENEFICIAL INTEREST See **interest.**

BENEFICIALLY ENTITLED Having a **beneficial interest** in property.

BENEFICIAL USE With respect to property, such right to its enjoyment as exists where the legal **title** is in one person while the right to such use or interest is in another. A person who has beneficial use does not hold legal title of property. Legal title is held in **trust** by another. See **beneficial interest; mortgage; trust; use.**

BENEFICIARY In general, the person receiving or designated to receive a benefit or advantage. **1.** The person having the beneficial enjoyment of property rather than the legal possession—for example, the person for the benefit of whom a **trust** is created, or, in other words, the CESTUI QUE TRUST [see **trust**] in a trust relationship; **2.** the third party who is designated as the receiver of benefits from a **contract; 3.** the person named in an **insurance** policy as the one to receive any benefits accruing under it; **4.** the person named in a **will** to receive property under the will.

INCIDENTAL BENEFICIARY A person who may incidentally benefit from the creation of a trust. Such a person has no actual interest in the trust and cannot enforce any right to incidental benefit.

BEQUEATH To make a gift of personalty by means of a **will.** Strictly, it signifies a gift of **personal property,** which distinguishes it from a **devise,** which is a gift of **real property.** A DISPOSITION is the generic name encompassing both a bequest of **personalty** and a devise of realty.

BEQUEST A **gift** or disposition of **personalty** contained in a **will.** A **devise** ordinarily passes **real property,** and a bequest, personal property. Compare **legacy.** *Re Booth and Merriam* (1910), 1 O.W.N. 646 (H.C.).

CONDITIONAL BEQUEST One that will take effect or continue only if a certain event occurs or fails to occur.

EXECUTORY BEQUEST A bequest of **personalty** or money that does not take effect until the happening of a possible or certain future event upon which it is thus said to be contingent.

RESIDUARY BEQUEST A bequest consisting of that which is left in an **estate** after payment of **debts** and general legacies and other specific gifts. *Higgins* v. *Dawson,* [1902] A.C. 1 (H.L.).

SPECIFIC BEQUEST A bequest of particular items of a testator's estate or all property of a certain class or kind. *Shepheard* v. *Beetham* (1877), 6 Ch.D. 597.

BEST EVIDENCE RULE A rule of evidence law requiring that the most persuasive **evidence** available be used to prove the terms of a writing. "The best evidence the circumstances of the case will allow must be given." *Villiers* v. *Villiers* (1740), 2 Atk. 71, 26 E.R. 444 (Ch.).

BESTIALITY Human sexual intercourse with an animal. Anyone who commits **buggery** or bestiality is guilty of a **hybrid offence.** *Criminal Code*, R.S.C. 1985, c. C–46, s. 160. See also *R.* v. *Triller* (1980), 55 C.C.C. (2d) 411 (B.C.Co.Ct.). See also **sodomy.**

BEYOND A REASONABLE DOUBT See **reasonable doubt.**

BFOR See **bona fide occupational requirement.**

BID An offer by an intending purchaser to buy goods or services at a stated price, or an offer by an intended seller to sell his goods or services for a stated price. In the context of building contracts, contractors usually solicit bids based on building specifications from several subcontractors in order to complete the project. Governmental units may be required by law to construct highways and buildings and to buy goods and services in accordance with a procedure wherein competitive bids are solicited by advertisement from the public, with the lowest competent bid winning the contract.

BIGAMY Under s. 290(1) of the *Criminal Code*, R.S.C. 1985, c. C–46, everyone commits bigamy who, in Canada, is already married and marries another person, or knowing that another person is married, marries that person, or on the same day or simultaneously goes through a form of marriage with more than one person. Also under s. 290(1), everyone commits bigamy who, being a Canadian citizen resident in Canada, leaves Canada intending to do any of the above and in fact does any of the above outside Canada. *R. v. Howard*, [1966] 3 C.C.C. 91 (B.C.Co.Ct.).

Section 290(2) of the Code lists four sets of circumstances, any one of which, if met, would mean bigamy had not been committed. These sets of circumstances are that *(a)* the person "in good faith and on reasonable grounds" believes his spouse is dead, *(b)* the spouse of the person has been continuously absent for seven years immediately preceding the time when he goes through the marriage, unless he knew his spouse was alive at any time during those seven years, *(c)* the person has been divorced from the bond of the just marriage, and *(d)* the former marriage has been declared void by a court of competent jurisdiction. Section 291(1) states that everyone who commits bigamy is guilty of an **indictable offence** and is liable to imprisonment for five years. A bigamous marriage is **void.**

BILATERAL CONTRACT See **contract.**

BILL A proposition or statement reduced to writing. **1.** In commercial law, an account of goods sold, services rendered and work done, or a written statement of the terms of contract or specification of the items of a transaction; a charge or invoice.
2. In legislation, a document submitted to **Parliament** or a provincial **legislature** for its consideration and/ or enactment. If approved, it becomes law in the form of a **statute.**

BILL OF ATTAINDER An abolished bill that declared persons charged with certain crimes—e.g., treason—to be *attainted,* involving the forfeiture of land, the **confiscation** of property, and the **corruption of blood.** Any traces of attainder have been removed from Canadian law by the *Criminal Code,* first enacted in 1892.

BILL OF COST An account of a lawyer's charges and disbursements incurred in the conduct of his client's business. The lawyer is obliged to deliver a statement of account to the client in order to give the client an opportunity of taxing it, i.e., having it examined by an appointed official or taxing master and possibly reduced. See **costs.**

BILL OF EXCEPTIONS A writing setting out the objections to rulings made or instructions given by a trial judge. The matter is determined in a court of error. If the objections are well argued, the result is a trial **de novo.** By Ord. LVIII, r. 1 of the English *Supreme Court of Judicature Act, 1875,* bills of exception were abolished.

BILL OF EXCHANGE As defined in the *Bills of Exchange Act,* R.S.C. 1985, c. B–4, s. 16(1), a bill of exchange is an unconditional order in writing, addressed by one person to another, signed by the person giving it, requiring the person to whom it is addressed to pay, on demand or at a fixed or determinable future time, a sum certain in money to or to the order of a specified person, or to bearer. It is assignable, at common law, by mere endorsement. Many names may possibly be attached to one bill as endorsers, and each of them is liable to be sued upon the bill, if it is not paid in due time. The person who makes or draws the bill is called the DRAWER; the person to whom it is addressed is, before acceptance, the

DRAWEE, and, after acceptance, the AC-CEPTOR; the person in whose favour it is drawn is the PAYEE; if he endorses the bill to another, he is called the ENDORSER, and the person to whom it is thus assigned, or negotiated, is the ENDORSEE, or HOLDER. See **bearer instrument; draft; negotiable instrument.**

BILL OF LADING A written acknowledgement of receipt of goods. It represents the **contract** of carriage and serves as evidence of the conditions of carriage agreed upon between the two parties, and it is a document of title to the goods described therein. *Can. Gen. Electric Co. Ltd.* v. *Les Armateurs du St.-Laurent Inc.*, [1977] 1 F.C. 215. An important function served by a bill of lading is to express the conditions under which the carrier seeks to limit the **liability** that would otherwise be imposed on it under common law.

BILL OF PARTICULARS A bill served on an opposing party to enable the party asking for the particulars to know what **claim, defence,** or other matter stated in pleadings he has to meet at **trial,** to save unnecessary expense and to avoid parties from being taken by surprise. *Spedding* v. *Fitzpatrick* (1888), 38 Ch.D. 410. The rules of civil procedure entitle an opposing party to apply for further and better particulars or facts of any matter stated in a **pleading.** A party would be entitled to particulars if it were necessary for him to know what case he had to meet. Particulars narrow the generality of the propositions contained in the statement of material facts, thereby further limiting and defining the issues to be tried. Particulars also determine the scope of discovery and govern the admission of evidence at the trial. *Bruce* v. *Odhams Press Ltd.*, [1936] 1 K.B. 697 (C.A.).

In criminal law, an **accused** who is unable to prepare his defence properly because the **charge** does not contain sufficient information may submit to the court an APPLICATION FOR PARTICULARS. The court may order the prosecutor at its discretion to furnish the accused or his counsel with the particulars requested. *Criminal Code*, R.S.C. 1985, c. C–46, s. 587, *Regina* v. *Canadian General Electric Co. Ltd. (No. 1)* (1974), 17 C.C.C. (2d) 433 (Ont.H.C.).

BILL OF RIGHTS A declaration delivered by the English Lords and Commons to the Prince and Princess of Orange in 1689 and afterwards enacted in Parliament when they became king and queen (1 W. & M., c. 2). It set forth that King James, by the assistance of evil counsellors, endeavoured to subvert the laws of the kingdom by, **inter alia,** levying money for the use of the Crown without consent of Parliament, by violent prosecutions, by excessive bail and by the infliction of cruel punishments—all of which were declared to be illegal. The Act of Parliament recognises all the rights and liberties asserted to be "the true, ancient, indisputable rights of the people of this kingdom."

The Bill of Rights is recognised as a landmark in the struggle of the individual and Parliament for control of the **executive.** It is also regarded as one of the fundamental traditions of government and constitutional law that Canada inherited from England. See, e.g., *R.* v. *Hess No. 2,* [1949] 4 D.L.R. 199 (B.C.C.A.) at 208–09: "[T]he purported powers...to deny an acquitted person bail, to obstruct and delay his application therefore, and to detain him in custody for an offence of which the Court has acquitted him and when there is no offence charged against him are all contrary to the written constitution of the United Kingdom, as reflected in Magna Carta (1215), the Petition of Right (1628), the Bill of Rights (1689) and the Act of Settlement (1700–1701)." See **Canadian Bill of Rights.**

BILL OF SALE A written agreement under which **title** to personal **chattels** is transferred; in a more technical sense, a document evidencing a **contract** of the sale of goods that may be required to be registered under the various provincial *Bill of Sale* statutes. In certain cases, a bill of sale must be registered; otherwise the sale may be treated as **void** as regards third parties, e.g., the creditors of the seller, as well as subsequent buyers and mortgagees in good faith. See, e.g., *Bills of Sale Act,* R.S.N.S. 1989, c. 39.

BIND Something that obligates or constrains the bound individual. A bind places one under legal duties and obligations. One can bind oneself as in a **contract** or one can be bound by a **judgment.**

BINDER A **contract** for temporary insurance; a written memorandum of the most important items of a preliminary contract, one that covers the insured and puts the **underwriter** on risk for the period while the insurance proposal is being considered and until a policy is either granted or refused. Also termed a COVER NOTE. *Wallace* v. *Co-Operative Fire & Casualty Co.* (1968), 68 D.L.R. (2d) 744 (N.B.S.C.A.D.).

BINDING As used in a statute, commonly means obligatory. At common law, a superior court's decision on a point of law is binding on an inferior court.

BINDING AGREEMENT A conclusive agreement.

BINDING INSTRUCTION An instruction that directs the jury how to determine an issue in the case if the condition stated in that instruction is shown to exist. See **directed verdict.**

BIND OVER The power exercisable by a magistrate, on facts established to his satisfaction, to order anyone to enter into a recognizance to keep the peace. *Regina* v. *White, Ex parte Chohan*, [1969] 1 C.C.C. 19 at 22 (B.C.S.C.).

BLASPHEMY At common law, the **misdemeanour** of reviling or ridiculing the established religion (Christianity) and the existence of God; *Gathercole's Case* (1838), 2 Lewin 237; 168 E.R. 1140. Under s. 296 of the *Criminal Code*, R.S.C. 1985, c. C–46, everyone who publishes a blasphemous libel is guilty of an **indictable offence** and is liable to imprisonment for two years. However, arguments upon a religious subject that are expressed in good faith and in decent language are allowable, and no one can be convicted of an offence for arguing in this manner. See s. 296(3). See also *John William Gott* (1922), 16 Cr.App.R. 87: *Rex* v. *Rahard* (1935), 65 C.C.C. 344 (Que.Ct. of Sess.).

BLOOD, CORRUPTION OF See **corruption of blood; bill of attainder.**

BLUE SKY LAWS Legislation imposing strict standards beyond mere disclosure on issues of securities. Under blue sky laws, the administrator of securities has the responsibility to decide whether it is fair for the public to be allowed to buy questionable securities; disclosure is not enough. See D. Johnston, *Canadian Securities Regulation* 10–11 (1977). See also *Securities Act*, R.S.O. 1990, c. S.5, s. 61(2).

BONA *(bō'-nà)* Lat.: good, virtuous. Also, goods and **chattels;** property moveable and immoveable (civil law).

BONA FIDE *(bō'-nà fīd)* Lat.: in or with **good faith;** without fraud or deceit.

BONA FIDE OCCUPATIONAL REQUIREMENT (BFOR) In human rights legislation, a refusal, expulsion, suspension, or preference deemed *not* to be discrimination if the employer has established that the characteristic (e.g., height, weight) is necessary for the safe and adequate performance of a job. *Canadian Human Rights Act*, R.S.C. 1985, c. H–6, s. 15 (*a*); *Ontario Human Rights Commission* v. *Borough of Etobicoke*, [1982] 1 S.C.R. 202.

BONA FIDE PURCHASER One who in **good faith** acquires legal **title** to **property** by paying valuable **consideration** and has no notice of third party claims. *Burns* v. *Young* (1900), 40 N.S.R. 199 (S.C.); *Stubbert* v. *Scott & Temple*, [1931] 1 W.W.R. 598 (B.C.S.C.).

BONA FIDE PURCHASE One made in **good faith** for valuable **consideration** and without notice of a competing claim. The plea of a purchase of a legal estate for value without notice is an absolute defence against the claims of any prior equitable owner. *Pilcher* v. *Rawlins* (1872), 7 Ch.App. 259 (C.A.).

BOND "[A] written **instrument** under **seal** whereby the person executing it [the obligor] makes a promise or incurs a personal liability to another [the obligee]." *Grimmer* v. *County of Gloucester* (1902), 32 S.C.R. 305 at 310. Usually, as well as binding the person who has executed it, the instrument binds his **heirs, executors** and **administrators** or if a **corporation,** their **successors,** to a specified act. The term is also applied to instruments of indebtedness issued by governments and companies to secure repayment of money borrowed by them. This obligation may be represented by a certificate for **principal** and by detachable coupons for current interest. *Re Emerson Election* (1887), 4 Man.L.R. 287 (Q.B.). The term includes all interest-bearing obligations of persons, corporations, and governments.

BONDSMAN A **surety;** one who is bound or gives surety for another; a person who obtains surety bonds for others for a fee; also, the individual who arranges for the defendant in a criminal case to be released from jail by posting a **bail bond.**

BOYCOTT To refrain by concerted effort from commercial dealing with someone; the refusal by a person or group to work for, purchase from, or handle the products of an employer. Boycotting is not necessarily illegal. *Ken Miller & Associates Bakery Distributors Ltd.* v. *Bakery & Confectionery Workers International Union, Local 468 and Kemmis,* [1971] 5 W.W.R. 460 (B.C.S.C.); *Slade & Stewart Ltd.* v. *Retail, Wholesale & Department Store Union Local 580* (1969), 69 W.W.R. 374 (B.C.S.C.).

BREACH 1. The failure of **performance** by a **party** of some contracted-for or agreed-upon act; **2.** the invasion of a right as in a breach of a DUTY OF CARE (see **duty**) in **negligence** law. A breach of a contractual or other right converts it into a right to obtain a remedy for the breach, generally a right of **action.** See **anticipatory breach; material breach.**

BREACH OF CONTRACT A wrongful non-performance of any contractual duty that results in the entitlement of the innocent party to maintain an action for **damages.** In certain instances the innocent party has the right to treat the contract as **discharged.** See S. Waddams, *The Law of Contracts* (3d ed. 1993), chap. 16. See **anticipatory breach; material breach.**

BREACH OF DUTY Failure to perform a duty owed to another or to society; e.g., the violation by a **trustee** of any duty he owes, in his capacity as trustee, to the **beneficiary.**

BREACH OF THE PEACE This offence embraces a great variety of conduct destroying or menacing public order and tranquility. Although breach of the peace has not been authoritatively defined, it includes not only violent acts, but acts and words likely to produce violence in others. The term is generally used to refer to any act that tends to disturb the quiet and tranquility of the realm or the ordinary peaceful state of the country. A riot, a disturbance, a fight or affray, or an **assault** is each a breach of the peace. The offence is one calculated to put one in fear of bodily harm. It is sufficient to constitute the offence if the conduct arouses the passions and induces personal violence. Sections 30, 31, 49 and 810 of the *Criminal Code,* R.S.C. 1985, c. C–46, deal with breaches of the peace. See *Frey* v. *Fedoruk,* [1950] S.C.R. 517; *Rex* v. *Zwicker,* [1938] 1 D.L.R. 461 (N.S.Co.Ct.). See also **disturbance of the peace; slander.**

BREACH OF PROMISE Often used as short form of breach of the promise of marriage. Breach of promise to marry gives rise to a right of action for damages at common law. A promise to marry need not be in writing nor need it be evidenced by writing. Either the man or the woman may sue for the breach. *LeBlanc* v. *Wetmore,* [1944] 2 D.L.R. 130 (N.B.S.C.A.D.); *Grant* v. *Cornock* (1888), 16 O.R. 406 (Q.B.).

BREACH OF TRUST A violation by a **trustee** of a **duty** that **equity** lays upon him, in disregard of either the terms of the **trust** or the rules of equity. This would include acts done by a trustee in contravention of his fiduciary duties, or in excess of them, or by way of neglect or omission of them. The concurrence or acquiescence of co-trustees is also a breach of trust. However, a mere error of judgment does not constitute a breach of trust. *Dover* v. *Denne* (1902), 3 O.L.R. 664 (C.A.); *Brown* v. *Brown,* [1932] 2 D.L.R. 819 (Ont.C.A.). For the applicable statute governing trusts, one should see the *Trustee Act* (or equivalent) in the appropriate jurisdiction.

BREACH OF WARRANTY A **warranty** is a **guarantee** and is breached when the thing so guaranteed is deficient according to the terms of the warranty. A warranty in contract law must be distinguished from a **condition.** A warranty is a provision that is subsidiary or collateral to the main purpose of the contract. In distinguishing between a condition and a warranty, see *Hong Kong Fir Shipping Co. Ltd.* v. *Kawasaki Kisen Kaisha Ltd.,* [1962] 2 Q.B. 26 at 70 (C.A.), where it was held that obligations could not satisfactorily be classified without taking into account the "nature of the event to which the breach gives rise." Breach of warranty entitles the innocent party only to **damages,** whereas breach of condition entitles him to treat the contract as at an end.

In the sale of goods, a warranty is defined by statute in the appropriate provincial *Sale of Goods Act:* e.g., in s. 2(0) of the Nova Scotia statute (R.S.N.S. 1989, c. 408) warranty is defined as "an agreement with reference to goods which are the subject of a contract of sale, but collateral to the main purpose of such contract, the breach of which gives rise to a claim for damages, but not a right to reject the goods and treat the contract as repudiated." *Bezanson* v. *Kaintz* (1967), 61 D.L.R. (2d) 410 (N.S.S.C.).

BREAKING A CLOSE [BREACH OF CLOSE] The **common-law trespass** of unlawful entering upon the land of another. See **quare clausum fregit.**

BREAKING AND ENTERING See **burglary.**

BREATHALYZER (BREATH ANALYSIS INSTRUMENT) "[A]n instrument . . . designed to receive and make an analysis of a sample of the breath of a person in order to measure the concentration of alcohol in the blood of that person." SI/85–201, *Canada Gazette*, Part II, 27/11/85, p. 4692. See also *Criminal Code,* R.S.C. 1985, c. C–46, s. 254.

BRIBERY At common law, bribery is the receiving or offering of any undue reward by or to any person in a public office in order to influence his behaviour in office and induce him to act contrary to the known rules of honesty and integrity. *Rex* v. *Hogg* (1914), 19 D.L.R. 113 (Sask.S.C.). Bribery is now a statutory offence. See *Criminal Code,* R.S.C. 1985, c. C–46, ss. 119–125, 139, and 426.

BRIEF A written argument concentrating upon legal points and authorities, which is used by the lawyer to convey to the court (trial or appellate) the essential facts of his client's case, a statement of the questions of law involved, the law he would have applied and the application he desires made of it by the court; it is submitted in connection with an application, motion, trial, or appeal. Compare **memorandum.**

A brief is often referred to as a **factum** in Canadian law. It includes a concise statement of facts, a list of issues, arguments, order or relief sought, and appendices containing a list of case citations, statutes and regulations. See, e.g., *Nova Scotia Civil Procedure Rules* (1983), r. 62.15.

BRITISH NORTH AMERICA [B.N.A.] ACT, 1867 [CONSTITUTION ACT, 1867] The principal document of the Canadian constitution until the enactment of the *Constitution Act, 1982.* The Act, a statute of the British Parliament, in its preamble proclaimed the desire of the four founding provinces (Nova Scotia, New Brunswick, Quebec, and Ontario) to be "federally united into one Dominion" with a constitution "similar in principle to that of the United Kingdom." In the key sections 91 and 92, legislative powers were divided between the Federal Parliament and the provincial legislatures.

See **constitution.**

BROKER A person who, for a commission or a fee brings parties together and assists in negotiating contracts between them for the purchase and sale of goods, stocks, shares, or policies of insurance. Under the *Canada Business Corporations Act,* R.S.C. 1985, c. C–44, s. 63, a broker gives to his customer, to the issuer of securities, and to a purchaser certain **warranties** as provided for in the section. Compare **jobber.**

BRUTUM FULMEN *(brū'-tŭm fŭl'-mĕn)* Lat.: inert thunder. An empty threat or charge. Sometimes used to refer to a **void judgment,** which in legal effect is no judgment.

BUGGERY Also termed **sodomy.** The provision that previously made buggery an indictable offence (*Criminal Code,* R.S.C. 1985, c. C–46, s. 156) was repealed in 1983. Under the provision of s. 159, anal intercourse is an indictable offence, punishable for a term not exceeding 10 years, or on summary conviction, unless engaged in, in private, between a husband and wife, or two consenting persons, each of whom is eighteen years or older. See also **bestiality.**

BULK SALES ACT Each of the common-law provinces has enacted a *Bulk Sales Act,* the object of which is to protect the **creditors** of a person who makes a bulk sale, by preventing the secret sale in bulk of substantially all of the **debtor** merchant's stock of goods. A bulk sale, as defined by the provincial statutes, is a sale of essentially all the stock-in-trade of a business or of the **fixtures,** goods, and **chattels** with which a person carries on a business. A bulk sale is of concern to creditors because the proceeds of the sale may not be retained within the business. The seller, for example, may abscond with the money or apply it in such ways that the creditors cannot recover it. See appropriate provincial legislation.

BURDEN OF PROOF [ONUS PROBANDI] The duty or onus to prove one's case. There are two principal burdens: (1) The LEGAL BURDEN, or BURDEN OF PROOF SIMPLICITER, "is the obligation of a party to meet the requirement of a rule of law that a fact in **issue** be proved (or disproved) either by a **preponderance of the evidence** or beyond **reasonable doubt** as the case may be." R. Cross & C. Tapper, *Cross on Evidence* 112 (7th ed. 1990). In **civil law,** a plaintiff must prove his case on a balance of probabilities, whereas, in criminal law, the Crown must prove each and every element of the case beyond a reasonable doubt. In other words, at the close of the evidence, if the trier of fact has a reasonable doubt as to the guilt of the accused, the accused must be acquitted. (2) The EVIDENTIAL BURDEN, or BURDEN OF ADDUCING EVIDENCE, "is the obligation to show, if called upon to do so, that there is sufficient evidence to raise an issue as to the existence or non-existence of a fact in issue, due regard being had to the standard of proof demanded of the party under such obligation. The concluding clause is designed to meet the point that the amount of evidence required to induce a judge to leave an issue

to the jury varies according to whether the case is civil or criminal, and whether the party bearing the burden is **plaintiff, prosecutor, defendant** or **accused.**" *Id.* at 113.

See generally *id.,* chap. 3, *Sutton* v. *Sadler* (1857), 3 C.B. 87 (N.S.); 140 E.R. 671; *Woolmington* v. *Director of Public Prosecutions,* [1935] A.C. 462 (H.L.). See also the various burdens of proof in the *Criminal Code,* R.S.C. 1985, c. C–46. See also **moral certainty; presumption; res ipsa loquitur.**

BURGLARY [BREAKING AND ENTERING] At common law, "the breaking and entering of the **dwelling house** of another, in the night time, with the intent to commit a felony therein whether or not the felony is committed." 3 Coke Inst. 63, 4 Bl.Comm. 224.

In the *Criminal Code,* R.S.C. 1985, c. C–46, the term *break and enter* is used. The Code has extended break and enter offences to include some that do not amount to burglaries at common law. The offence now extends to structures other than dwelling houses, and there is no distinction between breaking and entering by day or by night. See *id.,* ss. 348–351; *Regina* v. *Govedarov, Popovic & Askov* (1974), 3 O.R. (2d) 23 (C.A.).

BUSINESS RECORDS EXCEPTION See **hearsay rule.**

BY OPERATION OF LAW See **operation of law.**

BY THE ENTIRETY See **tenancy** [TENANCY BY THE ENTIRETY].

BY-LAWS 1. Rules and regulations pertaining to corporations; **2.** A form of subordinate legislation made by some authority subordinate to a **legislature** for the purposes of regulation, administration, or control—e.g., the by-laws of a municipal government.

C

CABINET Section 11 of the *Constitution Act, 1867* provides that "there shall be a Council to aid and advise in the Government of Canada." This council, known as the Cabinet, is composed of Ministers of the **Crown,** who serve as confidential advisers to the Sovereign and meet, on the instance of the Prime Minister, to advise the Sovereign collectively on policy. Since the powers of the Crown are, with rare exceptions, exercised on the advice and responsibility of ministers—either individually or as the Cabinet—the Cabinet is the centre of the **executive** government. Its functions are not, however, confined to executive acts. As a body that leads the majority party in the House of Commons, it is able to act as a ruling committee controlling the business of the House of Commons. Nearly all **legislation** passed through **Parliament** originates with the Cabinet. Thus the Cabinet formulates and introduces the legislation that represents the policy of the ruling party in the House of Commons, and also shapes and supervises the execution of the acts that are governed by the principles laid down in legislation. The Cabinet also has extensive lawmaking powers. Statutes frequently delegate the power to make rules and regulations, in furtherance of the legislative purpose, to the Governor-General, a government minister, etc.; in reality, these regulations are usually made or approved by the Cabinet. The term "Cabinet" is equally applicable to the body that represents the leadership of the majority party in a provincial legislature.

CALL In corporate law, a term that applies to partially paid **shares.** It is a demand by a **corporation** on a **shareholder** to pay any outstanding amount owing proportionate to his share of **stock.** However, shares are nearly always issued as fully paid and non-assessable, so that the partly paid share has fallen into disuse. Also, the *Canada Business Corporations Act,* R.S.C. 1985, c. C–44, s. 2(1), defines *call* as "an option transferable by delivery to demand delivery of a specified number or amount of securities at a fixed price within a specified time but does not include an option or right to acquire **securities** of the corporation that granted the option or right to acquire...."

CALUMNY Slander, defamation; false or malicious prosecution or accusation. For merly used in **civil law** to indicate unjust prosecution or defence of a suit.

CANADA ACT See **constitution.**

CANADA GAZETTE The official gazette of Canada, authorized by the *Statutory Instruments Act,* R.S.C. 1985, c. S–22, s. 10. The *Canada Gazette* is published in three parts:
Part I: all items required by federal statute or regulation to be published in the *Canada Gazette*
Part II: statutory instruments (**regulations**) and other statutory instruments and documents
Part III: Public Acts of Parliament and their enactment regulations.

CANADIAN BILL OF RIGHTS An Act for the recognition and protection of human rights and fundamental freedoms, passed by the federal Parliament in 1960. (see R.S.C. 1985, Appendix III). However, this legislation was enacted as a federal statute, rather than entrenched—by amendment of the **British North America Act**—in the **constitution;** hence, the *Canadian Bill of Rights* can be directly amended or repealed by Parliament and is limited in its application to federal laws. See **Canadian Charter of Rights and Freedoms.** For the text of the *Canadian Bill of Rights* see **Appendix II.**

CANADIAN CHARTER OF RIGHTS AND FREEDOMS Part I of the *Constitution Act 1982.* A bill of rights that is entrenched as part of the Constitution, and can therefore be altered only by constitutional amendment; this gives it more force than the existing **Canadian Bill of Rights** R.S.C. 1985, Appendix III, which has only the force of a statute.

The *Constitution Act 1982* was an appendix to the *Canada Act 1982* (U.K.), c. 11. The *Act* was passed by the British Parliament as its final legislative act for Canada. The *Charter* came into force on April 17, 1982 (with the exception of s. 15, which came into force on April 17, 1985 as provided by s. 32(2) of the *Charter*), and operates prospectively from that day.

The *Charter* reiterates the fundamental freedoms (freedom of religion, expression, assembly, and association) and legal rights (the rights of life, liberty, and security of the person) set out in the **Canadian Bill of Rights,** but includes additional rights.

The major provisions of the *Charter* are:

GUARANTEE OF RIGHTS AND FREEDOMS s. 1

See **Oakes test**

FUNDAMENTAL FREEDOMS S. 2

Freedom of conscience and religion (*R. v. Big M Drug Mart Ltd.*, [1985] 1 S.C.R. 295); freedom of thought, opinion, and expression (includes freedom of the press and other media of communication) (*Irwin Toy Ltd* v. *Quebec*, [1989] 1 S.C.R. 927); freedom of peaceful assembly (*R. v. Collins* (1982), 31 C.R. (3d) 283 (Ont. Co. Ct.)); freedom of association (*R. v. Skinner* (1990), 56 C.C.C. (3d) 1 (S.C.C.)).

DEMOCRATIC RIGHTS SS. 3–5

The right to vote in the election of the members of the Canadian House of Commons and of a provincial legislative assembly (s. 3) (*Badger* v. *Canada (A.G.)* (1988), 55 D.L.R. (4th) 177 (Man. C.A.)); the right to stand for office in either of these institutions; the requirement that no House of Commons and no legislative assembly continue for longer than five years, except in extraordinary circumstances (s. 4); the requirement that there be an annual sitting of Parliament and each legislature (s. 5);

MOBILITY RIGHTS S. 6

The right of every citizen of Canada to enter, remain in, and leave Canada; the right of every citizen of Canada, or any person having the status of a permanent resident, to move and take up residence in any province, and to pursue the gaining of a livelihood in any province (*Black* v. *Law Society of Alberta* (1989), 93 N.R. 266 (S.C.C.));

LEGAL RIGHTS SS. 7–14

The right to life, liberty, and security of the person (s. 7) *Morgentaler, Smoling and Scott* v. *The Queen* (1988), 37 C.C.C. (3d) 449 (S.C.C.)); protection against unreasonable **search and seizure** (s. 8) (*Hunter* v. *Southam Inc.*, [1984] 2 S.C.R. 145) or arbitrary detention or imprisonment (s. 9) (*R. v. Ladouceur*, [1990] 1 S.C.R. 1257);

on arrest or detention, the right to be informed without unreasonable delay of the charge (*R. v. Evans* (1991), 63 C.C.C. (3d) 289 (S.C.C.), the right to legal **counsel** (*Clarkson* v. *The Queen*, [1986] 1 S.C.R. 383), and the right to have the validity of the detention determined by *habeas corpus* (s. 10), (*Olson* v. *The Queen*, [1989] 1 S.C.R. 296);

on being charged with an offence, the rights in proceedings in criminal and penal matters include the right to the **presumption of innocence** (*R. v. Oakes*, [1986] 1 S.C.R. 103), and the right not to be denied **bail** without just cause (s. 11) (*R. v. Bray* (1983), 2 C.C.C. (3d) 325 (Ont. C.A.));

the right not to be subjected to any **cruel and unusual punishment** (s. 12) (*Smith* v. *The Queen*, [1987] 1 S.C.R. 1045);

protection against self-incrimination (s. 13) (*R. v. Altseimer* (1982), 142 D.L.R. (3d) 246);

and the right to an interpreter when a party or witness to a proceeding (s. 14) (*R. v. Petrovic* (1984), 10 D.L.R. (4th) 697 (Ont. C.A.)).

EQUALITY RIGHTS S.15

The guarantee of equality to every individual before and under the law, and the right to equal protection and benefit of the law without **discrimination.** See also **equality.**

Section 15(2) states that 15(1) does not preclude any program that has as its object the amelioration of conditions of disadvantaged persons or groups. See **affirmative action.**

OFFICIAL LANGUAGES OF CANADA SS. 16–22

Includes official language provisions for Canada and New Brunswick.

MINORITY LANGUAGE EDUCATIONAL RIGHTS S. 23

Lavoie v. *Nova Scotia (Attorney-General)* (1988), 50 D.L.R. (4th) 405 (N.S.S.C.);

ENFORCEMENT (INCLUDING EXCLUSION OF EVIDENCE) s.24

Collins v. *The Queen*, [1987] 1 S.C.R. 265.

PROTECTION OF ABORIGINAL RIGHTS AND FREEDOMS s. 25
(See also *Constitution Act 1982*, Part II, Rights of the Aboriginal Peoples of Canada, s. 35);
PRESERVATION OF MULTICULTURAL HERITAGE s. 27
R. v. Keegstra, [1990] 3 S.C.R. 697.
GUARANTEE OF EQUAL RIGHTS AND FREEDOMS TO MALE AND FEMALE PERSONS s. 28
Re Shewchuk and Ricard (1986), 28 D.L.R. (4th) 429 (B.C.C.A.).
PROTECTION OF NOMINATIONAL, SEPARATE, AND DISSENTIENT SCHOOLS s. 29
Reference re s. 79(3), (4) and (7) of the Public Schools Act (Manitoba), [1990] 2 W.W.R. 289 (Man. C.A.).
APPLICATION OF CHARTER s. 33
See also **override**
For the full text of the *Charter*, see **Appendix I.**

CANADIAN HUMAN RIGHTS ACT Federal antidiscrimination legislation. The *Canadian Human Rights Act*, R.S.C. 1985, c. H-6, prohibits discrimination (e.g., based on sex, religion, marital status, etc.) in areas including the provision of goods, services, facilities, accommodations, and employment (see **Appendix III**). While similar rights are entrenched in the **Canadian Charter of Rights and Freedoms** (see **Appendix I**), this "shall not be construed as denying the existence of any other rights and freedoms that exist in Canada." G. Gall, *The Canadian Legal System* 80 (3d ed. 1990). See **human rights [legislation].** For text of *Canadian Human Rights Act,* see Appendix III.

CANON **1.** A rule of ecclesiastical law, primarily concerning the clergy, but also at times embracing lay members of a congregation. **2.** A rule of **construction;** one of an aggregate of rules indicating the proper way to construe **statutes** and other pieces of **legislation. 3.** An ecclesiastical dignitary. *Randolph* v. *Milman* (1868), 4 L.R.C.P. 107· *Middleton et ux.* v. *Croft* (1737), 2 Strange 1056; 93 E.R. 1030 (K.B.). **4.** A professional canon is a rule or standard of conduct adopted by a professional group to guide or discipline the professional conduct of its members; e.g., the canons contained in the *Code of Judicial Conduct.*

CAPITAL Broadly, all the money and other property of a **corporation** or other enterprise used in transacting its business; each investment. A corporation's legal **liability** is ordinarily limited by its capital.
NOMINAL or AUTHORIZED CAPITAL is the number of **shares** or the aggregate **par** value that the company is authorized to **issue.** SUBSCRIBED CAPITAL is the number of shares taken or agreed to be taken by subscribers. ISSUED CAPITAL is the number of shares issued and allotted. PAID-UP CAPITAL is the amount paid up by subscribers, whether for all or part of issued or subscribed capital. See *Canada Business Corporations Act*, R.S.C. 1985, c. C–44.
WORKING CAPITAL is the amount required by a corporation to actually carry on its business. UNCALLED CAPITAL is the amount that has not yet been called for payment.
FIXED CAPITAL is "that which a company retains, in the shape of assets upon which the subscribed capital has been expended, and which assets either themselves produce income, independent of any further action by the company, or being retained by the company are made use of to produce income or gain profits." *Ammonia Soda Co.* v. *Chamberlain*, [1918] 1 Ch. 266 at 286. On the other hand, CIRCULATING CAPITAL "is a portion of the subscribed capital of the company intended to be used by being temporarily parted with and circulated in business, in the form of money, goods or other assets, and which, or the proceeds of which, are intended to return to the company with an increment, and are intended to be used again and again, and to always return with some accretion." *Id.*, at 286–87.

CAPITAL COST ALLOWANCE In calculating the taxable income of a taxpayer, a deduction allowed for depreciation on many tangible fixed assets and some intangible fixed assets. See E. Harris, *Canadian Income Taxation* 200 ff. (4th ed. 1986). Also see *Income Tax Act,* S.C. 1970–71–72, c. 63, s. 29(1)(*a*), *Income Tax Reg.* Part XI, Sch. II.

CAPITAL EXPENDITURE Expenditure from which benefits may be expected over a relatively long period; expenditure made for the improvement or betterment of a capital asset. *Minister of*

National Revenue v. *Dominion Natural Gas Co. Ltd.,* [1941] S.C.R. 19.

CAPITAL GAIN "Unforeseen increases in the real value of a man's existing property not directly attributable to his efforts, intelligence, capital or risk-taking" (as distinct from income). Seltzer, *The Nature of Tax Treatment of Capital Gains and Losses,* as quoted in *Wood* v. *M.N.R.,* [1967] C.T.C. 66 at 74. However, for taxation purposes certain proportions of capital gains are treated as income. See *Income Tax Act,* S.C. 1970–71–72, c. 63, ss. 38, 39.

CAPITAL PROPERTY The assets of an individual or corporation that are not consumed with use. See further E. Harris, *Canadian Income Taxation* 262 ff. (4th ed. 1986).

CAPITAL OFFENCE A criminal offence punishable by death. The following were formerly capital offences under the Criminal Code, R.S.C. 1970, c. C–34: **treason, piracy** involving murder or attempted murder or an act endangering life, and capital murder.

In 1976, the *Criminal Code,* S.C. 1974–75–76, c. 105, s. 21 abolished **capital punishment,** and all capital offences became punishable by life imprisonment.

CAPITAL PUNISHMENT The punishment of death for commission of a **capital offence.** Capital punishment was abolished in 1976 under the Criminal Code, S.C. 1974–75–76, c. 105, s. 21.

For the specific legislative provisions dealing with capital punishment, see *Criminal Code* R.S.C. 1970, c. C–34, ss. 669–681.

CAPTION 1. The heading of a legal document, containing the names of the **parties,** the court, index or **docket** number of the case, etc. 2. The act of seizing, which, together with ASPORTATION (the act of carrying away), was a necessary element of common-law **larceny.**

CARTEL A group of independent industrial **corporations,** usually operating on an international scale, that agree to restrict trade to their mutual benefit. See **monopoly; oligopoly.**

CASE An **action, cause, suit** or controversy at **law** or in **equity;** a **trial;** the evi-

dence and argument on behalf of one of the parties. Also, an abbreviation of **trespass on the case.** See *Letang* v. *Cooper,* [1965] 1 Q.B. 232 (C.A.). A judicial proceeding for the determination of a disagreement between two or more parties.

CASE AT BAR See **bar.**

CASE DISMISSED See **dismiss.**

CASE, ON THE See **trespass** [TRESPASS ON THE CASE].

CASE LAW See **common law.**

CASE OF FIRST IMPRESSION See **first impression.**

CASE OR CONTROVERSY See **controversy.**

CASH VALUE See **market value.**

CAUSA *(kâw'-zà)* Lat.: cause. A lawsuit or case; grounds, motive, purpose, reason; pretext, inducement, occasion.

CAUSA CAUSANS *(kaw'-zà kaw'-zănz)* Lat.: the immediate cause; the last link in the chain of causation. Must be distinguished from CAUSA SINE QUA NON (following), which refers to a preceding link but for which the causa causans could not have become operative. *Nicholson* v. *Debuse,* [1927] 3 W.W.R. 799 (Alta.S.C.A.D.).

CAUSA MORTIS *(môr'-tĭs)* Lat.: in anticipation of approaching death. See **gift** [GIFT MORTIS CAUSA].

CAUSA PROXIMA *(prŏk'-sĭ-mà)* Lat.: proximate cause, most closely related cause; used to indicate legal cause. That which is sufficiently related to the result as to justify imposing liability on the actor who produces the cause, or likewise, to relieve from liability the actor who produces a less closely related cause. See **cause** [PROXIMATE CAUSE].

CAUSA SINE QUA NON *(sē'-nà kwä nŏn)* Lat.: a cause without which it would not have occurred. see CAUSA CAUSANS.

CAUSE 1. That which effects a result; 2. A **suit,** matter pending or **action;** 3. A motive or reason. In law, *cause* is not a constant and agreed-upon term. *Canadian Southern Ry. Co.* v. *Phelps* (1884), 14 S.C.R. 132.

CAUSE IN FACT Whether something is a *cause in fact* depends on whether "the relation between the defendant's **breach of duty** [in negligence law] and the plaintiff's injury is one of cause and effect in accordance with 'scientific' or 'objective' notions of physical sequence. If such a causal relation does not exist, that puts an end to the plaintiff's case: to impose liability for loss to which the defendant's conduct has not *in fact* contributed would be incompatible with the principle of individual responsibility on which the law of torts has been traditionally based." J. Fleming, *The Law of Torts* 193 (8th ed. 1992).

DIRECT CAUSE The active, efficient cause that sets in motion a train of events that brings about a result without the intervention of any other independent source. Often used interchangeably with PROXIMATE CAUSE. *Buffet* v. *Waller & Lazarnick,* [1920] 2 W.W.R. 404 (Man.C.A.).

INTERVENING OR SUPERVENING CAUSE A cause that comes into operation in producing the result and is a later event occurring after the **negligence** of the defendant.

Depending on whether the new event is viewed as breaking the chain of causation between the negligence of the defendant and the final event that has been caused, the intervening or supervening cause may or may not exonerate the defendant. *Thompson* v. *Toorenburgh* (1972), 29 D.L.R. (3d) 608 (B.C.S.C.). *Bradford* v. *Kanellos,* [1971] 2 O.R. 393 (C.A.); affirmed by (1973), 40 D.L.R. (3d) 578 (S.C.C.).

PROBABLE CAUSE See **reasonable and probable cause.**

PROXIMATE CAUSE That which in natural and continuous sequence, unbroken by any new independent cause, produces an event, or without which the injury would not have occurred. In criminal and **tort** law, the defendant's **liability** is generally limited to results proximately caused by his conduct or omission. That the defendant's negligence has been established as a causal faction of the injury does not necessarily suffice for legal liability. See further J. Fleming, *The Law of Torts* 202 (8th ed. 1992).

SUPERSEDING CAUSE The doctrine of NOVUS ACTUS INTERVENIENS—i.e., an intervening cause that is so substantially responsible for the ultimate injury that it acts to cut off the liability of preceding actors regardless of whether their prior negligence was or was not a substantial factor in bringing about the injury complained of. This doctrine will not be available if the intervening act was a foreseeable consequence of the original actor's **negligence.** See dissenting judgment of Spence, J., in *Bradford* v. *Kanellos,* (1973), 40 D.L.R. (3d) 578 at 580 (S.C.C.).

CAUSE OF ACTION A claim in law and fact sufficient to demand judicial attention; the composite of facts necessary to give rise to the enforcement of a right. A RIGHT OF ACTION is the legal right to sue; a cause of action is the set of facts that give rise to a right of action. Should a cause of action not be disclosed in the documentation, the case will be **dismissed.**

The violation of any legal right committed knowingly constitutes **prima facie** a cause of action. *Sleuter* v. *Scott* (1914), 6 W.W.R. 451 (B.C.S.C.). Also see *Read* v. *Brown* (1888), 22 Q.B.D. 128 (C.A.).

CAVEAT *(kā'-vē-ăt)* Lat.: let him beware. In general, a warning for caution. It is a notice to some officer or judge to make an entry in order that a certain step in **proceedings** will not be taken without prior notice to the individual (CAVEATOR) who lodges the caveat. An example of a caveat would be a notice in writing that no **grant** is to be sealed in the estate of the deceased named (in the case of a **will**) without notice to the caveator. The main object of a caveat in this case is to enable a person who is considering opposing a grant to obtain evidence or legal advice on the matter. *Re McDevitt* (1913), 5 O.W.N. 333 (S.C.); *Grace* v. *Kuebler & Brunner* (1917), 56 S.C.R. 1.

CAVEAT EMPTOR *(kā'-vē-ăt ĕmp'-tôr)* Lat.: let the buyer beware. The rule of law that a purchaser buys at his own risk. In the areas of commercial and consumer law, the provincial legislatures have modified this harsh principle. Consumers now have certain rights respecting the purchase of goods—for example, warranties and conditions of fitness, merchantability (except where goods are bought expressly "as is"). *Public Utilities Commission for City of Waterloo* v. *Burroughs Business Machines Ltd.,* [1973] 2 O.R. 472 (H.C.J.); *Venus Electric Ltd.* v. *Brevel Products Ltd.* (1978), 19 O.R. (2d) 417 (C.A.).

CERTIFICATE OF DEPOSIT A bank's acknowledgement of receipt of money, with an engagement to repay it, establishing a debtor-creditor relationship between bank and depositor. The writing may or may not be a **negotiable instrument,** depending on whether it meets the requirements of negotiability. See *Bills of Exchange Act*, R.S.C. 1985, c. B–4.

CERTIFICATION In accordance with the appropriate provincial and federal legislation, a board may certify a trade union as a bargaining agent of employees of a unit and give the union full bargaining rights. The basis of certification by the board is that the **trade union** has the support of the majority of the employees in the unit. See, e.g., *Canada Labour Code*, R.S.C. 1985, c. L–2, s. 12.

CERTIORARI *(sêr'-shē-ô-rä'-rē)* A means of achieving judical review; a **common-law writ** issued from a superior court to one of inferior **jurisdiction,** inquiring into the validity of the proceedings of the latter. The writ is issued in either **civil** or **criminal** proceedings and it is commonly used for the purpose of **quashing** orders, alleged to be erroneous, of courts of summary jurisdiction. The writ is used to determine whether there have been any irregularities in the proceedings of the inferior **tribunal.** *R.* v. *Titchmarsh* (1914), 32 O.L.R. 569 (S.C.A.D.). Many provinces have codified judicial review procedure. See *Judicial Review Procedure Act,* R.S.O. 1990, c. J. 1.

CHAIN OF TITLE The successive **conveyances** of a certain property, commencing with the Crown **grant** or other original source, each being a perfect conveyance of the **title** down to and including the conveyance to the present holder. The recorded chain of title consists only of the documents affecting title that are recorded in a manner that makes the fact of their existence readily available to a **bona fide purchaser.** In Canada, there are two

major systems for recording land documents. The first is the REGISTRY SYSTEM, in which the instruments concerning land are registered in the appropriate registry office in grantor/grantee indices from which one can trace the title to land. This system is governed by statute in each province. See e.g., *Registry Act*, R.S.N.S. 1989, c. 392; *Registry Act*, R.S.O. 1990, c. R. 20; *Registry Act*, R.S.N.S. 1973, R–6.

See **registry [of deeds].** This system is slowly being supplanted by the LAND TITLES SYSTEM (or Torrens system, as it is known in some countries). A main distinction between land titles and registration is that under land titles the Government in effect guarantees the accuracy of the title as shown on the record. See e.g., *Land Titles Act*, R.S.O. 1990, c. L. 5; *Land Titles Act*, R.S.A. 1980, c. L–5. See **abstract of title; clear title; registry acts; title search; warranty deed.**

CHALLENGE Generally, the right to take exception to the jurors selected for a civil or criminal action. A challenge may be made by either party in a civil action. In criminal actions challenges may be made on the part of either the Crown or the accused. Challenges are of two kinds: a "challenge to the array" or a "challenge to the polls." A challenge to the array is an exception taken to the panel of jurors collectively on the grounds of partiality, fraud or willful misconduct on the part of the sheriff or his deputies by whom the jurors were returned. A challenge to the polls is an exception taken to one or more of the jurors who have appeared individually. See, e.g., *Criminal Code*, R.S.C. 1985, c. C–34, ss. 629–644. See **peremptory.**

CHAMPERTY See **maintenance.**

CHANCELLOR 1. In early English law, the name of the King's minister who would dispense justice in the King's name by extraordinary equitable relief (see **relief**) where the remedy at law was inadequate to do substantial justice. 2. Later, the name given to the chief judge of the Court of **Chancery,** i.e., the court of equity. In Canada and England, the courts of equity and law have been fused by the **judicature acts** of the provinces.

CHANCERY The jurisprudence that is

exercised in a **court of equity,** originally by the **chancellor;** synonymous with **equity,** or equitable jurisdiction. See *In re K. (Infant),* [1965] A.C. 201 (H.L.).

Equitable jurisdiction also existed in many of the provinces. In Ontario, a court of chancery was created in 1837. A judge known as the Vice-Chancellor exercised judicial powers over matters such as fraud, deceit, partnership, lunacy, trust, account, and guardianship.

CHARGE **1.** In criminal law, the underlying substantive offence contained in an **accusation** or **indictment. 2.** In trial practice, an address delivered by the court to the **jury** at the close of the **case,** instructing the jury as to the principles of law they are required to apply in reaching a decision. The judge may express his own opinion as to the importance of the evidence offered and as to the credibility of any particular witness; however, in this latter respect the judge must make it clear to the jury that they are not bound to accept his opinion concerning the facts. *Rex* v. *Gouin* (1926), 41 Que.K.B. 157. See also Robinette, *Charge to the Jury,* Special Lectures of the Law Society of Upper Canada 147 (1959).

3. In property law, a charge is an **encumbrance, lien,** or claim, a burden on the land. As such, it is a form of security for the satisfaction of a debt or performance of an obligation.

4. In its broadest sense, it means simply to entrust with, by way of responsibility, duty, etc. *F. C. Richert Co.* v. *Larkin,* [1928] 3 W.W.R. 305 (Alta.S.C.A.D.); *Dominion Creosoting Co.* v. *T. R. Nickerson Co.* (1917), 55 S.C.R. 303.

CHARTER **1.** A document issued that establishes a corporate entity; the governing instrument of a company that, among other things, contains the company name and purposes, its **capital,** and the number of **shares** into which that capital is divided. See **association, memorandum of.**

2. In earlier law, the term referred to a grant from the Sovereign guaranteeing to the person or persons therein named certain rights, privileges, and powers.

The Magna Carta, or Great Charter, granted by King John to the English barons in 1215, established the basis for English constitutional government. *Miller* v. *Thompson* (1866), 16 U.C.C.P. 513. Canada has the **Canadian Charter of Rights**

and Freedoms contained in the *Constitution Act, 1982.*

CHATTEL In general, any property less than **freehold.** A CHATTEL PERSONAL is any tangible, moveable thing. CHATTELS REAL are interests in land less than freehold—for example, **leasehold.** *Davidson* v. *Reynolds* (1865), 16 U.C.C.P. 140. *Re Estate of Isabella McMillan* (1902) 4 O.L.R. 415 (in chambers). See **personal property.**

CHATTEL MORTGAGE See **mortgage.**

CHEQUE The *Bills of Exchange Act,* R.S.C. 1985, c. B–4, ss. 165(1), defines a cheque as a **bill of exchange** (see s. 16(1)) drawn on a bank and payable on demand. *McLellan* v. *McLellan* (1911), 25 O.L.R. 214 (Div.Ct.); *Northern Bank* v. *Yuen* (1909), 11 W.L.R. 698.

CERTIFIED CHEQUE A cheque containing a certification that the drawer of the cheque has sufficient funds to cover payment of the cheque. It indicates that the bank will retain a sufficient amount of the drawer's funds to cover payment of the cheque on demand.

CHILD SUPPORT See **maintenance.**

CHOSE *(shōz)* Fr.: thing. A thing either presently possessed [CHOSE IN POSSESSION] or claimed [CHOSE IN ACTION].

CHOSE IN ACTION "A chose in action ... is an **incorporeal right** to something not in one's possession and, accordingly, it is not possible for the debtor to have possession of it." *Re Attorney-General for Ontario and Royal Bank of Canada,* [1970] 2 O.R. 467 at 470 (C.A.). The right to recover money **(debt)** or **damages** in a legal action; merely a right to sue. It becomes a CHOSE IN POSSESSION only upon successful completion of a lawsuit. *Re Dominion Coal Co. Ltd.* (1974), 9 N.S.R. (2d) 312 (S.C.A.D.).

CHOSE IN POSSESSION As opposed to a chose in action, a thing actually possessed (or possessable).

C.I.F. Cost, insurance, and freight; also written c.f.i. In a **contract** of sale, it means that the cost of the goods, the insurance thereon, and the freight to the destination are included in the contract price. The seller's responsibilities in this sort of contract are the following: "firstly to ship at the port of shipment goods of the description contained in the contract;

CIRCUIT COURT 41 CIVIL RIGHTS

secondly to procure a contract of af-freightment, under which the goods will be delivered at the destination contemplated by the contract; thirdly to arrange for an insurance upon the terms current in the trade which will be available for the benefit of the buyer; fourthly, to make out an invoice ... and finally to tender these documents to the buyer so that he may know what freight he has to pay and obtain delivery of the goods, if they arrive, or recover for their loss if they are lost on the voyage." *Schmidt* v. *Wilson & Canham Ltd.* (1920), 47 O.L.R. 194 (H.C.).

CIRCUIT COURT In Canada, refers to the practice of the superior court of the province travelling to various points in the province for sitting.

CIRCUMSTANTIAL EVIDENCE Indirect evidence; secondary facts by which a principal fact may be rationally inferred. Sometimes a fact in **issue** cannot be proved by direct evidence and must be established by proof of other facts. If sufficient other facts are proved, the court may from the circumstances infer that the fact in issue exists or does not exist. In this case proof is made by the circumstantial evidence. For a judicial consideration of circumstantial evidence, see *The King* v. *Edward Cook* (1914), 48 N.S.R. 150 (S.C.). It should be added that, in criminal cases where circumstantial evidence is involved, the rule in *Hodge's Case* (1838), 2 Lewin 227; 168 E.R. 1136 (Crown), must be satisfied. This rule states that in a criminal case based on circumstantial evidence the circumstances must be consistent with the conclusion that the act was committed by the accused and inconsistent with any other rational conclusion.

CITATION **1.** A reference to a source of legal authority, e.g., a citation to a **statute** or **case.** See further the Key to Effective Use of This Dictionary for examples of such citations. **2.** A **writ** that may be issued calling upon a person who is not a party to an **action** or **proceeding** to appear before the court. Compare **subpoena.**

CIVIL **1.** The branch of law that pertains to suits other than criminal practice and is concerned with the rights and duties of persons in **contract, tort,** etc.; **2. civil law** as opposed to **common law.**

CIVIL ACTION An action to protect a private, **civil** right or to compel a civil remedy in a dispute between private parties, as distinguished from a criminal **prosecution.**

CIVIL CONTEMPT See **contempt of court.**

CIVIL LAW **1.** Roman law embodied in the *Justinian Code (Codex Justinianeus)* and presently prevailing in most western European states and in Louisiana in the United States. The private law of the province of Quebec is governed by two major civil codes: the *Civil Code* of the province of Quebec and the *Code of Civil Procedure.* The former is an exhaustive code containing rules and principles governing virtually all areas of **substantive law.** The latter contains approximately 950 articles and sets out the rules of civil procedure for Quebec. **2.** The part of the law concerned with non-criminal matters. **3.** The body of laws prescribed by the supreme power of the state, as distinguished from **natural law.**

CIVIL LIABILITY Amenability to **civil action,** as distinguished from criminal action; liability relating to actions seeking private remedies or the enforcement of personal rights, based on **contract, tort,** etc.

CIVIL LIBERTIES See **civil rights.**

CIVIL RIGHTS From the Latin *civilis;* a citizen as distinguished from a barbarian. In general, civil rights mean the rights that are the outgrowth of civilization, that arise from the needs of civil as distinguished from barbaric communities, and that are given, defined, and circumscribed by such positive laws, enacted by such communities, as are necessary to the maintenance of organized government. *Hill* v. *Hill,* [1929] 2 W.W.R. 41 at 47 (Alta.S.C.A.D.).

Section 92(13) of the *Constitution Act, 1867,* confers upon the provincial legislature the power to make laws in relation to "property and civil rights in the province." A distinction is to be drawn here between civil rights and civil liberties as understood in a Canadian context: the former, as employed in the *Constitution Act, 1867,* refers to those proprietary, contractual, and tortious rights between individuals in society, while the latter refers to those democratic rights and freedoms that govern the relationship between the individual and the institutions—whether social, political, or economic—of society. P. Hogg, *Constitutional Law of Canada* 540 (3d ed. 1992). Historically, civil liberties in Canada were accorded no direct constitutional protection. The passage in 1960 of the **Canadian Bill of Rights** did not alter this situation, for, as a federal statute, the *Canadian Bill of Rights* could be amended or repealed by Parliament and was limited in its application to federal laws. Consequently, civil liberties were deemed to "exist when there is an absence of legal rules: whatever is not forbidden is a civil liberty." *Id.* However, a direct constitutional safeguard for Canadian civil liberties was effected by the passage of the *Constitution Act, 1982,* for that legislation, **inter alia,** entrenched the **Canadian Charter of Rights and Freedoms** in the constitution. See **Human Rights.**

CIVITAS *(sĭ'-vĭ-täs)* Lat.: the citizenry; the community. In Roman Law, any body of people living under the same laws; a state, commonwealth, community.

CLAIM **1.** The assertion of a right to money or **property. 2.** The aggregate of operative facts giving rise to a right enforceable in the courts. A claim must show the existence of a right, an injury, and a **prayer** for **damages.** One who makes a claim is the CLAIMANT.

CLASS ACTION A lawsuit brought by representative member(s) of a large group of persons on behalf of all members of the group. The number of persons represented must be so numerous that it is not practicable to join them as plaintiffs. The class must be ascertainable, the members must share a common interest in the issues of law and fact raised by the plaintiff(s) and the action must satisfy other special requirements applicable to class actions before the trial court will specifically certify the **action** to be one maintainable as a class action.

For the procedures to be taken in the case of a class action, see G. Watson, *Canadian Civil Procedure* 711–21 (3d ed. 1988). See also *Shaw* v. *Real Estate Board of Greater Vancouver* (1973), 36 D.L.R. (3d) 250 (B.C.C.A.); *Farnham* v. *Fingold,* [1973] 2 O.R. 132 (C.A.); *Ontario*

Rules of Civil Procedure, R.R.O. 1990, Reg. 194 r. 12.

CLEAN HANDS The concept in **equity** that claimants who seek equitable **relief** must not themselves have indulged in any impropriety in relation to the transaction in which relief is sought. A party with "unclean hands" cannot ask a court of conscience [the equity court] to come to his aid. *Klemkowich* v. *Klemkowich* (1954), 14 W.W.R. 418 (Man.Q.B.).

CLEAR TITLE Also termed **good title. A** clear or good **title** is one that is free from any **encumbrance,** obstruction, burden, or limitation that presents a doubtful or even a reasonable question of law or fact. *Canadian Northern Ry.* v. *Peterson* (1914), 6 W.W.R. 1194 (Sask.S.C.D.). See **marketable title.**

CLEMENCY See **pardon.**

CLERICAL ERROR An immediately correctable mistake resulting from the copying or transmission of legal documents. As distinguished from a **judicial error, a** clerical error is known by the character of the error and is not dependent on who makes the error, be it clerk or judge. See also **rectification.**

CLOSE **1.** An ancient term referring to an enclosure, whether surrounded by a visible or an invisible boundary. **2.** Land rightfully owned by a party, the **trespass** upon which is **actionable** at law. See **breaking a close. 3.** To terminate or complete—for example, to close an account, a **bargain,** an **estate.**

CODE A systematic compilation of the laws of one particular jurisdiction or of one area of law—for example, the Ontario *Human Rights Code,* R.S.O. 1990, c. H. 19. Codification is more prevalent in American jurisdictions; however, a notable exception is the **civil law** of Quebec encompassed in the Civil Code. See also **criminal code.**

CODICIL A supplement to a **will** or an addition made by the **testator** and annexed to and to be taken as part of a testament. A reference to the will carries with it a reference to that which is merely a supplement to it, and the mere fact that the testator describes the will only to its original date is not sufficient to exclude the inference that the will referred to is the will as modified by the codicils. *Re Hunter* (1911), 24 O.L.R. 5 (Div.Ct.).

COERCION The use of physical or moral force in an attempt to interfere with the exercise of free choice. *Hodges* v. *Webb*, [1920] 2 Ch. 70. See **duress; undue influence.**

COGENT Appealing forcibly to the mind; convincing. The word *cogent* is frequently used to describe the quality of a particular legal argument.

COGNIZABLE Within the **jurisdiction** of the court. An interest is cognizable in a court of law when that court has power to **adjudicate** the interest in controversy.

COHABITATION "The state of dwelling or living together as husband and wife; often with reference to persons who are not legally married, and usually but not always implying sexual intercourse. It is most generally used for the purpose of implying intercourse and is even commonly used as such in the Courts on examination of witnesses and is taken to include actual sexual intercourse." *Mitchell* v. *Mitchell*, [1941] 3 W.W.R. 152 at 153 (Man.K.B.).

"Cohabitation may be of two sorts, one continuous, the other intermittent. The parties may reside together constantly, or there may be only occasional intercourse between them, which may nevertheless, amount to cohabitation in the legal sense of the term." *Huxtable* v. *Huxtable* (1899), 68 L.J.P. 83 at 85 (Div.Ct.).

CO-HEIR One who inherits property jointly with another or others, either by **will** or upon **intestacy.**

CO-INSURANCE A plan of **insurance** wherein the **insurer** provides **indemnity** for only a certain percentage of the insured's loss. The plan reflects the division of risk between insurer and **insured.** This division is dependent on the relative amount of the policy and the actual value of the property insured. *Eckhardt* v. *Lancashire Insurance Co.* (1900), 27 O.A.R. 373 at 382–83 (C.A.), affirmed by 31 S.C.R. 72.

COLLATERAL **1.** Situated at the side; parallel or additional. Usually does not mean secondary or auxiliary unless specifically implied by the context. *The Royal Bank of Canada* v. *Slack,* [1958] O.R. 262 (C.A.).

2. In commercial transactions, collateral security "is any property which is **assigned** or pledged to secure the performance of an obligation and as additional thereto, and which upon the performance of the obligation is to be surrendered or discharged." *Id.,* at 273 (C.A.). To obtain credit, it is sometimes necessary to offer some collateral, i.e., to place within the legal control of the lender some property that in the event of a default may be sold and applied to the amount owing.

COLLATERAL CONTRACT A **contract** that is additional to another contract, as "a contract the consideration for which is the making of some other contract....It is collateral to the main contract, but each has an independent existence, and they do not differ in respect of their possessing to the full the character and status of a contract." *Heilbut, Symons & Co.* v. *Buckleton,* [1913] A.C. 30 at 47 (H.L.).

COLLATERAL WARRANTY A **warranty** collateral to the main contract.

COLLATERAL ATTACK A challenge to the integrity of a **judgment,** brought in a special **proceeding** intended for that express purpose. A DIRECT ATTACK, on the other hand, is an attempt to impeach a judgment within the same **action** in which the judgment was obtained, through an appeal, request for a new trial, etc. Lack of proper **jurisdiction** is often grounds for a collateral attack. **Habeas corpus** is a collateral attack remedy.

COLLATERAL ESTOPPEL The doctrine that recognizes that the determination of facts **litigated** between two **parties** in a **proceeding** is binding on those parties in all future proceedings against each other. In a subsequent **action** between the parties on a different **claim,** the judgment is conclusive as to the **issues** raised in the subsequent action, if these issues were actually litigated and determined in the prior action. See **estoppel.** See also **bar; res judicata.**

COLLECTIVE AGREEMENT See **collective bargaining agreement.**

COLLECTIVE BARGAINING In general, negotiating with a view to the conclusion of a collective agreement, or the renewal or revision of an existing collective agreement. See the appropriate federal or provincial labour **legislation.** *Otis Elevator Co. Ltd.* v. *Int'l Union of Elevator Constructors, Local No. 82,* [1973] 4 W.W.R. 355 (B.C.C.A.).

COLLECTIVE BARGAINING AGREEMENT Also termed "collective agreement." An agreement between an employer and a **trade union** setting forth terms and conditions of employment. *Otis Elevator Co. Ltd.* v. *Int'l Union of Elevator Constructors, Local No. 82,* [1973] 4 W.W.R. 355 (B.C.C.A.).

COLLOQUIUM An old term in **pleading.** Words in a **declaration** or complaint of **libel** under **common-law** pleadings, which purport to connect the libelous words with the **plaintiff** by setting forth extrinsic facts, showing that they applied to him and were so intended by the **defendant.**

COLLUSION 1. The making of an agreement with another for the purposes of perpetrating a **fraud,** or engaging in illegal activity, or in legal activity while having an illegal end in mind. Compare **conspiracy. 2.** In the context of divorce law, the *Divorce Act,* R.S.C. 1985 (2nd Supp.), c. 3, s. 11(4) defines collusion as ". . . an agreement or conspiracy to which an applicant for a divorce is either directly or indirectly a party for the purpose of subverting the administration of justice, and includes any agreement, understanding, or arrangement to fabricate or suppress evidence or to deceive the court, but does not include an agreement to the extent that it provides for separation between the parties, financial support, division of property or the custody of any child of the marriage."

Under s. 11(1)(*a*) of the Act, it is the duty of the court to satisfy itself that there has been no collusion when an application for divorce is made, and to dismiss the application if there has been collusion.

COLLUSIVE ACTION An impermissible **action** maintained by non-**adversary parties** to determine a hypothetical point of law or to produce a desired legal **precedent.** Because such a suit does not contain an actual **controversy,** it will not be entertained by a court. Compare **declaratory judgment.**

COLOUR Semblance; disguise. Often used to designate the hiding of a set of facts behind a deceptive, but technically proper, legal theory.

COLOURABLE Presenting an appearance that does not correspond with reality, or an appearance intended to conceal or deceive. *Etherington* v. *Wilson* (1875), 1 Ch.D. 160.

COLOUR OF LAW Mere semblance of a legal right. An action done under colour of law is one done with the apparent authority of law but actually in contravention of law.

COLOUR OF RIGHT "The term ... generally, although not exclusively, refers to a situation where there is an assertion of a proprietary or possessory right to the thing which is the subject matter of the [alleged offence]. One who is honestly asserting what he believes to be an honest claim cannot be said to act 'without colour of right,' even though it may be unfounded in law or fact....The term 'colour of right' is also used to denote an honest belief in a state of facts which if it actually existed would at law justify or excuse the act done....The term when used in the latter sense is merely a particular application of the doctrine of mistake of fact." *Regina* v. *DeMarco* (1973), 22 C.R.N.S. 258 at 260 (Ont.C.A.). See **mistake** [MISTAKE OF FACT]. See also *Criminal Code,* R.S.C. 1985, c. C-46, s. 429(2).

COLOUR OF TITLE Something lending the appearance of **title,** when in reality there is no title at all; said of an **instrument** that, on its face, professes to pass title and that one relies on as passing title, but that fails to do so, either because title is lacking in the person conveying or because the **conveyance** itself is defective. Thus, one possessing a forged or false **deed** has mere colour of title. Colour of title is sometimes an element of **adverse possession.** A person is said to hold under colour of title when he occupies land in the belief that he has legal title to the land but in fact does not. There are numerous ways in which such a mistake as to title may arise. The most common is where a deed is improperly executed or registered. A party does *not* hold under colour of title when he believes he has been given permission to occupy the land and in fact has not. See *Walker* v. *Russell,* [1966] 1 O.R. 197 (H.C.); *Wood* v. *LeBlanc* (1904), 34 S.C.R. 627; *Harris* v. *Mudie* (1882), 7 O.A.R. 414 (C.A.).

COMBINES [LEGISLATION] In Canada, most restraint of trade offences are dealt with under the *Competition Act,* R.S.C.

1985. c. C–34, as amended by R.S.C. 1985 (2nd Supp.), c. 19. This Act attempts to prevent monopolies or illegal trade practices, such as resale price maintenance, misleading advertising, conspiracy to prevent competition, etc., making each an offence under the Act. Proceedings are undertaken in either the criminal courts or the Federal Court, and the court may impose as a penalty a fine or imprisonment or both. See *Criminal Code*, R.S.C. 1985, c. C–46, ss. 466–467. In the United States, legislation designed to prevent monopolies by insuring freedom of competition are termed antitrust laws. designed to prevent monopolies by insuring freedom of competition are termed antitrust laws.

COMITY [COMITAS] Courtesy; compatibility; respect. The informal and non-mandatory courtesy sometimes referred to as a set of rules to which the courts of one **jurisdiction** often defer in determining questions where the laws or interests of another jurisdiction are involved. *C.N.R.* v. *Lewis*, [1930] 4 D.L.R. 537 (Ex.Ct.).

COMMENT The statement made by a judge or counsel concerning the defendant, such a statement not being based on fact, but rather on **alleged** facts. It should be noted that a judge may comment on the weight of the evidence and the credibility of witnesses provided that the **jury** understands it is their province to decide such questions. By s. 4(5) of the *Canada Evidence Act*, R.S.C. 1985, c. C–5, "the failure of the person charged or of the wife or husband of such person, to testify, shall not be made the subject of comment by the judge, or by counsel for the prosecution." Also, a prosecutor may not comment on the refusal to testify of a defendant in a criminal proceeding, and the court may not instruct a jury that such silence is evidence of guilt. *The King* v. *Charles King* (1905), 9 C.C.C. 426 (N.W.T.S.C.). *Rex* v. *Portigal*, [1923] 2 W.W.R. 289 (Man.C.A.).

COMMERCIAL PAPER A **negotiable instrument**; i.e., a writing **endorsed** by the **maker** or **drawee,** containing an unconditional promise or order to pay a certain sum on demand or at a specified time, made payable to order or to bearer. The term comprehends **bills of exchange, cheques,** notes, and **certificates of deposit.**

In common, untechnical usage, it also **may be used to refer to bills of sale** (chattel mortgages) and **conditional sales contracts.** See also **bearer instrument; mortgage** [CHATTEL MORTGAGE].

COMMITTEE 1. "[A]n individual or a body to which others have committed or delegated a particular duty, or have taken on themselves to perform it in the expectation of their act being confirmed by the body they profess to represent or act for." *Reynell* v. *Lewis* (1846), 153 E.R. 959 at 959 (Ex.). **2.** Frequently used to refer to a person to whom the **custody** of another or the **estate** of an insane person has been committed.

COMMODITY "Something produced for use or **sale,** all things, which have prices and are offered for sale, everything moveable which is bought and sold, anything moveable that is the subject of trade and commerce...." *Underwriters' Survey Bureau Ltd.* v. *Massie & Renwick Ltd.,* [1937] Ex.C.R. 15 at 21; varied without reference to this point, [1937] S.C.R. 265.

COMMON LAW The system of **jurisprudence,** which originated in England and was later applied in Canada, that is based on judicial **precedent** rather than legislative enactments; it is to be contrasted with **civil law** (the descendant of Roman law prevalent in other Western countries and in Quebec) and **equity** (the body of rules administered by the Court of Chancery). Common law depends for its authority upon the recognition given by the courts to principles, customs, and rules of conduct previously existing among the people. It is now recorded in the law reports that embody the decisions of the judges, together with the reasons they assigned for their decisions. *The King* v. *Mason* (1918), 39 D.L.R. 54 (Que. Police Mag.Ct.).

COMMON MISTAKE See **mistake** [MUTUAL MISTAKE].

COMMON NUISANCE See **nuisance.**

COMMON PROPERTY See **property.**

COMMONS 1. Land set aside for public use, e.g., public parks. **2.** The untitled class of Great Britain, represented in Parliament by the House of Commons. **3.** As a carry-over from the British parliamentary system, the term **House of Commons** is also applied to the main Canadian federal legislative body (i.e., the federal **legislature**).

COMMUTATION Substitution; change. **1.** The change to a lesser penalty from a greater one, such as life imprisonment instead of death, or a shorter term instead of a longer one. The Governor-General in Council has the power of clemency, which includes the broad power in his discretion to commute a sentence. See **pardon** and **reprieve. 2.** The **conversion** of the right to receive a variable or periodic payment into the right to receive a fixed or gross payment.

COMPANY Broadly, any group of people voluntarily united for performing jointly any activity, business, or commercial enterprise. The terms *company* and *corporation* are today often used interchangeably. "The word 'company' has no strictly technical meaning. It involves ... two ideas ... first that the association is of persons so numerous as not to be aptly described as a firm; and secondly, that the consent of all the other members is not required to the transfer of a member's interest." *In re Stanley, Tennant* v. *Stanley,* [1906] 1 Ch. 131 at 134. Historically, the term has been employed to cover a wide range of organizations, including **corporations, joint stock companies, partnerships,** etc., and usually implies an enterprise for purposes of gain. In the modern context, a company is usually regarded as a business entity incorporated under the *Companies* or *Corporations Acts* of the provincial and federal jurisdictions.

HOLDING COMPANY See **holding company.**

JOINT STOCK COMPANY See **joint stock company.**

COMPENSATION Remuneration for work done; indemnification for injury sustained; that which constitutes, or is regarded as, an equivalent or recompense; that which compensates for loss or privation. Often used with reference to the expropriation of property for public use; a FAIR COMPENSATION is just both to the owner of the property taken and to the public. See also **damages.**

COMPETENT Capable of doing a certain thing; having the capacity to understand and to act reasonably. Competent **evidence** is relevant to the issues being lit-

igated; a competent court has proper **jurisdiction** over the person or property at issue. An individual is competent to make a **will** if he is "of sound mind, memory and understanding." "When a will is contested on the ground of mental incapacity, the **executors** must prove that the **testator** had a sound disposing mind. This means that they must show that the testator was not only able to understand what he was doing, but that he was able to comprehend and recollect what property he had and remember the persons that he might be expected to benefit. He must understand, too, the extent of what he is giving to each beneficiary and the nature of the claim of others, whom he is excluding." 1 T. Feeney, *The Canadian Law of Wills: Probate* 31 (3d ed. 1987). See *Murphy* v. *Lamphier* (1914), 31 O.L.R. 287 (H.C.)

In a criminal proceeding, a court may "order an assessment of the **accused**'s mental condition if it has reasonable grounds to believe that such **evidence** is necessary to determine: . . . whether the accused is unfit to stand trial; . . . [to determine] the appropriate **disposition** to be made, where a **verdict** of not criminally responsible on account of **mental disorder** or unfit to stand trial has been rendered in respect of the accused . . . The court may order the assessment at any stage of the **proceedings** against the accused of its own **motion** or on the application of the accused or the **prosecutor.**" R. Salhany, *Canadian Criminal Procedure* c. 6 at 145 (6th ed. 1994). See *Criminal Code,* R.S.C. 1985 c. 46, ss. 672.11–12, 672.22–33.

Section 2 of the *Criminal Code* defines "unfit to stand trial" to mean "unable on account of mental disorder to (a) understand the nature or object of the proceedings, (b) understand the possible consequences of the proceedings, or (c) communicate with **counsel.**" Thus *competent* may refer to the accused's fitness to stand trial.

COMPLAINANT 1. Generally, the person who initiates the complaint in an **action** or **proceeding. 2.** The person against whom it is alleged that the offence was committed. Synonymous with **petitioner** and **plaintiff.**

COMPLAINT 1. A statement of fact, being the initiating step in a civil proceeding. **2.** An **allegation** against a person. **3.** A statement made to a third party by a person against whom a sexual offence has been committed. The fact of making a complaint and the complaint itself, although admissible, do not constitute corroboration of the act complained of. *R.* v. *Ball* (1957), 117 C.C.C. 366 (B.C.C.A.).

COMPOS MENTIS *(kŏm'-pōs mĕn'-tĭs)* Lat.: mentally competent. Compare **non compos mentis.**

COMPOUNDING A FELONY See **compounding an indictable offence.**

COMPOUNDING AN INDICTABLE OF-FENCE Section 141 of the *Criminal Code*, R.S.C. 1985, c. C–46, states that "everyone who asks or obtains or agrees to receive or obtain any valuable consideration for himself or any other person, by agreeing to compound [not cause criminal charges to be laid] or conceal an **indictable offence** is guilty of an indictable offence and is liable to imprisonment for two years." Compare **accessory.**

COMPULSION See **duress.**

COMPULSORY APPEARANCE See **appearance; appearance notice.**

COMPULSORY JOINDER See **joinder.**

CONCERTED ACTION [CONCERT OF AC-TION] 1. Action done in pursuance of some scheme, which has been planned and agreed upon between the parties acting together. Thus, in criminal law, concerted action is found only where there has been a **conspiracy** to commit an illegal act, i.e., all must share the criminal intent of the actual perpetrator. **2.** The term also applies to **joint tortfeasors** where there is **tort** liability for conspiracy. *Southam Co. Ltd.* v. *Gouthro*, [1948] 1 W.W.R. 593 (B.C.S.C.).

CONCLUSION OF FACT A conclusion reached solely through use of facts and natural reasoning, without resort to rules of law; inferences from evidentiary facts.

CONCLUSION OF LAW A conclusion reached through application of rules of law. In a case where one can arrive at the ultimate conclusion only by applying a rule of law, the result reached embodies a conclusion of law rather than fact.

CONCLUSIVE PRESUMPTION See **presumption.**

CONCUR To agree. A concurring opinion states agreement with the conclusion of the majority but may give different reasons why such a conclusion is reached. An opinion "concurring in the result only" is one that implies no agreement with the reasoning of the prevailing opinion but fails to state reasons of its own. Compare **dissent.**

CONCURRENT Running together; in conjunction with; existing together. In criminal law, the words *concurrent* and *consecutive* are generally used to indicate the intentions of the Court with respect to **sentencing.** When adapted to **judgments** in criminal cases, the opposite of concurrent is *consecutive* and *accumulative:* If sentences are not concurrent, they are consecutive and they accumulate. "Although the discretion whether to order the sentences to be served concurrently or consecutively rests with the trial judge, the general practice of the court in the past has been to order concurrent sentences where the offences are committed together within a short period of time and are in reality one transaction. Here the court should approach the problem by setting one over-all sentence rather than passing a multiplicity of short consecutive sentences adding up to a substantial sentence. On the other hand, if the offences are totally unrelated and took place at separate times and places, the court will consider imposing consecutive sentences." R. Salhany, *Canadian Criminal Procedure* c. 8 at 30 (6th ed. 1994). See *Criminal Code*, R.S.C. 1985, c. C–46, s. 717(4). See also *Regina* v. *Chisholm,* [1965] 4 C.C.C. 289 (Ont.C.A.); *Regina* v. *Courtney* (1956), 115 C.C.C. 260 (B.C.C.A.).

CONCURRENT CONDITION See **condition.**

CONCURRENT JURISDICTION See **jurisdiction.**

CONCURRING OPINION See **opinion.**

CONDEMN 1. To declare to be wrong; to convict of guilt; to sentence judicially. **2.** To pronounce unfit for use—e.g., an unsafe building. **3.** To declare forfeited or taken for public use—e.g., the adjudging of a captured vessel to be a lawful prize. See also **confiscate.**

CONDITION A term of a **contract** that goes so directly to the root of the contract or is so essential to its nature that, if the circumstances are, or become, inconsistent with the condition, all **executory** obligations under the contract may be treated as discharged by a party who is not in **default.** See *Wallis* v. *Pratt,* [1910] 2 K.B. 1003 at 1012. See **warranty.**

A condition may be EXPRESS or IMPLIED. Whether a particular term is to be implied depends, as a rule, solely upon the intention of the parties, as gathered from all the circumstances "with the object of giving to the transaction such efficacy as both parties must have intended that at all events it should have." *The Moorcock* (1889), 14 P.D. 64 at 68 (C.A.).

CONCURRENT CONDITION A condition precedent that exists when the obligation of each party to a contract, consisting of mutual promises, is conditional upon performance by the other.

CONDITION PRECEDENT A condition, express or implied, that the contract shall not bind one or both of the parties until or unless some event has happened.

CONDITION SUBSEQUENT A condition, express or implied, that, upon the occurrence of some event after the contract has become binding, it shall cease to be binding, or that one party or both parties shall have the right to avoid it.

CONDITIONAL Dependent upon the happening or non-happening of the **condition;** implies a type of **encumbrance.**

CONDITIONAL BEQUEST See **bequest.**

CONDITIONAL FEE [ESTATE] A **fee simple** [complete ownership of **real property**] that is limited in that it must eventually pass from the **donee** to certain **heirs** or the **issue** [children] of the donee [**heirs of the body**]. Should the designated heir fail to be in existence at the time of the death of the donee, the property **reverts** [goes back] to the donor or his **estate.** However, the entire estate rests with the donee until his death, the donor having the mere **possibility of a reverter.** Such a reverter may be released to the donee, thereby converting his estate from a fee simple conditional to a fee simple absolute. See also **determinable fee; life estate.**

CONDITIONAL SALES CONTRACT A **contract** for the sale of goods or land under which the purchase price is payable by installments and the property in the goods or land is to remain in the seller until the installments are paid.

CONDITION PRECEDENT An event or **condition** [express or **implied**] that must happen or be performed before an **estate** can **vest** or be enlarged, or before a **contract** is performed.

CONDITION SUBSEQUENT See **condition.**

CONDOMINIUM A type of ownership of individual units, generally in a multi-unit development or project—e.g., an apartment condominium. The owner will normally receive a deed upon purchase describing the scope of his ownership and the interest he possesses as **tenant in common** with other owners, such as hallways, elevators, gardens, etc. See, e.g., *Condominium Act,* R.S.O. 1990, c. C.26; R.S.N.S. 1989, c. 85. A condominium is distinguished from a COOPERATIVE form of occupancy when the **title** to the unit **premises** is not in the individual occupant, but in another entity such as a **corporation.**

CONDONATION "Condonation of a matrimonial offence means the forgiveness of the offence with a full knowledge of the circumstances followed by a reinstatement of the offending party to his or her former position." C. Davies, *Family Law in Canada* 417–18 (4th ed. 1984).

Section 11(1)(c) of the *Divorce Act,* R.S.C. 1985 (2nd Supp.), c. 3 provides that "where a divorce is sought in circumstances described in paragraph 8(2)(b)[adultery, or physical or mental cruelty] to satisfy itself that there has been no condonation or **connivance** on the part of the spouse bringing the proceeding, and to dismiss the application for a divorce if that spouse has condoned or connived at the act or conduct complained of unless, in the opinion of the court, the public interest would be better satisfied by granting the divorce."

CONFESSION An acknowledgement in express words, by the **accused** in a criminal case, of the truth of the main fact

charged, or of some essential part of it. An acknowledgement of a subordinate fact, not directly involving guilt, or in other words not essential to the crime charged, is not a confession, because the supposed ground of untrustworthiness of confessions is that a strong motive impels the accused to expose and declare his guilt as the price of purchasing immunity from present pain or subsequent punishment; and thus, by hypothesis, there must be some quality of guilt in the fact acknowledged. Confessions are only one species of **admissions.** *Rex* v. *Mandzuk,* [1945] 3 W.W.R. 280 (B.C.C.A.); *Rex* v. *Hurd* (1913), 4 W.W.R. 185 (Alta.S.C. en banc). See ss. 541, 542, 655, and 657 of the *Criminal Code,* R.S.C. 1985, c. C–46, relating to confessions.

With regard to the law concerning the admissibility of confessions into **evidence,** "it has long been established as a positive rule of ... criminal law, that no statement by an accused is admissible in evidence against him unless it is shown by the prosecution to have been a voluntary statement, in the sense that it has not been obtained from him either by fear of prejudice or hope of advantage exercised or held out by a person in authority." *Ibrahim* v. *The King,* [1914] A.C. 599 at 609 (P.C.). See also *Boudreau* v. *The King,* [1949] S.C.R. 262.

CONFESSION AND AVOIDANCE A **pleading** by which a **party** admits the **allegations** against him, either expressly or by implication, but which presents **new matter** that avoids the effect of the failure to deny those allegations. Thus a **litigant** "confesses" rather than denies the allegation, but his presentation of new matter acts to "avoid" a **judgment** against him. See G. Watson, *Canadian Civil Procedure* 369–370 (3d ed. 1988). See **defence.** Compare **denial.**

CONFISCATE To take private property without just **compensation;** to transfer property from a private use to a public use. See also **condemn.**

CONFLICT OF LAWS [CHOICE OF LAWS] The body of law by which the court where the **action** is maintained determines or chooses which law to apply where a diversity exists between the applicable law of that court's state [the **forum** state] and the applicable law of another **jurisdiction** connected with the controversy. The considerations comprising that decision formerly rested on simple and traditional rules such as LEX LOCI CONTRACTUS (law of the place where a contract is made) and LEX LOCI DELICTI (law of the place where the wrong is committed) in tort. More modern doctrine focuses on an interest analysis that very often arrives at the same choice but includes, along with the traditional considerations of place of contracting and place of the wrong, the public policy of the forum and, in general, which jurisdiction maintains the most significant relationship or contacts with the subject matter of the controversy. The interest analysis is referred to as CENTER OF GRAVITY or CONTACTS APPROACH. As a general rule, the forum state will apply its own law on questions of **procedure** regardless of a conflict. See J. G. Castel, *Canadian Conflict of Laws* 24 (3d ed. 1994); M. Hertz, *Introduction to Conflict of Laws* 1–12 (1978). See also **comity.**

CONFUSION OF GOODS The mixing together of **personal property** belonging to two or more owners to the point when the property of any of them no longer can be identified except as part of a mass of like goods.

CONGLOMERATE A group of **corporations** engaged in unrelated businesses and controlled by a single corporate entity.

CONJUGAL RIGHTS The rights of married persons, which include the enjoyment of association, sympathy, confidence, domestic happiness, the comforts of dwelling together in the same habitation, eating meals at the same table and profiting by the joint property rights, as well as the intimacies of domestic relations. See also **consortium.**

CONNIVANCE "Connivance means that the adultery of one spouse has been caused by or has been knowingly, willfully, or recklessly permitted by the other as an accessory. It is of the essence of connivance that it precedes the event, and generally, the material event is the inception of the adultery, and not its repetition." C. Davies, *Family Law in Canada* 426–27 (4th ed. 1984). *Maddock* v. *Maddock,* [1958] O.R. 810 (C.A.)

Section 11(1)(c) of the *Divorce Act,* R.S.C. 1985 (2nd Supp.), c. 3 provides that "where a divorce is sought in circumstances described in paragraph 8(2)(*b*) [adultery, or physical or mental cruelty] to satisfy itself that there has been no **condonation** or connivance on the part of the spouse bringing the proceeding, and to dismiss the application for a divorce if that spouse has condoned or connived at the act or conduct complained of unless, in the opinion of the court, the public interest would be better satisfied by granting the divorce.

Compare **collusion.**

CONSANGUINITY Relationship by blood; it is a requirement of a valid marriage in Canada that the parties must not be within prohibited degrees of consanguinity or **affinity** (relationship by marriage). The *Marriage (Prohibited Degrees) Act*, S.C. 1990, c. 46, s. 2(2) prohibits marriage between persons related "(a) lineally by consanguinity or adoption; (b) as brother and sister by consanguinity, whether by the whole blood or by the half-blood; or (c) as brother and sister by adoption." Under s. 3(2) of the *Act*, such marriages are void.

Archbishop Parker's Table of 1563, printed in the Book of Common Prayer of the Church of England, lists the degrees of prohibited relationship for male and female persons (17 each). The table specifies that the prohibited degrees are "by the whole or the half blood, and whether legitimate or illegitimate."

CONSENSUS AD IDEM *(kän-sĕn'-sŭs äd ē'-dĕm)* Lat.: agreement as to the same thing. Of the same mind; similar in all essential matters. A binding contract requires consensus ad idem [mutual agreement on the same subject matter] by both parties—i.e., a meeting of the minds.

CONSENT A deliberate and free act of the mind; an act of reason accompanied by deliberation. Thus an instrument such as a **will** may be invalidated if consent is obtained by fraud or **undue influence.** In **tort** law, the phrase *informed consent* is sometimes used with respect to the requirement that a patient be apprised of the nature and risks of a medical procedure before the physician can validly claim exemption from liability for **battery** or from responsibility for medical complications.

In **criminal** law, true consent of the complainant to the activity that forms the substance of the charge is a **defence** to the charge, if the consent is not consent to death, not excluded by the nature of the offence, freely given, and informed.

An honest belief, even if it is a mistaken and unreasonable belief, that the complainant was consenting to the activity that forms the substance of a charge of **assault** (Criminal Code, R.S.C. 1985, c. C–46, s. 265) is a defence, with the reasonableness of the belief to be considered only as to whether the belief was really held by the accused *Pappajohn* v. *The Queen*, [1980] 2 S.C.R. 120. See also *Criminal Code* s. 265(4) (honest belief in consent as a defence).

CONSEQUENTIAL DAMAGES See **damages.**

CONSERVATOR Temporary court-appointed guardian or custodian of **property.**

CONSIDERATION Something of value given in return for a performance or a promise of performance by another, for the purpose of forming a **contract;** one element of a contract that is generally required to make a promise binding and to make the agreement of the parties enforceable as a contract. To find consideration, there must be a performance or a return promise that has been bargained for by the parties. Restatement, *Contracts* 2d s. 75 (as adopted and promulgated May 1979). Consideration represents the element of bargaining, to indicate that each party agrees to surrender something in return for what it is to receive. It is consideration that distinguishes a contract from a mere **gift.**

"A valuable consideration may consist either in some right, interest, profit or benefit occurring to the one party or in some forbearance, detriment, loss or responsibility given, suffered or undertaken by the other." *Currie* v. *Misa* (1875), L.R. 10 Ex. 153 at 162.

"[T]o establish a valid contract each party must give or promise something in return for the other's act or promise. A bare, voluntary, gratuitous act or promise, unsupported by any reciprocal undertaking will not be enough. There must be mutuality; a contract must show that *both* parties are bound in some way. The act or promise of one party must be performed or given in exchange for something actually done or promised by the other." G. Fridman, *The Law of Contract in Canada*, 77–8 (2d ed. 1986).

Courts have used the word *consideration* with many different meanings. It is often used merely to express the legal conclusion that a promise is enforceable. Historically, its primary meaning may have been that the conditions were met under which an action of **assumpsit** [an early form of contract action] would lie. It was also used as the equivalent of the **quid pro quo** required in an action of **debt**. A **seal**, it has been said, imports a consideration, although the law was clear that no element of bargain was necessary to enforcement of a promise under seal. On the other hand, consideration has sometimes been used to refer to almost any reason asserted for enforcing a promise, even though the reason was insufficient [as in] promises in consideration of love and affection, illegal consideration, past consideration, and consideration furnished by reliance on a gratuitous promise where in fact there has been no consideration at all.

The phrase SUFFICIENT CONSIDERATION is used by some courts to express the legal conclusion that one requirement for an enforceable bargain has been met. This is redundant and misleading, however, since any performance or return promise that has been bargained for and received is legally sufficient to satisfy the consideration element of a contract. The law will not in general inquire into the adequacy of "consideration," and hence the term does not add anything of substance to the word *consideration*. So long as the bargained-for promise is not illusory or the performance a sham pretext, a sufficient exchange will have taken place to justify the enforcement of the agreement so far as consideration is at issue.

The performance may be any lawful act done for the benefit of the other contracting party or a third person and may include an act of forbearance. A MORAL CONSIDERATION will not generally qualify as consideration so as to render the promise enforceable.

FAILURE OF CONSIDERATION refers to the circumstances in which consideration was bargained for but either has become worthless, has ceased to exist or has not been performed as promised. Failure of consideration may be partial or total and is often used interchangeably with WANT OF CONSIDERATION. See further *id.*, Chapter 3.

CONSIGNMENT 1. The act of consigning; the act of sending off goods to an **agent** for **sale. 2.** Goods sent or delivered to an agent for sale.

CONSOLIDATION See **merger.**

CONSORTIUM The conjugal fellowship of husband and wife, and the right of each to the company, cooperation and aid of the other. Where a person willfully interferes with this relation, depriving one spouse of the consortium of the other, he may be liable in **damages.** Loss of consortium often figures in an award of damages in a **tort** action for injury or wrongful death of a spouse. See, e.g., *Best* v. *Samuel Fox & Co.*, [1952] A.C. 716 (H.L.). In some Canadian jurisdictions, purposeful interference with consortium may also give rise to an action for **alienation of affection.** See also **conjugal rights.**

CONSPIRACY "A conspiracy consists not merely in the intention of two or more, but in the agreement of two or more to do an unlawful act, or to do a lawful act by unlawful means. So long as such a design rests in intention only, it is not **indictable.** When two agree to carry it into effect, the very plot is an act in itself, and the act of each of the parties ... punishable if for a criminal object." *Mulcahy* v. *The Queen* (1868), L.R. 3 H.L. 306 at 317, as quoted in *The Queen* v. *O'Brien*, [1954] S.C.R. 666 at 669.

And further, "it is, of course, essential that the **conspirators** have the *intention to agree*, and this agreement must be complete. There must also be a common design to do something unlawful, or something lawful by illegal means. Although it is not necessary that there should be an overt act in furtherance of the conspiracy, to complete the crime,... there must exist *an intention to put the common design into effect*. A common design necessarily involves an intention. Both are synonymous. The intention cannot be anything else but the will to attain the object of the agreement." *Id.* at 668. There must obviously be at least two people for a conspiracy since otherwise there can be no agreement. See *Criminal Code*, R.S.C. 1985, c. C–46, ss. 465–467, for a statement of specific conspiracy offences. Compare **accessory; accomplice; aid, and abet.**

A conspiracy to injure another is an actionable **tort.** See R. Heuston & R. Chambers, *Salmond and Heuston on the Law of Torts.*

CONSPIRATOR One involved in a **conspiracy.** There must be at least two conspirators in order for there to be a conspiracy. Otherwise there can be no agreement. "But it is not necessary that two people be convicted—A may be convicted of conspiring with B even though B is dead or not **prosecuted.** Or A may be convicted of conspiring only with persons unknown. But if A and B are charged with conspiring only with each other and B is acquitted then A cannot be convicted. This is not the same where A, B and C are charged with conspiracy, for if B is acquitted, A and C may still have conspired with each other. If both B and C are acquitted, it seems that A must be acquitted but,...the **verdict** may only mean that A conspired with B or C but the jury cannot be satisfied as to which of these two it was." A. Mewett & M. Manning, *Criminal Law* 180–81 (2d ed. 1985).

CONSTITUTION The construct of rules, regulations and laws—either written or unwritten—that establishes and orders the political, governmental, and legal structure of the state. A constitution defines the state's mode of political organization (e.g., republic, monarchy, oligarchy), establishes the state's principal institutions (e.g., legislative, executive, and judicial), regulates the functions of the various departments of the state apparatus and governs the relationship between the individual and the state. P. Hogg, *Constitutional Law of Canada,* (3d ed. 1992).

In Canada, the central constitutional document is the **British North America Act** of 1867 (as of 1982, renamed *Constitution Act, 1867).* This act united the three colonies of Nova Scotia, New Brunswick and Canada (Ontario and Quebec) as the Dominion of Canada, and provided for the admission of other British North American colonies and territories into the Dominion. But the *Constitution Act, 1867* was not a declaration of Canadian independence; rather, it established Canada as an internally self-governing subordinate within the British imperial system. As such, the *Constitution Act, 1867* is not and was never intended to be a definitive constitutional

document: for example, it does not mention such entrenched features of the Canadian political structure as the office of the Prime Minister, the federal Cabinet or the party system. Thus, the *Constitution Act, 1867* is "only part of our whole working Constitution," the rest of which has been added by imperial amendment, by federal legislation, by custom, by the judgments of the courts and by joint federal-provincial agreements. E. Forsey, *How Canadians Govern Themselves* 10 (3d ed. 1991).

The *Constitution Act, 1867,* contained no provision for its own amendment, for, as an act of the British Parliament, the amending process of the *Constitution Act, 1867* was vested in that legislative body. To remedy this situation, the Canadian House of Commons and the Senate approved, in December of 1981, a Joint Address to the Crown requesting the patriation—i.e., the transfer of the amending process to the Canadian Parliament—of the Canadian constitution. Following this request, the British Parliament enacted the CANADA ACT, which ended British legislative powers over Canada. Parliament simultaneously passed the *Constitution Act, 1982,* which incorporated the following new provisions into the Canadian Constitution: an indigenous amending procedure, a Charter of Rights and Freedoms, an affirmation of the existing rights of native peoples, an entrenchment of the principle of equalization and a delineation of provincial powers over resources. E. Forsey, *The Constitution and You* 10 (1982).

CONSTITUTION ACTS, 1867–1982 See **constitution.**

CONSTITUTIONAL CONVENTIONS Those rules, values, and principles—either written or unwritten—based on custom or precedent but lacking direct constitutional authority, which "regulate the working of the various parts of the constitution, their relations to one another, and to the subject." Holdsworth, *The Conventions of the Eighteenth Century Constitution,* 17 Iowa L. Rev. 161 at 162 (1932). Constitutional conventions govern the exercise of legal powers accorded by the **constitution** to the various offices, institutions, and branches (bodies) of the political structure; thus, some conventions have the effect of transferring effective power from one political office to another, while other conventions limit an apparently broad legal power or even prescribe that a legal power shall not be exercised at all. P. Hogg, *Constitutional Law of Canada* 17 (3d ed. 1992). For example, the Queen, or her representative (in Canada, the Governor-General or the Lieutenant-Governor) is empowered to veto any bill in Parliament or a provincial legislature, but by constitutional convention consent cannot be refused (this veto power cannot be exercised). This situation dramatizes the relationship between **law** and convention; for here is a constitutional law creating wide **discretionary** powers, which is limited and neutralized by a countervailing constitutional convention. *Reference Re Amendment of the Constitution of Canada* (1981), 125 D.L.R. (3d) 1 (S.C.C.). See also *Gallant* v. *The King* (1949), 2 D.L.R. 425; (1949), 23 M.P.R. 48 (P.E.I.S.C.). However, constitutional conventions derive their authority from neither judicial nor statutory sources, but rather from the institutions of government themselves. Hence a convention is legally unenforceable; for, in the breach of convention, no illegality has been committed. *Reference Re Amendment of the Constitution of Canada* (1981), 125 D.L.R. (3d) 1 (S.C.C.). Thus, the remedy for the breach of convention is political rather than legal in nature.

CONSTRUCTION The giving of an interpretation to something that is less than totally clear—e.g., to determine the construction of a **statute** or **constitution** is to determine the meaning of an ambiguous part of it; the act of construing. See also **strict construction.**

CONSTRUCTIVE Not actual but accepted in law as a substitute for whatever is otherwise required. Thus, anything the law finds to exist constructively will be treated by the law as though it were actually so. If an object is not in a person's actual **possession** but he intentionally and knowingly has dominion and control over it, the law will treat it as though it were in his actual possession by finding a constructive possession. The same is true in many other contexts.

CONSTRUCTIVE DELIVERY See **delivery.**

CONSTRUCTIVE FRAUD See **fraud.**

CONSTRUCTIVE NOTICE See **notice.**

CONSTRUCTIVE POSSESSION See **possession.**

CONTEMPT OF COURT An act or omission tending to obstruct or interfere with the orderly administration of justice or to impair the dignity of the Court or respect for its authority. In Canada, two classifications of contempt exist. One is STATUTORY [CRIMINAL] CONTEMPT, found in the *Criminal Code*, R.S.C. 1985, c. C–46, and in other federal statutes containing express references to certain forms of contempt—notably, obstructing justice, disobeying a court order and the offences covered by the sections beginning with s. 118 of the Code. The other classification is CIVIL CONTEMPT, which consists largely of disobeying a **judgment** or court order. It includes disobeying an **injunction,** refusing to testify when ordered to do so or failing to appear as a witness. Thus, in civil matters, contempt has a primarily coercive dimension, in that it obliges one party to submit to a court order issued for the benefit of another. Criminal contempt, on the other hand, results from words, acts or writings that constitute an obstruction or discredit to the administration of justice. Examples are bribing a witness or a juror, attempting to influence a judge, falsely accusing a judge of bias, or disobeying a court order in a criminal case.

CONTIGUOUS Near to or in close proximity to.

CONTINGENT[CY] Something related to a possible future and uncertain event. See **lawyer's fees.**

CONTINGENT ESTATE An **interest** in land that might or might not begin in the future, depending upon the occurrence of a specific but uncertain event or depending on the determination or existence of the person(s) to whom the estate is limited. Thus, if property is granted "to A for life and then to the heirs of B," there is a contingent estate (a contingent **remainder**) in the heirs of B, which will **vest** [become certain] at the death of A unless B is without heirs. If B is without heirs, the estate **reverts** [goes back] to the original grantor. Because a contingent estate was regarded as a mere possibility or expectancy, it was not ALIENABLE INTER VIVOS [transferable during one's lifetime] at common law. Contingent remainders were made alienable in England in 1845 and are freely alienable today in the majority of common-law jurisdictions. C. Moynihan, *Introduction to the Law of Real Property* 139–40 (2d ed. 1988). Compare **conditional fee; determinable fee.** See also **condition; future interest.**

CONTINUANCE An adjournment or postponement to a specified subsequent date of the proceedings in an **action.**

CONTRA *(kän'-trä)* Lat.: against, in opposition to, contrary to; the reverse of; in violation of; in answer to, in reply to; in defiance of. Thus, "the Court's most recent decision is contra an established line of **precedent.**"

CONTRA BONOS MORES *(kän'-trä bô'-nōs mô'-räz)* Lat.: against good morals. Refers to conduct that offends the average conscience and commonly accepted standards.

CONTRACT "[T]he branch of law that determines the circumstances in which a promise shall be legally binding on the person making it." A. Guest, *Anson's Law of Contract* 1 (26th ed. 1984). "A contract is a legally recognized agreement between two or more persons, giving rise to obligations that may be enforced in the courts. By such an agreement the parties not only restrict their present or future freedom to act, by the limitations imposed upon themselves by the agreement, they are creating a . . . set of legal rules . . . binding as regards themselves and only themselves." G. Fridman, *The Law of Contract in Canada* 3 (2d ed. 1986).

The persons entering into a contract are called the **parties** to the contract: he who makes a promise is the PROMISOR; he to whom a promise is made is the PROMISEE. If both parties promise mutually to perform or not to perform different acts, the contract is called a BILATERAL CONTRACT. If only one party makes a promise (the other party merely performing or not performing some act), it is known as a UNILATERAL CONTRACT.

A contract may be under **seal** (a formal contract or **deed**) or simple (an informal contract). A simple contract may be made orally or in writing. However, in order to be enforceable, a simple contract may be required by the various **statutes of fraud** to be evidenced in writing that is signed by the party to be **charged.** The three

essential elements of a simple contract are often said to be **offer, acceptance,** and **consideration.** In addition, the parties must have the capacity to contract, an intention to create legal relations, and a legal purpose, and the terms of the contract must be sufficiently certain.

See **quasi** [QUASI-CONTRACT]. See also **breach of contract.**

CONTRACT OF ADHESION See **adhesion contract.**

CONTRACTOR 1. One who is party to a **contract.** 2. One who contracts to do work for another. In tort law, "an INDEPENDENT CONTRACTOR is one who is his own master . . . engaged to do certain work, but to exercise his own discretion as to the mode and time of doing it—he is bound by his contract, but not by his employer's orders." R. Heuston & R. Buckley, *Salmond & Heuston on the Law of Torts* 449 (20th ed. 1992). A GENERAL BUILDING CONTRACTOR is one who contracts directly with the owner of the property upon which the construction occurs, as distinguished from a **subcontractor,** who would deal only with one of the general contractors.

CONTRACTUAL BREACH See **breach of contract.**

CONTRACT UNDER SEAL A **contract** that is signed and has the **seal** of the signer attached. The term **deed** is also applied to an instrument under seal. A sealed contract is sometimes called a FORMAL CONTRACT as distinguished from a contract without a seal, or SIMPLE CONTRACT. At common law, a contract under seal did not require **consideration,** and this was the principal distinction between it and the simple contract. See further G. Fridman, *The Law of Contract in Canada* 105–7 (2d ed. 1986). The formal requirement of delivery may be by actually handing over the instrument to the other party or to someone on his behalf, or by doing any act or using words showing an intention to treat the instrument as a presently binding deed. *Xenos* v. *Wickham* (1867), L.R. 2 H.L. 296 at 312. See **sealed instrument.**

CONTRA PACEM *(kän'-trä pä'-kĕm)* Lat.: against the peace. This phrase was used in the Latin forms of **indictments** and also in **actions** for **trespass** to signify that the alleged offence was committed against the public peace.

CONTRIBUTION A right to demand that a person jointly responsible with someone else for an injury to another person contribute to the one required to compensate the victim; the equal sharing of a common burden. In the law of **torts,** a right of contribution exists, if at all, generally by statutes although some courts have upheld the right of contribution upon the broad equitable principle that persons who are equals in the duty of bearing a common burden may be compelled by their associates to bear their share of that burden. The duty generally involves an equal sharing of the loss, but in some **jurisdictions** it may be apportioned among the **joint tortfeasors** according to their degrees of relative fault. Compare **indemnity.**

CONTRIBUTORY NEGLIGENCE See **negligence.**

CONTROVERSY A dispute that occurs when there are adversaries on a particular **issue;** an **allegation** on one side and a **denial** on the other. It is distinguished from an opinion advising what the law would be upon a hypothetical state of facts. Compare **advisory opinion; reference case.** See also **justiciable; standing.**

CONTUMACY Willful disobedience to the **summons** or orders of a court; signifies overt defiance of authority. Contumacious conduct may result in a finding of **contempt of court.**

CONVERSION The **tortious** deprivation of another's property without his authorization. "An act of wilful interference, without lawful **justification,** with any **chattel** in a manner inconsistent with the right of another, whereby that other is deprived of the use and possession of it. Two elements are combined in such reference: (1) a dealing with the chattel in a manner inconsistent with the right of the person entitled to it, and (2) an intention in so doing to deny that person's right or to assert a right which is in fact inconsistent with such right. But where the act done is necessarily a denial of the other's right or an assertion of a right inconsistent with it, intention does not matter. Conversion may consist in an act deliberately done inconsistent with another's right, though the doer may not know of or intend to challenge the property or pos-

session of that other." R. Heuston, *Salmond on the Law of Torts* 143 (14th ed. 1965), as approved in *Toronto Dominion Bank* v. *Dearborn Motors Ltd. and Reid Motors Ltd.* (1986), 64 W.W.R. 577 (B.C.S.C.).

CONVEY In the law of **real property,** to transfer property from one to another; broadly, the transfer of property or the **title** to property from one person to another by means of a written **instrument** and other formalities. Compare **alienation.** See also **grant.**

CONVEYANCE An instrument that transfers property from one person to another; "includes an **assignment,** appointment (see **power of appointment**), **lease, settlement** and other assurance, made by **deed,** on a **sale, mortgage, demise,** or settlement of any **property** or on any other dealing with or for any property, and 'convey' has a meaning corresponding with that of conveyance." *Conveyancing and Law of Property Act,* R.S.O. 1990, c. C. 34, s. 1(1). See similar provincial statutes.

CONVICT 1. One who has been determined by the court to be guilty of the crime charged. 2. To determine such guilt. One is convicted upon a valid plea of guilty or a verdict of guilty and judgment of conviction entered thereupon.

CONVICTION An equivocal word that may include both the adjudication of **guilt,** or "conviction" properly so called, and the adjudication of punishment, or **sentence** properly so called; or it may refer only to the adjudication of guilt. *Rex* v. *Vanek,* [1944] O.R. 428 (C.A.).

CO-OPERATIVE See **condominium.**

CO-OPERATIVE ASSOCIATION A union of individuals—commonly, labourers, farmers or small capitalists—formed for the pursuit in common of some productive enterprise, the profits being shared in proportion to the capital or labour contributed by each.

Organizing a company as, and calling it, a co-operative is not sufficient in law; it is the actual nature of its activities that governs its designation. So where an association holds profits other than on account for its member-producers, it is not a co-operative. See *Montreal Milk Producers' Co-op Agricultural Ass'n* v. *M.N.R.,* [1958] Ex.C.R. 19.

CO-ORDINATE JURISDICTION See **jurisdiction** [CONCURRENT JURISDICTION].

COPARCENERS Persons who, by virtue of **descent,** have become concurrent owners. See **parcener; co-heir; joint tenancy; tenancy** [TENANCY IN COMMON].

COPYRIGHT The protection by **statute** or **common law** of the works of authors and artists giving them the exclusive right to "publish" their works and to determine who may so publish. The *Copyright Act,* R.S.C. 1985, c. C–42, s. 6, as amended by S.C. 1993, c. 44, s. 58, provides that copyright subsists for the life of the author, the remainder of the calendar year in which the author dies, plus fifty years after the end of that calendar year. There is no copyright in ideas or information; only the expression of the idea is protected. See *Stevenson* v. *Crook,* [1938] Ex.C.R. 299. Copyright exists in literary, dramatic, musical, and artistic works and such other works as provided in the *Copyright Act.* Compare **plagiarism.**

CORAM NOBIS, WRIT OF See **writ of coram nobis.**

COROLLARY RELIEF See **maintenance.**

CORONER A judicial officer who investigates the cause and circumstances of a suspicious death that occurs within his **jurisdiction** and makes a finding in a coroner's **inquest.** See also **post mortem.** A coroner's court is a court of record, and the coroner is a judge of a court of record. See *Davidson* v. *Garrett* (1899), 30 O.R. 653 (Div.Ct.).

CORONER'S WARRANT An authorization by the **coroner** directing that a person alleged by the coroner's inquisition to have committed **murder** or **manslaughter** be taken before a justice or entered into a **recognizance** to appear before a justice. See *Criminal Code,* R.S.C. 1985, c. C–46, s. 529.

CORPORAL PUNISHMENT Punishment inflicted upon the body (such as whipping, which was abolished in Canada in 1972). The term may or may not include imprisonment.

CORPORATION An association of **shareholders** created under law and regarded as an **artificial person** by the courts and thus "treated like any other independent person with its rights and liabilities appropriate to itself, and ... the motives of those who took part in the promotion of the company are absolutely irrelevant in discussing what those rights and liabilities are." *Salomon* v. *Salomon & Co.,* [1897] A.C. 22 at 30 (H.L.). A corporation has the capacity of taking, holding and conveying **property,** suing and being sued, and exercising such other powers as may be conferred on it by law, just as a **natural person.**

A corporation's **liability** is normally limited to its **assets;** thus **shareholders** are protected against personal liability in connection with the affairs of the corporation. (But see **piercing the corporate veil.**) The corporation is taxed at special corporate tax rates, and shareholders must pay an additional tax upon **dividends** or other profits from the corporation. Corporations are subject to regulation by the province of incorporation (see, e.g., *Corporations Act,* R.S.O. 1990, c. C. 38) and by the **jurisdictions** in which they carry on business. The federal government has the power of incorporation of companies with objects "other than provincial." *Citizens Insurance Co. of Canada* v. *Parsons* (1881–82), 7 A.C. 96 at 116 (P.C.). See further 1 J. Ziegel, *Studies in Canadian Company Law* 244 (1967).

CORPOREAL HEREDITAMENT See **hereditaments.**

CORPUS DELICTI *(kôr′-pŭs dĕ-lĭk′-tī)* Lat.: body of the crime. The ingredients of the offence. In a murder trial, the discovery of the body affords the best evidence of the fact of death, and the term *corpus delicti* has popularly come to mean the dead body. *R.* v. *McNicholl,* [1917] 2 I.R. 557 (Cr.Ca.R.). If it is not possible to find the body, the accused may still be convicted if the fact of death is proved by **circumstantial evidence** to be a moral certainty. *R.* v. *Huculak,* [1963] 2 C.C.C. 1 (S.C.C.).

Corpus delicti applies to every crime. In rape it means proving the lack of consent and the sexual act.

CORPUS JURIS *(kôr′-pŭs, jūr′-ĭs)* Lat.: body of law. A series of texts containing much of the **civil** and **canon** [ecclesiastical] law.

CORRUPTION OF BLOOD Incapacity to **inherit** or pass **property,** usually because of attainder, such as for **treason.** (See **bill**

of attainder.) According to this feudal doctrine, which was abolished in England in 1870, the blood of the attainted person was deemed to be corrupt, so that neither could he transmit his **estate** to his **heirs** nor could they take by **descent** from him.

COST OF COMPLETION In a **breach of contract** situation, a measure of **damages** representing the total amount of additional expense, over and above the **contract** price, that the injured party would have to incur in order to obtain a substituted **performance** that would place him in the same position he would have been in if the contract had not been breached; often used as a measure of damages for breaches of construction contracts. Compare **diminution in value; damages; specific performance.**

COSTS [TO ABIDE THE EVENT] A court order requiring the losing party to pay legal expenses of the prevailing party. Costs are in the discretion of the trial court, and the order does not mean that a **litigant** shall necessarily have full costs, but "that he shall have such costs as under the statutes and rules of court, a plaintiff recovering the amount that he recovers by the event is entitled to." *Watson* v. *Garrett* (1860), 3 P.R. 70 (Ont.).

CO-TENANCY Possession of a unit of property by two or more persons. The term does not refer to an **estate**, but rather to a relationship between persons as to their **holding** of property. It encompasses both tenancy in common and **joint tenancy** [and, thus, tenancy by the entirety as well]. See **tenancy.**

COUNSEL   1. A person retained by a client to plead his cause in a court of law; a barrister; an advocate. See **barrister and solicitor. 2.** The advice given in respect of the matters or things that barristers and solicitors are authorized by law to do or perform.

COUNT A distinct statement of **plaintiff's cause of action.** In indictments, a count, like a **charge**, is an **allegation** of a distinct offence. A complaint or indictment may contain one or more counts. There is no restriction under the *Criminal Code*, R.S.C. 1985, c. C–46, as to the number of counts that may be included in a single indictment. Section 591(1) provides that any number of counts for any number of **indictable offences** may be joined in the same indictment; but where they are so joined, each count may be treated as a separate indictment (s. 591(2)). However, where the offence charged is **murder**, no count charging any other offence may be included in the same indictment (s.589). Nevertheless, this does not preclude two counts of murder in the same indictment although it is not generally considered desirable. *Regina* v. *Haase*, [1965] 2 C.C.C. 56 (B.C.C.A.), affirmed [1965] 2 C.C.C. 123 (S.C.C.).

COUNTERCLAIM A counter-demand made by **defendant** in his favor against the **plaintiff.** It is not a mere **answer** or **denial** of plaintiff's **allegations,** but rather asserts an independent **cause of action,** the purpose of which is to oppose or deduct from plaintiff's claim. "Today a **defendant** can assert any claim against the **plaintiff** by counterclaim, subject only to the power of the court to exclude the defendant's claim where it cannot be conveniently dealt with in the plaintiff's action." G. Watson, *Canadian Civil Procedure* 638 (3d ed. 1988). The counterclaim is pleaded separately as part of the statement of defence, and the defendant may counterclaim against the plaintiff in respect of any cause of action, whenever and however arising. See **set-off.**

COUNTERFEIT An imitation of something made without lawful authority and with a view to defraud by passing the false copy as genuine or original; e.g., counterfeit coins, paper money, bonds, deeds, shares. See *Criminal Code*, R.S.C. 1985, c. C–46, ss. 376, 458.

COUNTY COURT A federally appointed court that heard intermediate civil cases and most serious criminal cases—in particular, **indictable offences** by election, appeals of **summary conviction offences,** appeals from small claims courts and family courts, and cases involving permanent wardship or adoption. County courts are now abolished in all of the provinces of Canada, with Nova Scotia being the last to do so in 1993. R. Salhany, *Canadian Criminal Procedure* 1–3 (6th ed. 1994).

COURSE OF EMPLOYMENT See **scope of employment.**

COURT-MARTIAL A court for the trial of a member of Her Majesty's Forces upon a charge of having committed any service offence. A service offence is defined in the *National Defence Act*, R.S.C. 1985, c. N–5, as "an offence under this Act, the **Criminal Code,** or any other Act of the Parliament of Canada, committed by a person while subject to the Code of Service Discipline." The Act provides for various kinds of court-martial: general courts-martial, disciplinary courts-martial, standing courts-martial, special general courts-martial. See *National Defence Act*, ss. 165–178; 230; 234–237; 245. The right to appeal is provided in s. 230; appeals may be heard by a court-martial appeal court (s. 234(1)) and the Supreme Court of Canada (s. 245(1)).

COURT OF APPEAL See **appellate court.**

COURT OF ASSIZE AND NISI PRIUS In English law, a court "composed of two or more commissioners, who [were] twice in every year sent by the king's special commission all around the kingdom to try by jury cases under their jurisdiction." See 3 Bl.Comm. *58, *59.

COURT OF EQUITY Historically, a court having **jurisdiction** where an adequate remedy was not available in the courts of **common law.** A court of equity would be one that applied the system of law developed by the English Court of **Chancery.** Courts guided primarily by equitable doctrine are said to be courts of equity. Courts of equity had their own principles (e.g., the **clean hands** doctrine) and their own unique remedies (e.g., **injunction, specific performance**). In England the courts of law and equity were merged by the *Judicature Act*, modelled on the English *Judicature Acts of 1873–75*, and the equity court as a distinct tribunal was abolished. Some Canadian jurisdictions also had a separate court of equity. In Nova Scotia, e.g., the courts of law and equity were merged in 1884 by a *Judicature Act* modelled on the English Acts.

COURT OF KING'S [QUEEN'S] BENCH See **King's Bench.**

COURT OF RECORD A phrase used to refer to a court, the records of which are maintained and preserved, and which may punish for **contempt of court.**

COURT OF STAR CHAMBER See **Star Chamber.**

COVENANT **1.** To enter into a formal agreement; to **bind** oneself in **contract;** to make a stipulation. **2.** An agreement or promise to do or not to do a particular thing; a promise incidental to a **deed** or contract, either express or implied; an agreement, convention, or promise of two or more parties, by written **deed** signed and delivered, by whichever of the parties pledges himself to the other that something is either done or shall be done or stipulates for the truth of certain facts.

Covenants for **title** are frequently termed *real* covenants. Examples of such covenants are that the vendor is **seised in fee;** has power to **convey;** for **quiet enjoyment** by the purchaser, his **heirs** and **assigns;** that the land shall be held free from **encumbrance;** and for further assurance (which obligates the **covenantor** to perform whatever acts are reasonably demanded by the **covenantee** for the purpose of perfecting or "assuming" the title). All covenants for the benefit of the **estate run with the land,** as he who has the one is subject to the other; they bind those who come in by act of law (as personal representatives) and those who come in by act of the parties. See **restrictive covenant.**

COVENANTEE One who receives the **covenant,** or for whom it is made.

COVENANTOR One who makes a **covenant.**

COVERTURE At **common law,** a married woman's legal condition; "under the cover," influence and protection of her husband. In effect, the **real property** of which the woman was **seised** at the time of marriage, or afterwards, **vested** in both husband and wife during coverture, in right of the wife, and the husband was entitled to the profits therefrom and had sole control and management. As to personal property (see **personalty**), at common law the husband became absolute owner of his wife's personal **chattels.** The disabilities of coverture in respect of property were eliminated by the English *Married Women's Property Act,* 1882, and equivalent statutes in the Canadian provinces.

CREDIT That which is extended to a buyer or borrower on the seller or lender's belief that what is given will be repaid. The term can be applied to unlimited types of transactions. In accounting, a credit is money owing and due to one, and is considered an **asset.** The word is also used with respect to one's reputation or business standing in a given community. For example, a person who has a healthy, profitable business and who has always repaid debts in the past will be considered a good "credit risk" by a prospective lender.

CREDITOR One to whom money is owed by the **debtor;** one to whom an obligation exists. In a strict legal sense, a creditor is one who voluntarily gives **credit** to another for money or other property; in a more general sense, he is one who has a legal right to demand and recover from another a sum of money.

CREDITOR'S BILL [SUIT] A proceeding in **equity** in which a **judgment creditor** (a creditor who has secured **judgment** against a **debtor** and whose **claim** has not been satisfied) attempts to gain a discovery, accounting, and deliverance of **property** owed to him by the **judgment debtor,** which property cannot be reached by **execution** (seizure and forced sale) at law; commonly referred to as **discovery** in aid of execution.

CRIME Any act the sovereign has deemed contrary to public good; a wrong the federal Parliament has determined is injurious to the public and, hence, prosecutable in a **criminal proceeding.** A common-law crime was one declared to be an offence by the developed case-law method of the **common-law** courts. Today, nearly all criminal offences are statutory and are contained in the Canadian **Criminal Code,** R.S.C. 1985, c. C–46. Some crimes are found in other federal statutes, e.g., the *Narcotic Control Act,* R.S.C. 1985, c. N–1. The provinces are permitted under the *Constitution Act, 1867,* s. 92(15), to impose punishment by way of fine, penalty, or imprisonment for enforcement of provincial laws. However, these provincial offences, while sometimes termed "quasi-crimes," are not strictly crimes, as the exclusive criminal law power is given to the federal Parliament by this Act (s. 91(27)). The same Act provides that the administration of justice in the provinces is a provincial matter, including the "Organization of Provincial Courts, both of Civil and of Criminal Jurisdiction" (s. 92(14)). Thus, most prosecutions of crimes are carried out by Crown attorneys appointed by the provinces. A distinction is drawn between **summary offences** and **indictable offences.** Summary offences are regarded as lesser offences and carry less stringent penalties. Indictable offences are more serious and usually carry more severe penalties.

CRIME AGAINST NATURE Sexual deviations that were considered crimes at **common law** and have been carried over by statute into the **Criminal Code;** includes **sodomy, bestiality,** and **buggery.**

CRIMEN FALSI *(krĭ′-mĕn fäl′-sē)* Lat.: a **crime** of deceit. At **common law,** a *crimen falsi* was a crime containing the elements of falsehood and fraud. Examples of *crimen falsi* include **forgery** and **perjury.**

CRIMINAL 1. An adjective denoting an act done with malicious intent. See **malice; malice aforethought. 2.** One who has been convicted of a violation of the criminal law. After the criminal has satisfied whatever sanction has been imposed upon him and is released, he is called an **EX-OFFENDER.** A person who re-offends after having been judicially dealt with for one offence is called a **recidivist.**

CRIMINAL CODE A federal **statute,** first enacted in 1892 (currently R.S.C. 1985, c. C–46), which substantially embodies the criminal law of Canada. It is amended, usually more than once in each session of Parliament, to take account of necessary changes and innovations in the criminal law. The Criminal Code is not, however, a complete delimitation of the criminal law of Canada and has no privileged status other than as a statute. See **crime.**

CRIMINAL CONTEMPT See **contempt of court.**

CRIMINAL CONVERSATION An action for **damages** in **tort** brought by one spouse against a third party and based on an act of **adultery.** To maintain such an action, proof of adultery is necessary, and the action may be brought even though there occurs no consequential loss of the wife's affection, society, and services (as in **alienation of affection**). *Mowder* v. *Roy,* [1946] 2 D.L.R. 427 at 439 (Ont.C.A.). As a cause of action, criminal conversation varies from province to province and in some jurisdictions has been deleted from family law and matrimonial causes legislation. It is rapidly becoming passé as a common-law **cause of action** or tort. See *Legare* v. *Clark,* [1978] 2 W.W.R. 195 (Sask.Q.B.); *Skinner* v. *Allen* (1978), 18 O.R. (2d) 3 (C.A.).

CRIMINAL NEGLIGENCE See **negligence.**

CROSS-EXAMINATION Questioning of a witness in a **trial** by the lawyer for the party who did not call him, after examination of the **witness** by the lawyer for the party calling him, which is known as the EXAMINATION-IN-CHIEF. The main purposes of cross-examination are to test the veracity of the witness and to obtain answers that assist the case of the cross-examining party.

CROWN A term frequently used when speaking of the Sovereign, or the rights, duties and prerogatives belonging to her. However, the royal prerogative powers are for the most part exercised by the Government in the name of the Queen. In practice, "the Crown" means "the Government of the day and its various departments." The phrase covers "all the departments of State and the official activities of all servants and agents of the State." G. Borrie, *Public Law* 57–58 (2d ed. 1970). With reference to the distribution of Crown rights and prerogatives under the *Constitution Act, 1867,* see *Bonanza Creek Gold Mining Co.* v. *R.,* [1916] 1 A.C. 566 (P.C.).

CROWN ATTORNEY A counsel appointed by the Attorney-General, under the provisions of provincial statutes, to take charge of and conduct, on behalf of the **Crown,** the **prosecution** of criminals. See **prosecutor.**

CRUEL AND UNUSUAL PUNISHMENT Section 12 of the **Canadian Charter of Rights and Freedoms** provides that "everyone has the right not to be subjected to any cruel and unusual treatment or punishment." There has been no judicial ruling that clearly defines the limits of such punishment, but the Supreme Court of Canada has considered the gravity of the offence, the personal characteristics of the offender, and the particular characteristics of the case when evaluating the treatment and its

effects. See *R.* v. *Smith,* [1987] 1 S.C.R. 1045.
The *Canadian Bill of Rights,* R.S.C. 1985, Appendix III, s. 2(b) provides similar protection. Under this provision, the Court stated that the punishment would have to be so excessive as to outrage standards of decency. *Miller and Cockriell* v. *The Queen,* [1977] 2 S.C.R. 680.

CULPABLE Deserving of moral blame or punishment; "criminal". Implies, in addition to intention, recklessness as well as an indifference or disregard for the consequences that might ensue from an act, as in "culpable" **homicide.** See, e.g., *Criminal Code,* R.S.C. 1985, c. C–46, ss. 222, 229–230. See also **constructive murder.**

CUMULATIVE DIVIDEND See **dividend.**

CURIA REGIS *(kyū'-rē-à rā'-gĭs)* Lat.: the King's Court. See **King's Bench.**

CURTESY The husband's right, at **common law,** upon the death of his wife, to a **life estate** in all the **estates** of **inheritance** in land that his wife possessed during their marriage; "a life estate to which the husband was entitled in all lands of which his wife was **seised** in **fee simple** or in **fee tail** at any time during the marriage, provided that there was **issue** born alive capable of inheriting the estate. On the birth of such qualified issue the husband's **tenancy** by the marital right was enlarged to an estate for his own life....Although ... the husband's estate for his life was called 'curtesy initiate' prior to his wife's death and 'curtesy consummate' after her death, he had a present life estate in both situations and there was no substantial difference between the two types of curtesy." C. Moynihan, *Introduction to the Law of Real Property* 48–9 (2d ed. 1988). Compare **dower.**

CURTILAGE At **common law,** the land around the **dwelling house;** a piece of ground within the common enclosure belonging to a dwelling house, and enjoyed with it, for its more convenient occupation.

CUSTODY **1.** As applied to property, it is not **ownership,** but a keeping, guarding, care, watching, inspection, preservation, or security of a thing, which carries with it the idea of the thing being within the immediate personal care and control of the person to whose custody it is subjected. **2.** As applied to persons, it is such restraint and physical control over the person as to insure his presence at any **hearing,** or the actual imprisonment resulting from a criminal **conviction. 3.** Custody of children is legal guardianship, often an **issue** between parents in a divorce action. See **joint custody.** Compare **possession.**

CUSTOM An unwritten law established by long usage. In England after the Norman Conquest, the judges recognized certain Anglo-Saxon laws and customs as appropriate for general application throughout the realm, and thus these became part of the **common law.** Some special and local customs remained and will be recognized even today if certain difficulties of proof and reasonableness are satisfied. For example, to be recognized as law, the custom must have existed "before legal memory" (before 1189, the first year of the reign of Richard I). The party alleging the custom must prove it, but in practice the courts raise a presumption in his favour if he can prove the custom as far back as living memory. See *Mercer* v. *Denne,* [1905] 2 Ch. 538 (C.A.).

In Canada, the notion of customary rights has sometimes been raised with reference to the aboriginal peoples. For example, in *R.* v. *Kogogolak* (1959), 31 C.R. 12 (N.W.T.), Sissons, J. held that an Eskimo who shot a musk-ox had not violated a game ordinance of the Northwest Territories. He said, **inter alia:** "Traditionally, this is the land of the Eskimos—the Innuit,...and from time immemorial they have lived by hunting and fishing."

Custom is an important source of **international law.** In this context, custom connotes a feeling of obligation on the part of states and is distinguished from mere habit or usage. "Evidence that a custom in this sense exists ... can be found only by examining the practice of states; that is to say, we must look at what states do in their relations with one another and attempt to understand why they do it and in particular whether they recognize an obligation to adopt a certain course, or, in the words of Article 38 (of the Statute of the International Court of Justice), we must examine whether the alleged custom shows 'a general practice accepted as law'." J. Brierly, *The Law of Nations* 59–60 (6th ed. 1963).

CUSTOMS Duties charged on commodities upon their importation into or exportation out of a country. *Attorney-General for B.C.* v. *MacDonald Murphy Lumber Co.,* [1930] 1 W.W.R. 830 at 834 (P.C.). The power to legislate with respect to customs matters is exercised by the federal Parliament. See, e.g., *Customs Act,* R.S.C. 1985 (2nd Supp.), c. 1; *Customs Tariff,* R.S.C. (3rd Supp.), c. 41. See **excise.**

CY-PRÈS *(sī'-prĕ)* Fr.: so near, as near. In the law of **trusts** and **wills,** the principle that **equity** will, when a charity bequest is illegal or later becomes impossible or impracticable of fulfillment, substitute another charitable object that is believed to approach the original purpose of the **testator** or **settlor** as closely as possible. The courts will exercise this power, however, only when the purpose for which the fund was established cannot be carried out and diversion of the income to some other purpose can be found to fall within the general intent of the donor expressed in the **instrument** establishing the trust.

DAMAGES Monetary **compensation** the law awards to one who has suffered damage, loss, or injury by the wrong of another; recompense for a legal wrong such as **breach of contract** or a **tortious** act. See, e.g., *Leistikow* v. *Liggett Co. Ltd.*, [1925] 1 D.L.R. 210 (Man.K.B.). It is one of several forms of relief that can be obtained from the court. Compare **specific performance.**

ACTUAL DAMAGES Losses that can readily be proven to have been sustained, and for which the injured party should be compensated as a matter of right.

AGGRAVATED DAMAGES See EXEM-PLARY [PUNITIVE] DAMAGES following.

CONSEQUENTIAL [SPECIAL] DAMAGES A loss or injury that is indirect or mediate. In contract law, consequential damages are recoverable if it was reasonably foreseeable at the time of contract that the injury or loss was probable if the contract were broken. *Hadley* v. *Baxendale* (1854), 9 Ex. 341; 156 E.R. 145. They are damages that follow because of knowledge of special conditions imputed to the defaulting party and increase the standard of **liability.** Thus they are synonymous with SPECIAL DAMAGES (see following).

DOUBLE [TREBLE] DAMAGES Twice [or three times] the amount of damages that a court or jury would normally find a party entitled to, which is recoverable by an injured party for certain kinds of injuries pursuant to a statute authorizing the double [or treble] recovery. See, e.g., *Landlord and Tenant Act,* R.S.O. 1990, c. L. 7, ss. 58, 59, 112. These damages are intended in certain instances as a punishment for improper behaviour.

EXEMPLARY [PUNITIVE] DAMAGES Compensation in excess of actual damages that "may be awarded where there is a wanton or intentional act, that is, an act which intended the result. Exemplary damages can be awarded whenever it is necessary to teach the wrongdoer that tort does not pay. They are

preventative or deterrent in character and are over and above compensation....The words 'aggravated' and 'exemplary' have been used interchangeably ... and mean one and the same type of damages." *S.* v. *Mundy*, [1970] 1 O.R. 764 at 767–68 (Middlesex Co.Ct.).

EXPECTATION DAMAGES A measure of the money **damages** available to the **plaintiff** in an action for **breach of contract,** based on the value of the benefit he would have received from the contract if the **defendant** had not breached but had completed **performance** as agreed. The amount is generally computed on the basis of the monetary value of the contract to the plaintiff, based on full performance thereof minus whatever costs the plaintiff was able to avoid by not performing his own part of the contract. When the buyer breaches, the expectation damages will ordinarily be the contract price, less costs saved; when the seller breaches, the buyer's expectation damages will be measured by the fair **market value** of the promised performance at the time and place of promised **tender** [delivery]. Compare **cost of completion; diminution in value; specific performance.**

GENERAL DAMAGES Those that the law will presume to be the direct natural or probable consequence of the act complained of, as in negligence claims for personal injuries. For example, where the element of continuance of health, employment, or disposition to work enters into the computation, the damages are general and include bodily pain and suffering and personal inconvenience. *Wersh* v. *Wersh and Wersh,* [1945] 1 W.W.R. 609 (Man.C.A.). Compare SPECIAL DAMAGES (see following).

INCIDENTAL DAMAGES Damages that include losses reasonably incident to, or conduct giving rise to, a claim for ACTUAL DAMAGES. A buyer's incidental damages would include expenses reasonably incurred in inspection, receipt, transportation, and care and custody of goods rightfully rejected. A seller's incidental damages would include any commercially reasonable charges, expenses or commissions incurred in stopping delivery, in the transportation, care and custody of goods after the buyer's **breach,** in connection with return or resale of the goods.

LIQUIDATED DAMAGES The genuine, reasonable, pre-estimate of the damages, agreed upon in advance by parties to a contract, that will be paid in the event of a **breach.** "Where such agreement is made and the parties are bound thereby, the result is that, regardless of the amount of the actual loss, the defaulting party's **liability** to pay damages is limited to the amount agreed upon, and the **aggrieved party** may not recover more than that amount." *Mitchell* v. *Paddington Homes Ltd.* (1977), 3 B.C.L.R. 330 at 332 (S.C.). Compare **penalty.**

NOMINAL DAMAGES The amount (usually, a trivial sum) paid to the plaintiff who has "proved the infraction of a legal right, but has failed to prove what damage, if any, was caused thereby. Nevertheless [the defendant] has been guilty of breaches of the agreement, and these breaches entitle [the plaintiff] to nominal damages." *Hudson's Bay Oil & Gas Co. Ltd.* v. *Dynamic Petroleums Ltd.* (1958), 26 W.W.R. 504 (Alta.S.C.).

SPECIAL DAMAGES Such damages as are capable of exact computation. *Gruden* v. *McLean,* [1972] 1 O.R. 860 at 861 (C.A.).

DAMNUM ABSQUE INJURIA *(däm'-nŭm äb'-skwā ĭn-jŭ-rē'-ä)* Lat.: loss without **injury.** The gist of this maxim is that if there is loss or damage without a legally recognized injury, the law provides no **cause of action** and consequently no legal remedy. See, e.g., *The Trustees of the St. John Y.M.C.A.* v. *Hutchison* (1879), 18 N.B.R. 523 (S.C.). Compare **injuria absque damno.**

DANGEROUS OFFENDER See **habitual criminal.**

DANGEROUS [DEADLY] WEAPON See **offensive weapon.**

DAY IN COURT A time when a person who is a party to a lawsuit has been duly cited to appear before the court and be heard. See also **appearance; due process of law.**

DEBAUCH "[T]he verb 'debauch,' as defined in ordinary dictionaries, means entice, lead astray, vitiate or corrupt.

When used as a legal term it has more signification, *viz.,* to seduce and violate a woman." *Guiry* v. *Wheeler,* [1952] O.W.N. 657 at 659 (H.C.).

DE BENE ESSE *(dĕ bĕ'-nĕ ĕs'-sĕ)* Lat.: conditionally; provisionally. "To do a thing de bene esse signifies allowing or accepting certain evidence for the present until more fully examined, *valeat quantum valere potest.* It is regarded as an additional examination to be utilized if necessary only in the event that witnesses cannot be examined later in the action in the regular way. This evidence therefore was taken 'for what it was worth.' " *C. T. Gogstad & Co.* v. *The S.S. "Camosun"* (1941), 56 B.C.R. 156 at 157 (Admiralty).

DEBENTURE " ... a debenture is a **contract** evidencing or acknowledging a **debt** which might, or might not have charging provisions relating to the **grantor's** property. That is, the terms of the debenture are to be negotiated between the parties as in any contract." *Re Selmas-Cromie Ltd.; Gardner* v. *M/S Apparel Ltd.* (1976), 21 C.B.R. (N.S.) 10 at 21 (B.C.S.C.). See further W. Grover & D. Ross, *Materials on Corporate Finance* 221 (1975); D. Horsley, H. Sutherland, and J. M. Edmiston, *Fraser's Handbook on Canadian Company Law* 310 (7th ed. 1985). See **bond.**

DEBT "[A] sum payable in respect of a liquidated money demand, recoverable by an action." *Diewold* v. *Diewold,* [1941] 1 D.L.R. 561 (S.C.C.). "[T]hat which is owed or due; anything, as money, goods or service, which one person is under obligation to pay or render another." *Secretary of State of Canada* v. *Neitzke* (1921), 62 S.C.R. 262. See **bankruptcy; creditor; insolvency.**

DEBTOR One who has the obligation of paying a **debt;** one who owes a debt. "The relation of debtor and creditor arises whenever one person, by contract or law, is liable and bound to pay another an amount of money certain or uncertain, as between a bank and its customer." *The Royal Bank of Canada* v. *Slack,* [1958] O.R. 262 at 276 (C.A.).

DECEASED One who has died; in property, the alternate term DECEDENT is generally used. In criminal law, "the deceased" refers to the victim of a **homicide.**

DECEDENT See **deceased.**

DECEIT The **tort** of **fraudulent** representation. "To succeed in the common-law action of deceit the plaintiff must show actual fraud, that is, an intention to deceive or that the statements complained of were made recklessly without regard for their truth or falsity." *McCusker* v. *O'Day*, [1975] W.W.D. 86 (B.C.C.A.). "Every person must be held responsible for the consequences of a false representation made by him to another, upon which a third person acts, and, so acting, is injured or damnified—provided it appear that such false representation was made with the intent that it should be acted upon by such third person in the manner that occasions the injury or loss...." *Barry* v. *Croskey* (1861), 2 Johns & Hem. 1 at 23–4, 70 E.R. 945 at 955, cited and followed in *Cherewick* v. *Moore*, [1955] 2 D.L.R. 492 at 494 (B.C.S.C.).

DECISION A conclusion; a determination; a formal **judgment.** A decision presupposes an existing dispute between two or more **parties** and involves presentation of the case by the parties to the dispute, ascertainment of facts by means of **evidence** adduced by the parties, submission of legal arguments, and the decision itself, which disposes of the matter by a finding on disputed facts and an application of the law of the land to the facts so found including, where necessary, ruling on any disputed **questions of law.**

DECISION ON THE MERITS See **on the merits.**

DECLARATION See **complaint.**

DECLARATION OF TRUST An acknowledgment by a person that he holds **property** in **trust** for another. It may be implied from conduct. *Gee* v. *Liddell* (1866), 55 E.R. 1038 (Rolls Ct.).

DECLARATORY JUDGMENT A **judgment** of the court granting relief to an applicant, in the form of a **declaration** stating "the legal position concerning a matter in dispute, so that the remedy ... is not in itself an order of the court and is thus non-coercive. Applicants do, however, frequently apply for an **injunction** as well as a declaration, so that the relief obtained is, so far as the injunction is concerned, enforceable." H. Hanbury, R. Maudsley, & J. Martin, *Hanbury and*

Maudsley Modern Equity 153 (11th ed. 1981). See, e.g., the *Courts of Justice Act*, R.S.O. 1990, c. C. 43, s. 97, or corresponding provincial Supreme Court rules. See also Mullan, *The Declaratory Judgment: Its Place as an Administrative Law Remedy in Nova Scotia*, 2 Dalhousie L.J. 91 (1975). Compare **advisory opinion.**

DECLARATORY STATUTE One that merely declares the existing law without proposing any additions or changes, for the purpose of resolving conflicts or doubts concerning a particular point of the **common law** or the meaning of a **statute.**

DECREE A law; a **judgment** or order of the court. In relation to dissolution of marriage, DECREE ABSOLUTE is the decree that finally dissolves the marriage. It may be issued after three months from the day following the grant of a **decree nisi** (a type of conditional decree requiring something further to be done to make it absolute).

DECREE NISI A provisional decree of **divorce**. The decree nisi and decree absolute (which took effect three months after the granting of the decree, if the court was satisfied that all rights of appeal had been exhausted) are no longer used in Canada.

Under the *Divorce Act*, R.S.C. 1985 (2nd Supp.), c. 3, s. 12(1), a divorce takes effect on the thirty-first day after the day on which the judgment granting the divorce is rendered, subject to special circumstances and appeals.

DEDICATION A **conveyance** of land by a private owner in the nature of a **gift** or **grant,** and an **acceptance** of that land by or on behalf of the public; "the setting apart of land for the public use," such as streets acquired by a town through a dedication to the public of the property comprising the streets (*Van Campenhout* v. *Government of Saskatchewan* (1959), 30 W.W.R. 485 (Sask.C.A.)).

DEED An **instrument** in writing that **conveys** an **interest** in land from the **grantor** to the **grantee;** an instrument used to effect a transfer of **realty.** Its main function is to pass **title** to land. See **bargain and sale; quitclaim deed; specialty; warranty** [WARRANTY DEED]. See also **inter vivos.**

DEED OF TRUST A transfer of legal **title** to property from the **trustor** to the **trustee,** for the purpose of placing the legal **title** with the trustee as **security** for the **performance** of certain obligations, monetary or otherwise. Compare **mortgage.**

DEEMED "... in deciding whether or not the use of the words 'deem' or 'deemed' establishes a conclusive or a rebuttable **presumption** depends largely upon the context in which they are used, always bearing in mind the purpose to be served by the **statute** and the necessity of ensuring that such purpose is served." *St. Leon Village Consolidated School District No. 1425* v. *Ronceray* (1960), 31 W.W.R. 385 at 391 (Man.C.A.).

DE FACTO *(dĕ fäk'-tō)* Lat.: in fact; by virtue of the deed or accomplishment; in reality; actually. Used to qualify many legal terms—e.g., DE FACTO CORPORATION: one that has inadvertently failed to comply with all the provisions of the laws relating to the creation of a **corporation** but has made a good faith effort to do so and has in good faith exercised the franchise of a corporation. See *Williams* v. *Rice,* [1926] 3 D.L.R. 225 (Man.K.B.). Compare **de jure.**

DEFALCATION The failure of one entrusted with money to pay it when it is due to another. Similar to misappropriation and **embezzlement** but wider in scope because it does not imply any criminal **fraud.** See, e.g., *Criminal Code,* R.S.C. 1985, c. C–46, ss. 330–332. See also **misapplication of property.**

DEFAMATION The publication of anything that is injurious to the good name or reputation of another or tends to bring him into disrepute. "A defamatory **libel** is matter published, without lawful justification or excuse, that is likely to injure the reputation of any person by exposing him to hatred, contempt or ridicule, or that is designed to insult the person of or concerning whom it is published." *Criminal Code,* R.S.C. 1985, c. C–46, s. 298(1). See also ss. 299–317. An oral defamation is a **slander.** A **tort** action under libel, slander, or defamation may be brought to recover **damages.**

DEFAULT Failure to discharge a duty, to one's own disadvantage; an omission to do that which ought to have been done by one of the parties. See *Alsip* v. *Robinson* (1911), 18 W.L.R. 39 (Man.T.D.).

The term is most often used to describe the occurrence of an event that cuts short the rights or **remedies** of one of the parties to an agreement or a legal dispute. It is often used in the context of **mortgages** to describe the failure of the MORTGAGOR (see **mortgage**) to pay **installments** when due and in the context of judicial **proceedings** to describe the failure of one of the parties to take the procedural steps necessary to prevent entry of a **judgment** against him (called a DEFAULT JUDGMENT or judgment by default).

DEFAULT JUDGMENT See **judgment** [DEFAULT JUDGMENT].

DEFEASANCE An **instrument** that, in effect, negates the effectiveness of a **deed** or **will;** a **collateral** deed that defeats the force of another deed upon the performance of certain conditions.

DEFEASIBLE Subject to **revocation** if certain **conditions** are not met; capable of being avoided or annulled or liable to such avoidance or annulment. Used in context of estates in **real property.**

DEFECTIVE **1.** Wanting as to an essential; incomplete, deficient, faulty. For example, in the provisions for interception of communications ("wiretap" legislation), the admissibility of an intercepted private communication as evidence may be affected by the existence of a substantive defect or irregularity on the face of the authorization allowing the interception. *Criminal Code,* R.S.C. 1985, c. C–46, s. 189(5). If the authorization does not comply with the requirements of s. 186(4), it is defective. See, e.g., *R.* v. *Douglas* (1977), 33 C.C.C. (2d) 395 (Ont.C.A.); *Grabowski* v. *The Queen* (1985), 22 C.C.C. (3d) 449 (S.C.C.); *R.* v. *Welsh & Iannuzzi (No. 6)* (1977), 32 C.C.C. (2d) 363 (Ont.C.A.). **2.** Not reasonably safe for a use that can be reasonably anticipated. See, e.g., *McMorran* v. *Dominion Stores Ltd.* (1977), 74 D.L.R. (3d) 186 (Ont.H.C.). See also **products liability; strict liability; warranty.**

DEFECTIVE TITLE One that is unmarketable. **1.** With reference to **title** in land, it means that the person making the **conveyance,** claiming to own **good title,** is actually subject to the partial or complete

ownership of the title by someone else. **2.** As to **negotiable instruments,** the term denotes title obtained through illegal means or means that amount to **fraud.**

DEFENCE A denial, answer, or plea (by the **defendant,** or **accused**) opposing the truth or validity of the **plaintiff's** case or the charge against the accused. "The defendant, in answer thereto [to the plaintiff's statement of claim] in his **statement of defence** may adopt all or any of the following courses: (1) he may deny or refuse to admit the facts stated by the plaintiff; (2) he may confess or admit them, and avoid their effect by asserting fresh facts which afford an answer thereto; (3) he may admit the facts stated by the plaintiff and may raise a question of law as to their legal effect...." *Webb* v. *Hamilton Cataract Power Light & Traction Co. (Ltd.)* (1904), 7 O.L.R. 607 at 609–10 (in chambers). See **affirmative defence.**

EQUITABLE DEFENCE A defence that is recognized by **courts of equity** acting solely upon inherent rules and principles of **equity.** Examples of such defence include **fraud, duress,** illegality. Such defences can now be asserted in courts of law as well. The term also refers to equitable doctrines such as **unclean hands** that may operate to **bar** a plaintiff from pursuing an equity action and thus constitute equitable defences to such an action.

DEFENDANT 1. In **civil proceedings,** the party responding to the claim of the **plaintiff;** the party sued in an **action. 2.** In **criminal** proceedings, the **accused.** See also **respondent.**

DEFERRED PAYMENTS Payments extended over a period of time or put off to a future date. Installment payments are usually a series of equal deferred payments made over a course of time.

DEFRAUD To deprive a person of **property** or **interest, estate** or right by fraud, **deceit,** or **artifice.** "To defraud is to deprive by deceit; it is by deceit to induce a man to act to his injury. More tersely it may be put, that to deceive is by falsehood to induce a state of mind; to defraud is by deceit to induce a course of action." *Re London and Globe Finance Corp. Ltd.,* [1903] 1 Ch. 728 at 732, cited in *Scott* v. *Metropolitan Police Commissioner* (1974), 60 Cr.App.R. 124 at 127, 130 (H.L.), "... to deprive a person

dishonestly of something which is his or of something to which he is or would or might but for the perpetration of the fraud, be entitled."

DE JURE *(dĕ jū'-rā)* Lat.: by right; by justice; lawful; legitimate. Generally used in contrast to **de facto** in that *de jure* connotes "as a matter of law" whereas *de facto* connotes "as a matter of conduct or practice not founded on law."

DELEGATED LEGISLATION See **legislation; subordinate [delegated] legislation.**

DELINQUENT 1. In a monetary context, something that has been made payable and is overdue and unpaid; implies a previous opportunity to make payment. See **default. 2.** With reference to persons, *delinquency* implies carelessness or recklessness. See also **juvenile delinquent.**

DELIVERY A voluntary transfer of **title** or **possession** from one **party** to another; a legally recognized handing over of one's possessory rights to another. ACTUAL DELIVERY is sometimes very cumbersome or impossible, and in those circumstances the courts may find a CONSTRUCTIVE DELIVERY sufficient where there is no actual delivery, provided that the intention is clearly to transfer title. Thus, "where goods are ponderous and incapable ... of being handed from one to another, there need not be an actual delivery; but it may be done by that which is tantamount, such as delivery of the key of a warehouse in which the goods are lodged, or by delivery of some other **indicia** of property." *McLean* v. *McGhee,* [1920] 2 W.W.R. 394 at 397 (Man.C.A.). Such an action is also called a SYMBOLIC DELIVERY. See **gift; livery of seisin.** Compare **bailment; conveyance; grant.**

DEMAND NOTE A note payable on demand. **1.** A negotiable **instrument** that by its express terms is payable immediately on an agreed-upon date of **maturation;** the **maker** of the note acknowledges his **liability** as of the due date. **2.** An instrument payable upon presentation or one in which no time for payment is stated. See *Bills of Exchange Act,* R.S.C. 1985, c. B–4, ss. 176–187. See also J. Falconbridge, *The Law of Negotiable Instruments in Canada* 23 (1964).

DE MINIMIS NON CURAT LEX *(dĕ mǐ'-nǐ-mǐs nōn kyū'-ràt lĕks)* Lat.: the law does not concern itself with trifles. Something that is *de minimis* in interest is one that does not rise to a level of sufficient importance to be dealt with judicially. "The maxim is not confined in its application to civil matters between private litigants ... the maxim applies equally in criminal matters ... where the matter complained of is so trivial or technical that no sentence or retribution is necessary." *R.* v. *Overvold* (1973), 20 C.R.N.S. 327 (N.W.T.Mag.Ct.).

DEMISE A term used to describe the **conveyance** of an **estate** in **real property.** See, e.g., *Spears* v. *Miller* (1882), 32 U.C.C.P. 661; *Forrest* v. *Greaves*, [1923] 3 W.W.R. 658 (Sask.K.B.). Most commonly used in a **lease** as a synonym for "let"—i.e., to grant a lease. *Bowater Power Co. Ltd.* v. *M.N.R.*, [1971] C.T.C. 818 (F.).

DEMOCRATIC RIGHTS See **Canadian Charter of Rights and Freedoms.**

DEMURRER "A demurrer was a form of **pleading** under the old system by which a party objected that his opponent's pleading disclosed no **cause of action** or ground of defence. When a demurrer was pleaded the question raised was forthwith set down for argument and decision, and the **judgment** was given by the full court sitting *in banc*....If he lost the demurrer, he lost the case and the facts were never gone into at all." W. Williston & R. Rolls, *The Law of Civil Procedure* 686 (1970). See rr. 21.01(1), (2) of *Ontario Rules of Civil Procedure*, R.R.O. 1990, Reg. 194. Demurrer has been abolished, and alternative modes of procedure are now used. See, e.g., *Nova Scotia Civil Procedure Rules* (1983) r. 14.25. See *Stevens* v. *Moritz* (1913), 14 D.L.R. 699 (Ont.S.C.). Compare **summary judgment.**

DENIAL [or TRAVERSE] A defence by denial of an essential **allegation** of fact of the plaintiff's **statement of claim.** In a **statement of defence**, the defendant must admit or deny the plaintiff's allegations of fact; if he does not specifically admit them, they are deemed to be denied. See, e.g., *Nova Scotia Civil Procedure Rules* (1983), r. 14.14–14.17. See **traverse.** Compare **confession and avoidance.**

DE NOVO (dĕ nō′-vō) Lat.: new, young, fresh; renewed, revived; a second time. See **hearing** [HEARING DE NOVO]; **trial** [TRIAL DE NOVO].

DEPONENT A **witness;** one who gives information concerning some fact or facts known to him, under **oath** in a **deposition.**

DEPOSIT **1.** In banking, "when a customer pays money into his account in the usual way of business, he sells it to the banker....In exchange for the money the banker makes an entry of an equal sum in credit in favor of his customer. And it is the entry to the credit of the customer, which, in the technical language of modern banking, is termed a deposit." *Re Alberta Legislation*, [1938] 2 D.L.R. 81 at 99 (S.C.C.)

2. In the sale of goods or real property, "sometimes part of the price is prepaid by way of security, when the contract is entered into....The return of the deposit in case the sale goes off is usually a matter of agreement, but in the absence of a different agreement the deposit is forfeited if the sale goes off through the buyer's default." *Erickson* v. *Andrew*, [1943] 2 D.L.R. 732 at 736 (Alta.S.C.A.D.).

DEPOSITION A method used in pretrial examination for **discovery;** it consists of a statement of a **witness** under oath, taken in question-and-answer form as it would be in court, with opportunity given to the **adversary** to be present and cross-examined, with all this reported and transcribed stenographically.

Such statements are the most common form of discovery and may be taken of any witness (whether or not a **party** to the **action**). See *Nova Scotia Civil Procedure Rules* (1983), r. 18.01 (1). In Ontario, the "party to an action may examine for discovery any other party adverse in interest . . ." *Ontario Rules of Civil Procedure*, R.R.O. 1990, Reg. 194, r. 31.03(1). When taken in the form described, the statement is called an "oral deposition." Depositions may also be taken on written **interrogatories**, where the questions are served to the party in written form, to which a written answer to interrogatories is returned. See, e.g., *Nova Scotia Civil Procedure Rules* (1983), r. 19.

DEPRECIATION Loss in value of assets over a period of time.

DERELICT "A vessel [that] had been **abandoned** and deserted at sea by those who were in charge of it without hope on their part of recovering it and without intention of returning to it." *Davie* v. *Ship "Young Hustler No. 1"* (1962), 32 D.L.R. (2d) 470 at 474 (Ex.Ct.).

DERELICTION A recession of the waters of the sea, a navigable river or other stream, by which land that had been covered with water is left dry. In such case, if the alteration takes place suddenly and sensibly, the ownership remains according to former bounds; but if it is made gradually and imperceptibly, the derelict or dry land belongs to the **riparian** owner from whose shore or bank the water has receded. The term may also refer to the land itself that is thus left uncovered. In order for **contiguous** landowners to gain ownership of the newly uncovered land, the withdrawal of the water must appear permanent, not merely seasonal. Compare **accretion; avulsion; reliction.**

DERIVATIVE ACTION 1. "Where the majority of shares in a company are held by persons who are to be defendants in an action and who have themselves caused the injuries or committed the acts complained of, then a derivative **action** may be maintained in the names of one or more **shareholders** on behalf of themselves and all others, except the defendants, against the company and those persons whose acts are complained of. An individual shareholder or shareholders can maintain an action on behalf of himself or themselves and all other shareholders of the company to prevent the **corporation** from commencing or continuing to do something that is illegal or *beyond* **ultra vires** the powers of the corporation, or where the act complained of amounts to a fraud upon the minority shareholders." W. Williston & R. Rolls, *The Law of Civil Procedure* 196 (1970). See, e.g., *Goldex Mines Ltd.* v. *Revill,* [1973] 3 O.R. 869 (H.C.). See **stockholder's derivative action.**
2. Also used to describe a **cause of action** that is founded on an injury to another, as when a husband sues for loss of **consortium** or services of his wife because of an injury to her by the defendant, or when a father sues for the loss of services of his children.

DEROGATE To destroy; to prejudice; to evade a right or obligation, "An application of the principle that a man shall not 'derogate from his grant' is that if the

grantor intends to reserve any right over the **tenement** granted, other than rights of absolute necessity, it is his duty to reserve it expressly in the grant." *Wheeldon* v. *Burrows* (1897), 12 Ch.D. 31 at 49 (C.A.).

DESCENT "... the taking of **real estate** by **inheritance,** that is, as heir of the former holder.... 'Descent' is used in respect of real estate ... of an **intestate.**" *Re Stone,* [1925] 1 D.L.R. 60 at 70 (S.C.C.). See, e.g., the *Intestate Succession Act,* R.S.N.S. 1989, c. 236; *Estates Administration Act,* R.S.O. 1990, c. E. 22. Compare **devise.**

DESERTION 1. Continual absence from **cohabitation,** which may be a ground for a **decree** of **divorce** or judicial separation; separation without consent and just cause. *Pheasant* v. *Pheasant,* [1972] 1 All E.R. 587 (Fam.Div.). Cessation of cohabitation and the respondent's intention permanently to desert the petitioner must be proved. Desertion for a period of one year may be proof of irretrievable breakdown of marriage. **2.** Also, improper absence from one's place of duty with the Canadian Armed Forces with the intention of remaining permanently absent.

DESTRUCTIBILITY A **common-law** rule of **future interests** that "a **contingent remainder** must **vest** at or before the termination of the preceding **life estate** or be destroyed." A. Sinclair, *Introduction to Real Property Law* 97 (3d ed. 1987). "There are at least three ways that this life estate supporting the contingent remainder in freehold could be destroyed other than by natural means, viz., by (a) **forfeiture;** (b) **merger;** and (c) **disclaimer.**" *Id.* at 73.

DETAINER [FORCIBLE] See **forcible detainer.**

DETENTION As applied to s. 10 of the **Canadian Charter of Rights and Freedoms,** which guarantees rights "on arrest or detention," detention is restraint of liberty, by police or another agent of the state, other than arrest, where an individual may require the assistance of counsel. *R.* v. *Therens,* [1985] 1 S.C.R. 613. Compare *Chromack* v. *The Queen* (1979), 49 C.C.C. (2d) 257 (under the Bill of Rights, S.C. 1960, c. 44, s. 2(c), "detention" means compulsory restraint).

DETERMINABLE FEE [FEE SIMPLE DE-TERMINABLE] An **interest** in **property** that may last forever, but that will automatically terminate upon the happening or non-happening of a specified event; e.g., "'O grants Blackacre to A and his heirs as long as used for church purposes.' ... A receives a fee simple determinable and O retains a possibility of reverter. When (if ever) A fails to carry out the use specified, O will get the land back and assume his original position, of being the owner of a fee simple absolute." A. Sinclair, *Introduction To Real Property Law* 15 (3d ed. 1987).

DETINUE At **common law,** an **action** for the wrongful detention of **personal property (personalty);** "A continuing cause of action which accrues at the date of the wrongful refusal to deliver up goods and continues until the delivery up of the goods or judgment in the action for detinue." *General Finance Facilities Ltd.* v. *Cooks Cars (Romford) Ltd.,* [1963] 2 All E.R. 314, cited in *Schentag* v. *Gauthier* (1972), 27 D.L.R. (3d) 710 at 712 (Sask.Dist.Ct.). "Detinue is the proper action to bring if the plaintiff wishes to recover possession of his goods, and not merely their value." *Id.* at 713. Compare **conversion; detainer [forcible]; replevin; trover.**

DEVISE A gift of land or an interest in land (**real property**) made by **will.** "The **testator** has accurately distinguished between 'devise' and 'legacy,' using the former word in case of **realty,** the latter in the case of **personalty.**" *Re Read* (1909), 13 O.W.R. 508 at 509 (Ont.Wk.Ct.). Compare **bequest; legacy.**

DEVISEE One who is in receipt of a **gift** of **real property** by **will.**

DEVISOR One who makes a **gift** of **real property** by **will** to a **devisee.**

DEVOLVE To pass **property** from one person to another by **operation of law,** without any voluntary act of the previous owner. The **estate** does not devolve from one person to another as the result of some positive act or agreement between them. The word implies a result without the intervention of any voluntary actor.

DICTUM A statement, remark or observation in a judicial **opinion** not necessary to the decision of the case. *Dicta* differ from **holdings** in that they do not establish a rule binding on the courts in subsequent cases "unless they can be shown to express a legal proposition which is a necessary step to the **judgment**" pronounced by the Court in the case wherein the dicta are found. *Davidson & Co.* v. *M'Robb,* [1918] A.C. 304 at 322, cited and followed in *Michigan Trust Co.* v. *Canadian Puget Sound Lumber Co.,* [1918] 3 W.W.R. 273 at 280 (B.C.C.A.). See also *Davidner* v. *Schuster,* [1936] 1 D.L.R. 560 at 573 (Sask.C.A.). See **obiter dicta.**

DIE WITHOUT ISSUE See **failure of issue.**

DILATORY PLEA [PLEA IN ABATEMENT] At **common law,** "the defendant (could) interpose a dilatory plea. Such a **plea** did not dispute the justice of the **plaintiff's** claim **on the merits;** its aim was simply to show that the particular suit could not be maintained in that court at that time. If successful, it defeated the particular **action** but did not preclude the plaintiff from starting afresh if he could cure the defect. One such plea was a plea to the **jurisdiction,** by which the **defendant** challenged the jurisdiction of the court to entertain the action. Another, more common class of dilatory plea was a plea in **abatement,** by which several types of defect could be attacked, including lack of capacity of the plaintiff to sue or the defendant to be sued; **misjoinder** (too many) or nonjoinder (too few) of the plaintiffs or defendants; and pendancy of another action between the same parties for the same cause." G. Watson and N. Williams, *Canadian Civil Procedure* 6–10 (2d ed. 1977).

DIMINUTION IN VALUE A measure of **damages** for breach of contract that reflects a decrease, occasioned by the breach, in the value of property with which the **contract** was concerned. In a building contract, it is the difference between the value of the building as constructed and its value had it been constructed in conformance with the contract. There are two general rules with variations where there are damages to **realty** and, in some cases, **personalty** attached to realty. There is the before-and-after value of realty rule, sometimes referred to as the diminution rule. There is also the restoration or replacement rule, which will generally be applied by the court if the injury is temporary and replacement is possible, or if it involves an amount less than that derived from application of the diminution rule.

Compare **cost of completion; damages** [EXPECTATION DAMAGES]; **specific performance.**

DIRECT CAUSE See **cause.**

DIRECTED VERDICT The verdict returned by a **jury** at the direction of the trial judge, by whose instruction the jury is bound. In **civil proceedings,** either party may receive a directed verdict in its favour if the opposing party fails to present **a prima facie case** or a necessary **defence.** In **criminal** proceedings, while there may be a directed verdict of **acquittal** (sometimes called a judgment of acquittal), there may be no directed verdict of conviction, as such a procedure would violate a person's rights under s. 7 of the **Canadian Charter of Rights and Freedoms.**

DIRECTOR One who sits on a board of directors of a **company** or **corporation** and who has the legal responsibility of exercising control over the officers and affairs of that company or corporation. "Agents for the company for which they act." *Finnemore* v. *Underwood Ltd.*, [1930] 3 D.L.R. 939 (Alta.S.C.A.D.).

A director has a **fiduciary duty** to the corporation and its **shareholders** to manage the affairs of the corporation in a manner consistent with their interests. Any **breach** of his fiduciary duty may subject him to personal liability to both the shareholders and the corporation. See, e.g., *D'Amore* v. *McDonald*, [1973] 1 O.R. 845 (H.C.).

DIRECTOR OF PUBLIC PROSECUTIONS **[D.P.P.]** In England, the D.P.P. under the supervision of the **Attorney General** has the duty "to institute, undertake and carry on . . . criminal proceedings and to give . . . advice and assistance to persons concerned in criminal proceedings as may be prescribed by regulations or may be directed in a special case by the Attorney General." 8 *Halsbury's Laws of England* (4th ed.) para. 1289.

In Canada, it is one of the responsibilities of the Attorney General of Canada or of a province to prosecute criminal offences. See R. Salhany, *Canadian Criminal Procedure* 6–1ff. (6th ed. 1994). See

also C.B.A. *Code of Professional Conduct* (1988).

DISABILITY "[T]he absence of legal capacity to do certain acts or enjoy certain benefits, such as disability to sue, to enter into contracts, to alienate property etc.... Its other meaning ... refers rather to want of physical or mental ability, either native or by reason of intervening cause." *Grini* v. *Grini* (1969), 68 W.W.R. 591 at 595 (Man.K.B.). Any want of legal capacity such as **infancy** or **insanity** renders a person legally **incompetent.**

DISBAR To deprive a lawyer of the right to practice law by rescinding the certificate to so practice, as a result of illegal or unethical conduct. See, e.g., *Barristers and Solicitors Act,* R.S.N.S. 1989, c. 30, ss. 31–35.

DISCHARGE A general word covering the methods by which a legal **duty** is extinguished. The factors bringing about a discharge of contractual obligation include full **performance, rescission, release, annulment, dismissal,** informal written **renunciation,** and contract not to sue.

DISCHARGE OF AN ACCUSED "Where an accused ... pleads guilty to or is found guilty of an offence, other than an offence for which a minimum punishment is prescribed by law or an offence punishable ... by imprisonment for 14 years or for life, the court ... may, if it considers it to be in the best interests of the accused and not contrary to public interest, instead of convicting the accused, by order direct that the accused be discharged absolutely or upon the conditions prescribed in a probation order." *Criminal Code*, R.S.C. 1985, c. C–46, s. 736. See *R.* v. *Sanchez-Pino* (1973), 11 C.C.C. (2d) 53 (Ont.C.A.). See **acquit.**

DISCHARGE OF A BANKRUPT "An order of discharge releases the bankrupt from all claims provable in **bankruptcy**" (*Bankruptcy and Insolvency Act,* R.S.C. 1985, c. B–3, s. 178(2)), except such debts as alimony, maintenance, fines imposed by the court, liability for fraud, embezzlement, or misappropriation; or debts for goods supplied as necessaries for life (s. 148(1)). See generally ss. 139–152. See, e.g., *Re Mascherin* (1976), 22 C.B.R. (N.S.) 263 (Ont.S.C.).

DISCHARGE OF A CONTRACT The termination of obligations under a contract which can occur in four ways: (1) by performance by both parties of the contractual obligations (see **accord** and **satisfaction**); (2) by express agreement between the parties to the contract; (3) by frustration of the contract where a subsequent event makes the performance of the contract impossible; and (4) by breach of contract. G.H.L. Fridman, *The Law of Contract in Canada* 515ff. (2d ed. 1986).

DISCHARGE OF A DEBT Settlement of a **debt.** A debt is discharged and the **debtor** released when the **creditor** has received something, either money or its equivalent, from the debtor that satisfies him. It may consist of **offsetting** mutual demands or of wiping out mutual disputed **claims** by mutual concessions, in which event no money is required to pass from one to the other. See, e.g., *Garcelon* v. *Eaton*, (1857), 8 N.B.R. 411 (N.B.S.C.). See also **satisfaction.**

Discharge also refers to the termination of one's employment by his employer; dismissal.

DISCLAIMER 1. A denial or repudiation of a person's **claim** or right to a thing, though previously that person insisted on that claim or right; **2.** complete renunciation of right to **possess** and of claim of **title,** e.g., renunciation of a gift, devise or bequest. See, e.g., *Re McFaden,* [1937] O.W.N. 404 (H.C.).

DISCONTINUANCE 1. In practice, the cessation of **proceedings** in an **action** where the **plaintiff** voluntarily puts an end to it, with or without the leave of the court; judicial leave may be required depending upon each jurisdiction's rules of practice and procedure. See, e.g., *Nova Scotia Civil Procedure Rules* (1983), r. 40. See also **nonsuit.**

2. In real property, "the difference between dispossession and discontinuance of **possession** might be expressed in this way: the one is where a person comes in and drives out the others from possession; the other case is where a person in possession goes out and is followed into possession by other persons." *Rains* v. *Buxton* (1880), 14 Ch.D. 537 at 539–40, cited and followed in *Rooney* v. *Petry* (1910), 22 O.L.R. 101 at 103–04 (C.A.).

DISCOUNT A deduction from a specified sum. "To discount a negotiable security [instrument] is ... to buy it at a discount; or it may mean, using another sense of the word, to lend money on the security, deducting the interest in advance." *Jones* v. *Imperial Bank* (1876), 23 Gr. 262 at 270.

DISCOVERY A modern pre-trial procedure by which one **party** gains vital information held by the **adverse party** concerning the case; the disclosure by the adverse party of facts, deeds, documents and other such things that are exclusively within his knowledge or possession and that are necessary to the other party's defence. See, e.g., *Nova Scotia Civil Procedure Rules* (1983), r. 18 [examination for discovery]. Compare *Magna* v. *R.* (1978), 40 C.R.N.S. 1 (Que.S.C.). See **depositions; interrogatories.**

DISCRETION The reasonable exercise of a power or right to act in a judicial capacity. Discretion involves the idea of choice, so that **abuse of discretion** includes more than a difference in judicial opinion between the **trial** and **appellate courts;** in order to constitute an abuse of discretion, the **judgment** must demonstrate a perversity of will, a defiance of good judgment, or bias. "[T]here is no such thing as an absolute and untrammelled 'discretion' [in public regulation], that is that action can be taken on any ground for any reason that can be suggested to the mind of the administrator; no legislative Act can, without express language, be taken to contemplate an unlimited arbitrary power exercisable for any purpose, however capricious or irrelevant, regardless of the nature or purpose of the statute....'Discretion' necessarily implies good faith in discharging public duty." *Roncarelli* v. *Duplessis,* [1959] S.C.R. 121 at 140.

JUDICIAL DISCRETION The reasonable use of judicial power, i.e., discretion "exercised according to the rules of law." *Jones* v. *Murray* (1908), 9 W.L.R. 204 at 205 (Sask., in chambers).

LEGAL DISCRETION The use of one of several equally satisfactory provisions of law.

PROSECUTORIAL DISCRETION The wide range of alternatives available to the **prosecutor** in criminal cases, including decision to prosecute, particular charges to be brought, **plea bargaining,** mode of trial conduct, recommendations for sentencing, **parole,** etc.

DISCRIMINATION "Discrimination may be described as a distinction, whether intentional or not, but based on grounds relating to personal characteristics of the individual or group, which has the effect of imposing burdens, obligations, or disadvantages on such individual or group not imposed upon others, or which withholds or limits access to opportunities, benefits, and advantages available to other members of society." *Andrews* v. *Law Society of British Columbia*, [1989] 1 S.C.R. 143 (S.C.C.).

Section 15(1) of the **Canadian Charter of Rights and Freedoms** provides for equality before and under the law, and the right to equal protection and benefit of the law without discrimination. See also **Canadian Bill of Rights**, R.S.C. 1985, Appendix III, s. 1, and the **Canadian Human Rights Act**, R.S.C. 1985, c. H–6, s. 2 (purpose), and ss. 3–25 (proscribed discrimination, and discriminatory practices).

DISHONOUR To refuse to make payment on a **negotiable instrument** when such an instrument is duly presented for payment. See *Bills of Exchange Act*, R.S.C. 1985, c. B–4, ss. 80–81; 94; 95–107. When a bank, for example, refuses to pay a cheque that has been presented to it for payment, it may do so because there are not adequate funds in the **drawer's** account to "cover" the cheque, or it may do so for other reasons. When such an instrument is dishonoured, for whatever reason, the holder may pursue his **remedies** against either the principal party [drawer or **maker**] or any subsequent **endorser.** See *id.*, s. 82. See also J. Falconbridge, *The Law of Negotiable Instruments in Canada* 38–39, 84–94 (1964).

DISINHERITANCE The act by the **donor** that dissolves the right of a person to **inherit** the **property** to which he previously had such a right; the act of terminating another's right to inherit.

DISJUNCTIVE ALLEGATIONS Charges that the **defendant** did one thing or another. Whenever the word *or* would leave the **averment** uncertain as to which of two or more things is meant, it is inadmissible. An **allegation** that charges the commission of a **crime** by one act "or" another is **defective** if it does not sufficiently and clearly inform the defendant of the charge against him so that he can prepare a **defence.** The same standard is applied to **pleadings** in **civil** cases, where both disjunctive allegations and disjunctive denials generally constitute defective pleadings and are therefore inadmissible. Compare **alternative pleading; denial.** See also **negative pregnant.**

DISMISS In a legal context, to remove a **case** from court; to terminate a case before **trial** or without a complete trial. See **demurrer.** Compare **summary judgment.**

DISMISSAL A cancellation. Dismissal of a **motion** is a denial of the motion. Dismissal of an **appeal** places the parties in the same condition as if no appeal had been taken or allowed, and is thus a confirmation of the judgment of the lower court. Compare **summary judgment.**

DISMISSAL WITH PREJUDICE Usually an **adjudication** upon the **merits** that operates as a **bar** to future action. See **res judicata.**

DISMISSAL WITHOUT PREJUDICE Usually an indication that the dismissal affects no right or **remedy** of the parties, i.e., is not **on the merits** and does not bar a subsequent **suit** on the same **cause of action.** See **collateral; estoppel; res judicata.**

DISPARAGEMENT See **bait and switch.**

DISPOSITION 1. The giving up or the relinquishment of anything; often used in reference to a testamentary **proceeding,** e.g., "the disposition of the estate"; **satisfaction** of a debt. 2. Courts are also said to "dispose of" **cases,** i.e., finally determine the rights of the parties or otherwise terminate the proceedings. 3. In criminal law, the **sentence** the **accused** receives is the disposition; i.e., the post-adjudicative phase of the criminal proceeding is called the disposition or the dispositionary stage (process). See also **bequeath.**

DISPUTABLE PRESUMPTION See **presumption** [REBUTTABLE PRESUMPTION].

DISSEISIN The act of wrongfully depriving a person of **seisin** of land; the taking possession of land under claim or **colour of title.**

DISSENT To differ in opinion; to disagree; to be of contrary sentiment. The most common usage is in a situation where a judge's **opinion** of the **case** differs from that of the majority of the court and the "dissenting judge" writes a contrary opinion explicating the deficiencies of the majority opinion and his reasons for arriving at a contrary conclusion. Compare **concur.**

DISSENTING OPINION See **opinion.**

DISTRIBUTION The division of property of an **intestate** among the next of kin. See **intestate succession.**

DISTRICT COURT "[A]n inferior court created by statute [which] possesses only that **jurisdiction** expressly conferred by the Act." W. Williston & R. Rolls, *The Law of Civil Procedure* 56–57 (1970). There are no longer any district courts in Canada. R. Salhany, *Canadian Criminal Procedure* c. 1 at 3 (6th ed. 1994).

DISTURBANCE OF THE [PUBLIC] PEACE "[T]o cause [by one's conduct] some disorder or agitation to ensue or ... any interference with the ordinary and customary use by the public of a public place." *R.* v. *Wolgram* (1976), 29 C.C.C. (2d) 536 at 537 (B.C.S.C.). "[Conduct which causes] the peace and tranquility of persons in a public place [to] have been interfered with or interrupted." *R.* v. *Hennessey* (1977), 35 C.C.C. (2d) 299 at 302 (N.S.Co.Ct.). See *Criminal Code*, R.S.C. 1985, c. C–46, s. 175. See **breach of the peace.**

DIVERS Many, several, sundry; a grouping of unspecified persons, things, acts, etc.

DIVESTITURE A statutory remedy, by virtue of which the court orders an offending party to rid itself of property or assets gained by wrongful conduct. Compare **restitution.**

DIVIDEND A "distribution of the profits of the company among the **shareholders** in respect of their shares. Such distributions are usually made by resolution of the directors declaring a dividend of a certain sum per share or at a rate percentage upon their shares to be payable on a certain date to shareholders of record as of a specified date subsequent to the date when the resolution is passed." D. Horsley, H. Sutherland, and J. M. Edmiston, *Fraser's Handbook on Canadian Company Law* 413 (7th ed. 1985). See *Re Carson*, [1963] 1 O.R. 373 (H.C.).

CUMULATIVE DIVIDEND A dividend with regard to which it is agreed that if at any time it is not paid in full, the difference shall be added to the following payment.

LIQUIDATION DIVIDEND A dividend resulting from **winding up** the affairs of a firm or **corporation,** settling with its **creditors** and **debtors,** and appropriating and distributing to its shareholders a residue proportionate to the profit and loss.

PREFERRED DIVIDEND A dividend paid to one class of stockholders in priority to that to be paid to another class.

STOCK DIVIDEND A dividend paid not in cash, but in **stock** so that each stockholder obtains a greater absolute number of shares but the same relative number of shares. See *Hosmer* v. *Royal Trust Co.,* [1953] R.L. 502 (Que.S.C.).

DIVISIBLE CONTRACT See **severable contract.**

DIVORCE The dissolution of a valid marriage. Proceedings commence with the filing of a **petition,** in a prescribed form, which sets out the facts on which the petitioner relies as proof of the grounds for divorce, and which concludes with a request that the marriage be dissolved. See *Divorce Act,* R.S.C. 1985 (2nd Supp.), c. 3. Divorce pertains to laws "dealing with dissolution of the matrimonial tie. It does not extend to judicial separation." *Hurson* v. *Hurson and Johnson* (1970), 72 W.W.R. 318 at 320 (B.C.S.C.).

DOCKET 1. A list of cases on a court calendar; 2. a summary or list of court decisions.

DOCUMENT Any material substance on which the thoughts of men are represented by writing, or any other species of conventional mark or symbol. A photograph of a deceased person is a document subject to production [for the purposes of discovery]. *Fox* v. *Sleeman* (1897), 17 P.R. 492 at 494 (C.A.).

A tape recording may be regarded as a document for the purposes of discovery and, where relevant to the issues, it is proper on oral examination to require the plaintiff to listen to the tape and answer questions as to the identity of voices. *Mouammar* v. *Bruner* (1977), 17 O.R. (2d) 526 (S.C.).

DOCTRINE OF WORTHIER TITLE See **worthier title, doctrine of.**

DOMAIN 1. Absolute ownership of land. **2.** Land of which one is absolute owner. See also **eminent domain; public domain.**

DOMESDAY BOOK A record made in the time of William the Conqueror (1081–1086) consisting of accurate and detailed surveys of the lands in England and the means by which the alleged owners obtained title. See 2 Bl.Comm. (original pagination) 49.

DOMESTIC CONTRACT See **marriage contract.**

DOMICILE "[G]enerally speaking, it means the place where a person has his permanent home....A man may have several residences but he can have only one domicile, and it is clear and beyond controversy that to constitute an acquired domicile two things are requisite, viz., act and intention, *factum et animus.* These two things cover, first, the residence, and then the intention of making it home, which must concur to make the domicile legal. Domicile is also said to be of three kinds: (1) birth; (2) choice; (3) operation of law....Domicile of choice is the relation the law creates between an individual and a particular locality or country. It is a conclusion or inference which the law derives from the fact of a man fixing voluntarily his sole or chief residence in a particular place with the intention of continuing to reside there for an unlimited time." *Crosby* v. *Thomson,* [1926] 4 D.L.R. 56 at 69–70 (N.B.S.C.A.D.).

DOMINANT ESTATE [TENEMENT] An estate whose owners are entitled to the **beneficial use** of another's property; **property** retained by an original grantor when a particular tract is subdivided and a portion is **conveyed,** and to which certain rights or benefits are legally owed by the conveyed or **servient estate.** These rights

and benefits may be in the nature of an **easement,** so that the owner of the retained land (dominant estate) is said to have a right of easement in the servient estate.

DONATIO (*dō-nä'-shē-ō*) Lat.: a **gift;** donation.

DONATIO MORTIS CAUSA See **causa** [CAUSA MORTIS].

DONATIVE INTENT Voluntary intent on the part of the **donor** to make a **gift.**

DONEE The recipient of a **gift, trust, power, right,** or **interest;** one who takes without first giving **consideration.** See, e.g., *Wurtele Estate* v. *M.N.R.,* [1963] C.T.C. 167 at 173 (Ex.Ct.). Compare bailee; **trustee.**

DONOR One who gives or makes a **gift;** a creator of a **trust;** a party conferring a power, e.g., the **grantor** of a **power of appointment.**

DOUBLE JEOPARDY A "general principal of common law that no person is to be placed twice in jeopardy for the same or substantially the same cause. Thus, if prosecuted again, the accused can plead his former **conviction** [AUTRE FOIS CONVICT] or **acquittal** [AUTRE FOIS ACQUIT] as a complete defence to this second charge. . . . [T]he former conviction [must have been] entered or acquittal . . . granted by a court with the proper **jurisdiction** to do so. . . . To succeed on the **defence** of **autre fois acquit** or **autre fois convict**, the accused must establish two things: the first is that there was a final **verdict** on the first charge; the second is that the 'matter' in both charges is the same in whole or in part and the charge before the court is the same, or implicitly included in the earlier charge, either in law or on the **evidence** presented if it had been legally possible at the time to make the necessary amendments." R. Salhany, *Canadian Criminal Procedure* c. 6 at 57–8 (6th ed. 1994). The special pleas autre fois acquit and autre fois convict are based on this principle. See *Criminal Code,* R.S.C. 1985, c. C–46, ss. 607–613. See, e.g., *R.* v. *Feeley, McDermott & Wright,* [1963] 1 C.C.C. 254 (Ont.C.A.); *R.* v. *Prince* [1986] 2 S.C.R. 480. Compare **estoppel; res judicata.**

Section 11(*h*) of the **Canadian Charter of Rights and Freedoms** provides that any person finally acquitted of an offence, has the right not to be tried for it again, and, if found guilty of an offence and punished, not to be tried and punished for it again. *R*. v. *Wigglesworth* [1987] 2 S.C.R. 541.

DOWER At **common law,** the right of a wife on surviving her husband to a life **estate** in one-third of the **freehold estates** of **inheritance** of which her deceased husband was solely **seised** at any time during the marriage and which her issue by him might possibly have inherited. 2 Bl.Comm. 131. Dower is the estate that a wife has for her life in certain freehold estates of her deceased husband. Until his death, her right is said to be INCHOATE. *Allan* v. *Rever* (1902), 4 O.L.R. 309 (K.B.). During the lifetime of her husband, a wife nevertheless has an interest in all his **real property,** and that interest cannot be **alienated** or interfered with by the husband without the wife's consent. *Freedman* v. *Mason* (1956), 4 D.L.R. (2d) 576 (Ont.H.C.) 1 A.H. Oosterhoff & W.B. Rayner, *Anger and Honsberger: Law of Real Property* 173–75 (2d ed. 1985). Compare **curtesy.** *N.B.:* Dower has been abrogated or abolished in most Canadian jurisdictions.

DOWRY Money and **personalty** the wife brings to the husband to support the expenses of marriage; a donation to the maintenance and support of the marriage.

DRAFT **1.** An order in writing directing a person other than the **maker** to pay a specified sum of money to a named person; see **bill of exchange.** Drafts may or may not be **negotiable instruments** depending upon whether the elements of negotiability are satisfied. **2.** The preliminary form of a legal document (e.g., the draft of a contract—often called a "rough draft"). **3.** The process of preparing or DRAWING a legal document (e.g., drafting a will) or piece of proposed legislation. **4.** In a military context, the conscription of citizens into the military service.

DRAWEE One to whom a **bill of exchange** or a **cheque** directs a request to pay a certain sum of money specified therein. In the typical chequing account situation, the bank is the drawee, the person writing the cheque is the **maker** or **drawer,** and the person to whom the cheque is written is the PAYEE.

DRAWER A person by whom a **cheque** or **bill of exchange** is drawn.

DROIT *(drwä)* Fr.: a right. Law; the whole body of the law.

DUCES TECUM See **subpoena** [SUBPOENA DUCES TECUM].

DUE CARE See **duty** [DUTY OF CARE].

DUE DATE The time fixed for payment of a debt, tax, interest, etc.

DUE PROCESS OF LAW The **Canadian Bill of Rights,** s. 1, provides that the individual has a right not to be deprived of life, liberty, security of the person, or enjoyment of property, except by due process of law. 28 Edw. III, c. 3 (1354) made it clear that no man should be harmed in any way "except" by due process of law. The phrase made its way into American jurisprudence by way of the Fifth Amendment to the United States Constitution.

The Supreme Court of Canada avoided defining the phrase for some time after its enactment. The Alberta Appellate Division in *R.* v. *Martin* (1961), 35 C.R. 276, felt that "due process of law" meant "the law of the land as applied to all the rights and privileges of every person in Canada when suspected of or charged with a crime [in the case at bar]." In *Curr* v. *The Queen,* [1972] S.C.R. 889, the Supreme Court of Canada rejected the notion of "substantive due process" as being implied in the Canadian legislation and said that the main intent of the subsection was to govern procedure. Laskin, J., felt that it was difficult to see what more could be read into s. 1(*a*) (from a procedural standpoint) than was already comprehended by ss. 2(*e*) and (*f*)—a "fair hearing in accordance with the principles of fundamental justice and a fair and public hearing by an independent and impartial tribunal."

The phrase was adopted in s. 7 of the **Canadian Charter of Rights and Freedoms,** which guarantees that:

7. Everyone had the right to life, liberty, and security of the person and the right not to be deprived thereof except in accordance with the principles of fundamental justice.

In the context of the *Charter*, the Supreme Court of Canada defined the phrase "principles of fundamental justice" to refer to both procedural and substantive matters. Lamer, J., stated "the principles of fundamental justice are to be found in the basic tenets and principles, not only of our judicial process, but also of the other components of our legal system." *Reference re Section 94(2) of the Motor Vehicle Act* (1985), 48 C.R. (3d) 289 at 317 (S.C.C.).

DUPLICITOUS The adjective applied to a **pleading** open to objection for **duplicity.**

DUPLICITY An objection to a **pleading** that has more than one **claim, charge,** or **defence** contained in it. The objection is largely obsolete. See *R.* v. *Grizzard* (1913), 9 Cr.App.R. 268. See also **joinder; misjoinder.**

DURABLE POWER OF ATTORNEY See **power of attorney.**

DURABLE POWER OF ATTORNEY FOR HEALTH CARE See **living will; power of attorney.**

DURESS An action by a person that compels another to do what he need not otherwise do. It is a **defence** to any act, such as a **crime, tort,** or **breach of contract,** that must be voluntary in order to create **liability** in the actor.

Duress is known to the *Criminal Code,* R.S.C. 1985, c. C–46, as COMPULSION and is defined as "threats of immediate death or grievous bodily harm from a person who is present when the offence is committed...." (s. 17). It is a defence where the person against whom the threats were issued is not a **party** to a **conspiracy.** The defence does not apply to certain serious crimes such as **rape, arson, murder,** or **robbery.**

Duress will similarly provide a vitiating factor in contractual relations, provided that the threats are unlawful. Where, however, the threat is of a criminal prosecution that would be well-founded, it is not destructive of the contract so long as there is adequate consideration and no

agreement to stifle the prosecution. *Rogers* v. *Rogers,* [1938] 1 D.L.R. 99 (N.S.S.C.).

DUTY 1. An obligation imposed by law to do or refrain from doing an act. **2.** In **tort** law, a legally sanctioned obligation the **breach** of which results in the **liability** of the person owing the duty. See **due care. 3.** In tax law, a levy or tax on imports and exports.

DUTY OF CARE A concept used in **tort** law to indicate the standard of **legal duty** one owes to others. **Negligence** is the failure to use due care, which is the amount of care that would be taken by a **reasonable man** in the circumstances. See *R. v. Coté* (1974), 51 D.L.R. (3d) 244 at 252 (S.C.C.). "The duty of care ... is confined to reasonably foreseeable dangers, the broad general test being ... whether a reasonable person should have anticipated that what happened might be a natural result of that act or omission." *University Hospital Bd.* v. *Lepine,* [1966] S.C.R. 561 at 579.

STATUTORY DUTY A duty imposed by statute.

DUTY OF ADDUCING EVIDENCE See **burden of proof.**

DWELLING HOUSE One's residence or abode; a structure or apartment used as a home or family unit. A motel unit is a dwelling house. *R. v. Henderson,* [1975] 1 W.W.R. 360 (B.C.Prov.Ct.). In a **conveyance** the term may also refer to the surrounding land reasonably necessary to enjoyment of the building. *Olafson* v. *Melsted,* [1939] 3 W.W.R. 375 (B.C.S.C.).

In criminal law, evidence that a person was in or entered a dwelling house without lawful excuse is **prima facie** evidence that he intended to commit an **indictable offence** therein. *Criminal Code,* R.S.C. 1985, c. C–46, s. 349(2). The offence of breaking and entering a dwelling house, intending to commit or committing an indictable offence, is more severely punished than the same offence in relation to other buildings. *Id.,* s. 348.

DYING DECLARATIONS See **hearsay rule.**

EASEMENT An interest one has in the land of another, known as a privilege without a profit; an incorporeal **hereditament.** The owner of the dominant **tenement** has the right to compel the owner of the servient tenement to do or refrain from doing something in respect of the dominant tenement.

The characteristics of an easement are (1) there must be a dominant and a servient tenement, (2) an easement must accommodate the dominant tenement, (3) the dominant and servient owners must be different individuals, and (4) to amount to an easement, the right over land must be capable of definition and not be uncertain. *Re Ellenborough Park,* [1956] Ch. 131 (C.A.).

EASEMENTS OF NECESSITY are those without which enjoyment of the land or building would be impossible.

Easements may be created in a number of ways: first, by express **grant;** secondly, by implied grant usually through the notion that a man cannot derogate from his grant; thirdly, by **prescription.**

See also **public easement.**

EGRESS See **ingress and egress.**

EJECTMENT A mixed action combining real and personal **remedies.** It is real in the sense that it is an action for the recovery of land. *Point* v. *Dibblee Construction Co. Ltd.* [1934] O.R. 142 (S.C.). It is personal in that it also includes an action for damages for wrongful withholding of land.

Originally the action was applicable only to a **leaseholder** wrongfully dispossessed but was extended by way of legal fiction so that it might be used by one entitled to the **freehold.** Such a fiction necessarily developed because of the extremely complex nature of a real action for the recovery of land by the person entitled to the freehold.

The Common Law Procedure Act, 1852, s. 168, abolished this fiction and made the action of ejectment similar to other actions except that it had no **pleadings.** See also **adverse possession.** Compare **eviction.**

EJUSDEM GENERIS RULE *(ĕ-yūs'-dĕm jĕn'-ĕr-ĭs)* Lat.; of the same class. A rule of **construction** of documents, sometimes known as Lord Tenterden's rule. Where general words follow an enumeration of particular persons or things having a specific meaning, the general words are constructed as being limited to all other persons or articles of a like class or nature. *Re Ollman* [1925] 3 D.L.R. 1196 (Ont.S.C.). Therefore, the phrase "any other person whatsoever" in the *Lords. Day Act,* R.S.O. 1897, c. 246, is to be read *ejusdem generis* with the preceding enumeration and consequently does not include corporations and their servants.

This rule of interpretation is not universal in its application and must give way to the general intent of the enactment or document under consideration. This is true where the specific words exhaust the category or genus and the general words would be meaningless if governed by the rule of *ejusdem generis. R.* v. *Jasper,* [1945] 1 W.W.R. 49 (Sask.Dist.Ct.).

Of course, the *ejusdem generis* doctrine does not apply where there is no genus or category to which the subsequent general words could be limited. The most obvious example of this is where only one species is named, as in "clerk or other persons" in the *Winding-up Act,* R.S.C. 1906, c. 144, s. 70. *Re Dominion Shipbuilding and Repair Co. Ltd.* (1921), 50 O.L.R. 350 (S.C.).

ELECTION The exercise of choice by an unrestrained will to take or do one thing or another. The obligation conferred upon a person to choose between two inconsistent or alternative rights or claims. *Cooper* v. *Canadian Northern Ontario Ry. Co.* (1924), 55 O.L.R. 256 (S.C.).

A person charged with having committed an **indictable offence** may elect to be tried by a provincial court judge, a judge alone, or by judge and jury. See *Criminal Code,* R.S.C. 1985, c. C-46, s. 536(2).

An Act relating to the representation of the people is usually defined as the election of a member to serve in **Parliament** or the provincial assemblies. See *Canada Elections Act,* R.S.C. 1985, c. E-2; *Elections Act,* R.S.N.S. 1989, c. 140.

ELECTION OF REMEDIES A choice of **remedies** permitted by law for the enforcement of a right or the redress of a wrong. Where these remedies are inconsistent, in the sense that pursuit of one implies a negation of the other, a person who has unequivocally elected for one remedy and communicated this election to the other party cannot thereafter have the benefit of a different remedy. Alternative remedies may be pleaded but an election need not be made until the time of **judgment.** As well, if a party by his actions manifests an **election,** he will thereafter be bound by it. *Standard Trust Co. Ltd.* v. *Little* (1915), 24 D.L.R. 713 (Sask.S.C.).

ELECTION UNDER THE WILL By the equitable doctrine of **election,** to take a benefit under a will requires conformity to all provisions of the will and renunciation of every right inconsistent with those provisions. One cannot approbate and reprobate. *Rosborough* v. *Trustees of St. Andrews Church* (1917), 55 S.C.R. 360. Thus, if a **testator devises** *A*'s property to *B* as well as devising his own property to *A,* then *A* is put to an election. He can accept the legacy only if he gives his own property or its value to *B.* Otherwise he may reject the **gift** and keep his own property.

Similarly, when a testamentary **beneficiary** is left two inconsistent claims to benefits (e.g., a devise or **bequest** under a will and a statutory claim), the beneficiary must choose between the two claims and relinquish one.

ELECTIVE FRANCHISE See **franchise.**

EMANCIPATION The process of freeing someone from the control of another; derived from the Roman Law doctrine of emancipation, which was concerned with the act by which a father relinquished control over his child so that the child became **sui juris.**

Emancipation has never been judicially defined with any precision. It occurs where there ceases to be the exceptional influence of parent over child and is a **question of fact** to be decided on the circumstances of every case. *Lancashere Loans Ltd.* v. *Black,* [1934] 1 K.B. 380 (C.A.).

EMBEZZLEMENT The fraudulent appropriation to the use of a servant or agent of property received by him in the name of his employer or principal. *Cana-*

dian Surety Co. v. *Quebec Insurance Agencies Ltd.,* [1936] S.C.R. 281.

There is no crime in the *Criminal Code* known as embezzlement nor was it a crime at common law. It was first made a crime in England by the Statute 21 Hen. VIII, c. 7, which is not in force in Canada. *Canadian Surety Co.* v. *Doucett* (1936), 10 M.P.R. 403 (N.B.S.C.A.D.). Embezzlement in Canada is included under the definition of *theft.* Compare **defalcation; misapplication [misappropriation] of property.**

EMBRACERY Originally, a **common-law misdemeanour** committed by a person who by any means whatever, except the production of **evidence** and presentation of agreement in open court, attempted to influence a **juror.** The offence exists in Canada through s. 139(3) of the *Criminal Code,* 1985, c. C–46, in essentially its common-law form. *R.* v. *Leblanc* (1885), 8 L.N. 114 (Que.K.B.).

EMINENT DOMAIN The right of the government to take private property for public purposes or for the common good. The doctrine is unknown to the common law, and the term is of American origin. However, it has been given statutory effect in Canada. Compare **public domain.**

EMOLUMENT A profit or advantage; that is, anything by which a person is benefited. Consequently, the term is wider than mere remuneration.

EMPANELLING [IMPANELLING] 1. The process by which **jurors** are selected and sworn in. **2.** The listing of those selected to serve on a particular **jury.** A potential juror is empanelled when called unless either counsel challenges. See *Criminal Code,* R.S.C. 1985, c. C–46, ss. 631–644.

ENACTING CLAUSE Generally, the preamble of a **statute,** or the part that identifies the statute as a legislative act and authorizes it as law.

ENACTMENT The process of being enacted; something that has been enacted. Refers to all **statutes** but may equally well be used to describe a particular provision in a statute. Enactment does not mean the same thing as **"Act."** "Act" means the whole Act, whereas a section or part of a section in an *Act* may be an enactment. Refer to *Interpretation Act,* R.S.C. 1985, c. I–21.

EN BANC *(än bänk)* Fr.: By the full [bench of a] court. In English law, the term usually referred to the sittings of judges of a superior court sitting as a full court, as distinguished from the sittings of individual judges at **nisi prius** or on circuit. In the Canadian context, a supreme court sitting **in banco** [en banc] might refer to three or more judges sitting together on an appeal. The sittings of the Nova Scotia Supreme Court in banco were abolished in 1966, and a separate appellate division of the Supreme Court was created.

ENCLOSURE Land enclosed by something more than an imaginary boundary line—e.g., a wall, hedge, ditch, fence or other actual obstruction. Compare **close.**

ENCROACH To make gradual inroads on; to trench usurpingly on the property, rights or authority of another; to intrude beyond the natural or conventional limits—for example, a clause in a **trust settlement** that allows the **trustee** to "encroach" upon the **capital** sum in set circumstances.

ENCROACHMENT The unauthorized extension by a person of a right possessed by him. The term is usually used in reference to land such as where an owner of land takes in or adds to it other land adjoining or near to it so that it appears that the added land is part of the original holding. Similarly, with regard to **easements,** where the owner of the dominant tenement does something in relation to his land that places a further burden or restriction on the *servient* tenement, he is said to commit an encroachment. *Ankerson* v. *Connelly,* [1907] 1 Ch. 678 (C.A.).

ENCUMBRANCE A **claim, lien,** or **liability** that is attached to **property.** *Beaument Estate* v. *M.N.R.,* [1968] C.T.C. 558 (Ex.). In essence, the term means that a legal or equitable **estate** has had a burden or charge placed upon it by the owner or another interested party. *Greene* v. *Appleton* (1915), 25 D.L.R. 333 (Alta.S.C.). *Encumbrance* includes **mortgages** and other voluntary **charges** as well as liens, registered **judgments,** and **lites pendentes.**

ENDORSE Generally, to sign the back of the **document.** It is not essential to the validity of an endorsement of a **bill of exchange** or **promissory note,** however, that the endorsement be on the back of the document; it may equally well be on the face. *Endorse* is equivalent to *sign.*

ENDOWMENT 1. Properly, this signifies the giving or assigning of **dower** to a woman. **2.** More usually, it pertains to a permanent fund of **property** or money bestowed on a person, charity, or institution, the income from which is used to support the specific purpose for which the endowment was originally set up. For example, an endowment may be bestowed on a college for the support of that institution.

ENDURING POWER OF ATTORNEY See **power of attorney.**

ENFEOFF To create a **feoffment,** which was an early common-law method of **conveying freehold estates.**
ENFEOFFMENT The act of investing with any dignity or possession; also, the **instrument** or **deed** by which a person is invested with **possessions.**

ENFRANCHISE To set free. Now chiefly used to signify the admittance to political rights and, most importantly, the right to vote at elections.

ENJOIN To command or instruct with authority; to abate, suspend, or restrain. To prohibit or restrain from doing a specific act by way of an **injunction** issued by a court with equitable **jurisdiction.**

ENJOY[MENT] The taking of the **benefit** of some **right.**

ENTAIL To convert into a **fee tail.** To settle land on a number of persons in **succession** so that it cannot be dealt with by any one possessor as absolute owner of a **fee simple.** Originally, in England a device by which the family estate was maintained within a strict lineal descent and could not be alienated.

Creation of an **estate** tail was accomplished by **conveyance** to a man and "the heirs of his body." These words of limitation gave what was originally known as a fee simple conditional (see **conditional fee**) and later as a fee tail. The **condition** was that, if the line of heirs ceased, the land would revert to the original owner or his estate. The effect was to tie up land indeterminably. Therefore, the judiciary began to view the condition as fulfilled if **issue** were born and the estate became a fee simple absolute. The landowners in 1235 forced the passage of the statute *De Donis Conditionalibus*. Following passage of this enactment, a person who had been granted a fee simple conditional was forbidden from conveying a fee simple absolute. This was enforced by the **reversioner**, who was given certain **remedies**. Thus, the **donee** could not alienate the land; it could only pass to his issue.

Eventually, fictitious proceedings known as FRISE [dispossession by force] and **recoveries** were developed to **bar** estates tail so that the estate of a tenant in tail could be converted into a fee simple absolute against both the donee's issue and the reversioner in tail. By the *Fines and Recoveries Act, 1833*, a tenant in tail was able to bar the entail against his own issue and against the reversioner if he had the consent of the protector of the settlement.

A general entail exists where the gift is to *A* and the "heirs of his body." A specific entail exists where the "heirs of his body" must be by a certain wife or some other specific condition. The gift can be further limited by the restriction that the property goes to *A* and the male heirs of his body. If the restriction is to the female heirs, then a female entail is created.

The estate tail has been abolished in half the provinces of Canada, and all have statutory provisions for disentailing.

ENTICEMENT The action of enticement developed in the eighteenth century out of the action of **trespass** *per quod consortuim amisit*, which here itself did not apply because of the wife's complicity. The **tort** consists of deliberately inducing a wife to leave her husband with knowledge of her marital status and with intent to interfere with the spouses' mutual duty to give **consortium**. Originally, a reciprocal action by the wife was not possible. However, developments in some common-law countries have resulted in the wife's being allowed to bring an action for enticement. *Wener* v. *Davidson* (1970), 15 D.L.R. (3d) 631 (Alta.S.C.). On the other hand, the action has been abolished altogether in England and in South Australia.

ENTIRETY See **tenancy** [TENANCY BY THE ENTIRETY].

ENTRAPMENT A common-law **defence** to a criminal charge that has recently been adopted in Canada. *R.* v. *Kirzner* (1977), 18 N.R. 400 at 407 (S.C.C.). The defence only operates where the police or other governmental body has drawn the **accused** into the commission of the **offence**—i.e., where the police have gone beyond mere **solicitation** and have actively organized a scheme of ensnarement in order to **prosecute** the person so caught. See also *R.* v. *Amato* (1982), 42 N.R. 487 (S.C.C.); *R.* v. *Mack* (1988), 44 C.C.C. (3d) 513 (S.C.C.); *R.* v. *Barnes* (1991), 63 C.C.C. (3d) 1 (S.C.C.).

ENTRY, FORCIBLE See **forcible entry**.

ENURE See **inure**.

EN VENTRE SA MÈRE *(än vän'-tr' sà mär)* Fr.: in his mother's womb. A descriptive phrase used to indicate an unborn child. Such a child is capable of receiving property under a will, (*Re Burrows, Cleghorn* v. *Burrows*, [1895] 2 Ch. 497), and may have a guardian assigned to it.

EQUALITY Equality before and under the law, and the right to equal protection and benefit of the law, without discrimination is guaranteed to every individual in the **Canadian Charter of Rights and Freedoms**, s. 15 (Equality Rights), which came into effect on April 17, 1985. Previous to the equality provisions of the Charter, equality before the law and protection of the law was provided for in the **Canadian Bill of Rights**, R.S.C. 1985, Appendix III, s. 1(b).

In 1989, the Supreme Court of Canada ruled on *Andrews* v. *The Law Society of British Columbia*, [1989] 1 S.C.R. 143. Their ruling rejected the previous standard of pre-Charter equality—that persons similarly situated be similarly treated (i.e. *Bliss* v. *Attorney-General of Canada*, [1979] 1 S.C.R. 183)—and emphasized the impact of the law in question on the individual or group concerned. See also **discrimination**.

EQUALITY BEFORE THE LAW The *Canadian Bill of Rights*, S.C. 1960, c. 44, recognizes "the right of an individual to equality before the law." Those to whom a law applies or extends are entitled to have the law as it exists applied equally and without fear that some persons will be shown favour in the application of the law. *R. v. Gonzales* (1962), 37 W.W.R. 257 (B.C.C.A.); *R. v. Drybones,* [1970] S.C.R. 282. This right is reiterated in s. 15(1) of the *Canadian Charter of Rights and Freedoms* in the **Constitution Act, 1982:** "Every individual is equal before and under the law and has the right to the equal protection and equal benefit of the law without discrimination." See *R. v. Turpin*, [1989] 1 S.C.R. 1296.

EQUALITY RIGHTS See **Canadian Charter of Rights and Freedoms.**

EQUITABLE DEFENCE See **defence; equity.**

EQUITABLE ESTATE See **equity; estate.**

EQUITABLE ESTOPPEL See **equity; estoppel.**

EQUITABLE INTEREST See **equity; interest.**

EQUITABLE LIEN See **equity; lien.**

EQUITABLE MAXIMS Phrases meant to represent the cornerstones of the law of **equity.** They are: (1) He who comes to equity must do equity. (2) He who comes to equity must come with clean hands. (3) Equity aids the vigilant. (4) Equity acts specifically. (5) Equity acts **in personam.** (6) Equity follows the law. (7) Equity suffers no wrong without a remedy. (8) Equity regards that as done which ought to have been done. (9) Equity regards the substance and intent, not the form. (10) Equity imputes an intent to fulfil an obligation. (11) Equality is equity. (12) Where the equities are equal, the law will prevail. (13) Where the equities are equal, priority of time will prevail.

EQUITABLE RELIEF See **equity; relief.**

EQUITABLE SEISIN See **equity; seisin.**

EQUITABLE TITLE See **equity; title.**

EQUITY Primarily, justice or fairness. In a very broad philosophical sense, equity means to do to all men as we would have them do unto us. It may be used to mean the discretionary power to do justice in particular cases where strict rules of **common law** would cause hardship.

In England, this was supplied by exercise of the Chancellor, who was **petitioned** by subjects who could not obtain justice in the common-law courts. Originally, equity mitigated the rigours of the common law and was flexible. However, in more modern times equity became excessively rigid and incapable of forming new remedies.

The common-law and equity courts are now fused and administered through one body by the judicature acts of the various provinces. Where common-law and equitable principles conflict, equity will prevail.

The term *equity* is also used in accounting to denote the net value of the assets of a business, determined by subtracting **liabilities** from **assets.** For incorporated business enterprises, equity is owned by the common and preferred **shareholders.** If the corporation is publicly held, the shares will be traded on a stock exchange or over-the-counter, which together comprise the EQUITY MARKET. In the case of a **partnership,** equity denotes the total net value of **capital** and current accounts.

EQUITABLE INTEREST refers to the **interest** a person is **beneficially entitled** to in a **property** with a **mortgage.** See *Bednarsky v. Weleschuk* (1961), 29 D.L.R. (2d) 270 (Alta.S.C.A.D.).

EQUITY OF REDEMPTION An **estate** in land; the person entitled to redeem is in **equity** the **owner** of the land. Where land is **mortgaged,** the mortgagor instantly acquires a contractual right to redeem on the date set for **redemption.** There is also an equitable right to redeem where the mortgagor has fallen into **default** on the payments of the mortgage. Strictly, the term *equity of redemption* only becomes appropriate after the legal or contractual right has been forfeited, *Garrow v. Baird,* [1931] 1 W.W.R. 129 (Man.K.B.), but generally the **interest** the mortgagor has in his mortgaged land is referred to as his equity of redemption.

The mortgagor cannot **contract** out of his equity of redemption at the time of making the mortgage, but he may agree that the mortgage be not redeemed for a reasonable period of time. See *Stephens v. Gulf Oil Canada Ltd.* (1974) 45 D.L.R. (3d) 161 (Ont.H.C.). Also, the equity of redemption may be extinguished by a lapse of time, by **foreclosure** and judicial sale or by a sale under a power of **sale.**

Otherwise, the mortgagor, upon payment of the mortgage debt, is entitled to a reconveyance of the legal estate that had been **vested** in the mortgage by virtue of the mortgage.

EQUITY'S DARLING A **bona fide purchaser** for value without notice of a prior legal estate. Such a purchaser was protected in **equity.**

ERGO *(ĕr'-gō)* Lat.: therefore; consequently; because.

ERRONEOUS Involving a mistake. It signifies a deviation from the requirements of the law. It is to be distinguished from "illegal" in that it does not connote a lack of legal authority. *R.* v. *Roberts,* [1908] 1 K.B. 407 (C.A.).

ERROR OF LAW ON THE FACE OF THE RECORD An error that may be ascertained without recourse to the **evidence** adduced in the **proceedings** but merely on examination of the proceedings. For these purposes, the **record** consists of the reasons for the decision or **order** given, the **pleadings** or documents that initiated the proceedings and also, by incorporation, any documents referred to or mentioned in the decision. *R.* v. *Northumberland Compensation Appeal Tribunal, ex parte Shaw,* [1952] 1 K.B. 338 (C.A.).

Where a decision-maker in judicial proceedings makes such an error, the courts may intervene to set the decision aside. Error of law on the face of the record includes applying the incorrect onus of **proof,** wrongful admission of **evidence** and wrongful refusal to hear evidence. Compare **admissible evidence.**

ESCALATOR CLAUSE The part of a **lease** or **contract** that provides for an increase in the contract price upon the determination of certain acts or other factors beyond the parties' control, such as an increase in the cost of labour or of a necessary commodity, or the fixing of maximum prices by a government agency. For example, a wife's **maintenance** may have an escalator clause, so that as the cost of living increases or as her husband's income increases so will her maintenance.

ESCHEAT A type of **reversion** wherein **property** reverts to the state as the ultimate proprietor of land; originally a part of the English feudal system. Under escheat, the land reverted to the Crown or lord of the **fee** from when or from whose ancestor or predecessor the **estate** was derived, taking it on the failure, natural or legal, of the **intestate** tenant's family.

Escheat might occur in two ways. First, where a person was outlawed for a felony known as *propter delictum tenentis,* such a person became incapable of holding or inheriting land, and it escheated to the lord. The other form of escheat is *propter defictum sanguinis,* which applied where the tenant died without an heir. *Mercer* v. *Attorney-General of Ont.* (1881), 5 S.C.R. 538.

The following Canadian provinces have retained escheat by statutory enactment: British Columbia, Manitoba, New Brunswick, Nova Scotia, Ontario, Prince Edward Island and Saskatchewan. See **forfeiture.**

ESCROW A written **instrument** such as a **deed** temporarily deposited with a third party, a stranger to the transaction, by agreement of the parties directly involved. It is to be held by him until certain specified conditions are fulfilled and then delivered by him to the other party to take effect absolutely. *Terrapin International Ltd.* v. *Inland Revenue Commissioners,* [1976] 2 All E.R. 461 (Ch.Div.).

Originally, for a writing to be an escrow the word *escrow* had to be written on it. Now, a writing is an escrow if the circumstances of delivery are such as to indicate that it is conditional on the performance of prescribed stipulations. If the conditions are not fulfilled, the deed never takes effect.

Once a writing has been delivered in escrow it cannot be retrieved until there has been an unreasonable delay in performing the condition.

ESTATE A term that signifies the relation between a person and the **property** in which he has an **interest** (*Thompson* v. *Yockney* (1912), 8 D.L.R. 776 (Man.K.B.)) and also the interest itself. More technically, it refers to the degree, nature and extent of an interest or ownership in land. "Estate" is a derivation from the notion that no one can be the absolute owner of land and one can only have a limited estate or interest in it. The Crown is the ultimate proprietor of all land.

Estates were divisible by reference to the potential limit of their duration into **freehold estates** and less than freehold estates.

Freehold estates could be estates of **inheritance**—such as **fee simple, fee tail,** or **frankmarriage**—or estates not of inheritance. If the latter, they were created either by the act of the parties or by operation of law. Those created by the act of the parties included estates for life (see **life estate**) and estates **pur autre vie,** whereas those resulting from operation of law included the estate of a tenant in tail after possibility of issue extinct and estates arising through **dower.**

Less than freehold estates could be of either certain duration (estates for years) or uncertain duration (estates at will or at sufferance).

Estates were also distinguishable by their quality, that is, by whether they were absolute, determinable or conditional. An ABSOLUTE ESTATE is one granted without condition or termination, a FEE SIMPLE ABSOLUTE. A DETERMINABLE ESTATE is one that has the potential to continue as though it were absolute but determines on the happening of some event. A CONDITIONAL ESTATE is one liable to be defeated on the fulfilment of some condition. See **conditional fee; determinable fee.**

Estates may be further divided into ESTATES IN POSSESSION, where there is a present right of enjoyment, and ESTATES IN EXPECTANCY, which could not be enjoyed until some future time.

Estate has also come to mean property, particularly where speaking in regard to the estate of a deceased person. Estate has also acquired a fictitious entity as in the situation where a debt is owing to the estate of a bankrupt individual. The estate represents the individual to whom it originally belonged.

See **preceding estate.**

ESTATE AT SUFFERANCE See **tenancy** [TENANCY AT SUFFERANCE].

ESTATE AT WILL See **tenancy** [TENANCY AT WILL].

ESTATE BY THE ENTIRETY See **tenancy** [TENANCY BY THE ENTIRETY].

ESTATE FOR LIFE See **life estate.**

ESTATE FOR YEARS See **tenancy** [TENANCY FOR YEARS].

ESTATE FROM YEAR TO YEAR [PERIOD TO PERIOD] See **tenancy** [PERIODIC TENANCY].

ESTATE IN COMMON See **tenancy** [TENANCY IN COMMON].

ESTATE PUR AUTRE VIE See **pur autre vie.**

ESTATE TAX See **tax.**

ESTOPPEL Originally known as preclusion; a **bar;** an impairment whereby a **party** is precluded in any subsequent **proceedings** from alleging or proving that certain facts are otherwise than they were originally made to appear. *The People's Bank of Halifax* v. *Richard A. Estey* (1904), 34 S.C.R. 429. Estoppel has been described as a rule of evidence, and consequently an action cannot be founded on it. *Low* v. *Bouverie,* [1891] 3 Ch. 82 (C.A.). However, the whole concept is more precisely viewed as a substantive rule of law; a principle of justice and equity. *Canada and Dominion Sugar Co. Ltd.* v. *Canadian National West Indies Steamships Ltd.,* [1947] A.C. 46 at 56 (P.C).

There are four kinds of estoppel: estoppel by matter of record, estoppel by deed, estoppel **in pais** and promissory estoppel.

ESTOPPEL BY RECORD Sometimes referred to as **res judicata.** It arises where an issue of fact that had been judicially determined in a final manner by a **tribunal** having **jurisdiction** arises subsequently between the same parties. *Re Ontario Sugar Co. McKinnon's Case* (1910), 22 O.L.R. 621 at 623 (Ont. S.C.). Consequently, the issue must be taken as conclusively determined in the initial proceedings. *Harper* v. *Cameron* (1893), 2 B.C.R. 365 (Div.Ct.).

ESTOPPEL BY DEED An estoppel that arises where a statement of fact is made in a **deed** and verified by **seal.** The rule simply states that a man cannot deny the veracity of statements made in his deed. *Barton* v. *Bank of New South Wales* (1890), 15 A.C. 379 at 380 (P.C.). If on the construction of the deed the statement in contention is that of all the parties, then all are bound. Otherwise, it is only binding on the person making it.

ESTOPPEL **in pais** Also known as ESTOPPEL BY CONDUCT. The usual meaning of the word *estoppel:* When one person by his conduct leads another to believe that certain facts are true and these are acted upon, then in any subsequent **proceedings** this person cannot deny the truth of such facts. *Capital Trust Corporation Ltd.* v. *Gordon,* [1945] O.R. 277 at 286 (Ont.S.C.).

PROMISSORY ESTOPPEL A doctrine derived from a principle of **equity,** *Hughes* v. *The Directors of the Metropolitan Ry. Co.* (1877), 2 A.C. 439 at 443 (H.L.), which has seen considerable expansion in recent years. It comes into existence where one party by words or conduct gives an assurance to the other party with the intention of affecting the legal relations between them and where the other party acts on the assurance accordingly. The one making the assurance cannot now revert to the previous legal relation but must abide by the qualifications he introduced himself. *Combe* v. *Combe,* [1951] 2 K.B. 215 at 220 (C.A.).

The doctrine is subject to the limitation that the promisor can resile from his promise by giving reasonable notice to allow the promisee the opportunity to regain his original position. If such cannot be regained, then the promise is irrevocable. *Ajayi* v. *R. T. Briscoe (Nigeria) Ltd.,* [1964] 3 All E.R. 556 at 559 (P.C.).

ESTOVERS Generally, any kind of sustenance, but **1.** commonly used in reference to a **tenant's** right to remove wood from the landlord's estate in order to effect repairs. This was the right of any tenant for life or years unless the agreement between the parties specifically provided otherwise. Estovers were also known as BOTES and were sometimes divided into *house-bote* for repairs to the dwelling, *fire-bote* for taking fuel, *plough-bote* for making and repairing agricultural instruments and *hay-bote* for repairing fences.

2. Less frequently, it is used to denote **alimony** for a widow or for a wife separated from her husband and also **maintenance** for an imprisoned felon.

ET AL. *(ĕt ăl)* Lat: and others; abbreviation of *et alii.* Where there are a number of **plaintiffs, grantors,** persons addressed, etc., it is common to set out fully the name of the person first mentioned followed by the words *et al.,* thereby including all relevant persons.

ET NON *(ĕt nŏn)* Lat.: and not. This phrase is used primarily in introducing a special **traverse** in **pleading** and thus is called the "inducement to the traverse"; synonymous in use with **absque hoc,** which means "without this."

ET. SEQ. *(ĕt sĕk)* Lat.: and the following; an abbreviation of *et sequentes* or *et sequentia.* Usually used to denote a reference to a certain page and the following pages: page 13 *et seq.*

ET UX. *(ĕt ŭks)* Lat.: and wife; abbreviation of *et uxor.* Used in old legal documents such as **wills** and other **instruments** that purport to **grant** or **convey.**

EUTHANASIA Also known as mercy killing; the suggested practice of painlessly putting to death those persons suffering from terminal diseases. See *Rodriguez* v. *British Columbia (A-G),* [1993] 3 S.C.R. 519.

EVICTION 1. Dispossession of a **tenant** by his **landlord.** A mere **trespass** will not be sufficient to constitute an eviction. Rather the act must be of a grave and permanent character done with the intention of depriving the tenant of enjoyment of the whole of the **demised premises.** *Cross* v. *Piggott,* [1922] 2 W.W.R. 662 (Man.K.B.). **2.** Generally, the recovery of land by operation of law. Compare **ejectment; ouster.**

EVIDENCE Any species of proof or probative matter legally presented by the acts of **parties** and through the medium of **witnesses, records,** documents, exhibits, or other concrete objects for the purpose of inducing belief in the minds of the court or jury as to their content. The rules of evidence (see **admissible evidence**) control the presentation of facts before the court. The purpose is to facilitate the introduction of all logically relevant facts without sacrificing any fundamental policy of the law which may be of more importance than the ascertainment of the truth. *Rex* v. *Whittaker,* [1924] 3 D.L.R. 63 (Alta. S.C.). Partially governed by legislation. See *Canada Evidence Act,* R.S.C. 1985, c. C–5, and provincial evidence statutes. See **circumstantial**

evidence; hearsay rule; presumptive evidence.

INADMISSIBLE EVIDENCE Generally, evidence that is logically **probative** is admissible unless explicitly disallowed by some specific rule of exclusion—for example, **hearsay rule.** Inadmissible evidence should not be considered in any form or for any purpose by the jury. *Savard* v. *R.,* [1946] S.C.R. 20. Evidence may also be found to be inadmissable under s. 24(2) of the **Canadian Charter of Rights and Freedoms** where the admitting of such evidence would bring the system of justice into disrepute. See *Collins* v. *The Queen* (1987), 33 C.C.C. (3d) 1 (S.C.C.).

EVIDENCE ALIUNDE See **aliunde.**

EVIDENTIAL BURDEN See **burden of proof.**

EXAMINATION-IN-CHIEF See **cross-examine.**

EXCEPTION 1. An objection or challenge taken to an answer contained in the **pleadings.** For example, a **plaintiff** might file an exception to a **defendant's** answer if it were insufficient or scandalous. See **demurrer. 2.** A clause in a **deed** preventing the thing excepted from passing in the **grant.**

EXCISE Broadly, any kind of tax that is not directly on property or the rents or incomes of real estate. Usually, though not exclusively, used to indicate a duty imposed on goods manufactured in another country before they reach the consumer. *Atlantic Smoke Shops Ltd.* v. *Conlon & Attorney-General for Canada,* [1943] A.C. 550 (P.C.).

EXCLUSIONARY RULE A statutory rule of law that provides that otherwise **admissible evidence** may not be used in evidence against the **witness** in some other proceedings.

EXCULPATORY Refers to **evidence** and/or statements that tend to clear, justify or excuse a **defendant** from alleged fault or **guilt.** Compare **incriminate; inculpatory.**

EX DEBITO JUSTITIAE (*ĕks dĕ'-bĭ-tō jŭs-tĭ'-shē-ĭ*) Lat.: because of the demands of justice. A **remedy** granted as of right, where the action is proved, as opposed to a discretionary remedy such as **certiorari.**

EXECUTE To complete or carry into effect. **1.** Where a legal **instrument** is involved, to complete all the formalities necessary in order to give validity thereto. Thus, to execute a deed requires that it be signed, sealed and delivered. **2.** To carry into effect or to enforce a judgment of the court. **3.** To put a person to death by authority of the state.

EXECUTED Fully accomplished, leaving nothing to be performed. *Redican* v. *Nesbitt,* [1924] S.C.R. 135. Compare **executory.**

EXECUTED INTEREST See **interest.**

EXECUTIVE The Crown in its administrative aspect; the branch of government that puts laws into execution as distinguished from the legislative branch, which enacts the laws, and the judiciary, which interprets them.

In the broad sense, the executive consists of the Government departments and their officers under the respective Ministers. The principal executive body is the Cabinet; the Prime Minister is its head.

EXECUTIVE AGREEMENT See **treaty.**

EXECUTOR [EXECUTRIX] The person to whom the execution of a **will** is entrusted, that is, the duty to carry out its provisions. Anyone capable of making a will can be an executor; a **corporation** may also be appointed to act as executor. The duties of an executor include seeing that the deceased is buried; proving the will; collecting the **estate** and, if required, converting it into money; and distributing **legacies** and any residue to those entitled. *Re Adamson* (1875), L.R. 3 P. & D. 253. The executor is usually given one year to wind up the estate of the deceased person. *Mc. Cargar* v. *McKinnon* (1868), 15 Gr. 361.

It is not essential that the executor be expressly named provided the implication is obvious. Such an executor is known as an "executor according to the tenor," and to constitute an executor of this nature, it must be evident on a reasonable construction of the will that the **testator** intended this person to carry out the duties of an executor. *Re Adamson* (1875), L.R. 3 P. & D. 253.

Compare **administrator.**

EXECUTOR DE SON TORT (*ĕg-zĕk'-yū-tôr dĕ sōn tôr*) One who assumes the office of executor, despite the lack of appointment to that position by the deceased or by the court, on the failure of the deceased to make such a selection. *Pickering* v. *Thompson* (1911), 24 O.L.R. 378 (Div.Ct.). Meddling with the goods of the deceased is sufficient to render one an executor de son tort. An executor *de son tort* "becomes liable to the rightful representatives and other interested persons, to the extent of such assets as he has received less any proper payments he has made." S. Bailey, *The Law of Wills* 294–95 (7th ed. 1973).

EXECUTORY That which remains to be carried into effect; the opposite of **executed**. For example, an EXECUTORY CONTRACT is one in which some performance remains to be completed. *Redican* v. *Nesbitt*, [1924] S.C.R. 135.

EXECUTORY BEQUEST See **bequest**.

EXEMPLARY DAMAGES See **damages**.

EX GRATIA (*ĕks grä'-shē-à*) Lat.: out of grace; gratuitously. That which is done as a favour rather than as a required task or as of right. Payments made to avoid litigation are often made *ex gratia*, that is, without admission of liability. *Edwards* v. *Skyways Ltd.*, [1964] 1 All E.R. 494 (Q.B.D.).

EX-OFFENDER See **criminal**.

EX OFFICIO (*ĕks ō-fĭ'-shĕ-ō*) Lat.: by virtue of his office. Powers that are a concomitant of holding a certain office may be exercised without any further instrument conferring such authority. For example, the Lord Mayor of London is *ex officio* a justice of the peace for the City of London.

EX PARTE (*ĕks pär'-tā*) Lat.: on behalf of. **1.** In its precise sense, an *ex parte* application in a judicial proceeding is made by a person who is not a party to the proceeding but who has a sufficient interest entitling him to make the application. *Stewart* v. *Braun Ex parte Patterson*, [1924] 3 D.L.R. 941 (Man.K.B.). **2.** More usually, the term indicates an application made by one party to a proceeding in the absence of the other party. Generally, such an application is only made in cases of emergency where it is not possible to give the adverse party **notice** of the **proceed-**ing. Where the other party was given notice but has chosen not to appear, the application is not properly called *ex parte*.

EXPECTANCY Contingency as to **possession** or **enjoyment**. In the law of **property**, **estates** may be either in possession or in expectancy; if an expectancy is created by the parties, it is a **remainder**; if by **operation of law**, is is a **reversion**. See **future interest; vested**.

EXPECTATION DAMAGES See **damages**.

EXPERT TESTIMONY [EVIDENCE] See **expert witness**.

EXPERT WITNESS A person possessed of a special skill or knowledge acquired through study or experience that entitles him to give an opinion or evidence concerning his area of expertise. *Rice* v. *Sockett* (1912), 4 O.W.N. 397 (H.C.). The opinion of such an expert is only admissible where the subject in issue before the court is such that competency to form an opinion on it can only be acquired by a course of specific study or by experience. *R.* v. *Kuzmack* (1955), 20 C.R. 365 (Alta.A.D.). The *Canada Evidence Act*, R.S.C. 1985, c. C–5, s. 7, allows only five such witnesses to be called by each party.

EX POST FACTO (*ĕks pōst fäk'-tō*) Lat.: after the fact; by a subsequent act. It signifies something done subsequently that affects another thing committed earlier. The most common usage is in regard to a statute that makes punishable an act that when committed was not punishable. Similarly, the term also applies to a statute that imposes a greater punishment for a crime than was possible at the time the crime was committed.

EXPRESSIO UNIUS EST EXCLUSIO ALTERIUS (*ĕks-prĕ-sē-ō ū'-nē-ūs ĕst ĕks-klū'-sē-ō äl-tĕr'-ē-ūs*) Lat.: the express mention of one person or thing is the exclusion of another. For example, an agreement of purchase and **sale** of a home that expressly includes the dining room chandelier will, however, exclude the hall chandelier. The phrase is a maxim for interpreting **statutes** and other written **instruments** but should not be applied without scrutiny of the specific circumstances. It has been said to be a valuable servant but a dangerous master to follow, because strict adherence to the rule may pervert the intentions of the draughtsman. *Docksteader* v. *Clark* (1903), 11 B.C.R. 37, affirmed (1905), 36 S.C.R. 622.

EXPROPRIATION Compulsorily depriving a person of a right of property belonging to him; a present manifestation of the **eminent domain** of the Crown or state. **Compensation** may be promised or paid.

EX REL. *(ĕks rĕl)* Lat.: from a narrative or information; abbreviation of *ex relatione.* When a report of a decision is made by one who derives his knowledge, not from having been present in court, but indirectly from notes or information disclosed to him by a barrister or, occasionally, a solicitor who heard the proceeding, the decision is said to be reported in *ex relatione.*

An action brought to restrain interference with a public right or to compel performance of a public duty must have the Attorney-General as a party unless there is at the same time interference with a private right or special damage is suffered over and above that of the general public. Where the Attorney-General is a necessary party, the action is brought by him at the relation *(ex relatione)* of the person seeking either to enforce the public duty or to restrain interference with that right. The relator is liable for the costs of the action. *Attorney-General* v. *Scott,* [1905] 2 K.B. 160 (C.A.).

EXTENUATING CIRCUMSTANCES Unusual factors related to and tending to contribute to the consummation of an illegal act, but over which the actor had little or no control. These factors therefore reduce the responsibility of the actor and serve to mitigate his punishment or his payment of **damages.** See **mitigating circumstances.** Compare **justification.**

EXTINGUISHMENT The termination or discharge of an obligation or right. Thus, the obligation to pay a **debt** is extinguished when the debt is in fact paid or when the **creditor** releases the **debtor** from his **liability.** Similarly, an easement

may be extinguished by express or implied agreement or by **unity of possession**—that is, where the dominant and servient **tenements** become united in the same person for an **estate in fee simple.**

Extinguishment can also refer to **aboriginal rights** that can be extinguished by legislation or through the consent of **aboriginal peoples.** See *R.* v. *Denny* (1990), 55 C.C.C. (3d) 322 at 331–32 (N.S.S.C.).

EXTORTION **1.** In common law, a **misdemeanour** committed by a holder of public office who by virtue of his office wrongfully received from another any money or valuable things. **2.** The inducing of a person to do anything by the use of threats, **accusations,** menaces, or violence without reasonable justification. *R.* v. *Natarelli and Volpe,* [1968] 1 C.C.C. 154 (S.C.C.). In Canada extortion is an **indictable offence** carrying a maximum penalty of life imprisonment. *Criminal Code,* R.S.C. 1985, c. C–46, s. 346.

EXTRADITION The surrendering by one state, at the request of another, of a person accused of a crime under the laws of the requesting state. It is usually regulated by reciprocal extradition **treaties** between states. Extradition may be barred unless for an offence punishable in the surrendering state. *Tzu-Tsai Chong* v. *Governor of Pentville Prison,* [1973] 2 All E.R. 204 (H.L.).

EXTREMIS See **in extremis.**

EXTRINSIC FRAUD See **fraud.**

EX TURPI CAUSA NON ORITUR ACTIO *(ĕks tūr'-pē kaw'-zà nòn órətər áeksh(iy)ow)* Lat.: no disgraceful [foul, immoral, obscene] matter can give rise to an **action.** Sometimes known as the illegality **defence,** it was used predominantly in **contract** cases but has recently been adopted in **tort** law. According to the doctrine, a **plaintiff** who has been engaged in criminal activity while injured will be denied **recovery.** *Tomlinson* v. *Harrison,* [1972] 1 O.R. 670 (H.C.).

FACINUS QUOS INQUINAT AEQUAT *(fä'-sĭ-nŭs kwōs ĭn'-kwĭ-nät ī'-kwät)* Lat.: villainy and guilt make all those whom they contaminate equal in character.

FACTA SUNT POTENTIORI VERBIS *(fäk'-tä sŭnt pō-tĕn'-tē-ô'-rē vĕr'-bēs)* Lat.: facts, deeds or accomplishments are more powerful than words.

FACT FINDER In a judicial or administrative **proceeding**, the person or group of persons that has the responsibility of determining the facts relevant to decide a controversy. In a jury trial, it is the role of a **jury**; in a non-jury trial, the judge sits as both fact finder and trier of law; in administrative proceedings, it may be a hearing officer or a hearing body. The term TRIER OF FACT generally denotes the same function.

FACTO *(fäk'-tō)* Lat.: in fact; by a deed, accomplishment or exploit. See also **de facto.**

FACTOR A type of mercantile **agent** to whom goods or documents of **title** are entrusted for the purpose of being sold. *Stevens v. Biller* (1883), 25 Ch.D. 31. The commission received by the factor for his services is known as FACTORAGE. A factor has a **lien** on the goods entrusted to him for his remuneration. Sales by a factor will bind the **principal** whether or not they are in derogation of private instructions by the principal unless the purchaser has knowledge of such instructions prior to the sale. See also **Factors Act.** Compare **jobber.**

FACTORS ACT A statute of English origin, which has been adopted in most Canadian provinces, e.g., *Factors Act,* R.S.N.S. 1989, c. 157. The general purpose and effect of such an enactment is to protect **bona fide purchasers** from mercantile **agents (factors)** who may have lost the capacity to dispose of goods that nonetheless remain in their **possession.** Such incapacity may result where the **agency** has been revoked, where the goods have already been sold or where goods have been entrusted for a different purpose. The *Factors Act* protects the bona fide purchaser for value without notice by validating sales to such a person where there appears to be no limit on the factor's power to deal with the goods in his possession.

FACTUM *(fäk'-tūm)* Lat.: literally, a deed, act, exploit, or accomplishment. Also, the written argument submitted by a lawyer to the court. See **brief.**

FACTUM PROBANDUM (pl.: **FACTA PROBANDA**) *(fäk'tūm prō'-băn'-dūm; fäk'-tà prō-băn'-dà)* Lat.: in the law of **evidence,** the principal fact, the fact in issue. The fact that must be proved and, therefore, the fact to which evidence is directed.

FACTUM PROBANS (pl.: **FACTA PROBANTIA**) *(fäk'-tūm prō'-bănz; fäk'-tà prō-băn'-tē-à)* Lat.: a fact given in **evidence** in order to prove the **factum probandum.** Also known as an EVIDENTIARY FACT.

FAILURE OF CONSIDERATION See **consideration.**

FAILURE OF ISSUE A phrase used in a **will** or **deed** to refer to a **condition** that operates in the event no children survive the decedent. An equivalent expression sometimes used is "die without **issue.**" The words may fix a condition whereby an estate, instead of being alienable and therefore capable of being conveyed to a third person, will, in the event of failure of issue, pass automatically to an alternative designated in the original **instrument.** Unless there was a contrary intention, the common law interpreted this condition as continuing *ad infinitum.*

Such a **construction** was termed INDEFINITE FAILURE OF ISSUE. Thus, if children of the first taker themselves fail to leave children, the estate will still go to the alternative. The first taker has a **fee tail** and his descendants are TENANTS IN TAIL. This common-law presumption has been reversed in all the common-law provinces of Canada (e.g., *Wills Act,* R.S.N.S. 1989, c. 505, s. 28), so that the condition is fulfilled where the first taker has issue surviving at his death.

FAIR COMMENT A **defence** to an **action** for **defamation** wherein the **defendant** shows that the comments, regardless of whether they were defamatory, were made without **malice,** *Sutherland v. Stopes* [1925] A.C. 47 (H.L.), and were "fair" in the sense that a fair-minded person could have formed such an opinion, *McQuire* v. *Western Morning News Ltd.* [1903] 2 K.B. 100 (C.A.). Furthermore, in order for the defence to succeed, it is necessary that the facts on which the comments were based be substantially true. *Barltrop* v. *Canadian Broadcasting Corp.* (1975), 86 D.L.R. (3d) 61 (N.S.S.C.A.D.). However, it is not essential that these facts appear alongside the expression of opinion provided these facts may be implied from the impugned comment. Finally, the comments must be made on a matter of general public interest. *Mack* v. *North Hill News Ltd., McIntosh* v. *North Hill News Ltd.* (1964), 44 D.L.R. (2d) 147 (Alta. S.C.).

FAIR HEARING Sometimes referred to as a principle or rule of "natural justice." Most frequently used in connection with the procedure followed by courts and quasi-judicial bodies (such as an **administrative tribunal**). The courts "have developed a presumption of interpretation ... that a fair procedure must be followed as a condition to the valid exercise of the [decision-making] power." Ontario Royal Commission, *Inquiry into Civil Rights* (McRuer Commission, 1968) at 136–47. In *Board of Education* v. *Rice,* [1911] A.C. 179 at 182 (H.L.)., Lord Loreburn, L.C. refers to the notion that where there is a conflict of interest between two parties a fair hearing entails the opportunity of each side to make his submission: "I need not add that ... [a Court] must act in good faith and *fairly listen to both sides for that is a duty lying upon everyone who decides anything.*" To give each side the opportunity of adequately presenting its case is also referred to as the principle of *audi alteram partem.* Other elements of a fair hearing often mentioned are the right to reasonable notice of the hearing, the right to counsel, the right to examine witnesses and the right to written reasons for the decision. An attempt to outline the procedures governing tribunals at or following a **hearing** may be embodied in a statute, e.g., *The Statutory Powers Procedure Act,* R.S.O. 1990, c. S. 22. See also *Re Toronto Newspaper Guild, Local 87,* [1951] O.R. 435 at 447 (S.C.); affirmed [1952] O.R. 345 (C.A.); affirmed [1953] 2 S.C.R. 18.

FAIR MARKET VALUE See **market value.**

FALSE ARREST Unlawful **arrest.** If one is restrained and detained without lawful authority, he may have a **civil action** for **damages.** Generally, where the police arrest without a **warrant** (*Criminal Code,* R.S.C. 1985, c. C–46, s. 495), they must have reasonable grounds for suspecting the person arrested of having committed an **indictable offence** or being about to commit an indictable offence. If such reasonable grounds do not exist, the police are guilty of false arrest. *Koechlin* v. *Waugh and Hamilton* (1958), 11 D.L.R. (2d) 447 (Ont.C.A.). See **false imprisonment.**

FALSE IMPRISONMENT A **tort** "action for false imprisonment lies when the liberty of a person has been restrained against his will without the authority of law. As soon as imprisonment is proved, the **defendant** must establish that the imprisonment was not his act or was justified." *Washburn* v. *Robertson* (1912), 3 W.W.R. 209 at 211 (Sask.C.A.). See also *Frey* v. *Fedoruk,* [1950] S.C.R. 517.

Furthermore, the restraint need only be for an appreciable amount of time; therefore, if the restraint is only momentary, the tort will still have been committed. *Bird* v. *Jones* (1845), 7 Q.B. 742; 115 E.R. 668.

The restraint may be accomplished by the direct application of force or by threat of force. A plaintiff is imprisoned where he submits to such threats rather than risk violence. *Sinclair* v. *Woodward's Store Ltd.,* [1942] 2 D.L.R. 395 (B.C.S.C.). Similarly, when a person submits to restraint in order to avoid embarrassment, there is an imprisonment. Finally, it is not necessary that the person confined be aware of the restraint. *Meering* v. *Grahame-White Aviation Co. Ltd.* (1919), 122 L.T. 44 (C.A.). Compare **kidnapping.**

FALSE VERDICT A manifestly unjust verdict; one inconsistent with the evidence. Originally, if a jury gave a false verdict, the party injured by the decision might sue out a writ of attaint either under the common law or by the Statute of 1495, 11 Hen. VII, c. 24, in order to reverse the verdict and at the same time punish the jurors. Such a practice was superseded early in the seventeenth century by the custom of setting aside verdicts and granting new trials.

FALSI CRIMEN See **crimen falsi.**

FAMOSUS LIBELLUS *(fă-mō'sŭs lē-bĕl'-ŭs)* Lat.: an infamous **libel;** a **slanderous** or libelous letter, handbill, advertisement, petition, written **accusation** or **indictment.** Its legal usage connotes a libelous writing.

FAULT A failing; a responsibility for failure or wrongdoing. For example, a falling below the care or skill of a competent and experienced driver, in relation to the manner of the driving and to the relevant circumstances of the case. *R.* v. *Gosney,* [1971] 3 All E.R. 220 (C.A.).

FAVOURED BENEFICIARY One who, in the circumstances of the particular case, has been favoured over others having equal claim to the **testator's** bounty. Confidential relations, accompanied with activity of a favoured beneficiary in the preparation and execution of a will, raises a presumption of **undue influence.**

FEALTY The vassal oath of fidelity between lord and **tenant;** the essential feudal bond. Fealty involved a number of obligations: that the tenant do no bodily harm to his lord; that he do no secret damage to him in his house; that he not injure his lord's reputation; that he render it easy for the lord to do any good and not make it impossible to be done that which was before in his lord's power to do.

Fealty was a seignorial incident and was therefore due on every change of tenancy of the seignory.

See also **homage.**

FEDERAL COURT Created in 1970 by the *Federal Court Act,* R.S.C. 1985, c. F–7, the Federal Court is a continuation of the Exchequer Court of Canada and the Citizenship Appeal Court, with an extended jurisdiction.

The Federal Court of Canada consists of two divisions, a Trial Division and an Appeal Division, the latter acting as a Federal Court of Appeal and sitting with four judges. In total, the Court consists of twelve judges, of whom four must be chosen from the Quebec bar or must have been judges of the Court of Queen's Bench or of the Superior Court of the Province of Quebec.

The jurisdiction of the Federal Court extends to suits against the Crown in right of Canada, patents and trademarks, copyright, Admiralty matters, and cases involving appeals from federal boards and tribunals.

FEDERALISM A system of government wherein governmental power is divided between two or more sovereign, independent authorities. Canada is a federal state with the division of law-making powers between the Parliament of Canada and the respective provincial legislatures. The division of powers is achieved principally by ss. 91 and 92 of the *Constitution Act, 1867.* "The essence of a federation is that the citizen is ruled partly by the central government and partly by the government of his region or province. This means two things. First, powers must be divided between the two levels of government. Second, the legal instrument responsible for such division must put it beyond the power of either level of government to usurp the authority of the other." P. Fitzgerald & K. McShane, *Looking at Law* 30 (2d ed. 1982).

In a true federal state, the central and regional governments are neither superior nor subordinate to one another. Rather, they are coordinate in the sense of being independent and autonomous. That is, neither is capable of altering the form of the other. This is opposed to a unitary state such as England or New Zealand, where local or regional authorities are essential to the proper governing of the state but are clearly subordinate to the central authority in the sense that power delegated to them can be retracted or modified unilaterally.

FEE **1.** A reward or recompense for services rendered; **2.** frequently used in reference to **real property** to indicate an **estate** in land that is capable of being **inherited** or **devised.**

"Fee" derives from "feudal" or *feodor,* meaning "land," importing that such land is held by some superior to whom certain **services** are due. Fee, **fee simple,** and fee simple absolute are often used as equivalents. The word *fee* indicates that it is an estate of **inheritance;** the word *simple* signifies that there are no restrictions on the inheritable characteristics of the estate. But a fee may be qualified, such as a **conditional** or **determinable fee,** which could continue forever but would be discontinued upon the happening of a certain event.

FEE SIMPLE An estate of virtually infinite duration **conveyed** or **granted** absolutely to a person and his heirs forever; also known as FEE SIMPLE ABSOLUTE. There are no conditions, restrictions, or limitations on the holder of such an estate, and the **property** is freely alienable or hereditable.

The holder of the estate is known as the tenant in fee simple (see **tenant**) because, technically, he is merely a tenant of the **Crown,** though he has the highest and most extensive estate possible. However, to all intents and purposes he is the absolute owner.

At **common law,** it was necessary to use the words "to A and his heirs" in order to convey a fee simple. *Re Airey* (1921), 21 O.W.N. 190 (H.C.). Without the phrase "and his heirs," only a **life estate** was created. At present the presumption is in favour of the conveyance of a fee simple unless there is manifest an intention to create a more limited estate. *Bartrop* v. *Blackstock* (1957), 10 D.L.R. (2d) 192 (Sask.C.A.). Furthermore, it is no longer necessary in some Canadian jurisdictions to use the word *heirs* to convey a fee simple. It may suffice if the words *in fee simple* are used or other words sufficiently indicative of that intention (e.g., *Conveyancing Act,* R.S.N. 1989, c. 97, s. 13). See further A. Sinclair, *Introduction to Real Property Law* 13–17 (3d ed. 1987).

See **words of limitation.** Compare **fee tail.**

FEE SIMPLE CONDITIONAL See **conditional fee.**

FEE SIMPLE DEFEASIBLE See **defeasible; fee simple.**

FEE SIMPLE DETERMINABLE See **determinable fee.**

FEE TAIL The estate created by **deed** or **will,** to a person "and the **heirs of his body.**" A fee tail establishes a fixed line of inheritable **succession** and cuts off the regular succession of **heirs** at law. It is a limited estate in that **inheritance** is through lineal descent only, which if exclusively through males is called FEE TAIL MALE or if exclusively through females is called FEE TAIL FEMALE. If the family line runs out **(failure of issue),** the fee **reverts** to the grantor or his successors in **interest.** See **words of limitation.** See further A. Sinclair, *Introduction to Real Property Law* 17–19 (3d ed. 1987).

FELLOW SERVANT A co-worker; defined for the doctrine of common employment, which relieved an employer of **liability** for **injury** caused to one servant by the **negligence** of a fellow servant. *Priestly* v. *Fowler* (1857), 3 M. & W. 1; 150 E. R. 1030. Because of the hardship inflicted by the doctrine, it fell into disrepute as social conditions altered and has been abrogated by statute, e.g., **Workmen's Compensation** statutes. *Cooperators Insurance Ass'n* v. *Kearney* (1965), 48 D.L.R. (2d) 1 (S.C.C.).

FELON One who has been convicted of a **felony.** See **criminal.**

FELONY A generic term employed to distinguish certain high crimes from minor offences known as **misdemeanours.** The distinction between felony and misdemeanour does not exist in the *Criminal Code of Canada,* R.S.C. 1985, c. C–46. Instead, serious crimes are those designated as punishable by **indictment** and lesser crimes as those punishable by **summary conviction.** See **indictable offence.**

FEOFFMENT Originally, the **conveyance** of **freehold** land through public or overt delivery by the owner to the purchaser, including **livery of seisin,** a cumbersome ceremony in which both parties to the transfer (FEOFFOR [owner] and FEOFFEE [purchaser]) entered onto the land and **seisin** was delivered when the feoffor symbolically transferred the land by conveying to the feoffee a twig or piece of sod or by appropriate words and then leaving the feoffee in possession.

Gradually, it became the practise to record such a transaction in writing, and this gained statutory force in England by passage of the **Statute of Frauds,** 1677, s. 1. Feoffment came to be known as the **deed** evidencing the transfer of possession of the freehold estate. See further A. Sinclair, *Introduction to Real Property Law* 89 (3d ed. 1987).

FERAE NATURAE *(fĕr'-ī nä-tūr'-ī)* Lat.: wild beasts of nature. **Animals** are described as *ferae naturae* when they are wild by nature and it is impossible to completely domesticate them: consequently, it requires the continuous exercise of force to subjugate them. *Campbell* v.

Hedley (1917), 39 O.L.R. 528 at 533 (A.D.).

A wild animal not tamed or ordinarily kept in captivity cannot be stolen unless it has been sufficiently reduced into possession or is in the course of being reduced into possession. *M.V. "Polar Star"* v. *Arsenault* (1964), 43 D.L.R. (2d) 354 (P.E.I.S.C.).

FERTILE OCTOGENARIAN A legal fiction created in regard to the **Rule Against Perpetuities,** conclusively presuming that an adult of any age is capable of having children regardless of such physiological facts as change of life, impotence, or surgical removal of reproductive organs. See *Re Fasken* (1959), 19 D.L.R. (2d) 182 (Ont.C.A.); *Ward* v. *Van der Loeff,* [1924] A.C. 653 (H.L.).

FEUDALISM A system of government and a means of holding property in England and Western Europe that grew out of the chaos of the Dark Ages (the fifth to tenth centuries). Through a ceremony called **homage,** in which mutual duties of support and protection were promised, the vassal in effect gave his land to the lord and the lord then had a duty to protect it and the vassal. Though the vassal thenceforth owned no land, he held the land of the lord as a **tenant** and retained a **use** in that land. This method of holding land was very different from the modern landlord-tenant situation. The land that the vassal held was called his feud, fief or feudum. The relationship between the lord and his vassal could become more indirect by the process of **subinfeudation,** so that theoretically there could be placed between the lord and his vassal any number of persons at different levels, each serving as a link in the chain of relations between the lord at the top and the least of the vassals. Eventually, the king became the ultimate lord over all, and all land in England was held of him. Only in England was feudalism the sole method of holding land, although it was the general method elsewhere in Western Europe See further A. Sinclair, *Introduction to Real Property Law* 1–7 (3d ed. 1987).

FIAT JUSTITIA *(fē'ät jūs-ti'-shē-à)* Lat.: let justice be done.

FIDUCIARY Relating to or proceeding from trust or confidence. One stands in a fiduciary relationship with regard to another person when he has rights and powers he must exercise for the benefit of that other person. Consequently, a fiduciary is not allowed himself to benefit in any way from the position he holds unless he has the requisite consent. *Boardman* v. *Phipps,* [1966] 3 All E.R. 721 (H.L.).

The number of circumstances in which a fiduciary relationship exists is indefinite and open-ended. Nonetheless, the following relationships are considered to be fiduciary: **trustee** and **beneficiary,** guardian and ward, **solicitor** and client, **principal** and **agent,** and wherever one reposes confidence in another. *Plowright* v. *Lambert* (1885), 52 L.T. 646 (Ch.).

FINAL DECREE See **decree.**

FINAL HEARING See **hearing.**

FINAL JUDGMENT See **judgment.**

FINAL ORDER See **order.**

FINDING Any conclusion upon an inquiry of fact made in a judicial proceeding. Findings of fact are made by a **jury** or, in the absence of a jury, by a judge sitting alone.

FIRST DEGREE MURDER See **murder.**

FIRST DEVISEE The first person who is to receive an **estate devised** by **will.** "Next devisee" refers to those who will receive the **remainder** in tail (see **fee tail).**

FIRST IMPRESSION First discussion or consideration. A case that presents to a court a **question of law** never before considered, and consequently one for which there is no **precedent,** is said to be a case of first impression. *Ultravite Laboratories Ltd.* v. *Whitehall Laboratories Ltd.* (1965), 53 D.L.R. (2d) 1 (S.C.C.).

FISCAL Of or pertaining to financial matters—as in FISCAL YEAR, meaning the financial year.

FIXTURES Articles of **personalty** that have been annexed to land to such an extent that they are thereafter regarded as part of the **realty** (i.e., PERMANENT). A lighting fixture will not be a fixture in the legal sense if it can be easily removed. Area carpets are not fixtures, but wall-to-wall carpeting may be. Articles attached to the land only by their weight are not considered fixtures unless such an intent is apparent. However, articles even slightly affixed are considered part of the land in the absence of a contrary intention. In determining whether an article has become a fixture, regard must be had to the degree and object of the annexation, and to the purpose to which the article will be put. *Stack* v. *T. Eaton Co.* (1902), 4 O.L.R. 335 (Div.Ct.). That is, whether it is for the better and more effectual use of the land as realty or for the better use of the article as a **chattel.** *La Salle Recreation Ltd.* v. *Canadian Candex Investments Ltd., Chester, Sigurdson and White Spot No. 12 Ltd.* (1969), 4 D.L.R. (3d) 549 (B.C.C.A.).

Fixtures are divided into two categories: (1) **landlord's** fixtures, or those that belong to the landlord, and (2) **tenant's** fixtures, which can be removed by the tenant. Tenant's fixtures can be further subdivided into **(a)** TRADE FIXTURES, which are articles annexed to land simply for purposes of trade, and **(b)** ORNAMENTAL FIXTURES, which are articles placed for domestic use or because of their ornamental value.

FORCIBLE DETAINER A **hybrid offence** committed by anyone who in **possession** of **real property** detains it without **colour of right** against a person entitled to possession in such a manner as to cause **breach of the peace** or reasonble apprehension of such. Punishment is up to two years' imprisonment. See *Criminal Code,* R.S.C. 1985, c. C–46, ss. 72, 73.

Compare **tenancy** [TENANCY AT SUFFERANCE].

FORCIBLE ENTRY Entry onto land in the **possession** of another in a manner likely to cause a **breach of the peace** or reasonable apprehension of such; a **hybrid offence** under the *Criminal Code,* R.S.C. 1985, c. C–46, s. 73. *R.* v. *Campey* (1910), 20 C.C.C. 492 (Alta.Dist.Ct.). Under s. 72(1.1), "it is immaterial whether or not a person is entitled to enter the real property or whether or not that person has any intention of taking possession of the real property." See also **trespass.**

FORCIBLE ENTRY AND DETAINER The violent taking and keeping possession of any lands and tenements occupied by another, by means of threats, force or arms, and without authority of law.

FORECLOSURE Generally, the termination of a right to **property.** When there is a default by the mortgagor in a **mortgage** agreement, the right to foreclosure arises, but only if there is a forfeiture by breach of **condition.** *Sampson* v. *Pattison* (1842), 1 Hare 533, 66 E.R. 1143 (Ch.). The foreclosure proceeding itself is any proceeding by which the mortgagor's **equity of redemption** is **barred** or **extinguished** beyond the possibility of recall, thus **vesting** the property absolutely in the mortgagee.

FORESEEABILITY A concept used in various areas of the law to limit the **liability** of a party for the consequences of his acts to the consequences that are within the scope of a FORESEEABLE RISK, i.e., a risk whose consequences a person of ordinary prudence would reasonably expect might occur as a result of his actions. "You must take reasonable care to avoid acts or omissions which you can reasonably foresee would injure your neighbour—persons who are so closely and directly affected by my act that I ought reasonably to have them in contemplation as being so affected when I am directing my mind to the acts or omissions which are called in question." *Donoghue* v. *Stevenson,* [1932] A.C. 562 at 579 (H.L.).

To be liable for **negligence,** the effects of a person's acts must have been foreseeable. *Overseas Tankship (U.K.) Ltd.* v. *Morts Dock and Engineering Co. Ltd., The Wagon Mound (No. 1),* [1961] A.C. 388 (P.C.).

In a contract setting, under the rule in *Hadley* v. *Baxendale* (1854), 9 Ex. 341, 156 E.R. 145, a party's liability for special or consequential **damage** is limited to the damages arising from the foreseeable consequences of his **breach.** See also *Victoria Laundry (Windsor) Ltd.* v. *Newman Industries Ltd.,* [1949] 2 K.B. 528 (C.A.).

FORFEITURE 1. A punishment whereby a person or offender loses all or some of his **interests** in his **property.** Thus, the **goods** and **chattels** of a criminal were, prior to the English *Forfeiture Act, 1870,* forfeited to the Crown. **2.** In a **lease,** a forfeiture clause reserves to the **lessor** a right of **reentry,** upon which the lease is forfeited. **3. Shares** may be forfeited by resolution of the board of directors of a **corporation** if such power is given in the **Articles of Association**—e.g., where a member fails to pay a **call** properly made on him.

FORGERY Defined in the *Criminal Code*, R.S.C. 1985, c. C–46, s. 366(1) as the making of a false document, with knowledge that it is false, intending that it will be acted upon as genuine, to the prejudice of anyone within or without Canada, or with the intent that someone will be induced to do or refrain from doing anything, whether within Canada or not. See *Cowan* v. *The Queen* (1962), 132 C.C.C. 352 (S.C.C.).

FORM A model of a **document** containing the phrases and **words of art** that are needed to make the document technically correct for **procedural** purposes. Forms are used by lawyers in drafting legal documents.

FORMS OF ACTION Technical categories of personal **actions** developed at **common law,** containing the entire course of legal proceedings particular to those actions. The forms of actions are no longer required, but they continue to affect modern civil procedure and **tort** law.

Forms of action consisted of proceedings for recovery of debts and for recovery of money **damages** resulting from **breach of contract** or injury to one's person, property, or relations. The forms can be classified as (*a*) actions in form *ex contractu,* including **assumpsit, covenant, debt,** and **account;** and (*b*) actions in form *ex delicto* (i.e., those not based on contracts), including **trespass, trover, case, detinue,** and **replevin.** See B. Shipman, *Handbook on Common Law Pleading* (3d ed. 1923), chap. 2.

"In the early English law, remedies for wrongs depended upon the issuance of **writs** to bring the defendant into court. . . . The number of such writs available was very limited, and their forms were strictly prescribed; and unless the cause of action could be fitted into the form of some recognized writ, the plaintiff was without a remedy. The result was a highly formal and artificial system of procedure." W.P. Keeton, *Prosser and Keeton on Torts* 29 (5th ed. 1984).

FORNICATION Generally, sexual intercourse between two unmarried people of different sexes. If either party is married, the proper term is **adultery.**

In Canada, fornication is not, in itself, an offence, unless it necessarily involves

the commission of another offence such as sexual exploitation of a young person fourteen years of age or over, but under the age of eighteen years (See *Criminal Code*, R.S.C. 1985, c. C–46, s. 153); or incest (s. 155).

FORUM A court; a place where disputes are settled according to the dictates of law and justice and where **remedies** afforded by law are pursued. The term is also used to indicate the country, state, province, etc., in which **jurisdiction** is exercised. A *forum competens* (or *incompetens*) is a court that has (or has not) the jurisdiction to deal with a matter. See also **venue.**

FORUM NON CONVENIENTS *(fôr'-ŭm nŏn kŏn-vē'-nē-ĕns)* Lat.: an inconvenient court. Under this doctrine a court, though it has **jurisdiction** of a case, may decide not to exercise it where there is no legitimate reason for the case to be brought there, or where presentation of the case in that court will create a hardship on the **defendants** or relevant **witnesses** because of its distance from them. The court will not **dismiss** the case under the doctrine unless the **plaintiff** has another **forum** open to him.

FOUR UNITIES See **unities.**

FRANCHISE **1.** A special privilege that is conferred by the government upon an individual and that does not belong to the citizens of the country generally, of common right. For example, a municipality may grant a franchise to a local bus company giving it sole authority to operate buses in the municipality for a certain number of years. **2.** Also, the right given to a private person or corporations to market another's product within a certain area. Thus, gas stations that sell brand-name gasoline often operate the station through a franchise granted by an oil company.

ELECTIVE FRANCHISE The right of citizens to vote in public elections; sometimes called simply "the franchise."

FRANKMARRIAGE A gift to a prospective bride and groom that was free of services to the donor. When land was given to a woman and her prospective husband "in frankmarriage" by a blood relation, the husband and wife held the land to them and their issue, free of services to the donor, although no words of inheritance or procreation were used in the gift.

FRAUD Intentional deception resulting in **injury** to another. Elements of fraud are a false and material **misrepresentation** made by one who either knows it is falsity or is ignorant of its truth; the maker's intent that the representation be relied on by the person and in a manner reasonably contemplated; the person's ignorance of the falsity of the representation; the person's rightful or justified reliance; and proximate injury to the person.

Fraud usually consists of a misrepresentation, concealment or nondisclosure of a material fact, or at least misleading conduct, devices or contrivance. It embraces all the **multifarious** means human ingenuity can devise to secure an advantage over another person. It includes all surprise, trick, cunning, dissembling, and unfair ways by which another is cheated. At **law,** fraud must be proved; in **equity,** one must only show fact and circumstances from which fraud may be presumed. *R.* v. *Brasso* (1977), 39 C.R.N.S. 1 (Alta.S.C.). See also **deceit.**

CONSTRUCTIVE FRAUD [LEGAL FRAUD] Any act, omission, or concealment involving **breach** of **equitable** or **legal duty,** trust or confidence and resulting in damage to another; no **scienter** is required. It consists of a material misrepresentation, though innocently made, that is relied upon and acted upon by the party to whom it is made, and that causes him injury. Thus, the party who makes the misrepresentation need not know it is false.

CRIMINAL FRAUD Depriving a person dishonestly of something that is his or of something to which he is or would or might, but for the perpetuation of the fraud, be entitled. *Scott* v. *Metropolitan Police Commissioner* (1974), 60 Cr.App.R. 124 (H.L.). *Criminal Code*, R.S.C. 1985, c. C–46, ss. 380–402.

EXTRINSIC FRAUD [COLLATERAL FRAUD] Fraud that prevents a party from knowing about his rights or **defences** or from having a fair opportunity to present them at a trial, or from fully **litigating** at the trial all the rights or defences he was entitled to assert. It is a ground for equitable **relief** from a **judgment.**

FRAUD IN FACT [POSITIVE FRAUD] Actual fraud; deceit; the concealing of something or making a false representation with an evil intent [scienter] when it causes injury to another. Used in contrast to CONSTRUCTIVE FRAUD, which does not require evil **intent.**

FRAUD IN LAW Fraud that is presumed from circumstances, where the one who commits it need not have evil intent to commit fraud. It is a CONSTRUCTIVE FRAUD—e.g., if a **debtor's transfer of assets** impairs the rights of her **creditors,** then the transfer might be a fraud in law and the **conveyance** could be set aside, although the debtor had no intention of prejudicing the creditor's rights.

FRAUD IN THE FACTUM Generally, fraud that arises from a lack of identity or a disparity between the **instrument** executed and the one intended to be executed, or from circumstances that go to the question as to whether the instrument ever had any legal existence; as, for example, when a blind or illiterate person executes a deed when it has been read falsely to him after he asked to have it read.

FRAUD IN THE INDUCEMENT Fraud that is intended to and that does cause one to execute an **instrument** or make an agreement or render a **judgment.** The misrepresentation involved does not mislead one as to the paper he signs but rather misleads as to the true facts of a situation, and the false impression it causes is a basis of a decision to sign or render a judgment. It renders an agreement **voidable.**

INTRINSIC FRAUD Fraudulent representation that is presented and considered in rendering a **judgment.** Generally, intrinsic fraud is not a sufficient ground for granting equitable **relief** from a judgment. For example, **perjury** is only intrinsic fraud because it does not prevent a completely **adversary proceeding.** It only influences the judgment, so it will not be a ground for equitable relief from a judgment resulting from it.

FRAUDULENT See **fraud.**

FREE AND CLEAR Unencumbered. In property law, one **conveys** land free and clear if he transfers a **good title** or **marketable title** unencumbered by any **interest** held by another in the land.

FREEDOM OF ASSEMBLY See **Assembly, Freedom of.**

FREEDOM OF CONTRACT The ability of parties to agree to the most advantageous bargain between them without interference from the courts. In the eighteenth century there was little restriction placed on this freedom, the philosophy being that men could pursue their interests in the way they saw fit and that the duty of the law was merely to give effect to the intention of the parties. See, e.g., *Printing and Numerical Registering Co.* v. *Sampson* (1875), L.R. 19 Eq. 462 (C.A.). This position still finds expression today; see, e.g., *Esso Petroleum Co.* v. *Harper's Garage (Stourport) Ltd.*, [1967] 1 All E.R. 699 (H.L.). However, there are significant areas in the law of **contract** where the courts are disposed to grant relief from contractual arrangements seen to be unreasonable or **unconscionable.** "I take the view that the Courts are not bound to accept all contracts at face value and enforce those contracts without some regard to the surrounding circumstances. I do not think that mere formal consensus is enough. I am of the opinion that the terms of a contract may be declared to be void as being unreasonable where it can be said that in all the circumstances it is unreasonable and unconscionable to bind the parties to their formal bargain." *Davidson* v. *Three Spruces Realty Ltd.*, [1977] 6 W.W.R. 460 at 476 (B.C.S.C.). Similarly, the courts will frequently strictly construe a **disclaimer** or exemption from liability clause in a contract. See further S. Waddams, *The Law of Contracts* (3d ed. 1993), chap. 14. Legislation may also permit interference with a contract where a court finds its terms to be harsh or unconscionable. See, e.g., *Unconscionable Transactions Relief Act,* R.S.A. 1980, c. U–2; *Consumer Protection Act,* R.S.O. 1990, c. C. 31.

FREEDOM OF INFORMATION "Freedom of information legislation . . . is designed to give a citizen access to government information. . . . [It] relates not to personal information but to government information in the nature of 'public business'." G. Gall, *The Canadian Legal System* 373 (3d ed. 1990). See *Access to Information Act,* R.S.C. 1985, c. A–1. Compare **privacy.**

FREEDOMS, FUNDAMENTAL See **Canadian Charter of Rights and Freedoms.**

FREEHOLD An estate in **fee** or a **life estate.**

FREEHOLD ESTATE An **estate** or **interest** in **real property** of infinite duration; a legal right as against all the world. It is an estate of **inheritance** or for life in either a corporeal or an incorporeal **hereditament** existing in or arising from real property of free **tenure.** Estates created under the **common law** could only be **conveyed** by engaging in the **livery of seisin;** upon assuming title by such livery, the **tenant** [or owner] became **seised** to the land and established ownership. Although a charter of **enfeoffment** may have recorded the ceremonious livery of seisin, under the common law, initially, no writing was required to transfer a freehold estate. See further A. Sinclair, *Introduction to Real Property Law* (3d ed. 1987), chap. 2.

At common law, "freehold" referred to those interests in land that could be associated with one who was considered a free man (*viz.*, the nobility); he who was free from servile requirements and received the right to possession of land for an indefinite period was a "freeholder." In the early period of English common law, only the freeholder was entitled to full protection of the remedies available in the common-law courts—e.g., the chance of legally getting back the land if wrongfully dispossessed. Those with possession for a definite period of time (i.e., an estate less than freehold) would have to be content with obtaining whatever **damages** might have been suffered. *Id.* at 10.

FRESH PURSUIT **1.** In criminal law, a term that refers to the **common-law** right of a police officer to cross jurisdictional lines in order to arrest a **felon. 2.** The term, as found in s. 494(1)(b)(ii) of the *Criminal Code,* R.S.C. 1985, c. C–46, also refers to the fact that "[a]nyone may arrest without **warrant** a person who, on reasonable and probable grounds, he believes is escaping from and freshly pursued by persons who have lawful authority to arrest that person."

FRIENDLY SUIT An action brought by agreement between the **parties** in order to obtain a **judgment** that will have a binding effect in circumstances where a mere agreement or settlement will not. For example, the friendly suit is employed when a **claim** in favour of an infant is settled because the infant cannot effectively **release** the claim by a release **contract,** though the entry of a judgment does bind him. The friendly suit is usually brought without formal **process,** but the court will demand some kind of proof (often **affidavits** are sufficient) that the settlement is a just and fair one. Suits that are "collusive" that is, those wherein the parties purport to have a controversy but do not, or where they agree to certain facts in order to obtain a certain legal result (as in divorce cases), will be **dismissed.** See **collusion.** Compare **adversary proceeding; controversy; declaratory judgment.**

FRIEND OF THE COURT See **amicus curiae.**

FRIVOLOUS Clearly insufficient as a matter of law; presenting no debatable question. A case may be dismissed as frivolous where it is clearly unsupported on the facts or is one for which the law provides no **remedy.** Thus, for a case to be considered frivolous, **vexatious** or an **abuse of process,** the alleged **cause of action** must be such that no reasonable person could treat it as **bona fide** and contend that he was entitled to approach the court with such a complaint. *MacDonald* v. *Pier,* [1923] S.C.R. 107.

FRUSTRATION The inability to complete or discharge a contract because of circumstances beyond the control of the contracting parties and outside of their contemplation. Prior to 1863, contracts were considered absolute (unless a contrary intention was expressed) so that a person was strictly bound by his contract despite the fact that changed circumstances made performance impossible. In 1803, in *Taylor* v. *Caldwell* (1863), 122 E.R. 309 (K.B.) [applied, e.g., in *Kerrigan* v. *Harrison* (1921), 62 S.C.R. 374], the doctrine of frustration was introduced by implying a **condition** that the contract was subject to the continued existence of the subject matter. This was extended to cover the situation where the transaction envisaged by the parties was frustrated. *Jackson* v. *Union Marine Insurance Co. Ltd.* (1874), L.R. 10 C.P. 125 (C.P.). It is a question of **construction** of the contract as to whether a particular event frustrates a contract. Money paid out before discharge of the contract may be recover-

able, as in QUASI-CONTRACT (see **quasi**). *Fibrosa Spolka Akcyjna* v. *Fairbairn Lawson Combe Barbour Ltd.,* [1943] A.C. 32 (H.L.). The doctrine will not be applied where the party seeking to introduce and rely on any such term has himself brought about the event or occurrence that he now claims for termination of the contract. See *Maritime National Fish Co.* v. *Ocean Trawlers Ltd.,* [1935] A.C. 524; [1935] 3 D.L.R. 12 (P.C.).

In spite of the *Fibrosa* decision, the common law did not completely cover the question of the amount recoverable for expenditures incurred before the frustration. As a result, a *Frustrated Contracts Act* was enacted in England in 1943. Similar statutes have been enacted in most Canadian jurisdictions. See, e.g., R.S.O. 1990, c. F. 34.

See **impossibility.**

FUGITIVE One who flees from justice. *Beim* v. *Goyer* (1965), 57 D.L.R. (2d) 253 (S.C.C.). Under the *Extradition Act,* R.S.C. 1985, c. E–23, s. 2, a fugitive or fugitive criminal is a person in or suspected of being in Canada who is **accused** or **convicted** of an extradition crime committed in a foreign state. Similarly, "fugitive" under the *Fugitive Offenders Act,* R.S.C. 1985, c. F–32, s. 2, refers to a person who is accused of committing any crime to which the act applies in any of Her Majesty's Realms and Territories except Canada and who has left that area. Any fugitive is **liable** to be apprehended and returned to the part of Her Majesty's Realm and Territories from which he is a fugitive.

FUNDAMENTAL FREEDOMS See **Canadian Charter of Rights and Freedoms.**

FUTURE INTEREST An **interest** in presently existing **real property** or **personal property** that is limited so as to commence in the future. Future interests are **estates** in expectancy as opposed to estates in **possession** and may be subclassified into two categories, **reversions** and **remainders.** If by **deed** the holder of a **fee simple** grants a particular estate to one person and a subsequent estate to another person, the subsequent estate is known as a remainder since it remains away from the original grantor. Where no subsequent estate is granted, the residue remains with the grantor and is known as a reversion to the grantor on the expiration of the particular estate.

FUTURES Agreements where one person says that he will sell a commodity at a certain time in the future for a certain price. The buyer agrees to pay that price, knowing that the person has nothing to deliver at the time, but with the understanding that when the time arrives for **delivery** the buyer is to pay him the difference between the **market value** of that commodity and the price agreed upon if the commodity's value declines; if it advances, the seller is to pay the buyer the difference between the agreed-upon price and the market price. Thus, if the price of the commodity rises, the buyer makes a profit, and if the price declines, the buyer suffers a loss.

Formerly, such speculative agreements were generally unenforceable in courts of law as being against public policy because they were a form of gambling. Today, futures are traded on commodity futures exchanges. In order to make the transaction legal, the parties must intend to deliver or receive delivery of the commodity, each party being obligated to make delivery or accept delivery of the commodity unless the contract has been **liquidated** by offset on the exchange. If a trader insists on literal satisfaction of his contract rights, it must be fulfilled by conveyance of the physical commodity. Thus the fundamental principle underlying all commodity exchanges is that a person who buys or sells a futures contract and does not offset it by a contra-transaction on the exchange must receive the commodity or be called on to deliver it. The fact that most persons who trade on a commodity exchange expect to offset their contracts before the date of delivery or receipt is not a denial of this principle.

G

GAINFUL EMPLOYMENT [OCCUPATION]
Work that is lucrative, remunerative, or based on gain. A person is said to be gainfully employed when he receives remuneration from his employer in return for the services he supplies under the contract of employment. The criterion for determining whether work is gainful is personal advantage to the employee, not the value of the work to the community. *R. Jazewsky (No.2),* [1945] 1 W.W.R. 107 (Sask.Dist.Ct.).

GAOL, GAOLER Variant spellings of jail and jailer. Though both forms are correct, recent dictionaries have preferred the *jail/jailer* form.

GARAGEMAN'S LIEN See **lien** [MECHANICS' LIEN].

GARNISH To bring a **garnishment** proceeding or to **attach** wages or other property pursuant to such a proceeding. In old English law, garnish meant to warn, that is, by giving notice of the proceedings.

GARNISHEE 1. A person who receives notice to retain **custody** of the **assets** of another until he receives further notice from the court. The garnishee merely holds the assets until legal **proceedings** determine who is entitled to the property. The term thus signifies one on whom process of **garnishment** has been served.
2. A **debtor** in whose hands a debt has been **attached,** who has been warned not to pay a debt to his **creditor** but to a third party who has obtained a **final judgment** against the creditor.

GARNISHMENT A statutory proceeding whereby a person's **property,** money or credits in possession or under control of, or owing by, another are applied to payment of the former's debt to a third person by proper statutory process against **debtor** and garnisher. See, e.g., *Court Order Enforcement Act,* R.S.B.C. 1979, c. 75; a process in which money or goods in the hands of a third person that are owed to a **defendant** are attached by a **plaintiff:** the **garnishee** is warned not to pay over the property to anyone except the plaintiff.

Under the statutory **remedy** the third party is notified to retain something he has that belongs to the defendant (debtor), to make disclosure to the court concerning it and to dispose of it as the court shall direct.
See also **attachment.**

GENERAL CONTRACTOR See **contractor.**

GENERAL INTENT See **intent.**

GENERIC A term referring to a group or class of related things, whereas *specific* is limited to a particular, definite or precise thing. In commercial law, where the contract is for a part of a specified whole, generic goods do not become ascertained, and therefore the property does not pass until they have been **appropriated** to the contract.

GENOCIDE An offence under the *Criminal Code,* R.S.C. 1985, c. C–46, s. 318, directed toward the destruction in whole or in part of any group identifiable by colour, race, religion, or ethnic origin, by killing members thereof or "deliberately inflicting on the group conditions of life calculated to bring about its physical destruction."

GERIOJURISPRUDENCE The study of law as it specifically affects older persons in society.

GERRYMANDER A method of arranging electoral districts in an unnatural manner so that one political party will be capable of electing more representatives than would have been likely under a fair system of division. The practice was originally employed by Elbridge Gerry, from whom the name is derived, and who utilized it in 1812 in Massachusetts in order to gain an unfair electoral advantage.

GIFT A gratuitous, voluntary transfer of **property** from the owner to another. To be valid, the gift must be fully completed, as the courts will not compel a **donor** to perfect his gift where the intention is unfulfilled. *McIntyre* v. *Royal Trust Co.* (1945), 53 Man.R. 353 (C.A.). There are two forms of gifts, **inter vivos** and **mortis causa:**
GIFT INTER VIVOS A gratuitous transfer of **property** from the owner to another person, with the full intention of each that the thing given shall not be re-

turned but shall be retained by the do-nee as his own. There are but three modes by which such a gift can be made: (1) by deed or instrument in writing; (2) by delivery to the **donee**, in cases where the subject matter admits of delivery; and (3) by declaration of trust in favour of the donee. In all these modes, a present **transfer,** or the equivalent of a transfer, is required. *McIntyre* v. *Royal Trust Co.,* [1945] 2 W.W.R. 364 at 367–68 (Man.K.B.).

GIFT MORTIS CAUSA [DONATIO MORTIS CAUSA] A gift made in contemplation of impending death. Besides being in contemplation (not expectation) of death, the donor must die while he is suffering from the condition that prompted the contemplation. *Thompson* v. *Mechan,* [1958] O.R. 357 (C.A.). There must be an intention that should the donor survive the condition, the gift will be **revocable,** *Cain* v. *Moon,* [1896] 2 Q.B. 283 (C.A.), and the condition must be one that when measured objectively would inspire a contemplation of death in the reasonable man. See *Thompson* v. *Mechan,* [1958] O.R. 357 (C.A.). There must be a **delivery** of the subject matter of the gift by the donor or by his direction, "so that possession of the thing will have passed from the donor to the donee to **vest,** upon the death of the donor, absolutely in the donee." *McDonald* v. *McDonald* (1903), 33 S.C.R. 145 at 161 (S.C.C.).

GIFT OVER An **estate** created upon the expiration of a **preceding estate**—e.g., a gift over to *C* is established when in **default** of the exercise of a **power of appointment** by *B,* the **donor** *A* has provided that *C* take in default, rather than have the property that is the subject matter of the power **revert** to *A*'s estate.

GOOD CAUSE Substantial or legally sufficient reason for doing something. For example, in most provinces the rules of court provide that, **prima facie,** costs should follow the event unless the judge is satisfied that there is good cause to order otherwise. Where it would be unfair or unjust for costs to follow the event, then good cause has been shown. However, no exhaustive definition of good cause is possible, and the court is not bound by any formulated rules defining what should be regarded as "good cause." *Whonnock Lumber Co. Ltd.* v. *Bain* (1958), 24 W.W.R. 519 (B.C.S.C.).

GOOD FAITH A standard implying absence of intent to take advantage of or **defraud** another party; absence of ulterior motive. *Central Estates (Belgravia) Ltd.* v. *Woolgar,* [1971] 3 All E.R. 647 (C.A.). An absence of bad faith [MALE FIDES].

To act in good faith, one must act openly, fairly and honestly, and the existence of **negligence** is irrelevant. In property law, a good faith purchaser is a person without knowledge of any alleged defect in **title** or any **encumbrance** on the property that would put a reasonably prudent man on notice. See **bona fide; bona fide purchaser.**

GOODS All **chattels** personal, other than things in action and money. In effect, therefore, all things in **possession,** save money used as currency of the realm. FUTURE GOODS are those to be manufactured or acquired by the seller following the making of the **contract** of sale. SPECIFIC GOODS are those identified and agreed upon at the time a contract of sale is made.

GOOD SAMARITAN LEGISLATION Statutes intended to protect would-be rescuers (i.e. at an accident scene) from liability, in the case that their efforts lead to further injury or damage. e.g. Alberta *Emergency Medical Aid Act,* R.S.A. 1980, c. E–9, s. 2. See also *Horsley* v. *MacLaren,* [1970] 2 O.R. 487 (C.A.).

GOOD TITLE A **title** free from present **litigation,** defects, or doubts concerning its validity or merchantability. In a property **conveyance,** if the **vendor** shows that he has the title that he is bound to convey, then he is said to have good title. The term is frequently employed in place of **marketable title** or clear title.

GOVERNOR-GENERAL OF CANADA [GOVERNOR-IN-COUNCIL] The Head of State in Canada; the personal representative of the Queen. He holds in all essential respects, the same position in relation to the administration of public affairs in Canada as is held by the Queen in Great Britain. The position of Governor-General and the powers given to him are created and contained in the

British North America (now *Constitution*) **Act, 1867.** Although the powers of the Governor-General are mainly formal, he performs such important functions as the proroguing and dissolution of **Parliament.** The Prime Minister and the **Cabinet** receive their power from him, and no federal **bill** can become **law** without his assent. The provincial counterpart of the Governor-General is the **Lieutenant-Governor.** See further P. Hogg, *Constitutional Law of Canada* 244ff. (3d ed. 1992).

GRACE PERIOD A period following the date or time when a particular duty that should have been performed will be permitted to be done **without prejudice.** Such days of grace are often given on insurance policies.

GRAFT The fraudulent obtaining of public money by the corruption of public officials; a dishonest transaction in relation to public or official acts; also commonly used to designate an advantage that one person by reason of his peculiar position or superior influence or trust acquires from another.

GRANDFATHER PERIOD A two-year period during which persons who were already employed within a trade that now requires **certification** may submit an application for a certificate without examination.

GRAND JURY See **jury** [GRAND JURY].

GRANT 1. To agree or consent to; to allow, as in granting a request. **2.** The allocation of rights to a particular person generally for a particular purpose. A common-law **conveyance. 3.** The **transfer** of **ownership** of **property** as distinguished from the **delivery** or transfer of the property itself. A conveyance is a **deed** of grant. **4.** The **gift** of money out of public funds by virtue of the authority of government to a private or commercial interest because it is deemed to be beneficial to the public interest. *G.T.E. Sylvania Canada Ltd.* v. *The Queen*, [1974] C.T.C. 408 (F.C.T.D.).

GRANTEE A person to whom a **grant** is made. See **chain of title.**

GRANTOR A person who gives a **grant.** See **chain of title.**

GRATIS (*gră'-tĭs*) Lat.: free; given or performed without reward.

GRATIS DICTUM (*gră'-tĭs dĭk'-tŭm*) Mere assertion.

GRATUITOUS BAILMENT See **bailment.**

GRATUITOUS PROMISE A promise by which a person states his intention to do or refrain from doing something without requiring any **consideration** in return. Such a promise is generally not enforceable except when made under **seal.** See *Royal Bank of Canada* v. *Kiska* (1967), 63 D.L.R. (2d) 582 (Ont.C.A.).

GRAVAMEN The **grievance** particularly complained of. The material part, substance or essence of a **complaint, charge, grievance, cause of action,** etc. The essence of a grievance bears most heavily on the person accused.

GRIEVANCE An allegation that something imposes an illegal obligation or burden, or denies some equitable or legal right, or causes injustice.

It is most commonly used to describe a complaint by an employer or employee that a term of a **collective bargaining agreement** is being breached. Most collective agreements establish a grievance procedure to be followed pursuant to such an allegation.

GROUND RENT An **estate of inheritance** in the **rent** of lands, an inheritable **interest** in and right to the rent collected through the **leasing** of certain lands. It is a **freehold estate,** and as such is subject to **encumbrance** by **mortgage** or **judgment** (**lien, attachment,** etc.). An incorporeal **hereditament,** the ground rent is an interest distinct from that held by the owner of the property, whose estate is in the land itself and is therefore corporeal.

GUARANTEE 1. The person in whose favour the **guarantor** binds himself. **2.** To agree or promise to be reponsible for the **debt, default,** or miscarriage of another. **3.** [also **guaranty**] A **contract collateral** to the **principal** contract by which a person engages to answer for the **debt,** default, or miscarriage of another. *Campbell* v. *McIsaac* (1985), 9 N.S.R. 287 (N.S.S.C.). The contract of guaranty is dependent on the unchanged continuance of the primary obligation, and any substantial alteration of the principal agreement (i.e., extension of time, partial release of security) renders the guaranty unenforceable.

Western Dominion Investment Co. Ltd. v. *MacMillan,* [1925] 1 W.W.R. 852 (Man.K.B.).

GUARANTOR A **surety.** One who binds himself by a **contract** of guaranty and agrees to pay the **debt** of another should that other **default.**

GUARANTY See **guarantee** (sense 3).

GUARDIAN A person appointed to take care of another person, his affairs and property. A person who has in law or in fact the **custody** or control of any child and is under a legal duty to provide necessaries for such child. Guardian "includes a head of a family and any other person who has in law or in fact the custody or care of a child." *Family Maintenance Act,* R.S.N.S. 1989, c. 160, s. 2(e). See also, e.g., *Stoakley* v. *Stoakley* (1976), 20 N.S.R. (2d) 675 (N.S.S.C.). See also **next friend.**

GUEST One to whom hospitality is extended, often in the form of entertainment, lodging, and refreshment and usually in return for monetary compensation. The keeper of guests is at common law only required to inform his guests of any concealed danger of which he has knowledge.

Formerly, at common law, an innkeeper was **prima facie** liable for the loss of the guests' goods. This has generally been amended by provincial statute so that the innkeeper will only be liable where the loss is a result of the innkeeper's willful act, **default,** or **negligence.** See *Innkeepers Act,* R.S.N.S. 1989, c. 229.

GUEST PASSENGER [GRATUITOUS PASSENGER] The driver of a motor vehicle may now be liable to a guest passenger where he has been negligent, the degree of negligence required depending on provincial statutes. *Motor Vehicle Act,* R.S.N.S. 1989, c. 293, s. 248(2). To determine whether a person is a guest within the meaning of the statute, regard must be had as to whether the purpose of the transportation is merely social or in performance of a contractual obligation or for business or commercial purposes. *Manuge* v. *Dominion Atlantic Railway Co.,* [1973] S.C.R. 232.

GUILTY **1.** The condition of having been found by the court to have committed the **crime** with which one was **charged** or some lesser **indictable offence. 2.** Also, the commission of a **civil** wrong or **tort,** but seldom used in this context. *Criminal Code,* R.S.C. 1985, c. C–46, ss. 606–613. **3.** The word used by a prisoner to **confess** his crime when **pleading** to an **indictment.**

HABEAS CORPUS *(hă'-bē-ŭs kôr'-pŭs)*
Lat.: you have the body. Known as the
"GREAT WRIT," *habeas corpus* is a **prerogative writ** with a varied use in criminal
and civil contexts. It is basically a procedure for obtaining a judicial determination of the legality of an individual's **custody.** *In re John Henderson,* [1930]
S.C.R. 45 at 55. In the criminal law context, it is used to bring the **petitioner**
before the court to inquire into the legality of his confinement. In the civil context, the **writ** is used to challenge the
validity of child custody and deporta-
tions. *In re Fred Storgoff,* [1945] S.C.R.
526. *Habeas corpus* is a safeguard of the
liberty of the subject. As a procedural
writ, it is not a new **suit** different from the
one dealt with at trial nor is it a means of
appealing. It is a writ to which any person
detained in prison is entitled and which is
granted for the sole purpose of having a
superior court determine whether the detention is legal. The judge's only **jurisdiction** under the writ is whether to order the
release of the accused. *Habeas corpus*
cannot be used to **nullify** the administration of criminal law. The right of *habeas
corpus* is now recognized in the **Canadian
Charter of Rights and Freedoms, s.**
10(*c*)

HABENDUM *(hă-běn'-dŭm)* Lat.: to
have. The clause in a **deed** that determines what **estate** or **interest** is granted by
the deed. *Re Gold and Rowe* (1913), 4
O.W.N. 642 at 643 (H.C.). It begins with
the words "to have and to hold." The
habendum may reduce, enlarge, explain,
or qualify, but not contradict or be repugnant to the estate granted. It is not essential to the deed. *Dunlap* v. *Dunlap*
(1883), 6 O.R. 141 (Ch.). In modern **conveyancing,** the inclusion of the *habendum*
clause has become somewhat redundant,
since its function is normally performed
by the granting clause in a conveyance.
The deed's validity is not affected by the
absence of the *habendum.*

**HABITUAL CRIMINAL [DANGEROUS OF-
FENDER]** One who is subject to an indeterminate period of imprisonment if

the court is satisfied that the requirements
of the *Criminal Code* have been fulfilled.
See *Criminal Code,* R.S.C. 1985, c. C–
46, s. 753. An accused can be said to be
leading a persistently **criminal** life when
it is proved, beyond a **reasonable doubt,**
that the nature of his crimes and the
circumstances surrounding their commission display **premeditation,** planning, preparation, and audacity and that
any periods of "honest life" have been
overshadowed by his reversion to crime.
R. v. *Ashton* (1964), 44 C.R. 85
(B.C.Co.Ct.). The crime must be a
serious personal injury offence defined
in s. 752 of the *Criminal Code,* and the
offender must constitute a threat to the
life, safety, or physical or mental well-
being of other persons. See **recidivist.**

HARD CASES **Cases** that, in order to
meet the exigencies presented by the extreme hardship of one **party,** produce decisions that may deviate from the true
principles of law.
  It is sometimes said that "hard cases
make bad law" because logic is often de-
emphasized in a hard case, and later attempts to justify the new law thus created
often compound the original inadequacy
of reasoning.

HARDSHIP, UNNECESSARY [UNDUE]
A relevant phrase in debtor-creditor relations. Where, despite a court order, a
debtor has refused payment to a **creditor,**
the creditor may, by the rules of civil procedure as well as by statute, have the
debtor committed to jail for up to twelve
months through application to the
court.

HARMLESS ERROR A term infrequently used by Canadian courts for an
error committed at trial that is not prejudicial to the **defendant,** so that the result
of the trial would not be reversed, or that
is prejudicial to the defendant but in no
way influenced the outcome of the case,
nor would its **reversal** change the court's
decision.

HEADNOTE A summary of the relevant
facts of a **case** and a concise synopsis of
the points of law decided therein. Placed
at the beginning of a case report, the
headnote is not an official portion of the
reported **judgment** but is compiled by a
commercial writer who extracts from the
judgment the salient points in the areas of

facts, issues, and decision. Despite the non-official status of headnotes, modern judges have been known to quote them in their judgments.

HEARING A proceeding held by a judicial, quasi-judicial (see **quasi**) or **administrative tribunal** to determine **questions of law** and **questions of fact**. See also **fair hearing**.

Originally applied to **chancery** proceedings, where a judge sat without a **jury**, it is now loosely applied to any **common-law** trial whether **civil** or **criminal**. *R*. v. *McKenzie*, [1929] 1 W.W.R. 249 (Man.K.B.).

FINAL HEARING The final **arbitration** of a decision on the facts. Determination of a **suit** on its **merits** as distinguished from a hearing of preliminary questions. Compare **preliminary hearing**.

HEARING DE NOVO A new hearing. In **administrative law**, a Board may have a second hearing to cure the defects of the first. This is a hearing **de novo**, not an **appeal**.

In criminal law, TRIAL DE NOVO (see **trial**) is a method of appeal where the judge adjudicates on both the facts and the law. This is distinguished from an appeal by way of stated case. See "trial de novo," *Criminal Code*, R.S.C. 1985, c. C–46, s. 822.

HEARSAY RULE Written or oral statements or communicative conduct made other than by a **witness** testifying at a **hearing**, offered as proof either of their truth or of assertions implicit therein, is hearsay **evidence** and **inadmissible**. *Dalrymple* v. *Sun Life Assurance Co. of Canada*, [1966] 2 O.R. 227 at 231 (C.A.).

The term *hearsay* in this connection imparts a purpose, not a quality. A statement is original or **circumstantial evidence**, and therefore not hearsay, if its materiality depends on the fact that it was made, and not on its being true. *R*. v. *Container Materials Ltd.*, [1940] 4 D.L.R. 293 (Ont.S.C.). For example: Witness *W* is asked, "What did *Y* tell you?" If *Y's* statement is elicited for the truth of the matter it asserted, it is hearsay. If, however, it is elicited merely to show that the words were spoken, it is not hearsay. *W's* answer will be admissible only for the fact that *Y* may have made a statement and not for the truth of that statement.

The basis of the rule is that the credibility of the assertor is the key ingredient in weighing the truth of his statement, and thus when that statement is made out of court, without benefit of cross-examination and without declarant's demeanour being exposed to the trier of fact (judge or jury), there is an unwillingness to permit the statement to be admitted.

Exceptions to the rule: (1) DYING DECLARATIONS, where the declarant has lost all hope of recovery; (2) declarations against the declarant's interest; (3) declarations in the course of duty; (4) declarations as to pedigree made before the **action**; (5) declarations as to physical or mental condition; (6) reputation evidence; (7) recitals and statements in ancient deeds; (8) official statements and records; (9) certificates and public registers; (10) testimony in former proceedings.

HEIR APPARENT That person who, should he survive his ancestor, will become the ancestor's heir. He does not become heir until the death of the ancestor, as no living person can have **heirs** (*nemo est haeres viventis*). The concept of heir apparent is also a reference to the heir to a throne.

HEIRS Strictly, those who would be designated by statute to inherit an **estate**, or portion of an estate, of an ancestor who dies without a **will** (i.e., **intestate**); in the law of wills, "heirs" in a **bequest** mean **devisees** and **legatees**. *Re Bolton* (1918), 14 O.W.N. 87 (S.C.). The term may be used to refer to **issue** of the **testator**, next of kin, devisees or legatees by will, **heirs of the body**, or persons who take on intestacy.

An heir is (at **common law**) one appointed by law to succeed to an estate in an intestacy situation, or the person set out by **statute** to succeed, or in popular terms, a successor by will. See **intestate succession**.

HEIRS OF THE BODY Natural heirs; **lineal** descendants of the deceased, excluding, therefore, the spouse, adopted children, in-laws, etc.; used in **conveyances** to create an **estate** in **fee tail**, a concept abolished in most Canadian provinces; **words of limitation** used by a **grantor** when attempting to keep the land granted within the family for succeeding generations.

HEREDITAMENTS Anything that can be inherited. It is not just **property** a person has by **descent** from an ancestor, but also that which he has by purchase, and which his **heirs** can inherit from him. The term applies to both **real property** and **personal property.** There are two kinds of hereditaments: CORPOREAL and INCOR-POREAL. The former generally are tangible things, such as land or houses. The latter are less tangible rights growing out of or connected to land, such as an **ease-ment** or right to **rent.**

HEREDITARY SUCCESSION The pass-ing of **title** according to the laws of **de-scent;** the acquisition of title to an **estate** by a person by **operation of law** upon the death of an ancestor without a valid **will** affecting the property inherited. See **in-heritance.** Compare **devise.**

HIGH COURT OF JUSTICE A superior **court of record** in England created by the *Judicature Acts of 1875.* In itself it per-forms no judicial function. The high court was a consolidation of both law and **equi-ty jurisdictions** and presently consists of three divisions: Chancery division, Queen's Bench division, and the Family division.

HIGH COURT OF JUSTICE OF ONTARIO
 The trial division at the Supreme Court level in Ontario. It is the only court in Canada so named.

HIGHWAY TRAFFIC ACTS See **Motor Vehicle Acts.**

HOLDER A person in possession of a document of **title** or an **instrument** or an investment **security** drawn, issued, or **de-vised** to him or to his **order** or to bearer or in blank. See *Bills of Exchange Act,* R.S.C. 1985, c. B–4, s. 2, governing the law of **negotiable instruments.** "Holder" means the payee or endorsee of a **bill of exchange** or **promissory note** who is in possession of it, or the bearer thereof, (*id.* s. 2). See **holder in due course.**

HOLDER IN DUE COURSE A **holder,** who has taken a **bill of exchange;** a holder free of most defences of prior parties to the **negotiable instrument** and free of con-flicting title **claims** to the instrument it-self. Under the *Bills of Exchange Act,* R.S.C. 1985, c. B–4, s. 55(1), a holder is one who has taken a bill, complete and regular on its face, under the following conditions: (*a*) that he became the holder of it before it was overdue and without

notice that it had been previously dishon-oured, if such was the fact; (*b*) that he took the bill in **good faith** and for value, and that at the time the bill was negoti-ated to him he had no notice of any defect in title of the person who negotiated it.

HOLDING 1. In commercial and prop-erty law, **property** in which one has legal **title** and of which one is in **possession;** the term may be used to refer specifically to ownership of stocks or **shares** of **corpora-tions. 2.** In **procedure,** any ruling of the court, including rulings upon the **admissi-bility** of **evidence** or other questions pre-sented during trial. Compare **dictum.**

HOLDING COMPANY 1. A **corporation** that owns or controls other corporations through its majority **interest; 2.** a corpora-tion organized to hold the **stock** of other companies; **3.** a corporation that can in-fluence the management of other compa-nies by ownership of **securities** in the lat-ter.

HOLDOVER TENANCY See **tenancy** [TENANCY AT SUFFERANCE].

HOLOGRAPHIC WILL A **will** wholly in the handwriting of and dated and signed by the **testator** requiring none of the other formalities essential for the validity of a conventional will. In particular, witnesses are not required. Most Canadian prov-inces now recognize holographic wills. See, e.g., *The Wills Act,* R.S.S. 1978, c. W-14, s. 7(2).

HOMAGE During the **feudal** period, the ceremony "wherein the vassal knelt be-fore the lord, acknowledged himself to be his man, and swore **fealty** to him. It was frequently accompanied by a **grant** of land from the lord to the vassal, the land to be held of the lord by the vassal as **tenant.**" C. Moynihan, *Introduction to the Law of Real Property* 3 (2d ed. 1988). As a con-sequence, any attempt by the vassal to **convey** more than the **estate** granted him was not only **tortious** conduct with regard to the lord, but was also **treasonous.**

HOMESTEAD LEGISLATION See **mat-rimonial property.**

HOMICIDE The killing of a human be-ing by another, directly or indirectly, by any means. It is either **culpable** (a **crime**) or non-culpable. If the former, it is classed as either **murder, manslaughter** or infanticide. *Criminal Code,* R.S.C. 1985, c. C–46, ss. 222–228.

JUSTIFIABLE HOMICIDE The killing of a human being by commandment of the law, in the execution of public justice, in **self-defence,** in lawful defence of habitation, property or person, etc. See, e.g., *Criminal Code,* R.S.C. 1985, c. C–46, ss. 25–42.

HORS *(ôr')* Fr.: outside of, besides, other than [sometimes *dehors* (dĕ-ôr')].

HOSTILE POSSESSION See **adverse possession.** See also **notorious possession.**

HOSTILE WITNESS See **witness.**

HOTCHPOT A type of clause in a **will** used when a parent does not wish to rely on the **presumption** against double portions with respect to his children to whom he has conferred benefits under a will. He then provides specifically in the will that benefits conferred in his lifetime on the **beneficiary** under the will are to be brought into the **estate** and accounted for accordingly. *In re Arbuthnot,* [1915] 1 Ch. 422.

HOUSE OF COMMONS The Canadian legislative lower house elected on the basis of universal adult suffrage. It is headed by the Prime Minister, who with his **Cabinet** operates solely through support of a majority of the members. That support is normally forthcoming from the party in power by virtue of party solidarity. See P. Hogg, *Constitutional Law of Canada* 238–40 (3d ed. 1992).

HOUSE OF LORDS The assembly of lords spiritual and temporal, forming the second branch of the British Parliament. It is the Supreme Court of Appeal from the Court of Appeal in England and the Superior Courts of Scotland and Northern Ireland.

HUMAN RIGHTS [LEGISLATION] Antidiscrimination law. Legislation "intended to give rise, amongst other things, to individual rights of vital importance, rights capable of enforcement . . . in a court of law." *Action Travail des Femmes* v. *Canadian National Railway Co.,* [1987] 1 S.C.R. 1114 at 1134. This type of legislation "is of a special nature and declares public policy regarding matters of general concern. It is not constitutional in nature in the sense that it may not be altered, amended or repealed by the Legislature. It is, however, of such nature that it may not be altered, amended, or repealed, nor may exceptions be created to its provisions, save by clear legislative pronouncement." *Winnipeg School Division No. 1* v. *Craton,* [1985] 2 S.C.R. 150 at 156.

In Canada, human rights legislation is embodied in the federal **Canadian Human Rights Act** and various provincial and territorial antidiscrimination statutes (see **Appendices III–V**). These human rights statutes compliment the **Canadian Charter of Rights and Freedoms** providing protection from discrimination to individuals in private activity, whereas the *Charter* protects individuals from discrimination in the area of governmental activity. *Retail, Wholesale & Department Union, Local 580* v. *Dolphin Delivery Ltd.,* [1986] 2 S.C.R. 573. See **civil rights.**

HUNG JURY A colloquialism describing a jury that cannot reach a **verdict** by the degree of agreement required of the members. The jury is then dismissed, a new one is impanelled and the case is tried again **de novo.**

HYBRID OFFENCE An offence "where the **prosecution** has a choice as to whether it proceeds by way of alleging that the accused committed an **indictable offence** or an offence punishable on **summary conviction.**" A. Mewett & M. Manning, *Criminal Law* 26 (2d ed. 1985). See e.g., *Criminal Code,* R.S.C. 1985, c. C–46, s. 140 (public mischief); s. 266 (assault); s. 437 (false alarm of fire).

I

IBID. *(ĭb'-ĭd)* Lat.: in the same place; abbreviation of *ibidem*. Used to mean "in the same book" or "on the same page." It avoids repetition of source data in the reference immediately preceding.

ID. *(ĭd)* Lat.: the same; abbreviation of *idem*. Used in citations to avoid repetition of the author's name and the title when a reference to an item immediately follows another to the same item.

ID CERTUM EST QUOD CERTUM REDDI POTEST *(ĭd sêr'-tŭm ĕst kwŏd sêr'-tŭm rĕd'-ē pō'-tĕst)* Lat.: that is certain which can be made certain.

ID EST *(ĭd ĕst)* Lat.: that is, that is to say. Abbreviated **i.e.**

I.E. Abbreviation of **id est.**

IGNORANTIA LEGIS NON EXCUSAT *(ĭg-nō-rän'-shē-à lā'-gĭs nŏn ĕks-kū'-zät)* Lat.: ignorance of the law is no excuse; i.e., the fact that a **defendant** did not think his act was against the law does not prevent the law from punishing him for the prohibited act. "Ignorance of the law by a person who commits an offence is not an excuse for committing that offence." *Criminal Code*, R.S.C. 1985, c. C–46, s. 19. But ignorance of fact may prove to be a **defence**, as where lack of knowledge of the automatic suspension of a driver's licence constituted a defence to a charge of driving with a suspended license. In addition, lack of knowledge may constitute a defence to an offence where it is necessary for the Crown to prove the existence of **mens rea.** See *R.* v. *Prue; R.* v. *Baril* (1979), 46 C.C.C. (2d) 257 (S.C.C.).

ILLEGITIMATE Illegal or improper; applied to children, it means born out of wedlock, **bastards.**

IMMIGRATION The movement of persons from one country into a country foreign to them for the purpose of permanently residing there. It is governed by the *Immigration Act*, R.S.C. 1985, c. I–2, which authorizes the annual establishment of immigration levels to satisfy demographic and labour conditions. The provinces, by s. 95 of the *B.N.A. Act*

(now the *Constitution Act, 1867*), have concurrent **jurisdiction** to legislate as long as the legislation is not repugnant to that of Parliament.

IMMORAL CONDUCT Conduct inconsistent with the standards considered acceptable by the community as a whole. Immoral conduct may provide the basis for suspension or dismissal from certain professions, such as law, medicine, teaching, etc.

IMMUNITY A right of exemption from a **duty** or penalty; a favour or benefit granted in exception to the general rule.

DIPLOMATIC IMMUNITY Immunity from **suit** and legal process, accorded to an envoy or other public minister of a foreign sovereign power, or to the family or official or domestic staff of such an envoy or minister or to the families of such staff. "[T]he function of the diplomatic agent can be effectively exercised and ... he can accomplish the delicate mission with which he is charged, only if he enjoys complete liberty in the foreign State, [or] only if he is free from all subjection to the State in which he temporarily resides. And the sovereignty of the State which he represents would suffer a certain dependence if its diplomatic envoys did not remain subjects of the sovereign whom they were called upon to represent and serve. It is upon this necessity that the principle of the privilege of diplomatic immunity is founded...." *Rose* v. *The King*, [1947] 3 D.L.R. 618 at 640 (Que.K.B., Appeal Side).

OFFICIAL IMMUNITY The personal immunity accorded to a public official from liability to anyone injured by any of his actions that are the consequence of the exercise of his official authority or duty. This immunity is complete for judges, so long as they act within the jurisdiction of their respective courts; administrative officers, however, are generally immune only for **discretionary** as opposed to **ministerial acts** that are done honestly and in **good faith.** W. P. Keeton, *Prosser and Keeton on Torts* (5th ed. 1984), s. 132.

SOVEREIGN IMMUNITY See **sovereign immunity.**
See *Foreign Missions and International Organizations Act*, S.C. 1991, c. 41.

IMPAIRED [DRIVING] Under section 253 of the *Criminal Code*, R.S.C. 1985, c.

C–46, it is an offence to operate or have care and control of a motor vehicle, vessel, aircraft, or railway equipment while impaired by alcohol or a drug. The **mens rea** of an impairment offence "need not necessarily be present in relation both to the act of driving and to the state of being impaired . . . [A] man who becomes impaired as the result of taking a drug on medical advice without knowing its effect cannot escape liability if he became aware of his impaired condition before he started to drive his car just as a man who did not appreciate his impaired condition when he started to drive cannot escape liability on the ground that his lack of appreciation was brought about by voluntary consumption of liquor or drug." *R.* v. *King* (1962), 133 C.C.C. 1 at 19 (S.C.C.). See also *R.* v. *Smith* (1992), 73 C.C.C. (3d) 285 (Alta. C.A.) (proof of impairment); *Ford* v. *The Queen* (1982), 65 C.C.C. (2d) 392 (S.C.C.) (proof of care and control). See **breathalyzer; intoxication.**

IMPANELLING See **empanelling.**

IMPEACHMENT 1. Used most often in the law of **evidence** to indicate a process whereby evidence is adduced in order to question a **witness's** credibility. The **discovery** of witnesses permits counsel to solicit or adduce evidence that may later be used at trial to impeach the witness's veracity by pointing out discrepancies in the **testimony. 2.** Also, a solemn **accusation** of great public offence, especially against a minister of the **Crown.** In Canada, impeachment is practically obsolete, though it is still used extensively in the United States to indicate the procedure taken after an accusation of grave import has been made against a public officer.

"The object of prosecutions of impeachment [in England and the United States] is to reach high potent offenders, such as might be presumed to escape punishment in the ordinary tribunals, either from their own extraordinary influence, or from the imperfect organization and powers of those tribunals. These prosecutions are, therefore, conducted by the representatives of the nation, in their public capacity in the face of the nation, and upon a responsibility which is at once felt and reverenced by the whole community." J. Story, *Commentaries on the Constitution of the United States* 250 (1833).

IMPLICATION Intention, meaning; that which is inferred; though not expressly stated, a state of mind or facts that is deduced.

NECESSARY IMPLICATION In statutory **construction,** a rule that the **Crown,** in the absence of express reference, can only be bound by necessary implication, i.e., "so strong a probability of **intention,** that an intention contrary to that which is imputed to the **testator** cannot be supposed." *Cork County Council* v. *Eire,* [1945] I.R. 561 at 573 (S.C.).

IMPLIED The antithesis of express; not explicitly written or stated; referring, e.g., to a condition, consent, power, warranty, state of mind, or fact that is determined by deduction or **inference** from known facts and circumstances.

IMPOSSIBILITY 1. A defence of nonperformance of **contract** that arises when **performance** is impossible because of the destruction of the subject matter of the contract (as, for example, by fire) or the death of a person necessary for its performance; performance is then excused and the contract **duty** terminated. At common law, impossibility did not reach the cases where performance simply became expensive or difficult, and it has no application at all if the promise has been made expressly unconditional even as against unforeseen difficulties. But "the essence of the [modern] defence of 'impossibility' is that the promised performance was at the making of the contract, or thereafter became impracticable owing to some extreme or unreasonable difficulty, expense, injury or loss involved, rather than that it is scientifically or actually impossible." 18 W. Jaeger, *Williston on Contracts* (3d ed. 1978), s. 1931, p. 6–7. The plea can only avail as an excuse for non-performance where the event that causes the impossibility cannot reasonably be supposed to have been in the contemplation of the parties when the contract was made; where the event was or might have been guarded against in the contract, **relief** will not be granted on account of it. *Canadian Merchant Marine* v. *Canadian Trading Co.* (1922), 68 D.L.R. 544 (S.C.C.). **2.** In criminal law, the term applies to situations in which one does an act that would be criminal but is not because the facts or circumstances render the crime impossible to commit. Thus it is impossible to **murder** someone already dead.

See **frustration.**

IMPROVEMENT The act or process by which the quality and hence the value of a thing is increased. *Re Canadian Anthracite Coal Co. and McNeill* (1912), 4 D.L.R. 784 (Alta.S.C.). Any development of land or buildings through the expenditure of money or labour that is designed to do more than merely repair, replace, or restore to the original condition. Generally, "improvements" refer to structures of a permanent nature that are attached and by concomitant necessity become part of **realty.**

IMPUTE To assign to a person or other entity the legal responsibility for the act of another, because of the relationship between the person so made liable and the actor, rather than because of actual participation in or knowledge of the act. See **vicarious liability.**

INADMISSIBLE EVIDENCE See **evidence.**

IN CAMERA *(ĭn kă'-mĕ-rà)* Lat.: in private; heard in a judge's chambers or a courtroom from which all spectators have been excluded. In general, court matters are of public record and are therefore open to the public; however, some matters—e.g., in family court—are *in camera,* and permission of the court and the **parties** is essential for attendance by others.

Section 486 of the *Criminal Code,* R.S.C. 1985, c. C–46 provides for in camera proceedings where it is ruled to be in the interest of public morals, the maintenance of order, or the proper administration of justice; see also s. 537.

INCAPACITY Lack of ability; the quality or state of being incapable; the lack of legal, physical, or intellectual power; inability. See **incompetency;** minor; **non compos mentis.** Compare **insanity.**

INCARCERATION Confinement in a jail, prison, or penitentiary.

INCENDIARY Arsonist; one who willfully and for a fraudulent purpose sets another's property on fire. **Arson** is an **indictable offence** under the *Criminal*

Code, R.S.C. 1985, c. C–46, ss. 433–434.1. See, e.g., *R.* v. *Varbeff* (1979), 24 N.S.R. (2d) 279 (N.S.S.C.A.D.). **2.** An object capable of starting and sustaining a fire; an incendiary device.

INCEST An **indictable offence** involving sexual intercourse between a man and woman related to each other where the tables of **affinity** and consanguinity would forbid marriage, e.g., parent and child, brother and sister, half-brother and sister, grandparent and grandchild. It is immaterial whether the relationship is traced through lawful wedlock, but the **accused** must know of the relationship. *R.* v. *Schmidt* (1948), 90 C.C.C. 297 (Ont.C.A.). See *Criminal Code,* R.S.C. 1985, c. C–46, s. 155(1).

INCHOATE DOWER See **dower.**

INCIDENTAL BENEFICIARY See **beneficiary.**

INCIDENTAL DAMAGES See **damages.**

INCLOSURE See **enclosure.**

INCLUDED OFFENCE See **lesser included offence.**

INCOMPETENCY Lack of ability, qualification, fitness, or capacity to perform certain duties. **1.** "In contracts for personal service, the incompetence of the employee to perform the services which he has undertaken is a sufficient ground for discharge, though he was hired for a definite period; the word 'competency' implies nothing more than reasonable skill." *Allman* v. *Yukon Consolidated Gold Fields Co.* (1907), 7 W.L.R. 318 at 332 (Y.T.). **2.** The term may also be applied where one lacks the legal, physical, or intellectual fitness to discharge a particular duty or function.

When a person is adjudicated incompetent, a **guardian** may be appointed to manage the incompetent's affairs. An adjudicated incompetent lacks capacity to contract, and his contracts are **void.** In the case of one not formally declared incompetent, a contract may be **voidable** only. See S. Waddans, *The Law of Contracts* (3d ed. 1993), chap. 19.

See **incapacity; minor; non compos mentis.** Compare **competent.**

INCORPORATE To combine together or unite to form a whole. To form a **corporation;** to organize and be granted status as a corporation by following procedures prescribed by law. See **association, memorandum of.**

INCORPOREAL Intangible, not material in nature. Incorporeal **property** or **chattels** cannot be seen or touched—they are rights only. **Copyrights** and **patent** rights are incorporeal, or CHOSES IN ACTION (see **chose**), enforceable only by an action. Compare **corporeal.**

INCORPOREAL HEREDITAMENT See **hereditaments.**

INCORPOREAL RIGHT A right issuing out of and annexed to or exercised with corporeal **inheritances,** as, e.g., **annuities** and rights of way. *Re Registration of a Transfer of Coal Rights* (1914), 7 W.W.R. 769 at 771 (Sask.M.T.).

INCORRIGIBLE Uncorrectable; a person, usually a juvenile, whose behaviour cannot be made to conform to standards dictated by law. See **habitual criminal; recidivist.**

INCREMENT An amount of increase in number, amount, or value. As to salaries, increments are the periodic, consecutive additions or increases that do not become part of salary until they accrue under the rule making such provision.

INCRIMINATE 1. To hold another, or oneself, responsible for **criminal** misconduct. 2. To involve someone, or oneself, in an **accusation** of a crime.

INCULPATORY That which tends to **incriminate** or bring about a criminal conviction. Compare **exculpatory.**

INCUMBRANCE See **encumbrance.**

INDECENCY That which tends to deprave and corrupt those whose minds are open to such immoral influence. *R.* v. *McAuliffe* (1904), 8 C.C.C. 21 (N.S.Co.Ct.). See *Criminal Code,* R.S.C. 1985, c. C–46, s. 175 [indecent exhibition], s. 173 [indecent act], s. 174 [nudity], and s. 372 [telephone calls]. See **gross indecency.**

INDEFEASIBLE Incapable of being defeated or altered. "A **gift** that is subject to being defeated or terminated on an event such as remarriage is **defeasible.**" *The Estate of Paul Dontigny* v. *The Queen,* [1974] 1 F.C. 418 at 420 (C.A.). In **real property,** indefeasible implies an **estate in fee simple,** or a perfect **title.**

IN DELICTO *(ĭn dĕ-lĭk'-tō)* Lat.: In fault,

though not in equal fault. Compare **in pari delicto.**

INDEMNIFY 1. To secure against loss or **damage** that may occur in the future; to **insure.** 2. To provide compensation for loss or damage already suffered.

INDEMNITY The obligation resting on one to make good any loss another person has incurred or may incur by acting at the former's request or for his benefit. 2. The right that the person suffering the loss or damage is entitled to claim. Refers to a total shifting of economic loss onto the party chiefly or primarily responsible for that loss. Compare **contribution.**

INDENTURE A **deed** between two parties **conveying real estate** by which both **parties** assume obligations; implies a **sealed instrument.** Historically, it referred to a crease or wavy cut made in duplicates of the deed so their authenticity could be verified later.

INDEPENDENT CONTRACTOR See **contractor.**

INDIANS See **aboriginal peoples**.

INDICIA *(ĭn-dĭ'-shē-à)* Lat.: indications, signs. In insurance law, e.g., an **agent** has *indicia* of his authority by having pink cards that may be delivered to persons seeking automobile insurance. The issue of the pink card manifests an intention on the part of the insurer to cover the insured. Any private instructions limiting the agent's authority but not known by the insured will be of no avail to the insurer. *Wassink* v. *Western Union Insurance Co.* (1964), 49 W.W.R. 404.

INDICTABLE OFFENCE Generally, a more serious criminal **charge** as distinguished from a **summary offence.** However, in Canada, the distinction between indictable offences and summary offences is somewhat blurred. In some instances, according to the provisions of the *Criminal Code,* the Crown may determine whether an offence will be tried "summarily" or by **"indictment."** An indictable offence is nonetheless indictable because, if the prosecution chose, it could proceed in respect of it summarily. *Regina* v. *Reed* (1975), 23 C.C.C. (2d) 121 (B.C.S.C.). Originally, indictable offences were tried only by the higher courts. This is still the case with reference to offences such as **murder** and **treason**

under s. 469 of the *Criminal Code,* R.S.C. 1985, c. C–46. However, other indictable offences can only be tried by a magistrate or provincial court judge, while still others may, at the option of the **accused,** be tried by a magistrate or county court judge, either alone or with a jury. See further P. Fitzgerald & K. McShane, *Looking at Law* 71–72 (2d ed. 1982). See **crime.** Compare **misdemeanor.**

INDICTMENT An accusation in writing of a serious, i.e., **indictable offence.** It sets out the **charges** against the **accused,** and each **count** therein must be comprised of only one transaction or offence. It includes "(*a*) information or a count therein, (*b*), a **plea,** replication or other **pleading,** and (*c*) any record." *Criminal Code,* R.S.C. 1985, c. C–46, s. 2. By s. 673, it includes "an information or charge in respect of which a person has been tried for an indictable offence under Part XIX."

INDISPENSABLE EVIDENCE Evidence that is necessary to prove a submitted fact.

INDISPENSABLE PARTY See **necessary party.**

INDIVIDUAL A person. Under the **Canadian Bill of Rights,** R.S.C. 1985, c. 44, "the right of the individual" extends to natural persons only, and not to corporations. *R.* v. *Colgate-Palmolive Ltd.* (1972), 8 C.C.C. (2d) 40 (Ont.Co.Ct.).

Section 15(1) of the **Canadian Charter of Rights and Freedoms** provides that "Every individual is equal before the law...." It has been ruled that *Charter* equality rights extend only to natural persons. *Parkdale Hotel Ltd.* v. *Attorney-General of Canada.* (1986), 1 F.T.R. 190 (F.C., T.D.)

The scope and meaning of individual has also been interpreted for other statutes, e.g. *Bankruptcy and Insolvency Act,* R.S.C. 1985, c. B–3 (see *Re, Witchekan Lake Farms Ltd.,* [1975] 1 W.W.R. 471 (C.A.)); and the *Income Tax Act,* S.C. 1970–71–72, c. 63 (see *In Re Saskatchewan Co-operative Elevator Co. Ltd.* [1933] 3 W.W.R. 669).

INDORSE See **endorse.**

INEVITABLE ACCIDENT Originally, a term in admiralty law for "that which a party charged with an offence could not possibly prevent by exercise of ordinary care, caution and maritime skill." *The Bolina* (1844), 3 Notes of Cases, 208; later applicable to motor vehicle accidents such that a person relying on the defence must satisfy a two-step test: (1) that the alleged cause of the accident could not have been prevented by the exercise of reasonable care, and (2) that, assuming such cause operated without **negligence** on the defendant's part, he could not, by the exercise of reasonable care, have avoided the accident. *Rintoul* v. *X-ray and Radium Industries Ltd.* [1956] S.C.R. 674 at 678.

"Today, defendants in negligence cases normally do not need to avail themselves of the plea of inevitable accident; all they have to do is deny that they were negligent." A. Linden, *Canadian Tort Law* 254 (5th ed. 1993). See **duty** [DUTY OF CARE].

IN EXTREMIS *(ĭn ĕks-trē'-mĭs)* Lat.: in the last stages (especially of illness); in contemplation of death.

INFANT One not having reached the age of legal **majority;** a **minor;** a child. An infant's contracts are generally **voidable,** at the option of the infant. However, the law has held that an infant can validly contract for necessities (see, e.g., the various *Sale of Goods* statutes) and contracts made while an infant can be ratified after reaching the **age of majority.** See S. Waddams, *The Law of Contracts* (3d ed. 1993), chap. 18.

An infant is **liable** for his own **torts** although special rules relating to the capacity of a very young actor to form the necessary **intent** may protect him to some extent. For example, while a child of tender years is not normally charged with CONTRIBUTORY NEGLIGENCE (see **negligence**), mere age is not in itself the test, but rather the capacity of the infant to understand and appreciate danger; "it is a question for the jury in each case whether the infant exercised the care to be expected from a child of like age, intelligence and experience." *McEllistrum* v. *Etches,* [1956] S.C.R. 787 at 793. See A. Linden, *Canadian Tort Law* 127–33 (5th ed. 1993).

The *Criminal Code,* R.S.C. 1985, c. C–46, s. 13, prohibits **conviction** of anyone for an offence committed while under the age of twelve years. Provincial child welfare legislation may apply to children who are under the age of twelve and commit criminal offences. E. Greenspan, *Martin's Annual Criminal Code, 1994* 42 (1993). See **young offender.**

IN FEE [IN FEE SIMPLE] Absolute ownership of an **estate** in land. It is not used to describe a quality of a title to an **easement,** or other appurtenance or incorporeal interest.

INFERENCE A deduction from the **evidence** presented that, if reasonable, may have the validity of legal **proof.** *McLaren* v. *C.P.R.,* [1938] 4 D.L.R. 620 at 625 (Sask.C.A.). A deduction of an ultimate fact from other proved facts, which proved facts, by virtue of the common experience of man, will support but not compel such a deduction. Compare **presumption.**

INFIRM sickly; a weak person. In particular circumstances, the **testimony** of an infirm person may be obtained in a manner that differs from regular procedure to prevent its loss through his death. See **de bene esse.**

IN FLAGRANTE DELICTO *(ĭn-flă-grănt'-ē dĕ-lĭk'-tō)* Lat.: in the very act of committing a crime; "red-handed."

IN FORMA PAUPERIS *(ĭn fôr'-mà paw-pĕr'-ĭs)* Lat.: in the manner of a pauper. In **pleadings,** *in forma pauperis* grants a party the right to sue without assuming the burden of **costs** or the formalities of pleading, such as the page size and number of copies required.

INFORMATION A statement by which a magistrate is informed of the **offence** for which a **summons** or **warrant** is required. In general, any person may lay an information, unless there is a statutory rule to the contrary. An information will suffice if it merely describes the alleged offence in ordinary, non-technical language. It is usually in writing and may be substantiated on oath.

INFORMATION AND BELIEF Verification of information to a degree of certainty that may fall short of actual knowledge, but is based on reasonable, good faith efforts to determine its truth or falsity. The term is used with reference to documents requiring verification, such as **affidavits.** See *Adams* v. *Adams* (1921), 62 D.L.R. 721 (Alta.S.C.A.D.).

INFORMED CONSENT Consent given only after full disclosure of what is being agreed to. A phrase used in **tort** law with respect to the requirement that a patient be apprised of the nature and risks of a medical procedure before the physician can validly claim exception from **liability** for **battery** or from responsibility for medical complications. See *Reibl* v. *Hughes,* [1980] 2 S.C.R. 880.

INFRA *(ĭn'-frà)* Lat.: below, beneath. In text, *infra* refers to a discussion or a citation appearing subsequently; the opposite of **supra** ["above"].

INFRINGEMENT An encroachment; interference with or violation of the right of another. The **remedy** is an **injunction** to restrain future infringements and an action for recovery of damages or profits made by past infringements.

INFRINGEMENT OF COPYRIGHT See **plagiarism.**

INFRINGEMENT OF PATENT See **patent [PATENT INFRINGEMENT].**

IN FUTURO *(ĭn fu-tū'-rō)* Lat.: in the future; at a later date. Compare **in praesenti.**

IN GENERE *(ĭn gĕ'-nĕ-rā)* Lat.: in kind; in the same class or species. Articles or things in the same genus are *in genere;* expresses any class relationship. Laws in the same subject are likewise said to be *in genere.* However, an *in genere* relationship between two **statutes** does not mean they are identical. Thus, laws in one area, though broadly designed to regulate one general field, may be aimed at different portions of that field and still be *in genere.* The term imports singleness in general purpose but permits diversity of individual purposes.

INGRESS AND EGRESS 1. The entering upon and departure from; 2. the means of entering and leaving; 3. the right of **lessee** to enter and leave the **leasehold.** See **easement.**

Ingress to and from the road is "the right of going from the **close** on to the road, or the right of going from the road on to the close." Egress from the road is "going out from the road—going forth from the road." *Somerset* v. *The Great Western Ry. Co.* (1882), 46 L.T. 883 at 884 (Q.B.).

INHERIT 1. Technically, to take as an heir at law solely by **descent,** rather than by **devise**; "in its strictly legal meaning, [the term] is used in contradistinction to acquiring by **will**, but in popular use this distinction is often disregarded" **2.** it also includes acquiring by will. *Perry* v. *Perry* (1918), 40 D.L.R. 628 (Man.C.A.).

INHERITANCE 1. Real property or **personal property** that is inherited by **heirs** according to the laws of **descent** and distribution. **2.** Popular use of the word includes property passed by **will.**

IN HOC *(ĭn hŏk)* Lat.: in this; in reference to this.

INJUNCTION A judicial **remedy** awarded for the purpose of requiring a party to refrain from doing a particular act or thing. Injunctions were first used by the **courts of equity** to restrain parties from conduct contrary to **equity** and good conscience. Today, with the merger of law and equity, they are also used in general courts of law, whereas law courts formerly were constrained to use the writ of **mandamus.**

A preventive measure, an injunction guards against future **injuries** rather than affording a remedy for past injuries. The court must be satisfied that there is a serious question to be tried and that on the facts the **plaintiff** is probably entitled to **relief.** Types of injunctions include:

INTERLOCUTORY INJUNCTIONS One that preserves the **status quo** until the case can be tried; the party applying for this injunction must give an undertaking in damages [covenant to reimburse the defendant] in case he is found in the wrong.

INTERIM INJUNCTION Usually **ex parte,** one that restrains the defendant until some specified date.

MANDATORY INJUNCTION See **mandatory injunction.**

PERMANENT INJUNCTION One that may be issued upon completion of a trial in which the injunction has been actively sought by a party.
See generally J. Martin, *Hanbury & Martin Modern Equity* 718–803 (14th ed. 1993).

INJURIA ABSQUE DAMNO *(ĭn-jū'-rē-à äb'-skwā däm'-nō)* Lat.: wrong or insult without damage. "Injuria" refers to a **tortious** act. Where a **cause of action** requires that **damages** be **pleaded** as an element, this maxim expresses the rule that a

wrong that causes no legally recognized damage cannot give rise to a cause of action. Although this is true in a **negligence** suit, it is not true in any cause of action in which NOMINAL DAMAGES (see **damages**) can be recovered, e.g., in intentional **torts** and actions for **breach of contract.** Compare damnum absque injuria.

INJURIA NON EXCUSAT INJURIAM *(ĭn-jū'-rē-à nŏn ĕks-kū'-zät ĭn-jū'-rē-äm)* Lat.: one wrong does not justify another.

INJURY Any wrong or damage done another, either to his person, rights, reputation, or **property.** The *infringement* of some right considered as having a money value. *Hildon Hotel* v. *Dominion Insurance* (1968), 1 D.L.R. (3d) 214 (B.C.S.C.).

"Injuries" means and includes "bodily injuries." *C.P.R.* v. *Robinson* (1891), 19 S.C.R. 292. However, unlike the ordinary meaning of injury, a LEGAL INJURY is any **damage** resulting from a violation of a legal right that gives rise to an **action** at law. See **damnum absque injuria; irreparable injury.**

IN KIND 1. Of the same or similar type or quality, though not necessarily the identical article; **2.** in the same or similar manner.

IN LOCO PARENTIS *(ĭn lō'-kō pä-rĕn'-tĭs)* Lat.: in the place of a parent. "A person *in loco parentis* to a child is one who has acted so as to evidence his intention of placing himself towards the child in the situation which is ordinarily occupied by the father for the provision of the child's pecuniary wants." *Shtitz* v. *C.N.R.,* [1927] 1 W.W.R. 193 at 201 (Sask.C.A.).

INNUENDO 1. The part of a **pleading** in an **action** for **libel** that explains words spoken or written that are the basis of the action, thereby attaching to those words their proper meaning; **2.** the meaning given to the alleged libelous words. Innuendo cannot enlarge the meaning of the words complained of. See *Higgins* v. *Walkem,* (1889) 17 S.C.R. 225; *Pherrill* v. *Sewell* (1908), 12 O.W.R. 63 (Div.Ct.).

Since the purpose of innuendo is to explain the application of words used, words that are not libelous in themselves cannot be made so by innuendo.

IN OMNIBUS *(ĭn ŏm'-nĭ-būs)* Lat.: in all things; in all the world; in all nature; in all respects.

IN PAIS *(ĭn pā'-es)* Fr.: in the country. Applies to a transaction handled outside the court or without a legal **proceeding.**

IN PARI DELICTO *(ĭn pä'-rē dĕ-lĭk'-tō)* Lat.: in equal fault. Used with reference to an exception to the general rule that illegal transactions or **contracts** are not legally enforceable; thus, where the parties to an illegal agreement are not *in pari delicto,* the agreement may nevertheless be enforceable at **equity** by the less guilty party.

"The true test for determining whether or not the **plaintiff** and **defendant** were *in pari delicto,* is by considering whether the plaintiff could make out his case otherwise than through the medium of the illegal transaction to which he was himself a party." *Clark* v. *Hagar* (1894), 22 S.C.R. 510 at 524, citing *Taylor* v. *Chester* (1869), L.R. 4 Q.B. 309.

The term may also be used with reference to **liability** in **tort,** where the party most **negligent** may be required to bear the entire burden of the loss or **injury.** See also **clean hands; duress.** Compare **in delicto.**

IN PARI MATERIA *(ĭn pä'-rē mă-tĕr'-ē-à)* Lat.: on like subject matter. **Statutes** *in pari materia* are those that relate to the same **person** or things. In the **construction** of a particular statute or in the interpretation of any of the provisions, all acts relating to the same subject or having **the** same general purpose should be read in connection with it, as together constituting one law.

IN PERPETUITY Existing forever.

IN PERSONAM *(ĭn pĕr-sō'-năm)* Lat.: against the person. In **pleading,** an **action** against a person or persons, founded on personal **liability,** and requiring **jurisdiction** by the court over the **defendant;** an action whereby the plaintiff either seeks to subject defendant's general **assets** to **execution** in order to satisfy a money **judgment** or to obtain a judgment directing defendant to do an act or refrain from doing an act under sanction of the court's contempt power. Distinguished from an action **in rem,** where a valid judgment may be obtained, so far as it affects the **res,** without personal **service** of **process.** In an action to recover a judgment *in per-*

sonam, process must usually be personally served or there must be compliance with the substituted service specifically provided by some **statutes.** A judgment *in rem* is conclusive upon all who may have or claim any **interest** in the subject matter of the litigation.

IN PRAESENTI *(ĭn prā-zĕn'-tē)* Lat.: in the present. For example, when a grant of land is made *in praesenti,* it imports the transfer, subject to the limitations mentioned, of a present **interest** in the lands designated. Compare **in futuro.**

IN QUANTUM MERUIT See **quantum meruit.**

INQUEST An inquiry; an inquisition. Inquest "has at least three meanings, one being 'a body of men appointed by law to inquire into certain matters: as, the inquest examined into the facts connected with the alleged murder. The grand jury is sometimes called the grand inquest.' Another, 'The judicial inquiry itself by a jury summoned for the purpose, is called an inquest. The finding of such men, upon an investigation, is also called an inquest, or an inquisition.' " *Davidson* v. *Garrett* (1899), 30 O.R. 653 at 661 (Div.Ct.). A coroner's inquest is in no sense a trial but is simply an inquisition into the cause of a death conducted largely for the benefit of the **Crown** and, such being the case, there is no right in **counsel** to appear for interested parties and examine or cross-examine **witnesses** in the Coroner's Court except by leave of the **coroner.** Although the discretion of the latter should be exercised with wisdom and common sense, it will not be interfered with unless it amounts to a deliberate suppression of the facts. *Wolfe* v. *Robinson,* [1961] O.R. 250 (H.C.).

IN RE *(ĭn rā)* Lat.: in the matter of. Usually signifies a legal proceeding where there is no opponent, but rather some judicial disposition of a thing, or **res,** such as the **estate** of a **decedent.**

IN REM *(ĭn rĕm)* Lat.: against the thing. Signifies an action that is against the **res,** or thing, rather than against the person. A proceeding taken *in rem* is one taken against **property** and has for its object the disposition of the property, without reference to the **title** of individual **claimants.** Compare **in personam.**

INSANITY A term previously used in the *Criminal Code,* R.S.C. 1985, c. C–46, s.

16, to mean a "disease of the mind." Under new provisions in 1992, it was replaced by the term **mental disorder.** These new provisions "are effectively identical to the previous s. 16 except for terminology which replaces the concept of insanity with the phraseology mental disorder. The new terminology still codifies the common law test of insanity, now termed mental disorder." E. Greenspan, *Martin's Annual Criminal Code, 1994* 44 (1993).

IN SE *(ĭn sā)* Lat.: in and of itself. For example, **malum in se** refers to that which is evil in and of itself.

INSIDER 1. Generally, one **privy** to ordinarily nondisclosed information. **2.** In corporate law, one with confidential information or access thereto, often relating to corporate acts to be carried out that will likely affect the market value of the **securities** of the **corporation.**

The *Canada Business Corporations Act*, R.S.C. 1985, c. C–44, s. 131(1), defines *insider* as (*a*) the corporation; (*b*) an affiliate of the corporation; (*c*) a **director** or an **officer** of the corporation; (*d*) a person who **beneficially** owns more than ten percent of the shares of the corporation or who exercises control or direction over more than ten percent of the votes attached to the **shares** of the corporation; (*e*) a person employed or retained by the corporation; and (*f*) a person who receives specific confidential information from a person described in this subsection or in subsection (3), including a person described in this paragraph, and who has knowledge that the person giving the information is a person described in this subsection or in subsection (3), including a person described in this paragraph."

Subsection (3) deals with **persons** deemed to be insiders. For the purpose of this section, (*a*) if a body corporate becomes an insider of a corporation, or enters into a business combination with a corporation, a director or officer of the body corporate is **deemed** to have been an insider of the corporation for the previous six months or for such shorter period as he was a director or an officer of the body corporate; and (*b*) if a corporation becomes an insider of a body corporate, or enters into a business combination with a body corporate, a director or an officer of the body corporate is deemed to have been an insider of the corporation for the

previous six months or for such shorter period as he was a director or officer of the body corporate.

INSOLVENCY 1. Inability to meet financial **obligations** as they mature in the ordinary course of business; **2.** excess of **liabilities** over **assets** at any given time.

The federal government has jurisdiction for the administrative control of **bankruptcy** and insolvency under s. 42 of the *Constitution Act, 1867.* The *Bankruptcy and Insolvency Act,* R.S.C. 1985, c. B–3, s. 2, defines an "insolvent person" as "a person who is not bankrupt and who resides or carries on business in Canada, whose liabilities to **creditors** provable as **claims** under this Act amount to one thousand dollars, and

(*a*) who is for any reason unable to meet his obligations as they generally become due, or

(*b*) who has ceased paying his current obligations in the ordinary course of business as they generally become due, or

(*c*) the aggregate of whose **property** is not, at a fair valuation, sufficient, or, if disposed of at a fairly conducted sale under legal process, would not be sufficient to enable payment of all his obligations, due and accruing due."

INSOLVENCY   PROCEEDINGS See **bankruptcy.**

IN SPECIE *(ĭn spē'-shē)* Lat.: in kind; in like form. For example, to repay a loan *in specie* is to return the same kind of goods to the lender as were borrowed.

INSPECTION OF DOCUMENTS The right of a **party** to view and copy documents in the possession of the court or of the adverse party essential to the adverse party's **cause of action.** This is done as part of the **discovery** process before trial; but, apart from the production for pretrial inspection, a party may by the use of a SUBPOENA DUCES TECUM (see **subpoena**) require the production of documents at the time of trial for the purpose of introducing them into **evidence.** See, e.g., r. 30.10, *Ontario Rules of Civil Procedure*, R.R.O. 1990, Reg. 194.

Inspection of documents in criminal matters is governed by the *Criminal Code*, R.S.C. 1985, c. C–46, ss. 603–604; inspection of exhibits comes under ss. 490(15) and 605.

INSTALLMENT A portion of a **debt;** a part or portion of the total sum or quantity due. When a debt is divided into two or more parts, payable at different times, each part is called an installment, and the debt is said to be payable by installments.

On whether a discontinuity in the installments amounts to a **breach of contract** to such an extent that the innocent party has a right to repudiate the contract as a whole, it has been said that the chief considerations are "first, the ratio quantitatively which the breach bears to the contract as a whole, and secondly, the degree of probability or improbability that such a breach will be repeated." *Maple Flock Co. Ltd.* v. *Universal Furniture Products (Wembley) Ltd.,* [1934] 1 K.B. 148 at 157 (C.A.). It has also been recognised that the further the parties have proceeded in the performance of the contract the more difficult it is to infer that a breach represents a complete repudiation of the contract. *Cornwall* v. *Henson,* [1900] 2 Ch. 298 at 304; followed in *Webber* v. *Havill* (1965), 47 D.L.R. (2d) 36 (N.S.S.C.).

IN STATU QUO (*in stă'-tū kwō*) Lat.: in the former situation or condition. For example, in a **contract,** "in statu quo [ante]" means being placed in the same position in which a **party** was at the time of the inception of the contract sought to be **rescinded.**

INSTRUCTION Directions given by the judge to the **jury** prior to its deliberations, informing them of the law applicable to the facts of the **case** before them, to guide them in reaching a correct verdict according to law and the **evidence;** the **charge** to the jury by the judge.

INSTRUMENT 1. "[A] formal legal document whereby a right is created or confirmed, or a fact recorded; a formal writing of any kind as an agreement, **deed,** charter, or record drawn up and executed in technical form." *Re Lambert Island Ltd. & Attorney-General of Ont.,* [1972] 2 O.R. 659 at 666 (H.C.). **2.** In the law of **evidence,** the term has a still wider meaning, including also **witnesses** and things animate and inanimate that may be presented for inspection by the **tribunal.**

INSURABLE INTEREST The pecuniary relationship that a person has in the subject matter of an insurance policy, which is necessary to support the issuance of the policy. "Any **title** or **interest** in the **property,** legal or equitable, will support a **contract** of **insurance** on such property. The term 'interest' as used in the phrase 'insurable interest' is not limited to property or ownership in the subject matter of the insurance. Where the interest of the **insured** in, or his relation to, the property is such that he will be benefited by its continued existence or suffer a direct pecuniary injury by its loss, his contract of insurance will be upheld, although he has no legal or equitable **title**." *Barcha* v. *Atlas Assurance Co. Ltd.,* [1924] 2 W.W.R. 467 at 471 (Alta.S.C.).

INSURANCE "[A]n undertaking [by] one [party] to **indemnify** another [party] for an agreed **consideration,** from loss or liability in respect of an event, the happening of which is uncertain." It is not essential that the insured party have an interest in the thing insured. *Re Bendix Automotive Ltd. & U.A.W.* (1971), 20 D.L.R. (3d) 151 at 157 (Ont.H.C.). "[A]n **insurer** taking the risk of loss in consideration of the **insured** paying a premium." *McClenaghan* v. *City of Edmonton,* [1926] 1 D.L.R. 1042 at 1052 (Alta.S.C.).

"Insurance is a **contract** upon speculation. The special facts upon which the contingent chance is to be computed lie most commonly in the knowledge of the insured only: the **under-writer** trusts to his representation, and proceeds upon confidence that he does not keep back any circumstance in his knowledge, to mislead the under-writer into a belief that the circumstance does not exist, and to induce him to estimate the risk, as if it did not exist. The keeping back of such circumstance is a fraud, and therefore the policy is **void**." *Taylor* v. *London Assurance,* [1934] O.R. 273 at 280 (C.A.). See also, e.g., *The Insurance Act,* R.S.O. 1990, c. I. 8.

INSURED One who obtains **insurance** on **property** or upon whose life insurance is obtained. Includes one who claims or may later claim to be an insured even though such claim may already have been contested by the **insurer.** *Winfield* v. *Walker* (1968), 65 W.W.R. 176 (B.C.C.A.).

INSURER The **underwriter** or insurance company that issues the policy of **insur-**

ance for valuable **consideration.** "The person who undertakes or agrees or offers to undertake a contract" of insurance. *The Insurance Act,* R.S.O. 1990, c. I. 8, s. 1

INTANGIBLE PROPERTY Property that in itself has no value, but that simply represents value, e.g., **stock certificates, bonds, promissory notes, franchises,** etc.

INTEGRATION 1. The process by which the parties to an agreement adopt a writing or writings as the full and final expression of their agreement; **2.** the writing **or** writings so adopted. Thus where the parties to a contract have agreed to it as an integration, **parol evidence** is not **admissible** to supplement or vary its terms.

INTENT A state of mind wherein **the** person knows and desires the consequences of his act that, for purposes of criminal **liability,** must exist at the time the alleged offence is committed. It is also the existence of intelligent will, the mind being fully aware of the nature and consequence of the act that is about to be done and with such knowledge and with full liberty of action willing and electing to do it. *R.* v. *Morrison* (1916), 28 D.L.R. 113 at 117 (N.S.S.C.).

"Motive." *Ross Bros. Ltd.* v. *Pearson* (1905), 1 W.L.R. 338 at 342 (N.W.T.C.A.).

Two general classes of intent exist **in** the criminal law: GENERAL INTENT, which must exist in all crimes, and SPECIFIC INTENT, which is essential to certain crimes and which, as an essential element of the crime, must be proved **beyond a reasonable doubt.**

See *Criminal Code,* R.S.C. 1985, c. C–46, s. 21 (common intention) and s. 59 (seditious intention). See **animo; mens rea; scienter.**

INTER ALIA *(ĭn'-tĕr ā'-lē-â)* Lat.: among other things. "It is submitted that the words *'inter alia'* contemplate new terms ... we should not translate these Latin words by substituting the English words 'amongst others.' 'Alia' in classical Latin is an adjective and a fitting translation would be 'among other things.' It does not mean nor should we so translate it 'amongst other terms.' The draftsman did not intend to thrust upon the opposite party new terms not agreed to. He did expect that it would be necessary to amplify but not to alter." *British American*

Timber Co. Ltd. v. *Elk River Timber Co. Ltd.,* [1934] 2 W.W.R. 658 at 673 (B.C.C.A.).

INTEREST 1. In commercial law, **consideration** or **compensation** paid for the use of money loaned or forbearance in demanding it when due. "[A]s a class of subject within exclusive Federal competence under s. 91(19) of the B.N.A. Act [interest] is a precise and unambiguous term, and in the absence of any contrary indication should be expounded in its natural and ordinary sense. It is not restricted to compensation determinable by application of a rate *per centum* to the principal amount of a loan, but covers compensation for the use of money by way of a fixed sum whether denominated a bonus, discount or premium, provided it is referable to principal money or to an obligation to pay money." *Re Unconscionable Transactions Relief Act, etc.* (1962), 35 D.L.R. (2d) 449 (Ont.C.A.) per headnote. The term includes compensation for use of property other than money. *Singer* v. *Goldhar* (1924), 55 O.L.R. 267 at 270 (A.D.). See *Interest Act,* R.S.C. 1985, c. I–15. **2.** In legal practice, the term connotes concern for the advantage or disadvantage of a party to the cause of action. Interest is a factor affecting the credibility of **witnesses.** Having such a concern is a requirement for the intervention of a third party in a lawsuit; it is also a ground for disqualifying a judge or juror. **3.** "The relation of being objectively concerned in something, by having a right or **title** to, a claim upon, or a share in a Legal concern *in* a thing; especially right or title to **property....**" *Re Canequip Exports Ltd. and Smith* (1972), 8 C.C.C. (2d) 360 at 362 (Man.Q.B.).

ADVERSE IN INTEREST A flexible term meaning pecuniary interest or some other SUBSTANTIAL INTEREST (see following) in the subject matter of **litigation.** *Menzies* v. *McLeod* (1915), 34 O.L.R. 572 (in chambers).

BENEFICIAL INTEREST The benefit resulting from an interest in an estate that is less than legal ownership or control; the interest of the beneficiary as opposed to the interest of the **trustee** who holds legal **title;** the EQUITABLE INTEREST (see following) in property held in **trust** that the **beneficiary** may enforce against the trustee according to the terms of the trust. In a trust, the beneficial equitable interest must be distinct from the legal interest, or a **merger** will occur and the effort by the creator of the trust (**settlor**) to create separate legal and equitable interests in particular property will be ineffective. See *Re Rispin* (1912), 25 O.L.R. 633 (C.A.); *Elgin Loan & Savings Co.* v. *National Trust Co.* (1903), 7 O.L.R. 1, affirmed (1905), 10 O.L.R. 41 (C.A.). See also Waters, *The Nature of the Trust Beneficiary's Interest,* 45 Can. Bar Rev. 219 (1967).

EQUITABLE INTEREST "Such an interest as a **Court of Equity** can pursue and appropriate to the discharge of debts." "[A]n assignment for value of property to be acquired or to come into existence [at a later time] **binds** the property when it comes into existence, and confers an equitable interest. *Tennant* v. *Rhineland* (1917), 38 D.L.R. 271 at 275 (Man.C.A.).

EXECUTED INTEREST An interest in property presently enjoyed and possessed by a party.

EXECUTORY INTEREST One that may become actual at some future date or upon the happening of some contingency.

PROPRIETARY INTEREST Interest as an owner; a legal right or **title.** *Reid* v. *Morwick* (1918), 42 O.L.R. 224 at 237 (C.A.). Any right in relation to a **chattel** that enables one to retain its **possession** indefinitely or for a period of time.

PUBLIC INTEREST A flexible term whose meaning, depending on the circumstances, may refer to the public as a whole or to individual sectors. *Re City of Portage la Prairie and Inter-City Gas Utilities Ltd.* (1970), 12 D.L.R. (3d) 388 (Man.C.A.).

SHIFTING INTEREST An interest created by cutting short one **freehold estate** in favor of another (not the **grantor**) as may occur in estates subject to a **condition** subsequent if certain events occur. Such shifts were illegal at common law. See further A. Sinclair, *Introduction to Real Property Law* 69–70 (3d ed. 1987).

SPRINGING INTEREST "[O]ne that comes from a grantor in the future (as it must be where the **remainder** is **contingent** freehold and not preceded by a freehold in another **grantee**)." *Id.* at 69. Such springs were illegal at common law.

SUBSTANTIAL INTEREST In commercial law, a "large quantity" or "considerable amount of **shares**"; need not be a controlling interest. *Manning Timber Products Ltd.* v. *Min. of Nat. Revenue,* [1952] 2 S.C.R. 481.

VESTED INTEREST One in which there is a present fixed right of present or future **enjoyment** that carries with it a right of **alienation,** even though the right to possession or enjoyment may be postponed to some uncertain time in the future. See **interest.**

INTERIM Connotes a definite period of time with a fixed beginning and ending; not strictly interchangeable with **interlocutory.** *Century Eng'r Co.* v. *Greto,* [1961] O.R. 85 at 90 (H.C.).

INTERIM ORDER A temporary order, made until another or FINAL ORDER (see **order**) takes its place or a specific **event** occurs. See also **interlocutory.**

INTERIM RELEASE A judicially ordered conditional release or undertaking of the **accused** as directed by the justice. See *Criminal Code,* R.S.C. 1985, c. C–46, s. 515.

INTERLOCUTORY Not final. An order or judgment is interlocutory if it does not determine the **issues** at trial but directs some further **proceeding** preliminary to a final order or **decree.** Such order or judgment is subject to change by the court during the pendency of the action to meet the exigencies of the case.

INTERLOCUTORY DECREE See **decree.**

INTERLOCUTORY ORDER Any order made before the final disposition of the case. *Century Eng'r Co.* v. *Greto,* [1961] O.R. 85 at 90 (H.C.). Not merely an order between **writ** and **final judgment** but an order other than final judgment. *Nelles* v. *Windsor, Essex and Lake Shore Rapid Ry.* (1908), 16 O.L.R. 359 at 363 (Div.Ct.).

INTERNATIONAL LAW The system of law that governs relations between states; also known as "the law of nations" or "public international law." Article 38(1) of the Statute of the International Court of Justice provides:

The Court, whose function is to decide in accordance with international law such disputes as are submitted to it, shall apply:

(*a*) international conventions, whether general or particular, establishing rules expressly recognized by the contesting states;

(b) international custom, as evidence of a general practice accepted as law;

(c) the general principles of law recognized by civilized nations; ◡

(d) ... judicial decisions and the teachings of the most highly qualified publicists of the various nations, as subsidiary means for the determination of rules of law.

S. Rosenne, *Documents on the International Court of Justice* 61–89 (3d ed. 1991).

This is frequently regarded as the main statement of the sources of international law. See further M. Akehurst, *A Modern Introduction to International Law* (6th ed. 1987), chap. 3.

INTER PARES *(ĭn'-tĕr pär'-ās)* Lat.: among peers; among those of equal rank.

INTER PARTES *(ĭn'-tĕr pär'-tās)* Lat.: between the parties.

INTERPLEADER An equitable **action in** which a **debtor,** not knowing to whom among his **creditors** a certain debt is owed, and having no **claim** or stake in the property in dispute other than its proper disposition, will petition a court to require that creditors litigate the claim among themselves. It is used to avoid double or multiple **liability** on the part of the debtor. Interpleader is often used by insurance carriers, who deposit the proceeds of a policy in a court where several **persons** with conflicting rights have made claims.

Similarly, where goods, etc., taken in execution by a sheriff are claimed by a third person, the sheriff may apply for interpleader relief. Compare **joinder.**

INTERPROVINCIAL TRADE AND COMMERCE 1. Intercourse and traffic between citizens or inhabitants of different provinces; **2.** A federal head of power under the *Constitution Act, 1867.*

INTERROGATION An informal term used to describe the process by which suspects are rigorously questioned by police.

INTERROGATORIES In **civil actions** in some provinces, a pre-trial **discovery** tool in which written questions are propounded by a **party** to the action and served on another **person,** who must give written replies under oath. See, e.g., *Nova Scotia Civil Procedure Rules* (1983), r. 19.

INTERVENING CAUSE See **cause.**

INTER VIVOS *(ĭn'-tĕr vē'-vōs)* Lat.: between the living. Transactions *inter vivos* are those made while the **parties** are living, and not upon death (as in the case of **inheritance**) or upon contemplation of death (CAUSA MORTIS). A **deed,** therefore, is an **instrument** that conveys *inter vivos* a present **interest** in land or that conveys the **corpus** of a **trust** to the **trustees** [A DEED OF TRUST].

GIFT INTER VIVOS See **gift** [GIFT INTER VIVOS].

INTESTATE [INTESTACY] The condition of having died without leaving a valid **will.** Intestate property (i.e., undevised **property**) is that which a **testator** has failed to dispose of by will. Thus, an intestate estate is that left upon the death of a devisee to whom a testator willed a **life estate** without providing for the **remainder.**

INTESTATE SUCCESSION The disposition of property according to the laws of **descent** and distribution upon the death of a person who has left no **will** or who has left a portion of his **estate** unaccounted for. See **heirs; intestate.** See e.g., *Succession Law Reform Act,* R.S.O. 1990. c. S. 26.

IN TOTO *(ĭn tō'-tō)* Lat.: in entirety; e.g., to repay a debt *in toto.*

INTOXICATION State of drunkenness or inebriation. In the criminal law, voluntary intoxication is no **defence** against crimes of "general **intent,**" but may operate to refute the existence of **mens rea** necessary for crimes of "specific intent." *R.* v. *George,* [1960] S.C.R. 871. Intoxication may also be a mitigating factor reducing punishment meted out for certain crimes. Involuntary intoxication will render an actor's conduct involuntary and thereby allow him to avoid criminal **liability.** Compare **incompetency.** See *Criminal*

Code, R.S.C. 1985, c. C–46, ss. 253 (care and control of a motor vehicle, vessel, aircraft, or railway equipment while impaired by alcohol or drug); 212(1)(*i*) (use of intoxicating liquor to stupefy a person in order to have illicit sexual intercourse with that person). See **impaired [driving]**.

INTRA VIRES *(ĭn'-trà vī'-rāz)* Lat.: within the powers. See *ultra vires*.

INTRINSIC FRAUD See **fraud**.

INURE To take effect, to operate; to serve to the use, benefit, or advantage of someone, in **property**, to **vest**.

INVEST To place **capital** with a view to securing income or profit.

There are two connotations in which the word *investing* can be used: the purchase of articles or property (1) for the income that can be obtained from them and (2) with the view to their resale. *First Torland Investments Ltd.* v. *M.N.R.*, [1969] C.T.C. 134 at 151–52 (Ex.).

INVITEE One who comes upon another's land by the latter's express or implied invitation. The term "is reserved for those who are invited into the premises by the owner or occupier for some purpose of business or of material interest." *McLean* v. *Y.M.C.A.*, [1918] 3 W.W.R. 522 at 526 (Alta.C.A.). In **tort** law, the owner is not an insurer of the safety of invitees, but he owes a **duty** to them to exercise reasonable care for protection against latent defects in the premises that might cause injury. Compare **licensee; trespass**. See provincial *Occupiers Liability Acts*.

INVOLUNTARY BAILMENT See **bailment**.

IPSE DIXIT *(ĭp'-sā dĭks'-ĭt)* Lat.: he himself said it. An assertion the sole authority for which is that the speaker himself has said it.

IPSO FACTO *(ĭp'-sō făk'-tō)* Lat.: by the fact itself; in and of itself. "The sale of his property should ipso facto end any interest he may have in it."

IPSO JURE *(ĭp'-sō jū'-rä)* Lat.: by the law itself; merely by the law.

IRREPARABLE INJURY "All that is meant is that the injury would be a material one, and one which could not be ade-quately remedied by **damages**." The term does not mean there must be no physical possibility of repairing the injury. *Humphreys* v. *Pollock* (1946), 19 M.P.R. 72 at 74 (N.B.S.C.).

Where the **plaintiff** in an **injunction** action establishes that the acts of the **defendant** have caused damage of an unascertainable amount, it may be said he has made out a case of irreparable injury. *Spooner Oils Ltd.* v. *Turner Valley Gas Conservation Board (No. 2)*, [1932] 4 D.L.R. 681 at 687 (Alta.C.A.).

ISSUE **1.** As a verb, to put into circulation; to send out, as to a buyer. With reference to **shares**, it is a word with no definite legal import. *Anglo-American Lumber Co.* v. *McLellan* (1908), 14 B.C.R. 93 (C.A.).

2. In the law of wills and real property, *issue* means descendants—all persons **descended** from a common ancestor may be regarded as issue. Some jurisdictions restrict issue to only "lawful, lineal descendants . . ." See, e.g., *Wills Act*, R.S.N.S. 1989, c. 505. It became a matter of judicial interpretation whether a reference to "issue" or "child" could refer to an **illegitimate** child. See, e.g., *Re Brand* (1957), 7 D.L.R. (2d) 579 (Ont.H.C.). New rights are being accorded to the illegitimate child with respect to both wills and **intestacy** situations. The *Intestate Succession Act*, R.S.A. 1980, c I–9, as amended, provides issue to include "all lineal descendants, whether born within or outside marriage, of the ancestor." See also *Surette* v. *Harris* (1989), 91 N.S.R. (2d) 419, where section 15 of the *Intestate Succession Act*, R.S.N.S. 1967, c 153, was found unconstitutional because it discriminated against illegitimate children in intestacy situations.

3. In legal practice, an issue is a single certain point of fact or law disputed (or AT ISSUE) between **parties** to a **litigation**, generally composed of an affirmative assertion by one side and a denial by the other.

ISSUED CAPITAL "[T]he number of shares issued and alloted by a company . . ." D. Horsley, H. Sutherland & J.M. Edmiston, *Fraser's Handbook on Canadian Company Law* 41 (7th ed. 1985). See **capital**. See also *Business Corporations Act*, R.S.O. 1990, c. B. 16, s. 23.

J

JD Juris doctor. American undergraduate law degree (formerly conferred as an LL.B).

JOBBER A middleman in the sale of goods; one who sells to anyone at a fraction above the market price and buys off anyone at a fraction below market. *Mollett* v. *Robinson* (1872), L.R. 7 C.P. 84 at 104–05. Jobbing "possibly means something more than selling by retail and less than selling by wholesale." *Cook* v. *Shaw* (1895), 25 O.R. 124 at 126 (Ch.D.). As distinguished from a **broker** or **agent**, who sells goods on another's behalf, a jobber actually purchases the goods himself and then resells them. Compare **wholesaler.**

JOINDER 1. Uniting of two or more causes of action or parties in a single suit; 2. joining another party in a legal step or proceeding. See **class action; interpleader; real party in interest.** Compare **misjoinder.**

COMPULSORY JOINDER The mandatory joining of a **person** who must be made a party with others in an action under certain circumstances because his participation is necessary for a just adjudication of the **controversy.** See G. Watson, *Canadian Civil Procedure* 628 (3d ed. 1988). A party must join all of his related claims against another or face the possibility of being barred from litigating them separately on the grounds that such action constitutes **multiplicity of suits.** If he is the defendant, a party must raise related claims as compulsory **counterclaims** in an analogous situation.

JOINDER OF CAUSES OF ACTION The joining of several **causes of action** in one without leave where the plaintiff claims and defendant is **alleged** to be **liable** in the same capacity in respect of all causes of action *or* if plaintiff claims and defendant is alleged to be liable in the capacity of **executor** or **administrator** of an **estate** in respect of one or more causes of action and in his personal capacity with reference to the same estate in respect of others.

JOINDER OF PARTIES The joining of all persons in one action as plaintiffs or defendants where the claim is in respect of the same transaction or series of transactions and where common questions of law or fact arise. See *id.* at 610.

PERMISSIVE JOINDER The joining of persons under certain circumstances, as plaintiff or defendants, in an action until such persons can sue or be sued separately. The interests of judicial economy encourage a party to raise as many unrelated claims in a single lawsuit as he may have against another party, with the court "severing" those that ought not to be tried together. See *id.* at 615.

Also, see *Criminal Code,* R.S.C. 1985, c. C–46, ss. 592–593., referring to joinder of **accused** in certain criminal cases—e.g., ACCESSORIES AFTER THE FACT (see **accessory**), having in possession.

JOINT United, combined; a common as opposed to an individual interest or liability.

JOINT ACCOUNT A bank account in two or more names, consisting of funds held in **joint tenancy;** an account upon which cheques can be drawn or withdrawals made by both parties or either of them; such an account is incapable of being attached at common law for a judgment debt recovered against one party only. *Hirschorn* v. *Evans,* [1938] 2 K.B. 801 (C.A.).

JOINT AND SEVERAL The condition in which rights and **liabilities** are shared among a group of persons collectively and also individually . Thus, if **defendants** in a **negligence suit** are jointly and severally liable, all may be sued together or any one may be sued for full **satisfaction** to the injured party. Compare **severally.**

"[Jointly and severally liable] in ordinary cases means that all must be proceeded against in the one suit who are liable, or each one separately in his suit." *M'Kenzie* v. *Dewan* (1875), 36 U.C.Q.B. 512 at 522.

See **contribution; indemnity.**

JOINT CUSTODY An order by the court in which, for example, **custody** of a child is awarded to both parties, but care and control is awarded to only one.

JOINT LIABILITY Shared liability that results in the right of any one party sued to insist that others be sued with him;

e.g., see *Tortfeasors Act,* R.S.N. 1989, c. 471, s. 5.

JOINT STOCK COMPANY An older term suggesting a company of association, usually unincorporated, that has the capital of its members pooled in a common fund; the capital stock is divided into **shares** and distributed to represent ownership **interest** in the company. A form of partnership that is distinguished from a partnership in the ordinary sense in that the membership of a joint stock company is changeable, its shares are transferable, its members can be many and not necessarily known to each other and its members cannot act or speak for the company.

JOINT TENANCY See **tenancy.**

JOINT TORTFEASORS Two or more persons who owe to another person the same **duty** and whose **negligence** results in injury to such other person, thus rendering the tortfeasors both **jointly and severally** (individually) **liable** for the injury; the parties must either act in concert or by independent acts unite in causing a single injury. See *Tortfeasors Act,* R.S.N.S. 1989, c. 471; *Negligence Act,* R.S.O. 1990, c. N. 1. See also **concerted action; contribution.** Compare **conspiracy.**

JOINTURE An **estate** or **property** secured to a prospective wife as a marriage settlement, to be enjoyed by her after her husband's decease. The estate existed under the **common law** as a means of protecting the wife's future, upon her husband's death, in lieu of **dower.** Compare **curtesy.**

JOINT VENTURE A business undertaking by two or more parties in which profits, losses and control are shared. Though the term is often considered synonymous with **partnership,** a joint venture may connote an enterprise of a more limited scope and duration, though there is the same sort of mutual **liability.** Compare **corporation.**

JSD Doctor of Laws degree.

JUDGE-MADE LAW Law made in the **common-law** tradition; law arrived at by judicial **precedent** rather than by **statute.** See **stare decisis.** Also, judicial **construction** of statutes so different from their original legislative intent that the resulting application of them can be attributed to the **judiciary,** rather than to the legislature.

JUDGMENT The determination of a court of competent **jurisdiction** upon matters submitted to it. "The sentence of the law is pronounced by the Court upon the matter contained in the record." *Lang* v. *Victoria* (1898), 6 B.C.R. 117 at 119 (S.C.).

Also, "any decision made by a Judge in the course of a trial with or without a jury, which may materially affect its result and lead to an acquittal." (*R.* v. *Hutchinson,* [1939] 1 W.W.R. 545 at 550 (Sask.C.A.).

"In the judgment of the Magistrate ... means ... opinion, based upon something not necessarily technically legal evidence adduced by the prosecution or defence." *Rex* v. *Power* (1922), 62 D.L.R. 470 at 478 (Alta.S.C.A.D.).

"Judgment" in the phrase "the seller's skill or judgment" includes any knowledge the seller has acquired relating to the goods. *Winslow* v. *Jenson,* [1920] 3 W.W.R. 856 (Alta.C.A.).

DEFAULT JUDGMENT [JUDGMENT BY DEFAULT] "When served with the originating process in an **action** the **defendant** must respond within the time specified in the Rules. The nature of the required response will depend upon the rules of the particular **jurisdiction.** If the originating process is a **statement of claim** then the defendant will be required to **deliver** . . . a **statement of defence** within the specified time. Where the originating process is a **writ of summons** the defendant is required to file an **appearance.** . . . The failure of the defendant to make a timely response in the required manner has serious consequences. It permits the **plaintiff** to take **default proceedings.** . . . If the plaintiff's claim is for a debt or liquidated demand . . . or for the possession of property he or she will be entitled to an immediate **judgment in default**— without a trial or any consideration of the merits of his claim by the court." G. Watson, *Canadian Civil Procedure,* 352 (3d ed. 1988). Compare **ex parte.**

FINAL JUDGMENT One that fully determines any action or judicial proceeding so that all that remains to be done is **execute** the judgment. *Spelman* v. *Spelman,* [1943] 3 W.W.R. 181 (B.C.C.A.). As defined in the *Supreme Court Act,*

R.S.C. 1985, c. S–26, s. 2(1), a final judgment is a decision that determines in whole or in part any substantive right of parties to a dispute in a judicial proceeding.

A final judgment is conclusive against the plaintiff if awarded for the defendant, and vice versa; however, it does not mean that any other legal recourse is precluded. If a superior court exists, the matter may be taken up on **appeal.** See also *Wolverton & Co. Ltd.* v. *Hooper* (1972), 24 D.L.R. (3d) 567 (B.C.C.A.).

JUDGMENT IN REM An adjudication pronounced upon the status of some particular subject matter [as distinguished from one pronounced upon persons] by a tribunal having competent authority for that purpose. *Rex* v. *Ashall*, [1946] O.R. 397 at 402 (C.A.).

JUDGMENT N.O.V. [NON OBSTANTE VEREDICTO] *(nŏn ŏb-stăn'-tā vĕ-rĕ-dĭk'-tō)* Lat.: notwithstanding the verdict. A judgment reversing the determination of the jury that is granted when it is obvious that the jury verdict had no reasonable support in fact or was contrary to law—i.e., the jury verdict was perverse based on the evidence before it. The motion for a judgment n.o.v. provides a second chance for the trial court to render what is, in effect, a **directed verdict** for the moving party.

JUDGMENT OF CONVICTION The **sentence** in a criminal **case** formally entered in the clerk's records.

SUMMARY JUDGMENT "[A] **motion** for a final **judgment** in which the parties put forward **affidavit** evidence with the moving party attempting to establish that there is no 'triable issue' or no 'genuine issue of fact requiring a trial' and that he or she is entitled to judgment as a matter of law." G. Watson, *Canadian Civil Procedure* 426–27 (3d ed. 1988). One example is the procedure by which a court may dismiss an **action** considered to be frivolous or vexatious.

JUDGMENT CREDITOR A creditor who has obtained **judgment** against a **debtor** by which he can enforce **execution.**

JUDGMENT DEBTOR A debtor who has had a **judgment** entered against him by a **creditor** and who is liable to enforcement of the judgment by an order of **execution.**

JUDICATURE The judiciary; the area of government that was intended to interpret and administer the law.

JUDICATURE ACTS Statutes that organize the system of courts and delineate the **jurisdiction** thereof. The English *Supreme Court of Judicature Act, 1873* amalgamated the then existing superior courts into the Supreme Court of Judicature, consisting of the Court of Appeal and High Court of Justice. It also provided for the fusion of law and **equity,** with the supremacy of equity in case of conflict. See the provincial *Judicature Acts.*

JUDICIAL DECISION See **decision**.

JUDICIAL DISCRETION See **discretion.**

JUDICIAL ERROR A judgment erroneous in some aspect; an act performed by the court that is in error. Some mistake in the foundation, proceeding, **judgment,** execution of an **action** in a court of record requiring correction either by the court in which it occurred (error of fact) or by a superior court (**error of law**).

JUDICIAL NOTICE The court's recognition of certain facts that can be confirmed by consulting sources of indisputable accuracy, thereby relieving one party of the burden of producing **evidence** to prove these facts. A court can use this doctrine to admit as "proved" such facts that are common knowledge to a judicial professional or to an average, well-informed citizen—e.g., that the mail is not delivered New Year's Day.

"I take judicial notice to mean the taking a thing as proved without requiring or receiving any proof of that thing ... [A] judicial notice is not taken as a matter of evidence to be submitted to the jury, but as a matter of fact sufficiently taken to be established." *Junkin* v. *Davis* (1857), 6 U.C.C.P. 408 (C.A.).

JUDICIAL REVIEW A superior court's examination of the conduct of an inferior court, board, committee, or **tribunal,** to ensure the conduct was proper in law (distinct from **appeal**). The supervisory jurisdiction of the common-law courts existing before 1867 was continued by s. 129 of the **British North America Act** (now *Constitution Act, 1867*). Since Confederation, provincial legislation has conferred the power of judicial review on provincial superior courts. However, the Privy Council held in *Board* v. *Board*, [1919] A.C. 956, that such jurisdiction exists even in the absence of express legislative enactment. With respect to federal courts, the Privy Council held in *Bow, MacLachlan & Co.* v. *The Camosun*, [1909] A.C. 597, that, in the absence of federal legislative authority, there is no common-law jurisdiction for judicial review.

In the area of administrative law, the superior courts will intervene and grant a remedy where a statutory decision-maker has acted in an area outside the scope of authority conferred by the empowering statute. "The jurisdiction of the Supreme Court [of Ontario] over courts of inferior jurisdiction ... is for the purpose ... of compelling the tribunal to exercise its true function, and, ... to prevent any court of limited jurisdiction from exercising or attempting to assert a jurisdiction which it does not possess." *Rex* v. *Spence* (1919), 31 C.C.C. 365 at 378 (Ont.S.C.A.D.).

JUDICIAL SALE See **sheriff's sale.**

JUMP BAIL A colloquial expression meaning to leave the **jurisdiction** or to avoid **appearance** as a **defendant** in a **criminal** trial after **bail** has been posted, thus causing a forfeiture of bail; to **abscond** after the posting of bail.

JURAT *(jŭr′-ät)* Lat.: has been sworn. The clause at the end of an **affidavit** or other legal document stating when, where and by whom it was sworn.

JURISDICTION **1.** The power to hear and determine a case; the power of a court or judge to entertain an **action, petition** or other **proceeding. 2.** Also, the district or limits within which the **judgments** or orders of the court can be enforced or executed. In general, the court may take cognizance of acts committed or arising abroad, but, in practice, the defendant must be within the jurisdiction when the **writ** is served, except where leave is given for service out of the jurisdiction. Jurisdiction may be over subject matter, parties or location. In addition to having the power to adjudicate, a valid exercise of jurisdiction requires fair notice and an opportunity to be heard. The absence of any essential element of jurisdiction will render the judgment **void.** *Harris* v. *Law*

Society of Alberta, [1936] 1 D.L.R. 401 (S.C.C.).

In sense 2, the word is used to refer to particular legal systems, as in "the law varies in different jurisdictions," and to territorial entities (coupled with authority to reach conduct within the territory) as in "within the jurisdiction of *X* province."

Jurisdiction may be exercised through **actions in personam** and **actions in rem** judgments. With in personam judgments the jurisdiction is over the defendant's person where there is legal authority to enter money judgments against him. Judgments from in rem actions involve the jurisdiction of the court over property where the court has the legal authority to determine rights in the property. F. James, G. Hazard & J. Leubsdorf, *Civil Procedure* 58 (4th ed. 1992).

An action *in rem* is a proceeding to determine the status or condition of the thing itself. *Fry* v. *Botsford & MacQuillan* (1902), 9 B.C.R. 234 (S.C.).

ADMIRALTY AND MARITIME JURISDICTION See **admiralty and maritime jurisdiction.**

APELLATE JURISDICTION The power vested in a superior **tribunal** to correct legal errors of an inferior tribunal and to revise their **judgments** accordingly.

CONCURRENT JURISDICTION Equal jurisdiction; that jurisdiction exercised by different courts at the same time, over the same subject matter and within the same territory, and wherein litigants may, in the first instance, resort to either court indifferently. The phrase is also used in constitutional law to refer to the situation where both provincial and federal governments have power to legislate in a given area.

JURIS IGNORANTIA EST CUM JUS NOSTRAM IGNORAMUS *(jū′-rĭs ĭg-nō-rän′-shē-à ĕst kŭm jŭs nōs′-träm ĭg-nō-rä′-mŭs)* Lat.: it is ignorance of the law when we are unfamiliar with our own rights.

JURISPRUDENCE **1.** The science of law; the philosophy of law; the study of the structure of legal systems, i.e., of form, as distinguished from content. **2.** A term denoting the collective course of judicial decisions; **3.** incorrectly used as a synonym for "law." See R. Pound, 1 *Jurisprudence* 7–9 (1959).

JURIST 1. A legal scholar; one versed in law, particularly the **civil law** or the law of nations. 2. A judge.

JUROR A person sworn as a member of a jury. 2. A person selected for jury duty, but not yet chosen for a particular case.

JURY A group of people, composed of a cross-section of the community, summoned and sworn to decide on the facts at **issue** in a trial.

GRAND JURY As originally established in England in 1164, the grand jury was a body of local inhabitants required to report all suspected criminals in their district. Introduced into Canada (except Saskatchewan and Alberta) with English law, the grand jury is now abolished in England and Canada, except in Nova Scotia, where it functions as a body of persons, with no prior knowledge of the **crime** allegedly committed, which sits to decide whether the facts and **accusations** presented by the **prosecutor** warrant an **indictment** and eventual trial of the accused. Called "grand" because of the relatively large number of jurors **impaneled** (traditionally twenty-three) as compared with a PETIT JURY.

PETIT [PETTY] JURY An ordinary trial jury, as opposed to a grand jury. Its function is to determine issues of fact in civil and criminal cases and to reach a **verdict** in conjunction with those **findings**. Petit juries have been composed traditionally of twelve members, whose verdict was required to be unanimous. However, today the composition varies, and in some **jurisdictions** a jury hearing a civil matter may consist of six members.

S. 11(*f*) of the **Canadian Charter of Rights and Freedoms** guarantees an accused to a trial by jury, except in the case of an offence under military law. See *R.* v. *Lee*, [1990] 1 W.W.R. 289 (S.C.C.).

See also *Criminal Code* ss. 632-642 (challenge to jury); **hung jury.**

JUST COMPENSATION Full **indemnity** or remuneration for the loss or damage sustained by the owner of property taken or injured under the power of **eminent domain.** It comprises a settlement that leaves the owner no poorer and no richer than he was before the property was taken. The measure generally used is the fair **market value** of the property at the time of taking. Just compensation need not take account of anticipated or possible future profitability, or of sentimental or other non-objective values, but is to be based on the property's value to a willing seller and a willing buyer.

JUS TERTII *(jūs tĕr'-shē-ī)* Lat.: the right of a third **party;** the legal right of a third. The term often appears in the context of **actions** involving claims of **title** to **real property,** wherein it is said that, because a possessor's title is good against all the world except those with a better title, one seeking to **oust** a possessor must do so on the strength of his own title and may not rely on a *jus tertii,* or the better title held by a third party.

JUSTICE OF THE PEACE A judge appointed by the provincial **Lieutenant-Governor** within a certain district to perform a number of limited functions, such as issuing summonses and warrants, taking information, granting bail, etc. The duties of justices of the peace were at one time much more extensive. Consult the various pertinent provincial statutes, such as the *Justices of the Peace Act,* R.S.O. 1990, c. J. 4. Often empowered **ex officio** to be **notaries public** or commissioners of oaths, or to carry out some of the duties of **solicitors** when circumstances require.

JUSTICIABLE Capable of being tried in a court of law or equity. Justiciability is generally a question of feasibility—i.e., whether it is feasible for a court to carry out and enforce its decision—as distinguished from **jurisdiction**—whether a court has the power or authority to hear a case. A court can have jurisdiction but at the same time have a non-justiciable **issue** before it.

JUSTICIABLE CONTROVERSY A real and substantial **controversy** that is appropriate for judicial determination, as distinguished from a hypothetical, contingent or abstract dispute; a dispute that involves legal relations of parties who have real adverse **interests.**

JUSTIFIABLE HOMICIDE See **homicide.**

JUSTIFICATION   1. Just and lawful excuse for an act. **2.** Showing of a sufficient reason in court why **defendant** did what he is called upon to **answer** to, so as to excuse criminal or civil **liability.** The defence of justification or excuse in **criminal** law and **tort** law excuses the defendant from liability for an otherwise criminal or tortious act; e.g., the *Criminal Code*, R.S.C. 1985, c. C–46, stipulates that self-defence is a justifiable course of action to repel a provoked **assault** (s. 34).

In actions for **defamation,** justification is a plea that the words complained of are "true in substance and in fact," which may provide a complete defence to an action in **libel** or **slander.** The defendant must prove that the facts were truly stated and that the **innuendo** is true. He must justify every injurious imputation. *Augustine Automatic Rotary Engine Co.* v. *Saturday Night Ltd.* (1917), 38 O.L.R. 609 (C.A.).

Compare **necessity, defence of.**

JUVENILE COURT [YOUTH COURT] See **youth court.**

JUVENILE DELINQUENT [YOUNG OFFENDER] See **young offender.**

KIDNAP To unlawfully take and carry away a person against his will. Kidnapping is **false imprisonment** with the extra element of movement of the person from one place to another. *R.* v. *Oakley* (1977), 36 C.C.C. (2d) 436 (Alta.S.C.A.D.). See *Criminal Code*, R.S.C. 1985, c. C–46, s. 279.

The original common-law offence was characterized by the requirement that the victim be taken out of the country, hence the reference in the *Criminal Code* to "transported out of Canada against his will." However, the ambit of the offence has been widened considerably. Consent to removal may be vitiated by false statements. *R.* v. *Brown* (1972), 8 C.C.C (2d) 13 (Ont.C.A.). Kidnapping was only a **misdemeanour** at common law but is an **indictable offence** in Canada. Compare **abduction.**

KING'S [QUEEN'S] BENCH Court of King's Bench or Court of Queen's Bench (depending on the reigning monarch); the English **common-law** court, both civil and criminal, so called because the King or Queen formerly presided; now known as the King's Bench or Queen's Bench Division of the High Court of Justice, embracing the **jurisdiction** of the former Courts of Exchequer and Courts of Common Pleas.

KING'S COUNSEL [K.C.] See **Queen's Counsel.**

L

LABOUR UNION See **trade union.**

LACHES An equitable **defence** doctrine, which can be "defined as inexcusable delay in asserting a right, accompanied by some actual or presumable change of circumstances, rendering it inequitable to grant relief." *York* v. *Powell* (1909), 10 W.L.R. 407 at 410 (C.A.).

It "is not an arbitrary or a technical doctrine. Where it would be practically unjust to give a **remedy,** either because the party has by his conduct done that which might fairly be regarded as equivalent to a **waiver** of it, or where, by his conduct and neglect, he has, though perhaps not waiving that remedy, yet put the other party in a situation in which it would not be reasonable to place him if the remedy were afterwards to be asserted; in either of these cases, lapse of time and delay are most material. But in every case, if an argument against relief which otherwise would be just is founded upon mere delay, that delay, of course, not amounting to a **bar** by the Statute of Limitations, the validity of that defence must be tried upon principles substantially equitable. Two circumstances always important in such cases are the length of the delay and the nature of the acts done during the interval, which might affect either **party** and cause a balance of justice or injustice in taking the one course or the other so far as relates to the remedy." *Farrel* v. *Manchester* (1908), 40 S.C.R. 339 at 346.

LAND 1. Broadly, any ground, soil, or earth. 2. More specifically, **real estate** or **real property,** including, also, things of a permanent nature found on the earth or affixed thereto—**tenements, hereditaments,** houses and buildings, *R.* v. *Meunier* (1942), 80 C.C.C. 125 (Que.S.C.); trees, *Laidlaw* v. *Vaughan-Rhys* (1911), 44 S.C.R. 458; mines and minerals, *Re St. Eugene Mining Co.* (1900), 7 B.C.R. 288 (B.C.S.C.). 3. In a limited legal sense, the character of the **estate** or **interest** that the **tenant** owns. "Land" may comprehend rights and interests in land and easements over land. See, e.g., *A. J. Reach*

Co. v. *Crosland* (1918), 45 D.L.R. 140 (Ont.S.C.A.D.).

Thus, the word *land* includes land of any **tenure;** mines and minerals; buildings; parts of buildings; corporeal and incorporeal **hereditaments; easements;** rights; **privileges;** benefit in, over or derived from land but not an individual **share** in land.

LANDLORD One who **leases real property.** The person who is entitled to exact payment of the **rent.** *Re Calgary Brewing & Malting Co.* (1915), 9 W.W.R. 563 at 565 (Alta.S.C.).

See also statutory definitions; e.g., *Landlord and Tenant Act,* R.S.O. 1990, c. L. 7, s. 1: "includes a person who is **lessor,** owner, the person giving or permitting the occupation of the **premises** in question, and these persons' **heirs** and **assigns** and legal representatives, and . . . also includes the person entitled to possession of the premises."

LANGUAGE RIGHTS See **fundamental freedoms.**

LAPSE The termination of a right, privilege, or option through neglect to exercise same within a specified time limit or by failure of a contingency.

When the person to whom property has been **devised** or **bequeathed** dies before the **testator,** the devise or **bequest** fails or lapses, and **property** falls into the residue, except that a lapsed share of residue does not fall into residue but devolves upon **intestacy.**

Proceedings lapse in event of the death of a **defendant** in criminal matters or where no step is taken in an **action** within appropriate time.

LARCENY The common-law crime of stealing, at one time distinguished as grand or petty larceny according to the value of that which was taken. The term **larceny** has been replaced by **theft** and does not appear in the *Criminal Code,* R.S.C. 1985, c. C–46.

LAST ANTECEDENT DOCTRINE In statutory **construction,** the doctrine under which relative or modifying phrases are to be applied only to words immediately preceding them, and are not to be construed as extending to more remote phrases, unless this is clearly required by the context of the statute or the reading of it as a whole.

LAST CHANCE [LAST CLEAR CHANCE]
The doctrine that the person with the last clear chance to avoid the accident, damage, or injury to another is **liable.** A defendant may be liable in **negligence,** notwithstanding the plaintiff's contributory negligence, if he was aware of the plaintiff's negligence and did not exercise **due care** in avoiding it. See *Morris* v. *Hamilton Radial Electric Ry.* (1923), 54 O.L.R. 208 (A.D.); *Dowser* v. *C.N.R.,* [1929] 4 D.L.R. 233 (Alta.S.C.).

LAST WILL AND TESTAMENT See **will.**

LATENT DEFECT A defect that is hidden from knowledge as well as from sight and one that would not be discovered even by the exercise of due diligence or of ordinary and reasonable care. "[N]ot discernible by adequate inspection." *Scottish Metropolitan Ass'ce Co.* v. *Canada Steamship Lines Ltd.,* [1930] 1 D.L.R. 201 at 214 (S.C.C.). Generally, a purchaser assumes the risk for defects evident upon a cursory inspection. However, in contracts for the sale of goods, there are certain **warranties** given by **vendors** that goods sold are fit for the purpose and of merchantable quality. A seller may be held accountable for a latent defect even if he were honest and incapable of discovering the defect. *Chomyn* v. *American Fur Co.,* [1948] 2 W.W.R. 1110 (Sask.Dist.Ct.).

With regard to the sale of **real property,** "the law seems clear that ... there being no fraud ... a latent defect of quality not amounting to a breach of obligation to show a good title is no ground of objection on the purchasers' part unless the vendor expressly or impliedly warranted or promised that the property sold should have the quality [in] which it is deficient." *Scott-Polson and Scott-Polson* v. *Hope* (1958), 14 D.L.R. (2d) 333 at 336 (B.C.S.C.). See also **warranty** [WARRANTY OF HABITABILITY].

LAW A "statute or long-settled principles." *Re Ashley,* [1934] O.R. 421 at 428 (C.A.). "[A] general term which includes not only statutes but also Orders and Regulations made under statutes." *Cooperative Committee on Japanese Canadians* v. *Attorney-General for Canada,* [1947] 1 D.L.R. 577 at 580 (P.C.). "[The] law should be regarded as the core matter which those persons and those institutions in any legal system utilize in order to effect an ongoing process in regulating the affairs and conduct of persons in society." G. Gall, *The Canadian Legal System* 18 (3d ed. 1990). " 'Law' is a word and words have varying uses. Their meanings are to be discovered in the light of their uses . . . they must not be plucked from their contexts . . . Even the differences between speaking of 'law,' speaking of 'the law,' and speaking of 'a law' may be vital . . . The following are paraphrases of some of the definitions of law which have been advanced from time to time over many thousands of years. (1) Law is the will of God expressed in His commands revealed to man through His chosen instruments. Obedience to God's will is the supreme command. (2) Law is in two great parts: Divine law, and human law. They may conflict. Differing theories were developed to explain a person's duty if faced with a conflict between the dictates of the two. (3) Law is the product of humanity's capacity to reason, and it consists of all those principles and rules which, by the use of reason, can be seen to be necessary for, or which can be seen to promote, humanity's peaceful and happy life in a society of human beings. (4) Law is in two great parts: natural law and positive law. Natural law is the product of reason (as in (3) above) whereas positive law is made up of all the rules in force in actual legal systems. The two may sometimes conflict. Differing theories have been developed to explain a person's duty when faced with a conflict between the two. (5) Law is the command of the sovereign. The sovereign is that person, or group of persons, in any independent human society who, owing no obedience to any outside body or person, enjoys the habitual obedience of all persons in that society. (6) Law is the instrument humanity uses in its attempt to achieve justice in society. (7) Law is an instrument of social engineering. (8) Law is an instrument by which capitalist society ensures the suppression of the proletariat. With the establishment of communism law will wither away. (9) Law is what the courts declare to be the law." D. Derham, F. Maher & P. Waller, *An Introduction to Law* 177–78 (6th ed. 1991).

See further G. Gall, *The Canadian Legal System, supra,* chap. 1.

LAW MERCHANT A body of commercial law governing merchants in England, with similar rules existing in other European states. These laws were first enforced by special English mercantile courts and later enforced in **common-law** courts of **law** and **equity**. The law merchant is particularly noted for its contributions to the law of negotiable instruments. The law merchant was the common law's recognition of usages and procedures that had developed over a long period among merchants in England and other European countries. As part of the common law of England, it was incorporated into Canadian law but has been largely supplanted by common-law evolution and statutory enactment.

LAW OF ADMIRALTY See **maritime law.**

LAW OF THE LAND A phrase first used in the Magna Carta referring to the then established law of the Kingdom as distinguished from Roman or **civil law. 2.** Today, the fundamental principles of justice commensurate with **due process of law,** i.e., those rights that the **legislature** or **Parliament** of Canada cannot abolish or significantly limit because they are fundamental to our system of liberty and justice. **3.** The law as developed by the courts or in **statutes** in pursuance of those basic principles or rights. The **Canadian Charter of Rights and Freedoms** guarantees the rights and freedoms set out in it "subject only to such reasonable limits prescribed by law as can be demonstrably justified in a free and democratic society."

LAWSUIT See **suit.**

LAWYER'S FEES 1. In general, the charge made by the lawyer for his services in representing a client; **2.** also, the charge made by other professionals for services they have rendered in the course of preparing and trying a case. See C.B.A. *Code of Professional Conduct* (1988) chap. XI.

CONTINGENT FEE A charge made by a lawyer under an agreement with the client that the lawyer will take a percentage of the **damages** awarded, instead of an hourly rate. See Arlidge, *Contingent Fees,* 1974 Ottawa L.R. 374; *Monteith* v. *Calladine* (1963), 49 W.W.R. 641 (B.C.C.A.).

In Canada, a **barrister** or **solicitor** may sue his client for unpaid fees and may exercise a possessory lien on the client's property in his possession to encourage payment (SOLICITOR'S LIEN).

LEADING QUESTION In the law of evidence, a question that directly or indirectly suggests the answer the **witness** is to give (especially "yes" or "no" answers). It is permitted in cross-examination but not normally in direct examination. *Maves* v. *Grand Trunk Pacific Ry. Co.* (1913), 5 W.W.R. 212 (Alta.C.A.).

Leading questions may be asked of a witness who is hostile to the party examining. Other exceptions are recognized, including matters not in dispute. The trial judge has an overriding discretion to permit leading questions in the interests of justice. See *Reference re R.* v. *Coffin* (1956), 114 C.C.C. 1 at 22 (S.C.C.).

LEASE An agreement whereby one party, the **landlord,** relinquishes his right to immediate possession of **property** while retaining ultimate legal ownership **(title).** "A conveyance by which a person having an estate in **hereditaments** transfers a portion of his interest therein to another, usually in consideration for a certain periodical **rent** or other recompense, and it imports that exclusive possession is given to the premises **conveyed.**" *Garland Mfg. Co.* v. *Northumberland Paper etc. Co.* (1899), 31 O.R. 40 at 52 (Div.Ct.). The **interest** in the property remaining in the landlord is called the **reversion.** 1 A.H. Oosterhoff & W.B. Rayner, *Anger and Honsberger: Law of Real Property* 225 (2d ed. 1985).

The difference between a lease and a **licence** is that the latter does not create any right or interest in the **land** itself and does not confer a right to exclusive possession of the party. See *Kerrison* v. *Smith,* [1897] 2 Q.B. 445.

LEASEHOLD The **estate** in **real property** of a **lessee,** created by a **lease.** See, e.g., *Canadian Glassine Co. Ltd.* v. *Min. of Nat. Revenue,* [1974] C.T.C. 63 (Fed.Ct.). A leasehold interest is **personalty** and not **real property.**

It generally refers to an estate whose duration is fixed but may also be used to describe a **tenancy** at will, periodic tenancy, etc.

LEASEHOLDER One who possesses property.

LEGACY A disposition in a **testamentary instrument** of **personal property**. See *Re Tyhurst*, [1932] S.C.R. 713. Generally viewed as synonymous with **bequest**, it is properly distinguished from **devise**, which connotes a disposition of **real property**.

But " 'legacy' which **prima facie** refers to **personalty** only may contextually extend to realty." *In re Yost Estate*, [1927] 1 W.W.R. 925 at 926 (Alta.S.C.).

LEGAL BURDEN See **burden of proof.**

LEGAL CONSIDERATION See **consideration.**

LEGAL DUTY An obligation imposed by law to perform or refrain from an act, as the duty of **due care** in **negligence** law. May arise by virtue of either **statute** or **common law**. *R. v. Coyne* (1958), 124 C.C.C. 176 (N.B.S.C.A.D.). **Breach** of a legal duty owed another is an element of negligence and is the essence of most actions in **tort**. Legal duties not otherwise imposed may be created by a **contract** or by one's entering into some other relationship (**landlord-tenant, host-invitee,** etc.). See **duty.**

LEGAL RIGHTS See **Canadian Charter of Rights and Freedoms.**

LEGATEE One who takes a **legacy**; one beneficially entitled under the **will** to either **realty** or **personalty**. *Re Hord* (1916), 10 O.W.N. 278 (H.C.).

LEGISLATE 1. To make or enact laws, rules, etc.; 2. to exercise the power and function of making laws binding on those for whom they are made.

LEGISLATION Acts or **statutes** passed by a governing authority. Statutes and **instruments** of **Parliament** are referred to as federal legislation. Likewise, enactments of the provincial **legislatures** are referred to as provincial legislation. Rules made by an inferior body by virtue of the power vested in it by **Parliament** or a provincial legislature are referred to as **subordinate [delegated] legislation.**

LEGISLATURE A body of persons (**Parliament** or a provincial legislature) vested with constitutional power to pass **legislation** to govern the nation or province.

LESSEE One who holds an **estate** by virtue of a **lease** whether the original grantee of the lease or an assignee. *Haines* v. *Garson*, [1943] 2 D.L.R. 525 (N.B.S.C.); the **tenant** of a **landlord.**

LESSER INCLUDED OFFENCE An **offence** the elements of which constitute a part of a different, greater offence. *Fergusson* v. *R.* (1961), 132 C.C.C. 112 (S.C.C.). Where an **indictment** charges with the greater offence, a conviction for the lesser included offence may be entered. *R. v. Dupuis* (1941), 76 C.C.C. 347 (Que.K.B., Appeal Side); *Luckett* v. *R.* (1980), 50 C.C.C. (2d) 489 (S.C.C.); also *Criminal Code*, R.S.C. 1985, c. C–46, s. 662.

LESSOR One who grants a **lease** of property to another; **landlord.**

LET To **lease, demise** (*R. v. Wiskin,* [1942] O.W.N. 321 (Cty.Ct.)) or **rent** (*Daugherty* v. *Armaly* (1921), 58 D.L.R. 380 (Ont.S.C.A.D.)).

LETTERS ROGATORY A request to a foreign court to take **evidence** from a **witness** residing in that jurisdiction and remit it to the court making the request.

LEVY 1. To raise or collect. 2. To assess, as to levy a tax. 3. To seize land or **property** or rights through lawful **process** (see, e.g., *Execution Act*, R.S.O. 1990, c. E. 24, ss. 18, 19) or by force. See **writ** [WRIT OF EXECUTION] 4. To wage or carry on (war). To levy war against Canada is to commit the criminal offence of high **treason.** *Criminal Code*, R.S.C. 1985, c. C–46, s. 46. 5. An amount levied.

LEX LOCI CONTRACTUS *(lĕks lō′-kē kŏntrăk′-tŭs)* Lat.: the law of the place where the **contract** is made; the law by which the rights and obligations of the parties to the contract are to be governed (the proper law of the contract). See **conflict of laws.**

LEX LOCI DELICTI *(lĕks lō′-kē dĕ-lĭk′-tī)* Lat.: the law of the place where the wrong or **offence** is committed. See **conflict of laws.**

LEX LOCI DOMICILII *(lĕks lō′-kē dō-mĭsī′-lē-ī)* Lat.: the law of the place of a person's domicile.

LIABILITY 1. An obligation to do or refrain from doing something; 2. a duty that eventually must be performed; 3. an obligation to pay money; 4. money owed, as opposed to an **asset**; 5. responsibility for one's conduct, such as contractual liability, tort liability, or criminal liability. Held in *Butler* v. *Fairhall* (1927), 61 O.L.R., 305 (C.A.), to have no "absolute and adamantine" meaning in law. See **strict liability; vicarious [responsibility] liability.**

LIABLE Responsible for; obligated in law. See **liability.**

LIBEL Defamation in a printed or permanent form (e.g., printing, writing, signs or pictures) that tends to expose a person to public scorn, hatred, contempt or ridicule. Spoken defamation is called **slander.** The **tort** of libel is frequently deemed by statute to include "defamatory words in a newspaper or broadcast"; see, e.g., *Libel and Slander Act,* R.S.O. 1990, c. L. 12. s. 2. The truth of the published statement constitutes a total **defence** (justification) to an **action** for libel.

The *Criminal Code,* R.S.C.1985, c. C–46, identifies blasphemous libel (s. 296), defamatory libel (ss. 300, 301) and seditious libel (s. 61) as offences.

Certain types of publications—e.g., fair and accurate reports of judicial or parliamentary proceedings—are accorded ABSOLUTE PRIVILEGE, i.e., freedom from liability for libels they may contain; see, e.g., *Libel and Slander Act,* R.S.O. 1990, c. L. 12, s. 3, and *Criminal Code,* s. 307. In addition, qualified privilege arises in relation to statements made in the discharge of a social, legal, or moral duty, or between persons having a "common interest" (e.g., references written by former employers to prospective employers). See *Hebert* v. *Jackson,* [1950] O.R. 799 (C.A.) and *Criminal Code,* s. 309. See also **privilege.**

LICENCE "[A] grant of permission, a power or authority given to another to do some lawful act. It may be either written or verbal...." *Jenny Lind Co.* v. *Bradley-Nicholson* (1883), 1 B.C.R. (pt. II) 185 (B.C.S.C.). The grant by a **licenser** to a **licensee** may give permission to carry on a trade, to enter premises or to do some other particular thing. Licences may be granted by private persons or by government authority, such as in the case of a driver's licence, liquor licence, etc. See **franchise; monopoly.**

In the law of **property**, a licence is a personal **privilege** or permission with respect to some use of the land and is revocable at the will of the landowner. *Wood* v. *Ledbitter* (1845), 14 L.J.Ex. 161. The privilege attaches only to the party holding it and not to the land itself since, unlike an **easement,** a licence does not represent an **estate** or **interest** in land. Compare **lease.**

LICENSEE One to whom a **licence** has been granted; in **property,** "a person whom the proprietor has not in any way invited—he has no **interest** in his being there—but he has either expressly permitted him to use his lands or knowledge of his presence more or less habitual having been brought home to him, he has then either accorded permission or shown no practical anxiety to stop his further frequenting the lands." *Robert Addie and Sons (Collieries) Ltd.* v. *Dumbreck,* [1929] A.C. 358 at 371 (H.L.). In **tort** law, one's status as a licensee may affect the duty of care owed to him. See **due care; occupiers' liability.** Compare **invitee.**

LICENSER One who grants a **licence.**

LIEN The right to hold the **property** of another as **security** for the performance of an obligation. A **common-law** lien lasts only as long as possession is retained but is assertable for that time against all other interests. An equitable lien exists independently of possession but may not be asserted against the purchaser of a legal estate for value without notice of the lien.

MARITIME LIEN A privileged claim (i.e., taking priority over **mortgages,** etc.) upon maritime property for service done to it or injury caused by it accruing from the moment the claim attaches, travelling with the property unconditionally, and enforced by means of an **action in rem.** G. Price, *The Law of Maritime Liens* 1 (1940).

MECHANICS' LIEN A statutory claim to secure priority of payment for services rendered or performed or materials furnished by a mechanic or workman in the construction or repair of buildings and other structures on the land. Sometimes called GARAGEMAN'S LIEN. The **lien** attaches upon the **estate** or **interest** of the owner in the land, building, or structure. The law of mechanics' liens is entirely statutory. "Speaking generally, the object of the Mechanics' Lien

Act is to prevent owners of land getting the benefit of buildings erected and work done at their instance on their land without paying for them." *Hickey v. Stalker*, [1924] 1 D.L.R. 440 at 441 (Ont.S.C.A.D.). See *Earl F. Wakefield Co. v. Oil City Petroleums (Leduc) Ltd.*, [1958] S.C.R. 361 at 364; *Re Shields (Trustee of Estate of Harris Construction Co. Ltd.) & City of Winnipeg* (1964), 47 D.L.R. (2d) 346 at 357 (Man.Q.B.). For an example of mechanics' lien legislation, see also *Mechanics' Lien Act*, R.S.N.S. 1989, c. 277; *Repair and Storage Liens Act*, R.S.O. 1990, c. R. 25; *The Builders' Liens Act*, R.S.M. 1987, c. B91.

VENDOR'S LIEN The right of an unpaid seller to retain property until the purchase price is paid. See, e.g., *Sale of Goods Act*, R.S.O. 1990, c. S. 1, s. 38.

LIEN NOTE A sales-financing document for goods that is primarily used in western Canada and is comprised of two parts, a promissory note and a document reserving title in the goods to the seller to the amount of the purchase price or balance outstanding. See *Lucka v. Cirka* (1955), 63 Man.R. 308 (Q.B.). The counterpart in eastern Canada is the conditional sales agreement, under which the buyer may take possession, but the property in the goods does not vest in him until the price is paid. See, e.g., *Conditional Sales Act*, R.S.N.S. 1989, c. 84, s. 2(1)(b).

LIEN JURISDICTIONS Jurisdictions in which title to mortgaged premises remains with the mortgagor pending payment of the mortgage price. See mortgage.

LIEUTENANT-GOVERNOR [LIEUTEN-ANT-GOVERNOR-IN-COUNCIL] Traditionally, the Queen's representative in the various provinces (the Governor-General of Canada is the federal counterpart). The authority of the executive is vested at the provincial level in the Lieutenant-Governor. However, by convention the Lieutenant-Governor only acts upon the advice of the provincial Cabinet. One of the Lieutenant-Governor's most important functions is the granting of ROYAL ASSENT to bills approved by the legislature. Legally, this formal approval by the Lieutenant-Governor is a prerequisite to

a bill becoming a statute. See further G. Gall, *The Canadian Legal System*, 56 (3d ed. 1990).

LIFE ESTATE An estate whose duration is limited to or measured by the life of the person holding it or that of some other person [per autre vie].

LIMITATIONS, STATUTE OF See statute of limitations.

LIMITED PARTNERSHIP See partnership.

LINEAL Refers to descent by a direct line of succession in ancestry.

LIQUIDATE To settle; to determine the amount due and to whom due, and, having done so, to extinguish the indebtedness.

LIQUIDATE A BUSINESS To dissolve or wind up a limited company by having a liquidator convert all assets of a business into money, collect and pay all debts owed and owing, and distribute the balance among shareholders or owners. See *Canada Business Corporations Act*, R.S.C. 1985, c. C–44, ss. 207–228.

LIQUIDATE A CLAIM To determine by agreement or litigation the amount of a claim.

LIQUIDATED DAMAGES See damages.

LIQUIDATION DIVIDEND See dividend.

LIQUIDATOR The person charged by a court to liquidate a business upon its dissolution. See *Canada Business Corporations Act*, R.S.C. 1985, c. C–44, ss. 217–228. See receiver

LIS PENDENS *(lēs pĕn'-dĕns)* Lat.: a suspended lawsuit; a pending lawsuit. Legally, the term is equivalent to the maxim that, pending the suit, nothing should be changed. The doctrine of *lis pendens* is that one who has acquired an interest in property from a party to litigation respecting such property takes that interest subject to the decree or judgment in such litigation and is bound by it. *Bellamy v. Sabine* (1857), 1 De G. & J. 566; 44 E.R. 842 (Ch.). See also pendente lite.

CERTIFICATE OF LIS PENDENS A document registrable in land titles registries to warn persons (such as prospective purchasers) of the pending lawsuit. The certificate is, however, only an allegation of the fact that an action is pending and not a confirmation of it. *Granby Consolidated Mining, Smelting and Power Ltd.* v. *Esquimalt and Nanaimo Ry. Co.* (1919), 3 W.W.R. 331 (P.C.).

LITE PENDENTE See **pendente lite.**

LITIGANTS The **parties** involved in a lawsuit; those involved in **litigation;** refers to all parties whether **plaintiffs** or **defendants.** The term is usually limited to those actively involved in the suit.

LITIGATION A controversy in a court; a judicial contest through which legal rights are sought to be determined and enforced. The term refers to **civil actions.** See also **action; case; suit.**

LITIGIOUS Having a propensity to engage in **litigation.** Thus, a citizen who repeatedly sues his neighbour over various issues would be called litigious. Compare **malicious prosecution.** See also **vexatious litigation.**

LIVERY OF SEISIN A ceremony in feudal times signifying an **alienation** of land by **feoffment.** Either **title** or the right of immediate **possession** could be transferred by livery of seisin. The ceremony was necessary at **common law** to grant any **freehold** estate. The grantee was said to be **seised** of the legal estate in the land. A.H. Oosterhoff & W.B. Rayner, *Anger and Honsberger: Law of Real Property* 1259 (2d ed. 1985). See **seisin.**

LIVING WILL In the United States, there is widespread recognition of so-called "natural death acts" that enable an individual by means of a document called a "living will" to declare that she or he does not want certain life sustaining procedures carried out if the drafter is suffering from a terminal condition and is no longer mentally competent. In the absence of enabling legislation, the status of such documents is uncertain in Canadian jurisdictions even though many persons will request their lawyers to write living wills for them. L. Rozovsky and F. Rozovsky, *Canadian Law of Consent to Treatment* 97 (1990). A variation of the living will is an authorization permitting a person to authorize another to give future consent to medical treatment at any time when the person giving the authorization is no longer capable of giving such consent. See *Medical Consent Act*, R.S.N.S. 1989, c.

279. Such authorization is sometimes referred to as a **durable power of attorney for health care.**

LL.B. Bachelor of Laws degree; the undergraduate law degree conferred by Canadian law faculties.

LL.D. Doctor of Laws degree conferred *honoris causa tantum.* An honorary degree given by Canadian universities for significant contribution to society.

LL.M. Master of Laws Degree.

LOBBYIST One engaged in the business of persuading persons involved in the legislative process to enact, defeat, or amend legislation to suit his interests or those of his clients.

LOCKOUT The closing of a place of employment, the suspension of work, or the refusal by an employer to continue to employ a number of his employees, for the purpose of exerting pressure upon the employees or a **trade union** in connection with their employment or **collective bargaining agreement,** in order to compel employees to agree to conditions of employment or to refrain from exercising existing rights and privileges. See provincial trade union statutes, e.g., *Labour Relations Act*, R.S.O. 1990, c. L. 2.

A laying-off of enough employees effectively to halt the operation suffices. *Re Harrison and Alta. Coal Mining Co.* (1909), 10 W.L.R. 389 (Alta.Dist.Ct.).

LOCO PARENTIS See **in loco parentis.**

LOCUS *(lō'-kŭs)* Lat.: the place.

LOCUS IN QUO *(lō'-kŭs ĭn kwō)* Lat.: the place where or in which; refers to the locale where an **offence** was committed or a **cause of action** arose.

LOCUS STANDI *(lō'-kŭs stăn'-dī)* Lat.: a place of standing. The right of a **party** to an action to appear and be heard on the question before any tribunal.

LOITER To linger idly or unduly; to waste time when engaged in a particular task. Something less than "prowling" or "looking for trouble." *R.* v. *MacLean* (1970), 75 W.W.R. 157 at 160 (Alta.Mag.Ct.).

The doing of this in exercise of the right to strike is nonetheless loitering. *Re Rex* v. *Burt*, [1941] O.R. 35 (H.C.).

Criminal prohibitions against loitering include doing so in a public place and obstructing others in a public place (*Criminal Code*, R.S.C. 1985, c. C–46, s. 175(1)(*c*)); loitering upon the property of another person, near a **dwelling house** at night (*id.* s. 177). Dangerous offenders (*id.* s. 753) shall not loiter near schools, playgrounds, public parks, or bathing areas—s. 179(1)(*b*).

LOST PROPERTY Property with which the owner has involuntarily parted through neglect, carelessness, or inadvertence. **Mislaid property,** on the other hand, is property the owner intentionally placed where he could again resort to it, but then forgot where he placed it. Compare **abandonment.**

LSAT Law School Admission Test. A standardized written examination administered to candidates for law school in Canada and the United States. The LSAT is designed to test mental abilities necessary for the study of law.

MAGISTRATE A judicial officer appointed under provincial legislation who exercises summary **jurisdiction** in matters of a **criminal** nature. The term *magistrate* commonly refers to a **justice of the peace** or a stipendiary magistrate. STIPENDIARY MAGISTRATES are appointed to act in certain populous places such as a town or county and are entitled to receive a salary for their services.

MAIL BOX RULE [POST BOX RULE] In the law of contract, a rule that where an **offer** is sent through the mail or is in some other way communicated to the offeree and where the method of communication of **acceptance** is not prescribed by the offeror, when the offeree responds by mailing the acceptance, the **contract** is said to be effective at the time the acceptance is mailed even though it may not have been received by the offeror. Thus the offer cannot be revoked by a purported **revocation** sent by the offeror through the mail before the offeror receives the letter of acceptance mailed prior to the notice of revocation. See *Adams* v. *Lindsell* (1818), 1 B. & Ald. 681, 106 E.R. 250 (K.B.); *Henthorn* v. *Fraser,* [1892] 2 Ch. 27 (C.A.); *Magann* v. *Auger* (1901), 31 S.C.R. 186.

MAINTENANCE **1.** The act of keeping in good repair, in efficient working order, in an efficient state. **2.** An agreement to finance or in any way assist in the **litigation** of another person in **consideration** of having a share in the fruits of litigation giving rise to an **action** in **tort**. Also called CHAMPERTY. *Kroeker* v. *Harkema Express Lines Ltd.* (1974), 2 O.R. (2d) 210 (H.C.); *Newswander* v. *Giegerich* (1907), 39 S.C.R. 354 at 358–60; *Craig* v. *Thompson* (1907), 42 N.S.R. 150 at 155–57 (S.C.). **3.** The supply of the necessaries of life for a person, such as food, shelter, and clothing. Upon the granting of a **decree nisi** of **divorce**, an **order** of maintenance may be made requiring either the husband or the wife to pay such lump sums or periodic sums (either monthly or weekly)

as the court thinks reasonable for the maintenance of either spouse and any children of the marriage. See *Divorce Act,* R.S.C. 1985 (2nd Supp.), c. 3.

The court may make an **interim order** where a **petition** for divorce has been brought, requiring either spouse to pay **alimony** or an alimentary pension (one in which the capital is held in **trust** and the interest is paid out) for the maintenance of the other as well as for the care of any children of the marriage pending the hearing and determination of the petition. *Id.,* s. 10. See generally *Fergusson* v. *Fergusson* (1974), 19 R.F.L. 331 at 334–55 (B.C.S.C.); *Nash* v. *Nash* (1974), 2 N.R. 271 (S.C.C.); *Zacks* v. *Zacks,* [1973] S.C.R. 891 at 901; *Redding* v. *Redding* (1976), 13 Nfld. & P.E.I.R. 214 (Nfld.S.C.).

Under various provincial **statutes,** maintenance may be sought from a parent for children in the custody of an agency (see, e.g., *Children and Family Services Act,* S.N.S. 1990, c. 5, s. 52; *Child Welfare Act,* S.A. 1984, c. C–8.1, s. 9), or for the support of one spouse by the other, as well as maintenance for dependent children and parents (see, e.g., *Family Maintenance Act,* R.S.N.S. 1989, c. 160; *Family Relations Act,* R.S.B.C. 1979, c. 121, s. 61).

MAJORITY, AGE OF See **age of majority.**

MAJORITY OPINION [MAJORITY RULE] The **opinion** or rule of the greatest number; rule by the majority of those who actually vote rather than those entitled to vote. Majority rule is a basic premise of corporate law. The courts will not interfere with the internal management of a company where the majority of **shareholders** have assented to its actions. Thus, in general, a **resolution** concerning a matter within the competence of the corporation to determine and supported by a majority of shareholders is binding on the minority and hence upon the corporation as a whole.

MAKER One who signs (**endorses**) a **promissory note.** By making the promissory note, the maker promises unconditionally to pay the note according to its tenor, i.e., the exact words of the **document.** See *Bills of Exchange Act,* R.S.C. 1985, c. B–4, ss. 176(1), 185.

MALA FIDE *(mă'-là fīd)* Lat.: in bad faith. See **bona fide.**

MALFEASANCE The commission of an act that is positively wrong and unlawful, e.g., **trespassing;** wrongful conduct; an improper act. Compare **misfeasance; nonfeasance.**

MALICE 1. Generally in criminal law, malice means willfully, intentionally, and in the absence of legal excuse. "Malice in law does not necessarily mean any ill-will against any person but is established by a wrongful act done intentionally without just **cause** or excuse." *Manning* v. *Nickerson,* [1927] 3 D.L.R. 728 at 737 (B.C.C.A.), affirmed *(sub nom. Nickerson* v. *Manning),* [1928] S.C.R. 91. If one acts maliciously, one intended to do the unlawful act with which one is charged. See also **malice aforethought.**
  2. In the law of **defamation,** which is generally defined here as an improper purpose or indirect motive, *Jerome* v. *Anderson,* [1964] S.C.R. 291 at 299; *Sun Life Assurance Co. of Canada* v. *Dalrymple,* [1965] S.C.R. 302 at 309, malice is implied from the mere publication of a false statement and can be rebutted by proving that the statement was made on an occasion of **privilege.** To overcome the **defence** of privilege, the **plaintiff** must establish that the **defendant** was actuated by what is known as actual malice. Actual malice "is not confined to personal spite or ill-will but includes every unjustifiable intention to inflict injury on the person defamed, and every wrong feeling in the man's mind." *English* v. *Lamb* (1900), 32 O.R. 73 at 77 (Div.Ct.). See also *Jerome* v. *Anderson,* [1964] S.C.R. 291 at 299; *Green* v. *Miller* (1903), 33 S.C.R. 193 at 209–11.
  3. Malice is also an element of the **tort** of **malicious prosecution,** which is the malicious institution of a criminal **prosecution** without **reasonable and probable cause.** "The malice which, in an action for malicious prosecution, a plaintiff has to prove is not malice in its legal sense, that is, such as may be assumed from a wrongful act done intentionally without just cause or excuse, but malice in fact, indicating that the defendant was actuated either by spite or ill-will against the plaintiff, or by indirect or improper motives, though these may be wholly unconnected with any uncharitable feeling against any-

body." *Landry* v. *The Bathurst Lumber Co. Ltd.* (1916), 44 N.B.R. 374 at 384–85 (S.C.A.D.). See also *The Mayor of the City of Montreal* v. *Hall* (1885), 12 S.C.R. 74 at 104–05; *Chute* v. *Stewart* (1907), 6 W.L.R. 569 (Y.T.C.A.).

MALICE AFORETHOUGHT In criminal law, the **intention** to commit **murder.** Malice aforethought may be either express or implied. Express malice exists where the accused deliberately deprives another of life or inflicts grievous bodily harm. Malice aforethought is implied by law where the accused intends to do an act that is likely to kill and from which death results. "Malice aforethought is a common name for all the following states of mind: (*a*) An intent preceding the act to kill or to do serious bodily injury to the person killed, or to any other person. (*b*) Knowledge that the act done is likely to produce such consequences, whether coupled with an intention to produce them or not. (*c*) An intent to commit any felony. (*d*) An intent to resist an officer of justice in the execution of his duty." *R.* v. *Graves* (1912), 9 D.L.R. 30 at 44 (N.S.S.C.), quoting from the Draft Code of England.
  In Canada, the term *malice aforethought* is not commonly used, being comprehended under the term **mens rea.** *Mens rea* is the mental element in most criminal offences and in relation to murder is the intentional killing of another or the intentional infliction of bodily harm that is likely to cause death whether by accident or mistake or where a person, for an unlawful object, does anything that he knows or ought to know is likely to cause death, and death results even though he may have sought to effect his object without causing death or bodily harm to any human being. See *Criminal Code,* R.S.C. 1985, c. C–46, s. 141. *R.*v. *Henry and Benzanson* (1974), 30 C.R.N.S. 15 (N.S.S.C.A.D.). *R.* v. *Tennant and Naccarato* (1975), 23 C.C.C. (2d) 80 at 89–96 (Ont. C.A.).
  Compare **manslaughter; premeditation.**

MALICIOUS ARREST The arresting of a person on a criminal **charge** without **probable cause** or with knowledge that the person did not commit the offence charged. See *Croft* v. *Dunphy,* [1932] 1 D.L.R. 749 at 751 (N.S.S.C.); *Delancey* v. *Dale S.*

Co. Ltd. (1959), 20 D.L.R. (2d) 12 (N.S.S.C.). Compare **false arrest.**

MALICIOUS PROSECUTION In the law of torts, the abuse of legal process by the malicious institution of a groundless **criminal** prosecution without reasonable and probable cause. The **plaintiff** must prove injury to either his character, person, or **pecuniary interests** in order to be able to recover **damages.** See *The Mayor of the City of Montreal* v. *Hall* (1885), 12 S.C.R. 74 at 104–05; *Meyer* v. *General Exchange Insurance Corporation*, [1962] S.C.R. 193 at 199–200; *Perry* v. *Fried* (1972), 32 D.L.R. (3d) 589 at 601–02 (N.S.S.C.).

See *Nelles* v. *Ontario* (1989), 60 D.L.R. (4th) 609 (S.C.C.) (re immunity of Crown Attorneys and the Attorney-General). See **malice.**

MALUM IN SE *(mă'-lŭm ĭn sā)* Lat.: evil in itself. Inherently evil, immoral; contrary to natural and moral law. For example, **murder** is *malum in se* because even without a specific criminal prohibition a civilized community would think it to be an evil and wrongful **act.** Compare **malum prohibitum.**

MALUM PROHIBITUM *(mă'-lŭm prō-hĭ'-bĭ-tŭm)* Lat.: wrong because it is prohibited. Made unlawful by **statute** for the public welfare, but not inherently evil and not involving **moral turpitude.** The term refers to an act that is wrong only because it is made so by statute. It is contradistinguished from **malum in se.** For example, speeding along the highway is *malum prohibitum* because it has been so designated by statute as a result of a legislative determination that it is dangerous to the community, though it may not be inherently dangerous, whereas reckless driving would be regarded as *malum in se.*

MANDAMUS *(măn-dā'-mŭs)* Lat.: we command. A discretionary **prerogative writ** issued by a **superior court** and used to compel public authorities to perform their duties, to ensure the proper exercise of **discretion,** or to compel observance of the rules of **natural justice** where a duty to observe those rules is required by **statute** or can be implied. Before mandamus will be granted, the applicant must show (*a*) a sufficient interest in the **performance of** the **duty;** (*b*) proof that the duty is due to be performed; (*c*) proof that the duty is

ministerial in nature, is imperative and not discretionary; (*d*) proof that there was a demand for performance of the duty and a refusal of that demand. See generally *R. ex. rel. Johannesson* v. *Rural Municipality of Cartier*, [1922] 2 W.W.R. 670 at 672–73 (Man.K.B.); *Karavos* v. *The City of Toronto and Gillies*, [1948] O.W.N. 17 at 18 (C.A.); *Re Ridge and Council of Saskatchewan Association of Architects* (1979), 108 D.L.R. (3d) 441 at 445–46 (Sask.C.A.); *Archibald* v. *The King* (1917), 56 S.C.R. 48 at 51; *R. ex rel. Canadian Wirevision Ltd.* v. *New Westminster* (1964), 50 W.W.R. (N.S.) 465 (B.C.S.C.).

An order of mandamus will not issue as of right and will not ordinarily be granted where another **remedy** is available. *Cheyenne Realty Ltd.* v. *Thompson* (1974), 15 C.C.C. (2d) 49 at 51 (S.C.C.); *Harelkin* v. *The University of Regina* (1979), 26 N.R. 364 (S.C.C.). Mandamus will also not issue against the Crown or any servant of the Crown acting in his capacity as servant. *Re Lofstrom and Murphy* (1971), 22 D.L.R. (3d) 120 (Sask.C.A.). *R. ex rel. Central Canada Potash Co. Ltd. and Schmitt* v. *Minister of Mineral Resources of Saskatchewan*, [1972] 6 W.W.R. 62 (Sask.Q.B.). A mandamus order is available in both **civil** and **criminal proceedings.** See the various provincial rules of court, e.g., *British Columbia Supreme Court Rules* (1990), r. 63; *Nova Scotia Civil Procedure Rules* (1983), rr. 56.15, 58.10; and *Criminal Code*, R.S.C. 1985, c. C–46, ss. 774, 784.

MANDATE 1. A direction, request, or authoritative command; e.g., a cheque is a mandate by the **drawer** to his banker to pay the amount to the **holder** of the cheque. The term "mandate" (or mandatum) also refers to the **bailment** of money or goods to one who is to carry them from place to place or to do something about them without reward. See *Harris* v. *Sheffield* (1875), 10 N.S.R. 1 (S.C.). *Wills* v. *Browne* (1912), 3 O.W.N. 580 at 581–82 (Co.Ct.), affirmed (1912), 3 O.W.N. 583 (Div.Ct.); *Remme* v. *Wall* (1978), 29 N.S.R. (2d) 39 (S.C.).

MANDATORY INJUNCTION An **injunction** that requires the performance of a positive act rather than restraint from doing a particular act. See *Cook* v. *MacLean* (1973), 9 N.B.R. (2d) 119 (S.C.); *Pele-*

shok Motors Ltd. v. *General Motors of Canada Ltd.* (1977), 2 B.L.R. 56 at 61 (Ont.H.C.).

MANSLAUGHTER The unlawful killing of another person without sufficient **intent** so as to constitute **murder.** Any **culpable homicide** that is not murder or infanticide. See *Criminal Code,* R.S.C. 1985, c. C–46, s. 234; *R.* v. *Kuzmack* (1955), 111 C.C.C. 1 (S.C.C.); *R.* v. *Mack* (1975), 22 C.C.C. (2d) 257 (Alta.S.C.A.D.).

The crime of manslaughter, as distinguished from murder, is designated for homicides that are not as extreme and are explainable. Although no such distinction is drawn in the *Criminal Code,* manslaughter is sometimes said to be either voluntary or involuntary. In general, VOLUNTARY MANSLAUGHTER is an intentional killing committed under circumstances that mitigate the homicide although they do not justify it. The classic example of voluntary manslaughter is where the accused killed in the heat of passion caused by the **deceased's provocation.** *Criminal Code*, ss. 232(1), (2). For provocation to be applicable to reduce to manslaughter the intentional killing that would otherwise be murder, there is a two-fold test: (1) Would the act or insult have deprived an ordinary man of his power of self-control and (2) if so, was the accused, in fact, deprived of his power of self-control? A. Mewett & M. Manning, *Criminal Law* 553–54 (2d ed. 1985). See generally *Wright* v. *The Queen,* [1969] S.C.R. 335; *Parnerkar* v. *The Queen* (1973), 10 C.C.C. (2d) 253 at 260–65 (S.C.C.); *Taylor* v. *The King,* [1947] S.C.R. 462.

INVOLUNTARY MANSLAUGHTER occurs where, through criminal **negligence** or some unlawful act of the accused, death results, although the accused clearly did not intend to kill his victim. See *Criminal Code,* ss. 220, 222(5)*(a), (b).* "If a person is engaged in doing a lawful act, and in the course of doing that lawful act behaves so negligently as to cause the death of some other person, then it is for the jury to say, upon a consideration of the whole of the facts of the case, whether the negligence proved against the accused person amounts to manslaughter, and it is the duty of the presiding Judge to tell them that it will not amount to manslaughter unless the negligence is

of a very high degree. The expression most commonly used is 'unless it shows the accused person to have been reckless as to the consequences of the act.' That is the law where the act is lawful. Where the act which a person is engaged in performing is unlawful, then if at the same time it is a dangerous act, that is, an act which is likely to injure another person, and quite inadvertently the doer of the act causes the death of that other person by that act, then he is guilty of manslaughter." *R.* v. *Larkin* (1942), 29 Cr.App.R. 18 at 23 (C.C.A.). An example of involuntary manslaughter through criminal negligence is where death results from the negligent operation of a motor vehicle. See *R.* v. *Connolly and Gulliver* (1979), 22 N. & P.E.I.R. 304 (Nfld.Dist.Ct.); *R.* v. *Darrach* (1978), 1 M.V.R. 130 (P.E.I.S.C. in banco). For examples of involuntary manslaughter caused by an unlawful act, see generally *R.* v. *Mack,* [1975] 4 W.W.R. 180 (Alta.S.C.A.D.); *R.* v. *Lelievre,* [1962] O.R. 522 (C.A.).

MARITAL DEDUCTION In income tax law, the amount prescribed by the Act and regulations that a taxpayer is permitted to deduct for a dependant spouse. See *Income Tax Act,* S.C. 1970–71–72, c. 63, s. 109(1)(*a*) as amended.

MARITIME LAW The traditional body of rules and practices particularly relating to commerce and navigation—to business transacted at sea or relating to navigation, ships, seamen, harbours, and general maritime affairs. See **admiralty and maritime jurisdiction.**

MARKETABLE TITLE A title that is free from plausible or reasonable objections and from material defects, called defects in title; a title permitting **quiet enjoyment;** a title acceptable to a reasonably well-informed and prudent **purchaser** or MORTGAGEE (see **mortgage**). "[E]very purchaser is entitled to require a marketable title; by which ... [is] meant a title, which, so far as its antecedents are concerned, may at all times, and under all circumstances, be forced upon an unwilling purchaser." *Pyrke* v. *Waddingham* (1852), 10 Hare 1 at 8; 68 E.R. 813 at 816 (Ch.). See also *Re Land Registry Act and Shaw* (1915), 24 D.L.R. 429 at 430–442 (B.C.C.A.). The term *marketable title* is generally synonymous with **good title.**

MARKET VALUE The price that goods or **property** would bring in a market of willing buyers and willing sellers, in the ordinary course of trade; the price an asset would bring in a fair and open market. See *Re Marshall* (1909), 20 O.L.R. 116 at 121 (C.A.); *The King* v. *Thomas Lawson and Sons Ltd.*, [1948] Ex.C.R. 44 at 80–82; *Sellers-Gough Fur Co. Ltd.* v. *The Minister of National Revenue*, [1954] Ex.C.R. 644 at 651.

Market value is generally established on the basis of sales of similar goods or property in the same locality, but where there have been no such prior sales, there is no single measure of value, and other evidence of value must be looked to. Market value is generally regarded as synonymous with ACTUAL VALUE, CASH VALUE, and FAIR MARKET VALUE.

MARRIAGE CONTRACT [DOMESTIC CONTRACT] A written contract providing for the rights and obligations of **spouses** during marriage, and on separation, which usually provides for financial arrangements and division of property. *Webster* v. *Webster* (1986) 4 R.F.L.(3d) 225, at 227 (annotation). The term "domestic contract" is used more commonly in reference to cohabitation.

Most provincial **matrimonial property** statutes make provision for the effect of marriage contracts i.e. *Marital Property Act* R.S.M. 1987, c. M–45, ss. 33–41; *Matrimonial Property Act*, R.S.N.S. 1989, c. 275, ss. 23–30; *Family Law Act*, R.S.D. 1990, c. F. 3, ss. 51–60.

MARRIED WOMEN'S ACTS General term describing provincial **statutes** (except those of Quebec) commonly referred to as Married Women's Property Acts, whereby married women are recognized in law as being capable of acquiring, holding, and disposing of **real** and **personal property** as separate from that of their husbands, and such property therefore may not be seized to extinguish the husband's debts. In Quebec, legislation of this type is covered by the Code Civil. See, e.g., *The Married Women's Act*, R.S.A. 1980, c. M–7; *Married Women's Property Act*, R.S.N.S. 1989, c. 272.

In addition, several provinces in Canada have enacted matrimonial property legislation governing the equitable division of matrimonial property between husband and wife upon termination of the marriage. Such legislation generally affects any **assets** acquired by the married woman before or during the marriage. See, e.g., *The Matrimonial Property Act*, R.S.A. 1980, c. M–9; *The Family Law Act*, R.S.O. 1990, c. F. 3; *Matrimonial Property Act*, R.S.N.S. 1989, c. 275.

MARSHALLING   [MARSHALING] Arranging or ranking in order. The equitable doctrine of marshalling applies where there are two **creditors** (*A* and *B*) of the same **debtor** and two funds (*X* and *Y*) out of which payment must be claimed, and where the first creditor (*A*) can resort to both funds (X,Y) for the satisfaction of his debt but the other creditor (*B*) can resort to only one fund (*Y*). In this instance, equity will intervene and, in order to prevent the first creditor *A* from depriving the other creditor (*B*) of his **security,** order *A* to be paid out of the *X* fund to which *B* is not entitled, resorting to the *Y* fund only in case of deficiency, while allowing *B* to be paid out of the *Y* fund. If *A* has already paid himself from the *Y* fund, the doctrine will apply to allow *B* to stand in *A*'s shoes and resort to the *X* fund to the extent to which the *Y* fund has been exhausted by *A*. See *Re Hingston-Smith, Ex parte MacPherson Estate,* [1924] 3 D.L.R. 844 (Man.K.B.); *In re Andrew Weatherwax* (1940), 22 C.B.R. 96 at 108–09 (Ont.S.C.); *Midland Loan & Savings Co.* v. *Genitti* (1916), 36 O.L.R. 163 (S.C.).

MARSHALLING ASSETS In the administration of the estate of a deceased person, arranging the assets so as to give effect to the priority of **debts.** In the distribution of an estate, ranking the assets in such a way as to achieve an equitable distribution of them among as many claims as possible according to the equities of the different parties. See generally *Re Steacy* (1917), 39 O.L.R. 548 at 550 (S.C.).

MARSHALLING LIENS The ranking or ordering of several parcels of land in order to satisfy a **judgment** or **mortgage** to which they are liable even though the estates were successively sold by the debtor. For example, in relation to mortgages, where a mortgage covers several lots and the owner sells the lots at different times to different purchasers who have no notice of the mortgage, the lots are liable to the charge of the mortgage debt in reverse order to which they were sold, i.e., the lot last sold is charged first under the mortgage. See generally *Collins* v. *Cunningham* (1892), 21 S.C.R. 139 at 150; *Ernst Bros. Co.* v. *Canada Permanent Mortgage Corp.* (1920), 47 O.L.R. 362 at 367–68 (S.C.).

MARTIAL LAW System of law, arbitrary in character, implemented in time of actual war by which officers of the Crown or military authorities exercise control over civilians in domestic territory in order to maintain public order and security.

In England, when a state of actual war, riot, insurrection or rebellion exists, the Crown by proclamation, or the military authorities by notice, may supersede the ordinary law and government of the country or parts of the country by using force to restore order. This use of force is sometimes termed martial law. During the time of actual war, military tribunals are given jurisdiction to try and to punish certain offenses, and civil courts have no authority to review the actions of military authorities. However, the powers of military authorities cease and those of civil courts are restored once the state of war ends. See generally *Ex parte Marais*, [1902] A.C. 109 at 114–16 (P.C.) (Cape of Good Hope).

The so-called military courts established under martial law are not really courts; and "[i]t is by this time a very familiar observation that what is called 'martial law' is no law at all. The notion that 'martial law' exists by reason of the proclamation ... is an entire delusion. The right to administer force against force in actual war does not depend upon the proclamation of martial law at all. It depends upon the question whether there is war or not. If there is war, there is the right to repel force by force, but it is found convenient and decorous, from time to time to authorize what are called 'courts' to administer punishments, and to restrain by acts of repression the violence that is committed in time of war ... But to attempt to make these proceedings of so called '**courts-martial,**' administering summary justice under the supervision of a military commander, analogous to the regular proceedings of Courts of justice is quite illusory." *Tilonko* v. *The Attorney-General of the Colony of Natal*, [1907] A.C. 93 at 94–95 (P.C.).

In Canada the term *martial law* is not used. However, under the *Emergencies Act*, R.S.C. 1985 (4th Supp.), c. 22, the issue of a proclamation by the **Governor-in-Council,** in the belief based on reasonable grounds, that a public welfare emergency (ss. 5–15), public order emergency (ss. 16–26), international emergency (ss. 27–36), or war emergency (ss. 37–45) exists in respect of Canada gives the Governor-in-Council sweeping powers. Depending on the class of emergency, orders and regulations may be issued to: regulate and control the distribution and availability of essential goods, services, and resources; prohibit public assembly and travel; control public utilities, industry and use of property; authorize the entry and search of any dwelling house or conveyance; deport persons; as well as arrest those in contravention of such orders and regulations made under the *Act*. The powers of the Governor-in-Council under this Act in time of a national emergency may broadly conform to what is generally described as martial law.

MASTER [MASTER IN CHANCERY] In England, a senior official of the Court of Chancery who assisted the Chancellor in dealing with petitions, issuing original writs and hearing witnesses. Judicial functions were in time delegated to the Master, who would hear and report on cases to the Chancellor. The Master of the Rolls was chief among all the Masters in Chancery and, from the sixteenth century, was the chief assistant and deputy of the Chancellor. The offices of the Masters in Chancery were abolished in 1852 and were replaced by eight appointed Chief Clerks who, since 1897, have been called Masters of the Supreme Court.

In Ontario, a Master is a provincially appointed judicial officer exercising jurisdiction over **interlocutory** matters either as a Master of the Supreme Court of Ontario or as a County Court judge sitting in the capacity as a Local Judge or Local Master. See generally *Ontario Rules of Civil Procedure*, R.R.O. 1990, Reg. 194, rr. 37.02, 37.11–37.14.

MATERIAL Important, necessary; relating to a given matter.
MATERIAL ALTERATION Any alteration in a written **instrument** that changes its tenor or effect. Important alterations

that materially or substantially change the legal nature of the instrument See *Clement* v. *Renaud*, [1956] O.W.N. 222 (C.A.) *Bills of Exchange Act*, R.S.C. 1985, c. B–4, s. 144, 145.

MATERIAL FACTS   In pleadings, the facts upon which the party pleading relies but not the evidence by which they are to be proved; facts that are relevant to or have a bearing upon the issues in question. Material facts are those that the party to an action must plead and prove in order to obtain a judgment in his favour. See *Hammell* v. *The British American Oil Co. Ltd.*, [1945] O.W.N. 742 (H.C.); *Dennison* v. *Sanderson*, [1944] O.W.N. 264 at 266 (H.C.).

In the law of insurance, a material fact is one that, if disclosed to a reasonable insurer, would influence him either to decline the risk altogether or not to accept it unless a higher premium is paid. See *Ontario Metal Products Co. Ltd.* v. *Mutual Life Insurance Co. of New York*, [1925] 1 W.W.R. 362 at 368 (P.C.) (Ont.); *McCammon* v. *Alliance Assurance Co. Ltd.*, [1931] 2 W.W.R. 621 at 626–27 (Sask.C.A.); *Melvin* v. *The British American Assurance Co. Ltd.* (1933), 6 M.P.R. 438 at 444 (N.S.S.C. in banco).

MATRIMONIAL HOME   The residence(s) occupied by the married spouses as their family home. On divorce and application for division, each spouse has an equal right of possession to the matrimonial home, regardless of ownership. *Family Law Act,* R.S.O. 1990, c. F. 3, ss. 17–28. See also *Family Law Act*, R.S.N. 1990, c. F–2, ss. 6–17 (s. 8, statutory joint tenancy in the matrimonial home).

Alberta, British Columbia, Saskatchewan, and Manitoba have enacted several acts that encompass the three elements in American homestead legislation: the protection of the home from execution creditors; the requirement of the wife's consent before any disposition or encumbrance of the home; and the right of the widow (and sometimes the children) to remain in the home after the owner's death. See e.g. *Homesteads Act* S.S. 1989, c. H–5.1; *The Dower Act,* R.S.A. 1980, c. D–38.

MATRIMONIAL PROPERTY [FAMILY PROPERTY]   **Property** of the marriage that is divisible between divorced spouses on application by one of the spouses. The particulars of matrimonial property are governed by provincial statute, i.e., *Matrimonial Property Act,* R.S.N.S. 1989, c. 275, ss, 4, 12; *Family Law Act* R.S.O. 1990, c. F. 3, ss. 4–16 ("Matrimonial property" is referred to in Ontario as "family property").

MATTER OF FACT   See **question of fact.**

MATTER OF LAW   See **question of law.**

MATURITY   The date at which legal rights in an entity ripen; e.g., in relation to **negotiable instruments** it is the time when a **bill of exchange** or **promissory note** becomes due.

MECHANICS' LIEN   See **lien.**

MEDIATE DATA   Facts from which ultimate facts may be inferred for purposes of **collateral estoppel.**

MEDIATELY   Indirectly; deduced from proven facts.

MEECH LAKE ACCORD, THE   The *Constitution Amendment, 1987* (commonly known as "The Meech Lake Accord") was signed by the Prime Minister of Canada and the ten provincial premiers on April 30, 1987. The central purpose of the Accord was to bring about the full and active participation of Quebec in Canada's constitutional evolution. To that end, the **Constitution** of Canada was to be interpreted in a manner consistent with "the recognition that Quebec constitutes within Canada a distinct society" (s. 1). Other provisions related to the appointment of senators (s. 2); provincial control over immigration matters (s. 3); changes in the appointment of judges to the **Supreme Court of Canada** (s. 6); changes in the administration of cost-shared programs between federal and provincial governments (s. 7); and future amendments to the Constitution of Canada (s. 9).

It was commonly understood that the Accord would not take effect unless ratified by the **Parliament** of Canada, and the ten provincial **legislatures,** by June 23, 1990 (three years after the first legislative approval by Quebec on June 23, 1987). Neither Manitoba nor Newfoundland met the June 23 deadline for ratification. On June 23, 1990, then Prime Minister Brian Mulroney confirmed the demise of the Accord.

MEETING OF MINDS See **consensus ad idem.**

MEMORANDUM An informal record; a note of the particulars of any transaction or matter. An agreement set down in writing with a particular purpose, e.g., memorandum of association of a company. Some written evidence of a contract or deed sufficient to satisfy the Statute of Frauds. See *Adam* v. *General Paper Co. Ltd.* (1978), 19 O.R. (2d) 574 (H.C.).

A legal memorandum is an informal note discussing the law in relation to a given factual problem, usually written by a law clerk or junior partner for the benefit of a senior partner of a law firm.

In a marine insurance policy, the memorandum is a clause inserted to prevent the underwriters from being liable for injury or minor damage to goods of a peculiarly perishable nature.

See also **association, memorandum of.**

MENS REA (*mĕnz rē'-à*) Lat.: guilty mind. A culpable state of mind. Mens rea indicates the mental element or intent required for the commission of a criminal act. Mens rea encompasses several criminal states of mind knowingly, recklessly, **fraudulently,** or **maliciously** doing an act. In some statutory offences the mens rea may be described as a general intent or a specific intent. A crime of GENERAL INTENT—e.g., **sexual assault**—requires proof of the intention to do the prohibited act, whereas a SPECIFIC INTENT offence— e.g., theft—requires proof of a special mental element (in the case of theft, the taking of something with the intent to deprive, temporarily or absolutely, the owner or other person who has a special property or interest in it of the thing, or of his property or interest in it). See *Criminal Code*, R.S.C. 1985, c. C–46, s. 322. Crimes of **strict liability** do not require the existence of mens rea as an element of the offence. In a criminal prosecution, the Crown must prove beyond a reasonable doubt that the required mental state (mens rea) coexisted with the doing of the proscribed act (**actus reus**). The defences of **mental disorder,** drunkenness, or **mistake** may be raised to rebut the existence of mens rea on a charge involving a crime of specific intent. See generally *The King* v. *Crowe* (1941), 16 M.P.R. 101 at 106–11 (N.S.S.C. in banco); *Watts & Gaunt* v. *The Queen*, [1953] 1 S.C.R. 505 at 511;

R. v. *George*, [1960] S.C.R. 871 at 877.

MENTAL ANGUISH [MENTAL SUFFERING] Compensable **injury** embracing all forms of mental pain, as distinguished from mere physical pain, including deep grief, distress, anxiety, and fright. See generally *Austin* v. *Mascarin*, [1942] O.R. 165 (H.C.); *Edmonds* v. *Armstrong Funeral Home Ltd.*, [1930] 3 W.W.R. 649 (Alta.S.C.A.D.). The **tort** of intentional infliction of mental suffering is not actionable without proof of "recognizable physical or psychopathological harm." *Frame* v. *Smith*, [1987] 2 S.C.R. 99 at 128. Compare **nervous shock; pain and suffering.**

MENTAL CRUELTY A course of behaviour of one spouse that endangers the other spouse's mental or physical well-being to such an extent that it renders intolerable the continued marriage relationship. Under the *Divorce Act*, mental cruelty constitutes grounds for **divorce.** See *Divorce Act*, R.S.C. 1985 (2nd Supp.), c. 3, s. 8(2)(b)(ii).

In determining what acts constitute mental cruelty, the court will look at all the circumstances of each case, including the physical and mental condition of the parties, their education and cultural development, as well as age, attitude toward the marriage and social convention. C. Davies, *Family Law in Canada* 365–66 (4th ed. 1984). See generally *Zalesky* v. *Zalesky* (1968), 67 W.W.R. 104 (Man.Q.B.); *Hawthorne* v. *Hawthorne* (1969), 1 N.B.R. (2d) 803 (N.B.S.C.); *Bramley* v. *Bramley* (1974), 48 D.L.R. (3d) 367 (Ont.S.C.).

MENTAL DISORDER A disease of the mind or mental illness; used as a **defence** to criminal **charges.** Under s. 16(1) of the *Criminal Code*, R.S.C. 1985, c. C–46, no one " is criminally responsible for an act committed or an omission made while suffering from a mental disorder that rendered the person incapable of appreciating the nature and quality of the act or omission or of knowing that it was wrong."

The term "disease of the mind" is broadly interpreted. It "embraces any illness, disorder or abnormal condition which impairs the human mind and its functioning, excluding, however, self-induced states caused by alcohol or drugs, as well as transitory mental states such as hysteria or concussion. Thus, personality disorders may constitute disease of the mind. The word *appreciates* imports a requirement beyond mere knowledge of the physical quality of the act and requires a capacity to apprehend the nature of the act and its consequences." E. Greenspan, *Martin's Annual Criminal Code*, 1994 44ff. (1993). See also *Cooper* v. *The Queen* (1980), 51 C.C.C. (2d) 129 (S.C.C.).

Previous to 1992, the term **insanity** was used in the *Code*. Now, it has been removed and the provisions dealing with insanity and fitness to stand trial have been consolidated under Part XX.I of the *Code* with the heading "Mental Disorder." See R. Salhany, *Canadian Criminal Procedure* 6–144ff. (6th ed. 1994).

See **competent; M'Naghten Rule.** Compare **incompetency; non compos mentis.**

MERCANTILE LAW The branch of law (often called commercial law) that deals with the rules and institutions of commercial transactions. It is derived from the **law merchant.** See *Pearse & Edworthy Bros.* v. *Rur. Mun. Bjorkdale*, [1929] 2 D.L.R. 537 at 539 (Sask.C.A.).

MERCHANTABLE Saleable and fit for the market. "[W]hatever else merchantable may mean, it does mean that the article sold, if only meant for one particular use in ordinary course, is fit for that use; merchantable does not mean that the thing is saleable in the market simply because it looks all right." *Grant* v. *Australian Knitting Mills Ltd.*, [1936] A.C. 85 at 99–100 (P.C.) (Austl.). See also *Porter* v. *Dead River Ltd.* (1951), 29 M.P.R. 40 at 50 (N.B.S.C.A.D.).

MERCHANTABLE QUALITY The various provincial *Sale of Goods Acts* provide that where goods are bought by description from a seller who deals in goods of that description, whether or not he is the manufacturer, there is an **implied condition** that the goods shall be of merchantable quality. Merchantable quality means "that the article is of such quality and in such condition that a reasonable man acting reasonably would after a full examination accept it under the circumstances of the case in performance of his offer to buy that article whether he buys for his own use or to sell again." *Bristol Tramways Carriage Co. Ltd.* v. *Fiat Motors Ltd.*, [1910] 2 K.B. 831 at 841 (C.A.). See

also *Int'l Business Machines Co. Ltd.* v. *Shcherban*, [1925] 1 D.L.R. 864 at 868 (Sask.C.A.); *Farmer* v. *Canada Packers Ltd.*, [1956] O.R. 657 at 670 (H.C.).

MERCY KILLING See **euthanasia.**

MERGER The amalgamation of one thing into another; a consolidation.

1. In the law of **corporations,** the terms *merger* and *amalgamation* are often used interchangeably, although only the latter term has a specific legal meaning. AMALGAMATION is the fusion of two or more corporations and their continuance as one corporation. Such an amalgamation, or, popularly, a merger, is accomplished in several ways: (1) A sale of the assets of one (or more than one) corporation to an existing corporation in consideration of the issuance of paid-up shares or securities of the latter. The vendor corporation will then pay its liabilities and distribute its assets among its own shareholders and surrender its charter or in some other manner be dissolved; (2) a lease of the whole or a substantial part of the assets and business of one or more corporations to another corporation. In this case the **lessor** corporation remains in existence and distributes, by way of dividends among its shareholders, the rentals paid by the **lessee** corporation; (3) acquisition of shares of two or more corporations by a new corporation or by an existing corporation; (4) amalgamation by agreement between the corporations pursuant to special statutory provisions. This last-named method of effecting amalgamations is governed by both federal and provincial companies legislation. See, e.g., *Canada Business Corporations Act*, R.S.C. 1985, c. C–44, ss. 181, 182; *Companies Act*, R.S.N.S. 1989, c. 81, s. 134; *The Corporations Act*, R.S.O. 1990, c. C. 38, s. 113; *The Business Corporations Act*, R.S.O. 1990, c. B. 16, s. 174. See also *R.* v. *Black & Decker Manufacturing Co. Ltd.* (1974), 43 D.L.R. (3d) 393 at 399–400 (S.C.C.); *Attorney-General for Ontario* v. *Electrical Development Co. Ltd.* (1919), 45 O.L.R. 186 at 190 (H.C.).

2. In the law of **real property,** it is a general rule that where two estates in land become vested in one person and there is no intervening estate in another person, the lesser estate is merged, extinguished or drowned, by operation of law, in the greater estate. For example, if **A** becomes vested of a TENANCY FOR YEARS (see **tenancy**) and subsequently acquires, either by purchase or by inheritance, a **reversion** in **fee simple,** then the tenancy for years, being the lesser estate, is merged in the fee simple and therefore no longer exists. See *Doe Dem. McPherson* v. *Hunter* (1848), 4 U.C.Q.B. 449; *Wigle* v. *Merrick* (1858), 8 U.C.C.P. 307; *Dalye* v. *Robertson* (1860), 19 U.C.Q.B. 411. In **equity,** the merger of a lesser **estate** in a greater, or the merger of a charge in the land, is a question of the intention, actual or presumed, of the person in whom the interest in the estates are united. Thus the lesser estate is not merged in the greater if there is an express or presumed intention that it shall be kept alive. Similarly, if a person acquires a charge upon land to which he is entitled and expresses his intention that the charge shall not merge, it remains alive. However, if there is an express or presumed intention in favour of merger, the charge will be extinguished. See *Henry* v. *Low* (1862), 9 Gr. 265.

3. Generally, in the law of **contracts,** where a **creditor** takes from his **debtor** a **security** of a higher nature than that already owing him—e.g., if he takes a bond or recovers **judgment** in respect of a simple contract debt—then his remedies on the lower security are merged, by operation of law, in the higher remedy and are thereby extinguished. The merger of the lower security in the higher only occurs with respect to the same debt and must involve the same parties. See *Gore Bank* v. *McWhirter* (1868), 18 U.C.C.P. 293; *Shenkman* v. *Steinbook* (1915), 7 W.W.R. 1051 at 1052 (Alta.Dist.Ct.). The term *merger* is also used in relation to an agreement that requires the execution of a deed—e.g., an agreement for the sale of land—where it is said that the agreement is superseded by the deed, or "merged" in it. See *Knight Sugar Co.* v. *Alberta Ry. & Irrigation Co.,* [1938] 1 D.L.R. 321 at 324 (P.C.).

MERITS The various elements that enter into or qualify the plaintiff's right to the **relief** sought or the defendant's right to prevail in his defence; the real matters in question rather than technicalities; the substance of a **litigant's** claim or refutation of a claim; the totality of the elements of a party's claim that tend to establish or refute the validity or credibility of his cause; the grounds of an action or defence. A person may be said to have a good cause of action or defence **on the merits.**

MESNE *(mēn)* Intermediate; between two extremes, especially in rank or time.

MESNE LORD In English feudal law a mesne lord was one who held lands under the authority of the King and who stood between the King and the tenants who occupied the land, known as tenants in demesne, thereby becoming a lord to the tenants.

MESNE PROFITS Rents and profits obtained from the land by one who is in unlawful possession of the land and who holds it against the true owner. See *Vivian* v. *Tizard,* [1918] 2 W.W.R. 765 at 766 (Sask.S.C.).

METES AND BOUNDS The limits or boundaries of property as marked by natural features or man-made structures. A method of describing the territorial limits of property by means of measuring distances and angles from designated landmarks and in relation to adjoining properties.

MINISTERIAL ACT [MINISTERIAL FUNCTION] The performance of acts, the making of decisions or the issuance of orders by a public servant or official, in which there is little or no element of discretion or independent judgment. The performance of a ministerial act, as required by statute or otherwise, may be enforced through an order of **mandamus.** The term is to be distinguished from **judicial** or **legislative acts** and **executive** or **administrative** acts, which involve the exercise of a substantial amount of **discretion** and individual judgment. See *M. Gordon & Son Ltd.* v. *Debly* (1956), 3 D.L.R. (2d) 1 at 5 (S.C.C.); *McDonald* v. *Attorney-General for Alberta* (1968), 66 W.W.R. 111 (Alta.S.C.A.D.); *Canadian Financial Co.* v. *O'Neill* (1977), 26 N.B.R. (2d) 221 at 223 (Co.Ct.).

MINOR A person not of full legal capacity; one under the **age of majority;** an infant.

MINORITY LANGUAGE EDUCATION RIGHTS See **Canadian Charter of Rights and Freedoms.**

MISAPPLICATION [MISAPPROPRIATION] OF PROPERTY Generally, the use of funds or property for a wrongful purpose. The term is commonly used in relation to persons who, while acting in a **fiduciary** capacity—e.g., as a banker, trustee, director of a corporation, etc.— misapply funds intended for another purpose or who convert another's funds for their own benefit. "Misappropriation does not necessarily mean **peculation,** though it may mean that." *Hanna* v. *De-Blaquiere* (1853), 11 U.C.Q.B. 310 at 314.

In Canada, the misappropriation of money or valuable security by one under direction to apply such money or security to a particular purpose or to pay it to a person specified in the direction is treated as theft under s. 332(1) of the *Criminal Code,* R.S.C. 1985, c. C–46. See also s. 336. See, e.g., *R.* v. *Legare* (1977), 36 C.C.C. (2d) 463 (S.C.C.). See **larceny.**

MISCARRIAGE OF JUSTICE A term of indefinite meaning, usually referring to a failure of justice or a situation where, upon the determination or outcome of a legal proceeding, the substantial rights of a party are prejudiced. The expression *miscarriage of justice* "means such departure from the rules which permeate all judicial procedure as to make that which happened not in the proper use of the word judicial procedure at all." *Robins* v. *National Trust Co. Ltd.,* [1927] 2 D.L.R. 97 at 99 (P.C.) (Ont.).

The *Criminal Code,* R.S.C. 1985, c. C–46, s. 686(1)(a)(iii), provides: "(1) On the hearing of an appeal against a conviction or against a verdict that the appellant is unfit to stand trial or not criminally responsible on account of **mental disorder,** the court of appeal (*a*) may allow the appeal where it is of the opinion that (iii) on any ground there was a miscarriage of justice." By allowing the appeal on a finding that there was a miscarriage of justice, the court of appeal shall quash the conviction and either direct that a judgment or a verdict of acquittal be entered, or order a new trial. *Id.,* s. 686(2). See *R.* v. *Wong (No. 2),* [1978] 4 W.W.R. 468 at 476 (B.C.C.A.);

R. v. *Ignat,* [1950] 1 W.W.R. 304 at 307–08 (Man. C.A.).

MISDEMEANOUR At common law, all crimes were divided into felonies, misdemeanours, and **treason.** Generally, misdemeanours were less serious offences than felonies and were sanctioned by less severe penalties. In Canada, the distinction between felonies and misdemeanours was abolished by the *Criminal Code,* S.C. 1892, c. 29, being replaced by **indictable offences** and offences punishable upon **summary conviction.** Indictable offences are generally understood to be more serious crimes (e.g., **murder, aggravated sexual assault, manslaughter**), whereas summary conviction offences are less serious (e.g., common **assault,** operation of a vessel while impaired by alcohol or a drug, willful destruction or damage of property not exceeding fifty dollars). The distinction between felonies and misdemeanours remains important in the United States.

MISFEASANCE The doing of an act in a wrongful or injurious manner; the improper performance of a lawful act; "active misconduct working positive injury to others." J. Fleming, *The Law of Torts* 146 (8th ed. 1992). See *Corporation of Richmond* v. *Evans* (1919), 48 D.L.R. 209 (P.C. (B.C.); *Moose Jaw Bread Co. Ltd.* v. *City of Moose Jaw,* [1920] 2 W.W.R. 917 (Sask.C.A.); *Crawford* v. *Municipality of Franklin,* [1924] 2 W.W.R. 1073 at 1078 (Man.K.B.). Compare **malfeasance; nonfeasance.**

MISJOINDER Improper joining of plaintiffs or defendants in a single action, i.e., where persons are made parties who ought not to be. Compare **joinder.**

MISLAID PROPERTY Property that the owner has intentionally placed where he can resort to it, but which place is then forgotten. The finder of mislaid property acquires no **interest** or right to **possession,** and thus the proprietor of the place in which the mislaid object is found is the only one entitled to retain possession pending the search for the true owner. Compare **abandonment; lost property.**

MISNOMER A misnaming; a term applied to a mistake in the word or combination of words constituting a person's name and distinguishing him from other

individuals. The giving of a wrong name to a person in pleadings.

MISREPRESENTATION Words or conduct that convey a false or misleading impression. A misrepresentation may be fraudulent, innocent, or negligent. A FRAUDULENT MISREPRESENTATION is one made with the knowledge it is false and with the intent to deceive the party to whom it is made. A fradulent misrepresentation is actionable as a **tort** when it is made with the knowledge that the plaintiff will rely on the misrepresentation, as he in fact did, to his detriment. An INNOCENT MISREPRESENTATION is an untrue statement of fact made in the honest belief that it is true. A NEGLIGENT MISREPRESENTATION is one made carelessly and with no reasonable grounds for believing it to be true. Such a misrepresentation may give rise to a **cause of action** in tort if a special relationship exists between the parties, one of whom is engaged in the business of providing information or advice of a kind requiring special skill (e.g., a doctor or an accountant) and consequently negligently provides misleading advice to the other who he knows, or ought to know, will rely on such advice to his financial detriment. *Hedley Byrne & Co. Ltd.* v. *Heller & Partners Ltd.*, [1964] A.C. 465 (H.L.). See also *Haig* v. *Bamford*, [1977] 1 S.C.R. 466; *Smith* v. *Mattacchione*, [1970] 3 O.R. 541 (York Co.Ct.); *Cherewick* v. *Moore & Dean*, [1955] 2 D.L.R. 492 at 494 (B.C.S.C.); *Lee* v. *Durand* (1939), 14 M.P.R. 161 (N.S.S.C. in banco).

Where a person has been induced to enter into a contract on the basis of a material misrepresentation, either fraudulent or innocent, he may either (*a*) affirm the contract and seek damages for the misrepresentation; (*b*) rescind the contract, if it is still executory; or (*c*) rely upon the misrepresentation as a defence to an action to enforce the contract. See *Redican* v. *Nesbitt*, [1924] S.C.R. 135 at 147–56; *Morash* v. *Morash* (1977), 27 N.S.R. (2d) 47 (N.S.S.C.); *Put on Products Ltd.* v. *Johnson* (1978), 22 N.B.R. (2d) 400 (N.B.S.C.).

MISTAKE An unintentional act involving misapprehension or error in the existence of a thing, arising either from ignorance or from a false belief on the point. Mere forgetfulness is not a mistake

against which the court will grant relief. *Lovejoy* v. *Mercer* (1911), 23 O.L.R. 29 at 31 (H.C.).

A distinction is often drawn between unilateral mistake, common mistake, and mutual mistake in the law of contract.

UNILATERAL MISTAKE A mistake by only one of the parties to the contract as to its terms or object. **Rectification** or alteration of the contract is available as a remedy for this type of mistake only if it can be shown that the other party was aware of the mistake and that his taking advantage of it would amount to **fraud** or constitute misrepresentation amounting to fraud. The contract may, however, be **rescinded** if the mistake is of a fundamental character. See *Sykes* v. *The King*, [1939] Ex.C.R. 77 at 85; *McMillen* v. *Chapman and S. S. Kresge Company Ltd.*, [1953] O.R. 399 at 405–06 (C.A.); *McMaster University* v. *Wilchar Construction Ltd.*, [1971] 3 O.R. 801 (H.C.); *Pacific Petroleums Ltd.* v. *Concordia Propane Gas Marketers Ltd.* (1977), 5 A.R. 421 (Alta.S.C.).

COMMON MISTAKE A mistake made when both parties are contracting under an error and share the same mistaken belief. "Each knows the intention of the other and accepts it, but each is mistaken about some underlying and fundamental fact." M. Furmston, *Cheshire, Fifoot and Furmston's Law of Contract* 229 (12th ed. 1991). For example, in contracting for the sale of a cow, A and B both believe the cow to be a breeder, when in fact it is barren.

MUTUAL MISTAKE A mistake made when "the [contracting] parties misunderstand each other and are at cross purposes. A, for example, intends to offer his Ford Sierra car for sale, but B believes that the offer relates to the Ford Granada [car] also owned by A." *Id.* at 229–230.

A distinction is made by some courts and writers between "common" and "mutual" mistake. Sometimes the terms are used interchangeably. Fridman suggests that "little, if any, theoretical or practical effect may flow from the differentiation of common and mutual mistake." It was stated in *McMaster University* v. *Wilchar Const. Ltd.* [1971]

3 O.R. 801 at 809 (H.C.): "In mutual or common mistake the error or mistake in order to avoid the contract at law, must have been based either upon a fundamental mistaken assumption as to the subject-matter of the contract or upon a mistake relating to a fundamental term of the contract." See G. Fridman, *The Law of Contract in Canada* 240ff. (2d ed. 1986).

A further distinction is drawn between a mistake of law and a mistake of fact. In the law of contract, a MISTAKE OF FACT is "a mistake not caused by the neglect of legal duty on the part of the person making the mistake, and consisting in an unconscientiousness, ignorance, or forgetfulness of a fact past or present material to the transaction; or in the belief in the present existence of a thing material to the transaction which does not exist, or in the past existence of a thing which has not existed." *Black* v. *The Bank of Nova Scotia* (1889), 21 N.S.R. 448 at 460–61 (C.A.). A mistake of fact will justify rescission of the contract if the mistake is material to the nature of the transaction. However, a MISTAKE OF LAW—which consists of one's ignorance of the legal consequences of his conduct, though he is fully cognizant of the facts and substance of that conduct—is not generally regarded as sufficient to justify rescission or reformation of a contract, unless the mistake is a mutual one concerning the parties' relative and respective legal rights under the contract. See *U.S.A.* v. *Motor Trucks Ltd.* (1922), 52 O.L.R. 262 at 271–72 (S.C.A.D.); *Thompson* v. *Crawford*, [1932] O.R. 281, affirmed 41 O.W.N. 231 (C.A.). Compare **ignorantia legis non excusat.**

The criminal law has traditionally recognized the same dichotomy, allowing a mistake of fact in some cases to constitute a valid defence to a criminal prosecution, but relying on the maxim "Ignorance of the law is no excuse" with regard to mistakes of law. This maxim is now incorporated in s. 19 of the *Criminal Code,* R.S.C. 1985, c. C–46. Generally, only a mistake of fact is, in Canada, a valid defence since it negates one of the essential elements of those offences requiring a culpable state of mind, i.e., **mens rea.** However, although a mistake of law is no defence, a mistake of fact may arise from a misinterpretation of the law and may

operate as a valid defence to a criminal prosecution. A. Mewett & M. Manning, *Criminal Law* 333 (2d ed. 1985).

Recently, in Canada, officially induced mistake of law has been recognized as a defence to a criminal charge. "[A]n officially induced error of law may, in some circumstances, constitute a valid defence. This will of course depend on whether the opinion of the official was reasonable in the circumstances and whether it was reasonable for the accused to follow it." *R.* v. *Cancoil Thermal Corp. and Parkinson* (1986), 52 C.R. (3d) 188 at 200 (Ont.C.A.).

MISTRIAL An erroneous or **nugatory trial.** A trial that is ended because of lack of **jurisdiction,** error in **procedure** or disregard of some other fundamental process before or during the trial. It does not result in a **judgment** for any party, but merely indicates a failure of the trial. See, e.g., *R.* v. *Armstrong* (1969), 7 C.R.N.S. 227 (N.S.S.C.A.D.).

MITIGATING CIRCUMSTANCES Circumstances that, while not completely exonerating the person charged, at least reduce the penalty connected to the offence, or the **damages** arising from the offence; e.g., **murder** may be reduced to **manslaughter** where there were mitigating circumstances, i.e., that the killing was committed in a sudden heat of passion caused by legally adequate provocation. Mitigating circumstances may also influence the choice of sanction by the court so that a defendant pleading mitigating circumstances might receive a more lenient **sentence.** See *R.* v. *Johnston & Tremayne,* [1970] 4 C.C.C. 64 (Ont.C.A.); *R.* v. *Shanower* (1972), 8 C.C.C. (2d) 527 (Ont.C.A.).

MITIGATION OF DAMAGES A requirement that one who seeks to recover damages by reason of a **breach of contract** or another's **tort** exercise reasonable diligence and care to avoid aggravating the injury or increasing the **damages.** The duty to mitigate damages, though not a duty in the sense that its breach will give rise to a **cause of action** against the person who violates it, expresses the general rule that one who was wronged must act reasonably to avoid or limit losses because he cannot recover damages that could reasonably have been avoided. See generally

Hamilton Gas & Light Co. and United Gas & Fuel Co. v. *Gest* (1916), 37 O.L.R. 132 at 134 (A.D.); *Karas* v. *Rowlett,* [1944] S.C.R. 1 at 7–8; *Jones* v. *Fabbi; Jones* v. *Fleck* (1974), 49 D.L.R. (3d) 316 (B.C.S.C.).

M'NAGHTEN RULE The **common-law** rule or test to be applied in establishing a defence of **mental disorder** as announced by the House of Lords in *M'Naghten's Case* (1843), 10 Cl. & Fin. 200; 8 E.R. 718 (H.L.). Under this rule an accused person is not criminally responsible if, at the time of committing the act, he was suffering from such mental disease or defect that he was unable to understand what he was doing or that it was wrong or if he committed an offence while laboring under a partial delusion (but is not in other respects insane) that, if true, would have provided a good defence. Thus an accused person was entitled to be acquitted by reason of insanity if he did not understand at all what he was doing or did not know that it was wrong. He was likewise excused if because of an insane delusion he thought he was acting in self-defence. It is the law in Canada that a person who commits a criminal act under an uncontrollable or irresistible impulse, knowing what he is doing and with the knowledge it is wrong, is criminally responsible for the consequences of that act. *The King* v. *Creighton* (1908), 14 C.C.C. 349 (Ont.H.C.); *R.* v. *Jessamine* (1912), 21 O.W.R. 392 (C.A.). The test of mental disorder as a defence for purposes of Canadian criminal law is now covered by s. 16 of the *Criminal Code,* R.S.C. 1985, c. C–46.

MOBILITY RIGHTS See **Canadian Charter of Rights and Freedoms.**

MODUS OPERANDI *(mō'-dŭs ŏp-ĕr-än'-dē)* Lat.: the manner of operation. The means of accomplishing an act; the mode or manner in which the offence was committed. Police officers frequently refer to this concept as the "M.O."

MOIETY A term used generally to denote the half part in contrast to *entirety,* which denotes the whole. To hold a moiety is to hold a half part. See *In re Angus' Will Trusts,* [1960] 1 W.L.R. 1296 at 1300 (Ch.D.).

MOLLITER MANUS IMPOSUIT *(mō'-lĭ-tĕr mä'-nŭs ĭm-pō'-zū-ĭt)* Lat.: the gentle laying of hands upon. At common law, a plea in defence to an action for **battery** whereby the defendant claimed that the battery was lawful and that he "laid hands upon the plaintiff gently," thereby using no more force than was necessary. Compare **self-defence.**

MONOPOLY The exclusive power vested in an individual, a combination of individuals, or a company to control a particular business or trade or the sale of a given commodity so as to prevent competition, restrict trade, and create exclusive control over prices.

The investigation and control of monopolies in Canada is governed by the *Competition Act,* R.S.C. 1985, c. C–34, as amended by R.S.C. 1985 (2nd Supp.), c. 19, which now uses the terms "abuse of dominant position" and "anti-competitive acts" when referring to the regulation of monopolies under the *Act.* See *Canada (Director of Investigation and Research)* v. *NutraSweet Co.* (1990), 32 C.P.R. (3d) 1 (Comp. Trib.). See **combines.**

MOOT CASE A case that seeks the determination of an abstract question not arising from already existing facts or rights; an unsettled case presenting a topic for dispute.

MOOT COURT A court established for the purpose of arguing a **moot case.** Law students are usually required to argue fictional cases before such courts as part of their legal education.

MORAL CERTAINTY Certainty beyond a **reasonable doubt;** a conviction based on convincing reasons and excluding all doubts that a contrary or opposite conclusion can exist. A juror is said to be morally certain of the truth of a fact sought to be proved when he would act in reliance upon its truth in matters of greatest importance to himself.

The term is sometimes used to express the criminal law standard of proof (proof "beyond a reasonable doubt") but may also be used to indicate an even higher standard, as in regard to an allegation that an unlawful **homicide** has been committed when the victim's body is missing. Compare **preponderance of the evidence.**

MORAL CONSIDERATION See **consideration.**

MORAL TURPITUDE Baseness, vileness or dishonesty of a high degree. Conduct contrary to justice, honesty, modesty, and good morals. For example, the offence of theft under s. 322 of the *Criminal Code*, R.S.C. 1985, c. C–46, may be said to be a crime involving moral turpitude. See generally *King v. Brooks and Minister of Citizenship & Immigration* (1960), 24 D.L.R. (2d) 567 at 572–73 (Man.Q.B.).

MORTGAGE A conditional **conveyance** of a legal **estate** or **interest** in land or other **property** as **security** for the payment of a **debt.** The debt usually takes the form of a loan of money representing the purchase price (or a part thereof) of the property so conveyed. The party who conveys the property as security is called the MORTGAGOR whereas the party who receives the interest in such property is called the MORTGAGEE. The mortgage operates so as to rest legal ownership of the property in the mortgagee while equitable **title** remains vested in the mortgagor. Once the mortgagor has repaid the debt to the mortgagee, the mortgagor is entitled to have the security redeemed, i.e., to have the legal interest in the property transferred back to the mortgagor. This right in the mortgagor to have the legal interest in the property revert to him upon repayment of the debt to the mortgagee is known as the **equity of redemption**. See *In re Order in Council, In re Crop Payments Act, In re Bills of Sale and Chattel Mortgage Act,* [1926] 2 W.W.R. 844 at 849 (Man.C.A.).

In several provincial jurisdictions, most notably in Western Canada, a mortgage under the Land Titles or Torrens system operates as a form of security, creating a charge on land, and does not vest in the mortgagee any legal estate, registered title remaining vested in the mortgagor. See, e.g., *The Real Property Act,* R.S.M. 1988, c. R30, s. 1; *The Land Titles Act,* R.S.A. 1980, c. L–5, s. 1(*p*); *The Land Titles Act,* R.S.O. 1990, c. L. 5, uses the term *charge,* but this term is not defined. See also *Smith v. National Trust Co.* (1912), 1 D.L.R. 698 at 711–13 (S.C.C.).

CHATTEL MORTGAGE Conveyance of a present interest in **personal property,** also generally made as security for the payment of money, such as the purchase price of the property, or for the performance of some other act. The mortgage operates as a transfer of a property interest in the **chattels** to the mortgagee subject to the mortgagor's right to retain possession of the chattels. See *O'Brien v. Stebbins,* [1927] 3 D.L.R. 274 at 278 (Sask. C.A.). Chattel mortgages are governed by provincial Bills of Sale Acts. See, e.g., *Bills of Sale Act,* R.S.N.S. 1989, c. 39; *The Personal Property Security Act,* R.S.O. 1990, c. P. 10; *Personal Property Security Act,* S.A. 1988, c. P–4. 05.

EQUITABLE MORTGAGE A contract that creates an equitable charge on the property but does not transfer the legal estate to the mortgagee. Such a mortgage is enforceable under the equitable jurisdiction of the court. An equitable mortgage may be created (1) where only an equitable interest is mortgaged, (2) where the instrument executed by the mortgagor is not sufficient to transfer a legal estate or interest in the property, or (3) by a deposit of title deeds. W. Rayner & R. McLaren, *Falconbridge on Mortgages* 81 (4th ed. 1977). See *London County & Westminister Bank Ltd. v. Tompkins,* [1918] 1 K.B. 515 at 528 (C.A.); *Zimmerman v. Sproat* (1912), 26 O.L.R. 448 (H.C.); *Royal Bank of Canada v. Grobman* (1977), 2 B.L.R. 145 at 156–61 (Ont.H.C.).

MORTGAGEE/MORTGAGOR See **mortgage.**

MORTIS CAUSA (*môr'-tĭs kaw'-zà*) Lat.: by reason of death. In contemplation of death. See **gift** [GIFT MORTIS CAUSA].

MORTMAIN Literally, dead hand; applies to all **property** that, from the nature of the purposes to which it is devoted, or the character of the **ownership** to which it is subjected, is for every practical purpose in a dead or unserving hand (not freely alienable). In England, *Mortmain Acts,* restricting any **alienation** of property that would limit its free circulation by means of **possession** or control by one **corporation** perpetually, constituted a response to such possession and control over lands by the Church and other ecclesiastical bodies; but the concept has been used with reference to any corporation that may hold property in perpetuity, and thus with a "dead hand."

MOTION An application to a court or judge for a direction or **order** that something be done that is for the benefit of the applicant. Generally, a motion is made by oral request of counsel in open court.

MOTOR VEHICLE ACTS Various provincial acts that regulate the operation of motor vehicles on public highways and impose civil and quasi-**criminal** duties and liabilities on persons associated with the operation, ownership, and use of motor vehicles. Also called Highway Traffic Acts in some provinces. See, e.g., *Motor Vehicle Act*, R.S.N.S. 1989, c. 293; *Motor Vehicle Administration Act*, R.S.A. 1980, c. M–22; *Highway Traffic Act*, R.S.A. 1980, c. H–7.

MOVANT The moving party; the applicant for an **order** by way of **motion** before a court.

MOVE To make a **motion;** to make application to a court or other tribunal for a ruling, **order,** or particular **relief.**

MULTIFARIOUS Characterized by **misjoinder** of parties or **causes of action** in a proceeding; the joining of wholly distinct and unconnected matters in the same action against one or more **defendants.** Modern practice favours the joining of several causes of action in the same proceeding in the interests of economy and the avoidance of a multiplicity of actions. See, e.g., *Nova Scotia Civil Procedure Rules* (1983), *Ontario Rules of Civil Procedure*, R.R.O. 1990, Reg. 194, r. 5.01.

MULTIPARTITE Consisting of two or more parts or parties, as where several nations join in a treaty.

MULTIPLICITY OF SUITS [OR ACTIONS] The bringing of several different legal suits or actions against the same defendant on the same issue.

MUNICIPAL COURT An inferior court of limited **jurisdiction** established in towns or cities in some provinces, generally having jurisdiction in matters arising under municipal by-laws and over certain **civil** matters.

MURDER At common law, the unlawful killing of another human being with **malice aforethought.** *R.* v. *Elnick, R.* v. *Clements, R.* v. *Burdie,* [1920] 2 W.W.R. 606 at 614–15 (Man.C.A.).

In Canada, if a person, directly or indirectly, by any means, causes the death of a human being, he has committed a **homicide.** *Criminal Code,* R.S.C. 1985, c. C–46, s. 222(1). Homicide is either **culpable** or not culpable, and only culpable homicide is an **offence.** To amount to murder, culpable homicide must be within the provisions of either s. 229 or s. 230 of the *Criminal Code (id.).*

Murder in the first degree may be defined as an unlawful killing that is planned and deliberate or the victim of which is a police officer, prison employee, or other person employed for the preservation and maintenance of the public peace, while he was acting in the course of his duties. *Id.,* s. 231(4).

All murder that does not come within the definition of first degree murder is second degree murder. *Id.,* s. 231(7).

Both first and second degree murder are **indictable offences** punishable by a mandatory sentence of life imprisonment. A person convicted of first degree murder must serve at least twenty-five years' imprisonment before being eligible for parole, while a person convicted of second degree murder is subject to a minimum term of ten years' imprisonment without eligibility for parole, or such longer period, up to twenty-five years, as the trial judge, in his discretion, may impose. See *id.,* s. 742 and s. 744. See also *id.,* s. 744.1.

The attempt to commit murder is also an indictable offence, and everyone who so attempts, by any means, to commit murder is liable to imprisonment for life. *Id.,* s. 239.

Culpable homicide that otherwise would be murder may be reduced to **manslaughter** if the person who committed it did so in the heat of passion caused by sudden provocation. *Id.,* s. 232(1).

MUTUALITY OF OBLIGATION The responsibilities imposed on each of the parties to a **contract,** requiring each to do something in **consideration** of the other party's act or promise. Neither party to the contract is bound unless both are bound. See *Young* v. *C.N.R.,* [1930] 3 D.L.R. 352 at 357 (Man.C.A.); *Schrader* v. *Lillis* (1885), 10 O.R. 358 (Ch.D.).

MUTUAL MISTAKE See **mistake.**

NATIVE PEOPLES See **aboriginal peoples.**

NATIVE RIGHTS See **aboriginal rights.**

NATURAL DEATH ACT [STATUTE] See **living will.**

NATURAL JUSTICE "[A] duty of procedural fairness to persons in the course of lawful interference with various of their interests, including interests in property." *Walters* v. *Essex County Board of Education* (1973), 38 D.L.R. (3d) 693 at 697 (S.C.C.). The term is generally understood to apply to statutory **tribunals** charged with adjudicating disputes between others where legal rights and **interests** may be affected. These bodies must adhere to and apply the principles of natural justice—that is, give persons specially affected by the decision a reasonable opportunity of presenting their case, listen fairly to both sides (*audi alteram partem*) and reach a decision untainted by bias. See *Wiswell* v. *The Metropolitan Corp. of Greater Winnipeg*, [1965] S.C.R. 512. *The Queen (Ex parte Municipal Spraying & Contracting Ltd.)* v. *Labour Relations Board (Nova Scotia)*, [1955] 2 D.L.R. 681 at 688 (N.S.S.C.). *Nicholson* v. *Haldimand-Norfolk Regional Board of Commissioners of Police*, [1979] 1 S.C.R. 311.

Although the matter remains unsettled, it is generally understood that the principles of natural justice apply to statutory boards exercising only **judicial** or quasi-judicial functions, while the duty of fairness (which may be something less than natural justice) applies to those bodies exercising administrative functions. See *Calgary Power Ltd.* v. *Copithorne*, [1959] S.C.R. 24. *Coopers & Lybrand* v. *Minister of National Revenue* (1978), 24 N.R. 163 (S.C.C.). *Nicholson* v. *Haldimand-Norfolk Regional Board of Commissioners of Police*, [1979] 1 S.C.R. 311 at 324–28.

NATURAL LAW The law of nature. This law, which is different from man-made law, is set forth by God through human reason to conform man's human nature, meaning his whole mental, moral, and physical constitution. Knowledge of natural laws may be attained merely by the light of reason, from the facts of their essential aggreeableness with the constitution of human nature. Natural law exists regardless of whether it is enacted as **positive law.** See also **positivism.** *Chabot* v. *Les Commissaires D'Ecoles de Lamorandiere*, [1957] B.R. 707 at 721–22 (Que.C.A.).

NATURAL LAW THEORY In jurisprudence, the view that the nature and value of any legal order is best understood by studying how the **positive law** of that legal order agrees or contrasts with **natural law.**

NATURAL PERSON "A natural person is a human being that has the capacity for rights or duties." *Hague* v. *Cancer Relief & Research Institute*, [1939] 4 D.L.R. 191 at 194 (Man.K.B.). Compare **artificial person; corporation.**

NECESSARY INFERENCE The only inevitable inference that can be deduced from a proposition. It is not a "necessary inference" if one can deduce another reasonable inference. Compare **presumption.**

NECESSARY PARTY A person whose **joinder** to an action is necessary in order that complete relief may be obtained by the **party** (either plaintiff or defendant) who is joining them. "[T]hen the court in its discretion may allow him to be added as a party....It enables all matters in dispute 'to be effectually and completely determined and adjudicated upon' between all those directly concerned in the outcome." *Gurtner* v. *Circuit*, [1968] 1 All E.R. 328 at 332 (C.A.). See also *Harron* v. *Crown Trust Co.*, [1955] O.W.N. 48 (H.C.).

NECESSITY, DEFENCE OF In **criminal** law, excusing the defendant of **guilt** for an **offence** that was committed under circumstances of great urgency and where there was no opportunity to pursue an alternative course of action that did not involve a breach of the law. The **defence** is available in the criminal law context by virtue of s. 8(3) of the *Criminal Code*, R.S.C. 1985, c. C–46, which preserves **common-law** defences. Necessity differs from **self-defence** in that the person whose interests are adversely affected by the defendant's conduct is innocent of any responsibility for the creation of danger to the defendant.

The limitation on this defence is that "[w]here an accused believes upon reasonable and probable grounds that serious harm will befall himself or some other person, he is justified in committing a criminal offence to avert that harm if there is such an emergency that no other course of conduct is reasonably possible in order to prevent that harm; but this defence does not apply where the offence committed gives rise to more serious harm than that sought to be prevented." A. Mewett & M. Manning, *Criminal Law* 351 (2d ed. 1985).

"A defence of necessity at the very least must rest upon evidence from which a jury could find (i) that the accused in good faith considered the situation so emergent that failure to terminate the pregnancy immediately could endanger life or health and (ii) that upon any reasonable view of the facts compliance with the law was impossible." *Morgentaler* v. *The Queen* (1975), 20 C.C.C. (2d) 449 at 500 (S.C.C.).

In **tort** law, there are two types of necessity—public and private. PUBLIC NECESSITY involves the interference with private rights for the safety and convenience of the public. The individual who suffers loss receives no compensation. PRIVATE NECESSITY exists when the defendant acts to protect his own interest, whether to preserve his own life, health or property, as long as no damage occurs to another's property. When damage does occur to another's property as the result of a claim of private necessity, there is a conflict of authority. One line of authority holds that you may cause property damage in order to save lives or property of greater value. *Bell Canada* v. *The Ship "Mar-Tirenno"* (1974), 52 D.L.R. (3d) 702 (F.C.). The other line of authority recognizes an incomplete **privilege**. The intrusion on another's property under claim of private necessity is protected as long as it is a technical tort and no damage is committed. Once damage occurs, the party who incurs the damage must be compensated by the party who received the benefit of the intrusion. *Read* v. *Smith* (1836), 2 N.B.R. 173 (S.C.).

Compare **justification.**

NEGATIVE PREGNANT In **pleading,** a **denial** that implies an affirmation of a substantial fact and hence is beneficial to opponent. Thus, when only a qualification or modification is denied while the fact itself remains undenied, the denial is pregnant with the affirmation of that fact.

NEGLIGENCE "Negligence is the omitting to do something that a **reasonable man** would do or the doing something which a reasonable man would not do....It is really the absence of such care as it was the duty of the defendant to use....The care taken by a prudent man has always been the rule laid down—a regard to caution such as a man of ordinary prudence would observe." *Bishop* v. *McDonald* (1942), 16 M.P.R. 455 at 467 (N.B.S.C.A.D.). Compare **reckless disregard.**

CONTRIBUTORY NEGLIGENCE Conduct on the part of plaintiff that falls below the standard of care to which he should conform for his own protection and that, when combined with defendant's negligence, was a legally contributing cause bringing about the plaintiff's harm or injury. At common law the defendant can raise contributory negligence as a defence to a negligence action brought by the plaintiff against him, thereby alleging that the plaintiff's own negligence directly caused or contributed to his own injuries. "The defence of contributory negligence has but two elements, namely, that the injured person did not in his own interest take reasonable care of himself, and by this want of care contributed to his own injury." *Branley* v. *Gugins and Mac-Donald,* [1952] 4 D.L.R. 646 at 649 (Alta.S.C.). See also *Winnipeg Oil Co.* v. *Canadian Northern Ry. Co.* (1911), 18 W.L.R. 424 at 441 (Man.C.A.). *Hendricks* v. *The Queen* (1969), 9 D.L.R. (3d) 454 (S.C.C.). *Lepine* v. *Demeule* (1973), 36 D.L.R. (3d) 388 (N.W.T.C.A.). Contributory negligence legislation has been enacted in all the common-law provinces. See, e.g., *The Negligence Act,* R.S.O. 1990, c. N.1. As a defence the **burden of proof** is on the defendant. Compare **assumption of the risk.** A. Linden, *Canadian Tort Law* 439 (5th ed. 1993).

CRIMINAL [CULPABLE] NEGLIGENCE Such negligence as is necessary to incur criminal liability. "(1) Everyone is criminally negligent who (a) in doing anything, or (b) in omitting to do anything that it is his duty to do, shows wanton or reckless disregard for the lives or safety of other persons. (2) For the purposes of this section, 'duty' means a duty imposed by law." *Criminal Code*, R.S.C., 1985, c. C–46, s. 219 *R.* v. *Sharp* (1984), 12 C.C.C. (3d) 428 (Ont. C.A.). See also *R.* v. *Waite*, [1989] 1 S.C.R. 1436; *R.* v. *Tutton*, [1989] 1 S.C.R. 1392.

NEGLIGENCE PER SE Negligence as a matter of law. Frequently used in relation to a breach of a safety statute where violation would be regarded as "statutory negligence." J. Fleming, *The Law of Torts* 124 (8th ed. 1992). The terms *negligence per se* and *statutory negligence* are sometimes used interchangeably. *Ritchie and Colvin* v. *Ptaff*, [1954] O.W.N. 865 (C.A.); *The Lionel* v. *The Manchester Merchant*, [1970] S.C.R. 538.

NEGOTIATE In reference to a bill of exchange, to transfer for value by delivery or endorsement for a valuable consideration. In contract law, the process preceding contract formation in a bilateral relationship. Negotiation ends when one or both parties terminate the interaction short of contract formation or when a contract is formed.

NEGOTIABLE INSTRUMENT An instrument that passes by delivery giving the bona fide holder for value a good title. A bona fide holder of the instrument for value is known as a holder in due course, and he holds it free from any claims, defects, or equities affecting the title of the transferor. A negotiable instrument usually contains an obligation or unconditional promise by the maker to pay a certain sum of money at a definite time to the holder or bearer of the instrument. A transfer of the instrument may operate as a complete legal transfer of the document and obligation which is enforceable by the transferee. Bills of exchange, cheques, and promissory notes are the most important kind of negotiable instruments. *Martin* v. *National Union Fire Insurance Co. of Pittsburg*, [1923] 3 D.L.R. 220

(Alta.S.C.), affirmed [1923] 4 D.L.R. 574 (Alta.S.C.A.D.), affirmed [1924] S.C.R. 348; *The Provincial Treasurer of Manitoba* v. *Bennett*, [1937] S.C.R. 138.

NEMO EST SUPRA LEGIS *(nā'-mō ĕst sū'-prà lā'-gĭs)* Lat.: nobody is above the law.

NEMO JUDEX IN CAUSA SUA DEBET ESSE *(nā'-mō jū'-dĕks ĭn kaw'-zà sū'-à dĕ'-bĕt ĕ'-sĕ)* Lat.: no one ought to be a judge in his own cause. Usually referred to as the second limb of the principles of natural justice, the rules against bias do not require the courts to look for proof of actual bias. The most common test used by the courts is to ask whether a reasonable man in the applicant's position, conversant with all the facts, would have considered there was a real likelihood that the decision-maker was biased. D. Mullan, *Administrative Law* 53 (3d ed. 1979); *Minister of Highways, British Columbia* v. *Shaw* (1970), 18 D.L.R. (3d) 636 at 638 (B.C.S.C.).

NERVOUS SHOCK Substantial damage to the state of mind of a person suffered through the means of one or more of the senses for which a plaintiff can have a cause of action in tort as physical injury. "If impact be not necessary, and if, as must be assumed here, the fear is proved to have naturally and directly produced physical effects, so that the ill results of the negligence which caused the fear are as measurable in damages as the same results would be if they arose from an actual impact, why should not an action for those damages lie just as well as it lies where there has been an actual impact." *Dulieu* v. *White & Sons*, [1901] 2 K.B. 669 at 675. See also *Austin* v. *Mascarin*, [1942] O.R. 165 (S.C.); *Vana* v. *Tosta*, [1968] S.C.R. 71 at 80–82; *Pollard* v. *Makarchuk* (1958), 16 D.L.R. (2d) 225 (Alta.S.C.); *Horne* v. *New Glasgow*, [1954] 1 D.L.R. 832 (N.S.S.C.).

NET ESTATE *In re Barker Estate*, [1946] 2 W.W.R. 543 at 547–48 (Man.Surr.Ct.), held "net estate" to be that which was defined in *The Dower Act*, R.S.M. 1940, c. 55, s. 2(*d*), as follows: "all the net real and personal property of a testator, together with all moneys paid or payable after the testator's death under or by virtue of insurance policies on the life of the testator to and for the benefit of the wife

... and together with any property owned at the time of the testator's death by the wife ... which is property (or the proceeds or investments of property) which the testator had during his life after marriage conveyed to his wife ... as a gift or by way of advancement."

NET INCOME Gross income after all deductions and exemptions. See *Oryx Realty Corp.* v. *M.N.R.,* [1974] C.T.C. 430 (F.C.A.); *Samson* v. *M.N.R.,* [1943] C.T.C. 47 at 58–59 (Ex.); *Re Caulfield,* [1933] O.W.N. 233 at 234 (H.C.).

NEW MATTER In pleading, issues raised by the **defendant,** which are more than denials of the **plaintiff's** allegations, encompassing new issues and new facts to be proven. New matter implies that the alleged **cause of action** never did exist and that the essential allegations are not the truth.

NEXT FRIEND [I]n all cases where a party cannot sue for himself, the court employs a prochein amy as its officer to conduct the suit for him...." *Morgan* v. *Thorne* (1841), 7 M. & W. 400 at 409; 151 E.R. 821 at 825 (Ex.). This officer of the court, originally known as a "prochein amy," was later named by the Chancery Division *next friend,* and the term became applied universally. Generally, persons under legal disability, such as infants, could only bring an action by their next friend. See, e.g., *Weir* v. *Weir,* [1939] 1 D.L.R. 57 (Man.K.B.) The term *next friend* is not used often in Canada, being replaced in many jurisdictions by GUARDIAN AD LITEM. The **guardian** ad litem performs the same functions as the next friend; i.e., he commences or defends proceedings on behalf of a minor or a mentally incompetent person. See *British Columbia Supreme Court Rules* (1990) r. 6(2); *Nova Scotia Civil Procedure Rules* (1983), r. 6.02(1).

NEXT OF KIN Refers to the nearest in blood, "... and not to the statutory next of kin, unless the testator has in some way referred to the statutory as distinct from common law kinship." *Re Young* (1928), 62 O.L.R. 275 at 278 (Ont.S.C.). See also *Fasken* v. *Fasken,* [1953] 2 S.C.R. 10 at 14–15; *Re Jardin Estate, Re Carey Estate, Royal Trust Company* v. *Jardine* (1956), 18 W.W.R. (N.S.) 445 at 449–50 (Alta.S.C.A.D.).

NIHIL *(nĭ'-hĭl)* Lat.: nothing, not at all, in no respect. Nil is an often used form to express the noun.

NIL See **nihil.**

NISI PRIUS *(nī'-sī prē'-ŭs)* Lat.: unless before. A trial at *nisi prius* was a jury trial before a single judge as opposed to actions tried at the bar, that is, before the full court, which consisted of several judges. Trial at nisi prius followed after the sheriff was commanded to bring the jurors from the county where the cause of action arose to the court at Westminster "unless before" that day [*nisi prius*] the justices of assize came to that county.

NO FORCE AND EFFECT Under s. 52 of the *Constitution Act, 1982,* any law which is inconsistent with the provisions of the *Constitution Act, 1982* (which includes the **Canadian Charter of Rights and Freedoms)** is, to the extent of the inconsistency, of no force and effect. Laws and provisions which are of no force and effect are commonly referred to as being "struck down." See *R.* v. *Wholesale Travel Group Inc.* (1991), 8 C.R. (4th) 145 (S.C.C.).

NOLLE PROSEQUI *(nŏl'-ā prŏs'-ē-kwē)* Lat.: unwilling to proceed. The authority conferred by the *Criminal Code,* R.S.C. 1985, c. C–46, s. 579(1), upon the **Attorney-General** to grant a stay of proceedings upon an indictment is what was termed under the common law "entering a *nolle prosequi.*" This proceeding does not operate as an acquittal but merely suspends the proceedings. *R.* v. *Imperial Tobacco Co. of Canada Ltd.,* [1942] 1 W.W.R. 363 at 368–69 (Alta S.C.A.D.). *R.* v. *Spence* (1919), 31 C.C.C. 365 (Ont. S.C.A.D.). Any proceedings stayed may be recommenced without laying a new charge or preferring a new indictment by the Crown giving notice to the clerk of the court in which the stay of proceedings was entered. However, notice must be given within one year after the entry of the stay; otherwise the proceedings shall be deemed never to have been commenced. *Criminal Code,* R.S.C. 1985, c. C–46, s. 579(2).

NOLO CONTENDERE *(nō'-lō kŏn-těn'-dě-rā)* Lat.: I do not wish to contend, fight, or maintain (a **defence**); not strictly a **plea**

charge made by the government. Like a **demurrer** to an **indictment,** it admits all facts stated in the indictment for the purposes of a particular **case,** but it cannot be used as an **admission** elsewhere, as it is an implied **confession** only of the **offence** charged. Thus corporations often plead *nolo contendere* in order to avoid any **collateral** civil effects from their plea in criminal antitrust cases. The plea of *nolo contendere* is equivalent to a plea of guilty for the purposes of the criminal matter and is accepted only in the discretion of the trial court, which must be satisfied that the plea is voluntarily and intelligently entered and that there is factual basis to support it.

NOMINAL DAMAGES   See **damages.**

NOMINAL PARTY   See **party.**

NON COMPOS MENTIS *(nŏn kŏm'-pōs mĕn'-tĭs)* Lat.: of unsound mind; insane. *Ex parte Barnsley* (1744), 3 Atk. 168 at 171; 26 E.R. 899 at 900 (Ch.); *Re Kelly* (1875), 6 P.R. 220 (Ch.Cham.).

NON-CONFORMING USE   A **use** of land or buildings that lawfully existed prior to the enactment of a **zoning** by-law and that does not conform to the by-law enacted but may continue to exist as a "nonconforming use." *Rex ex rel. Rodgers* v. *Clark Brothers & Hughes Ltd.* (1924), 34 Man.R. 521 (C.A.); *Town of Richmond Hill* v. *Miller Paving Ltd.* (1978), 22 O.R. (2d) 779 (H.C.). Many provinces have enacted planning acts or similar legislation that gives protection to a non-conforming use of land or buildings. See, e.g., *The Planning Act*, R.S.N.S. 1989, c. 346, s. 90; *The Planning Act*, R.S.O. 1990, c. P.13. Holding or occupying the land, *Re Davis and The City of Toronto* (1891), 21 O.R. 243 at 247 (Q.B.), or making use of it "... for enjoyment, revenue or profit without in any way otherwise diminishing or impairing the property itself" constitutes a use of the land. *Pickering Twp.* v. *Godfrey*, [1958] O.R. 429 at 437 (C.A.). See also **grandfather period.** Compare **variance.**

NON-CUSTODIAL SENTENCE   See **probation.**

NON-DISCLOSURE   In insurance law, the failure of the assured to bring to the notice of the insurers a material fact he is under a duty to reveal. When the failure to reveal the fact is not intentional and the assured deals **bona fide** with the insurers, the term *non-disclosure* is used. E. Ivamy, *General Principles of Insurance Law* 122 (5th ed. 1986).

"Disclosure" has a specific **administrative law** meaning, i.e., the disclosure to parties of information the agency or board has about the decision to be made that will affect the interests of the party or parties. It is part of the rules of **natural justice.**

NON EST FACTUM *(nŏn ĕst fäk'-tŭm)* Lat.: it is not his deed. The old common-law defence that allows a person who has signed a written document in ignorance of its character to plead that, notwithstanding his signature, "it is not his deed." See *Prudential Trust Co. Ltd.* v. *Cugnet*, [1956] S.C.R. 914 at 921–26; *Marvco Color Research* v. *Harris*, [1982] 2 S.C.R. 774.

NON-EXCULPATORY DEFENCES   "Defences" that afford an accused with the means to avoid conviction for reasons unrelated to his/her guilt; i.e. **de minimis, abuse of process.**

NON-FEASANCE   The neglect or failure to do some act that ought to be done; *e.g.,* failing to clear a sidewalk of ice and snow. *Brooks* v. *Whyte*, [1934] O.R. 55 at 58 (C.A.); *The City of Saint John* v. *Jane Campbell* (1896), 26 S.C.R. 1. It differs from **misfeasance,** which is the improper performance of an act one may lawfully do.

NON OBSTANTE VEREDICTO [N.O.V.] *(nŏn ŏb-stän'-tā vĕr-ĕ-dĭk'-tō)* Lat.: notwithstanding the verdict. See **judgment** [JUDGMENT N.O.V.].

NON-PERFORMANCE   Generally, the failure to keep the terms of a **contract** rendering the party failing to do so liable to the innocent party in damages for breach of contract.

NON-REBUTTABLE PRESUMPTION See **presumption** [CONCLUSIVE PRESUMPTION].

NON-REPAIR   In *Armour* v. *Town of Peterborough* (1905), 10 O.L.R. 306 at 308 (in chambers), the court interpreted s. 104 of the *Judicature Act*, R.S.O. 1897, c. 51, in the following way: " 'non-repair' seems to mean any omission of duty on the part of the municipality which makes the highway unsafe. Making a new road or walk defectively and having it in such unsafe condition would seem to be 'non-repair'...."

"[Non-repair] in my view, is an abstract noun, being the name of a state or condition of the street, and not a verbal noun meaning 'not repairing.' " *Brown* v. *City of Toronto* (1910), 21 O.L.R. 230 at 236 (Div.Ct.).

NON-RESIDENCE, NON-RESIDENT Non-resident is the condition applied to a person who is not ordinarily resident in Canada. For the correct meaning of "ordinarily resident" under s. 3(1) of the *Divorce Act*, R.S.C. 1985 (2nd Supp.), c. 3, see *Marsellus* v. *Marsellus* (1970), 75 W.W.R. 746 (B.C.S.C.); *Graves* v. *Graves* (1973), 11 R.F.L. (N.S.S.C.); *Anema* v. *Anema and Foss*, (1976), R.F.L. 156 (Man.Q.B.). Non-resident means not resident in Canada. *Income Tax Act*, S.C. 1970–71–72, c. 63, s. 248(1) as amended; *Erikson* v. *M.N.R.* [1980] C.T.C. 2117 (T.R.B.). Residence sometimes represents one of the qualifications of a director of a corporation. See *Canadian Business Corporations Act*, R.S.C. 1985, c. C–44, s. 105(3).

NON SEQUITUR *(nŏn sĕ'-kwĭ-tūr)* Lat.: it does not follow; often abbreviated non seq. When an action or decree is non sequitur, it is unrelated to the preceding events. A non sequitur is something that has no logical or temporal purpose for its place in the progression of events; it is logically, temporally, and spatially incoherent.

NON SUI JURIS *(nŏn sū'-ē jū'-rĭs)* Lat.: not by his own authority or legal right. This maxim refers to those who are not legally **competent** to manage their own affairs as regards **contracts** and other causes in which this **incompetency** restricts their granting **power of attorney** or otherwise exercising self-judgment. Compare **non compos mentis.**

NONSUIT A **judgment** rendered against a **plaintiff** who fails to proceed to trial or is unable to prove his case. Since the adjudication is made when the **complainant** has simply failed to provide evidence sufficient to make out a case, it does not decide the **merits** of his **cause of action** and thus does not preclude his bringing it again. Strictly, there is no longer such a thing as a nonsuit. *Fox* v. *Star Newspaper Co. Ltd.,* [1900] A.C. 19. But the word is now used to denote the act of the judge when he withdraws the case from the jury and directs judgment to be entered for the defendant without (or in spite of) their verdict. *Mars* v. *Drury* (1913), 3 W.W.R. 1143 at 1144 (Sask.S.C. en banc).

Before 1883, the term was used to mean the abandonment of a case at the trial before the jury gave their verdict, and judgment of nonsuit was given against the plaintiff, when he failed to prove his case or proceed to trial.

NON-USER A person who may lose a right acquired by use. The term is mainly used with reference to **easements,** profits **à prendre** (the right to take the production of another's land), and similar rights. Such rights may be extinguished by the non-user for a certain number of years, but not fewer than twenty years. The non-user must show an intention to cease to exercise a right or must neglect to use it.

NOSCITUR A SOCIIS *(nŏ'-sī-tūr à sŏ'-sĕ-ĭs)* Lat.: The meaning of a word can be understood by its companions. One can get the meaning of a word from its accompanying words or by reference to the meaning of words or phrases associated with it. "English words derive colour from those which surround them." *Bourne* v. *Norwich Crematorium Ltd.,* [1967] 2 All E.R. 576 at 578 (Ch.). The maxim is generally applied as an aid to interpretation of statutory language. "When two or more words susceptible of analogous meaning, are coupled together, *noscitur a sociis*; they are understood to be used in their cognate sense. They take, as it were, their colour from each other; that is the more general is restricted to a sense analogous to the less general." *Fraser* v. *Pere Marquette R.W. Co.* (1908), 18 O.L.R. 589 at 602 (C.A.); *The Queen* v. *France* (1898), 1 C.C.C. 321 at 331–32 (Que.Q.B.).

NOTA BENE *(nŏ'-tà bā'-nā)* Lat.: note or mark well. Usually written *N.B.*, it is used to call attention to something important in a text.

NOTARY PUBLIC A person authorized to administer oaths, take affidavits, and execute, authenticate or certify documents. In most provincial jurisdictions private persons may receive permission to act as notaries or may be appointed a notary public by the provincial Lieutenant-Governor. In some provinces a lawyer admitted to practice within the jurisdiction can act as a notary public. See, e.g., *Notaries and Commissioners Act*, R.S.N.S. 1989, c. 312, s. 11; *Notarial Act*, R.S.Q. 1977, c. N–2, ss. 107, 113. For variations in appointment of notaries compare *Notaries and Commissioners Act*, R.S.N.S. 1989, c. 312; *The Notaries Public Act*, R.S.A. 1980, c. N–11; *The Notaries Public Act*, R.S.S. 1978, c. N–8; *Notaries Act*, S.B.C. 1981, c. 23.

NOT GUILTY The **plea** to an indictment by which the prisoner wishes to deny everything, letting the **prosecution** make and prove the case as best they can.

The plea denies the entire case of the prosecution and places the burden on them to prove the facts and case in issue beyond a **reasonable doubt.**

See *Criminal Code* R.S.C. 1985, C–46, s. 613.

NOTICE 1. Information or knowledge regarding a fact actually brought to a person's attention; **2.** also, the **service** of a document on a **defendant** in an action that has been commenced against him.

Notice may be *actual (express)*, *constructive*, or *implied*. Actual notice is express notice when any fact is conveyed to a person either in writing or by oral communication.

ACTUAL NOTICE "[A]ctual notice [is] knowledge, not presumed as in the case of constructive notice, but shown to be actually brought home to the party charged with it, either by proof of his own admission or by the evidence of witnesses who are able to establish that the very fact, of which notice is to be established, not something which would have led to the discovery of the fact if an enquiry had been pursued, was brought to his knowledge." *Rose* v. *Peterkin* (1885), 13 S.C.R. 677 at 694; *Harrington* v. *Spring Creek Cheese Manufacturing Co.* (1904), 7 O.L.R. 319 at 325 (C.A.); *Sherboneau* v. *Jeffs* (1869), 15. Gr. 574 at 576 (Ch.). In some provincial jurisdictions in relation to the **conveyance** of any **interest** in

land, where the conveyance is registered in the proper Land Registry or Land Titles office, all persons who receive an interest in the same lands after such registration are conclusively deemed to have actual notice of any previous conveyance. See, e.g., *The Registry Act*, R.S.O. 1990, c. R. 20, s. 74; *The Registry Act*, R.S.M. 1987, c. R–50, s. 53.

CONSTRUCTIVE NOTICE Knowledge of a fact imputed by law to a person, even though he may not have actual knowledge of it, since the circumstances should have put him on inquiry. "Constructive notice, properly so called, is the knowledge which the Courts impute to a person upon a presumption so strong of the existence of the knowledge, that it cannot be allowed to be rebutted, either from his knowing something which ought to have put him upon further inquiry, or from his willfully abstaining from inquiry, to avoid notice." *Espin* v. *Pemberton* (1859), 3 De G. & J. 547 at 554; 44 E.R. 1380 at 1383 (Ch.). "Constructive notice is defined as notice of such facts as should have put one on his guard." *Ferguson* v. *Zinn*, [1933] O.R. 9 at 17 (S.C.). See also *Bishop* v. *Western Trust Co.* [1922] 3 W.W.R. 818 at 822 (Sask.K.B.); *Ross* v. *Hunter* (1882), 7 S.C.R. 289 at 304–05.

IMPLIED NOTICE A variety of actual notice that arises where the existence of a fact is within the knowledge of a party so that he is put upon inquiry and can discover the true facts by making reasonable inquiry. For example, in the law of **agency,** notice can be implied or imputed by law to the **principal** when notice of any issue or matter is given to an **agent** when the matter is within the scope of his agency. The principal cannot deny notice except to charge that the agent is in collusion with the party claiming such notice. See generally *Cave* v. *Cave* (1880), 15 Ch.D. 639 at 643–44; *Berwick & Co.* v. *Price*, [1905] 1 Ch. 632 at 639.

JUDICIAL NOTICE See **judicial notice.**

NOTICE OF APPEAL A written notice that follows the Rules of Practice of the appropriate appellate court, given by a **litigant** to the other party and listing the grounds of his appeal from a court's verdict. See *Re Favretto,* [1938] 1 D.L.R. 230 at 237 (N.S.S.C.).

NOTICE OF ASSESSMENT A notice from a taxing authority—for example, the Minister of Revenue under the Income Tax Act or, in a municipal corporation, the clerk in regard to real property situated within the boundaries of the municipal unit—whereby a taxpayer is informed of the tax assessment owed by him. See *Income Tax Act,* S.C. 1970–71–72, c. 63, s. 152(2); *Pure Spring Co. Ltd.* v. *M.N.R.,* [1946] C.T.C. 169 at 198 (Ex.); *Morch* v. *M.N.R.,* [1949] C.T.C. 250 at 258 (Ex.); *Pupatello* v. *M.N.R.,* [1977] C.T.C. 499 at 503–05 (F.).

NOTICE OF DISHONOUR In regard to **bills of exchange,** a notice given by the payee or endorsee thereof, to all concerned other than the acceptor that the bill was not honoured at presentment. Notice of dishonour is required in order that parties to the bill can protect themselves by taking up the bill and commencing action against the party ultimately responsible upon it. See *Bills of Exchange Act,* R.S.C. 1985, c. B–4, s. 101; *Bank of Nova Scotia* v. *Sharp,* [1975] 6 W.W.R. 97 (B.C.C.A.) reversing [1974] 6 W.W.R. 481 (B.C.S.C.).

NOTICE OF MOTION In an action, a written notice that one party wishing to undertake an **interlocutory** proceeding serves on other interested parties to the litigation instructing the others of the relief that is sought from the court, and including the time, date, and location where his motion is to be heard. The form and particulars of such notice are regulated by the Rules of Practice of the appropriate courts. See, e.g. *Ontario Rules of Civil Procedure,* R.R.O. 1990, Reg. 194, r. 37.06; *British Columbia Supreme Court Rules* (1990), rr. 44(3), 44(7); *Rules of Court, New Brunswick,* (1981), N.B. Reg. 82–73, r. 37. Not all provincial rules make use of this term. For example, in Nova Scotia, interlocutory proceedings are commenced not by filing a notice of motion but by either an interlocutory notice (application **inter partes**) or an interlocutory notice (**ex parte** application). See *Nova Scotia Civil Procedure Rules* (1983), r. 37.03.

NOTICE TO QUIT A notice of the termination of a tenancy given by either a landlord or a tenant. "A notice to quit ... must ... be unambiguous and certain in its terms, and it must indicate an intention to put an end to the tenancy." *Gemeroy* v. *Proverbs,* [1924] 2 W.W.R. 764 at 765 (Sask.C.A.). See also *Burquitlam Co-operative Housing Ass'n* v. *Romund* (1976), 1 B.C.L.R. 229 (Co.Ct.). The form and particulars of such notices are regulated by the relevant provincial statutes relating to landlords and tenants. See, e.g., *Residential Tenancies Act,* R.S.N.S. 1989, c. 401, s. 10; *Landlord and Tenant Act,* R.S.N.B. 1973, c. L-1, s. 19; *Landlord and Tenant Act,* R.S.P.E.I. 1989, c. L-4, s. 77. In some provincial jurisdictions the term *notice of termination* is used. See *Residential Tenancy Act,* S.B.C. 1984, c. 15, ss. 23–27; *Residential Tenancies Act,* R.S.A. 1980, c. R–15.3, ss. 4–9; *The Residential Tenancies Act,* R.S.S. 1978, c. R–22, ss. 22, 23.

NOTORIOUS POSSESSION Occupation of **real property** in an open undisguised and conspicuous manner, so that such possession is well known and recognized. The term is one of the elements in defining or determining a claim of **adverse possession** that involves an assertion of a right to property not by legal **title** but by possession and occupation for a period of time governed by statute (at least twenty years under provincial Statutes of Limitations). The possession is required to be actual, continuous and notorious so that the titleholder without actual **notice** of such possession may be presumed in law to have received notice. See *Sherren* v. *Pearson* (1886), 14 S.C.R. 581 at 585–86; *Wood* v. *LeBlanc* (1904), 34 S.C.R. 627 at 638–39.

Where an **interest** in an **easement** is claimed to have been acquired by **prescription** (having acquired an interest through continuous use for a period of twenty years rather than by legal right or title), it must be shown, in addition to use for the required period, that use of the easement was such that it could be said to be *nec vi, nec clam, nec precario*—i.e., not by violence, not secretly but by open and notorious use, and not by request or permission of the owner of the land over which the claim is being asserted. See

McLachlin v. *Schlievert* (1911), 18 O.W.R. 457 at 457–58 (Div.Ct.); *Adams* v. *Fairweather* (1906), 13 O.L.R. 490 at 495–96 (Div.Ct.); *Garfinkel* v. *Kleinberg and Kleinberg*, [1955] O.R. 388 at 393–94 (C.A.).

NOTWITHSTANDING CLAUSE See **override clause.**

N.O.V. See **judgment** [JUDGMENT N.O.V.].

NOVATION Agreement of one **party** to a **contract** to the substitution of a new party to replace one of the original parties to the contract. The result is a new contract on the same terms as the old, but with a new party. A common example is where a creditor at the request of the debtor agrees to the substitution of another party as debtor in place of the original debtor. "[N]ovation ... means this—the term being derived from the Civil Law—that there being a contract in existence, some new contract is substituted for it, either between the same parties (for that might be) or between different parties; the consideration mutually being the discharge of the old contract." *West* v. *Occidental Fire Ins. Co.*, [1927] 3 D.L.R. 260 at 263 (Sask.K.B.), quoting Lord Selborne, L.C., in *Scarf* v. *Jardine* (1882), 7 App.Cas. 345 at 351 (H.L.). See also *In re Abernethy-Lougheed Logging Co.; Attorney-General for British Columbia* v. *Salter*, [1940] 1 W.W.R. 319 at 326–27 (B.C.C.A.); *Irwin* v. *Kelly* (1908), 8 W.L.R. 95 at 101 (Y.T.).

NOVUS ACTUS INTERVENIENS See **cause** [SUPERSEDING CAUSE].

NUDUM PACTUM *(nū'-dŭm păk'-tŭm)* Lat.: a nude **contract.** A bare agreement; a bare **promise** made without **consideration.** A bare contract is not enforceable unless made under **seal.** *Brayfield* v. *Cardiff* (1893), 9 Man.R. 302 (Q.B.); *Stewart* v. *Rennie* (1836), 5 U.C.Q.B. (O.S.) 151.

NUGATORY Void; of no effect; invalid. For example, **judicial proceedings** in a court that lacks **jurisdiction** are sometimes considered nugatory. Compare **voidable.**

NUISANCE An act or omission, causing injury to a person's health, comfort, or convenience, or impairing the **use** and enjoyment of one's property and giving rise to an action for damages. Unlike **negligence,** where the damage must be shown to have been caused by some want of care, in nuisance it is the injury itself that gives rise to an action for damages.

There are two kinds of nuisance, public and private. A PUBLIC NUISANCE is an act that interferes with a right enjoyed by all members of the community. A PRIVATE NUISANCE is an interference with the use or enjoyment of a person's land or of rights in the land. "Now, to be a nuisance, the act must be unlawful. A public nuisance must affect the welfare of the community. A private nuisance must specially affect the welfare of an individual and moreover, a nuisance, whether public or private, must have some element of continuity." *Hutson* v. *United Motor Service Ltd.*, [1936] O.R. 225 at 228–29 (C.A.), affirmed *(sub nom.) United Motors Service, Inc.* v. *Hutson*, [1937] S.C.R. 294. See generally *Muirhead* v. *Timbers Bros. Sand & Gravel Ltd.* (1977), 3 C.C.L.T. 1 (Ont.H.C.).

Common nuisance means a public nuisance. See *R.* v. *McGregor*, [1979] 3 W.W.R. 651 at 656–57 (B.C.Prov.Ct.). A COMMON NUISANCE occurs where one commits an unlawful act or fails to discharge a legal duty and thereby endangers the lives, safety, health, property, or comfort of the public or obstructs the public in the exercise or enjoyment of any right that is common to all the subjects of Her Majesty in Canada. *Criminal Code,* R.S.C. 1985, c. C–46, s. 180(2). Under s 180(1), everyone who commits a common nuisance and thereby endangers the lives, safety, or health of the public or causes physical injury to any person is guilty of an **indictable offence** and is liable to two years' imprisonment. See also **abatable nuisance.**

NULLITY Of no legal force or effect; invalid. See *Trusts & Guarantee Co.* v. *Trustee of the Property of National Debenture Corp. Ltd.*, [1946] 3 D.L.R. 28 at 36–37 (Ont.C.A.); *Elloway* v. *British Columbia Electric Ry. Co. Ltd.* (1956), 19 W.W.R. (N.S.) 408 at 413 (B.C.S.C.); *R.* v. *Dupuis* (1975), 23 C.C.C. (2d) 358 at 360 (Ont.C.A.).

NUNC PRO TUNC *(nŭnk prō tŭnk)* Lat.: now for then. A judgment *nunc pro tunc* is entered when the court directs a proceeding to be dated as of an earlier date than that on which it was actually taken. A **judgment** that was delayed by act of the court can be antedated, or if the plaintiff has died between the hearing and date when the judgment was given, a judgment *nunc pro tunc* may be entered.

"Leave of the court must be obtained to do things *nunc pro tunc;* and this is granted to answer the purposes of justice, but never to do an injustice. A judgment *nunc pro tunc* can be entered only when the delay has arisen from the act of the court." *Carey* v. *Beardsley* (1973), 6 N.S.R. (2d) 46 at 48 (Co.Ct.), quoting from 11 *Bouvier's Law Dictionary* 247 (1875).

O

OAKES TEST A standard inquiry articulated by the Supreme Court of Canada in *R.* v. *Oakes* [1986] 1 S.C.R. 103 for the interpretation of s. 1 of The **Canadian Charter of Rights and Freedoms,** which guarantees the Charter rights and freedoms "subject only to such reasonable limits prescribed by law as can be demonstrably justified in a free and democratic society."

"To establish that a limit is reasonable and demonstrably justified, two central criteria must be satisfied. First, the objective which the measures responsible for a limit on a Charter right or freedom are designed to serve, must be 'of sufficient importance' to warrant overriding a constitutionally protected right or freedom...

"Second, once a sufficiently significant objective is recognized, then the party invoking s. 1 must show that the means chosen are reasonable and demonstrably justified...First, the measures adopted must be carefully designed to achieve the objective in question... Second, the means, even if rationally connected to the objective in this first sense, should impair 'as little as possible' the right or freedom in question...Third, there must be a proportionality between the effects of the measures which are responsible for limiting the Charter right or freedom, and the objective which has been identified as of 'sufficient importance'..."

OATH An affirmation of the truth of a statement that, if made by a person who knows it to be false, may subject him to prosecution for **perjury** or other legal proceeding. See *Criminal Code, R.S.C.* 1985, c. C–46, ss. 133, 134. The form of the oath is immaterial provided that it involves in the mind of the **witness** the apprehension of punishment (by a Supreme Being). See *Crown Lumber Co.* v. *Hickle,* [1925] 1 D.L.R. 626 (Alta. S.C.A.D.). Writings (e.g., **affidavits**) as well as oral **testimony** may be made "under oath."

OBITER DICTUM *(ŏ′-bǐ-têr dǐk′-tŭm)* Lat.: a saying by the way; a passing or incidental statement. A statement made or decision reached in a court **opinion** that is not essential for disposition of the case. See *Davidner* v. *Schuster,* [1936] 1 D.L.R. 560 at 569 (Sask.C.A.). See **dictum.**

OBLIGATION A legal duty. **1.** It "refers to something in the nature of a **contract,** such as a **covenant, bond** or **agreement.**" *Stokes* v. *Leavens* (1918), 40 D.L.R. 23 at 24 (Man.C.A.). **2.** In the law of **tort** it refers to the bond created as a result of the special relationship existing between two or more persons, giving rise, e.g., to a duty to exercise **due care.**

OBLIGATION OF A CONTRACT The civil obligation, binding efficacy, coercive power, or legal duty of performing a contract. Thus the term refers not to any duty that arises out of the contract itself, but to the legal requirements that bind the contracting parties to the performance of their undertaking. But except where **specific performance** is available as a remedy, one cannot be compelled to actually perform a contract obligation; rather, he merely subjects himself to liability in **damages** if he fails to honor the obligation of a contract.

OBSCENE MATERIAL Material a dominant characteristic of which is "the undue exploitation of sex, or of sex and any one or more of the following subjects, namely, crime, horror, cruelty and violence." *Criminal Code,* R.S.C. 1985, c. C–46, s. 163(8). The standard set for judging whether material is obscene is a standard of tolerance "What matters is not what Canadians think is right for themselves to see. What matters is what Canadians would not abide other Canadians seeing because it would be beyond the contemporary Canadian standard of tolerance to see it." *Towne Cinema Theatres Ltd.* v. *The Queen* (1985), 18 C.C.C. (3d) 193(S.C.C.).

Section 163(8) does not violate section 2(b) (freedom of expression) of the **Canadian Charter of Rights and Freedoms,** and is not so vague as to violate s. 7 of the Charter. *R.* v. *Red Hot Video Ltd.* (1985), 18 C.C.C. (3d) 1 (B.C.C.A.).

OBSTRUCTION OF JUSTICE Acting to "obstruct, pervert or defeat the course of justice"; it is a criminal offence. Among acts that constitute an obstruction of justice are dissuading a person by threats from giving evidence; influencing a person in his capacity as a **juror;** or, being a person who may give evidence or act as a juror, accepting bribes or threats in connection with those duties. *Criminal Code*, R.S.C. 1985, c. C–46, s. 139. See **embracery.**

Obstructing the course of justice has been interpreted broadly to include an attempt to interfere with the normal enforcement by police of the contravention of a municipal by-law. *R.* v. *Zeck* (1980), 53 C.C.C. (2d) 551 (Ont.C.A.). Also, an attempt to dissuade a person from reporting an incident to the police may constitute the offence. *R.* v. *Whalen* (1974), 17 C.C.C. (2d) 217 (Ont.Co.Ct.).

OCCUPANT One who takes **possession;** one who has the actual use or possession of a thing; one who holds possession and exercises control over a thing; see *Purdy* v. *Rural Municipality of Langenburg*, [1918] 3 W.W.R. 161 (Sask.K.B.). The person with actual possession, such as a **tenant,** as distinguished from **landlord,** who retains the legal **ownership.**

OCCUPATIONAL DISEASE [INDUSTRIAL DISEASE] A disease peculiar to or characteristic of a particular industrial process, trade, or occupation; "a condition that results from exposure in a work place to a physical, chemical or biological agent to the extent that the normal physiological mechanisms are affected and the health of the worker is impaired thereby." *Occupational Health and Safety Act*, R.S.O. 1990, c. 0.1, s. 1. It usually arises after long and continued exposure to conditions of employment that are more dangerous than those found in employment and living conditions in general and frequently includes such diseases as silicosis, coal miners' pneumonoconiosis, lead poisoning, and frost-bite, among others. *Workmen's Compensation Act*, R.S.N.S. 1989, c. 508, ss. 84–94 and Sched. A. Where an employee suffers from one of these diseases as a result of his work, there arises, subject to statutory conditions, an entitlement to compensation. See, e.g., *Workmen's Compensation Act*, R.S.O. 1990, c. W.12, s. 134. See also **workmen's compensation acts.**

OCCUPATIONAL HAZARD A risk that is peculiar to a particular type of employ-

ment or work place and that arises as a natural incident of such employment or of employment in such a place.

OCCUPIERS' LIABILITY "The [common law] rules concerning occupiers' liability are those legal rules governing the **liability** of an occupier of land or other premises....The hallmark of occupiers' liability law is the fact that the occupier's **obligation** to persons visiting his premises depends on the legal class into which the visitor falls....Associated with each category is a different standard of care owed by the occupier to the visitor, each standard having its own peculiar intricacies." M. Hertz, *Occupiers' Liability Law: A Study Paper* 1 (1976). The three general categories of visitors to premises are **invitee, licensee,** and **trespasser.** See *Robert Addie & Sons (Collieries) Ltd.* v. *Dumbreck*, [1929] A.C. 358 (H.L.).

Statutory changes to the law include an elimination of some or all of the previous categories with a single standard of care owed to all persons entering premises. See, e.g., *Occupiers' Liability Act*, R.S.A. 1980, c. O-3; *Occupiers' Liability Act*, R.S.O. 1990, c. 0.2.

OCCUPYING THE FIELD See **paramountcy; pre-emption.**

OFFENCE Generally, an act or omission punishable under the criminal law; a "crime." *Horsfield* v. *Brown*, [1932] 1 K.B. 355 at 367. See **indictable offence; misdemeanour; summary offence.**

OFFENSIVE WEAPON A class of weapon divided by the *Criminal Code*, R.S.C., 1985, c. C–46, s. 84(1), into prohibited weapons and restricted weapons, notwithstanding the exceptions listed in s. 84(1) of the *Criminal Code*:

" '[P]rohibited weapon' means (*a*) any device or contrivance designed or intended to muffle or stop the sound or report of a firearm, (*b*) any knife that has a blade that opens automatically by gravity or centrifugal force or by hand pressure applied to a button, spring or other device in or attached to the handle of the knife, (*c*) any firearm, not being a restricted weapon described in paragraph (c) (c.1) of the definition of that expression in this subsection, that is capable of, or assembled or designed and manufactured with the capability of, firing projectiles in rapid succession during one pressure of the trigger, whether or not it has been altered to fire only one projectile with one such pressure, (d) any firearm adapted from a rifle or shotgun, whether by sawing, cutting or other alteration or modification, that, as so adapted, has a barrel that is less than 457 mm in length or that is less than 660 mm in overall length, (e) a weapon of any kind, not being an antique firearm or a firearm of a kind commonly used in Canada for hunting or sporting purposes, that is declared by order of the **Governor in Council** to be a prohibited weapon; . . .

" '[R]estricted weapon' means (a) any firearm, not being a prohibited weapon, designed, altered or intended to be aimed and fired by the action of one hand, (b) any firearm that (i) is not a prohibited weapon, has a barrel that is less than 470 mm in length and is capable of discharging centre-fire ammunition in a semi-automatic manner, or (ii) is designed or adapted to be fired when reduced to a length of less than 660 mm by folding, telescoping or otherwise, or (c) any firearm that is designed, altered or intended to fire bullets in rapid succession during one pressure of the trigger and that, on January 1, 1978 was registered as a restricted weapon and formed part of a gun collection in Canada of a genuine gun collector, (c.1) any firearm that is assembled or designed and manufactured with the capability of firing projectiles in rapid succession with one pressure of the trigger, to the extent that (i) the firearm is altered to fire only one projectile with one such pressure, (ii) on October 1, 1992, the firearm was registered as a restricted weapon . . . and the firearm formed part of a gun collection in Canada of a genuine gun collector . . . or (d) a weapon of any kind, not being a prohibited weapon or a shotgun or rifle of a kind that, in the opinion of the Governor in Council, is reasonable for use in Canada for hunting or sporting purposes, that is declared by order of the Governor in Council to be a restricted weapon."

OFFER "[A] manifestation of willingness to be bound by one party [to a contract] that has a certain legal result, namely, that of giving the other party the power to conclude a binding contract by accep-

tance." S. Waddams, *The Law of Contracts* 19 (3d ed. 1993).

A communication addressed to numerous persons will not generally be an offer but will rather be considered an invitation for offers (which may then become **contracts** through acceptance). This is the case in most mail-order settings and in newspaper advertisements.

To constitute an offer there must be "language of promise" (i.e., "I may" or "I want" is not as likely to be construed as an offer as is a communication using the language "I will") and a sufficiently definite statement of terms so that an acceptance may be made without suggesting new terms.

OFFEREE In **contract** law, the **party** to whom an **offer** is addressed and who may be bound upon **acceptance** of the offer.

OFFEROR In **contract** law, the **party** who makes the **offer** and indicates a willingness to enter into legal relations.

OFFICER 1. A person invested with the authority of a particular position or office. The term embraces the idea of **tenure,** duration, **emoluments** and duties, the last-named being continuing and permanent and not occasional or temporary. An officer may be either public or private in that the office he occupies may or may not be invested with a public trust. 2. Corporate personnel appointed by the directors and charged with the duty of managing the day-to-day affairs of the corporation. See *Elliott* v. *Holmwood* (1915), 25 D.L.R. 765 (B.C.S.C.). See **peace officer.**

OFFICIAL IMMUNITY See **immunity.**

OFFICIOUS INTERMEDDLER One who performs an act that confers a benefit upon another, although he had neither a contractual duty nor a legally recognized interest in performing the act, and who may nevertheless expect payment or **restitution** for the benefit conferred.

OFFSET See **setoff.**

OK The endorsement of "OK" on an agreement may be used as evidence that the agreement is satisfactory to the parties concerned; nevertheless, the endorsement may be explained by other evidence. See *Saperstein* v. *Drury,* [1943] 4 D.L.R. 191 (B.C.C.A.).

OLIGOPOLY An industry in which a few large sellers of substantially identical products dominate the market, e.g., the automobile industry. An oligopolistic industry is more concentrated than a competitive one but is less concentrated than a monopoly.

OMBUDSMAN A government official appointed to receive, investigate, and report on grievances of the public against the government's acts, omissions, decisions, and recommendations.

OMISSION A neglect or failure to do something; that which is left undone. The neglect will not give rise to liability unless there is a **duty** to act. Thus, since a parent owes a duty of protection to a child, if the parent fails to do what is required to protect the child, the parent may face criminal liability; a nurse who neglects a patient may face **tort** and/or **criminal** liability. Thus, an omission, though it consists of a failure to act, will constitute the **actus reus** that is a component of criminal liability. See *Re Bayack,* [1929] 3 D.L.R. 480 (Ont.S.C.A.D.). See also *Criminal Code,* R.S.C. 1985, c. C–46, ss. 217–219.

ON DEMAND When requested. For example, a note payable on demand is payable when the sum is requested. Such a note is called a **demand note** if no due date is stated in the obligation.

A demand note is mature on the day it is given. *Royal Bank of Canada* v. *Dwigans,* [1933] 3 D.L.R. 178 (Alta. S.C.A.D.). But other evidence may imply a requirement that reasonable notice be given. *Davies* v. *Funston* (1880), 45 U.C.Q.B. 369.

A demand note includes a bill in which no time for payment is expressed. *Bills of Exchange Act,* R.S.C. 1985, c. B–4, s. 22(1).

ON THE MERITS Refers to a decision or **judgment** based upon the essential facts of the case rather than upon a technical rule of practice, such as a failure of proper **service** or other **jurisdictional** defect. A DECISION ON THE MERITS is rendered by the TRIER OF FACT (see **fact finder**) after a full presentation of the **evidence** and determines finally the rights of the party, barring appeal or relitigation. A **summary judgment** may also be on the merits. See **res judicata.** See generally *R.* v. *Trainer,* [1945] 3 W.W.R. 223 at 230–31 (Alta.Dist.Ct.).

A **conviction** quashed on the merits of the evidence must be treated as equivalent to an acquittal. *R.* v. *Young Kee,* [1917] 2 W.W.R. 654 at 657 (Alta.S.C. in chambers).

ONUS PROBANDI (*ō'-nŭs prō-băn'-dē*) Lat.: the onus or **burden of proof.**

OPEN COURT A court or place that the public knows is a court and to which they may resort and have free access. *Robinson* v. *Robinson and Schmitke,* [1942] 2 W.W.R. 565 at 569 (Man.K.B.). Most legal proceedings take place in open court except where confidentiality is a recognized interest (e.g., in **divorce** or **juvenile delinquency** proceedings).

OPEN POSSESSION See **notorious possession.**

OPERATION OF LAW By or through law; refers to the determination of rights and obligations through the automatic effects of the law and not by any direct act of the party affected. Thus, when one dies **intestate,** one's **heirs** take according to the provincial statute of **descent** and **distribution,** "by operation of law." So, too, in certain instances the law will impose a constructive **trust** upon a transaction "by operation of law" to protect certain classes of persons.

OPINION The reason given for a court's **judgment, finding** or conclusion, as distinguished from the decision, which is the judgment itself. An opinion of a court implies its adoption by a "carrying vote" of the judges. Opinions are usually written by a single judge, and if there were more than one judge deciding the matter, other judges will join in the opinion. If a majority of a multi-judge tribunal joins in the opinion, it is a **majority opinion** or simply "the opinion," whereas a PLURALITY OPINION is one agreed to by less than a majority of the court, but that is concurred in by a majority for the result only so that the **appellate court** can dispose of the matter in accordance with the majority wishes of the court with respect to result if not with respect to the reasoning. A plurality opinion carries less weight under **stare decisis** than does a majority opinion.

CONCURRING OPINION   A view that is basically in accord with the majority opinion but is written to express a somewhat different perception of the issues, to eliminate a particular judge's reasoning or to expound a principle held in high esteem. An opinion that concurs "in the result only" is one that entirely rejects the reasoning and conclusions concerning the law and/or the facts on the basis of which the majority reached its decision, and that expresses a different view that has coincidentally led the judge writing it to recommend the same **disposition** of the case as was agreed upon by the majority (or plurality).

DISSENTING OPINION   A view that disagrees with the disposition made of the case by the court, with the facts or law on the basis of which the court arrived at its decision and/or with the principles of law announced by the court in deciding the case. Opinions may also be written expressing a dissent "in part."

PER CURIAM OPINION   An opinion "by the court" that expresses its decision in the case without identifying the author.

Opinion also refers to the conclusions reached by a witness that are drawn from his observations of the facts. See **expert witness.**

The use of the word **opinion** in statute would seem to imply even a more restricted freedom of determination than does the statutory use of the word **discretion.** Where such an opinion has the effect of authorization to perform a judicial act, it should, more than other opinions, be justified by appropriate reasons. *Rex ex rel. Wilson* v. *Holmes,* [1931]   2   W.W.R.   41   at   45 (Sask.C.A.).

"The nice philological distinctions between the words 'opinion' and 'belief' are too subtle and refined to form a basis on which to ground substantial justice." *Cook* v. *Shaw* (1921), 62 D.L.R. 546 at 547 (N.S.S.C.), quoting *Day* v. *Southwell* (1854), 3 Wis. 657 at 661.

ORAL CONTRACT   See **contract.**

ORDER   **1.** A direction of the court on some matter incidental to the main proceeding that adjudicates a preliminary point or directs some step in the proceed-ing. See *Fawkes* v. *Swayzie* (1899), 31 O.R. 256 (Div.Ct.).

2. In commercial law, an order "for particular goods given either under a contract previously made or sent in the form of a request for a specific quantity of named" goods. *White* v. *National Paper Co.* (1914), 6 O.W.N. 521 at 522 (C.A.).

3. " 'Orders' and 'Regulations' are merely the terms used to designate the mode of exercising the powers conferred on the **Governor-in-Council.**" *Re George Edwin Gray* (1918), 57 S.C.R. 150 at 155. " 'Order' is a proper term for describing an act of the Governor-in-Council by which he exercises a law-making power, whether the power exist as part of the prerogative or devolve upon him by statute." *Id.* at 167.

Order is generally understood as comprising subordinate legislation issued for a particular situation, as distinct from regulation, which is generally taken to comprise subordinate legislation of general and substantive effect.

A FINAL ORDER is one that finally disposes of the rights of the parties. *Goverdhandas Vishindas Ratanchand* v. *Ramchand Manjimal,* [1920] 1 W.W.R. 850 (J.C.P.C.).

See **interlocutory order; restraining order.**

ORDER PAPER   A negotiable instrument that is payable to order, i.e., payable to whomever the payee directs in his **endorsement.** An instrument will be negotiable only if it is payable to **order** or to bearer. Compare **bearer instrument.**

ORDINANCE   A local law that applies to persons and things subject to the local **jurisdiction.** "The word 'ordinance' has no technical significations; it means no more than an instrument embodying an order or direction." *R.* v. *Markin* (1969), 2 D.L.R. (3d) 606 at 607 (B.C.S.C.), quoting *Metcalfe* v. *Cox,* [1895] A.C. 328 at 338.

Usually the word is used in its municipal law context to mean an act of a city council or similar body that has the same force and effect as a statute when it is duly enacted. It is a form of subordinate legislation differing from laws (**statutes**) enacted by the federal or provincial **legislatures.** Ordinances are enacted to regulate **zoning,** highway speed, parking, refuse disposal and other matters typically and traditionally of local concern.

ORIGINAL DOCUMENT RULE A rule requiring that where the contents of a writing are relevant to certain proceedings, the person putting forward the document will be allowed to prove them only by tender of the original document, in preference to evidence about the document, unless a satisfactory reason is established for its absence. *Evans* v. *Evans* (1911), 19 W.L.R. 237 (Alta.S.C. en banc); affirmed by (1912), 50 S.C.R. 262. See also **best evidence rule.**

OSTENSIBLE AUTHORITY See **apparent authority.**

OUSTER The wrongful dispossession or exclusion of a person from property, usually associated with the acts of a co-tenant that exclude other co-tenants from their legal right to share **possession.** The ouster of co-tenants with proper **notice** will commence the running of the **statute of limitations** for purposes of **adverse possession.**

OVERREACHING In commercial law, the taking of unfair advantage over another through cunning, cheating, or generally fraudulent practices; synonymous with **fraud.** See *Stocks* v. *Boulter* (1912), 3 O.W.N. 1397 (C.A.). Contracts that are the product of overreaching in an unequal bargaining context may be unenforceable today under modern concepts of fraud or the **unconscionability** doctrine.

OVERRIDE CLAUSE Section 33 of the **Canadian Charter of Rights and Freedoms** permits **Parliament** or a provincial **legislature** to declare that a **statute** (or a provision thereof) shall operate notwithstanding a provision included in s. 2 of the *Charter* (re **Fundamental Freedoms**) or ss. 7–15 (re **Legal Rights** and **Equality** Rights). Section 33(3) sets a five-year limitation period on the operation of such a statute (or provision), but the limitation may be extended (s. 33(4)).

Section 33 was used by the government of Quebec in 1988 to permit French-only business signs in that province, thus "overriding" the *Charter* guarantee of "freedom of expression."

See *Ford* v. *Quebec (A–G)* (1988) 54 D.L.R. (4th) 577 (S.C.C.).

OVERRULE 1. To overturn or make **void** the **holding** (decision) of a prior **case;** generally accomplished by a court in a different and subsequent case, when it makes a decision on a point of law exactly opposite to that made in the prior case. A decision can be overruled only by the same court or a higher court within the same **jurisdiction.** The overruling of a decision generally destroys its value as **precedent.** The term should be distinguished from **reverse,** which applies to a higher court's overturning of a lower court's decision in the same case, though sometimes the distinction is not made.
2. To deny a position, objection, or other point raised to the court, such as in "overruling a motion for a new trial" or "objection overruled."

OVERT ACT Open, non-secretive act. An overt act is required to find criminal liability for **treason.** See *Criminal Code*, R.S.C. 1985, c. C–46, s. 46(4).

OWNERSHIP "[T]he right of enjoying and disposing of things in the most absolute manner, provided that no use be made of them which is prohibited by law or by regulations." *Johnston* v. *Minister & Trustees of St. Andrew's Church, Montreal* (1877), 1 S.C.R. 235 at 317.

The term has been given a wide range of meanings but is often said to comprehend both the concept of **possession** and, further, that of **title,** and thus to be broader than either.

ALLODIAL OWNERSHIP Free ownership, not subject to the restrictions or obligations associated with **feudal tenures.**

TENURIAL OWNERSHIP The holding of land subject to specific **services** or obligations owed to another.

OYER AND TERMINER Special tribunals empowered to hear and determine cases within their criminal **jurisdiction,** commissioned by the Crown when the delay involved in ordinary prosecution could not be tolerated, as in the case of sudden insurrection.

P

PACTUM *(păk'-tŭm)* Lat.: pact, **contract,** agreement. An agreement that is unenforceable because it lacks **consideration** is said to be **nudum pactum,** meaning a naked or bare agreement.

PAIN AND SUFFERING One of the basic heads of **damages** in **contract** and **tort.** Now a term of art with no precise difference between pain on the one hand and suffering on the other. It has been suggested that pain is the immediately felt effects on the nerves and brain as a consequence of some lesion or injury to part of the body, while suffering is distress that is not felt directly as being connected with any bodily condition. It includes fright at the time of injury, fear of future incapacity, possible death, insanity, or inability to make a living. H. McGregor, *McGregor on Damages* 1214 (14th ed. 1980). See *Fick* v. *B.C. Electric R. Co.,* [1951] 1 D.L.R. 81 (S.C.C.).

PAR Equal to the established value; denotes the face amount or stated value of a **negotiable instrument,** stock or bond, not the actual value it would receive on the open market. **Bills of exchange, stocks** and the like are AT PAR when they sell at their nominal value, above or below par when they sell for more or less.

PARAMOUNTCY The condition of being superior to all others; supreme. "The rule which has been adopted by the courts is the doctrine of 'federal paramountcy': where there are inconsistent (or conflicting) federal and provincial laws, it is the federal law which prevails. A similar rule has been adopted in the United States and Australia, and apparently by all modern federal constitutions. The doctrine of paramountcy applies where there is a federal law and a provincial law which are (1) each valid, and (2) inconsistent. . . . Validity depends upon the principles . . . does the 'matter' (or pith and substance) of the law come within the 'class of subject' (or heads of power) allocated to the enacting Parliament or Legislature? [In Canada by the *Constitution Act, 1867,* ss. 91, 92 . . .] It is only if each law independently passes the test of validity that it is necessary to determine if the laws are inconsistent." P. Hogg, *Constitutional Law of Canada* 418–19 (3d ed. 1992).

In *Tennant* v. *Union Bank of Canada,* [1894] A.C. 31 at 45 (P.C.), Lord Watson stated that "the exclusive legislative authority of the Parliament of Canada shall extend to all matters coming within the enumerated classes [of s. 91, *Constitution Act, 1867*] which plainly indicates that the legislation of that Parliament, so long as it strictly relates to these matters, is to be of paramount authority."

PARAMOUNT TITLE A **title** that will prevail over another asserted against it. It signifies an immediate right of **possession** and is generally referred to as the basis for **eviction** of a **tenant** by one with a right of possession superior to that of the tenant.

PARAMOUR One's lover; one who stands in the place of a husband or wife, but without the legal rights attached to the marital relationship.

PARCENER One who holds an **estate** jointly with others, usually by virtue of **descent** or **inheritance.** The term is no longer widely used, since it is now said to be indistinguishable from TENANCY IN COMMON (see **tenancy**).

PARDON An exercise of mercy through the sovereign's prerogative. "The effect of a pardon under the great seal is to clear the person from all infamy and from all consequences of the offence for which it is granted, and from all statutory or other disqualifications following upon conviction." 8 *Halsbury's Laws of England* (4th ed.), para. 952.

In Canada, the *Criminal Code,* R.S.C. 1985, c. C–46, authorizes the **Governor-in-Council** to reduce a sentence of imprisonment by granting a free pardon or a conditional pardon or to remit, in whole or in part, any pecuniary penalty, fine or forfeiture (ss. 749 and 750). The **Governor-General of Canada,** acting on the advice of a member of the **Cabinet,** may grant a pardon to an **accused** who is serving a term of imprisonment (s. 751). A FREE PARDON will be granted where the innocence of the accused is established; and, for all purposes thereafter, he is deemed never to have committed the offence (s. 749(3)). A CONDITIONAL PARDON, on the other hand, which imposes some condition, has no effect on the guilt or innocence of the accused and is usually granted on compassionate grounds. See **amnesty; commutation.**

PARENS PATRIAE (pā′-rĕnz pā′-trē-ī) Lat.: "parent of the country." Originally the duty of the English sovereign to protect his or her subjects. At present, it is the power of the superior court to deal with matters involving persons under disability, particularly children; in some provinces, this power is preserved by the Judicature Act (e.g., R.S.N.S. 1989, c. 240, s. 43(10) & (11)). See *Beson* v. *Director of Child Welfare*, [1982] 2 S.C.R. 716 (S.C.C.).

PARENT CORPORATION A company owning over 50 percent of the voting shares in another company, called the **subsidiary.** The term also refers to a large organization that subdivides itself internally into a number of departments each of which is technically a separate organization. *Royal Bank of Canada* v. *Wallace Investments Ltd.* (1961), 30 D.L.R. (2d) 280 (B.C.Co.Ct.).

PARI DELICTO See **in pari delicto.**

PARLIAMENT The federal legislature of Canada consisting of the **Queen,** the Senate and the **House of Commons.** Its life is fixed for five years, divided into sessions (one or more each year), except in time of real or apprehended war, invasion or insurrections. Legislation usually necessitates the concurrence of the Queen, by and with the advice and consent of the Senate and House of Commons. *Reference Re Legislative Authority of Parliament to Alter or Replace the Senate* (1979), 102 D.L.R. (3d) 1 (S.C.C.).

PAROLE 1. Conditional release from imprisonment or other confinement after actually serving part of the **sentence.** In Canada, there is a distinction between day parole and full parole. Under s. 99(1) of the *Corrections and Conditional Release Act,* S.C. 1992, c. 20, day parole is the authority granted an offender to be at large during his term of imprisonment in preparation for full parole or statutory release upon the condition that the offender "return to a penitentiary, a community-based residential facility or a provincial correctional facility each night. . . ." Full parole grants the authority to the offender

to be at large during the term of imprisonment. See *Frankie* v. *Commissioner of Corrections (Can.)* (1993), 61 F.T.R. 274 (Fed. T.D.). Compare **probation.**

2. In international law a promise given by a prisoner of war, when he has leave to depart from custody, that unless discharged, he will return at the appointed time and will not take up arms against the government whose forces captured him.

PAROL EVIDENCE **Evidence** that is oral rather than written; the ordinary kind of evidence given by a witness in court. Such evidence usually becomes an issue when relating to a transaction contained in a written **instrument** such as a **will, deed,** or **contract.**

PAROL EVIDENCE RULE A rule of **substantive law** that operates to prevent parties to a **contract** from altering, contradicting or varying the terms of a written document considered to be the final expression of their agreement. However, parol evidence is admissible to prove **fraud, duress, mistake, misrepresentation,** lack of capacity, the existence of a separate oral agreement that modifies or rescinds the main contract, the existence of a separate oral agreement to a matter on which the document is silent and which is not inconsistent with its terms, or to prove that the parties did not intend the document to be a complete and final statement of the entire transaction. See further S. Waddams, *The Law of Contracts* 209ff. (3d ed. 1993).

PARTIALLY DISCLOSED PRINCIPAL See **principal.**

PARTICULARS, BILL OF See **bill of particulars.**

PARTITION Judicial division of property interests jointly held, usually land; "the division of lands, **tenements,** and **hereditament** belonging to co-owners, and the allotment among them of the parts, so as to put an end to community of ownership between some or all of them." 32 *Halsbury's Laws of England* (3d ed.), para. 539.

PARTNERSHIP "[T]he relation that subsists between parties carrying on business in common with a view to profit. It is a relationship resulting from **contract,** and the fundamental rule to be observed in determining the existence of a partnership is, that regard must be paid to the true contract and the intention of the parties...." *Sproule* v. *McConnell,* [1925] 1 W.W.R. 609 (Sask.C.A.).

Each partner is authorized by his fellow-partners to bind the members of the partnership for acts done in the normal course of carrying on business. A partner is liable for the extent of any loss unless he is a member of a publicly registered limited liability partnership.

LIMITED PARTNERSHIP A form of business organization in the nature of a partnership involving two or more persons in which one or more of the partners have limited their liability for debts to the amount they have agreed to invest in the business by registering a prescribed form. See *Limited Partnerships Act,* R.S.O. 1990, c. L. 16. Not permitted in all provinces.

PART PERFORMANCE A doctrine that the statute of frauds does not apply where there has been performance or part performance of an oral contract or where otherwise the result would be a fraud against or injustice to the other party. *Re Landlord and Tenant Act; Int'l Associated Hairdressers Ltd.* v. *Glasgow* (1956), 65 Man.R. 374 (Man.C.A.).

PARTY A participant who is directly interested in any affair, contract, or conveyance, or who is actively concerned in the prosecution and defence of any legal proceeding as plaintiff or defendant.

NECESSARY PARTY See **necessary party.**

NOMINAL PARTY A party appearing on the record not because he has any real interest in the case, but because technical rules of pleading require his presence in the record.

PARTIES TO A CRIME See accessory; accomplice.

THIRD PARTY A procedural method whereby a defendant in an action may join additional parties to the action. *Pharmacie Belisle Pharmacy Ltd.* v. *Mineau* (1977), 4 C.P.C. 203 (Ont.C.A.).

PARTY WALL A wall erected on a property boundary as common support to structures on both sides that are under different ownerships. "The words party wall may be used in four different senses ... [1] a wall of which the two adjoining owners are tenants in common ... [2] a

wall divided longitudinally into two strips, one belonging to each of the neighbouring owners ... [3] a wall that belongs entirely to one of the adjoining owners, but is subject to an easement or right in the other to have it maintained as a dividing wall between the two tenements ... [4] a wall divided longitudinally into two [halves] each [half] being subject to a cross easement in favour of the owner of the other moiety" *Lewis* v. *Allison* (1899), 30 S.C.R. 173 at 181 (S.C.C.).

PATENT 1. Apparent on the face of an instrument. **2.** By statute, "letters patent" for an invention. Patents are monopolies, a limited exclusive privilege the law allows a patentee in his own invention as a natural right arising from production and differs from ownership in that the owner is required to hand it over to the public after a seventeen-year period. *Patent Act,* R.S.C. 1985, c. P–4. A patent may be granted for invention of any new and useful art, process, machine, manufacture, or composition of matter or any new and useful improvements in any art, process, machine, manufacture or composition of matter. No patent can be obtained for a scientific principle or abstract theorem. The inventor must apply for a grant of a patent and, upon application, there is a presumption of novelty that may be disproved by an opposing party attacking the grant by showing prior common general knowledge of the subject matter of the patent. The design of the patent law is to reward those who make a substantial discovery or invention that adds to our knowledge and advances the useful arts. See *Canada Gypsum Co. Ltd.* v. *Gypsum, Lime, & Alabastine, Canada Ltd.,* [1931] Ex.C.R. 180.

PATENT INFRINGEMENT The act of a person who, without license from the patentee, either directly or indirectly makes, uses, or puts into practice the invention or any part of it that is embraced by the claims. It includes doing one of the things that, by terms of the grant, a person is not entitled to do, or colourably imitating the invention in any way or taking its substance. Infringement is determined by the state of the prior art at the time the patent was issued. See *Consolidated Car Heating Co.* v. *Came,* [1903] A.C. 509 (P.C.).

PATENT PENDING A phrase that describes the state of a patent that has been applied for but has not yet been granted.

PATENT DEFECT A defect that could be recognized upon reasonably careful inspection or through ordinary diligence and care. Compare **latent defect.**

PATERNITY SUIT An action to prove the father of an illegitimate child and to provide **maintenance** for the child. Proof of paternity is usually accomplished by oral evidence and a blood test on the possible father. The suspect father does not necessarily always have to be proved the father but must be one of the possible putative fathers. See, e.g., *R.* v. *P.H.* (1978), 5 R.F.L. 254 (N.S.Co.Ct.).

PAT. PEND. [PATENT PENDING] See **patent.**

PATRIATE Although there is no exact definition of "patriation," the term is commonly used in the context of the "bringing home" of the **Constitution** to Canada. As its final legislative act for Canada, the British Parliament passed the Canada Act 1982 (U.K.), c. 11, with the Constitution Act 1982 appended as Schedule B., ensuring Canada a certain autonomy from the United Kingdom. See P. Hogg, *Constitutional Law of Canada* 53 (3d ed. 1992).

PATRICIDE The killing of one's own father.

PAWN To give **personal property** to another as **security** for a loan; property deposited with another as security for payment of a **debt.**

PAY EQUITY An employment policy which requires the payment of equal pay for work of equal value to men and women. In Canada, the federal government and some provinces have passed pay equity legislation, which establishes pay equity commissions and outlines the administration of pay equity programs for employers within their jurisdiction.

Pay equity legislation extends previous policies of equal pay for equal work, i.e. where female clerks must be paid the same as their male counterparts. Pay equity considers skill, effort, responsibility, and working conditions in evaluating which different job categories should be paid on the same level. See *Pay Equity Act*, R.S.N.S. 1989, c. 337; *Pay Equity Act*, R.S.O. 1990, c. P.7.

PAYABLE TO BEARER See **bearer instrument.**

PEACEABLE POSSESSION Possession that is continuous and not interrupted by adverse **suits** or other hostile action intended to oust the possessor from the land. The term often refers to parties in **adverse possession** of land, and thus has nothing to do with actual **ownership.** The existence of adverse claims is not precluded, so long as no actual attempt to dispossess is made. An action to **quiet title** generally requires a showing of peaceable possession by the one bringing the action.

PEACEFUL ENJOYMENT See **quiet enjoyment.**

PEACE OFFICER A person employed for the preservation and maintenance of the public peace or for the service or execution of civil process; under the *Criminal Code*, R.S.C. 1985, c. C–46, s. 2, the term includes mayors, wardens, reeves, sheriffs, deputy sheriffs, sheriff's officers, justice of the peace, prison officials, police officers, customs officials, fisheries officers, pilots in command of aircraft and members of the armed forces under certain conditions.

A peace officer is limited territorially by the jurisdiction of the authority that appoints him. *R.* v. *Soucy* (1975), 23 C.C.C. (2d) 561 (N.B.S.C.A.D.).

PECULATION The fraudulent **misappropriation** to one's own use of money or goods entrusted to his care. See **embezzlement; larceny.**

PECUNIARY Relating to money and monetary affairs; consisting of money or that which can be valued in money. Many fatal injury statutes limit recovery to PECUNIARY LOSS, i.e., a loss of money or of something that can be translated into an economic loss. The loss of affection that a parent suffers by the **negligent** death of a child is not such a loss, whereas the loss of actual or anticipated financial support by the deceased child is pecuniary loss.

PENAL INSTITUTION A place of confinement for **convicted** criminals. Penal institutions include local and county jails and workhouses, reformatories, penitentiaries, prison camps and farms, as well as the modern CORRECTIONAL INSTITU-TIONS (nomenclature now used to describe many penal institutions previously called prisons).

PENAL LAW A law enacted to preserve the public order, which defines an offence against the public and inflicts a penalty for its violation. **Statutes** that grant a private [**civil**] **action** against a wrongdoer are not considered penal, but remedial in nature.

PENALTY 1. A punishment, particularly a monetary payment. The *Criminal Code*, R.S.C. 1985, c. C–46, s. 722(5), defines penalty as being all the sums of money, including fines, in default of payment of which a term of imprisonment is imposed.

2. The nominal sum specified payable by a party in breach of a contract. " 'The essence of liquidated damages is a genuine covenanted pre-estimate of the damages' likely to accrue; while the 'essence of a penalty is a payment of money stipulated as in terrorem of the offending party.' ... Whether the sum stipulated to be paid is a penalty or **liquidated damages** is to be decided upon [the construction of] the terms of the contract, the circumstances under which it was entered into, [the] nature of the undertaking, and the loss which at the time the contract was made the parties might have considered as flowing from its breach." *Sask. Co-op Wheat Producers Ltd.* v. *Zurowski,* [1926] 3 D.L.R. 810 at 819 (Sask.C.A.).

As **equity** will afford **relief** against a penalty, only a sum representing the actual loss incurred can be recovered. Compare also **damages** [EXEMPLARY DAMAGES].

PENDENTE LITE [LITE PENDENTE] *(pĕn-dĕn'-tā lē'-tā)* Lat.: pending the **suit;** contingent upon the determination of a pending lawsuit. Thus, funds may be deposited with the clerk of the court *pendente lite*—i.e., so that those funds can be used to make payment to the opposing party if the depositing party loses the lawsuit. See also **lis pendens.**

PER ANNUM *(pĕr ăn'-ŭm)* Lat.: through the course of a year; annually. Anything (e.g., interest, wages, rent) calculated per annum is calculated on the basis of a year in time; sometimes a per annum rate will be fixed at 1/360th (or 1/364th) per day. See **year.**

PER [PUR] AUTRE VIE *(pĕr [pûr] ō'-tr vē)* Fr.: for another's life. A life **estate** that terminates on the death of another person or persons who may be the **grantor** or a third party called the CESTUI QUE VIE. An estate *per autre vie* may be created by express limitation by **deed** or **will** or by the **assignment** of an existing life estate.

PER CAPITA *(pĕr kăp'-ĭ-tà)* Lat.: through the head, top, summit. Through the leader or capital (of a country); defined by the heads or polls according to the number of individuals, share and share alike. Anything figured per capita is calculated by the number of individuals (heads) involved and is divided equally among all. Compare **per stirpes.**

PER CURIAM *(pĕr kyū'-rē'-ăm)* Lat.: by the court. Used to distinguish an opinion of the whole court from an opinion written by one judge. See **opinion.**

PER DIEM *(pĕr dē'-ĕm)* Lat.: by the day. Used in connection with a means of calculating compensation or expenses.

PEREMPTORY Absolute, conclusive, positive, not admitting of question or appeal. A peremptory trial date may be established by the court on its own **motion** or at the request of a **party** to insure timely disposition of the case. In the selection of a jury, each side has a right to a fixed number of peremptory **challenges** to the seating of potential jurors.

PEREMPTORY WRIT At common law, an original writ requiring the presence of the defendant in **civil actions** for certain cases including **trespass.**

PERFECTED Completed, executed, enforceable, merchantable; refers especially to the status ascribed to **security interests** after certain events have occurred. The necessary events in order to achieve PERFECTION can be broken down into two categories.

Certain security interests are perfected by no more than the creation of the security interest itself. An example of such an automatic perfected security interest is a purchase money security interest in consumer goods.

Other security interests require the creditor to take certain steps to perfect, including taking possession of the collateral, or filing.

There are many consequences that flow

from perfection. The most important is that a perfected security interest has **priority** over an unperfected interest. The date of perfection is also the time from which courts judge priority contests with other perfected creditors.

PERFORMANCE The fulfillment of an obligation or a promise; especially, completion of one's obligation under a **contract**. See **specific performance; substantial performance.**

PERIODIC TENANCY See **tenancy.**

PERJURY Section 131 of the *Criminal Code*, R.S.C.1985, c. C–46, defines the act of perjury as a false statement by a person, with an intent to mislead, knowing that the statement is false whether or not such a statement is made in a judicial **proceeding.** The **burden of proof** is on the Crown to prove the statement false. See *R.* v. *Noftle* (1976), 12 Nfld. & P.E.I.R. 1 (Nfld.Dist.Ct.). It is no defence that the accused's statements are true if he knew and intended that they would be taken in another sense. *Farris* v. *The Queen,* [1965] 3 C.C.C. 245 (Ont.C.A.). See also **subornation of perjury.**

PERMANENT FIXTURE See **fixtures.**

PERMANENT INJUNCTION See **injunction.**

PER MY ET PER TOUT *(pĕr mē ā pĕr tū)* Law Fr.: by half and by whole. In **joint tenancy,** each tenant's share is the whole, for purposes of **tenure** and **survivorship** [tout], and each share is an **aliquot** portion for purposes of **alienation** [my].

PERPETUITIES, RULE AGAINST See **rule against perpetuities.**

PERPETUITY See **in perpetuity.**

PER QUOD *(pĕr kwŏd)* Lat.: through which; by which; whereby. False imputations may be **actionable per se**—in themselves—or *per quod*—on allegation and proof of special **damage.** In a **libel** or **slander** action, words used that are not on their face, in their usual and natural usage, injurious, but that become so as a consequence of extrinsic facts and that require an **innuendo,** are actionable *per quod.*

PER SE *(pĕr sā)* Lat.: through itself, by means of itself. Not requiring extraneous evidence or support to establish its exist-

ence. For example, **negligence** *per se* refers to acts that are inherently negligent, i.e., that implicitly involve a **breach** of duty, obviating the need to expressly allege the existence of the duty.

PERSON In law, an individual or incorporated group having certain legal rights and responsibilities. This has been held to include foreign and domestic **corporations.** Compare artificial person; **natural person.**

PERSONAL JUDGMENT Judgment imposed on a defendant requiring sums to be advanced from whatever assets he has within the **jurisdiction** of the issuing court, as distinguished from a judgment directed against particular property (called an **in rem** judgment) or a judgment against a **corporate** entity.

PERSONAL PROPERTY See **personalty.**

PERSONAL SERVICE See **service.**

PERSONALTY The class of property that deals with the right in **chattels.** Chattels are property of a temporary character and can be easily moved about; also, they can be handled, transferred, altered and destroyed without much difficulty. The distinguishing feature from **real property** is that the forms of action lie **in personam** in the form of **conversion, detinue** and **replevin.** R. Brown, *The Law of Personal Property* (3d ed. 1975).

PERSONS CASE In the case of *Henrietta Muir Edwards et al* v. *Attorney General for Canada* (the "Persons Case") [1930] A.C. 124 the Judicial Committee of the Privy Council held that women were "persons" as designated in s. 24 of the **Constitution** Act 1967 [B.N.A. Act] and could therefore be summoned to and become members of the Senate of Canada.

PER STIRPES *(pĕr stûr'-pāz)* Lat.: or stock; by family stock representation. Denotes how an **estate,** or portion of an estate, should be distributed on an **intestacy.** The essential characteristic of an intestate's estate *per stirpes* is that each distributee inherits in a representative capacity and stands in the place of a deceased ancestor. Thus each beneficiary receives a share in the property to be distributed, not necessarily equal, but the proper fraction of the fraction to which the person through whom he claims from the ancestor would have been entitled. It is distinguished from a distribution **per capita,** which is a provision for equal division among the beneficiaries, each receiving the same share as the others without reference to the intermediate course of descent from the ancestor. See, e.g., *In re Smith Estate* (1919), 3 W.W.R. 745 (Man.K.B.).

PER TOUT ET NON PER MY *(pĕr tū ā nŏn pĕr mē)* Law Fr.: by the whole and not by half. A term applied to a tenancy by the entirety or a joint tenancy (see **tenancy**); e.g., joint tenants or a husband and wife who own property by the entirety own an **undivided interest** in the whole of the property but not an individual interest in half the property.

PETITION A prayer (formal request) from a person or group to a power or person for the exercise of his authority in the redress of some wrong. In old English law, a petition was addressed to the King and later to the Chancellor in a situation where a case was beyond the ordinary **writ** system. In present day, a divorce proceeding is started by petitioning the court.

PETITIONER One who presents a petition to a court or other body in order to either institute an **equity** proceeding or take an **appeal** from a **judgment.** The adverse party is called the **respondent.**

PETIT JURY See **jury.**

PICKETING The practice, often used in labour disputes, of patrolling, usually with placards, to publicize a dispute or to secure support for a cause.

PIERCING THE CORPORATE VEIL The process of disregarding the corporate entity and imposing liability on a person or entity other than the offending **corporation** itself.

Generally the corporate form isolates both individuals and **parent corporations** [see **subsidiary**] from liability for corporate misdeeds. However, there are times (such as when incorporation itself was accomplished to perpetrate a **fraud**) when the court will ignore the corporate entity and strip the organizers and managers of the corporation of the limited liability they usually enjoy. See, e.g., *Jones* v. *Lipman,* [1962] 1 All E.R. 442 (Ch.D.); *Saskatchewan* v. *Patterson-Boyd* (1981), 6 Sask.R. 325 (C.A.).

PIRACY 1. In the context of commercial **tort,** the **misappropriation** or theft of a trade secret or an idea (under certain circumstances), or of a **trademark. 2.** Also, the illicit representing or reproduction of a copyrighted writing or article as a sound recording or work of art. See **copyright; infringement. 3.** Considered a crime under **international law** and under the *Criminal Code,* R.S.C. 1985, c. C–46, s.74. In the criminal context, piracy is an **indictable offence** involving, inter alia, theft of a Canadian ship or its cargo, or a mutinous act on board a Canadian ship.

PLAGIARISM Appropriation of the literary composition of another and passing off as one's own the product of the mind and language of another. An example of the offence of plagiarism in the law is INFRINGEMENT OF COPYRIGHT, which comes into being when the work allegedly copied is protected by **copyright.**

PLAINTIFF The one who initially brings the **suit;** a person who brings an **action.** Also, a **defendant** who brings a **counterclaim** will be considered a plaintiff as relating to his counterclaim. See **complainant.**

PLEA 1. In **equity,** a special answer showing or relying upon one or more things as a cause why the **suit** should be dismissed, delayed or barred. **2.** At **law,** broadly, any one of the common-law **pleadings. 3.** Technically, the defendant's answer by matter of fact to the plaintiff's **declaration,** as distinguished from a **demurrer,** which is an answer by a matter of law. In criminal procedure, at his **arraignment,** the defendant will enter a plea of not guilty, guilty or some other defence, e.g., AUTREFOIS ACQUIT (see **double jeopardy**).

PLEA BARGAINING An informal practice where the **accused** uses his right both to plead not guilty and to demand a full trial in order to bargain for a benefit that is usually related to a **charge** or the **sentence.** A bargain can be with a judge or prosecutor, or both. It may involve a reduction in the charge, a withdrawal of other charges or a promise not to institute other proceedings. The accused may agree to testify against other co-accused persons or may agree not to appeal. The Crown may bargain because of weakness in the evidence, or to save time or money. See *R.* v. *Wood* (1976), 26 C.C.C. (2d) 100 (Alta. C.A.)

PLEBISCITE The means of securing an expression of popular view from the common people on particular issues, usually by a yes/no response. The plebiscite has been used widely in many Canadian provinces in seeking local views, particularly concerning the sale of liquor. See **referendum.**

PLEAD 1. To make a **pleading; 2.** to answer **plaintiff's common-law declaration; 3.** in criminal law, to answer to the **charge,** either by admitting or by denying guilt.

PLEADINGS Statements in writing served by each party alternatively to his opponent, stating the facts relied on to support his case and giving all details his opponent needs to know in order to prepare his case in answer. The usual pleadings in an action are the **statement of claim,** the **defence,** any **counterclaim,** a reply to the counterclaim, and any demands for further and better particulars.

PLENARY Full; complete; absolute; perfect; unqualified. In judicial proceedings, the term denotes a complete, formally **pleaded** suit wherein a **bill** or **petition** or **complaint** is filed by one or more persons against one or more other persons who file an **answer** or a response. Compare **summary proceeding.**

POLITICAL ASYLUM See **asylum.**

POLITICAL QUESTION A question that a court determines is not properly subject to judicial determination because resolution of it is committed exclusively to the jurisdiction of another branch of government or because adequate standards of judicial review are lacking or because there is no way to insure enforcement of the court's judgment.

POLL TAX An equal tax or a tax of a fixed amount upon all persons, or all persons of a particular category, without reference to property or lack of it.

POLYGAMY The offence, under s. 293 of the *Criminal Code,* R.S.C. 1985, c. C–46, of having more than one husband or wife at one time.

POSITIVE LAW Law enacted and adopted by proper authority for the government of an organized jural society;

"law set by political superiors to political inferiors." J. Austin, *The Province of Jurisprudence Determined* 9 (2d ed. 1954).

POSITIVISM In **jurisprudence,** the view that any legal system is best studied by concentrating on the **positive law** of that system; formed in reaction to **natural law** theory that claims that some principles or rules of human conduct are discoverable by reason alone and that there is a necessary connection between law and morals.

POSSE COMITATUS *(pŏ'-sā kŏm'-ĭ-tä'-tūs)* Lat.: power or force of a country. The authority of the sheriff to assemble all able-bodied male inhabitants above the age of fifteen, except peers and clergymen, to defend the country against enemies of the Crown, to keep the peace, to pursue felons, or to enforce the royal writ. The term has become obsolete since the establishment of police forces.

POSSESSION The right to **custody,** dominion and control of **property.** The term imports manual custody and physical control, coupled with the intention of exercising such control. ACTUAL POSSESSION occurs when a person has direct physical control over the thing at a given time. CONSTRUCTIVE POSSESSION occurs when a person, although not in actual possession, knowingly has both the power and the intention at a given time to exercise control over the thing, either directly or through another person.

In criminal law, by s. 4(3) of the *Criminal Code,* R.S.C. 1985, c. C–46, a person has custody when he has anything in his possession or knowingly in the actual possession or custody of another person or has it in any place, whether or not that place belongs to or is occupied by him, for use or benefit of himself or another person. To constitute possession within the criminal law there must be knowledge of what the thing is and some act of control. *Beaver* v. *R.* (1957), 118 C.C.C. 129 (S.C.C.).

POSSESSORY ACTION A lawsuit brought for the purpose of obtaining or maintaining possession of **real property.** In a common instance, a landlord will bring a possessory action to evict holdover tenants (see **tenancy [**TENANCY AT SUFFERANCE**]**), praying that the court will issue a writ of possession against the holdover tenants.

POSSESSORY INTEREST A right to exert control over certain land to the exclusion of others, coupled with an intent to exercise that right. It is this "privilege of exclusive occupation" that distinguishes possessory from non-possessory interests. One holding a non-possessory interest is subject to specific restrictions with respect to the use he may make of land, but the holder of a possessory interest is limited only by the rights of others (including co-owners, neighbors, **remaindermen**). Examples of non-possessory interests include **easements, remainders,** and the rights retained by the grantor of a **life estate.** See **adverse possession.**

POSSIBILITY OF A REVERTER The possibility of the return of an **estate** to the **grantor,** should a specified event occur or a particular act be performed in the future. The **interest** that remains in a grantor or **testator** after the **conveyance** or devise of a fee simple determinable (see **determinable fee**) and that permits the grantor to be revested automatically of his **estate** on, for example, **breach** of a condition. *Re Tilbury West Public School Board and Hastie,* [1966] 2 O.R. 20 (H.C.). Compare **re-entry [right of].**

POST FACTO See **ex post facto.**

POST MORTEM *(pōst môr'-tĕm)* Lat.: after death. An autopsy or examination of a dead body to ascertain the cause of death.

POWER OF APPOINTMENT The legal authority given by a **grantor** (the **donor** of the power) to the **donee** of the power (also called the APPOINTOR) to appoint **property,** or an **interest** therein, to some person (the APPOINTEE). The power may be created by **deed** or **will.** A power may be (1) GENERAL, where the appointor may appoint anyone including himself, (2) SPECIAL, where the choice of appointees is restricted by the terms of the power, or (3) HYBRID, where the appointor is given power to appoint anyone except certain people or groups of people. A power of appointment is distinguished from a trust power in that a power of appointment is discretionary whereas a trust power is obligatory upon the appointor. A bare power is usually coupled with a **gift over** in default of appointment. *Higginson* v. *Kerr* (1898), 30 O.R. 62 (H.C.).

POWER OF ATTORNEY An instrument in writing authorizing another to act as one's **agent** or attorney. It confers upon the agent the authority to perform certain specified acts or kinds of acts on behalf of his **principal.** Its primary purpose is to evidence the authority of the agent to third parties with whom the agent deals.

The traditional power of attorney ceases to be effective if the principle becomes incapacitated. Legislation has been enacted in some jurisdictions to provide for an **enduring** or **durable power of attorney.** In such cases, the enduring power of attorney authorizes the management of the estate of the **donor**, and is not terminated by reason of the donor's legal incapacity. See e.g., *Powers of Attorney Act,* R.S.N.S. 1989, c. 352.

PRAYER FOR RELIEF That part of the **pleading** where the type of **relief** and **remedies** sought are enumerated (money **damages, injunction,** etc.). It is common to add a general request for "such other and further relief as to the court may seem just and proper" to enable the court to grant whatever relief it feels is appropriate.

PREAMBLE A preliminary clause in a **treaty, constitution, statute,** or other legal **instrument** that states the intent, purpose or spirit of the instrument. The preamble may be looked at to ascertain the intention of the legislation, but the enacting clauses are the ones that ultimately govern interpretation of the Act. "[A] preamble may afford useful light as to what a statute intends to reach, and ... if an enactment is itself clear and unambiguous, no preamble can clarify or cut down the enactment." *Powell* v. *The Kempton Park Racecourse Co. Ltd.,* [1899] A.C. 143 (H.L.). Compare **purview.**

PRECATORY Advisory; in the nature of a prayer, request, recommendation or entreaty; conveying or embodying a recommendation or advice or the expression of a wish, but not a positive command or direction. The term is applied to language, usually in a **trust** or a **will,** by which the **settlor** or **testator** expresses a wish or a desire to benefit another but does not impose an enforceable obligation upon any party to carry out his wish.
PRECATORY TRUST See **trust.**

PRECEDENT **1.** The doctrine [of judicial precedent] whereby a previously decided case is recognized as authority for the disposition of future cases. In the **common law,** precedents are regarded as a major source of law. A precedent may involve a novel question of common law or it may involve the interpretation of a **statute.** In either event, to the extent that future cases rely upon the precedent or distinguish it from themselves without disapproving of it, the case will serve as a precedent for future cases under the doctrine of **stare decisis.** See further G. Gall, *The Canadian Legal System,* (3d ed. 1990), chap. 10. **2.** The term is also used to denote a copy of an instrument used as a guide in preparing another instrument of similar description.

PRECEDENT CONDITION See **condition precedent.**

PRECEDING ESTATE A prior **estate** upon which a **future interest** is limited. Thus, a **remainder** is said to **vest** upon the termination of a preceding estate, such as a **life estate.**

PRE-EMPTION 1. A doctrine concerning federal judicial treatment of provincial legislation related to the same subject matter as federal [Parliamentary enacted] legislation; it rests upon the powers conferred in s. 91 of the *Constitution Act, 1867,* and deprives a province of **jurisdiction** over matters embraced by a Parliamentary Act, regardless of whether the provincial Act coincides with, is complementary to or opposes the federal legislation. When Parliament legislates in an area of federal concern, it may specifically pre-empt all provincial legislation, thus OCCUPYING THE FIELD, or may bar only inconsistent legislation; where Parliament does not directly indicate its intention in this regard, the court will determine that intention based on the nature and legislative history of the enactment.
Provincial legislatures may also pre-empt local governments in the same manner. **2.** At common law, the term expressed the King's right to buy provisions and other necessities for the use of his household in preference to others. **3.** In international law, it expresses the right of a nation to detain goods of a stranger in transit so as to afford its subjects a preference of purchase. See **paramountcy.**

PREFERENCE A priority of payment given by an **insolvent** person to one creditor or to a certain class of his creditors over others. The primary and natural import of the word means "a voluntary act on the part of the debtor and therefore [is] a term which is not applicable to an act brought about by the active influence of the creditor." *Stephens* v. *McArthur & Worthington* (1891), 19 S.C.R. 446 at 453.

PREFERRED DIVIDEND See **dividend.**

PREFERRED SHARES Shares that confer on the holders some preference over other classes of shares in respect of either dividend or repayment of capital or both. L. Gower, *Modern Company Law,* 370 (5th ed. 1992).

PREFERRED STOCK A class of stock entailing certain rights beyond those attached to common stock; corporate stock having preference rights. It represents a contribution to the capital of the corporation and is in no sense a loan of money. By general definition, preferred stock is stock entitled to a preference over other kinds of stock in the payment of **dividends.** The dividends come out of earnings [income] and not out of **capital.** Unless there are net earnings, there is no right to dividends.

PREJUDICE Bias, preconceived opinion; favouring one cause as opposed to another, without justification; deprivation of some legal right or interest without just cause. The notion of a **fair hearing** involves a duty upon the members of a tribunal or court to deal with the question referred to them without prejudice or bias. See, e.g., *Local Government Bd.* v. *Arlidge,* [1915] A.C. 120 at 132 (H.L.).

PREJUDICIAL ERROR An error that affects or presumptively affects the final results of the trial; an error substantively affecting the parties' legal rights and obligations. See **reversible error.**

PRELIMINARY HEARING "[Not] a trial but simply an enquiry or investigation or inquisition that is made by the magistrate with a view to satisfying himself as to whether or not there is sufficient evidence for him to commit the accused for trial to a higher Court, the powers of the magistrate in this respect being almost unfettered." *R.* v. *Myers,* [1925] 2 W.W.R. 445 at 446 (Man.Police Ct.). See *Crimi-*

nal Code, R.S.C. 1985, c. C–46, ss. 535–551. Compare **arraignment.**

PRELIMINARY INQUIRY See **preliminary hearing.**

PREMEDITATION 1. Forethought; the act of meditating in advance, considering and contemplating prior to acting. It is a prior determination to do an act, but such determination need not exist for any particular period before it is carried out. **2.** In criminal law, forethought to the commission of a crime, such as **murder.** See also **mens rea.**

PREMISES In the ordinary meaning of the term, the grounds immediately surrounding a house. *Martin* v. *Martin* (1904), 8 O.L.R. 462 (C.A.). Sometimes the term includes **appurtenances,** buildings and other structures, in addition to the grounds.

In **conveyancing,** the part of a **deed** that precedes the **habendum** and includes the introduction, date, persons executing the instrument, recitals and other operative parts.

PREPONDERANCE OF THE EVIDENCE The evidence with the most weight; the standard of proof used in most **civil** cases. It refers to the proof that leads the trier of fact (see **fact finder**) to find that the existence of the fact in issue is more probable than not. The general rule in civil cases is that the party having the **burden of proof** must produce a preponderance of evidence or that such evidence (when weighed with that opposed to it) has more convincing force, from which results the greater probability in favour of the party upon whom the burden rests.

PREROGATIVE WRIT A class of writs granted by a court in its discretion if the matter so merits. Generally, the writs are a method by which the courts can exercise control over **administrative tribunals,** even in the absence of a specific right of appeal. The most common of these "extraordinary remedies" are the **writ of prohibition, mandamus, quo warranto, habeas corpus,** or **certiorari.**

PRESCRIPTION In real estate law, one of the principal methods of creating or acquiring an **easement.** It signifies the use of land that has been enjoyed as of right and without interruption, openly and peacefully, for a certain period of time prescribed by provincial statutes. See further 2 A.H. Oosterhoff & W.B. Rayner, *Anger and Honsberger: Law of Real Property* 935ff. (2d ed. 1985).

PRESENTMENT 1. In criminal law, a written accusation of **crime** made and returned by the **grand jury** upon its own initiative in the exercise of its lawful inquisitorial powers.

2. In commercial law, the presenting of a **bill of exchange** or **promissory note** to the party on whom is **drawn,** for his acceptance, or to the person bound to pay, for payment. Where the instrument has been **executed** and the parties bound thereby, presentment means presentment for payment, as distinguished from presentment for **acceptance,** which is made before the instrument is due.

PRESUMPTION An assumption arising from a given set of facts that has sufficient evidentiary weight to require the production of further **evidence** to overcome the assumption thereby established. A presumption may be one of law or of fact. A PRESUMPTION OF LAW has been defined as "an arbitrary consequence expressly annexed by law to particular facts." See *Re Claresholm Provincial Election: McVaught* v. *McKenzie* (1912), 3 W.W.R. 133 at 137 (Alta.S.C.). A PRESUMPTION OF FACT has been defined as "an **inference** which the mind naturally and logically draws from given facts irrespective of their legal effect." *Id.*

CONCLUSIVE [NON-REBUTTABLE] PRESUMPTION One that no evidence, however strong, no argument, or consideration will be permitted to overcome.

REBUTTABLE PRESUMPTION An ordinary presumption that must, as a matter of law, be made once certain facts have been proved, and that is thus said to establish a certain conclusion **prima facie** once those facts have been adduced; but it is one that may be rebutted. If it is not overcome through introduction of contrary evidence, **it** becomes conclusive.

PRESUMPTION OF INNOCENCE In the **Canadian Charter of Rights and Freedoms,** section 11(d) provides that anyone charged with an offence has the right "to be presumed innocent until proven guilty according to law in a fair and public hearing by an independent and impartial tribunal." Speaking of the right enumerated in s. 11(*d*), in *R.* v. *Oakes,* [1986] 1 S.C.R. 103, the Supreme Court stated that the right was "crucial." "It ensures that until the State proves an accused's guilt beyond all reasonable doubt, he or she is innocent. This is essential in a society committed to fairness and social justice. The presumption of innocence confirms our faith in humankind; it reflects our belief that individuals are decent and law-abiding members of the community until proven otherwise."

The presumption of innocence existed at common law. See *Woolmington* v. *Director of Public Prosecutions* [1935] A.C. 462 (H.L.).

PRESUMPTIVE EVIDENCE Evidence that is indirect or **circumstantial; prima facie** evidence; evidence that is not conclusive and admits of explanation or contradiction; evidence that must be treated as true and sufficient until and unless rebutted by other evidence, i.e., evidence that a statute deems to be presumptive of another fact unless rebutted. See, e.g., s. 348(2), *Criminal Code,* R.S.C. 1985, c. C–46. See **presumption.**

PRICE FIXING The cooperative setting of price levels or ranges by competing firms; an illegal trade practice involving a **conspiracy** or agreement among sellers to raise, depress, fix, peg, or stabilize prices. See *Competition Act,* R.S.C. 1985, c. C–34, s. 50.

PRIMA FACIE *(prī'-mà fā'-shà)* Lat.: at first sight; on the face of it. A fact presumed to be true unless disproved by contrary evidence. See *Craig* v. *McKay* (1906), 12 O.L.R. 121 (C.A.).

PRIMA FACIE CASE A case sufficient on its face, being supported by at least the requisite minimum of **evidence;** one that will usually prevail in the absence of contradictory evidence; "the Crown, in a criminal case, is not required to do more than produce evidence which, if unanswered, and believed, is sufficient to raise a 'prima facie' case upon which the jury might be justified in finding a verdict." *Girvin* v. *The King* (1911), 45 S.C.R. 167 at 169.

PRIMA FACIE EVIDENCE "Prima facie evidence is evidence which, if accepted by the tribunal, establishes a fact in the absence of acceptable evidence to the contrary." 15 *Halsbury's Laws of England,* (3d ed.), para. 506.

Prima facie evidence is evidence that, until its effect is overcome by other evidence, will suffice as proof of fact in issue. See, e.g., *R.* v. *Davis and Dorion* (1954), 108 C.C.C 257 (N.B.S.C.).

PRIMOGENITURE Ancient common law of descent in which the eldest son takes all property of his decedent father. The opposite of primogeniture, BOROUGH ENGLISH, where the youngest son inherited on the death of the father, existed under local custom in at least one jurisdiction even while primogeniture prevailed elsewhere in England. Under the local custom of GAVELKIND, all sons took equally. In the event all issue of the decedent were daughters, they took equal shares in coparceny. See generally 2 F. Pollack & F. Maitland, *History of English Law* 261–66 (2nd ed. 1903).

PRINCIPAL Most important; primary; highest in rank, authority, character, degree or importance.

1. In criminal law, the person who actually committed the **offence.** PRINCIPALS OF THE FIRST DEGREE were the actual perpetrators of the crime, and PRINCIPALS OF THE SECOND DEGREE were those who were present, aiding and abetting the act to be done. These common-law distinctions are not preserved in the *Criminal Code,* R.S.C. 1985, c. C–46 (s. 21). The distinction between principals of the first and second degree has been abrogated and now both are regarded as parties to the offence.

2. In the law of agency, "one who has permitted or directed another to act for his benefit and subject to his direction or control." W. Seavey, *Law of Agency* s. 3 (1964). **Master** is a species of principal. *Id.* "In a transaction conducted by an **agent,** the principal is DISCLOSED if the other party has notice of his identity; he is PARTIALLY DISCLOSED if the other party has notice of his existence but not his identity; he is UNDISCLOSED if the other party has no notice that the agent is acting for a principal." *Id.* at s. 4.

3. In commercial law, the amount that is received in the case of a loan, or the amount upon which interest is charged.

PRIORITY Preference; the condition of coming before, or of coming first; e.g., in a **bankruptcy** proceeding, the right to be paid before other **creditors** out of the assets of the bankrupt party. The term may also be used with reference to a **prior lien,** prior **mortgage,** etc.

PRIOR LIEN A first or superior **lien,** though not necessarily one antecedent to others.

PRIVACY Provisions in federal and some provincial legislation that "relate to an individual's access to and use of personal information in government data banks concerning himself. . . ." G. Gall, *The Canadian Legal System* 373 (3d ed. 1990). See e.g., *Privacy Act,* R.S.C. 1985, c. P-21; *Privacy Act,* R.S.N. 1990, c. P-22. Compare **freedom of information.**

PRIVILEGE 1. A particular advantage or benefit enjoyed by a person, company or class, beyond the common advantages of other citizens; "an advantage conferred over and above ordinary law." *Re Turner* (1922), 65 D.L.R. 130 (Sask.K.B.). Examples include the personal privilege of an ambassador from arrest, exemption from jury duty among certain professionals, and special immunities and advantages given to persons within special relationships such as attorney/client, doctor/patient, etc. **2.** In the law of **libel** and **slander,** a defence that impliedly admits the defamatory nature of the words complained of but seeks to defend it on the grounds that the words were published on a privileged occasion exempting the defendant from liability. Privilege may be absolute, e.g., that enjoyed by judges in a judicial proceedings. See, e.g., *O'Connor* v. *Waldron,* [1935] A.C. 76 at 81 (P.C.). It may also be qualified, as in a defence of **fair comment.** "The defamatory statement ... is only protected when it is fairly warranted by some reasonable occasion or exigency, and when it is fairly made in discharge of some public or private duty or in the conduct of the defendant's own affairs in matters in which his interests are concerned." *Halls* v. *Mitchell,* [1928] S.C.R. 125 at 133. See also the various provincial **defamation** or libel and slander statutes.

PRIVILEGED [CONFIDENTIAL] COMMU-NICATIONS Communications that occur between husband and wife and in certain other relationshps usually of a professional nature, e.g., solicitor and client, priest and penitent. Designating a com-

munication as privileged allows the speaker to resist legal pressure to disclose its contents. See J. Sopinka & S. Lederman, *The Law of Evidence in Civil Cases* 157 (1974).

PRIVITY A relationship between parties arising out of a mutuality of interest.

In the law of **judgments,** the doctrine of **res judicata** applies not only to the actual parties to **litigation** but also to those whose interests are so related as to be affected by the judgment.

PRIVITY OF CONTRACT The doctrine whereby one can enforce contractual rights against another only if one was a party to the contract. Under the general doctrine of privity of contract, no one who is not original party to a contract is entitled to seek to enforce the terms of the contract or is bound by any of its provisions. *Great Northern Ry. Co.* v. *Cole Agencies Ltd.* (1964), 49 W.W.R. 153 at 159 (Sask.Q.B.)

PRIVITY OF ESTATE The relationship between persons who have property interest in the same estate, such as **lessor** and **lessee** or **joint tenants.**

PRIVY Persons who have an interest in some matter, action or thing, and the relation is other than that of actual **contract.**

PRIVY COUNCIL, CANADA According to s. 11 of the *Constitution Act, 1867,* "There shall be a council to aid and advise in the Government of Canada, to be styled the Queen's Privy Council for Canada; and the persons who are to be members of that council shall be from time to time chosen and summoned by the **Governor General** and sworn in as Privy Councillors, and members thereof may be from time to time removed by the Governor General." In Canada the Privy Council is by convention the federal **cabinet,** and its advice to the Governor-General is tantamount to a direction. P. Hogg, *Canada Act Annotated* 99 (1982). The cabinet ministers are all appointed to the Queen's Privy Council for Canada. Appointments are for life, so that its membership also includes ministers of past governments as well as some honourary appointments for persons of distinction. The cabinet, however, constitutes the only active part of the Privy Council, and it exercises all the powers of that body except certain powers reserved specifically unto the Governor-General or the Prime Minister.

PROBABLE CAUSE See **reasonable and probable cause.**

PROBATE The procedure for determining the validity of a **will** and for the proper distribution of an **estate.** The surrogate or probate court of the province has jurisdiction to issue certificates of probate to acknowledging that the will has been proved and registered and that the **administration** of the estate will be **executed.**

PROBATION In criminal law, a non-custodial sentence; the release of an accused into the community under the supervision of a probation officer. The release is conditional on the accused acting in a manner stipulated by his special officer. Compare **parole.**

PROBATIVE Tending to prove or proving facts, evidence and issues. If evidence is probative it is admissible even if obtained illegally unless it is indirect through confession or unless its PROBATIVE VALUE (its relative weight as evidence) is negligible in relation to its prejudicial effect. *R.* v. *Wray*, [1971] S.C.R. 272.

PRO BONO *(prō bō'-nō)* Lat.: for the good of; i.e., pro bono publico: for the public good or welfare.

PROCEDURE The mode of proceeding by which a legal right is enforced, including the whole law of evidence, the enforcement of a right, rules of limitation, methods of execution and formal steps in an action. The rules of procedure do not extend to the substantive right. See **substantive law.**

PROCEEDING "[T]he form in which actions are brought and defended, the manner of intervening in suits and of conducting them." *Eddy* v. *Stewart*, [1932] 3 W.W.R. 71 at 74 (Sask.C.A.). The term is usually broader in meaning than **action** and is also applied to any step in an action. In its derivative sense, the term means the action of going onward, advancing.

PROCESS 1. A formal writing **(writ)** used by the court to exercise **jurisdiction** over a person; usually refers to the method used to compel attendance of a

defendant in court in a **civil** suit. See **service; service of process. 2.** Also, the **proceeding** in any action from beginning to end.

3. In patent law, the method by which certain subject matter is transformed into a different state of thing. Patent law protects not only the thing produced but also the process of producing the same. *The Commissioner of Patents* v. *CIBA Ltd.,* [1959] S.C.R. 378.

PROCTOR 1. One who manages another's affairs, acting as that person's **agent. 2.** Also, a lawyer who **probates** an **estate** on behalf of the **executor** of a **will.** Compare **administrator.**

PRODUCTS LIABILITY A concept in the law of **torts** regarding the circumstances in which a manufacturer who designs and puts a product on the market is liable to the ultimate consumer to ensure that the goods so marketed are free from defects arising from **negligence** or lack of care on the part of the manufacturer. See, e.g., *Donoghue* v. *Stevenson*, [1932] A.C. 562 (H.L.); *Grant* v. *Australian Knitting Mills Ltd.*, [1936] A.C. 85 (P.C.); *Phillips* v. *Ford Motor Co. of Can.*, [1970] 2 O.R. 714 (Ont.H.C.). See **warranty.**

PRO FORMA *(prō fôr'-mà)* Lat.: for the sake of form. As a matter of form. In an appealable **decree** or **judgment,** the term usually means that the decision was rendered, not upon intellectual conviction that the decree was right, but merely to facilitate further proceedings.

PROHIBITION See **writ** [WRIT OF PROHIBITION].

PROMISE A declaration that binds the person who makes it, either in honour, conscience or law, to do or forbear a certain specific act, and that gives the person to whom it is made a right to expect or claim performance of the thing promised. It is an essential element of an **offer** in **contract.** See also **covenant.**

PROMISEE A person who receives a **promise** or undertaking relating to some event.

PROMISOR One who makes a **promise** or gives an undertaking relating to some event.

PROMISSORY ESTOPPEL See **estoppel.**

PROMISSORY NOTE A kind of **negotiable instrument** wherein the **maker** agrees **(promises)** to pay a specific sum at a definite time.

PROOF The quantity or quality of **evidence** that tends to establish the existence of a fact in issue; the persuasion of the TRIER OF FACT (see **fact finder**) by the production of evidence of the truth of a fact alleged; the production of a sufficient quantity of evidence to prevent the **judge** from withdrawing the **issue** from the **jury.** It includes the **burden of proof** borne by a party, who will lose on the issue if after reviewing all the evidence the judge or jury entertains the appropriate degree of doubt. See also **inference; preponderance of the evidence; presumption; reasonable doubt.**

PROOF BEYOND A REASONABLE DOUBT See **reasonable doubt.**

PROPERTY That which belongs exclusively to a person; in a legal sense, the aggregate of rights or **interests** that are subject to **ownership.** The term may denote the thing or object to which the rights or interests apply or the legal relation that exists with respect to those rights. Property may be an object having physical existence or it may be an intangible thing such as a **patent** right. Property is usually divided into two classes, real and personal. Compare **possession.** See **real property; personalty.**

COMMON PROPERTY That which belongs to the citizenry as a whole; property owned by TENANTS IN COMMON (see **tenancy),** or in some jurisdictions, where designated by statute, that owned by husband and wife.

PROPRIETARY INTEREST See **interest.**

PRO RATA *(prō rā'-tà)* Lat.: according to the rate, i.e., in proportion; according to a measure that fixes proportions. It has no meaning unless referable to some rule or standard. Thus, a lease terminated by agreement before the expiration of the full term may call for payment of rent on a *pro rata* basis for the expired term of the lease; an adjudicated bankrupt, after establishing **insolvency,** is relieved of liability to all tested creditors after engaging in a *pro rata* distribution of his assets among those creditors.

PROROGATION The bringing of a session of **Parliament** (or a provincial legislature) to an end. This, like dissolution that brings Parliament to an end, can be done only by an exercise of the royal prerogative. Adjournment to a future hour on the same day, or to a future day, can be effected by Parliament's own motion; all business lapses upon prorogation and must be reintroduced in the new session or the new Parliament.

PRO SE *(prō sā)* Lat.: for himself; in one's own behalf. For example, one represents himself *pro se* in a legal **action** when he does so without aid of **counsel.**

PROSECUTION The act of pursuing a criminal **trial** by the Crown. Where the Crown fails to move the case towards final resolution or trial as required by the court schedule, the matter may be dismissed for "want of prosecution."

PROSECUTOR A public official who prepares and conducts the prosecution of persons accused of crime. The provincial prosecutors are usually called Crown prosecutors. The basic role of the prosecutor is to seek justice and not convictions. His office is charged with the duty to see that the laws of the jurisdiction are faithfully executed and enforced. In the enforcement of laws, the prosecutor has the responsibility of making a decision of who and when to prosecute, a decision with respect to which the prosecution has broad directions. See **Crown Attorney.**

PRO TANTO *(prō tän'-tō)* Lat.: to such extent; for so much; as far as it goes.

PROVINCIAL COURTS According to s. 92(14) of the *Constitution Act, 1867,* each provincial legislature may make laws in relation to "Administration of Justice in the Province, including the Constitution, Maintenance, and Organization of Provincial Courts, both of Civil and of Criminal Jurisdiction, and including Procedure in Civil Matters in those Courts."

"Canada's court system is a cross between the unitary system of England and the federal system of the U.S.A. . . . .

"This complexity results from three provisions in the *Constitution Act.* First, the Act gave responsibility for the administration of justice in the provinces to the provinces (s. 92(14)). Second, it authorized Parliament to establish a court of appeal for Canada and any additional courts needed for "the better administration" of our federal laws (s. 101). Third, and most curious, it entrusted to federal authority the appointment, remuneration and dismissal of judges of the higher provincial courts, i.e., superior, district and county courts (ss. 96, 99 and 100).

"In consequence our court system has three distinctive features. Most matters under both federal and provincial law are dealt with by provincial courts, which were in large part retained as they had been when the province in question entered Confederation. Some matters, however, are dealt with in federal courts, established after Confederation—final appeals may lie to the Supreme Court of Canada and certain items under federal law fall under the jurisdiction of the Federal Court. And the judges (except for those in the lower provincial courts) are all federally appointed and paid." P. Fitzgerald & K. McShane, *Looking at Law* 33–4 (2d ed. 1982). See further G. Gall, *The Canadian Legal System* 105–6 (3d ed. 1990).

PROVISO A condition or stipulation. Its general function is to except something from the basic provision, to qualify or restrain its general scope, or to prevent misinterpretation.

PROVOCATION Any act inciting irrational response. As an element in a case of homicide, provocation may reduce the offence from **murder** to **manslaughter.** See *Criminal Code*, R.S.C. 1985, c. C–46, s. 232. Also *R.* v. *Hill* (1985), 51 C.R. (3d) 97 (S.C.C.)

PROXIMATE CAUSE See **cause.**

PROXY A term used to describe both the agent and the instrument appointing him that enables an individual to vote in the place of another at a company's shareholders' meeting. A two-way proxy enables members to direct the proxy to vote for or against a resolution. Usually the **articles of incorporation** of the company provide for proxy votes. See *Montreal Trust Co.* v. *The Oxford Pipe Line Co. Ltd.*, [1942] O.R. 490 (C.A.).

PUBLIC DOMAIN 1. Lands owned by the government, e.g., Indian reserves and national parks.

2. Information that is generally available to the public and cannot be **copyrighted** is said to be in the public domain.

PUBLIC EASEMENT A public right of way. A right exercisable by anyone, whether he owns land or not, merely by nature of the general law—e.g., the public right of way over a highway or a footpath. See *Williams-Ellis* v. *Cobb,* [1935] 1 K.B. 310.

PUBLIC NUISANCE See **nuisance.**

PUBLIC OFFICER 1. A position created to fulfil a public function or duty. 2. An officer of a joint stock company or corporation.

The *Interpretation Act*, R.S.C. 1985, c. I–21, states: A "'public officer' includes any person in the public service of Canada who is authorized by or under an enactment to do or enforce the doing of an act or thing or to exercise a power, or on whom a duty is imposed by or under an enactment."

PUBLIC PROPERTY Property dedicated to the use of the public, and over which the government (municipal, provincial or federal) has dominion and control. Thus the term may be used either to describe the use to which the property is put or to describe the character of its ownership. See also **public domain.**

PUBLIC SALE See **sale.**

PURCHASER One who acquires goods or lands in exchange for money. One to whom land is expressly transferred other than by **descent,** e.g., by the act of the parties, by **conveyance** on **sale,** by **will** or by **gift.** A purchaser for value is one who obtains a property for a valuable, as distinguished from a merely good, **consideration.** *Crossett* v. *Haycock* (1904), 7 O.L.R. 655 (H.C.).

PURLOIN To steal; to commit theft.

PURVIEW The enacting part or body of a **statute** as distinguished from other parts of it, such as the **preamble.** Conduct is said to be WITHIN THE PURVIEW of a statute when such conduct properly comes within the statute's purpose, operation or effect.

PUTATIVE Alleged; supposed; commonly used in family law. Thus, a putative father is a person declared to be the father of an illegitimate child in an **affiliation** proceeding.

Q

QUAERE *(kwē'-rē)* See **query.**

QUANTUM MERUIT *(kwän'-tŭm mě'-rū-ĭt)* Lat.: wherefore; on what account. As much as he has earned. Where one renders service or performs work for another, under a **contract,** express or implied, and the party gaining the benefit of such service or work fails to pay for such benefit, the other party is said to be entitled to recover a reasonable price for his services on the basis of quantum meruit— as much as he deserves. Quantum meruit is based on an implied promise to pay where one party has performed work for another, in whole or in part, without remuneration, and the other party has thereby unjustly gained the benefit of the services rendered. See *Racette* v. *Bearden,* [1977] 5 W.W.R. 762 (Sask.Q.B.); *Renton* v. *Renton* (1925), 52 N.B.R. 356 (S.C.A.D.).

The principle of quantum meruit is generally subsumed in the law of **restitution** or **unjust enrichment** that permits a **plaintiff** to recover where the defendant has been unjustly enriched by the receipt of a benefit at the plaintiff's expense. See *Deglman* v. *Guaranty Trust Co.,* [1954] S.C.R. 725 at 728.

QUARE CLAUSUM FREGIT *(kwä'-rā klàu'-zŭm frä'-gĭt)* Lat.: wherefore he broke the close. An early form of **trespass** designed to obtain **damages** for unlawful entry upon another's **land.** The **form of action** was called trespass quare clausum fregit or trespass qu. cl. fr. **Breaking a close** was the technical **common-law** expression for unlawful entry upon land. Even without an actual fence the **complainant** would **plead** that the "defendant with force and arms broke and entered the close of the **plaintiff,**" since in the eyes of the common law, every unauthorized entry upon the soil of another was trespass.

QUASH To annul, set aside, discharge or vacate by judicial decision. For example, a wrongful **conviction** on a criminal charge in an inferior court may be quashed by an appellate court. See *Gray*

v. *City of Oshawa,* [1971] 3 O.R. 112 at 115 (H.C.).

QUASI *(kwä'-zī)* Lat.: as it were; so to speak; about, nearly, almost, like.

QUASI-CONTRACTS The class of **contracts** where the law imposes an obligation on one who has retained money that belongs to another or who has gained some benefit from another without reward, to return to the other party the monies lawfully belonging to him or to properly pay such party for the benefit gained. Thus, for example, an action for money had and received or for recovery of money paid under mistake of fact was said to be based on implied or quasi-contract. See *Dominion Distillery Products Co. Ltd.* v. *The King,* [1937] Ex.C.R. 145 at 163–65; *Re Grand River Motors Ltd.,* [1932] O.R. 712 at 721–22 (C.A.). The more modern and widely accepted view in Canada is that these are cases of **unjust enrichment** for which an action will lie in **quantum meruit** or **restitution.**

QUASI-CRIMINAL Describes a **proceeding** that although not actually a criminal **prosecution** is sufficiently similar in terms of the "grievous loss" (civil fine, loss of employment, loss of license, suspension from school, etc.) or the stigma to be attached to warrant some of the special procedural safeguards of a criminal proceeding. See *Beaurone* v. *Beaurone* (1972), 11 R.F.L. 211 at 213 (Ont.Co.Ct.).

QUASI-JUDICIAL A term used to describe the acts of persons, bodies, or tribunals that are not strictly judicial, in the sense of performing the functions of courts or judges, but are similar in that they have authority or discretion to decide important issues affecting the rights and obligations of opposing parties, and whose decisions have the effect of imposing serious sanctions or consequences on the parties directly or indirectly affected thereby. Generally, quasi-judicial boards and tribunals are under a duty to act in accordance with the rules of **natural justice.** See *Nicolson* v. *Haldimand-Norfolk Regional Board of Commissioners of Police,* [1979] 1 S.C.R. 311 at 324–28; *Coopers & Lybrand* v. *Minister of National Revenue* (1978), 24 N.R. 163 at 172–73 (S.C.C.); *Re Abel and Director, Pene-*

tanguishene Mental Health Centre; Re Abel and Advisory Review Board (1979), 46 C.C.C. (2d) 342 at 357–59 (Ont.H.C.).

QUEEN In Canada, Queen Elizabeth II (or the present reigning British monarch) is the formal head of state. Section 9 of the *Constitutional Act, 1867* states: "The Executive Government and Authority of and over Canada is hereby declared to continue and to be vested in the Queen." In reality, however, the Queen is only the nominal head of state. The powers vested in her are delegated at the federal level to the **Governor-General** of Canada and at the provincial level to the **Lieutenant-Governor** of the province. See further P. Hogg, *Constitutional Law of Canada* (3d ed. 1992) at, e.g., 229–32. See **Crown.**

QUEEN'S BENCH See **King's Bench.**

QUEEN'S [KING'S] COUNSEL [Q.C., K.C.] In England, near the end of the sixteenth century, one or two senior **barristers** were appointed King's or Queen's Counsel (depending upon the sex of the monarch). They were required to give services to the **Crown** when requested. By the nineteenth century they had become more numerous, and their duties to the Crown merely nominal. The title today is basically one of distinction conferred on prominent barristers. See L. Curzon, *English Legal History* (2d ed. 1979).

In Canada the title "is awarded to solicitors who have never argued a case in court, to law teachers, and even to politicians who have no more than nominal membership in the legal profession. Certain formal privileges survive, such as the right to wear a silk gown and to argue cases from within the Bar in court (that is, from a position closer to the judge). But by and large, in Canada it has become a mere honorary appendage, indicating little more than a certain degree of seniority and a certain degree of acceptability to the government that has awarded the title." S. Waddams, *Introduction to the Study of Law* 134 (4th ed. 1992).

QUERY Question; indicates that the proposition or rule it introduces is unsettled or is open to some question.

QUESTION OF FACT Disputed factual contention that is traditionally left for the **jury** to decide. For example, in a **battery** case, a question of fact would be whether A touched B. The legal significance of the touching of B by A is left for the judge to decide since it amounts to a **question of law.** See *Curlett* v. *Canadian Fire Insurance Co.,* [1938] 3 W.W.R. 357 at 364 (Alta.S.C.).

QUESTION OF LAW Disputed legal contentions that are traditionally left for the judge to decide. The occurrence or non-occurrence of an event is a **question of fact;** its legal significance is a question of law. Questions of law are generally determined by considering legal authorities and arguments. Generally, only questions of law can be raised on the appeal of a case.

It is often difficult to decide whether a question is one of fact or of law. In some cases, questions of mixed fact and law arise. For example, in a trial on a charge of manslaughter the question of what the accused did is a question of fact while the issue of whether these facts are also consistent with the legal definition of manslaughter is a question of law. See *R.* v. *Fillmore* (1975), 11 N.B.R. (2d) 257 (S.C.A.D.); *Roy* v. *The King,* [1938] S.C.R. 32 at 42–46; *Loblaw Groceterias Co. Ltd.* v. *The Corp. of the City of Toronto,* [1936] S.C.R. 249 at 254.

QUIA EMPTORES, STATUTE OF *(kwē'-à ĕmp-tô'-rēz)* Lat.: an English statute passed in 1290 that terminated the process of **subinfeudation** [creation of new manors by the subject of a lord]. After that date, only the King was able to infeudate. The statute's practical effect on land transactions and ownership was that, after the land was sold, the seller had no further connection with it. See G. Cheshire & E. Burn, *The Modern Law of Real Property* 14-5 (14th ed. 1988). Thus subinfeudation was replaced by strict **alienation.**

QUID PRO QUO *(kwĭd prō kwō)* Lat.. what for what; something for something; in some legal contexts, synonymous with **consideration;** sometimes referred to simply as the "quid" and always indicating that which a party receives or is promised in return for something he promises, gives or does.

QUIET ENJOYMENT The right to unimpaired use and enjoyment of **property leased** or **conveyed.** As to leased premises a guarantee of quiet enjoyment is usually expressed by a **covenant** of quiet enjoyment in a written lease, but such a covenant may be implied from the landlord-tenant relationship where it is not so expressed. This covenant is violated if the tenant's enjoyment of the premises is substantially disturbed either by wrongful acts or omissions of the landlord or by persons claiming a **paramount title** to the landlord. The covenant may be and often is included in a **deed** conveying title to property, but in this context it does not arise by implication. See, e.g., *Walton v. Biggs* (1912), 7 D.L.R. 843 (Man.Cty.Ct.).

QUIET[ING] TITLE An equitable **action** to determine all adverse claims to the property in question; a **suit** in **equity** brought to obtain a final determination as the **title** of a specific piece of **property**; such a suit is usually the result of various individuals asserting contradictory rights to the same parcel of land. An action can be brought under statute in some provinces to have title to the property judicially investigated and to determine any adverse claims to such property. See, e.g., *Quieting Titles Act*, R.S.N.S. 1989, c. 382; *Quieting of Titles Act*, R.S.N.B. 1973, c. Q-4; *Quieting Titles Act*, R.S.P.E.I. 1988, c. Q-2.

QUITCLAIM DEED A **deed** that conveys only that right, **title**, or **interest** that the **grantor** has or may have, and that does not require that the grantor thereby pass a **good title**. The grantor of a quitclaim deed does not represent that he has any interest in the property for which he gives the deed—merely that whatever interest he may have he **conveys** to the **grantee**. Compare **warranty** [WARRANTY DEED].

QUORUM The minimum number of members of a body who must necessarily be present in order to transact the business of that body. Usually, but not necessarily, a quorum requires a majority.

A quorum is generally required to render legitimate any actions voted on or taken, for example, by directors or shareholders of limited companies or **corpora-**

tions. While a quorum is usually a majority of either the total membership or the members present, this general principle can be altered by the body to require or permit that more or less than a majority of the body is necessary to transact business. See, e.g., *Canada Business Corporations Act*, R.S.C. 1985, c. C–44, s. 114(2); 139(1).

QUOTATION 1. In commercial usage, a statement of the price of an item; also the price stated in response to an inquiry; **2.** more generally, the word-for-word repetition of a statement from some authority, case or law. See *Victoria Electrical Co. v. Monarch Electrical Co. Ltd.* (1917), 13 O.W.N. 141 (S.C.).

QUO WARRANTO *(kwō wä′-ràn-tō)* Lat.: by what right or authority. A prerogative remedy, now falling into disuse in most provincial jursidictions, by which one seeks to inquire or establish by what authority a person holds public office. The remedy is available against persons who hold public office created by royal charter, royal prerogative or by statute, and its purpose is to remove those who have usurped their office. A person could be found to have usurped his office by acting without statutory qualifications to hold the particular office or appointment or by losing the required qualifications during the term of office. There must be a purported exercise of the allegedly usurped office before this remedy will be issued, and the court may, in its discretion, refuse to grant this form of relief where other more appropriate remedies are available. In British Columbia, the *Judicial Review Procedure Act*, R.S.B.C. 1979, c. 209, s. 19, abolishes quo warranto and replaces it with injunctive relief. See generally *Bruce and Meadley v. Reynett*, [1979] 4 W.W.R. 408 at 417–20 (F.); *Regina ex rel. Hennigar v. Stevens* (1969), 3 D.L.R. (3d) 668 at 671–72 (N.S.S.C.); *Shaw v. Trainor* (1967), 53 M.P.R. 380 (P.E.I.S.C., in banco); *The King ex rel. The Township of Stamford v. McKeown*, [1934] O.R. 662 at 664 (S.C.). See also *Nova Scotia Civil Procedure Rules* (1983) rr. 56.09–56.14.

R

RAPE Commonly regarded as the act of unlawful sexual intercourse between persons not married to each other, accomplished through the use of force or threat of force by a male person and implying lack of consent, and resistance, by a female person. Under earlier versions of the *Criminal Code* (e.g., R.S.C. 1970, c. C–34), rape was an **indictable offence** with a maximum penalty of imprisonment for life. *An Act to amend the Criminal Code in relation to sexual offences*, S.C. 1980–81–82–83, c. 125, repealed the provisions dealing with rape and created new offences respecting sexual assault and aggravated sexual assault. See **sexual assault.**

RATIFICATION The act or process of formally ratifying, adopting or confirming a **contract,** treaty or other transaction by the parties, which they were not legally bound by originally.

1. In contract, it is the act of the **principal,** either by words or by conduct, that amounts to a manifestation of assent to the act of an **agent.** If the principal ratifies the agent's unauthorized act, he is taken to ratify the contract **in toto** and cannot select such provision as may operate to his advantage. See *Cornwal* v. *Wilson* (1750), 1 Ves.Sr. 509; 27 E.R. 1173 (Ch.). Ratification is said to relate back to the time of the transaction with the agent. See *Bolton Partners* v. *Lambert* (1888), 41 Ch.D. 295 (C.A.). The prerequisites of ratification are (1) the agent to the contract must profess at the time of making the contract to be acting on behalf of the persons who subsequently ratify the contract. See *Keighley, Maxsted & Co.* v. *Durant,* [1901] A.C. 240 (H.L.); (2) at the time when the contract was made the agent must have had a competent principal. See *Kelner* v. *Baxter* (1866), L.R. 2 C.P. 174.

Infants can ratify their contracts themselves after reaching the age of majority. The ratification is binding without new **consideration.** Ratification is presumed unless the infant disaffirms a long-standing contract within a reasonable time after reaching his **majority.** *Blackwell* v. *Farrow,* [1948] O.W.N. 7 (H.C.).

2. In international law, after a treaty has been signed, normally it is not binding until it is ratified. Ratification is a formal ceremony where the parties exchange solemn confirmations, adopting the treaty by their own internal law.

3. "Ratification by a Court of law may signify that the Court is to examine the transaction submitted to it and to decide, according to its discretion, whether the terms of the transaction are such that the parties ought or ought not, to be bound by the agreement which they have made, or it may mean that the court is to give its formal approval without reference to the terms of the transaction, on being satisfied that due provision has been made for protecting and securing the legal interests of third parties which would be prejudicially affected if no such provision were made." *Stewart* v. *Kennedy* (1890), 15 A.C. 75 at 99 (H.L.)

RATIO DECIDENDI *(rä'-shē-ō dā-sĭ-dĕn'-dē)* Lat.: the reason for the decision. The principle that the case establishes.

RATIO LEGIS *(rǎ'-shē-ō lĕ'-gĭs)* Lat.: legal reason or ground. The underlying principle; the theory, doctrine or science of law. Thus, the *ratio legis* of a loitering by-law is to allow law enforcement officers more latitude in attempting to prevent crime rather than to rely solely on apprehension and sentencing as a deterrent.

R.C.M.P. See **Royal Canadian Mounted Police.**

READ[ING] INTO A phrase commonly associated with a court's willingness in the process of interpreting the **Canadian Charter of Rights and Freedoms** to "read into" the equality requirements of section 15 certain assumptions regarded as fundamental to the Canadian democratic system. In other words, the courts may go beyond a strict narrow interpretation of a listed category to accomplish what is regarded as necessary for the broader public interest. See *Schachter* v. *Canada* (1992), 139 N.R. 1. For example, in several cases the courts have stated that while not expressly referred to in section 15 of the *Charter,* **sexual orientation** is an analogous category to those specifically enumerated. See e.g. *Veysey* v. *Canada (Correctional Services)* (1988), 64 O.R. (2d) 258 (H.C.); *Knodel* v. *British Columbia (Medical Services Commission)* (1991), 58

B.C.L.R. (2d) 356 (S.C.); *Vriend* v. *Alberta,* April 12, 1994 (Alta. Q.B.).

REAL ESTATE Every possible **interest** in land, except for a mere **chattel** interest; every estate, interest and right—legal and equitable—in **lands, tenements** and **hereditaments.**

REAL PARTY IN INTEREST The individual entitled to the benefits of a successful **action;** one who is essentially, fundamentally and truly interested in the subject matter, in contrast to a party who has only a small, formal or unimportant interest in or relation with the action.

REAL PROPERTY Lands, **tenements,** and **hereditaments;** in other words, land and buildings erected upon it. Generally, all interests in land are real property, except for **leaseholds** for a term of years, which are **personalty** or **chattels.**

The difference between real property and **personal property** is that real property (immovable property) can always be recovered by a real **action (action in rem)** and personal property (movable property, e.g., chattels) can be recovered by an **action in personam,** i.e., **conversion, detinue, replevin.**

To be classified as real property, a movable must be sufficiently incorporated into the constructions or buildings in which it is installed to form an integral part. It will not become unmovable by nature merely by reason of its forming part of a system. *City of St. Laurent* v. *Quebec Hydro-Electric Commission,* [1978] 2 S.C.R. 529.

Real property comprises two distinct classes called CORPOREAL and INCORPOREAL HEREDITAMENTS (see **hereditaments**). Corporeal hereditaments are physical matters such as land, over which ownership is exercised; incorporeal hereditaments are not things but rights, such as **easements.**

REALTY An **estate** in land; another word for **real property.**

REASONABLE AND PROBABLE CAUSE A cause that "depends in all cases not upon the actual existence, but upon the reasonable bona fide belief in the existence of such a state of things as would amount to a justification of the course pursued." *Hicks* v. *Faulkner* (1878), 8 Q.B.D. 167 at 173.

Reasonable and probable cause [GROUNDS] is usually referred to in relation to the law of arrest in Canada. Section 495, *Criminal Code,* R.S.C. 1985, c. C–46, states: "A **peace officer** may arrest without warrant a person who has committed an indictable offence or who, on reasonable grounds, he believes has committed or is about to commit an indictable offence, [also] a person in respect of whom he has reasonable grounds to believe that a warrant of arrest or committal, in any form set out in Part XXVIII in relation thereto, is in force within the territorial jurisdiction in which the person is found."

"For a peace officer to have reasonable and probable grounds for believing in someone's guilt, his belief must take into account all the information available to him. He is entitled to disregard only what he has good reason for believing not reliable." *Chartier* v. *Attorney-General of Quebec* (1979), 48 C.C.C. (2d) 34 at 56 (S.C.C.). The courts have been reluctant to rigidly define what is reasonable and probable, preferring to retain the flexibility required to make independent determinations on particular facts.

REASONABLE DOUBT Refers to the level of certainty needed by a juror to form a legally sound determination of the guilt of the **accused.** In the **instructions** to the jury at a criminal trial, these words signify that there is a **presumption** of innocence unless guilt is so manifestly proven that the jury can have no reasonable doubt of the guilt of the criminal **defendant.** Reasonable doubt is not just a mere presence in the mind, but neither does the notion require that the evidence be so certain that no chance of error can be present. It means that the evidence must be so complete and convincing that any reasonable doubts of the facts are erased from the minds of the jurors. "By reasonable doubt as to a person's guilt is meant that real doubt—real as distinguished from illusory—which an honest juror has after considering all the circumstances of the case and as a result of which he is unable to say: 'I am morally certain of his guilt.' Moral certainty does not mean absolute certainty. Absolute, that is, demonstrable certainty, is generally impossible and juries might well be told that in discharging their serious responsibilities their consciences need not be racked and tortured because of the fact that absolute certainty is impossible." *R. v. Sears,* [1948] O.R. 9 at 14 (C.A.). See also *R. v Latta,* [1972] 6 W.W.R. 147 (Alta.S.C.A.D.).

REASONABLE MAN See **reasonable person.**

REASONABLE PERSON An imaginary person who possesses and uses the qualities of carefulness, intelligence and judgment that society requires of its members for the protection of their own interest and the interests of others.

In *Arland* v. *Taylor,* [1955] O.R. 131 (C.A.) Mr. Justice Laidlaw noted at p. 142: "[The reasonable person is] a mythical creature of the law whose conduct is the standard by which the Courts measure the conduct of all other persons and find it to be proper or improper in particular circumstances as they may exist from time to time. He is not an extraordinary or unusual creature; he is not superhuman; he is not required to display the highest skill of which anyone is capable; he is not a genius who can perform uncommon feats, nor is he possessed of unusual powers of foresight. He is a person of normal intelligence who makes prudence a guide to his conduct. He does nothing that a prudent man would not do and does not omit to do anything a prudent man would do. He acts in accord with general and approved practice. His conduct is guided by considerations which ordinarily regulate the conduct of human affairs. His conduct is the standard, adopted in the community by persons of ordinary intelligence and prudence.' "

REBUTTAL EVIDENCE Evidence introduced by one **party** in an **action** to justify, repulse, counteract or dispose of the evidence given by the other party or a **witness.** Rebuttal evidence can also be employed to contradict other evidence or to rebut a **presumption.**

REBUTTER In **common law,** a pleading that was an answer of fact given by a **defendant** to the **plaintiff's** response to the defendant's **surrejoinder.** This form of pleading is seldom used, and many provincial **jurisdictions** have abandoned it with a reform to their Civil Procedure Rules.

RECEIVER An impartial person appointed by the court on an **interlocutory** application to collect and receive the benefits (**rents,** issues, and profits of land or personal **estate**), which it does not seem reasonable to the court that either party should collect or receive, or to enable the same to be distributed among the persons entitled. The reason for the appointment of a receiver is to safeguard the **property** until the rights of the **parties** have been determined. For example, in a proceeding to extinguish a **partnership** a receiver is frequently engaged to sell off the company assets.

Receivers have very broad powers in relation to the disputed property and may take possession of the subject matter and do all such acts of **ownership**—in relation to the receipts of rents, compelling payment of them, management, letting lands and houses, and otherwise making the property productive—for the parties ultimately declared to be entitled thereto.

During **bankruptcy,** the official receiver can be appointed INTERIM RECEIVER at any time after the presentation of the **petition** into the court. If he is so appointed, the receiver has the duty to act until a **trustee** is appointed. A mortgagee can engage a receiver of the mortgaged property when the **mortgage** becomes payable. *Re Cape Breton Cash Store* (1929), 10 C.B.R. 353 (N.S.S.C.).

By way of equitable **execution,** a receiver can be appointed by the court to allow a **judgment creditor** to obtain payment of his debt, when the possession of property is in the hand of the debtor or the ordinary process of execution cannot be used to get at an interest in land.

RECEIVERSHIP **1.** An equitable **remedy** whereby **property** is by court **order,** for the benefit of the affected parties, placed under the supervision and control of a **receiver.** Because of **action** by creditors, a failing business may be placed in receivership, but the business is often continued, subject to the power of the receiver. Receivership is usually not the main **relief** sought in an action but is ancillary to the main purpose of the action. Usually a receivership order is used to protect property during **litigation** concerning entitlement to the property. **2.** Receivership is also used to describe property affected by the remedy; for example, property is said to be IN RECEIVERSHIP. Compare **bankruptcy.**

RECESS 1. A temporary adjournment in the course of a **trial** or **hearing.** The adjournment can vary in length from minutes to days. **2.** Also, the time between sittings of the same legislative body at its usual or adjourned session, but not the time between the final adjournment of one body and the convening of another at the next regular session. Compare **sine die.**

RECIDIVIST A person who, after having been convicted of an offence and serving his sentence or being pardoned, commits another offence. When this is done more than twice, he may be classified as a **habitual criminal** and thus affected by habitual criminal statutes that lead to extended times of imprisonment. See *R. v. Pelletier* (1974), 18 C.C.C. (2d) 516 (Ont.C.A.).

RECIPROCITY A practice carried on between persons, **corporations,** provinces, or countries whereby courtesies or privileges given by one are reciprocated by the other. For example, if State X allows workers from State Y to work there, State Y in permitting workers from State X to work in Y would be participating in reciprocity. Other examples include **maintenance orders, custody** orders. See *Re Needham v. Needham,* [1964] 1 O.R. 645 (H.C.). Compare **comity.**

RECKLESS Marked by lack of proper caution; careless of the consequences. In some cases the term insinuates more than carelessness, even going as far as to imply willfulness. In this context the meaning may be indifferent to the consequences, mindless, not caring; very **negligent;** advertent negligence where the consequence was foreseen as possible but not desired. *Shawinigan Ltd. v. Vokins & Co. Ltd.,* [1961] 1 W.L.R. 1206 at 1214 (Q.B.D.): "reckless means grossly careless ... the doing of something which in fact involves a risk, whether the doer realizes it or not."

In criminal law, recklessness is recognized as an alternative to intention in nearly all crimes requiring **mens rea.** For crimes such as perjury the **defendant** may realize the possibility of the falsity of the statement yet affirm the statement as though it were true. A person is reckless if, knowing that there is a risk, that an event may result from his conduct, or that a circumstance may exist, he takes that risk even though it is unreasonable for him to take it having regard to the degree and nature of the risk he knows to be present. The risk must be of such a type and extent that the person's failure to appreciate it, taking into account the object of his conduct and the circumstances known by him, includes a gross deviation from the level of care that a reasonable and prudent individual would have undertaken in that person's circumstances. *R. v. Binus,* [1966] 2 O.R. 324 (C.A.).

RECKLESS DISREGARD In relation to behaviour, lack of heed, or regard for the results; especially, foolishly ignoring danger, rash, heedlessly neglectful or inattentive to consequences. This involves a realization of danger and a willingness to undertake the risk. Ordinary **negligence** is less severe than reckless disregard but the latter does not require a criminal intent to inflict injury. **Guest** passenger statutes and actions of drivers of motor vehicles are often associated with the phrase. See *Leblanc v. R.,* [1977] 1 S.C.R. 339, where a pilot injuring individuals on the ground by flying too low was found to show reckless disregard for their safety and the lives of his passengers.

RECOGNIZANCE The procedure by which a person is released and in the place of **bail** furnishes a promise to appear and respond to criminal charges against him. It is an acknowledgement of indebtedness to the Sovereign made orally before a court or a **magistrate.** The accused is bound by the recognizance to appear for his bail and continues to be bound until **sentenced** or **discharged,** notwithstanding that his trial has been adjourned. A recognizance is automatically discharged when the conditions upon which it was entered are fulfilled. See *R. v. Badman* (1956), 116 C.C.C. 212 (B.C.C.A.).

In deciding whether to grant **release,** the court takes into account the type and circumstances of the charged offence, the evidence against the accused, the family, the employment situation of the accused, his financial resources, as well as his mental condition.

RECORD 1. To maintain in written or printed form or by any alternate means such as tape, film or video. **2.** The precise chronicle of a trial (action) from its beginning to its termination, including the **conclusions of law** recorded by the proper officer of the court for the purpose of preserving the exact state of facts.

During an appeal, the **appellant** cannot go outside the RECORD OF APPEAL—that is, the items introduced in **evidence** in the lower court—in making his case.

In *R.* v. *Thompson* (1950), 99 C.C.C. 89 at 95 (B.C.S.C.), it was held that in a **preliminary hearing** the record consisted of the **information** (if any), the **depositions** of the **witnesses**, the exhibits thereto, the statements of the accused, all **recognizances** entered into and any deposition taken before a **coroner**, if any such have been sent to the justice.

Certiorari is an available remedy to **quash** a decision, on the ground that there is an error "on the face of the record." The record must contain at least the documents, the **pleadings**, if any, and the **adjudication**, but not the evidence nor the reasons for a decision, unless the **tribunal** chooses to incorporate them. *Id.*

RECOUPMENT The right of a **defendant** to have the **plaintiff's** award of **damages** against the defendant reduced; a right of deduction from the amount of the plaintiff's claim by reason of either a payment thereon or some loss sustained by the defendant because of the plaintiff's wrongful or defective **performance** of the **contract,** out of which his **claim** originated. It has been defined to be a keeping back of something that is due, because there is an equitable reason for withholding it. The word is nearly synonymous with discount, deduction or reduction. See also **counterclaim; setoff.**

RECOVERY 1. An individual's repossession of something wrongfully taken or detained from him, to which he is otherwise entitled.

2. The result of a **judgment** of the court that leads to the establishment of a right. The successful **party** in a **suit** to obtain a judgment recovers those things that the **tribunal** believes him to have been deprived of, although recovery does not necessarily mean restoration of the whole. **3.** Also, the amount collected and the amount of the judgment.

4. In the context of criminal law, recovery pertains to the recovery by an accused from **mental disorder,** s. 16 of the *Criminal Code,* R.S.C. 1985, c. C–46. See also ss. 672.5(10)(ii), 672.51(3), 672.86.

RECTIFICATION [REFORMATION] The rewording or rewriting of a **contract** in cases where the written form of the agreement does not express what was actually agreed upon. It is an equitable doctrine based on the notion of **unjust enrichment.** Because of this, rectification is only allowed upon the clear and satisfactory showing of a mutual **mistake.** See *Pepper* v. *Prudential Trust Co. Ltd.,* [1965] S.C.R. 417. It is an exception to the **parol evidence rule.** See *Alampi* v. *Swartz* (1964), 43 D.L.R. (2d) 11 (Ont.C.A.). It is important to distinguish cases of mistaken assumption where rectification does not apply. "In order to get rectification it is necessary to show that the parties were in complete agreement on the terms of their contract, but by an error wrote them down wrongly; and in this regard, in order to ascertain the terms of their contract, you do not look into the inner minds of the parties—into their intentions....You look at their outward acts, that is, at what they said or wrote to one another in coming to their agreement, and then compare it with the document which they have signed. If you can predicate with certainty what their contract was, and that it is by a common mistake, wrongly expressed in the document, then you can rectify the document; but nothing less will suffice." *Rose (London) Ltd.* v. *Pim Jnr. & Co. Ltd.,* [1953] 2 Q.B. 450 (C.A.).

Compare **rescission.**

REDEMPTION A right possessed by the mortgagor upon payment of the **mortgage** to regain legal **title** to the **property.** "This equity of redemption is an estate in land and the person entitled to it is in **equity** the owner of the land." *Fletcher* v. *Rodden* (1882), 1 O.R. 155 at 160 (Ch.D.).

REDUCTIO AD ABSURDUM (*rā-dŭk'-tē-ō ād āb-sûr'-dŭm*) Lat.: reduction to the absurd. The process whereby a legal argument is reduced to the absurd by showing that the argument ultimately follows to a preposterous position.

RE-ENTRY [RIGHT OF] The resumption of **possession** pursuant to a right reserved when the former possession was surrendered. It was a remedy given by feudal law for nonpayment of rent and also refers to a right reserved in the **conveyance** of a **fee** that is subject to a **condition** subsequent. See **conditional fee.** See, e.g., *Re Melville* (1886), 11 O.R. 626 (Ch.D.). Under **common law,** the right of re-entry was usually available to the **grantor** through self-help. Recent judicial decisions have for the most part denied this right even if reserved in the **deed** or **instrument** of conveyance. A **suit** to **quiet title** is the preferred course.

Landlord-tenant legislation in Canada generally allows the landlord to elect to terminate the **lease** when there has been default in payment of **rent,** and this may be done by peaceable 're-entry' without previous judicial **proceedings,** in the exercise of self-help. *Re Rexdale Investments Ltd. and Gibson,* [1967] 1 O.R. 251 (C.A.). See also *Prudential Insurance Co. of America* v. *McLean,* [1943] O.R. 377 (C.A.).

REFEREE   An **arbitrator.** A person appointed by a court; a quasi-judicial officer to whom the court refers a matter. The referee may take **testimony,** arbitrate a dispute between parties and report his findings to the court, upon which the court can base a judgment. See **Master.**

REFERENCE CASE   A case sent to a **referee** or court for a decision or recommendation on a point of law. "Each Canadian jurisdiction has conferred non-judicial functions on its courts, by enacting a statute which enables the government to refer a question of law to the courts for an **advisory opinion.** P. Hogg, *Constitutional Law of Canada* 215 (3d ed. 1992) "The *Supreme Court Act* [R.S.C. 1985, c. S-26] imposes on the Court the function of giving advisory opinions on questions referred to the Court by the federal government. . . . A provincial government has no power to direct a reference to the Supreme Court of Canada. However, each of the ten provinces has enacted legislation permitting the provincial government to direct a reference to the provincial court of appeal. . . . When the provincial court of appeal has rendered an opinion on a reference . . . there is an appeal as of right to the Supreme Court of Canada." *Id.* at 214–15.

REFERENDUM   1. Like the **plebiscite,** a method used for obtaining the community view on a particular issue. **2.** In western Canada, the referendum has also been used as a vehicle to permit voters to participate directly in law-making. In the latter sense the referendum is more than advisory in nature and might require that, on petition of a certain percentage of voters, certain provincial laws be suspended until the whole electorate has voted on them. Such provincial attempts at direct democracy have included the *Initiative and Referendum Act,* S.M. 1916, c. 59, which was found to be **ultra vires** the powers of the province in that it interfered with the office of the **Lieutenant-Governor** (Re *Initiative and Referendum Act,* [1919] A.C. 935 (P.C.)), and invested the primary powers of legislation in a body other than the Legislature (Re *Initiative and Referendum Act* (1916), 27 Man.R. 1 (C.A.)). See further P. Hogg, *Constitutional Law of Canada* 347ff. (3d ed. 1992).

REFORMATION   See **rectification.**

REGISTER   1. To record formally and exactly; to enroll; to enter precisely in a list or the like. **2.** A public record to establish matters of fact such as births, deaths, and marriages. **3.** Also, the books of a company incorporated under one of the various Companies Acts requiring certain matters of disclosure, e.g., the manner in which shares are held by directors of the company. See, e.g., *Re Kramer* v. *Humfrey* (1970), 17 D.L.R. (3d) 103 at 111 (Man.Q.B.).

REGISTRY ACTS   **Legislation** in each of the provinces of Canada providing for the registration of instruments affecting **real property (deeds, mortgages,** etc.) and for the effect of such registration. Such a statute affords a means of giving public notice of the nature of an interest in land that is claimed, and establishes priorities between claimants to enable the determination of the rights of all parties claiming an interest in a property and the exact limits of the property. In Canada, two systems of land registration are in existence, the registry office system and the land titles system, and reference must be made to the appropriate provincial legislation.

LAND TITLES SYSTEM A record system based upon the Torrens system of registration in Australia, which provides protection for a **bona fide purchaser** from a "registered" owner to the extent that the purchaser does not have to go behind the **register** and search the **vendor's title** in order to satisfy himself as to its validity. When land is transferred under this system, the transferee becomes the registered owner and earlier links in the **chain of title** are immaterial. See further 2 A.H. Oosterhoff & W.B Rayner, *Anger and Honsberger: Law of Real Property* 1606ff. (2d ed. 1985). See also the various provincial statutes, e.g., *Land Title Act,* R.S.B.C. 1979, c. 219. *Land Titles Act,* R.S.S. 1978, c. L-5; *Land Titles Act,* R.S.O., 1990, c. L. 5.

REGISTRY SYSTEM A record system that differs from the land titles system in that it is a "system of deed, not title, recordation. This means that the system attempts to compel registration of all interests in the land. If an interest is not registered it is liable to be defeated by a subsequent interest . . . Under the registry system practically any instrument may be registered. The registrar is not concerned with the intrinsic worth of the instrument but records it for what it is worth. It is also inevitable under a deed registration system that there be a continual lengthening of the title which must be searched by successive purchasers. Thus, not only does the search become more difficult, the risk of error increases." *Id.* at 1621, 1628–29.

REGISTRY [OF DEEDS] A system or delegated public office that serves to give notice to third parties of **inter alia** changes in the ownership of **real property** effected by **conveyance** of that property. See **registry acts.**

REGNAL YEAR The year of the reign of the monarch. Sessions of the federal **Parliament** and of most provincial legislatures have traditionally been designated by the regnal year or years of the monarch during which sessions were held. For example, instead of using the calendar year 1967, the designation 15 & 16 Eliz. II

might be used. The regnal year method was also the traditional method for the **citation** of **statutes.** It is no longer a common method of citation for Canadian statutes. However, the regnal year must still be used in citing British statutes prior to 1963.

REGULATIONS A form of SUBORDINATE LEGISLATION (see **legislation**). It is a normal practice for most modern **statutes** to confer lawmaking powers upon the **Governor-General** in Council or **Lieutenant-Governor** in Council for the further carrying out of the purposes of the statute in question. Such practice enables the government (federal or provincial) to act expeditiously and provide additional regulations without the necessity of enacting new statutes. The power to enact regulations may also be conferred upon a Minister or government official (e.g., a Registrar of Motor Vehicles), an administrative board, etc. The various provincial *Regulations Acts* and the federal *Statutory Instruments Act,* R.S.C. 1985, c. S–22, contain definitions of regulations and information concerning requirement of publication, etc. See further S. Waddams, *Introduction to the Study of Law* 100-1 (4th ed. 1992).

REGULATORY OFFENCE Crimes that are not inherently evil but are wrong only because prohibited by legislation. In general, a crime involving moral turpitude is **malum in se**; otherwise, it is **malum prohibitum.** Some examples of regulatory offences are exceeding the speed limit, selling intoxicating liquors, and public intoxication. Regulatory offences are also called STATUTORY OFFENCES and often impose **strict liability** upon the defendants for violation.

REHEARING A retrial or reconsideration of the issues by the same court or body in which the suit or matter was originally heard, and upon the **pleadings** and **depositions** already in the case.

REJOINDER In **pleadings**, at **common law,** an answer to **plaintiff's** replication by some matter of fact, in an **action at law.** This largely historical procedural device was prevalent prior to procedural reforms of the nineteenth century. See G. Watson, *Canadian Civil Procedure* 377 (3d ed. 1988).

RELATION BACK The principle that an act done at a later time is deemed by law to have occurred at a prior time.

RELEASE The act or writing by which some **claim,** right, or **interest** is given up to the person against whom the claim, right or interest could have been enforced. For example, a person may sign a release that ends his right to sue someone for an injury caused by that person.

In the law of property, the holder of a **fee simple** may convey to another a term of years and then subsequently release his **reversionary** interest (LEASE AND RELEASE) to the possessor of the term of years; conversely, should the possessor of the term of years quit the premises before the end of the term, he may be said to have surrendered the remainder of the term to the **grantor.**

RELEASE ON RECOGNIZANCE See **recognizance.**

RELEVANT Applying to the matter in question; affording something to the purpose. **Evidence** must be relevant to be admissible in a judicial proceeding. See **admissible evidence.**

RELIANCE Dependence, trust in what is deemed sufficient support or authority.

DETRIMENTAL RELIANCE Reliance by one party on the acts, representations or promises of another that causes the first party to allow a worsening of his position; an important element in many legal contexts. If such a detrimental change of position is established, and if the reliance appears to have been justified under the circumstances, it may preclude **revocation** of an offer of waiver, may support a promise as a **contract** even without **consideration** (see **estoppel** [PROMISSORY ESTOPPEL]), and is a necessary ingredient in an action to recover upon a claim of **fraud.** See further S. Waddams, *The Law of Contracts* 131–38 (3d ed. 1993).

RELICTION The gradual and imperceptible withdrawal of water from land that it covers by the lowering of its surface level from any cause. If the retreat of the waters is permanent—i.e., not merely seasonal—the owner of the contiguous property acquires ownership of the dry land thus created. Compare **dereliction.** See also **accretion; avulsion.**

RELIEF 1. The redress or assistance awarded to a **complainant,** by the court, especially a **court of equity,** including such remedies as **specific performance, injunction, rescission** of a contract, etc.; but the term may also comprehend an award of money **damages.** The term AFFIRMATIVE RELIEF is often used to indicate that the gist of relief is protection from future harm rather than compensation for past injury.

2. In feudal property law, a payment made by the **heir** of a deceased **tenant** to the lord in order to step into his ancestor's shoes and keep the family home and land intact. A. Sinclair, *Introduction to Real Property Law* 5 (3d ed. (1987). Thus, it operated as a kind of inheritance tax. Because inheritance was a privilege to be paid for, the lord possessed unlimited discretion in fixing the price payable by the tenant. Abuse of this prerogative led to the charging of exorbitant reliefs, which effectively disinherited the tenant's descendant and therefore inspired many ingenius efforts to avoid them. Inheritance later became a matter of right, but the payment of relief to the lord continued.

3. More generally, the assistance that society gives to those in need, usually that which is administered by a branch of the government. Relief in this sense is often called public assistance or welfare.

REMAINDER That part of an **estate** in land that is left upon the termination of the immediately preceding estate and that does not amount to a **reversion** to the original grantor or his heirs. The legal conditions for a remainder are that there must be a precedent particular estate, whose regular termination the remainder must await; the remainder must be created by the same **conveyance,** and at the same time, as a particular estate; the remainder must **vest** in right during the continuance of the particular estate; and no remainder can be limited after a **fee simple.** Thus, if A, being the owner of land [in fee simple] gives it by deed or will to B for life, and after the death of B, to C in fee, the estate given to C is called a remainder, because it is the remnant or remainder of the estate or title which is left after taking out the lesser estate [life estate] given to B.

See further A. Sinclair, *Introduction to Real Property Law* 63 ff. (3d ed. 1987).

CONTINGENT [EXECUTORY] REMAINDER "[A]ny remainder which is created in favor of an ascertained person but is subject to a **condition** precedent; is created in favor of an unborn person; or is created in favor of an existing but unascertained person. It was not, according to the older **common law** definition, an estate, but merely the possibility of an estate.... A contingent remainder becomes a **vested** remainder if any condition precedent is fulfilled and if the **remainderman** is ascertained before the termination of the preceding estate. Thus, A conveys to B for life, then to C and his heirs if C marries. At the time of the conveyance C is unmarried. The state of the title at that time is: life estate in B, contingent remainder in fee simple in C, reversion in fee simple in A. C marries while B is yet living. C's remainder becomes vested immediately on his marriage and all of the characteristics of a vested remainder attach thereto. The vesting of C's remainder operates to divest the **reversion** in A." C. Moynihan, *Introduction to the Law of Real Property* 129 (2d ed. 1988).

EXECUTED REMAINDER A remainder interest that is **vested** as of the present, though the enjoyment of it may be withheld until a future date.

VESTED REMAINDER A **remainder** that is limited to an ascertained person in being, whose right to the **estate** is fixed and certain, and that does not depend upon the happening of any future event, but whose **enjoyment** of the estate is postponed to some future time. See **remainder** [CONTINGENT REMAINDER].

"Remainders are either vested or contingent according to whether they are or are not, respectively, presently ready to take effect in possession upon the determination of the preceding estate or estates.

"A remainder is vested if the person entitled to it will obtain possession of the land upon the happening of no other contingency than the natural expiration of the prior estate (*Lundy* v. *Maloney* (1861), 11 U.C.C.P. 143 ...).

"In other words, a remainder limited to take effect automatically upon the expiration of the prior particular estate is a vested remainder because a present estate is conferred although it is not to be enjoyed until that future time. The estate granted by way of remainder does not depend for its existence upon any contingency, even though the time when it will come into possession may be uncertain when the estate is created. The remainder may actually end or be divested before the preceding estate ends and thus never come into possession, but that possibility does not prevent it from being vested. On the other hand, a contingent remainder is one limited to depend for its existence upon the happening of some event or the performance of some condition, which may never happen, or be performed, or may not happen or be performed until after the preceding estate ends." 1 A.H. Oosterhoff & W.B. Rayner, *Anger and Honsberger: Law of Real Property* 395 (2d ed. 1985).

REMAINDERMAN One who has an interest in land **in futuro;** one who has an interest in an estate that becomes possessory at some point in the future after the termination, by whatever reason, of a present possessory interest. Remainderman usually refers to one who holds an interest in a **remainder,** whether **vested** or **contingent.** It may also refer to one who holds an interest in an executory limitation.

REMAND To order or send back; a judicial order sending a prisoner back to **custody.** Remand is dealt with in various sections of the *Criminal Code*, R.S.C. 1985, c. C–46. For example, under s. 672.11, a court that has reasonable grounds to believe evidence is necessary to determine the mental condition of an accused found guilty of an offence may remand the accused for assessment to determine whether the accused should be detained in a treatment facility. See further R. Salhany, *Canadian Criminal Procedure* c. 7 at 20 (6th ed. 1994).

REMEDY The means employed to enforce or redress an injury. The most common remedy at law consists of money **damages.** The courts of **chancery** developed a number of equitable remedies where none could be had at **common law.** The remedies of **specific performance, injunction** and **recission** are important examples. Today a court will not normally employ an equitable remedy unless the evidence clearly indicates that such a remedy is necessary to preserve the rights of a party.

PREROGATIVE [EXTRAORDINARY] REMEDY A remedy available in the area of **administrative law** where a **tribunal** has exceeded its **jurisdiction** or breached a rule of natural justice. These remedies in the form of **writs** (known as PREROGATIVE WRITS) are granted by the courts and may have the effect of **quashing** a decision or prohibiting an administrative tribunal from hearing a particular matter. Examples include **certiorari, mandamus, prohibition,** etc. See further G. Gall, *The Canadian Legal System* 364–66 (3d ed. 1990).

REMITTER The act by which a person, who has **good title** to land, and enters upon the land with less than his original title, is restored to his original good title. See 3 Bl.Comm. 19. The doctrine whereby the law will relate back from a defective title to an earlier valid title.

REMITTITUR (*rē-mĭ´-tĭ-tūr*) Lat.: reduction. The **procedural** process by which the **verdict** of a **jury** is diminished by subtraction; generally, any reduction made by the court without the consent of the jury. The theory of ADDITUR is a corollary to that of *remittitur:* the former increases an inadequate verdict; the latter decreases an excessive verdict. It is a universal rule that a *remittitur* may not be granted by a court in lieu of a new trial unless consented to by the party unfavourably affected thereby.

REMOTENESS A judicial concept used to limit the extent of potential **liability** that may stem from a single act; a point in the continuum of events between the **defendant's** act and the **plaintiff's** injury beyond which the law will not allow **recovery.** Remoteness may be assessed by determining what was a reasonably foreseeable, or possibly direct, consequence of the defendant's **wrongful act.**

REMOTENESS OF DAMAGE In the law of **tort,** the notion that one's **liability** is limited to results PROXIMATELY CAUSED (see **cause**) by his conduct or omission. "Causation alone is not enough; it must be demonstrated that the conduct is the proximate cause of the damage. Put another way, the losses incurred by plaintiffs must not be 'too remote' a consequence of the act." See A. Linden, *Canadian Tort Law* (5th ed. 1993), chap. 10.

REMOVAL A change in place or position, as the removal of a **proceeding** to another court.

RENT Periodic payment by a **tenant** of land or of other corporeal **hereditament.** Payment is usually in money but may be a non-monetary compensation, e.g., in the form of goods or labour.

RENUNCIATION 1. In **contract** law, a party who by words or conduct refuses to perform, or who disables himself from performing a contract, is said to have broken or breached the contract by renunciation. See *Hochster* v. *de la Tour* (1853), 3 E. & B. 678; 118 E.R. 922. See further S. Waddams, *The Law of Contracts* 398 (3d ed. 1993).

2. Also, a disclaimer or refusal by a person to perform a legal function, e.g., to act as the **executor** or **administrator** of an **estate.**

RENVOI The rule in **conflict of laws** (or PRIVATE INTERNATIONAL LAW) that in some jurisdictions the capacity of a non-resident to sue upon a cause arising locally may be determined by the court looking to the law of his **domicile** rather than to the local law. An application of the renvoi doctrine occurs when the whole law of a foreign state, including its conflict of laws rules, is looked to for a solution. If reference is to the whole law, and not merely the internal law of the other state, then use of the renvoi concept is involved. Take, for example, the case of a citizen of Canada permanently residing in Germany who dies leaving personal property in Ontario. Assuming the Ontario conflict of laws rule to be that the law of the **decedent's** domicile will govern the matter, the Ontario **forum** would look to the "law" of Germany. If the forum should merely look to the law applicable to a German dying in Germany leaving personal property there, the court would be rejecting use of the renvoi. If, however, the forum looks to the whole law, i.e., including the German conflicts rule, this is making use of the renvoi. See further J.-G. Castel, *Introduction to Conflict of Laws* (2d ed. 1986), chap. 4.

REORGANIZATION The transfer of substantially all the assets of an old **corporation** to a newly formed corporation, in which the **shareholders** own the same proportion of **stock** as in the old corporation.

REPEAL 1. To abolish, rescind, annul by legislative act. **2.** The abrogation or annulling of a previously existing law by the enactment of a subsequent statute, which either declares that the former law shall be revoked and abrogated or contains provisions so contrary to or irreconcilable with those of the earlier law that only one of the two can stand in force. The latter is the IMPLIED REPEAL; the former, the EXPRESS REPEAL.

REPLEVIN An **action** that lies for the recovery of the thing taken, rather than for the value of that thing; a possessory remedy; a legal form of action ordinarily employed only to recover **possession** or the value of specific **personal property** unlawfully withheld from the plaintiff plus **damages** for its detention. Replevin is primarily a possessory action in which the issues ordinarily are limited to the plaintiff's title or right to possession of the goods. Compare **trespass; trover.**

REPLEVY To deliver to the owner; to redeliver goods that have been kept from the rightful owner. See **replevin.**

REPLY In pleadings the **plaintiff's** answer if the **defendant,** instead of merely resting his **defence** on a denial of the plaintiff's allegations, has raised **an** affirmative defence, i.e., pleaded in **confession and avoidance.** See G. Watson, *Canadian Civil Procedure* 370–71 (3d ed. 1988).

REPRESENTATION A statement made before or at the time of the entering into a contract. A representation may become a term of a contract (**condition** or **warranty**) if so intended by the parties. However, even if not a term of the contract, a rep-

resentation will, if it is false and if it induced the making of the contract, give a right to the party deceived by it to **rescind** the contract. See further S. Waddams, *The Law of Contracts* (3d ed. 1993), chap. 13. See **misrepresentation.**

REPRIEVE In criminal law, the suspension of execution of a criminal's **sentence.** It is merely the postponement of the sentence for a time.

RES *(räs)* Lat.: thing. The subject matter of **actions** that are primarily **in rem,** i.e., actions that establish rights in relation to an object, as opposed to a person, or **in personam.** For example, in an action that resolves a conflict over **title** to **real property,** the land in question is the *res.* Tangible **personal property** can also be a *res,* as in the corpus of a trust. In a **quasi in rem proceeding,** land or **chattels** that are seized and **attached** at the beginning of the action, in order that they may later be used to satisfy a personal **claim,** are the *res* of such suits. The term refers as well to the status of individuals. Thus, in a divorce suit, the marital status is the *res.* The purpose of a *res* is to establish a court's **jurisdiction;** if the property lies within the state where the action is brought, or an individual in a divorce action is a **domiciliary** of the state, then jurisdiction is established.

RESCIND To **abrogate** a **contract,** release the parties from further obligation to each other and restore the parties to the positions they would have occupied if the contract had never been made. For instance, in rescinding a sales contract, any monies paid or goods received would usually be returned to their original holders, though the parties could agree otherwise.

RESCISSION The cancellation of a **contract** and the return of the parties to the positions they would have occupied if the contract had not been made; "The right of one party, arising upon conduct by the other, by which he intimates his intention to abide by the contract no longer. It is a right to treat the contract as at an end, if he chooses, and to claim damages for its total breach, but it is a right in his option and does not depend in theory on any implied term providing for its exercise, but is given by law in vindication of a breach." *Hirji Mulji* v. *Cheong Yue S.S. Co.,* [1926] A.C. 497 at 509–10 (P.C.).

In addition to the right of a party in certain circumstances to treat a contract as at an end, rescission may be brought about by the mutual consent of the parties, or by a **decree** of a court exercising its equitable **jurisdiction** to grant rescission of a contract that has been entered into as a result, e.g., of a false **representation** or **fraud.** See further G. Fridman, *The Law of Contract* 729 ff. (2d ed. 1986).

RESCUE DOCTRINE Tort rule that holds a **tortfeasor** liable to his victim's rescuer, should the latter injure himself during a reasonable rescue attempt. The doctrine derives from the fact that "the wrong that imperils life is a wrong to the imperilled victim; it is a wrong also to the rescuer." See *Moddejonge* v. *Huron County Board of Education,* [1972] 2 O.R. 437 at 444 (H.C.). See also A. Linden, *Canadian Tort Law* 334–37 (5th ed. 1993).

RESERVATION 1. A clause in any **instrument** of **conveyance,** such as a **deed,** that creates a lesser **estate,** or some right, interest or profit in the estate granted, to be retained by the **grantor.** An example might be a conveyance of land wherein the grantor reserves the right to mines and minerals. See *Re C.P.R. and Reid* (1914), 6 W.W.R. 1160 (Sask.M.T.).

2. In practice, the term refers to the act of a court or other body in delaying a decision on a point of law. The court may reserve decision and proceed with the matter, or may adjourn the proceedings pending its decision. When the court "takes the matter under advisement," it in effect reserves decision, often so that it may render a written decision.

RES GESTAE *(rās gĕs′-tī)* Lat.: the thing done. Declarations that are subject to the **hearsay rule** may be admissible if they qualify as *res gestae,* i.e., if they constitute a part of the thing done, under a recognized exception to the hearsay rule. See *Gilbert* v. *Rex,* [1907] 38 S.C.R. 284. "There are many incidents, however, which, though not strictly constituting a fact in issue, may yet be regarded as forming a part of it, in the sense that they closely accompany and explain that fact. In testifying to the matters in issue, therefore, witnesses must state them not in

their barest possible form, but, with a reasonable fulness of detail and circumstance. These constituent or accompanying incidents are in law said to be admissible as forming part of the *res gesta* or main fact; and, when they consist of declarations accompanying an act, are subject to three important qualifications: (1) They must not be made at such an interval as to allow of fabrication, or to reduce them to the mere narrative of a past event; (2) they must relate to, and can only be used to explain, the act they accompany, and not independent facts prior or subsequent thereto; and (3) though admissible to explain, or corroborate, they are not, in general, to be taken as any proof of the truth of the matters stated: they are consequently not, in any strict sense, to be classed as exceptions to the hearsay rule." *Cassels* v. *T.C.C.,* [1938] O.R. 155 at 161–62 (C.A.), quoting 13 *Halsbury's Laws of England* 551 (2d ed.). See also Stone, *Res Gesta Reagitata,* 55 L.Q.R. 66 (1939).

RESIDENCE "[A]n elastic term ... [that] takes colour from the context in which it is used ... [and is] capable of various constructions according to the statute in which it appears." Generally, residence "means a person's permanent place of abode and not his temporary place of abode....The mere physical presence of a person in a place does not constitute his residence there but in addition he must have the present intention of remaining there for some time but not necessarily for all time." *Re Fulford and Townshend,* [1970] 3 O.R. 493 at 500 (Surr.Ct.).

"There is a difference between residence and domicile. The latter is more permanent and is the jurisdiction which a person regards or intends to make his permanent home for all time unless some unforeseen circumstances in future change that intention." *Id.* at 501. Compare **domicile.**

RESIDENT ALIEN See **residence; alien.**

RESIDUARY BEQUEST See **bequest; residuary legacy.**

RESIDUARY CLAUSE A clause in a **will** that conveys to the beneficiary of a **residuary legacy** everything in a **testator's estate** not **devised** to a specific **legatee.** It will include **legacies** that were originally

void either because the disposition was illegal or because for any other reason it was impossible that it should take effect. It operates to transfer to the residuary legatee such portion of his property as the testator has not perfectly disposed of. *In re Moody Estate* (1906), 12 O.L.R. 10 (H.C.).

RESIDUARY ESTATE The part of a **testator's** estate that remains undisposed of after all of the **estate** has been discharged through the satisfaction of all claims and specific legacies with the exception of the dispositions authorized by the **residuary clause;** the portion of the estate that remains after payment of debts and other classes of legacies.

RESIDUARY LEGACY A general **legacy** into which all the assets of the estate fall after the satisfaction of other legacies and payment of all debts of the estate and all costs of administration. However, the words *residuary legatee* by themselves **prima facie** do not apply to real estate, though their application might be extended so as to do so when the context requires. See *Re Wightman*, [1945] 4 D.L.R. 754 (Alta.S.C.).

RESIDUE The **remainder** of a **testator's** estate after payment of **debts** and **legacies.**

RES IPSA LOQUITUR *(rās ĭp'-sà lō'-kwĭ-tûr)* Lat.: the thing speaks for itself. A circumstantial rule of **evidence** based on the concept that, when an accident occurs under circumstances where it is so improbable that it could have happened without the negligence of the **defendant,** the mere happening of the accident gives rise to an inference that the defendant was **negligent.** When a **plaintiff** has established a **prima facie** case against a defendant through the doctrine of *res ipsa loquitur,* the evidentiary obligation on the defendant is to put forward an explanation of the accident that is consistent with the facts and shows no negligence on his part. *Res ipsa loquitur* does not have the effect of shifting the legal **burden of proof** to the defendant so that he must disprove negligence on his part. *MacDonald* v. *York County Hospital Corp.,* [1972] 3 O.R. 469 (H.C.).

RESISTING ARREST A common-law offence involving physical efforts to op-

pose a lawful arrest. In every case where one person has a right to arrest or restrain another, the other can have no rights to resist, since the two rights cannot co-exist. No right of **self-defence** can arise out of such a circumstance. The Crown must establish beyond a reasonable doubt that a police officer was engaged in the execution of his duty when he arrested the defendant. Once a reasonable doubt arises as to the lawfulness of the arrest the defendant cannot be guilty of resisting a peace officer in the execution of his duty when such duty is the arrest. *Regina* v. *Stevens* (1976), 33 C.C.C. (2d) 429 (N.S.S.C.A.D.).

RES JUDICATA *(rās jū-dĭ-kä'-tà)* Lat.: a thing decided. If the thing actually and directly in dispute has been already adjudicated upon, it cannot be litigated again. "The plea of *res judicata* applies, except in special cases, not only to points upon which the Court was actually required by the parties to form an **opinion** and pronounce a **judgment,** but to every point which properly belonged to the subject of litigation, and which the parties, exercising reasonable diligence, might have brought forward at the time." *Cameron* v. *Rounsefell*, [1933] 3 W.W.R. 121 at 125 (B.C.S.C.).

RESOLUTION An expression of opinion or intention passed at a meeting, often used in company management. See **by-laws; resolved.**

RESOLVED Points to unanimity of sentiment, as opposed to a formally paved **resolution.** *Anderson* v. *Municipality of South Vancouver* (1910), 13 W.L.R. 226 (B.C.S.C.).

RESPITE 1. A delay, postponement or **forbearance** of a **sentence,** not comprehending a permanent suspension of execution of the judgment; a respite of execution. See **reprieve. 2.** Also, a delay in repayment granted to a debtor by his creditor. See **grace period.**

RESPONDEAT SUPERIOR *(rā-spŏn'-dā-ät sū-pĕr'-ē-ôr)* Lat.: let the superior reply. A maxim in **contract** law where one who expects to derive an advantage from an act done by another person for him must answer for any injury that a third person may sustain from it. *Lavere* v. *Smith's Falls Public Hospital* (1915), 26

D.L.R. 346 (Ont.S.C.A.D.). See **scope of employment.** Compare **vicarious liability.**

RESPONDENT A person against whom a petition is presented, a summons is issued or an **appeal** is brought.

RESTITUTION Act of making good, or of giving the equivalent for, any loss, damage or injury; **indemnification.** As a remedy, restitution is available to prevent **unjust enrichment,** to correct an erroneous payment and to permit an **aggrieved party** to recover deposits advanced on a contract. At common law, a plaintiff would have to elect between restitution and **damages.** As a contract remedy, restitution is limited to the value of a performance rendered by the injured party and ordinarily requires that both parties to a transaction be returned to the **status quo.** *Wiley and Wiley* v. *Fortin,* [1946] 2 W.W.R. 93 (B.C.S.C.).

RESTRAINING ORDER An order granted without notice or hearing, demanding the preservation of the **status quo** until a hearing can be had to determine the propriety of **injunctive relief,** temporary or permanent. The restraining order is issued upon application of a plaintiff requesting the court to forbid an action or a threatened action of the defendant; the form of request will generally be upon an order to show cause why the injunctive relief the plaintiff seeks ought not be granted. After a hearing, a preliminary or permanent injunction may issue. Compare **injunction.**

RESTRAINT OF TRADE [UNREASONABLE] Contractual interference with free competition in business and commercial transactions that tends to restrict production, affect prices or otherwise control the market to the detriment of purchasers or consumers of goods and services. Ordinarily reasonable restraints of trade are made unreasonable if they are contrary to public policy. The usual theory of restraint of trade cannot be applied to **restrictive covenants** concerning the sale of land. *International Coal & Coke Co.* v. *Trelle* (1907), 7 W.L.R. 264 (Alta.S.C.).

RESTRAINT ON ALIENATION Restriction on the ability to **convey real property** interests, any attempt at which is in **derogation** of the **common-law** policy in favour of free alienability; interests thus created are **void** or **voidable** as unlawful restraints on alienation.

Although fees on condition subsequent and fee simple determinables are, in general, permissible **estates,** a condition that states, "but if any attempt is made to alienate the land, the **grantor** and his **heirs** reserve the right to re-enter and declare the estate forfeit," would be against the policy. As a consequence, a rule exists requiring that there be a person capable of transferring absolute interest in possession within a certain period of time. See **alienation; rule against perpetuities.** However, in estates created by short-term **leases** such restraints are permissible. The determination of validity is based upon the nature and quality (duration) of the restraint, the type of estate in question and the penalty imposed for violation of the restraint.

RESTRICTIVE COVENANT A promise existing as part of an agreement, restricting the use of **real property** or the kind of buildings that may be erected thereupon; the promise is usually expressed by the creation of an express **covenant, reservation** or exception in a **deed.** In order for a grantor to enforce the covenant against REMOTE GRANTEES, i.e., subsequent owners who take title from the first grantee, the covenant must **run with the land.** In **equity,** negative or restrictive covenants run with the land, except against a **bona fide purchaser** for value without notice. Positive covenants do not run with the land. See *Harrod* v. *Hadden* (1924), 25 O.W.N. 581 (H.C.); *Re Sullivan and Township of Bertie* (1927), 60 O.L.R. 107 (S.C.).

RESTRICTIVE ENDORSEMENT An endorsement on a **bill of exchange** that prohibits or inhibits further endorsement of the bill. See **endorse.**

RESULTING TRUST See **trust.**

RESULTING USE See **use.**

RETAINER 1. The appointment of a barrister or solicitor to take or defend proceedings, or to counsel or otherwise act for the client. **2.** The document by which such employment is evidenced. **3.** A preliminary fee given to a solicitor, which does not act to diminish future bills chargeable. *Re Solicitor* (1910), 22 O.L.R. 30 (C.A.).

RETIRE **1.** In reference to **bills of exchange,** to recover, redeem, regain by the payment of a sum of money; to withdraw from circulation or from the market.
2. Also, to withdraw voluntarily from office, a public station, business or other employment.
3. A **jury** is retired at the point when the judge has submitted the case to it for its consideration and **verdict.**

RETRACTION Withdrawal of a **renunciation,** declaration, **accusation,** premise, etc. As to a **defamation,** a retraction can be effective only if it is complete, unequivocal and without lurking insinuations or hesitant withdrawals. It must, in short, be an honest endeavour to repair all the wrong done by the defamatory imputation.

RETROACTIVE Refers to a rule of law, whether legislative or judicial, that relates to things already decided in the past. A RETROSPECTIVE law is one that relates back to a previous transaction and gives it some different legal effect from that which it had under the law when it occurred. Similarly, in respect to **ex post facto** laws, retroactivity refers to the imposition of **criminal** liability on behaviour that took place prior to the enactment of the statute. It should be noted, however, that judicially created law (common law) is often retroactive in its effects, the court's decision being made on the basis of a previously existent fact pattern wherein the actors could not possibly have predicted at the time of their actions the court's eventual interpretation of the law but are nevertheless held accountable to it. See *In re the Immigration Act, and In re Rahim* (1911), 1 W.W.R. 114 (B.C.S.C.).

RETROSPECTIVE See **retroactive.**

RETURN **1.** A report from an official, such as a sheriff, stating what he has done in respect to a command from the court, or why he has failed to do what was requested. A FALSE RETURN is a false or incorrect statement by an official that acts to the detriment of an interested party.
2. A report from an individual or cor-

poration as to its earnings, etc., for tax or other governmental purposes.

REVERSAL As used in **opinions, judgments** and **mandates,** the setting aside, annulling, **vacating** or changing to the contrary the decision of a lower court or other body. Compare **overrule; quash; remand.** See also **affirm.**

REVERSIBLE ERROR Error substantially affecting an **appellant's** legal rights and obligations that, if uncorrected, would result in a miscarriage of justice and that justifies reversing a judgment in the inferior court; synonymous with **prejudicial error.** Compare **harmless error.**

REVERSION "[T]he returning of the land to the **grantor** or his heirs after the grant is determined....Where the residue of the estate always continues in him who made the particular estate. The idea of a reversion is founded on the principle that where a person has not parted with his whole estate and interest in a piece of land, all that which he has not given away remains in him, and the possession of it reverts or returns to him upon the determination of the preceding estate." *Mercer* v. *Attorney-General for Ontario* (1881), 5 S.C.R. 538 at 626–27. Compare **remainder.**

REVERTER See **reversion.** See also **possibility of a reverter.**

REVIEW Judicial re-examination of the proceedings of a court or other body; a reconsideration of its former decision; often used to express what an **appellate court** does when it examines the **record** of a lower court or agency's determination that is on **appeal** before the court. *Regina* v. *West,* [1973] 1 O.R. 211 (C.A.).

REVISED STATUTES A publication by government authority of unrepealed public general statutes. Every ten or fifteen years, most Canadian jurisdictions revise and consolidate their public general acts in order to eliminate errors, consolidate amendments and generally tidy things up. When the revision is completed, the revised statutes are proclaimed in force and the former versions are repealed. See *Statute Revision Act,* R.S.C. 1985, c. S-20.

REVOCATION **1.** The recall of a power or authority conferred; 2. the cancellation of an **instrument** previously made; **3.** the cancellation of an **offer** by the offeror, which, if effective, terminates the offeree's power of **acceptance.** Synonymous with cancellation.

REVOCATION OF PAROLE Cancellation of **parole.**

REVOCATION OF PROBATION Cancellation of **probation.**

REVOKE To annul, repeal, rescind, cancel privileges; e.g., in many provinces a motorist who is convicted of manslaughter by reason of the operation of a motor vehicle may have his license revoked. See *Regina* v. *MacPhee,* [1970] 5 C.C.C. 131 (N.S.Co.Ct.).

RIGHT IN GROSS A right that exists on its own, independent of all other rights; a right not appendant to or otherwise annexed to land. See **à prendre.**

RIGHT OF ACTION See **cause of action.**

RIGHT OF REDEMPTION See **redemption.**

RIGHT OF RE-ENTRY See **re-entry, right of.**

RIGHT OF WAY The right to pass over another's land. A public right of way can be created by statute or by **dedication** and **acceptance.**

RIGHT OR WRONG TEST See **M'Naghten Rule.**

RIGOR MORTIS *(rĭ'-gôr môr'-tĭs)* Lat.: stiffness of death; medical terminology depicting the rigidity of the muscles after death. Medical authorities agree that it is not possible to fix the time of death from the onset of rigor mortis.

RIPARIAN RIGHTS Rights that accrue to owners of land on the banks of water ways, such as the use of such water, ownership of soil under the water, etc.; "rights which a riparian owner (one whose lands run to and are bounded by water) may have in respect to water may be divided into those rights which are natural rights of user ... and those rights which are acquired by **prescription.**" 2 A.H. Oosterhoff & W.B. Rayner, *Anger and Honsberger: Law of Real Property* 962 (2d ed. 1985). See also *Leahy* v. *North Sydney* (1906), 37 S.C.R. 464.

ROBBERY Forcible stealing; as defined in the *Criminal Code,* R.S.C. 1985, c. C–46, s. 343, "Every one commits robbery who (*a*) steals, and for the purpose of extorting whatever is stolen or to prevent or overcome resistance to the stealing, uses violence or threats of violence to a person or property; (*b*) steals from any person and, at the time he steals or immediately before or immediately thereafter, wounds, beats, strikes or uses any personal violence to that person; (*c*) assaults any person with intent to steal from him; or (*d*) steals from any person while armed with an offensive weapon or imitation thereof." Compare **burglary.**

ROYAL ASSENT An act of agreement that transforms a bill into an Act of Parliament (federal) or Act of the legislature (provincial) and instantly has the force and effect of law, unless some time for the commencement of its operation should have been specially appointed; an act by which the Crown agrees to a bill that has already been raised by Parliament or the legislature. Royal assent may be given by the Sovereign in person or by persons appointed by the Crown. See **Governor-General of Canada;** Lieutenant-Governor.

ROYAL CANADIAN MOUNTED POLICE [R.C.M.P.] The national police force of Canada established by federal statute (*Royal Canadian Mounted Police Act,* R.S.C. 1985, c. R–10). It is "responsible for policing the Yukon and the North West Territories, for enforcing particular areas of federal law generally, and by arrangement with ... eight provincial governments [excluding Ontario and Quebec] for law enforcement in those provinces." P. Fitzgerald & K. McShane, *Looking at Law* 48 (2d ed. 1982). Officers of the force are appointed and hold office at the pleasure of the **Governor-General-in-Council** and have the status of a **peace officer** in every part of Canada.

RULE AGAINST PERPETUITIES The rule in the law of **real property** that "a future **interest** is void unless it must **vest,** if at all, within a period measured by lives in being plus a further period of twenty-one years." A. Sinclair, *Introduction to Real Property Law* 99 (3d ed. 1987). The purpose of the rule is to prevent the possibility of remoteness of vesting and the problems that would be created by long tie-ups of property and unreasonable **restraints on alienation.** *Id.*

RULE IN SHELLEY'S CASE The rule that "where a deed or will gives a **freehold** to a person and then gives a **remainder** mediately or immediately to that person's **heirs,** or the heirs of his body, that remainder is transformed into a remainder in the first grantee if both estates, present and future, are legal or both are equitable." A. Sinclair, *Introduction to Real Property Law* 75–79 (3d ed. 1987). *Shelley's Case* (1581), 1 Co.Rep. 93f; 76 E.R. 206.

RULE IN WILD'S CASE In **real property** law, a rule of **construction** by which a **devise** to "B and his children," where B has no children at the time the gift **vests in** B, is read to mean a gift to B in **fee tail,** the words "and his children" thus being construed as **words of limitation** and not words of purchase. *Wild's Case* (1599), 6 Co. Rep. 16f; 77 E.R. 277. See further 1 A.H. Oosterhoff & W.B. Rayner, *Anger and Honsberger: Law of Real Property* 138–39 (2d ed. 1985).

RULE NISI Procedure by which one party by an **ex parte** application or an order to show cause calls upon another to show cause why the rule set forth in his proposed order should not be made final by the court. If no cause is shown, the court will enter an order rendering the rule "absolute" (final), thereby requiring whatever was sought to be accomplished.

RUN WITH THE LAND A phrase used with respect to **covenants** in the law of real property where the burden or benefit of the covenant passes to persons who succeed to the **estate** of the original contracting parties. For example, with respect to covenants made between a **lessor** and **lessee,** "A covenant is said to run . . . with the land when either the liability to perform it, or the right to take advantage of it, passes to the assignee of the tenant." See further 1 A.H. Oosterhoff & W.B. Rayner, *Anger and Honsberger: Law of Real Property* 253ff. (2d ed. 1985).

S

SALE A **contract** by which **property** real or personal is transferred from the seller (**vendor**) to the buyer (**vendee**) for a fixed price in money, paid or agreed to be paid by the buyer. See *Abbott* v. *Ridgeway Park Ltd.* (1915), 7 W.W.R 1280 at 1282 (Alta.S.C.A.D.). In Canada, a contract for the sale of goods must be distinguished from other contracts generally and from the law dealing with other kinds of sales (e.g., the sale of land). The distinction is important because contracts for the sale of goods are regulated by the *Sale of Goods* legislation in the common-law provinces and territories. See, e.g., *Sale of Goods Act*, R.S.O. 1990, c. S.1. Section 2(1) of this Ontario statute defines a contract for the sale of goods as "a contract whereby the seller transfers or agrees to transfer the property in the goods to the buyer for a money consideration called the price, and there may be a contract of sale between one part owner and another." See further G. Fridman, *Sale of Goods in Canada* (3d ed. 1986), chap. 1.

ABSOLUTE SALE Generally, a sale wherein the property passes to the buyer upon completion of the agreement between the parties. However, contracts for the sale of goods may be regarded as absolute, i.e., effective from the time they are made "though such terms as relate to the passing of property ... or the time for payment of the price may not take effect until the time or event fixed by the contract." *Id.* at 25ff.

CONDITIONAL SALE A sale in which the buyer receives **possession** and the right of use of the goods sold, but the transfer of title is not effectuated until performance of some condition, usually the complete payment of the purchase price. Such contracts may be governed by special **legislation** such as that concerned with conditional sales agreements, CHATTEL MORTGAGES (see **mortgage**), and **secured transactions**, and need not necessarily be governed by the *Sale of Goods* legislation. Under the latter, conditional sales would seem to be "contracts which are intended to be binding on the parties (and to pass property in the goods which are sold) only on the occurrence of some stipulated event or circumstance." *Id.* at 27.

EXECUTED SALE Status when nothing remains to be done by either party to effect a complete transfer of the **title** to the **property** concerned.

EXECUTION SALE See **sheriff's sale.**

EXECUTORY SALE An agreement to sell where something more remains to be done before all the terms of the agreement are performed.

PUBLIC SALE A sale upon notice to the public and in which members of the public may bid.

SALE BY DESCRIPTION By the *Sale of Goods Acts,* "where there is a contract for the sale of goods by description, there is an implied **condition** that the goods will correspond with the description. . . ." See, e.g., *Sale of Goods Act*, R.S.O. 1990, c. S.1, s. 14. There may be a sale by description, however, even if the buyer has actually seen the goods. See *Grant* v. *Australian Knitting Mills Ltd.*, [1936] A.C. 85 at 100 (P.C.) (Austl.).

SALE BY SAMPLE If the sale of goods "is by sample, as well as by description, it is not sufficient that the bulk of the goods corresponds with the sample if the goods do not also correspond with the description." See, e.g., *Sale of Goods Act*, R.S.O. 1980, c. 462, s. 14.

SHERIFF'S SALE See **sheriff's sale.**

TAX SALE A sale of land for non-payment of taxes.

SANCTION A consequence or punishment for violation of accepted norms of social conduct, which may be of two kinds: those that redress **civil** injuries (civil sanctions) and those that punish **crimes** (penal sanctions).

SATISFACTION The ending of an obligation by performance, e.g., the payment of a debt; a release and discharge of an obligation.

An **accord** is an agreement whereby an earlier obligation between the parties is discharged; the **consideration** that makes the agreement operative is the satisfaction. *Williams* v. *Enskat*, [1952] O.W.N.

628 at 631 (C.A.). See also **accord and satisfaction.**

SCIENTER *(sī'-ĕn-tûr)* Lat.: knowledge. Previous knowledge of an operative state of facts; a claim in **pleading** that a thing has been knowingly done by a **defendant** or **accused;** also the cognizance by an animal's owner of its disposition.

SCOPE OF EMPLOYMENT The range of activities encompassed by one's employment; generally the phrase is used to denote the area within which an employer will be liable for the **torts** of his **servants.** See, e.g., *Hall and Marlow* v. *Halifax Transfer Co. Ltd.* (1959), 18 D.L.R. (2d) 115 at 118ff. The master (employer) is **vicariously liable** only for those torts of the servant (employee) that are committed within the scope of his employment. See **respondeat superior.** See also **Workmen's Compensation Acts.**

SEAL 1. At common law, an impression on wax, wafer, or other tenacious substance capable of being impressed; **2.** a formal method of communicating assent to a written document.

Every corporation must have a COMMON SEAL, since such a body cannot exhibit its intention by acts or discourse of a personal nature, but acts and speaks through its common seal, except, e.g., in instances when it is represented by an officer, agent or attorney in the course of ordinary day-to-day business.

SEALED INSTRUMENT One that is signed and has the **seal** of the signer attached. An **instrument** is sufficiently sealed if the party, with intent to seal, places a die or stick or his finger on sealing wax or on a wafer, or merely on the paper or parchment. It is not necessary that any mark or impression be made, provided there is an intention to seal. See *In re Sandilands* (1871), L.R. 6 C.P. 411 at 413.

A sealed contract, or CONTRACT UNDER SEAL, is a FORMAL CONTRACT (as distinguished from a contract without a seal—a SIMPLE CONTRACT) that did not require **consideration** at **common law.**

SEARCH AND SEIZURE A police practice whereby premises are searched and property is seized that may be pertinent in the investigation and prosecution of a crime. A search and seizure is constitutionally limited by s. 8 of the *Canadian Charter of Rights and Freedoms,* which provides that "everyone has the right to be secure against unreasonable search or seizure." See *Hunter* v. *Southam Inc.,* [1984] 2 S.C.R. 145. In most instances a **search warrant** is required. *R.* v. *Lyons* (1892), 2 C.C.C. 218 (Ont.Co.Ct.). See further R. Salhany, *Canadian Criminal Procedure* c. 3 at 32ff. (6th ed. 1994).

SEARCH WARRANT Under the *Criminal Code,* R.S.C. 1985, c. C–46, an order issued by a justice that authorizes a peace officer (or person named in the warrant) to conduct a search of specified premises and to seize "(a) anything on or in respect of which any offence against this Act or any other Act of Parliament has been or is suspected to have been committed, (b) anything that there is reasonable ground to believe will afford evidence with respect to the commission of an offence against this Act or any other Act of Parliament, or (c) anything that there are reasonable grounds to believe is intended to be used for the purpose of committing any offence against the person for which a person may be arrested without warrant." See R. Salhany, *Canadian Criminal Procedure* c. 3 at 39ff. (6th ed. 1994). See further, e.g., *R.* v. *Debot* (1986), 30 C.C.C. (3d) 207 (Ont.C.A., aff'd [1989] 2 S.C.R. 140.

SECUNDUM *(sĕ-kūn'-dŭm)* Lat.: immediately after; beside; next to. In law publishing, the second series of a treatise may be called *secundum,* as in Corpus Juris Secundum (C.J.S.).

SECURED TRANSACTIONS See **credit.**

SECURITIES Stock certificates, bonds or other **evidence** of a secured indebtedness or of a right created in the holder to participate in profits or **assets** distribution of a profit-making enterprise; more generally, written assurances for the return or payment of money; **instruments** giving to their legal holders right to money or other property. They are therefore instruments that have value and are used as such in regular channels of commerce. The issuing and trading of securities are regulated by provincial legislation. See, e.g., *Securities Act,* R.S.O. 1990, c. S.5.

PUBLIC SECURITIES Those certificates and other **negotiable instruments** evidencing the debt of a governmental body.

SECURITY DEPOSIT Money that a **tenant** deposits with a **landlord** to insure the landlord that the tenant will abide by the **lease** agreements; a fund from which the landlord may obtain payment for **damages** caused by the tenant during his occupancy.

SECURITY INTEREST An **interest** in **real** or **personal property** that secures the payment of an obligation. At common law, security interests either are consensual or arise by **operation of law.** Those arising by operation of law include judgment **liens** and statutory liens.

The clearest examples of security interests are the **mortgage,** the pledge, and the CONDITIONAL SALE (see **sale**). The mortgage involves the situation wherein the mortgagor gives the mortgagee a security interest in a specific asset, which is usually real property. The pledge deals with the situation wherein the creditor takes possession of the property. The conditional sale involves the situation wherein the seller gives credit and takes a security interest.

SEDITION Under the *Criminal Code,* R.S.C. 1985, c. C–46, ss. 59 and 61, it is an **indictable offence** to speak seditious words, i.e., words expressive of a seditious intention. A seditious intention is an intention to raise disaffection and discontent among Her Majesty's subjects or to promote public disorder. See *Rex* v. *Felton* (1916), 25 C.C.C. 207 (Alta. S.C.A.D.). See also **seditious libel.**

SEDITIOUS LIBEL A libel that expresses a seditious intention, viz., teaching or advocating, publishing or circulating any writing that advocates the use of force as a means of accomplishing a governmental change in Canada. *Criminal Code,* R.S.C. 1985, c. C–46, s. 59(2). Words constitute a seditious libel "if they are expressive of a seditious intention, and ... are both calculated (likely) and intended to stir up and excite discontent and disaffection among His Majesty's subjects." *Rex* v. *Giesinger* (1916), 32 D.L.R. 325 at 330 (Sask.S.C.).

SEISED The condition of legally owning and possessing **realty.** A person seised of **real property** has a **freehold estate** with possession or a right to possession. The phrase imports legal **title** as opposed to a beneficial **interest.**

SEISIN A term that describes the **title** of a **freehold estate** with a right of immediate **possession,** the term really being synonymous with possession. "In feudal times the title or right of immediate possession of a freehold estate was transmissable by . . . **livery of seisin** . . . Now livery of seisin has been done away with by statute and replaced by transfer by deed." 2 A.H.Oosterhoff & W.B. Rayner, *Anger and Honsberger: Law of Real Property* 1259 (2d ed. 1985). Today, 'seisin' is generally considered synonymous with ownership. See also *Innes* v. *Ferguson* (1894), 21 O.A.R. 323.

SEIZURE A forcible taking of possession, *Pacific Finance Co.* v. *Ireland,* [1931] 2 W.W.R. 593 (Alta.S.C.A.D.); the act of forcibly dispossessing an owner of property, under actual or apparent authority of law; the taking of property into the **custody** of the court in **satisfaction** of a **judgment,** or in consequence of a violation of public law. When a **writ** of seizure is executed by a sheriff, **chattels** in possession of a **debtor** are taken away. See also **search and seizure.**

SELF-DEALING A type of trading in which a party acts upon secret information obtained by his or another's special position in the corporation; synonymous with INSIDER TRADING. It may involve sale or purchase of stock by the director, officers, and majority **shareholders** of a **corporation.** Under common iaw, most courts hold that **insiders** are under no **fiduciary** duty to disclose inside information to either purchaser or seller. See *Percival* v. *Wright,* [1902] 2 Ch. 421. Some courts have applied the so-called "special facts doctrine" under which disclosure is required if certain conditions are shown, such as the nature of the responsibility the director has assumed towards the shareholder. See *Coleman* v. *Myers* (1977), 2 N.Z.L.R. 298 (C.A.). See also provincial legislation, e.g., *Securities Act,* R.S.O. 1990, c.S.5, Part XXI.

SELF-DEFENCE The right that exists to protect one's person, or members of one's family, and, to a lesser extent, one's property, from harm by an aggressor. It may be a valid **defence** to a criminal **charge** or to **tort** liability. See generally *Criminal Code,* R.S.C. 1985, c. C–46, ss. 34–37 (defence of person), ss. 38–42 (defence of property). While one may use force to repel an attack, real or apprehended, such force must not be excessive. See *Wackett* v. *Calder* (1965), 51 D.L.R. (2d) 598 at 601 (B.C.C.A.). The defence is also available to a person who believes on reasonable grounds that he, a relative or friend "was in imminent danger, even though those reasonable grounds are founded on a genuine mistake of act." See *Gambriell* v. *Caparelli* (1974), 54 D.L.R. (3d) 661 at 665–66 (Ont.Co.Ct.).

SELF-INCRIMINATION, PRIVILEGE AGAINST Section 13 of the *Canadian Charter of Rights and Freedoms* provides, "A witness who testifies in any proceedings has the right not to have any incriminating evidence so given used to incriminate that witness in any other proceedings, except in a prosecution for perjury or for the giving of contradictory evidence." The provision would seem to give a constitutional guarantee from prosecution to an individual who in giving **testimony** incriminates himself in a crime. Such provision would thus override the provisions in the various federal or provincial *Evidence Acts* that might require, **inter alia,** that an individual specifically request protection before incriminating testimony is given.

SENILE DEMENTIA *(dĕ-mĕn'-shē-à)* Lat.: a state where mental faculties are enfeebled. Insanity that occurs as the result of old age and is progressive in character; an incurable form of fixed insanity resulting in a total collapse of mental faculties that, in its final state, necessarily deprives one of **testamentary** capacity because of loss of power to think, reason, or act sanely. See also **competent; incompetency; non compos mentis.**

SENTENCE The punishment ordered by a court to be inflicted upon a person convicted of a crime; also any **order** of the trial court made on conviction "in addition to or substitution for fine and imprisonment." See *Hall* v. *The Queen* (1954), 111 C.C.C. 181 at 184 (B.C.C.A.); *Criminal Code,* R.S.C. 1985, c. C–46, s. 673, 785(1).

CONCURRENT SENTENCE A sentence that overlaps with another for a period of time as opposed to a consecutive sentence that runs by itself, beginning after or ending before the running of another sentence.

CONSECUTIVE SENTENCE A sentence that runs separately from one or more other sentences to be served by the same individual. Under the *Criminal Code,* R.S.C. 1985, c. C–46, s. 717(4), the court that convicts the accused may direct that terms of imprisonment be served one after the other in the circumstances described. It is within the trial judge's discretion to determine whether sentences are to be served consecutively or concurrently. See R. Salhany, *Canadian Criminal Procedure* 8–28–30 (6th ed. 1994).

INDETERMINATE SENTENCE A sentence imposed for an indeterminate period up to a certain maximum, in addition to any other sentence. "Prior to 1978, there were provisions under the *Prisons and Reformatories Act* [R.S.C. 1985, c. P-20] which permitted the courts in certain provinces, such as British Columbia and Ontario, to impose indeterminate sentences . . . Those provisions were repealed by the Parliament of Canada in 1977." R. Salhany, *supra,* c. 8 at 35.

SUSPENDED SENTENCE A sentence whose imposition or execution has been withheld by the court on certain terms and conditions. Under s. 737(1) of the *Criminal Code,* the court may suspend the passing of sentence "having regard to the age and character of the accused, the nature of the offence and the circumstances surrounding its commission" and direct that the accused be released upon conditions prescribed in a **probation** order. See R. Salhany, *supra,* c. 8 at 40–41.

SEQUESTER To separate from, as in to sequester assets or to sequester witnesses during a trial. See **sequestration.**

SEQUESTRATION 1. In **equity,** the act of seizing or taking possession of the property belonging to another until he complies with an **order** or **judgment.** In some cases it might direct a sheriff to go on the **real property** and receive **rents** and profits therefrom until the debt concerned has been paid; "a **writ** of sequestration is an extraordinary remedy, only to be employed as a last resort...." *Cudmore* v. *Cudmore* (1921), 50 O.L.R. 489 at 490 (H.C.).

2. The term also applies to the common-law practice whereby **juries** (e.g., in **capital offence** cases) might be sequestered, or kept together throughout the trial and deliberations and guarded from improper contact, until they were discharged. The common-law practice concerning sequestration has been replaced by the provisions of the *Criminal Code,* R.S.C. 1985, c. C–46, s. 647, in which **discretion** is given to the trial judge to permit jurors to separate before the jury retires to consider a verdict.

3. Sequestration of **witnesses** may be ordered by the court in order to insure that in-court testimony of each witness not be coloured by what another witness said. The order of sequestration usually forbids the witnesses who have not yet testified from talking with witnesses who have testified.

SERIATIM *(sĕr-ē-ä'-tĭm)* Lat.: in due order, successively; in order, in succession; individually, one by one; separately; severally.

SERVANT One who works for, and is subject to, the control of his master; a person employed to "perform services in the affairs of another and who with respect to the physical conduct in the performance of the services is subject to the other's control or right to control.

"In determining whether one acting for another is a servant or an independent **contractor,** the following matters of fact, among others, are considered: (a) the extent of control which, by the agreement, the master may exercise over the details of the work; (b) whether or not the one employed is engaged in a distinct occupation or business; (c) the kind of occupation, with reference to whether, in the locality, the work is usually done under the direction of the employer or by a specialist without supervision; (d) the skill required in the particular occupation; (e) whether the employer or the workman supplies the instrumentalities, tools, and the place of work for the person doing the work; (f) the length of time for which the person is employed; (g) the method of payment, whether by the time or by the job; (h) whether or not the work is a part of the regular business of the employer; (i) whether or not the parties believe they are creating the relation of master and ser-

vant; and (j) whether the principal is or is not in business." *Restatement of Agency* (2d) s. 220, at 485–87. A master is in many instances liable, under the theory of **respondeat superior,** for the torts of his servant, but not for those of an independent contractor. See also **agent.**

See *T. B. Bright & Co. Ltd.* v. *Kerr,* [1939] S.C.R. 63; *Performing Right Society, Ltd.* v. *Mitchell,* [1924] 1 K.B. 762. See further G. Fridman, *The Law of Agency* (6th ed. 1990) esp. chap. 2 .

SERVICE Delivery of communication of a **pleading, notice,** or other paper in a **suit** to the opposite party, so as to charge him with receipt of it and subject him to its legal effect; the bringing to notice, either actually or constructively.

PERSONAL SERVICE Actual delivery to the party to be served; "the essential ingredient ... is that the process delivered to the defendant must be so delivered under circumstances which enable the court to conclude that he knew, or reasonably should have known, what it was, or, ...that he knew the document was a writ, issued against him by the plaintiff, and knew, in addition, the general nature of the claim therein advanced. ´ *Orazio* v. *Ciulla* (1966), 57 W.W.R. 641 at 646 (B.C.S.C.). See further G. Watson, *Canadian Civil Procedure* 357 (3d ed. 1988).

SUBSTITUTED SERVICE Service by a means other than on the defendant personally. Where a plaintiff is unable to effect prompt personal service, the court may order substituted service by a variety of methods, e.g., by mail at his last-known address; by leaving the writ with the defendant's spouse or other relative or his solicitor, etc. See further *id.* at 363ff.

SERVICE OF PROCESS The communication of the substance of the **process** to the defendant, either by actual delivery, or by other methods whereby defendant is furnished with reasonable notice of the proceedings against him to afford him opportunity to appear and be heard. For the types of service of process see **service.**

SERVICES At common law, the acts done by an English **feudal tenant** for the benefit of his lord, which formed the **consideration** for the property granted to him by his lord. Services were of several types, including knight's service, military service and the more varied kind of certain and determinate service called **socage.** See also **tenure.**

SERVIENT ESTATE [TENEMENT] In an **easement** situation, the estate that is subject to use in some way for the benefit of a **dominant estate,** the dominant estate being one to which certain rights or benefits are legally owed by the servient estate.

SESSION "[T]he period of time during which members of the Legislature are called together for the dispatch of public business." *Re Sessional Allowances under the Ontario Legislative Assembly Act,* [1945] 2 D.L.R. 631 at 636 (Ont.C.A.). The term refers **inter alia** to the sittings of **Parliament,** the courts, etc.

SET ASIDE To annul or make **void,** as to set aside a **judgment.** When **proceedings** are irregular, they may be set aside on **motion** of the **party** whom they injuriously affect. See also **reversal.**

SETOFF In civil procedure, a method by which a **defendant** in an **action** can plead a claim against the **plaintiff** without commencing a separate action; in effect, a **counterclaim** by the defendant against the plaintiff that diminishes the plaintiff's potential recovery. However, though setoff and counterclaim are similar in purpose, there are important procedural differences. See G. Watson *Canadian Civil Procedure* 638ff. (3d ed. 1988). "Where there are mutual debts between the plaintiff and defendant or, if either party sue or be sued as executor or administrator, where there are mutual debts between the testator or intestate and either party, one debt may be set against the other." See, e.g., *Courts of Justice Act,* R.S.O. 1990, c. C. 43, s. 111, and similar provisions in other common-law provinces. "There is, however, another **equity** which has sometimes been called 'set-off,' but which does not in any way depend upon the statute, which arises when the claims are upon the same **contract** or are so interwoven by the dealings between the parties that the Court can find that there has been established a mutual credit, or an agreement, express or implied, that the claims should be set one against the other." *Burman* v. *Rosin, Rosin* v. *Burman* (1915), 35 O.L.R. 134 at 136 (Ont.H.C.).

SETTLEMENT Generally, the conclusive fixing or resolving of a matter; the arrangement of a final disposition of it. A compromise achieved by the **adverse parties** in a **civil suit** before final **judgment** whereby they agree between themselves upon their respective rights and obligations, thus eliminating the necessity of judicial resolution of the controversy. Compare **plea bargaining** in the criminal context. See further, G. Watson, *Canadian Civil Procedure* 65–66, 275–284, 356–57 (3d ed. 1988).

SETTLOR One who creates a **trust** by giving **real** or **personal property** "in trust" to another (the **trustee**) for the benefit of a third person (the **beneficiary**). One who gives such money is said to "settle" it on, or bring **title** to rest with, the trustee, and is also called the **donor** or TRUSTOR.

SEVERABLE CONTRACT One that, in the event of a **breach** by one of the parties, may be justly considered as several independent agreements that have been expressed in a single **instrument.** Where a contract is deemed severable, a breach thereof may constitute a default as to only a part of the contract, saving the defaulting party from the necessity of responding in **damages** for a breach of the entire agreement. See further G. Fridman, *The Law of Contract* 505–06 (2d ed. 1986).

SEVERABLE STATUTE A statute the remainder of which remains valid when a portion has been declared invalid, because the statute is one whose parts are not wholly interdependent. After the invalid portion of the act has been stricken out, if that which remains is self-sustaining and capable of separate enforcement without regard to the portion of the statute that has been cast aside, the statute is said to be severable.

SEVERALLY Separate and apart from. **1.** In a **note,** each who severally promises to pay is responsible separately for the entire amount. **2.** In a **judgment** against more than one defendant, arising out of one **action,** each may be **liable** for the entire amount of the judgment, thereby permitting the successful plaintiff to recover the entire amount of the judgment from any defendant against whom he chooses to institute a suit. Compare **joint; joint and several; joint tortfeasors.**

SEVERALTY Refers to the holding of property solely, separately and individually. "A person who is sole owner of an estate is said to hold it in severalty because he holds it in his own right with no one having any interest jointly with him." 1 A.H. Oosterhoff & W.B. Rayner, *Anger and Honsberger: Law of Real Property* 787 (2d ed. 1985).

SEVERANCE The act of separating; the state of being disjoined or separated. In **contract** law, when a contract contains several distinct promises or a promise which is by its terms divisible into distinct promises, some of which are illegal and others legal, the court may enforce those that are legal and refuse to enforce those that are illegal. This is known as severance or the "doctrine of severability of promises." See, e.g., *Attwood* v. *Lamont*, [1920] 3 K.B. 571 (C.A.). See further G. Fridman, *The Law of Contract in Canada* 399–402 (2d ed. 1986).

SEXUAL ASSAULT *An Act to Amend the Criminal Code in Relation to Sexual Offences,* S.C. 1980–81–82–83, c. 125 repealed the provisions in the *Criminal Code,* R.S.C. 1970, c. C–34, dealing with rape, and created new offences dealing with sexual assault and aggravated sexual assault.

In *R.* v. *Chase,* [1987] 2 S.C.R. 293, the Supreme Court of Canada defined sexual assault under s. 271 of the *Criminal Code,* R.S.C. 1985, c. C–46, as "an assault within any one of the definitions of that concept in [s. 265(1)] of the *Criminal Code,* which is committed in circumstances of a sexual nature, such that the sexual integrity of the victim is violated." (Section 265(1) is the general assault provision of the *Code*).

Under s. 271 of the *Code,* sexual assault is either an **indictable** or **summary offence,** with a maximum penalty on **indictment** of 10 years imprisonment. The *Code* includes spousal sexual assault, regardless of whether or not the spouses were living together at the time of the assault (s. 278).

AGGRAVATED SEXUAL ASSAULT "Every one [*sic*] commits an aggravated sexual assault who, in committing a sexual assault, wounds, maims, disfigures, or endangers the life of the complainant." (s. 273(1)). Aggravated sexual assault is an indictable offence, with a maximum of life imprisonment.

Sexual assault is an offence of general **intent.** *Leary* v. *The Queen* [1978] 1 S.C.R. 29. See **rape.**

SEXUAL HARASSMENT Under s. 3(o) of the Nova Scotia *Human Rights Act,* R.S.N.S. 1989, c. 214, as amended by S.N.S. 1991, c. 12, sexual harassment means "(i) vexatious sexual conduct or a course of comment that is known or ought reasonably to be known as unwelcome, (ii) a sexual solicitation or advance made to an individual by another individual where the other individual is in a position to confer a benefit on, or deny a benefit to, the individual to whom the solicitation or advance is made, where the individual who makes the solicitation or advance knows or ought reasonably to know that it is unwelcome, or (iii) a reprisal or threat of reprisal against an individual for rejecting a sexual solicitation or advance." See *Janzen* v. *Platy Enterprises Ltd.,* [1989] 1 S.C.R. 1252.

SEXUAL ORIENTATION One's sexual preference. A term that means "heterosexual, homosexual or bi-sexual and refers only to consenting adults acting within the law." *Human Rights Act,* R.S.Y. 1986 (Supp.), c. 11, s. 34. Sexual orientation is a prohibited ground of discrimination in many provincial human rights acts. See e.g., Ontario *Human Rights Code,* R.S.O. 1990, c. H.19, s. 1 (see **Appendix IV**); Nova Scotia *Human Rights Act,* R.S.N.S. 1989, c. 214, s. 5(n), as amended by S.N.S. 1991, c 12. Although sexual orientation does not explicitly appear as a prohibited ground of discrimination in s. 3(1) of the *Canadian Human Rights Act,* R.S.C. 1985, c. H-6 (see **Appendix III**), it has been effectively **read into** the *Act. Haig* v. *Canada* (1992), 5 O.R. (3d) 495 at 508 (C.A.). See also McAllister, *Recent Sexual Orientation Cases,* 2 N.J.C.L. 354 (1992).

SHAM PLEADING One that is clearly and indisputably false and presents no real **issue** of fact to be determined; a **defence** wholly unsupported by the facts. Bad faith is not necessary. However, such a pleading may be resorted to for purposes of delay and annoyance.

SHARE A portion of something; an **interest in a corporation.** "A 'share of stock' is a right which the owner has in the management, profits, and ultimate assets of the corporation...." *Re Kootenay Valley Fruit Lands Co.* (1911), 18 W.L.R. 145 at 147 (Man.K.B.). See **stock certificate.**

SHAREHOLDER One who is holder or proprietor of one or more **shares** of stock of a **corporation.** To be a shareholder of an incorporated company is to be possessed of the evidence, usually **stock certificates,** that the holder is the real owner of a certain individual portion of the property in actual or potential existence held by the company in its name as a unit for the common benefit of all the owners of the entire **capital** stock of the company.

SHELLEY'S CASE See **Rule in Shelley's Case.**

SHERIFF An official appointed by the **Crown** who has numerous duties, including the serving of legal documents such as WRITS OF SUMMONS (see **writ**) and **subpoenas,** the maintaining of good order in Her Majesty's courts and the **seizure** and sale under court order of the property of judgment debtors.

SHERIFF'S SALE A sale of **property** by the **sheriff** under authority of a court's **judgment** and WRIT OF EXECUTION (see **writ**) in order to satisfy an unpaid judgment, **mortgage, lien** or other **debt** of the owner (**judgment debtor).** An EXECUTION SALE of **real property** has the same effect as a **conveyance** by **quitclaim deed,** in that only such **title** as the judgment debtor has at the time of the sale is passed. Any title or **interest** acquired after the time of sale is not conveyed.

SHIFTING INTEREST See **interest.**

SHIFTING USE See **use.** See also **interest** [EXECUTORY INTEREST].

SHOW CAUSE ORDER An **order,** made upon the **motion** of one party, requiring a party to appear and show cause [argue] why a certain thing should be permitted or not permitted. It requires the adverse party to meet the **prima facie case** made by the applicant's verified **complaint** or **affidavit.**

An order to show cause is an accelerated method of beginning a **litigation** by compelling the adverse party to respond in a much shorter period of time than he would normally have to respond to a **complaint.** The order may or may not contain temporary restraints [see **restraining orders**] but will generally be "returnable" in a few days, which means that the opposing party must prepare answering affidavits and persuade the court that an issue of a fact exists that requires a full, plenary trial proceeding or simply argue on the return date that even if the plaintiff's statements in his moving papers are true, they do not state a cause of action or justify the relief prayed for in the order to show cause.

Compare **summons.**

SIMPLE CONTRACT See **sealed instrument.**

SINE DIE *(sē′-nā dē′-ā)* Lat.: without day, without time. A legislative body adjourns *sine die* when it adjourns without appointing a day on which to appear or assemble again.

SINE QUA NON *(sē′-nā kwā nŏn)* Lat.: without which not; that without which the thing cannot be, i.e., the essence of something. For example, in **tort** law, the act of the defendant, without which there would not have been a tort. See **cause.**

SINKING FUND An accumulation, by a corporation or government body, of money invested for the purpose of repaying a **debt** or debts. In government bodies, a sinking fund is a fund arising from taxes, imposts or duties, which is appropriated toward the payment of interest due on a public loan and for the eventual payment of the **principal.**

SLANDER A **defamatory** statement. At common law, a distinction was drawn between **libel** and slander. The distinction lies in the manner of publication. "Broadly speaking, libel relates to defamatory statements that are written or otherwise in more permanent form; slander relates to spoken statements, or those which are more transitory in nature." G. Fridman, *Introduction to the Law of Torts* 153 (1978). "The importance of the manner in which defamatory matter was published lay at common law and still lies in jurisdictions which have made no generally significant change, such as Ontario, in the attitude of the law with regard to the actionability of the publication. If defamation were in the form of libel, it was and still is actionable without proof of damage, although the amount recoverable by the victim would depend upon the damage actually suffered by him.... If the publication were of a slander then no action would lie, and still will not lie ... without proof of what was termed 'special damage' unless the case fell within one of a number of exceptions." *Id.* at 154.

SOCAGE In feudal England, a type of tenure founded upon certain and designated services performed by the vassal for his lord, other than military or knight's service. Where the services were considered honourable, it was called FREE SOCAGE and where the services were of a baser nature, it was called VILLEIN SOCAGE. By the statute 12 Car. 2, c. 24, almost all **tenures** by knight-servants were converted into FREE AND COMMON SOCAGE. See 2 Bl.Comm. 79–80. See also **homage.**

SODOMY Unnatural sexual intercourse, a so-called **crime against nature.** Originally only an ecclesiastical offence, in Canada it is a **hybrid offence** under the *Criminal Code,* R.S.C. 1985 c. C–46, ss. 159, 160. Sodomy includes both **bestiality** and **buggery.** See, e.g., *Anonymous* (1869), 29 U.C.Q.B. 456.

SOLICITATION An offence developed by the later common-law courts to reach conduct whereby one enticed, incited or opportuned another to commit a **felony** or certain **misdemeanours** injurious to the public welfare. See *R.* v. *Higgins* (1801), 102 E.R. 269. Under the *Criminal Code,* R.S.C. 1985, c. C–46, s. 212, everyone who "procures, attempts to procure or solicits a person to have illicit sexual intercourse with another person" is guilty of an **indictable offence.** "It must be noted . . . that the word 'solicit' is not defined in the Criminal Code, therefore, the Courts below have taken what I am of the opinion was a proper course and have turned to English dictionaries for the purpose of defining the word. . . . [In the] Shorter Oxford Dictionary . . . the definition is exact and I quote it. 'c. of women; to accost and importune (men) for immoral purposes.' " See *Hutt* v. *The Queen* (1978), 82 D.L.R. (3d) 95 at 100 (S.C.C.).

SOLICITOR See **barrister and solicitor.**

SOLICITOR GENERAL [OF CANADA OR OF A PROVINCE] Minister of the **Cabinet** responsible for reformatories, prisons, penetentiaries, parole, remission and statutory release, the **Royal Canadian Mounted Police,** and the Canadian Security Intelligence Service. *Department of the Solicitor General Act,* R.S.C. 1985, c. S–13, s. 4.

SOLVENCY The ability to pay all **debts** and just claims as they come due. "In considering the question of whether a debtor is solvent or insolvent, I do not think his position can be properly considered from a more favourable point of view than this—to inquire whether all his **property,** both **real** and **personal,** subject to **execution** be sufficient if realised upon at the present time to pay his debts in full, and in considering the question of how much can be realised out of his property, both the land and personal property must be estimated not at what he thinks the property is worth, nor at what others say the property is worth, but at what the property will bring on the market at a forced sale; for the debtor is not in a position to wait for favourable opportunities to sell." *Wagner* v. *Hartows,* [1923] 1 D.L.R. 186 at 190 (Sask.C.A.).

SOUNDS IN Has a connection or association with; is concerned with; thus, though a party to a lawsuit has **pleaded damages** in **tort,** it may be said that the **action** nevertheless "sounds in" **contract** if the elements of the offence charged appear to constitute a contract, rather than a tort, action. Whether the court will consider it a tort or a contract may influence the damage measure since, for example, punitive damages (see **damages** [EXEMPLARY DAMAGES]) are recoverable in tort but not in contract. See, e.g., *Dominion Chain Co. Ltd.* v. *Eastern Construction Co.* (1976), 68 D.L.R. (3d) 385 (Ont.C.A.), where the court considered whether an action against an architect, engineer or builder for negligent performance of contractual duties "sounds only in" contract.

SOVEREIGN IMMUNITY A doctrine precluding the institution of a **suit** against the Sovereign [government] without the Sovereign's consent when the Sovereign is engaged in a governmental function; originally based on the maxim "the King can do no wrong." Another rationale is that the Sovereign is exempt from suit, not because of any formal conception or obsolete theory, but on the logical and practical ground that there can be no legal right against the authority that makes the law on which the right depends. In Canada, Her Majesty the Queen is the head of state and head of the executive government. While modern common-law doctrine is that the Sovereign, as the representative of executive authority, can incur liabilities in the same way as other persons (i.e., that "the **Crown** is subject to the law of the land"), still the Crown enjoys certain special and peculiar privileges, such as immunity from statutory control. See, e.g., *Interpretation Act,* R.S.O. 1990, c. I.11, s. 11: "No Act affects the rights of Her Majesty, Her heirs or successors, unless it is expressly stated therein that Her Majesty is bound thereby." See further C. McNairn, *Governmental and Intergovernmental Immunity in Australia and Canada* 3 (1977).

In the area of **international law** there are "general principles ... according to which a sovereign State is held to be immune from the **jurisdiction** of another sovereign State. This is sometimes said to flow from international **comity** or courtesy, but may now more properly be regarded as a rule of international law, accepted among the community of nations. It is binding on the municipal Courts of this country in the sense and to the extent that it has been received and enforced by these Courts." *Compania Naviera Vascongado* v. *S.S. Cristina,* [1938] A.C. 485 at 502 (H.L.). See further L. Green, *International Law Through the Cases,* (4th ed. 1978), chap. 12.

SPECIAL DAMAGES See damages [CONSEQUENTIAL DAMAGES].

SPECIAL TRAVERSE See traverse.

SPECIALTY A **contract** under seal. See **sealed instrument.**

SPECIE Money that has an intrinsic value, e.g., gold and silver coins. These are coins made of scarce metals that are usually minted in various denominations differentiated by weight and fineness. Most often these coins are stamped with government seals and insignias signifying their value as currency. See also **in specie.**

SPECIFIC BEQUEST [LEGACY] See **bequest** [SPECIFIC BEQUEST].

SPECIFIC DEVISE Generally, a **gift** by **will** of a particular piece of **real property.** Compare **specific bequest.**

SPECIFIC INTENT See **intent; mens rea.**

SPECIFIC PERFORMANCE An equitable **remedy** available to an **aggrieved party** when his remedy at law is inadequate, which consists of a requirement that the party guilty of a **breach of contract** undertake to perform or to complete performance of his obligations under the contract. It is grounded on the equitable maxim that **equity** regards as done what ought to have been done.

One can obtain a decree of specific performance for the purchase of a unique chattel such as a rare painting, and in all transactions involving land, which the law presumes to be unique. Once a purchaser of land has signed a contract he is said to have equitable title because he can enforce the contract through a decree of specific performance.

There are cases in which the court of equity will not specifically enforce a contract even though the remedy at law is inadequate. Personal service contracts and construction contracts are common examples, due to the difficulty of the court's overseeing proper performance by the defaulting party. See further S. Waddams, *The Law of Contracts* 459ff. (3d ed. 1993).

SPENDTHRIFT TRUST A **trust** created to provide a fund for maintenance of a **beneficiary** that is so restricted that it is secure against the beneficiary's improvidence and beyond the reach of his **creditors.**

SPLITTING A CAUSE OF ACTION Impermissible practice of bringing an **action** for only part of the **cause of action** in one **suit,** and initiating another suit for another part; consists in dividing a single or individual cause of action into several parts or claims and bringing several actions thereon. See G. Watson, *Canadian Civil Procedure* 567–68, 569 (3d ed. 1988). Under the general policy against splitting the causes of action, the law mandatorily requires that all **damages** sustained or accruing to one as a result of a single **wrongful act** be claimed and recovered in one action or not at all. See also **multiplicity of suits.** Compare **joinder; misjoinder.**

SPOUSE Under the *Divorce Act,* R.S.C. 1985 (2nd Supp.), c.3, s. 2, a "spouse" is a partner in marriage, making the Act applicable only to a man and woman who were legally married at the time proscribed by statute.

Under some provincial statutes, for the purpose of **maintenance** or support, "spouse" may include a man or woman who has co-habited for a prescribed period of time—e.g., *Family Maintenance Act,* R.S.N.S. 1989, c. 160, s. 2(m) (one year); *Family Law Act,* R.S.O. 1990, c. F.3, ss. 1(1), 29 (three years).

See also *Welk* v. *Saskatchewan Social Services Appeal Board* [1986] 2 W.W.R. 333 (Sask. Q.B.), where the court ruled that, in the absence of legislative definition of "spouse," it was not within the jurisdiction of the Board to assign it a meaning. Also *Fraser* v. *Haight* (1987), 36 D.L.R. (4th) 459 (Ont. H.C.) (Insurance policies).

In *Egan* v. *Canada,* [1992] 2 F.C. 687 (T.D.), it was held that the term "spouse" in the *Old Age Security Act,* R.S.C. 1985, c. 0–9, did not include same-sex couples. Thus, spousal benefits could not extend to a same-sex partner. Leave to appeal the decision to the Supreme Court of Canada was granted on October 14, 1993.

SPRINGING INTEREST See **interest.**

SPRINGING USE See **use.** See also **interest** [EXECUTORY INTEREST].

STAKEHOLDER A third party chosen by two or more persons to keep in deposit **property** or money the right or **possession** of which is in dispute, and to deliver the property or money to the one who establishes his right to it.

STANDING The legal right of a person or group to challenge in a judicial forum the conduct of another especially with respect to government conduct. The case of *Thorson* v. *Attorney-General of Canada,* [1975] 1 S.C.R. 138, e.g., upheld the standing of a federal taxpayer to challenge the constitutional validity of federal legislation. "[W]here all members of the public are affected alike ... and there is a

justiciable issue respecting the validity of legislation, the Court must be able to say that as between allowing a taxpayer's action and denying any standing at all when the Attorney General refuses to act, it may choose to hear the case on the merits." *Id.* at 161. See also *Nova Scotia Board of Censors* v. *McNeil* (1975), 55 D.L.R. (3d) 632 (S.C.C.).

STANDING MUTE In a criminal trial, refusing to **plead;** today equivalent to a **plea** of **not guilty.** Compare **self-incrimination, privilege against.**

STAR CHAMBER An ancient court of England that received its name because the ceiling was covered with stars; it sat with no jury and could administer any penalty but death. The Star Chamber was abolished when its **jurisdiction** was expanded to such an extent that it became too onerous for the people of England. See J. Baker, *An Introduction to English Legal History* 102 (2d ed. 1979).

STARE DECISIS *(stä'-rā dĕ-sī'-sĭs)* Lat.: to stand by that which was decided. The rule by which **common-law courts** tend to follow prior decisions or **precedents.** "Basically, under the doctrine of stare decisis, the decision of a higher court within the same jurisdiction acts as binding authority on a lower court within that same jurisdiction. The decision of a court of another jurisdiction only acts as persuasive authority." G. Gall, *The Canadian Legal System* 274 (3d ed. 1990). In *Stuart* v. *Bank of Montreal* (1909), 41 S.C.R. 516, the **Supreme Court of Canada** indicated that it felt bound by its own prior decisions. However, **dicta** in several more recent decisions suggest this may no longer be the prevailing attitude. For example, in *Binus* v. *The Queen,* [1967] S.C.R. 594 at 601, it was stated; "I do not doubt the power of this Court to depart from a previous judgment of its own but . . . I think that such a departure should be made only for compelling reasons." See generally G. Gall, *supra,* at chap. 10.

STATEMENT OF CLAIM The written statement of a **plaintiff** in a **cause of action** the purpose of which is to "set out the remedy claimed from the **defendant,** e.g., **damages** or **specific performance,** and describe the events that took place which would justify the court awarding this remedy. . . ." A part of the **pleadings** exchanged between plaintiff and defendant. See G. Watson, *Canadian Civil Procedure* 368 (3d ed. 1988).

STATEMENT OF DEFENCE In **pleading**, the **defendant's** reply to the **plaintiff's statement of claim.** See further G. Watson, *Canadian Civil Procedure* 369 (3d ed. 1988).

STATUS QUO (*stă'-tŭs kwō*) Lat.: the postures, positions, conditions or situations that existed.

STATUTE An act of the legislature; in Canada an act of a provincial legislature or the Federal **Parliament** adopted pursuant to constitutional authority. Statutes constitute a primary source of law and are enacted, for example, to prescribe conduct, define crimes, create inferior government bodies, appropriate public monies, and in general promote the public good and welfare. In Canada, the *Constitution Act, 1982* divides legislative power between the provincial legislatures and the Parliament of Canada. See **constitution.** Compare **common law; ordinances; regulations.** See further G. Gall, *The Canadian Legal System* 36ff. (3d ed. 1990).

STATUTE OF FRAUDS The statutory requirement that certain **contracts** be in writing to be enforceable. Most such statutes are patterned after the English statute enacted in 1677. Contracts to answer to a **creditor** for the **debt** of another, contracts made in **consideration** of marriage, contracts for the sale of land or affecting any **interest** in land (except short-term **leases**), and contracts not to be performed within one year from their making, must be evidenced by a written memorandum, and signed by the PARTY TO BE CHARGED, (i.e., by the defendant in an action for **breach**). Under a separate section of the English statute and as enacted in provincial legislation, a contract for the sale of goods where the contract price exceeds a certain specified amount (e.g., forty dollars or more) must likewise be in writing. See, e.g., *Sale of Goods Act,* R.S.O. 1990, c. S.1.

There are several exceptions to the statute. For example, PART PERFORMANCE is an important exception and operates to take an oral contract "out of the statute," i.e., to render it enforceable. In the case of a sale of goods within the statute, acceptance of part or all of the goods by the buyer or payment of all or part of the purchase price by the buyer suffices as part performance as to that portion of the contract.

See further, e.g., S. Waddams, *The Law of Contracts* (3d ed. 1993), chap. 6.

STATUTE OF LIMITATIONS Any law that fixes the time within which **parties** must take judicial action to enforce rights or else be thereafter barred from enforcing them.

Most every type of action at law has a statutory time beyond which the action may not be brought. *Equity* proceedings are governed by an independent equity doctrine called **laches.** These limitations are also an essential element of **adverse possession,** prescribing the time at which the adverse possessor's interest in the property becomes unassailable. The policy behind the enactment of such laws consists of the belief that there is a point beyond which a prospective defendant should no longer need to worry about the possible commencement in the future of an action against him, that the law disfavors "stale evidence," and that no one should be able to "sit on his rights" for an unreasonable amount of time without forfeiting his claims. See, e.g., *Limitations Act,* R.S.O. 1990, c. L.15.

STATUTE OF QUIA EMPTORES See **Quia Emptores, Statute of.**

STATUTE OF USES An English statute (27 Hen. VIII, C.10) enacted in 1535, for the purpose of preventing the separation of legal and equitable **estates** in land, a separation that arose whenever a **use** was created at **common law.** The purpose was to unite all legal and equitable estates in the **beneficiary** (the holder of the equitable estates) and to strip the **trustee** (the holder of the legal **title**) of all interest. (See **use** for a discussion of the statute's application.)

STATUTE OF WESTMINSTER, 1931 A statute of the **Parliament** of the United Kingdom intended to give full legislative autonomy to Canada and the other self-governing dominions that were former British colonies. The Statute provided **inter alia** that "(1) the U.K. Parliament could only legislate for a Dominion at its request and with its consent, and (2) the

Dominion could repeal any English Statute, imperial or otherwise." P. Fitzgerald & K. McShane, *Looking At Law* 26 (2d ed. 1982). The Statute of Westminster did not, however, give Canada authority to alter or repeal the *British North America Acts* because to that time no amending formula had been agreed upon between the provinces and the Parliament of Canada. Such an amending formula was not achieved until the British Parliament enacted the *Canada Act, 1982,* which incorporated the *Constitution Act, 1982*. The latter enactment provides in Part V a procedure for amending the Constitution of Canada.

STATUTE OF WILLS An early English statute prescribing the conditions necessary for a valid disposition through a **will.** Today, the term is used broadly to refer to the statutory provisions of a particular **jurisdiction** relating to the requirements for valid testamentary dispositions. See generally S. Bailey, *The Law of Wills* 21 (7th ed. 1973). See further the various provincial wills statutes, e.g., *Wills Act,* R.S.N.S. 1989, c. 505.

STATUTORY DECLARATION In effect, an oath; a written statement of facts signed and solemnly declared to be true by the person making it (the declarant) before a person with authority to take such declarations, such as a Commissioner of Oaths.

STATUTORY INSTRUMENT [STATUTORY ORDER] See **regulation;** see also **subordinate legislation.**

STAY A halt in a judicial **proceeding** where, by its **order,** the court will not take further action until the occurrence of some event. Inherent **jurisdiction** rests with the court to stay all proceedings that are, for example, frivolous or vexatious or an abuse of the process of the court. A stay may be temporary or permanent. Compare **adjournment; continuance; recess.**

STAY OF EXECUTION process whereby a **judgment** is precluded from being executed for a specific period of time.

STATUTORY OFFENCE See **regulatory offence.**

STIRPES See **per stirpes.**

STOCK CERTIFICATE A written **instru**ment evidencing a **share** in the ownership of a **corporation.**

STOCK DIVIDEND See **dividend.**

STOCKHOLDER See **shareholder.**

STOCKHOLDER'S DERIVATIVE ACTION In legal effect, a **suit** whereby "the minority **shareholders** themselves could bring an action in their own names (but in truth on behalf of the company) against the wrongdoing directors for the damage done by them to the company, provided always that it was impossible to get the company itself to sue them....The form of the action is always 'AB (a minority shareholder) on behalf of himself and all other shareholders of the Company' against the wrongdoing directors and company. That form of action was said by Lord Davey to be a 'mere matter of procedure in order to give a remedy for a wrong which would otherwise escape redress': see *Burland* v. *Earle,* [1902] A.C. 83 (P.C.). Stripped of mere procedure, the principle is that, where the wrongdoers themselves control the company, an action can be brought on behalf of the company by the minority shareholders, on the footing that they are its representatives, to obtain redress on its behalf. I am glad to find this principle well stated by Professor Gower in his book on companies in words which I would gratefully adopt:

> Where such an action is allowed the member is not really suing on his own behalf nor on behalf of the members generally, but on behalf of the company itself. Although ... he will have to frame his action as a representative one on behalf of himself and all the members other than the wrongdoers, this gives a misleading impression of what really occurs. The plaintiff shareholder is not acting as a representative of the other shareholders but as a representative of the company ... in the United States ... this type of action has been given the distinctive name of a 'derivative action,' recognizing that its true nature is that the individual member sues on behalf of the company to enforce rights derived from it."

Wallersteiner v. *Moir* (No. 2), [1975] 1 All E.R. 849 at 857–58 (C.A.).

In Canada, the derivative action has

been given legislative recognition. See, e.g., the *Canada Business Corporations Act,* R.S.C. 1985, c. C–44, s. 239.

STOCK OPTION The granting to an individual of the right to purchase a corporate **stock** at some future date at a price specified at the time the option is given rather than at the time the stock is purchased. Such options involve no commitments on the part of the individual to purchase the stock, and the option is usually exercised only if the price of the stock has risen above the price specified at the time the option was given.

Stock options are a form of incentive compensation. They are usually given by a corporation in an attempt to motivate an employee or **officer** to continue with the corporation or to improve corporate productivity in a manner that will cause the price of the corporation's stock to rise and thereby increase the value of the option. See also **dividend** [STOCK DIVIDEND].

STRAW MAN 1. A colloquial expression designating arguments in **briefs** or **opinions** created solely for the purpose of debunking or "discovering" them. Arguments so created are like straw men because they are, by nature, insubstantial. 2. In commerical and property contexts, the term may be used when a transfer is made to a third party, the straw man, simply to re-transfer to the transferror in order to accomplish some purpose not otherwise permitted. Thus, if a **covenant running with the land** must be included in the deed in the jurisdiction, such a covenant can be established subsequently by conveying the property to a straw man and obtaining from him a new grant with the desired convenant now in the **deed.**

STRICT CONSTRUCTION As to **statutes** or **contracts,** an interpretation by adherence to the literal meaning of the words used. "Statutes in derogation of the common law are to be construed strictly.... In *Rex* v. *Morris* ... Boyles, J. said: 'It is a sound rule to construe a statute in conformity with the **common law** rather than against it except where and so far as the statute is plainly intended to alter the course of the common law.' " *B. & R. Co.* v. *McLeod* (1912), 2 W.W.R. 1093 at 1096 (Alta.S.C.). But compare, e.g., *R.*

v. *Crown Zellerbach Canada Ltd.* (1954), 14 W.W.R. 433 at 440–41 (B.C.S.C.): "It is not for the court to approve or disapprove the policy embodied in an Act of parliament. In construing **criminal** statutes the presumption is that the representatives of the people in parliament assembled have in mind an evil prevalent in the land which should be corrected....The attitude of the courts towards the interpretation, **inter alia,** of criminal and taxation statutes has somewhat changed in recent years.... It is realized that criminal law is sane and humane and passed with an eye to the good of society. Doubtless Parliament is as anxious as any judge can be to deal kindly with offenders and to make their rehabilitation possible. The courts, sensing the intent of parliament, do not seek to render the provisions of our criminal law **nugatory** by strict interpretation, but rather to give them an honest and faithful construction. So, too, until comparatively recent times taxation measures were construed strictly, but today the courts realize that taxes are imposed for the good of society and, while the extracting process hurts, it is necessary that taxes be collected if society is to have those things for which it asks. Hence, a more liberal interpretation.... The purpose of the legislation is to be kept in mind and the statute is to be given such fair, large and liberal construction and interpretation as will best ensure the attainment of the object of the Act."

STRICT LIABILITY In **tort** and **criminal** law, **liability** without a showing of fault. It is often the case in tort law that one who engages in an activity that has an inherent risk of injury, something classified, for example, as ultra-hazardous, is liable for all injuries **proximately caused** by his enterprise, even without a showing of **negligence.** Thus, one who uses explosives or who harbours wild animals is liable for resulting injuries even if he uses utmost care. See, e.g., G. Fridman, *Introduction to the Law of Torts* 38, 49–53 (1978).

In the criminal law, offences sometimes do not require any specific or general **mens rea.** The conduct itself, even if innocently engaged in, results in criminal liability. Because of the possible harshness of holding people strictly accountable in this way, the courts require strong evidence of a legislative intent to statutorily create strict liability before the usual requirement of mens rea will be dispensed with; and strict liability crimes are usually limited to minor offences or **regulatory offences,** such as parking violations and violations of health codes.

Strict liability offences are also referred to as absolute liability, statutory, public welfare, and strict responsibility offences. *R.* v. *Sault Ste Marie* (1978), 3 C.R. (3d) 30 (S.C.C.)

SUA SPONTE *(sū'-à spŏn'-tā)* Lat.: of itself or of one's self; without being prompted, as where the court moves to declare a mistrial *sua sponte,* through its own volition, without a **motion** being made by either of the parties.

SUBCONTRACTOR One to whom the principal contractor sublets part of, or all of, a contract; also refers to portions obtained from other subcontractors. One who takes a part of a contract for the principal [general] contractor or another subcontractor.

SUBINFEUDATION The process that developed under **feudal** law whereby the **grantee** of an **estate** in land from his lord granted a smaller estate in the same land to another. In 1066, William the Conqueror claimed all the land of England for the Crown. Subsequently, he granted land to barons for their use in exchange for **services,** but retained ultimate **ownership,** this grant process being call infeudation. Such barons held land IN CAPITE (by direct grant from the king). Subinfeudation was the process by which barons further divided the land by making grants to knights in return for knight services, and the term also includes all subsequent grants and subdivisions by knights and their grantees. Owners under subinfeudation held land "in service" to their grantor and owed nothing directly to the king. G. Cheshire & E. Burn, *Modern Law of Real Property,* 14ff. (14th ed. 1988).

Subinfeudation was made illegal by the Statute of **Quia Emptores,** 18 Edw. I.C.I., and was replaced by the modern concept of **alienation.**

SUBJECT MATTER The thing in dispute; the nature of the **cause of action;** the real **issue** of fact or law presented for **trial** as between **parties;** the object of a **contract.**

SUB JUDICE *(sŭb jū'-dĭ-sā)* Lat.: under a court; before a court or judge for consideration. Thus, the "instant matter" or the "case at bar" will be called the "matter (case) *sub judice.*"

SUBLEASE A transaction whereby a **tenant** [one who has **leased premises** from the owner, or **landlord**] grants an **interest** in the leased premises less than his own, or reserves to himself a **reversionary** interest in the term. See **assignment,** which connotes the **conveyance** of the whole term of a lease.

SUBLET To make a **sublease** accompanied by a surrender of the **premises** or at least a part thereof. See **let.** Compare **assignment.**

SUB MODO *(sŭb mō'-dō)* Lat.: under a qualification; subject to a **condition** or qualification.

SUB NOMINE *(sŭb nō'-mē-nā)* Lat.: under the name. Used to indicate that the title of a case has been altered at a later stage in the proceedings; e.g., *A* v. *B, aff'd sub nom. C* v. *B.*

SUBORDINATE [DELEGATED] LEGISLATION Rules, **regulations,** by-laws, etc., made by persons or bodies under the authority given in a **statute.** There has been an ever-growing tendency in the twentieth century to enact **legislation** in general terms concerning many matters the detailed rules of which could not possibly be drawn up by the members of **Parliament** or a provincial legislature. The difficulty is surmounted by giving the power to make such rules to subordinate authorities such as boards or commissions, government departments, municipalities, etc. The power to make such laws is thus "delegated," and the rules that are made in this way are termed "delegated" or "subordinate" legislation. See further G. Gall, *The Canadian Legal System* 37–8 (3d ed. 1990).

SUBORNATION OF PERJURY "[T]he act of causing a witness to swear falsely in a judicial proceeding." *R.* v. *Picard* (1937), 68 C.C.C. 82 (Que.Mag.Ct.). Formerly, subornation of perjury was a specific offence in the *Criminal Code* and defined as "counselling or procuring a person to commit any perjury which is actually committed." *Id.* at 83. The offence would be included today under the Code provisions relating to obstructing justice. See *Criminal Code*, R.S.C. 1985, c. C–46, s. 139. See further *R.* v. *Savinkoff*, [1963] 3 C.C.C. 163 (B.C.C.A.).

SUBPOENA *(sŭ-pē'-nà)* Lat.: under penalty. A **writ** issued under authority of a court to compel the **appearance** of a **witness** at a judicial proceeding, the disobedience of which may be punishable as a **contempt of court.**

SUBPOENA AD TESTIFICANDUM *(äd tĕs'-tĭ-fĭ-kän'-dŭm)* Subpoena to testify. It is a technical and descriptive name for the ordinary subpoena. Compare **summons.**

SUBPOENA DUCES TECUM *(dū'-chĕs tā'-kŭm)* Under penalty you shall bring it with you. Type of subpoena issued by a court at the request of one of the parties to a **suit** which requires a witness having under his control documents or papers relevant to the controversy to bring such items to court during the trial.

SUBROGATION "[T]he right [of an insurer] to succeed to all the ways and means by which the person indemnified might have protected himself against or reimbursed himself for [a] loss. In other words, in dealing with subrogation, what the insured recovers against a third party must be credited upon or allowed against the amount sought to be recovered from the insurance company, if it is such that if he retain it he will be paid twice over." *Commercial Finance Corp. Ltd.* v. *Merchants Casualty Ins. Co. and Western Ass'ce Co.*, [1931] 1 D.L.R. 212 at 232 (Ont.S.C.A.D.).

Subrogation typically arises when an insurance company pays its insured under a collision protection feature of an insurance policy; in that event the company is subrogated to the cause of action of its insured. So too, under **Workmen's Compensation Acts** the board is subrogated to the injured worker's right (up to the amount of the board's payments) to sue the responsible party.

SUBROGEE One who, by **subrogation,** succeeds to the legal rights or claims of another.

SUBROGOR One whose legal rights or claims are acquired by another through **subrogation.**

SUBSIDIARY An inferior position or capacity; usually used in describing the relationship between **corporations.**

SUBSIDIARY CORPORATION One in which another corporation owns at least a majority of the shares and thus has control; it has all of the normal elements of a corporation (**charter, bylaws, directors,** etc.) but its **stock** is controlled by another corporation known as the **parent corporation.** This relationship of parent and subsidiary often becomes important for tax purposes and for determining whether a court will ignore the corporate existence of the subsidiary and **pierce the corporate veil.**

SUB SILENTIO *(sŭb sĭ-lĕn'-shē-ō)* Lat.: under silence; silently. When a later opinion reaches a result contrary to what would appear to be controlling authority, it is said that the later case, by necessary implication, overrules *sub silentio* the prior holding.

SUBSTANTIAL PERFORMANCE [COMPLIANCE] The **performance** of all the essential terms of a contract so that the purpose of the contract is accomplished; however, unimportant omissions and defects may exist in the strict performance of the contract. *Hoenig* v. *Isaacs,* [1952] 2 All E.R. 176 (C.A.). Whether entire performance is a **condition** precedent to payment "depends on the **construction** of the contract." "When a contract provides for a specific sum to be paid on completion of specified work, the courts lean against a construction of the contract which would deprive the contractor of any payment at all simply because there are some defects or omissions. The promise to complete the work is ... construed as a term of the contract, but not as a condition. It is not every breach of that term which absolves the employer from his promise to pay the price, but only a breach which goes to the root of the contract, such as an abandonment of the work when it is only half done. Unless the breach does go to the root of the matter, the employer cannot resist payment of the price. He must pay it and bring a cross-claim for the defects and omissions, or, alternatively, set them up in diminution of the price." *Id.* at 180–81. See **breach of contract.**

SUBSTANTIVE LAW The **positive law** that creates, defines and regulates the rights and duties of the **parties** and that may give rise to a **cause of action,** as distinguished from adjective law, which pertains to and prescribes the practice and **procedure** or the legal machinery by which the substantive law is determined or made effective. See *Carvell* v. *Carvell,* [1969] 2 O.R. 513 (C.A.).

SUBSTITUTED SERVICE See **service [of process].**

SUBTENANT One who **leases** all or part of rented **premises** from the original **lessee** for a term less than that held by the original lessee. The original lessee becomes the sublessor as to the subtenant. Most leases either prohibit subletting or require the lessor's permission in advance. The original lessee remains responsible for the subtenant's obligations to the lessor. Compare **assignment.**

SUCCESSION The process by which the property of a **decedent** is taken through **descent** or by **will.** See, e.g., *Attorney-General for Ontario* v. *Baby* (1926), 60 O.L.R. 1 (S.C.A.D.). It is a word that clearly excludes those who take by **deed, grant, gift,** or any form of purchase or **contract.** See **inheritance; intestate succession.**

SUICIDE The voluntary and intentional killing of oneself; the completed act was a **felony** at **common law.** Under the *Criminal Code,* R.S.C. 1985, c. C–46, s. 241, it is an **offence** to counsel or procure a person to commit suicide or to aid or abet a person to commit suicide. See *Stone* v. *World Newspaper Co.* (1918), 44 O.L.R. 33 (S.C.). Suicide by one in possession of his mental faculties is ordinarily excluded from insurance coverage. See *London Life Insurance Co.* v. *Lang Shirt Co.'s Trustee; Metro Life Insurance Co.* v. *Moore; Aetna Life Insurance Co.* v. *Moore,* [1929] S.C.R. 117.

SUI JURIS *(sū'-ē jūr'-ĭs)* Lat.: of his own right. Describes one who is no longer dependent, e.g., one who has reached the age of **majority** or has been removed from the care of a **guardian;** signifies one capable of caring for himself. Compare **emancipation; incompetency.**

SUIT Any **proceeding** in a court of justice by which an individual seeks a decision of the court or pursues a **remedy** that the law affords.

"[T]here are two basic elements of every law suit—the law and the facts. Though a party can establish the facts upon which the claim rests, the action will fail unless those facts entitle the litigant to a remedy in law. Whether or not the facts afford a remedy is a question of law for the judge to decide; the law does not give relief in every situation in which a citizen has been hurt or injured." G. Watson, *Canadian Civil Procedure* 2 (3d ed. 1988).

SUMMARY [CONVICTION] OFFENCE In Canada all crimes are classified as **indictable offences** or offences punishable on summary conviction. Generally speaking, summary offences, which may be federal or provincial, are those of a less serious nature and carry a lesser penalty. The procedure to try all summary conviction offences under the *Criminal Code* or other Act of **Parliament** is set out in Part XXVII of the *Criminal Code,* R.S.C. 1985, c. C–46. Summary offences are tried by justices or provincial court judges, and proceedings are generally quicker than, for example, in a trial by judge and jury, which is the most common form of trial for serious indictable offences. See further R. Salhany, *Canadian Criminal Procedures* (6th ed. 1994).

SUMMARY JUDGMENT See **judgment** [SUMMARY JUDGMENT].

SUMMARY JURISDICTION The **jurisdiction,** provided by statute, of a judge or **magistrate** to try an accused without a jury. Summary jurisdiction for the criminal law is provided by the *Criminal Code,* R.S.C. 1985, c. C–46, ss. 785–840. See also **summary offence; summary proceeding.**

SUMMARY PROCEEDING. A method by which the **parties** to a legal controversy may achieve a more expeditious disposition or determination of their case than is usual, by use of simplified **procedural** rules, usually involving more limited **discovery** or fact finding than is normally permitted in the particular type of proceeding; a form of **trial** in which the established course of legal **proceedings** is disregarded, especially in the matter of trial by **jury**. "In no case can the [matter] be tried summarily unless such proceedings are authorized by legislative authority, except perhaps in cases of contempts, for the common law is a stranger to such a mode of trial." J. Bouvier, *Bouvier's Law Dictionary*, 1066.

SUMMONS A call to appear in court; an order requiring the **appearance** of a **defendant** in an action under penalty of having **judgment** entered against him for failure to do so; in **criminal** law, an order to an accused informing him of an alleged offence and requiring him to appear in court to answer the allegation. See **writ** [WRIT OF SUMMONS]; **process**; **service**. Compare **subpoena**.

SUO NOMINE *(sū'-ō nō'-mē-nā)* Lat.: in his own name.

SUPERSEDING CAUSE See **cause**.

SUPERIOR COURT By s. 96 of the *B.N.A. Act, 1867* (now the *Constitution Act, 1867*) judges are appointed by federal authority to the higher provincial courts, i.e., superior and the former district and county courts. The courts of superior jurisdiction consist of "the supreme court of a province, including both the appellate and trial divisions, and both of those courts in those provinces where the two divisions are constituted as separate courts." G. Gall, *The Canadian Legal System* 147ff. (3d ed. 1990).

SUPERVENING CAUSE See **cause** [INTERVENING CAUSE].

SUPRA *(sū'-prà)* Lat.: above. In a written work, it refers the reader to a part preceding that which he is presently reading, as compared with the command **infra**, which directs the reader forward.

SUPREME COURT OF CANADA The final court of appeal for all **civil** and **criminal** cases in Canada. Section 101 of the *Constitution Act, 1867* authorized **Parliament** to enact laws establishing certain federal courts and tribunals. The **jurisdiction** of the Supreme Court of Canada is governed by the *Supreme Court Act*, R.S.C. 1985, c. S–26. "The Act was amended significantly in 1975 to abolish the prevailing civil monetary jurisdiction with the result that now the Supreme

Court is able to choose the cases it regards as raising matters of national importance or important issues of law, and to decide only those cases. The criminal appeal jurisdiction, however, remains unchanged." G. Gall, *The Canadian Legal System*, 107 (3d ed. 1990).

SURETY One who undertakes to pay money or perform other acts in the event that his **principal** fails therein; the surety is directly and immediately liable for the **debt**. Unlike an insurer, who might be found to pay a loss only on the happening of a defined **contingency**, a surety "became bound, it might be, unconditionally and without previous notice or demand, to pay the debt or make good the default which the principal was or should be liable to pay or make good, and the surety must see he did it." *Whalen v. Union Indemnity Co.* (1932), 41 O.W.N. 208 (H.C.)

SURREBUTTER In **common-law** pleading, a **plaintiff's** answer to the **defendant's** **rebuttal (rebutter)**.

SURREJOINDER In **common-law** pleading, a **plaintiff's** answer to the **defendant's** **rejoinder**.

SURROGATE A judicial officer of limited **jurisdiction**, who administers matters of **probate** and **intestate succession**.

SURROGATE COURT A provincial court of limited **jurisdiction** that is concerned with the **probate** of **wills** and the administration of **estates**. In some jurisdictions such a court may be known as the PROBATE COURT.

SURVIVAL STATUTE A statute that preserves for a **deceased's estate** or personal representatives a **cause of action** vested in the deceased. See, e.g., *Survival of Actions Act*, R.S.N.S. 1989, c. 453; *Fatal Injuries Act*, R.S.N.S. 1989, c. 163; *Family Law Act*, R.S.O. 1990, c. F.3. Part V.

SURVIVORSHIP A right whereby a person becomes entitled to property by reason of his having survived another person who had an interest in it. It is one of the elements of a **joint tenancy**. See also **survival statute**.

SUSPENDED SENTENCE See **sentence**.

TAIL, ESTATE IN See **fee tail.**

TANGIBLE PROPERTY Property, either **real** or **personal,** capable of being **possessed** and of being perceived by the senses; accessible; identifiable. Tangible property is **corporeal,** as distinguished from **intangible property** or **incorporeal rights** in property, such as **franchises, copyrights, easements** and goodwill.

TAX "[E]very contribution to a public purpose imposed by superior authority," *Les Ecclésiastiques de St. Sulpice de Montréal* v. *The City of Montreal* (1889), 16 S.C.R. 399 at 401; a rate or sum of money that people are compelled by a competent authority to pay for support of the government and that is commonly levied upon **assets** or **real property** (property tax), or income derived from office, employment, business or property (income tax), or upon the sale or purchase of **goods** (sales tax). It is essential that a tax be enforceable by law, be imposed by a public body under legislative authority and for a public purpose, and that it be compulsory. *A.-G. for Can.* v. *Registrar of Titles of Vancouver Land Registration District,* [1934] 3 W.W.R. 165 (B.C.C.A.).

Taxes can be direct or indirect. By section 92(2) of the *Constitution Act, 1867,* provincial legislatures are empowered to impose only DIRECT TAXATION, i.e., upon the individual from whom the tax is to be exacted. An INDIRECT TAX is one exacted from an individual with the understanding that he will indemnify himself at another's expense. *A.-G. for Manitoba* v. *A.-G. for Canada,* [1925] A.C. 561 (P.C.).

AD VALOREM TAX A tax on the value of the actual property subject to taxation laid as a percentage of that value, as opposed to a specific tax, which is applied as a fixed sum to all of a certain class of articles.

CAPITAL GAINS TAX See **capital** [CAPITAL GAIN].

ESTATE TAX A tax on the transfer of property, not on the property itself.

Estate taxes are based on the power to transmit or the transmission from the dead to the living, while **inheritance** taxes are based on the right to receive the property and are thus applied to the recipients thereof.

EXCISE TAX See **excise.**

POLL TAX See **poll tax.**

TAX SALE See **sale.**

TEMPORE *(tĕm'-pô-rā)* Lat.: for the time of.

TENANCY 1. Generally, a **tenant's** right to possess an **estate,** whether by **lease** or by **title.** A tenancy cannot be created unless exclusive **possession** is conferred on the tenant. *Furnishers Ltd.* v. *Booth,* [1933] 1 D.L.R. 54 (N.B.Co.Ct.). **2.** In a more limited sense, a holding in subordination to another's title, as in the **landlord**-tenant relationship.

HOLDOVER TENANCY See TENANCY AT SUFFERANCE.

JOINT TENANCY A tenancy "created where the same interest in **real** or **personal property** is passed by the same conveyance to two or more persons in the same right or by **construction** or **operation of law** jointly, with a right of ownership, i.e., the right of the survivor or survivors to the whole property." *R.* v. *Uniacke,* [1944] 3 W.W.R. 323 at 327 (Sask.C.A.). To have a joint tenancy, the four **unities** of time, **title, interest** and **possession** must be present. See A. Sinclair, *Introduction to Real Property Law* 56–58 (3d ed. 1987).

PERIODIC TENANCY In landlord-tenant law, a tenancy for a particular period (a week, month, year, or number of years), plus the expectancy or possibility that the period will be repeated. In contrast to a TENANCY FOR YEARS [see following], a periodic tenancy must be terminated by due **notice** to quit by either the landlord or the tenant, unless one party has failed to perform some part of his obligation. A periodic tenancy is considered a form of TENANCY AT WILL [see following] and is created either by express agreement or by implication from the manner in which rent is paid. For example, if A holds B's land with no express time limitation, and rent is paid yearly, it will be deemed a TENANCY FROM YEAR TO

YEAR. Provincial statutes govern the time necessary for due notice to be given. See, e.g., *Residential Tenancies Act*, R.S.N.S. 1989, c. 401, s.10.

from year to year is **alienable.** See A. Sinclair, *supra*, at 26–27.

TENANCY AT SUFFERANCE [HOLDOVER TENANCY] In landlord-tenant law, a tenancy that comes into existence when one at first lawfully possesses **land** as under a **lease** and subsequently holds over beyond the end of one term of such lease or occupies the land without such lawful authority. For example, if A has a TENANCY FOR YEARS [see following] for one month, at the end of that month, if A continues in **possession,** he becomes a tenant at sufferance [or holdover tenant]. Thus a tenancy at sufferance cannot arise from an agreement, which distinguishes it from a TENANCY AT WILL [see following]. A tenant at sufferance differs from a **trespasser** only in that he originally entered with the landlord's permission. The landlord has a right to establish a landlord-tenant relationship (i.e., extend the lease) of a tenant at sufferance. Reciprocally, a tenant cannot be sued for trespass as a tenant at sufferance before the landlord enters and demands possession. A tenant at sufferance cannot grant such an estate to a third person.

TENANCY AT WILL In landlord-tenant law, a leased **estate** that confers upon the tenant the right to **possession** for an indefinite period such as is agreed upon by both **parties.** A tenancy at will is characterized primarily by the uncertain term and the right of either party to terminate upon proper **notice.** A tenancy at will may arise out of an express **contract** or by **implication.** Because a tenancy at will is determinable at any time, the tenant cannot **assign** or **grant** his estate to another.

TENANCY BY THE ENTIRETY The ownership of property, real or personal, **tangible** or **intangible,** by a husband and wife together. In addition to the four unities of time, title, interest, and possession, there is a fifth unity, that of husband and wife. Neither is allowed to **alienate** any part of the property so held without consent of the other, and the survivor of the marriage is entitled to the whole property.

Upon the passage of statutes in all jurisdictions in Canada making a married woman, at law, a femme sole (see, e.g., *Married Women's Property Act*, R.S.N.S. 1989, c. 272), the doctrine has all but disappeared. See A. Sinclair, *supra*, at 58–59.

TENANCY FOR YEARS An estate in land created by a lease and limited to endure for any specified and definite term, whether in weeks, months, or years. It is DETERMINABLE (i.e., it ends) upon expiration of that term and does not require **notice** or **re-entry** by the landlord nor notice to quit by the tenant. However, if the tenant stays on, the tenancy may be converted into a TENANCY AT SUFFERANCE [which see], TENANCY AT WILL [which see] or PERIODIC TENANCY [which see], determinable as tenancies of those kinds. A tenancy for years is **alienable,** subject to lease restrictions against **assignment** or **sublease.** See A. Sinclair, *supra*, at 26.

TENANCY FROM MONTH TO MONTH See PERIODIC TENANCY.

TENANCY FROM YEAR TO YEAR See PERIODIC TENANCY.

TENANCY IN CAPITE *(ĭn kä'-pē-tā)* Lat.: in chief; tenancy-in-chief. In feudal law, the holding of land directly from the Crown.

TENANCY IN COMMON A form of tenancy that "arises when owners have community of possession but distinct and several **titles** to their **shares** which need not necessarily be equal: and there is no right of **survivorship** between owners in common." *R.* v. *Uniacke,* [1944] 3 W.W.R. 323 at 327 (Sask.C.A.).

See generally A. Sinclair, *supra*.

TENANT "[T]he person who, by reason of his **possession** or occupancy or his rights thereto, whether by **priority** of **contract** or **estate,** for the time being holds the premises under **title** immediately or mediately from the landlord or his predecessor in title, and by reason of his so holding is the person liable for the time being to pay the rent. Or, to put it still another way, during the course of the existence of a term of years, the persons who are respectively **landlord** and **tenant** may—one or both—change from time to time, and the enactment refers to the persons who, for the time being, stand in the relationship of landlord and tenant." *Re Calgary Brewing & Malting Co.* (1915), 9 W.W.R. 563 at 565 (Alta.S.C.).

The term may include "sub-tenant and the assigns of the tenant and any person in actual occupation of the premises under or with the assent of the tenant during the currency of the lease, or while the rent is due or in arrear, whether or not he has attorned to or become the tenant of the landlord." *Phalen* v. *Levitt,* [1923] 2 D.L.R. 600 at 602 (Alta.S.C.).

A tenant need not occupy the premises. *Anderson* v. *Scott* (1912), 8 D.L.R. 816 (Alta.S.C.A.D.).

"One who holds of another is a tenant but there is ordinarily associated with a tenancy the idea of the tenant doing, or delivering, or paying something as a symbol of and return for his holding." *Re Burns,* [1924] 1 D.L.R. 721 at 722 (Alta.S.C.).

TENANT IN FEE SIMPLE   A holder of an estate of **freehold,** the most extensive interest a man can have.

A tenant in fee simple has lands, tenements or **hereditaments** to hold to him and his heirs forever, generally, absolutely and simply, without mentioning what heirs, but leaving that to his own pleasure or to the disposition of the law. The word *fee* alone, without any qualifying words, serves to designate a **fee simple estate** and is not infrequently used in that sense.

See also **tenancy.**

TENDER   An unconditional offer to **perform** coupled with a manifested ability to carry out the offer and production of the subject matter (money, etc.), unless such production is waived by the creditor. See *Dunlop* v. *Haney* (1878), 6 B.C.R. 185; *Middleton* v. *Scott* (1902), 4 O.L.R. 459 (Div.Ct.).

Tender is an offer of performance that, if unjustifiably refused, places the refusing party in default and permits the party making tender to exercise his remedy for **breach of contract.**

LEGAL TENDER   An offer of payment in a form the creditor is obliged to accept, e.g., the currency of a country.

TENDER OFFER   A public offer made to **shareholders** of a particular **corporation** to purchase a specific number of shares of **stock** at a specific price. The price quoted in such an **offer** is payable only if the offeror is able to obtain the total amount of stock specified in the offer, usually the number of shares sufficient to give the offeror control of the corporation.

TENEMENT   1. A technical word applicable to all real estate, including offices and dignities that concern land and profits issuing out of land.
2. Strictly, property of a permanent and fixed nature including both **corporeal** and **incorporeal real property. 3.** In modern usage, any house, building, or structure attached to land, and also any kind of human habitation or dwelling inhabited by a **tenant.**

A **servient tenement** is the estate or land over which an **easement** or some other service exists in favour of the **dominant tenement.**

TENURE   Right to hold; manner of holding land or office. **1.** In real property law, since the monarch is absolute owner of land, the possessor is a mere **tenant** and his mode of possession is tenure while the extent of his interest is his **estate.**
2. Tenure refers also to a statutory or **contractual** right of certain public servants and teachers to retain their positions permanently, subject only to removal for adequate cause or economic necessity.

TERM OF COURT   A definite time period prescribed by law for a court to administer its duties. Term and session are often used interchangeably, but, technically, term is the statutory time prescribed for judicial business and session is the time a court actually sits to hear cases. In general, terms of court no longer have any special significance, fixed periods of days having replaced the stated terms of court.

TESTACY   The state or condition of leaving a valid **will** at one's death, as distinguished from **intestacy,** the condition of dying without leaving a will.

TESTAMENT   Strictly, a testimonial or just statement of a person's wishes concerning the disposition of his **personal property** after death, in contrast to a **will,**

which is strictly a **devise** of **real estate.** Commonly, however, will and testament are considered synonymous. The law of testaments is statutory. The word is rarely used today except in the formal heading of one's will, which reads "This is the last will and testament of ..."

TESTAMENTARY Relating to the grant and revocation of the **probate** of **wills** and of administration and incidental matters. *In re McElhinney Estate,* [1929] 3 W.W.R. 664 (Sask.C.A.).

TESTAMENTARY DISPOSITION A **gift** of property that takes effect at the time of the death of the person making the disposition. It can be effected by **deed,** by an **inter vivos** transaction, or by will. All **instruments** used to make testamentary dispositions must comply with the requirements of the **statute of wills.** See **causa** [CAUSA MORTIS].

TESTATOR [TESTATRIX] One who makes and executes a **testament** or **will,** testator applying to a man, testatrix to a woman. See also **intestate; testament; testamentary** [TESTAMENTARY DISPOSITION]. Compare **administrator; executor.**

TESTIMONY A statement made by a **witness,** under oath, usually related to a legal **proceeding** or legislative hearing; **evidence** given by a competent witness, under oath or affirmation, as distinguished from evidence derived from writing and other sources. Evidence is the broader term and includes all testimony, which is one species of evidence. See **expert witness.** See generally *Crown Lumber Co. Ltd.* v. *Hickle,* [1925] 1 W.W.R. 279 (Alta.S.C.A.D.).

THEFT A positive act of acquisition, without consent, by one without title, of another's **property** with an intent to deprive. The *Criminal Code,* R.S.C. 1985, c. C–46, s. 322, states that "[e]very one commits theft who fraudulently and without **colour of right** takes, or converts to his use, or the use of another person, any thing whether animate or inanimate, with intent to deprive, temporarily or absolutely, the owner of it or a person who has a special property or interest in it, of the thing or of his property or interest in it." "A thing cannot be said to be stolen unless it appears that the thing was taken or converted with intent to deprive."

Smith v. *The Queen* (1961), 131 C.C.C. 403 at 409 (S.C.C.). See **larceny.**

THIRD PARTY See **party.**

THIRD-PARTY BENEFICIARY A person recognized as having enforceable rights created in him by a **contract** to which he gives no **consideration.** The third person is a DONEE BENEFICIARY if the **promisee** who buys the promise expresses an intention and purpose to confer a benefit upon the third person as a **gift** in the shape of the promised performance. He is a CREDITOR BENEFICIARY "if the promisee, or some other person, is under an obligation (a duty or a liability) to him and the contract is so made that the promised performance or the making of the **executory** contract itself will discharge that obligation." A. Corbin, *Corbin on Contracts* 727 (1952).

The contract must be primarily for the third person's benefit, so that an incidental beneficiary of a contract would not have sufficient interest under which to enforce the promise.

A third person's interest may be cut off prior to **vesting** by **rescission** between the contracting parties. Once a third person's rights are vested, he may sue the promisor in the event of a **breach.** This prevents the **promisor** from **unjust enrichment** and avoids multiple litigation in the case of a creditor beneficiary. Any defences available to the promisor arising from the contract may be asserted against the beneficiary.

TIDE-LAND Land over which the tide ebbs and flows; land covered and uncovered by ordinary tides. The limit of the tide-land is usually the mean high tide. See also **avulsion; reliction.**

TITHE In old English law, a right of the clergy to extract for the use of the church one tenth of the produce of lands and personal industry of the people. Comparable to rent charges or **ground rents.**

TITLE Ownership. In property law, a term denoting the facts that, if proved, will enable a **plaintiff** to recover **possession** or a **defendant** to retain possession of a thing; the right to possess a thing, but entirely different from **property** in the thing. "One person may hold bare title to property while the whole beneficial ownership rests in some other person." *Hendrickson* v. *Mid-City Motors,* [1951] 3 D.L.R. 276 at 284 (Alta.S.C.).

"I take the word 'title' to mean a **vested** right or title, something to which the right is already acquired, though the enjoyment may be postponed." *O'Dell* v. *Gregory* (1895), 24 S.C.R. 661 at 663.

"The term title means on the one hand the right of ownership and on the other the instrument or evidence of such right." *Re Vancouver Improvement Co.* (1893), 3 B.C.R. 601 at 605 (B.C.S.C.).

ADVERSE TITLE   A title asserted in opposition to another; one claimed to have been acquired by **adverse possession.**

CLEAR TITLE   See **clear title.**

CLEAR TITLE OF RECORD   A title that the **record** shows to be an **indefeasible** unencumbered **estate.** It differs from a CLEAR TITLE in that the latter can be demonstrated by **evidence** independent of the record.

COLOUR OF TITLE   See **colour of title.**

DEFECTIVE TITLE   See **defective title.**

EQUITABLE TITLE   "[T]he right of the party to whom it belongs to have the legal title transferred to him." *Tennant* v. *Rhineland* (1918), 38 D.L.R. 271 at 279 *per* Cameron, J.A. dissenting (Man.C.A.).

Ownership that is recognized by a **court of equity** or founded upon equitable principles, as opposed to formal legal title. The purchaser of real property can specifically enforce his contract for purchase and as a result, prior to the actual **conveyance,** he has an enforceable equitable title, which can be terminated only by a **bona fide purchaser.** See **specific performance.**

GOOD TITLE   See **good title.**

MARKETABLE TITLE   See **marketable title.**

QUIET TITLE   See **quiet title.**

TITLE SEARCH   A search made through the records maintained in the **Registry of Deeds** to determine the state of a **title,** including all **liens, encumbrances, mortgages, future interests,** etc., affecting the property; the means by which a **chain of title** is ascertained.

TORT   "[I]njury; wrong. The **breach** of a **duty** imposed by law, whereby some per-

son acquires a right of action for damages." *Lawson* v. *Wellesley Hospital* (1976), 9 O.R. (2d) 677 at 681 (Ont.C.A.).

"Tort is not a noun which has both a popular meaning and a legal meaning. It only has a legal meaning and is not a word which is used in a popular sense." *Id.* at 681.

"In very general terms, a tort is a civil wrong, other than a breach of contract, which the law will redress by an award of damages." *Id.* at 682, quoting Fleming, *The Law of Torts,* 3d ed.

TORTFEASOR   One who is held liable or admits liability for a **tort.** In statutory construction, the term may include "a person who impliedly assumes or admits liability when he enters into a settlement ... A person does not pay anything in settlement of a claim or of an action unless he feels he is liable or may be held liable in some degree." *Marschler* v. *G. Masser's Garage* (1956), 2 D.L.R. (2d) 484 at 490 (Ont.H.C.).

JOINT TORTFEASORS   See **joint tortfeasors.**

TORTIOUS   Unlawful; an adjective describing conduct that subjects the actor(s) to **tort** liability.

TO WIT   Namely; that is to say.

TRADE FIXTURE   Property placed on or annexed to rented **real estate** by a **tenant** for the purpose of aiding himself in the conduct of a trade or business.

"The term 'trade' has been given a wide significance and seems to cover any calling for the purpose of pecuniary profit provided it is not exclusively agricultural in its nature, and so articles and things for the purpose of carrying on a trade are called trade **fixtures** and are removable by the tenant at the end of his term if the removal will not materially injure the premises." *Coleman* v. *Monahan,* [1927] 2 D.L.R. 209 at 214 (N.B.S.C.A.D.).

TRADEMARK   "... a mark that is used by a person for the purpose of distinguishing or so as to distinguish wares or services manufactured, sold, leased, hired or performed by him from those manufactured, sold, leased, hired or performed by others, (b) a certification mark, (c) a distinguishing guise, or (d) a proposed **trade**

mark." *Trade Marks Act,* R.S.C. 1985, c. T-13, S. 2.

TRADE UNION "[A]n organization of employees formed for purposes that include the regulation of relations between employees and employers and includes a provincial, national, or international trade union, a certified council of trade unions and a designated or certified employee bargaining agency." *Labour Relations Act,* R.S.O. 1990, c. L.2, s. 1(1). See similar provincial statutes and *Canada Labour Code,* R.S.C. 1985, c. L–2.

TRANSFER "[T]he act by which the owner of a thing delivers it to another person, with the intent of passing the rights which he has in it to the latter." *Langley* v. *Kahnert* (1904), 7 O.L.R. 356 at 363 (C.P.D.), quoting *Bouvier's Law Dictionary.*

"As a verb, [transfer] means 'to make over the legal **title** or ownership of to another.' As a noun, it means the making over of such title or ownership." *Re Gill Lumber Ltd. and United Bro. of Carpenters* (1973), 42 D.L.R. (3d) 271 at 274 (N.B.S.C.A.D.).

TRANSFEREE The person to whom something is **transferred.**

TRANSFEROR The person who **transfers.**

TRANSFERRED INTENT A concept in **tort** law that states that if defendant intends harm to A but harms B instead, the intent is said to be transferred to the harm befalling the actual victim, as far as defendant's liability to B in tort is concerned. This is only a "fiction," or a legal conclusion, created in order to accomplish the desired result in terms of liability.

TRAVERSE A **common-law pleading** that denies the opposing party's **allegations** of fact. "[T]he express contradiction of an allegation of fact in an opponent's pleading; it is generally a contradiction in the very terms of the allegation. It is, as a rule, framed in the negative, because the fact which it denies is, as a rule, alleged in the affirmative." D. Casson & I. Dennis, *Odgers' Principles of Pleading and Practice* 131 (1981). See **denial.**

GENERAL TRAVERSE   A blanket denial, stated in general terms, intended to cover all the allegations.

SPECIAL TRAVERSE   A denial that is not absolute, but that seeks to establish a denial through the presentation of supplementary facts that, if accurate, would render the allegations untenable. See **absque hoc; confession and avoidance.**

TREASON An **indictable offence** against the Queen's authority or person punishable by fourteen years' imprisonment or, for high treason, by life imprisonment. See *Criminal Code,* R.S.C. 1985, c. C–46, ss. 46–48.

Treason includes acts in Canada such as (*a*) use of force against a government; (*b*) communication of prejudicial information to a foreign state; (*c*) conspiracy to commit high treason or (*a*) above; (*d*) forms and overtly manifests on intention to commit high treason or (*a*) or (*b*) above.

HIGH TREASON   (*a*) Killing or harming or attempting to kill Her Majesty; (*b*) levying war against Canada or so preparing; or (*c*) assisting an enemy of Canada.

TREATY In **international law,** a compact made between two or more independent nations with a view to the public welfare. "The Statute of the International Court of Justice speaks of 'international conventions, whether general or particular, es-' tablishing rules expressly recognized by the contesting states.' The word 'convention' means a treaty, and that is the only meaning which the word possesses in international law, and in international relations generally." M. Akehurst, *A Modern Introduction to International Law* 23–24 (6th ed. 1987). "Other words used as a synonym for treaties, or for particular types of treaty, are agreement, pact, protocol, charter, **statute,** act, covenant, declaration, engagement, arrangement, accord, **regulations,** provisions. Some of these words have alternative meanings (that is, they can also mean something other than treaties), which makes the problem of terminology even more confusing." *Id.* at 23 fn.

"Contractual engagements between states are called by various names—treaties, conventions, pacts, acts, declarations, protocols. None of these terms has an absolutely fixed meaning; but a treaty suggests the most formal kind of agreement; a convention or a pact generally, but not always, an agreement less formal or less important; an act generally means an agreement resulting from a formal conference and summing up its results; a declaration is generally used of a law-declaring or law-making agreement ... but such agreements are equally often called conventions, e.g., the Hague Conventions; 'protocol' is a word with many meanings in diplomacy, denoting the minutes of the proceedings at an international conference, an agreement of a less formal kind, or often a supplementary or explanatory addendum to another treaty...." J. Brierly, *The Law of Nations* 317 (6th ed. 1963).

"An unconstrained act of independent powers" that, when in conflict with a statute, must follow the statute. *R.* v. *Syliboy,* [1929] 1 D.L.R. 307 at 313 (N.S.Co.Ct.).

"[A] treaty does not confer, as between the State and the subject, or as between subjects, any rights upon the latter, and ... under our constitution such rights can only be conferred by the **common law** of England or by legislative enactment of a duly competent legislature." *Re Arrow River and Tributaries Slide & Boom Co. Ltd.* (1930), 65 O.L.R. 575 at 585 (Ont.H.C.).

TREATY INDIANS "Native Canadians who entered into **treaties** with the Dominion government and who, by certain treaties, gave up certain rights and in return secured certain rights and who usually at the same time received reserves of land, they having given up their right to a larger domain." *R.* v. *Johns* (1961), 36 W.W.R. 403 at 406 (Sask.Q.B.). See **aboriginal rights.**

TREBLE DAMAGES See **damages** [DOUBLE DAMAGES].

TRESPASS 1. "At **common law,** every unauthorized entry upon land in the occupation or **possession** of another. [Any invasion of private **property,**] however minute is a trespass. No man can set foot upon [another's] ground without ... **license,** but he is liable to an action though the damage be nothing." *Sorlie* v. *McKee,* [1927] 1 D.L.R. 249 at 250 (Sask.C.A.).
2. A **form of action** instituted to recover

damages for any unlawful injury to the plaintiff's person, property or rights, involving immediate force or violence. **3.** Also used to signify the act itself that causes such injury. **4.** In modern usage the term most often connotes a wrongful interference with or disturbance of the possession of another and is applied to **personalty** as well as to **realty.**

CONTINUING TRESPASS An invasion of another's rights that is of a more than temporary nature, e.g., the erection of a structure or dumping of rubbish on another's land.

TRESPASS ON THE CASE One of the two early English actions at common law dealing with **torts** (the other being simply trespass). Trespass on the case, or simply "case," afforded remedy against injury to person or property indirectly resulting from the conduct of the defendant. The action of trespass covered only directly resulting injury. "The classic illustration of the difference between trespass and case is that of a log thrown into the highway. A person struck by the log as it fell could maintain trespass against the thrower, since injury was direct; but one who was hurt by stumbling over it as it lay in the road could maintain, not trespass, but an action on the case." W.P. Keeton, *Prosser and Keeton on Torts* 29 (5th ed. 1984).

TRESPASS QUARE CLAUSUM FREGIT *(kwä′-rā klaū′-zūm frā′-gĭt)* Lat.: wherefore he broke the **close.** An early form of trespass to **land;** "consists merely of personal entry by the defendant, or by some other person through his procurement, into land or buildings occupied by another, and is actionable **per se** without any proof of damage. *Sorlie* v. *McKee,* [1927] 1 D.L.R. 249 at 258 (Sask.C.A.).

TRESPASS VI ET ARMIS *(vē ĕt är′-mĭs)* **1.** Trespass with force and arms, or by an unlawful means; **2.** a remedy for injuries accompanied with force or violence, or where the act done is in itself an immediate injury to another person or property.

TRIAL "[T]he examination of a **cause,** civil or **criminal,** before a Judge who has jurisdiction over it, according to the laws of the land." *Dunlop* v. *Haney* (1899), 7 B.C.R. 300 at 302 (B.C.S.C.), quoting

Wharton's Law Dictionary.

"A trial is where the Judge (with the assistance of a jury) has to decide which of two parties is entitled to succeed." *Dunlop* v. *Haney* (1899), 7 B.C.R. 300 at 302.

TRIAL DE NOVO *(dē nō'-vo)* "Strictly ... a new trial before another tribunal than that which held the first trial, as distinguished from a rehearing before the same tribunal." *R.* v. *Rice*, [1930] 3 D.L.R. 911 at 914 (N.S.S.C.).

TRIBUNAL An officer or body having authority to **adjudicate** judicial or **quasi**-judicial matters. See also **forum.**

TRIER OF FACT See **fact finder.**

TROVER An early common-law **tort action** to recover **damages** for a wrongful **conversion** of **personal property** or to recover actual **possession** of such property. Originally, the action was limited to cases in which lost property had been found and converted by the finder to his own use. Later the action was expanded to include property not actually lost and found, but only wrongfully converted. At first, a fiction was created (when the facts revealed otherwise) that such property had been lost and found, but since the distinction was later abandoned, the use of such a fiction became unnecessary. Compare **detinue; replevin; trespass; detainer.**

TRUST A right of **property** held by one party for the benefit of another. It implies two interests, one legal and the other **equitable;** the **trustee** holding the legal title or interest, and the CESTUI QUE TRUST, or **beneficiary,** holding the equitable title or interest.

"The one thing necessary to give validity to a declaration of trust [is] that the donor, or grantor ... should have absolutely parted with that interest which had been his up to the time of the declaration, having effectually changed his right in that respect and put the property out of his power, at least in the way of interest." *In re Garden Estate,* [1931] 2 W.W.R. 849 at 857 (Alta.S.C.).

CESTUI QUE TRUST *(sĕs'-twē kā)* Old Fr.: one for whose benefit the trust is created; a beneficiary.

CONSTRUCTIVE TRUST "[A] constructive trust, apart from resulting trusts, may be defined as one which is not expressed in any instrument, but is imposed upon a person by a court of Equity upon the ground of public policy ... so as to prevent him from holding, for his own benefit, an advantage which he has gained by reason of some fiduciary relation subsisting between him and others, and for whose benefit only it is his duty to act." *Taylor* v. *Davis* (1917), 41 O.L.R. (A.D.). Contrast RESULTING TRUST [following].

EXPRESS TRUST A trust created by the free and deliberate acts of the parties, including an affirmative intention of the **settlor** (the one granting the property) to set up the trust, usually evidenced by some writing, **deed** or **will.** Trusts are generally classified as either express or implied, the latter class including RESULTING TRUSTS and CONSTRUCTIVE TRUSTS. A valid express trust requires the cooperation of three parties: the settlor, the **trustee,** and the beneficiary.

IMPLIED TRUST One that is inferred by **operation of law** from the parties' transactions, in contrast to an EXPRESS TRUST that is created by the parties' deliberate acts and/or expression of intent. Implied trusts may be either CONSTRUCTIVE or RESULTING.

PRECATORY TRUST "[A] trust established by precatory words, such as expressions of confidence, request or desire that property will or shall be applied for the benefit of a definite person or object, where these words are construed in **equity** as imperatively constituting a trust." 38 *Halsbury's Laws of England* (3d ed.) para. 1372.

There are three requisites of a precatory trust: (1) that the words used might be construed upon the whole as imperative, (2) that the subject of the recommendation or wish be certain, and (3) that the objects or persons intended to have the benefit of the recommendation or wish be also certain. The modern trend is to lean against precatory trust and not to construe words in a will, not being words of a strict definite legal character, or words that are beyond all doubt as creating a trust. *Johnson* v. *Farney* (1913), 29

O.L.R. 223 (A.D.).

RESULTING TRUST   A trust arising by implication of law when it appears from the nature of the transaction that it was the intention of the **parties** to create a trust. It is therefore to be distinguished from a constructive trust in that it arises automatically out of certain circumstances by **operation of law,** while a constructive trust is a **remedy** that **equity** applied in order to prevent injustice or in order to do justice. Thus a resulting trust involves the element of **intent,** which though implied, makes it more like an EXPRESS TRUST. A constructive trust, in contrast, is sometimes found contrary to the parties' intent, in order to work equity or frustrate **fraud.**

"The trust of a legal estate taken in the name of any person results to the man who advances the purchase money, but, as this resulting trust arises from an equitable presumption, it may be rebutted by **parol evidence,** showing that it was the intention, at the time of the purchase, of the person who advanced the purchase money that the person to whom the property is conveyed should take for his or her own benefit." *Dudgeon* v. *Dudgeon and Parsons* (1907), 13 B.C.R. 179 at 180 (B.C.S.C.).

TRUSTEE   1. One who holds legal **title** to **property** in **trust** for the benefit of another person, and who is required to carry out specific duties with regard to the property, or who has been given power affecting the disposition of property for another's benefit. **2.** Also used loosely as anyone who acts as a **guardian** or **fiduciary** in relationship to another, such as a **public officer** towards his constituents or a partner to his co-partner. See **use.** Compare **settlor.** Includes **executor** and **administrator.** *Armstrong* v. *McIntyre* (1915), 9 O.W.N. 240 at 241 (Ont.H.C.). See generally *Cape Breton Cold Storage* v. *Rowlings,* [1929] S.C.R. 505.

TRUSTEE IN BANKRUPTCY One appointed to hold in **trust** for a **bankrupt** in accordance with the *Bankruptcy and Insolvency Act,* R.S.C. 1985, c. B-3. ss. 13–41. He takes legal **title** to the property and/or money for equitable distribution among the bankrupt's **creditors.**

TRUST FUND   Real or **personal property** held in **trust** for the benefit of another person; the corpus [**res**] of a trust.

TRUSTOR   One who creates a **trust;** often called the **settlor.**

TRY TITLE   To submit to judicial scrutiny the legitimacy of **title** to property. See also **quiet title.**

ULTRAHAZARDOUS ACTIVITY An uncommon activity giving rise to **strict liability,** which necessarily involves risk of serious harm to the person, land or **chattels** of others and which cannot be eliminated by the exercise of utmost care. For example, blasting is universally recognized as an ultrahazardous activity. It should be noted that strict liability in this context means the duty owed cannot be delegated; e.g., an owner of property who hires an independent **contractor** to perform blasting cannot escape **liability** for damage resulting from the blasting operation.

ULTRA VIRES *(ŭl'-trà vī'-rāz)* Lat.: beyond, outside of, in excess of powers; that which is beyond the power authorized by law for an entity. The term applies, for example, to an action of a **corporation** that is beyond the powers conferred upon it by its charter, or by the **statute** under which it was created. See *Ontario Bank* v. *McAllister* (1910), 43 S.C.R. 338.

The doctrine of ultra vires was also enshrined in the Canadian constitutional system. Under the doctrine, "the *B.N.A. Act* possessed a supremacy over all statutes enacted by the **Parliament** of Canada and by the legislatures of the ten provinces. The result of this was that any Act passed by Parliament or a legislature had to conform to the jurisdictional constraints set out in ss. 91 and 92 of the *B.N.A. Act.*" G. Gall, *The Canadian Legal System* 61 (3d ed. 1990). This doctrine continues in the *Constitution Act, 1867.*

In the field of **administrative law,** "an administrative tribunal may only enact rules or make decisions only within the bounds of the authority granted to it by its governing statute." Action taken outside of its legal jurisdiction could be declared ultra vires by a court of law. *Id.* at 358.

UNCLEAN HANDS One of the equitable maxims embodying the principle that a party seeking equitable **relief** must not have done any dishonest or unethical act in the transaction upon which he maintains an action in **equity;** a court of con-

science will not grant relief to one guilty of **unconscionable** conduct. Compare **clean hands.**

UNCONSCIONABLE In **contract** law, terms so unreasonable to the interest of a contracting party as to render the contract unenforceable.

"It may be apparent from the intrinsic nature and subject of the bargain itself; such as no man in his senses and not under delusion would make on the one hand, and as no honest and fair man would accept on the other; which are unequitable and unconscientious bargains..." *Chesterfield (Earl)* v. *Janssen* (1751), 2 Ves.Sr. 125 at 155; 28 E.R. 82, app'd in *Gronbach* v. *Petty & Solicitor* (1951), 4 W.W.R. (N.S.) 49 at 55 (Man.K.B.).

UNDERLEASE See **sublease.**

UNDERWRITE To insure the satisfaction of an obligation, such as an **insurance** contract or the sale of **bonds.** To underwrite an insurance contract is to act as **insurer** for the life or property of another.

To underwrite a **stock** or bond issue is to insure the sale of stocks or bonds by agreeing that if they are not all taken up by the public, the underwriter will take what remains. See *Montreal Trust Co.* v. *Richardson,* [1922] 1 W.W.R. 548 (S.C.C.).

UNDISCLOSED PRINCIPAL See **principal.**

UNDIVIDED INTEREST [UNDIVIDED RIGHTS] That interest or right in **property** owned by TENANTS IN COMMON (see **tenancy**) or **joint tenants** whereby each tenant has an equal right to make use of and enjoy the entire property.

An undivided interest derives from UNITY OF POSSESSION (see **unities**), which is essential to the above tenancies. Undivided interests in property are to be distinguished from interests that have been **partitioned,** i.e., divided and distributed to the different owners for their use in **severalty.**

An undivided interest may be of only a fractional share, e.g., "an undivided one quarter interest," in which case the holder is entitled to one quarter of all profits and sale proceeds but has a right to possession of the whole.

UNDUE INFLUENCE   1. Influence of another that destroys the requisite free agency of a **testator** or **donor** and creates a ground for nullifying a **will** or invalidating an improvident **gift.** "To be undue influence in the eye of the law there must be ... coercion. It must not be a case in which a person has been induced by means such as I have suggested to you to come to a conclusion that he or she will make a will in a particular person's favour, because if the testator has only been persuaded or induced by considerations which you may condemn, really and truly to intend to give his property to another, though you may disapprove of the act, yet it is strictly legitimate in the sense of its being legal. It is only when the will of the person who becomes a testator is coerced into doing that which he or she does not desire to do, that it is undue influence." *Wingrove* v. *Wingrove* (1885), 11 P. 81 at 82. See also *Pare* v. *Cusson,* [1921] 2 W.W.R. 8 (Man.C.A.); *Hopkins* v. *Hopkins* (1900), 27 O.A.R. 658.

2. Also, influence of another that impedes, prevents or otherwise interferes with the free exercise of the franchise of any voter. *Re MacDonald Election* (1923), 23 Man.R. 542 (C.A.).

"[T]he burden of proof of undue influence is upon the party alleging it...." *National Trust Co.* v. *Taylor* (1922), 68 D.L.R. 339 at 379 (Man.K.B.).

Compare **duress.**

UNEXECUTED USE   See **use.**

UNILATERAL CONTRACT   "Under contracts which are unilateral—one party, whom I will call the **'promisor'** undertakes to do or to refrain from doing something on his part if another party, 'the **promisee**,' does or refrains from doing something, but the promisee does not himself undertake to do or to refrain from doing that thing.... A unilateral contract does not give rise to any immediate obligation on the part of either party to do or to refrain from doing anything except possibly an obligation on the part of the promisor to refrain from putting it out of his power to perform his undertaking in the future. This apart, a unilateral contract may never give rise to any obligation on the part of the promisor; it will only do so upon the occurrence of the event specified in the contract, viz., the doing (or

refraining from doing) by the promisee of a particular thing. But it never gives rise to any obligation upon the promisee to bring about the event by doing or refraining from doing that particular thing." *United Dominions Trust (Commercial) Ltd.* v. *Eagle Aircraft Services Ltd.,* [1968] 1 W.L.R. 74 at 83 (C.A.). App'd *Carlson, Carlson and Hettrick* v. *Big Bud Tractor of Canada Ltd.* (1981), 7 Sask.R. 337 at 351 (C.A.). See **contract.**

UNILATERAL MISTAKE   See **mistake.**

UNION   See **trade union.**

UNITIES   The **common-law** requirements necessary to create a **joint tenancy,** or a TENANCY BY THE ENTIRETY (see **tenancy**). A joint tenancy requires the FOUR UNITIES of **interest, possession,** time, and title, and, in addition, a tenancy by the entirety requires unity of person. See A. Sinclair, *Introduction to Real Property Law* 57–8 (3d ed. 1987). Tenants in common, as a result of the kind of **estate** they hold, have a unity of possession, but no unity is required to create such an interest.

UNITY OF INTEREST   The requirement that interests of the co-tenants in a joint tenancy be equal. An individual joint tenant cannot encumber his share by **mortgage** without destroying this unity; to preserve the joint tenancy the mortgage must be agreed to by all. Tenants in common are not subject to this unity of interest rule and may have unequal shares in the same property. See **tenancy** [TENANCY IN COMMON].

UNITY OF PERSON   The common law requirement for the creation of a tenancy by the entirety that the co-tenants be husband and wife, based on the conception that marriage created a unity of person. "Upon the passage of statutes in all jurisdictions effectively making a married woman, at law, a *femme sole,* the doctrine of tenancy by the entirety had to disappear, for the fifth unity, from a property viewpoint, had gone. While there are one or two cases to the contrary outstanding in Canada, it would appear only correct to say that a conveyance in this country today to A and B will create a tenancy in common in them; whether A and B are husband and wife will be immaterial for this determination. Modern legislation concerning matrimonial property, referred to earlier, will have greater control in the future as well." *Id.* at 59.

UNITY OF POSSESSION   The equal right of each co-owner of property to the **use** and possession of the whole property.

Unity of possession is necessary for each of the types of co-tenancies. See **undivided interest.**

UNITY OF TIME   The requirement that the interests of the co-tenants in a joint tenancy must commence (or **vest**) at the same moment in time.

UNITY OF TITLE   The requirement that all tenants of a joint tenancy acquire their interests under the same **title;** thus such co-tenants cannot hold by different **deeds.**

UNIVERSAL AGENT   One authorized to transact all the business of his **principal.** See **agent.**

UNJUST ENRICHMENT   The modern designation for the older doctrine of QUASI-CONTRACTS (see **quasi**), which are not true contracts, but are obligations created by the law when money, **property** or services have been obtained by one person at the expense of another under such circumstances that in **equity** and good conscience he ought not to retain it. See *Deglman* v. *Guaranty Trust Co.,* [1954] S.C.R. 725.

See also **quantum meruit.**

UNLAWFUL ASSEMBLY   Under s. 63(1) of the *Criminal Code,* R.S.C. 1985, c. C-46, "An unlawful assembly is an assembly of three or more persons who, with intent to carry out any common purpose, assemble in such a manner or so conduct themselves when they are assembled as to cause persons in the neighbourhood of the assembly to fear, on reasonable grounds, that they (*a*) will disturb the peace tumultuously, or (*b*) will by that assembly needlessly and without reasonable cause or provoke other persons to disturb the peace tumultuously."

"The provision of the Code prohibiting unlawful assemblies is for the purpose of drawing the line between a lawful meeting and an assembly, either unlawful in its inception, or which is deemed to have become unlawful either by reason of the action of those assembled, or by reason of the improper action of others having no

sympathy with the objects of the meeting." *Rex* v. *Patterson,* [1931] 3 D.L.R. 267 at 274 (Ont.A.D.).

"It will be seen that to constitute the offence there need be no intention on the part of any member of the assembly to commit an offence but it is the manner in which the assembly conducts itself that brings it within the purview of the section." *Rex* v. *Jones and Sheinin,* [1931] 3 W.W.R. 716 at 720 (Alta.S.C.A.D.).

UNLAWFUL DETAINER   The act of holding **possession** without right, as in the case of a tenant whose lease has expired. See **forcible detainer; tenancy** [TENANCY AT SUFFERANCE].

UNNATURAL ACT [OFFENCE]   See **crime against nature.**

USE   The right to enjoy the benefits flowing from **real** or **personal property.**

Uses, historically, have been created (1) by express provision in a valid **deed;** (2) by implication to the conveyor when **conveyance** is made without **consideration** (called a RESULTING USE); (3) by bargain and sale; (4) by covenant to stand **seised.** Under the **Statute of Uses,** the party in whom a use was created was deemed seised of a like **estate** as he had in the use; hence "A to B for the use of C for life" was operative under the statute to convey to C a life estate. It should be noted that not all uses were converted under the Statute to legal interests or estates. The Statute applied to PASSIVE USES, i.e., instances where the legal titleholder had no obligations with respect to the estate other than to hold title. Thus A to B for the use of C created a passive use that the Statute converted into a legal estate in C. Those not so converted, classified as UN-EXECUTED USES, were a use raised on a non-**freehold estate,** i.e., a **tenancy,** "A to B for 10 years for the use of C;" a USE ON A USE, "A to B for the use of C for life, then to the use of D;" and ACTIVE USES, which constitute the modern **trusts,** i.e., where a person holds legal title but unlike in passive use the legal titleholder has duties and obligations to perform in connection with his holding. Thus A to B to invest for the benefit of C creates an active use, and legal title does not merge with C's use. See C. Moynihan, *Introduction to the Law of Real Property* 199–204 (2d ed. 1988).

An important effect of the *Statute of Uses* was the validation of EXECUTORY INTERESTS (see **interest**), a species of **future interests** that had heretofore been recognized only in equity. Two kinds of executory interests so converted into legal estates were the springing and shifting uses. A SHIFTING USE is a use that arises in derogation of another, i.e., shifts from one beneficiary to another, depending on some future **contingency**. A SPRINGING USE is a use that arises upon the occurrence of a future event and that does not take effect in derogation of any interest other than that which results to the grantor, or remains to him in the meantime. Thus, A to B and his heirs to the use of C and his heirs beginning at some future date creates a legal estate in B, a resulting use for the interim period in A, and a springing use in C when his interest comes into effect. If A conveys property to B for the use of C unless a contingency occurs in which case D should have the use, C obtains an equitable estate but if the contingency occurs then the equitable estate shifts to D, who has a shifting use. "A shifting use is one which cuts short a prior use estate in a person other than the conveyor; a springing use is one which cuts short a use estate in the conveyor." *Id.* at 178.

The term *use* has frequently arisen in the matter of construction of **wills** where, for example, a **testator** gave his widow a **life estate** in his **residue** directing his trustees to "allow her to 'use' so much of it as she may wish during her lifetime." In *Re Claman Estate* (1963), 45 W.W.R. (N.S.) 193 (Sask.Q.B.) it was held that this did not mean that she could if she wished "take over the management of the entire residue." *Id.* at 175–6.

USUFRUCT A right originating in the **civil law** to use and enjoy, independent of ownership, certain advantages, benefits or profits attached to land, produced by, or incidental to it. For example, "The proprietor of **riparian** lands has a right incident to the land, independent of the ownership of the solum of the stream or river, to the flow of water through or by his land in its natural state, and if the stream is polluted or otherwise interfered with, so as to affect this right, by an upper riparian proprietor, the lower riparian proprietor who has suffered damage in law, though not in fact, may maintain an action for an injunction unless the person causing the interference with his right has a prescriptive right to do so." *McKie* v. *The K.V.P. Co. Ltd.*, [1948] 3 D.L.R. 201 at 209 (Ont.H.C.). Other examples of usufructuary rights include such things as the right to light, air, and water "which a man may occupy by means of his windows, his gardens, his mills, and other convenience...." *Id.* at 210.

USURY An unconscionable or exorbitant rate of **interest;** an excessive and illegal requirement of compensation for **forbearance** on a debt [**interest**].

UTTER To put forth; to execute; to offer a forged instrument with representations by words or acts, directly or indirectly, that the instrument is valid; defined in the *Criminal Code,* R.S.C. 1985, c. C–46, s. 448, to include "sell, pay, tender and put off." To utter **counterfeit** money or a coin that is not current are indictable offences relating to currency under ss. 452 and 453 of the *Criminal Code, id.* "The element of deception or dishonesty which, in general, the word 'utter' imports is inherent in the sale of counterfeit money to be circulated as currency since the inevitable consequence is the defrauding of the public...." *Regina* v. *Kelly and Lauzon* (1980), 48 C.C.C. (2d) 560 at 566 (Ont.C.A.).

V

VACATE **1.** To render **void**; to **set aside,** as "to vacate a **judgment.**" See **reversal.** A **pardon** under the *Criminal Records Act,* R.S.C. 1985, c. C–47, s. 5(b), as amended by S.C. 1992, c.22, s.5, "vacates the conviction in respect of which it is granted and . . . removes any disqualification to which the person so convicted is, by reason of the conviction, subject by virtue of the provisions of any Act of **Parliament,** other than section 100 or 259 of the Criminal Code, or of a **regulation** made under an Act of Parliament."

2. To move out; to render vacant as in "vacating **premises.**" See *Fefferman* v. *McCargar,* [1947] 2 W.W.R. 742 (Alta.S.C.), where an order to vacate signified the termination of the relationship of **landlord** and **tenant.**

See **abandonment.**

VAGRANCY A general term for a class of minor offences such as idleness without employment, having no visible means of support; roaming or **loitering;** wandering from place to place without any lawful purpose. Vagrancy statutes developed following the breaking of the English feudal estates. The downfall of the feudal system led to labour shortages. The *Statutes of Laborers,* 23 Edw. 3, c. 1 (1349); 25 Edw. 3, c. 1. (1350) were enacted to stabilize the working force by prohibiting increases in wages and prohibiting the movement of workers in search of improved conditions. Later, the poor laws included vagrancy provisions to prevent the movement of "wild rogues" and the "notorious brotherhood of beggars." See *Ledwith* v. *Roberts,* [1937] 1 K.B. 232 at 271. Vagrancy is now restricted to two offences under s. 179(1)(*a*) and (*b*) of the *Criminal Code,* R.S.C. 1985, c. C–46: supporting oneself in whole or in part by gaming or crime, having no lawful profession or calling; and (having been convicted of certain specified offences) being found loitering in or near a school ground, playground, public park or bathing area.

VALUABLE CONSIDERATION See **consideration.**

VARIANCE **1.** A lack of concordance between **allegations** contained in the **pleadings** and facts sought to be proven at trial. The court has it in its discretion, according to the desirability of doing justice to the parties, to allow amendment of the pleadings to incorporate allegation of the new fact. See G. Watson, *Canadian Civil Procedure* 6, 379ff. (3d ed. 1988). See *Sullivan* v. *Hoppmann Bros. Ltd.,* [1968] 2 O.R. 201 (H.C.).

2. In **zoning** law, it is an exemption from the application of a zoning ordinance or **regulation** permitting a use that varies from that otherwise permitted under the zoning regulation. The exception is granted by the appropriate authority in special circumstances to protect against an undue hardship wrought by strict enforcement of the zoning regulations. See **non-conforming use.**

VEL NON *(vĕl nŏn)* Lat.: or not. "The question of his being guilty, *vel non,* is for the **jury** to determine."

VENDEE Buyer; **purchaser,** especially in a **contract** for the **sale** of **realty.**

VENDOR Seller; especially person who sells **real property.** The word seller is used more often to describe a **personal property** transaction. See *R.* v. *Thomas Equipment Ltd.* (1979), 10 Alta.L.R. (2d) 1 (S.C.C.); *Cairns Construction Ltd.* v. *Government of Saskatchewan* (1960), 24 D.L.R. (2d) 1 (S.C.C.).

VENIRE *(vĕ-nē′-rā)* Lat.: to come. Refers to the common-law process by which jurors are summoned to try a case.

VENIRE DE NOVO *(dā nō′-vō)* Lat.: to come anew. "[A] **writ** issued by the Court of King's Bench when moved by a writ of error (i.e., alleging an error appearing on the face of the record of an inferior court), vacating the verdict and directing the sheriff to summon jurors anew (whence the name of the writ). Writ of error in **criminal** cases was abolished in England by the *Criminal Appeal Act* 1907, s. 20. *Venire de novo* was and still is available in some other circumstances ... its scope is highly technical." *D.P.P. of Jamaica* v. *White,* [1977] 3 All E.R. 1003 at 1007 (P.C.).

VENUE A neighbourhood, a neighbouring place; sometimes synonymous with place of trial. In general, it refers to a place or area where something is done or takes place. Venue may refer to the place of trial or the place where an alleged crime is said to have been committed, depending on the interpretation of relevant statutory provisions. *Rex* v. *Dunn*, [1945] 2 W.W.R. 495 (B.C.C.A.). At common law, "the accused had the right to be tried in the county where the offence was alleged to have been committed." *Id.* at 497. A statement of venue in a charge of conspiracy alleged the place at which the conspiracy was entered into. *R.* v. *Annunziello*, [1949] 1 W.W.R. 27 (B.C.C.A.).

VERDICT The opinion in either civil or criminal proceedings of a **jury,** or of a judge sitting as a jury, on a question of fact. A verdict differs from a **judgment** in that a verdict is not a judicial determination, but rather a finding of fact, such as a finding of the guilt or innocence of the accused, or a finding that the accused is competent to stand trial. See, e.g., *Morgantaler* v. *The Queen* (1975), 30 C.R. (N.S.) 209 (S.C.C.); *Rex* v. *Murray and Fairbairn* (1913), 27 O.L.R. 382 (C.A.).

DIRECTED VERDICT See **directed verdict.**

GENERAL VERDICT An ordinary verdict declaring simply which party prevails, or in a criminal case, a determination as to the guilt or innocence of the accused. "In the general verdict the jury found for one party or the other and if for the plaintiff (in personal actions) the amount of damages." *Rowan* v. *Toronto R.W. Co.* (1918), 43 O.L.R. 164 at 177 (A.D.).

SPECIAL VERDICT One rendered on certain specific factual issues posed by the courts. "For example, on a trial for publishing a defamatory libel the judge may give to the jury a direction or opinion on the matter in issue and they may find a special verdict on the issue. Again, where it is found that the accused committed the act but was at the time suffering from mental disorder so as to be exempt from criminal responsibility by virtue of s. 16(1), the jury are required to state in their verdict that the accused "committed the act or made the omission but is not criminally responsible on account of mental disorder." [Citing *Criminal Code*, R.S.C. 1985, c. C–46, ss. 317, 672.34.] R. Sal-

hany, *Canadian Criminal Procedure* 6 at 136 (6th ed. 1994). See *Rowan* v. *Toronto R.W. Co.* (1918), 43 O.L.R. 164 at 177 (A.D.).

VERIFICATION Confirmation of the correctness, truth, or authenticity of a **pleading** of other paper **affidavit,** oath, or **deposition.**

VESTED Fixed, accrued, or absolute; not contingent; generally used to describe any right or **title** to something that is not dependent upon the occurrence or failure to occur of some specified future event (**condition** precedent). Although sometimes used to refer to an immediate possessory **interest** in property, the more technically proper definition comprehends as well interests that will only become rights to actual **possession** of property at some later time [**in futuro**]. Originally applied in reference to estates in **real property,** it has come to be applied to other property interests, e.g., **personal property, trust.** Compare **contingent.**

VESTED ESTATE A property **interest** that will necessarily come into **possession** in the future merely upon the DETERMINATION (end) of the **preceding estate.** Thus for there to be a vested estate there must exist a known person who would have an immediate right to possession upon the expiration of the prior estate.

"When an estate commences or takes effect, it is said to be vested, the word vest being derived from the old French *vestir* and the Latin *vestire,* to clothe, that is, to clothe with a right. Therefore, a condition precedent is one to be performed before an estate can vest and a condition subsequent is one to be performed after it has vested. It is not necessary that the estate be in possession, for an interest can vest in right before it comes into possession and the event to which a condition subsequent refers need not be a **remainder** ... (*Cunliffe* v. *Brancker* (1876), 3 Ch.D. 393, (C.A.); *White* v. *Summers,* [1908] 2 Ch. 256, (265)." 1 A.H. Oosterhoff & W.B Rayner, *Anger and Honsberger: Law of Real Property* 301ff. (2d ed. 1985).

VESTED INTEREST See **interest.**

VESTED REMAINDER See **remainder.**

VESTED RIGHTS A right that has become so fixed that it is not subject to being divested without consent of the owner.

VEXATIOUS LITIGATION Civil action instituted for an ulterior motive other than to enforce a true legal claim or maliciously and without **probable cause.** See *Guilford Industries Ltd.* v. *Hankinson Management Services Ltd.* (1973), 40 D.L.R. (3d) 398 (B.C.S.C.); *Jones* v. *Swift Canadian Co.* (1922), 68 D.L.R. 751 (Man.K.B.). See **litigious; malicious prosecution.**

VICARIOUS LIABILITY The imputed responsibility of one person for the acts of another; occurs "when the law holds one person responsible for the misconduct of another, although he is himself free from personal blameworthiness or fault. It is therefore an instance of strict (no fault) liability." J. Fleming, *The Law of Torts* 366 (8th ed. 1992).

In tort law, if an employee, EE, while in the **scope of his employment** for employer, ER, drives a delivery truck, and hits and injures P crossing the street, ER will be vicariously liable, under the doctrine of **respondeat superior**, for injuries sustained by P. In criminal law, while **prima facie** a principal is not criminally responsible for the acts of his servants, **Parliament** or a **legislature** may make a prohibition or duty absolute, in which case the **principal** is liable even if, in fact, the act is done by his servants. See, e.g., *Allen* v. *Whitehead*, [1930] 1 K.B. 211. Compare **strict liability.**

VICINAGE Neighbourhood; vicinity. Its contemporary meaning denotes a particular area where a crime was committed, where a **trial** is being held or from which **jurors** are called.

VICTIM IMPACT STATEMENT A written statement from the victim of an **offence** describing "the harm done to, or loss suffered by, the victim arising from the commission of an offence." The statement may be included as evidence for use in determining the sentence imposed on the convicted offender. *Criminal Code,* R.S.C. 1985, c. C–46, s. 735.

VIDELICET *(vĭ-dĕl'-ĭ-sĕt)* Lat.: that is to say. See **viz.**

VI ET ARMIS *(vē ĕt är'-mĭs)* Lat.: by force and by arms. See **trespass** [TRESPASS VI ET ARMIS].

VILLEIN SOCAGE See **socage.**

VILLENAGE A menial form of feudal **tenure** in which the **tenant** [the VILLEIN] was required to perform all **services** demanded by the lord of the manor.

VIS MAJOR *(vĭz mä-yôr')* Lat.: a greater force, superior force. Used in civil law to mean an **act of God** and has reference to "every event which the prudence of man cannot foresee and which cannot be resisted when it is foreseen." See *Watt & Scott Ltd.* v. *City of Montreal* (1920), 60 S.C.R. 523 at 543 (S.C.C.). The term is synonymous with FORCE MAJEURE. *Id.*

"The decisions make it clear that it is a **question of fact** whether an occurrence of nature is so phenomenal or of such a magnitude as not to be reasonably foreseen and guarded against, the capacity to foresee being based on previous experience and knowledge of nature's law." See *Low* v. *C.P.R.,* [1949] 2 W.W.R. 433 at 453 (Alta.S.C.) app'd in *Frache* v *City of Lethbridge* (1954), 13 W.W.R (N.S.) 609 at 615 (Alta.S C.).

It is not necessary to sustain a plea of *vis major* that such an event should never have happened before. *Bénard* v. *Hingston* (1918), 39 D.L.R. 137 (S.C.C.).

VITIATE To void; to render a nullity; to impair.

VIVA VOCE *(vē'-vă vō'-chā)* Lat.: with the living voice; orally.

VIZ. Abbreviated form of the Latin word **videlicet,** meaning *namely, that is to say.* A term used in **pleadings** to particularize or explain what goes before it.

VOID Empty, having no legal force, ineffectual, unenforceable; incapable of being ratified. For example, a person declared **incompetent** loses all power to deal with his property, and any **instrument** he makes is void. *In re Marshall, Marshall* v. *Whateley,* [1920] 1 Ch. 284. A **contract** that is void "is without legal effect. . . ." G. Fridman, *The Law of Contract* 321 (2d ed. 1986). Certain contracts made by **infants** may be void on the basis of illegality, on the basis of lack of capacity to contract, by reason of the operation of **mistake** in contracting, etc. *Id.* at 128ff. Compare **voidable.**

VOIDABLE Capable of being later annulled; a valid act that, though it may be avoided, may accomplish the thing sought to be accomplished until the fatal defect in the transaction has been effectively asserted or judiciously ascertained and declared. For example, certain **contracts** made by infants "may be avoided or enforced at the option of the infant...." See *Rex* v. *Rash* (1927), 53 O.L.R. 245 at 256 (A.D.). "Contracts ... by which the infant undertakes to pay for goods supplied to him for use in trade are of this class...." *Id.* A contract made by a person when he is extremely intoxicated is voidable, and the contracting party may, if he takes prompt action, disaffirm the contract upon regaining sobriety. *Bawlf Grain Co.* v. *Ross* (1917), 37 D.L.R. 620 (S.C.C.).

VOIR DIRE *(vwär dēr)* Fr.: to speak the truth. **1.** A VOIR DIRE EXAMINATION may refer to a preliminary examination of a witness by the court requiring him "to speak the truth" with respect to questions put to him. **2.** A *voir dire* examination during a trial refers to a **hearing** out of the presence of the **jury** by the court upon some issue of fact or law that requires an initial determination by the court or upon which the court must rule as a matter of law alone. For example, if the prosecution seeks to admit a **confession** of the **accused,** the court must conduct a *voir dire* examination to determine if the statements were obtained. voluntarily. This determination must be made at least initially by the court before the jury is permitted to hear the confession.

VOLENTI NON FIT INJURIA *(vō-lĕn'-tē nŏn fĕt ĭn-jū'-rē-à)* Lat.: the volunteer suffers no wrong; no legal wrong is done to him who consents. In **torts,** a defence asserting that the plaintiff consented to the damage done or, in full knowledge of the nature and extent of the risk he was running, elected to take that risk. See, e.g., *MacGregor* v. *C.N.R. & Edmonton,* [1931] 1 D.L.R. 87 (Alta.S.C.A.D.); *Fred A. Campbell* v. *Regal Oil & Refining Co.,* [1936] S.C.R. 309.

VOLUNTARY WASTE See **waste.**

VOTING TRUST The accumulation in a single hand, or in a few hands, of **shares** of corporate **stock** belonging to many owners in order thereby to control the business of the **company.**

"Under the voting trust agreement the parties gave up a **property** right—the right to vote their shares as they saw fit at meetings of shareholders of the Company—and placed that property under the control of the majority. The property right created by the agreement was the right of the majority to vote the shares at the meeting of shareholders of the Company.... Under the voting **trust agreement** the parties had an obligation to act in good faith and make their decision at a meeting." *Field* v. *Bachynski* (1977), 1 Alta.R. 491 at 508, 510 (Alta.S.C.A.D.).

W

WAIVER The "act of waiving, or not insisting on some right, claim or privilege, a foregoing or giving up of some advantage," *Ross* v. *Imperial Life Assurance Co. Ltd.*, [1929] 1 D.L.R. 324 at 328 (Alta.S.C.A.D.); "an intentional relinquishment of a known right, or such conduct as warrants an inference of the relinquishment or waiver of such right; waiver involves both knowledge and intention." *Crump* v. *McNeill* (1918), 14 Alta.L.R. 206 at 211 (Alta.S.C.). Waiver "implies an intention to go on with an agreement while tacitly or expressly foregoing, i.e., not insisting upon, some condition thereof which prior thereto should have been fulfilled by the other party." *Hollister* v. *Porchet*, [1922] 1 W.W.R. 30, per Stuart, J.A. at 35 (Alta.S.C.A.D.). Also in *Hollister* v. *Porchet, id.* at 44, Hyndman, J.A. noted: "A clear and unequivocal intention must be shown on the evidence." Thus waiver will not be inferred from silence.

It has been claimed that the "so called 'waiver' " is in reality a branch of **estoppel.** *Teasdall* v. *Sun Life Assurance Co. of Canada*, [1927] 2 D.L.R. 502 at 509 (Ont.S.C.A.D.).

WANT OF CONSIDERATION See **consideration.**

WANTON Grossly **negligent** or careless; extremely **reckless.** " 'Wantonness' is perhaps a subclass of recklessness. It is a wild, mad or arrogant kind of recklessness and thus closely related to 'wilfulness.' " *R.* v. *Walker* (1974), 8 N.S.R. (2d) 300 at 306 (N.S.S.C.A.D.). Also, "conduct which [indicates] reckless indifference of consequences." *Regina* v. *Moroz*, [1972] 2 W.W.R. 307 at 316 (Alta.S.C.A.D.).

It is clearly wrong to define wanton conduct as "inhuman, merciless or malicious." *R.* v. *Knowlton* (1973), 5 Nfld. & P.E.I R. 209 at 211 (Nfld.S.C.A.D.).

To act wantonly is "to wander from moral rectitude and to do an act licentiously and dissolutely, unrestrained by law or morality, intentionally and without excuse." *R.* v. *Goodman* (1951), 99 C.C.C. 366 at 371 (B.C.C.A.).

WARRANT A written **order** directing the **arrest** of a person or persons, issued by a court, body or official having authority to issue warrants of arrest (see also **bench warrant**); also a **writ** from a competent authority directing the doing of a certain act.

SEARCH WARRANT An order that certain premises or property be searched for particularized items that if found are to be seized and used as **evidence** in a criminal **trial** or destroyed as contraband. See **search warrant.**

WARRANT OF COMMITTAL Section 734 of the *Criminal Code*, R.S.C. 1985, c. C–46 provides: "A **peace officer** or other person to whom a warrant of committal authorized by this or any other Act of Parliament is directed shall arrest the person named or described therein, if it is necessary to do so in order to take that person into custody, convey that person to the prison mentioned in the warrant and deliver him, together with the warrant, to the keeper of the prison..." See *Re Rombough's Detention* (1963), 43 W.W.R. 287 (Alta. S.C.).

The word *warrant* is also used in commercial and property law to refer to a particular kind of guarantee or assurance creating an express **warranty** as to the quality and validity of what is being conveyed. See **guarantee;** merchantable; **warranty.**

WARRANTY An assurance by one **party** to a **contract** of the existence of a fact upon which the other party may rely, intended precisely to relieve the **promisee** of any duty to ascertain the fact for himself; amounts to a **promise** to **indemnify** the promisee for any loss if the fact warranted proves untrue. Such warranties are made either overtly (EXPRESS WARRANTIES) or by implication (IMPLIED WARRANTIES).

A warranty is term of a contract that is collateral to the main purpose of the contract, i.e., that is not so vital as to effect a discharge of the contract, if the circumstances are or become inconsistent with it. *Wallis* v. *Pratt*, [1910] 2 K.B. 1003 at 1012 (C.A). Whether a term of a contract is a **condition** or a warranty depends upon the intention of the parties at the time of making the contract. *Heilbut, Symons & Co.* v. *Buckleton*, [1913] A.C. 30 (H.L.). The distinction between a condition and a warranty has found statutory codifiction in the various provincial statutes dealing with the sale of goods. For example, the *Sale of Goods Act,* R.S.O. 1990, c. S.1, s. 12(2), states: "Whether a stipulation in a contract of sale is a condition the breach of which may give rise to a right to treat the contract as repudiated, or a warranty, the breach of which may give rise to a claim for damages but not to a right to reject the goods and treat the contract as repudiated, depends in each case on the construction of the contract and a stipulation may be a condition, though called a warranty in the contract."

See further G. Fridman, *The Law of Contract* 460ff. (2d ed. 1986).

WARRANTY DEED The terms or clause in a deed that forms a **covenant running with the land,** insuring the continuing validity of **title,** the **breach** of which occurs at the time of **conveyance** and gives rise to an action by the last **vendee** against the first or any other warrantor. Compare **quitclaim deed.**

WARRANTY OF FITNESS A warranty that goods are suitable for the special purpose of the buyer. When goods are ordered for a particular purpose known to the vendor, the law implies a warranty by the vendor that they shall be fit for that purpose. *William Hamilton Mfg. Co.* v. *Victoria Lumber & Mfg. Co.* (1895), 4 B.C.R. 101 (C.A.).

WARRANTY OF HABITABILITY [More properly, an implied or express COVENANT OF HABITABILITY] A promise by a landlord that at the inception of the lease there are no **latent defects** in facilities vital to the use of premises for residential purposes, and that these facilities will remain in usable condition during the duration of the lease.

WARRANTY OF MERCHANTABILITY A warranty that the goods are reasonably fit for the general purposes for which they are sold.

WASTE Generally, an act, by one in rightful **possession** of land who has less than a **fee simple** interest in the land, which decreases the value of the land or the owner's **interest** or the interest of one who has an **estate** that may become possessory at some future time (such as a **remainderman, lessor, mortgagee, rever-**

sioner). "'Waste' is a spoil or destruction in houses, gardens, trees or other corporeal **hereditaments** to the disherison [**disheritance**] of him in **remainder** or **reversion,** etc., or to the prejudice of the **heir** or reversioner." *Drake* v. *Wigle* (1874), 24 U.C.C.P. 405 at 413.

"Waste seems to me to be an expression necessarily bearing upon an actual injury to the estate of the reversioner, as ... by diminishing the value, increasing the burden, or impairing the evidence of title." *Id.* at 414.

"The holder of an estate in fee simple has, as an incident of his estate, the right to exercise acts of ownership of all kinds, including the commission of 'waste,' such as felling trees, mining and pulling down buildings. Even when his estate comes to an end with an executory gift over, he is not impeachable for waste ... although . . . he is in the same position as a life tenant without impeachment for waste and may not commit 'equitable' waste, that is, **wanton** or malicious acts, such as destruction of houses or felling of trees left for ornament or shelter." 1 A.H. Oosterhoff & W.B Rayner, *Anger and Honsberger: Law of Real Property* 122 (2d ed. 1985).

AMELIORATING WASTE A change in "the character of the property is, technically waste. Ameliorating waste is that which results in benefit and not in an injury, so that it in fact improves the inheritance . . . Unless the character of the property is completely changed, it is unlikely that a court will award **damages** or grant an **injunction** for ameliorating waste as between a life tenant and a remainderman." *Id.* at 168.

EQUITABLE WASTE A "wanton, malicious or unconscientious destruction, such as of houses or trees planted or left for purposes of ornament or shelter. It is called equitable waste because, although it is voluntary waste, courts of **equity** would not allow it to be committed even by a tenant "who held 'without impeachment for waste.'" *Id.* at 172.

PERMISSIVE WASTE Injury to the inheritance caused by an act of omission or neglect of the tenant "such as allowing buildings to fall down or become dilapidated." *Id.* at 172. "Permissive waste can arise only in the case of an omission by the tenant to do some act which would prevent injury to the property, its very existence must depend upon his **negligence,** for manifestly a tenant would not be chargeable with the omission to do an act, for the performance of which he was in no way bound." *Cherry v. Smith,* [1933] 1 W.W.R. 205 at 211 (Sask.Dist.Ct.).

VOLUNTARY WASTE "[T]he commission of an act which is injurious to the inheritance or to those entitled in **remainder or reversion,** either (*a*) by diminishing the value of the **estate,** such as by felling trees, mining or destroying buildings or gardens, or (*b*) by increasing the burden on it, or (*c*) by impairing the evidence of title." A.H. Oosterhoff & W.B. Rayner, *supra* at 168. "Generally speaking . . . it seems . . . that the result of [the] authorities is that, any damage to the freehold or inheritance, which is the natural and probable consequence of some improper and positive act of the tenant, is voluntary waste, and it is immaterial, whether or not such act be negligent, since 'voluntary waste' could as easily flow from a negligent act." *Cherry* v. *Smith,* [1933] 1 W.W.R. 205 at 211 (Sask.Dist.Ct.).

WEIGHT OF THE EVIDENCE The relative value of the totality of **evidence** presented on one side of a judicial dispute, in light of the evidence presented on the other side; refers to the persuasiveness of the testimony of the **witnesses.** See **against the [manifest] [weight of the] evidence; burden of proof.** "The judge in weighing the evidence ... must ... decide whether it is admissible in accordance with the rules of common law ... he then must weigh it; if he decides, on the balance of probabilities, that to exclude the evidence on the particular issue would prevent the making of a just determination, he should allow it....In weighing the evidence, the judge should apply the ... standard ... proof on a preponderance of the evidence or a balance of probabilities...." *R.* v. *Moulton* (1979), 13 C.R. (3d) 143 at 160 (Alta.C.A.).

WESTMINSTER, STATUTE OF See **Statute of Westminster.**

WHIPLASH INJURY Neck injury commonly associated with rear-end-type au-

tomobile collisions; caused by a sudden and unexpected forced forward movement of the body while the unsupported head of an automobile occupant attempts to remain stationary consistent with the law of physics, subjecting the neck to a severe strain while in a relaxed position. It is a frequent claim in **tort** actions arising from such collisions.

Soft tissue damage to the neck. *O'Bray* v. *John Doe and Administrator of Motor Vehicle Accident Claims Act* (1978), 5 Alta.L.R. (2d) 286 (Alta.S.C.).

WHOLESALER Middleman; a person who buys large quantities of goods and resells to other distributors rather than to ultimate consumers; one who deals with the trade who buy to sell again, while the retail trader deals direct with the consumer. Compare **jobber.**

WILD'S CASE, RULE IN See **Rule in Wild's Case.**

WILL A person's declaration of how he desires his **property** to be disposed of after his death, which declaration is revocable during his lifetime, operative for no purpose until death, and applicable to the situation that exists at his death. A will may also contain other declarations of the **testator's** desires as to what is to be done after he dies but it must dispose of some property. See 1 T. Feeney, *The Canadian Law of Wills: Probate* (3d ed. 1987), chap. 1.

The difference between a will and a **deed** is that, by means of a deed, a present **interest** passes on **delivery,** while a will takes effect only upon the death of the testator. Will is generally used as synonymous with **testament,** but the latter is technically confined to the disposition of **personal property.** LAST WILL AND TESTAMENT is an expression commonly used to refer to the most recent document directing the disposition of the real and personal property of the party. See **causa** [CAUSA MORTIS]; **codicil; living will.** Compare **gift; testamentary** [TESTAMENTARY DISPOSITION].

WILLFUL [WILFUL] "[A]s used in courts of law, [willful] implies ... that the person of whose action or default the expression is used, is a free agent, and that what has been done arises from the spontaneous action of his will." *In re Young* *and Harston's Contract* (1886), 31 Ch.D. 168 at 174 (C.A.).

"Generally in penal statutes the word 'wilful' or 'wilfully' means something more than a voluntary or intentional act; it includes the idea of an action intentionally done with a bad motive or purpose, or as it is otherwise expressed 'with an evil intent.' " *Anderson and Eddy* v. *Canadian Northern Ry. Co.* (1917), 35 D.L.R. 473 at 480 (Sask.S.C.).

"The word 'willfully' has not been uniformly interpreted and its meaning to some extent depends upon the context in which it is used. Its primary meaning is 'intentionally', but it is also used to mean 'recklessly'." *R.* v. *Buzzanga & Durocher* (1979), 49 C.C.C. (2d) 369 at 379 (Ont.C.A.). See also *R.* v. *Muma* (1989), 51 C.C.C. (3d) 85 (Ont.C.A.).

WINDING UP The process of **liquidating** a corporation. The **assets** of the enterprise are used to discharge liabilities, and the resulting net assets are distributed to the **shareholders** on a **pro rata** basis, according to preference.

The term *winding up* usually refers to the procedures carried out by a liquidator, but the courts have used it to describe discontinuance of a business as well. *Merritt* v. *M.N.R.*, [1940–41] C.T.C. 226 (Ex.Ct.).; *Kennedy* v. *M.N.R.*, [1972] C.T.C. 429 (F.).

Liquidation procedures are usually prescribed and regulated by statute, e.g., the *Winding-up Act*, R.S.C. 1985, c. W–11.

WITHDRAW[AL] To remove; to take back. When a **charge** is withdrawn, the judicial process ceases to operate and the issue is removed from the **consideration** of the courts. A **stay** merely suspends proceedings, whereas the withdrawal of a charge ends them.

A provincial attorney-general, in withdrawing a charge, is exercising a judicial discretion in his capacity as chief law enforcement officer, with which discretion the courts are most reluctant to interfere. *Regina ex rel. Graham* v. *Leonard* (1962), 38 W.W.R. 300 (Alta.S.C.).

"When a charge has been withdrawn there is no charge on the record and in order to continue a prosecution a new charge would have to be laid. Withdrawing the charge has the effect of ending the **proceedings**." *Id.* at 303.

WITHOUT PREJUDICE A phrase that may have the effect of excluding from evidence the documents upon which it is written. "The claim of privilege for correspondence written without prejudice is applicable only to correspondence containing offers of compromise or respecting **bona fide** negotiations entered into for the settlement of disputes." *Sherren* v. *Boudreau* (1973), 6 N.B.R. (2d) 701 at 703 (N.B.S.C.A.D.).

"All communications expressed to be written without prejudice, and fairly made for the purposes of expressing the writer's view on the matter of litigation or dispute, as well as overtures for settlement or compromise, and which are not made with some other object in view and wrong motives are not admissible in evidence." *Pirie* v. *Wyld* (1886), 11 O.R. 422 at 429 (Common Pleas Div.).

WITNESS One who gives evidence in a cause before a court and who **attests** or swears to facts or gives or bears **testimony** under oath. Witness is defined in s. 118 of the *Criminal Code*, R.S.C. 1985, c.C-46 as "a person who gives **evidence** orally under **oath** or by **affidavit** in a judicial **proceeding,** whether or not he is competent to be a witness, and includes a child of tender years who gives evidence but does not give it under oath, because, in the opinion of the person presiding, the child does not understand the nature of an oath." See also *Canada Evidence Act,* R.S.C. 1985, c. C-5, ss. 3–16.

ADVERSE [HOSTILE] WITNESS One who has exhibited such a hostile animus towards the party calling him as to reveal a desire not to tell the truth. *Rex* v. *Marceniuk,* [1923] 3 W.W.R. 758 (Alta.S.C.A.D.).

WORDS OF ART Words that have a particular meaning in a particular area of study; e.g., in law, **last clear chance,** PROMISSORY ESTOPPEL (see **estoppel**), and **reliance** are all words of art, because they have either no meaning or different meanings outside a legal context.

WORDS OF LIMITATION Words used in an **instrument** conveying an **interest** in **property** that seem to indicate the party to whom a **conveyance** is made, but that actually indicate the type of **estate** taken by the **grantee;** e.g., in a conveyance from A "to B and his heirs," "and his heirs" are words of limitation, in that they de-limit the estate taken by B, namely, a **fee simple;** and since a fee simple vests in B an absolute power to **alienate** the fee, B is under no obligation to give his heirs any-thing.

"Following upon the Conveyancing and Law of Property Act, 1881, the sev-eral provinces passed statutes which gen-erally provide that in a deed it is not necessary to use the word 'heirs' to convey a fee simple but the words 'in fee simple' may be used, or other words sufficiently indicating the intention, and, further-more, if no words of limitation are used, a deed can pass all the estate or interest held by the grantor unless a contrary in-tention appears in the **deed** [Canadian provincial legislation cited]." 1 A.H. Oos-terhoff & W.B. Rayner, *Anger and Honsberger: Law of Real Property* 102 (2d ed. 1985). See generally *id.,* chaps. 5 & 6.

On the other hand, WORDS OF PUR-CHASE are those that indicate the grantees or persons who take, as they would seem to indicate; hence, in the preceding exam-ple, "to B" are words of purchase.

In *Re Bostock,* [1921] 2 Ch. 469 at 490 (C.A.), it was held: "An absolute estate can only be conferred by the use of the word 'heirs' or since the Conveyancing Act, 1881—but not before—by the addi-tion of the words 'in fee simple.' "

WORKERS' COMPENSATION ACTS (WORKMEN'S COMPENSATION) Stat-utes that in general establish the liability of an employer for injuries that arise out of and in the course of employment, e.g., the *Workers' Compensation Act,* R.S.O. 1990, c. W.11. In Canada, agencies known as workers' compensation boards have been created in every jurisdiction.

"Workers' compensation boards are public bodies created by statute. Em-ployers and employees governed by the scheme are required to participate. As the title suggests, workers' compensation is an activity-specific scheme which provides compensation for personal injuries that occur in the course of employment. Minor injuries are excluded from most schemes by a requirement that the employee must be disabled beyond the day of the acci-dent in order to make a claim. In part, the Canadian schemes are 'pure' no-fault, because the legislation prohibits the em-ployee from suing his employer in **tort.** The employee, however, has the option of either claiming from the fund or bring-ing a tort action against a person other than his employer. Nevertheless, the vast majority of work-related accident claims are dealt with by workers' compensation boards and not courts." R. Solomon, B. Feldthusen, & S. Mills, *Cases and Mate-rials on the Law of Torts* 524–25 (3d ed. 1991).

"The **damages** payable under workers' compensation schemes differ significantly from those awarded in **negligence.** For ex-ample, there is no recovery for pain and suffering or loss of amenities." *Id.* at 525.

See, e.g., *Kinney* v. *Workmen's Com-pensation Board* (1972), 4 N.B.R. (2d) 705 (N.B.S.C.A.D.); *Workmen's Com-pensation Board* v. *Pelletier* (1973), 5 N.B.R. (2d) 283 (N.B.Q.B.).

WORTHIER TITLE, DOCTRINE OF The rule that "where a **testator** (or **grantor**) **devises** (or **grants**) a **life estate** to a person and in the same instrument limits a **re-mainder** to the heirs of the testator (or grantor) the attempted remainder is void and the result is a **reversion** in the testator (or grantor)." A. Sinclair, *Introduction to Real Property Law* 79 (3d ed. 1987).

WRIT "[I]n law a written command, precept or formal order ... in the name of the sovereign." *McBrearty* v. *McBrearty,* [1941] 1 W.W.R. 590 at 591 (Sask.K.B.). It is a mandatory precept issued by the authority, and in the name of the sover-eign or the state for the purpose of com-pelling a person to do something therein mentioned. Issued by a court or other competent tribunal, it is directed to the sheriff or other officer authorized to exe-cute the same. In every case the writ itself contains directions as to what is required to be done. See **peremptory** [PEREMP-TORY WRIT]; **prerogative writ.**

WRIT OF ASSISTANCE See **assistance, writ of.**

WRIT OF CORAM NOBIS [WRIT OF ERROR CORAM NOBIS; CORAM NOBIS] *(kôr'-äm nō'-bĭs)* Lat.: before us; in our pres-ence, i.e., in our court. The purpose of the writ is to bring the attention of the court to, and obtain relief from, errors of fact, such as a valid **defence** existing in the facts of the case, that, without **negligence** on the part of the defendant, was not made, through either **duress, fraud** or excusable **mistake;** these facts not appearing on the face of the record and being such as, if known in season, would have prevented the rendition and entry of the **judgment** questioned. The writ does not correct errors of law. It is addressed to the court that rendered the judgment in which injustice was allegedly done, in contrast to **appeals** and review, which are directed to another court.

WRIT OF ERROR   An early common-law **writ** issued by the **Appellate Court,** directing the trial judge to send up the **record** in the case. The one seeking the review, whether the **plaintiff** or **defendant** in the trial court, is termed the plaintiff in error, while his opponent is called the defendant in error. The Appellate Court review only alleged errors of law. A writ of error is similar to a writ of **certiorari,** but, unlike a writ of certiorari, it is a writ of right and lies only where **jurisdiction** is exercised according to the course of the **common law.**

WRIT OF EXECUTION   A writ issued after the determination of an issue the object of which is to enforce the **judgment** of the Court. It authorizes the **sheriff** to **levy** on property belonging to the **judgment debtor** for the benefit of the plaintiff in whose favour the judgment has been granted. It "shall include writs of *fieri facias,* **sequestration** and **attachment** and all subsequent writs that may issue for giving effect thereto [to judgments]." *Ross* v. *Rogers and CNR,* [1927] 3 W.W.R. 169 at 171 (Sask.K.B.).

WRIT OF PROHIBITION   A **process** or writ issued by a superior court that prevents an inferior court or tribunal from exceeding its **jurisdiction** or usurping jurisdiction with which it has not been vested by law. It is an extraordinary writ because it issues only when the party seeking it is without other means of redress for the wrong about to be inflicted by the act of the inferior tribu-

nal. It is a **prerogative writ.** In addition, as noted by McGillivray, J.A. in *Rex* v. *Fodor,* [1938] 2 D.L.R. 290 at 302 (Alta.S.C.A.D.): "[In my opinion] prohibition lies not only in cases of lack of jurisidiction over the subject matter or over the person but also in cases in which the inferior court proceeds in circumstances that show bias or self-interest or a perversion of the principles of natural justice."

WRIT OF SUMMONS   A writ issued by a court in order to compel the defendant to appear if he wishes to reply to the charge made against him; a basic method for commencing court proceedings in civil matters. A writ of summons is "the traditional method of commencing an action . . . This is a command in the name of the sovereign, endorsed with a very brief statement of the plaintiff's claim, and warning the defendant to respond to the writ or suffer judgment by default." G. Watson, *Canadian Civil Procedure* 325 (3d ed. 1988). See generally *id.,* chap. 4. See **summons.**

WRONGFUL ACT   An act that, without necessarily being illegal, is contrary to moral or ethical standards and results in some harm being done to individuals or the community. The term is more comprehensive than the phrase *unlawful act,* but all unlawful acts are wrongs. Various sections of the *Criminal Code,* R.S.C. 1985, c. C–46, deal with "wrongful acts." However, where a statute imposed liability for "unlawful acts or default," it was stated: "The wrongful act or default so involved does not necessarily have to be of a **criminal** or **quasi**-criminal nature. It has been said that it can be a breach of legal duty of any degree which causes or contributes to the casualty.... Possibly as useful a test as any is that the wrongful act must be the doing of something ... 'plainly' [which the defendant] ought not to have done." *Belisle* v. *Minister of Transport,* [1967] 2 Ex.C.R. 141 at 149–50.

Y

YEAR In federal statutes, refers to "any period of twelve consecutive months, except that a reference to a 'calendar year' means a period of twelve consecutive months commencing on the first day of January and a reference by number to a Dominical year means the period of twelve consecutive months commencing on the first day of January of that year." *Interpretation Act,* R.S.C. 1985, c. I–21, s. 37.

FISCAL YEAR [FINANCIAL YEAR] "[I]n relation to money provided by **Parliament** or the Consolidated Revenue Fund, or the accounts, taxes or finances of Canada, the period beginning on and including the 1st day of April in one year and ending on and including the 31st day of March in the next year." *Id.*

TAXATION YEAR For the purpose of the *Income Tax Act,* S.C. 1970–71–72, c. 63, s. 249(1), (*a*) in the case of a corporation, a fiscal period, and (*b*) in the case of an individual, a calendar year, and when a taxation year is referred to by reference to a calendar year the reference is to the taxation year or years coinciding with, or ending in, that year.

In **contract** law, the meaning of the term *year* is a matter of **construction** and may or may not mean the calendar year current at the date of the contract. *Ozias* v. *Reeves & Co.* (1911), 1 W.W.R. 517 (S.C.C.). In a life insurance policy, the term *yearly* was interpreted to mean "yearly from the time provided by law for payment of the first installment." *Gill* v.

Great West Life Assurance Co. (1911), 2 O.W.N. 777 at 778 (Div.Ct.).

YEAR-BOOKS The reports of cases in England covering the period 1289 to 1537. Though invaluable to the legal historian, the Year-Books are of little value to the modern lawyer. Written in Anglo-Norman, they are largely concerned with the form of **pleadings,** often to the exclusion of the reasons for the decision.

YIELD To give way to another; to give the "right of way." In motor vehicle cases it has been held that the effect of a yield sign is to "give [the] other party the right of going through the intersection first." *Hammond* v. *Smith* (1964), 45 D.L.R. (2d) 762 at 766 (N.S.Co.Ct.). However, it has also been stated that the effect of such a sign is to warn drivers of potential danger and that the sign itself does not necessarily alter existing rules of right of way. *Johnson* v. *Semple and Mills* (1962), 36 D.L.R. (2d) 319 (P.E.I.S.C.).

YOUNG OFFENDER [YOUNG PERSON] "a person who is or, in the absence of evidence to the contrary, appears to be twelve years of age or more, but under eighteen years of age, where the context requires, includes any person who is charged under this Act with having committed an offence while he was a young person or is found guilty of an offence under this act." *Young Offenders Act,* R.S.C. 1985, c. Y–1, s. 2.

YOUTH COURT "[C]ourt established or designated by or under an Act of the legislature of a province, or designated by the Governor in Council or the Lieutenant Governor in Council of a province as a youth court for the purposes of this Act." *Young Offenders Act,* R.S.C. 1985, s. Y–1, s. 2.

Z

ZONE OF EMPLOYMENT See **scope of employment.**

ZONING Legislative action, usually on the municipal level, that separates or divides municipalities into districts for the purpose of regulating, controlling or in some way limiting the use of private property, and the construction and/or structural nature of buildings erected within the zones or districts established. "Zoning is one of several types of regulation of property by a local government... 'zoning is the regulation by districts of the build ing development and uses of property, and its essence is a territorial division according to the character of lands and structures and their peculiar suitability for particular uses and the uniformity of use within the division.' " *Ingram and Scott* v. *City of Lethbridge* (1962), 34 D.L.R. (2d) 490 at 493 (Alta.S.C.A.D.).

Zoning power is usually an aspect of DELEGATED LEGISLATION (see **legislation**). See, e.g., *Gulf Canada Ltd.* v. *Corp. of City of Vancouver* (1979), 17 B.C.L.R. 273 (B.C.S.C.).

Appendix I

Canadian Charter of Rights and Freedoms

Whereas Canada is founded upon principles that recognize the supremacy of God and the rule of law.

Guarantee of Rights and Freedoms

1. The *Canadian Charter of Rights and Freedoms* guarantees the rights and freedoms set out in it subject only to such reasonable limits prescribed by law as can be demonstrably justified in a free and democratic society.

Fundamental Freedoms

2. Everyone has the following fundamental freedoms:

   (a) freedom of conscience and religion;

   (b) freedom of thought, belief, opinion and expression, including freedom of the press and other media of communication;

   (c) freedom of peaceful assembly; and

   (d) freedom of association.

Democratic Rights

3. Every citizen of Canada has the right to vote in an election of members of the House of Commons or of a legislative assembly and to be qualified for membership therein.

4. (1) No House of Commons and no legislative assembly shall continue for longer than five years from the date fixed for the return of the writs at a general election of its members.

   (2) In time of real or apprehended war, invasion or insurrection, a House of Commons may be continued by Parliament and a legislative assembly may

be continued by the legislature beyond five years if such continuation is not opposed by the votes of more than one-third of the members of the House of Commons or the legislative assembly, as the case may be.

5. There shall be a sitting of Parliament and of each legislature at least once every twelve months.

Mobility Rights

6. (1) Every citizen of Canada has the right to enter, remain in and leave Canada.

(2) Every citizen of Canada and every person who has the status of a permanent resident of Canada has the right

(a) to move to and take up residence in any province; and

(b) to pursue the gaining of a livelihood in any province.

(3) The rights specified in subsection (2) are subject to

(a) any laws or practices of general application in force in a province other than those that discriminate among persons primarily on the basis of province of present or previous residence; and

(b) any laws providing for reasonable residency requirements as a qualification of the receipt of publicly provided social services.

(4) Subsections (2) and (3) do not preclude any law, program or activity that has as its object the amelioration in a province of conditions of individuals in that province who are socially or economically disadvantaged if the rate of employment in that province is below the rate of employment in Canada.

Legal Rights

7. Everyone has the right to life, liberty and security of the person and the right not to be deprived thereof except in accordance with the principles of fundamental justice.

8. Everyone has the right to be secure against unreasonable search or seizure.

9. Everyone has the right not to be arbitrarily detained or imprisoned.

10. Everyone has the right on arrest or detention

(a) to be informed promptly of the reasons therefor;

(b) to retain and instruct counsel without delay and to be informed of that right; and

(c) to have the validity of the detention determined by way of *habeas corpus* and to be released if the detention is not lawful.

11. Any person charged with an offence has the right

(a) to be informed without unreasonable delay of the specific offence;

(b) to be tried within a reasonable time;

(c) not to be compelled to be a witness in proceedings against that person in respect of the offence;

(d) to be presumed innocent until proven guilty according to law in a fair and public hearing by an independent and impartial tribunal;

(e) not to be denied reasonable bail without just cause;

(f) except in the case of an offence under military law tried before a military tribunal, to the benefit of trial by jury where the maximum punishment for the offence is imprisonment for five years or a more severe punishment;

(g) not to be found guilty on account of any act or omission unless, at the time of the act or omission, it constituted an offence under Canadian or international law or was criminal according to the general principles of law recognized by the community of nations;

(h) if finally acquitted of the offence, not to be tried for it again and, if finally found guilty and punished for the offence, not to be tried or punished for it again; and

(i) if found guilty of the offence and if the punishment for the offence has been varied between the time of commission and the time of sentencing, to the benefit of the lesser punishment.

12. Everyone has the right not to be subjected to any cruel and unusual treatment or punishment.

13. A witness who testifies in any proceedings has the right not to have any incriminating evidence so given used to incriminate that witness in any other proceedings, except in a prosecution for perjury or for the giving of contradictory evidence.

14. A party or witness in any proceedings who does not understand or speak the language in which the proceedings are conducted or who is deaf has the right to the assistance of an interpreter.

Equality Rights

15. (1) Every individual is equal before and under the law and has the right to the equal protection and equal benefit of the law without discrimination and, in particular, without discrimination based on race, national or ethnic origin, colour, religion, sex, age or mental or physical disability.

(2) Subsection (1) does not preclude any law, program or activity that has as its object the amelioration of conditions of disadvantaged individuals or groups including those that are disadvantaged because of race, national or ethnic origin, colour, religion, sex, age or mental or physical disability.

Official Languages of Canada

16. (1) English and French are the official languages of Canada and have equality of status and equal rights and privileges as to their use in all institutions of the Parliament and government of Canada.

(2) English and French are the official languages of New Brunswick and have equality of status and equal rights and privileges as to their use in all institutions of the legislature and government of New Brunswick.

(3) Nothing in this Charter limits the authority of Parliament or ,a legislature to advance the equality of status or use of English and French.

17. (1) Everyone has the right to use English or French in any debates and other proceedings of Parliament.

(2) Everyone has the right to use English or French in any debates and other proceedings of the legislature of New Brunswick.

18. (1) The statutes, records and journals of Parliament shall be printed and published in English and French and both language versions are equally authoritative.

(2) The statutes, records and journals of the legislature of New Brunswick shall be printed and published in English and French and both versions are equally authoritative.

19. (1) Either English or French may be used by any person in, or in any pleading in or process issuing from, any court established by Parliament.

(2) Either English or French may be used by any person in, or in any pleading in or process issuing from, any court of New Brunswick.

20. (1) Any member of the public in Canada has the right to communicate with, and to receive available services from, any head or central office of an

institution of the Parliament or government of Canada in English or French, and has the same right with respect to any other office of any such institution where

(a) there is significant demand for communications with and services from that office in such language; or

(b) due to the nature of the office, it is reasonable that communications with and services from the office be available in both English and French.

(2) Any member of the public in New Brunswick has the right to communicate with, and to receive available services from, any office of an institution of the legislature or government of New Brunswick in English or French.

21. Nothing in sections 16 to 20 abrogates or derogates from any right, privilege or obligation with respect to the English and French languages, or either of them, that exists or is continued by virtue of any other provision of the Constitution of Canada.

22. Nothing in sections 16 to 20 abrogates or derogates from any legal or customary right or privilege acquired or enjoyed either before or after the coming into force of this Charter with respect to any language that is not English or French.

Minority Language Educational Rights

23. (1) Citizens of Canada

(a) whose first language learned and still understood is that of the English or French linguistic minority population of the province in which they reside, or

(b) who have received their primary school instruction in Canada in English or French and reside in a province where the language in which they received that instruction is the language of the English or French linguistic minority population of the province.

have the right to have their children receive primary and secondary school instruction in that language in that province.

(2) Citizens of Canada of whom any child has received or is receiving primary or secondary school instruction in English or French in Canada, have the right to have all their children receive primary and secondary school instruction in the same language.

(3) The right of citizens of Canada under subsections (1) and (2) to have their children receive primary and secondary school instruction in the language of the English or French linguistic minority population of a province

(a) applies wherever in the province the number of children of citizens who have such a right is sufficient to warrant the provision to them out of public funds of minority language instruction; and

(b) includes, where the number of those children so warrants, the right to have them receive that instruction in minority language educational facilities provided out of public funds.

Enforcement

24. (1) Anyone whose rights or freedoms, as guaranteed by this Charter, have been infringed or denied may apply to a court of competent jurisdiction to obtain such remedy as the court considers appropriate and just in the circumstances.

(2) Where, in proceedings under subsection (1), a court concludes that evidence was obtained in a manner that infringed or denied any rights or freedoms guaranteed by this Charter, the evidence shall be excluded if it is established that, having regard to all the circumstances, the admission of it in the proceedings would bring the administration of justice into disrepute.

General

25. The guarantee in this Charter of certain rights and freedoms shall not be construed so as to abrogate or derogate from any aboriginal, treaty or other rights or freedoms that pertain to the aboriginal peoples of Canada including

(a) any rights or freedoms that have been recognized by the Royal Proclamation of October 7, 1763; and

(b) any rights or freedoms that may be acquired by the aboriginal peoples of Canada by way of land claims settlement.

26. The guarantee in this Charter of certain rights and freedoms shall not be construed as denying the existence of any other rights or freedoms that exist in Canada.

27. This Charter shall be interpreted in a manner consistent with the preservation and enhancement of the multicultural heritage of Canadians.

28. Notwithstanding anything in this Charter, the rights and freedoms referred to in it are guaranteed equally to male and female persons.

29. Nothing in this Charter abrogates or derogates from any rights or privileges guaranteed by or under the Constitution of Canada in respect of denominational, separate or dissentient schools.

30. A reference in this Charter to a province or to the legislative assembly or legislature of a province shall be deemed to include a reference to the Yukon Territory and the Northwest Territories, or to the appropriate legislative authority thereof, as the case may be.

31. Nothing in this Charter extends the legislative powers of any body or authority.

Application of Charter

32. (1) This Charter applies

    (a) to the Parliament and government of Canada in respect of all matters within the authority of Parliament including all matters relating to the Yukon Territory and Northwest Territories; and

    (b) to the legislature and government of each province in respect of all matters within the authority of the legislature of each province.

(2) Notwithstanding subsection (1), section 15 shall not have effect until three years after this section comes into force.

33. (1) Parliament or the legislature of a province may expressly declare in an Act of Parliament or of the legislature, as the case may be, that the Act or a provision thereof shall operate notwithstanding a provision included in section 2 or sections 7 to 15 of this Charter.

(2) An Act or a provision of an Act in respect of which a declaration made under this section is in effect shall have such operation as it would have but for the provision of this Charter referred to in the declaration.

(3) A declaration made under subsection (1) shall cease to have effect five years after it comes into force or on such earlier date as may be specified in the declaration.

(4) Parliament or a legislature of a province may re-enact a declaration made under subsection (1).

(5) Subsection (3) applies in respect of a re-enactment made under subsection (4).

Citation

34. This part may be cited as the *Canadian Charter of Rights and Freedoms*.

Appendix II

Canadian Bill of Rights (Abridged)

An Act for the Recognition and Protection of Human Rights and Fundamental Freedoms

8–9 Elizabeth II, c. 44 (Canada)

[Assented to 10th August 1960]

The Parliament of Canada, affirming that the Canadian Nation is founded upon principles that acknowledge the supremacy of God, the dignity and worth of the human person and the position of the family in a society of free men and free institutions;

Affirming also that men and institutions remain free only when freedom is founded upon respect for moral and spiritual values and the rule of law;

And being desirous of enshrining these principles and the human rights and fundamental freedoms derived from them, in a Bill of Rights which shall reflect the respect of Parliament for its constitutional authority and which shall ensure the protection of these rights and freedoms in Canada:

Therefore Her Majesty, by and with the advice and consent of the Senate and House of Commons of Canada, enacts as follows:

PART I

BILL OF RIGHTS

1. It is hereby recognized and declared that in Canada there have existed and shall continue to exist without discrimination by reason of race, national origin, colour, religion or sex, the following human rights and fundamental freedoms, namely,

(*a*) the right of the individual to life, liberty, security of the person and enjoyment of property, and the right not to be deprived thereof except by due process of law;

(*b*) the right of the individual to equality before the law and the protection of the law;

(*c*) freedom of religion;

(*d*) freedom of speech;

(*e*) freedom of assembly and association; and

(*f*) freedom of the press.

2. Every law of Canada shall, unless it is expressly declared by an Act of the Parliament of Canada that it shall operate notwithstanding the *Canadian Bill of Rights,* be so construed and applied as not to abrogate, abridge or infringe or to authorize the abrogation, abridgment or infringement or any of the rights or freedoms herein recognized and declared, and in particular, no law of Canada shall be construed or applied so as to

(*a*) authorize or effect the arbitrary detention, imprisonment or exile of any person;

(*b*) impose or authorize the imposition of cruel and unusual treatment or punishment;

(*c*) deprive a person who has been arrested or detained

(i) of the right to be informed promptly of the reason for his arrest or detention,

(ii) of the right to retain and instruct counsel without delay, or

(iii) of the remedy by way of *habeas corpus* for the determination of the validity of his detention and for his release if the detention is not lawful;

(*d*) authorize a court, tribunal, commission, board or other authority to compel a person to give evidence if he is denied counsel, protection against self crimination or other constitutional safeguards;

(*e*) deprive a person of the right to a fair hearing in accordance with the principles of fundamental justice for the determination of his rights and obligations;

(*f*) deprive a person charged with a criminal offence of the right to be presumed innocent until proved guilty according to law in a fair and public hearing by an independent and impartial tribunal, or of the right to reasonable bail without just cause; or

(*g*) deprive a person of the right to the assistance of an interpreter in any proceedings in which he is involved or in which he is a party or a witness, before a court, commission, board or other tribunal, if he does not understand or speak the language in which such proceedings arc conducted.

Appendix III

Canadian Human Rights Act (Abridged)

CHAPTER H-6

An Act to extend the laws in Canada that proscribe discrimination

SHORT TITLE

1. This Act may be cited as the *Canadian Human Rights Act.* 1976–77, c. 33, s. 1.

PURPOSE OF ACT

2. The purpose of this Act is to extend the laws in Canada to give effect, within the purview of matters coming within the legislative authority of Parliament, to the principle that every individual should have an equal opportunity with other individuals to make for himself or herself the life that he or she is able and wishes to have, consistent with his or her duties and obligations as a member of society, without being hindered in or prevented from doing so by discriminatory practices based on race, national or ethnic origin, colour, religion, age, sex, marital status, family status, disability or conviction for an offence for which a pardon has been granted. 1976–77, c. 33, s. 2; 1980–81–82–83, c. 143, ss. 1, 28.

PART I

PROSCRIBED DISCRIMINATION

General

3. (1) For all purposes of this Act, race, national or ethnic origin, colour, religion, age, sex, marital status, family status, disability and conviction for which a pardon has been granted are prohibited grounds of discrimination.

(2) Where the ground of discrimination is pregnancy or child-birth, the discrimination shall be deemed to be on the ground of sex. 1976–77, c. 33, s. 3; 1980–81–82–83, c. 143, s. 2.

4. A discriminatory practice, as described in sections 5 to 14, may be the subject of a complaint under Part III and anyone found to be engaging or to have engaged in a discriminatory practice may be made subject to an order as provided in sections 53 and 54. 1976–77, c. 33, s. 4; 1980–81–82–83, c. 143, s. 2.

Discriminatory Practices

5. It is a discriminatory practice in the provision of goods, services, facilities or accommodation customarily available to the general public

(*a*) to deny, or to deny access to, any such good, service, facility or accommodation to any individual, or

(*b*) to differentiate adversely in relation to any individual,

on a prohibited ground of discrimination. 1976–77, c. 33, s. 5.

6. It is a discriminatory practice in the provision of commercial premises or residential accommodation

(*a*) to deny occupancy of such premises or accommodation to any individual, or

(*b*) to differentiate adversely in relation to any individual,

on a prohibited ground of discrimination. 1976–77, c. 33, s. 6.

7. It is a discriminatory practice, directly or indirectly,

(*a*) to refuse to employ or continue to employ any individual, or

(*b*) in the course of employment, to differentiate adversely in relation to an employee,

on a prohibited ground of discrimination. 1976–77, c. 33, s. 7.

8. It is a discriminatory practice

(*a*) to use or circulate any form of application for employment, or

(*b*) in connection with employment or prospective employment, to publish any advertisement or to make any written or oral inquiry

that expresses or implies any limitation, specification or preference based on a prohibited ground of discrimination. 1976–77, c. 33, s. 8.

9. (1) It is a discriminatory practice for an employee organization on a prohibited ground of discrimination

(*a*) to exclude an individual from full membership in the organization;

(*b*) to expel or suspend a member of the organization; or

(*c*) to limit, segregate, classify or otherwise act in relation to an individual in a way that would deprive the individual of employment opportunities, or limit employment opportunities or otherwise adversely affect the status of the individual, where the individual is a member of the organization or where any of the obligations of the organization pursuant to a collective agreement relate to the individual.

(2) Notwithstanding subsection (1), it is not a discriminatory practice for an employee organization to exclude, expel or suspend an individual from membership in the organization because that individual has reached the normal age of retirement for individuals working in positions similar to the position of that individual.

(3) For the purposes of this section and sections 10 and 60, "employee organization" includes a trade union or other organization of employees or local thereof, the purposes of which include the negotiation, on behalf of employees, of the terms and conditions of employment with employers. 1976–77, c. 33, s. 9; 1980–81–82–83, c. 143, s. 4.

10. It is a discriminatory practice for an employer, employee organization or organization of employers

(*a*) to establish or pursue a policy or practice, or

(*b*) to enter into an agreement affecting recruitment, referral, hiring, promotion, training, apprenticeship, transfer or any other matter relating to employment or prospective employment,

that deprives or tends to deprive an individual or class of individuals of any employment opportunities on a prohibited ground of discrimination. 1976–77, c. 33, s. 10; 1980–81–82–83, c. 143, s. 5.

11. (1) It is a discriminatory practice for an employer to establish or maintain differences in wages between male and female employees employed in the same establishment who are performing work of equal value.

(2) In assessing the value of work performed by employees employed in the same establishment, the criterion to be applied is the composite of the skill, effort and responsibility required in the performance of the work and the conditions under which the work is performed.

(3) Separate establishments established or maintained by an employer solely or principally for the purpose of establishing or maintaining differences in wages between male and female employees shall be deemed for the purposes of this section to be the same establishment.

(4) Notwithstanding subsection (1), it is not a discriminatory practice to pay to male and female employees different wages if the difference is based on a factor prescribed by guidelines, issued by the Canadian Human Rights Commission pursuant to subsection 27(2), to be a reasonable factor that justifies the difference.

(5) For greater certainty, sex does not constitute a reasonable factor justifying a difference in wages.

(6) An employer shall not reduce wages in order to eliminate a discriminatory practice described in this section.

(7) For the purposes of this section, "wages" means any form of remuneration payable for work performed by an individual and includes

(*a*) salaries, commissions, vacation pay, dismissal wages and bonuses;

(*b*) reasonable value for board, rent, housing and lodging;

(*c*) payments in kind;

(*d*) employer contributions to pension funds or plans, long-term disability plans and all forms of health insurance plans; and

(*e*) any other advantage received directly or indirectly from the individual's employer. 1976–77, c. 33, s. 11.

12. It is a discriminatory practice to publish or display before the public or to cause to be published or displayed before the public any notice, sign, symbol, emblem or other representation that

(*a*) expresses or implies discrimination or an intention to discriminate, or

(*b*) incites or is calculated to incite others to discriminate

if the discrimination expressed or implied, intended to be expressed or implied or incited or calculated to be incited would otherwise, if engaged in, be a discriminatory practice described in any of sections 5 to 11 or in section 14. 1976–77, c. 33, s. 12; 1980–81–82–83, c. 143, s. 6.

13. (1) It is a discriminatory practice for a person or a group of persons acting in concert to communicate telephonically or to cause to be so communicated, repeatedly, in whole or in part by means of the facilities of a telecommunication undertaking within the legislative authority of Parliament, any matter that is likely to expose a person or persons to hatred or contempt by reason of the fact that that person or those persons are identifiable on the basis of a prohibited ground of discrimination.

(2) Subsection (1) does not apply in respect of any matter that is communicated in whole or in part by means of the facilities of a broadcasting undertaking.

(3) For the purposes of this section, no owner or operator of a telecommunication undertaking communicates or causes to be communicated any matter described in subsection (1) by reason only that the facilities of a telecommunication undertaking owned or operated by that person are used by other persons for the transmission of that matter. 1976–77, c. 33, s. 13.

14. (1) It is a discriminatory practice,

(*a*) in the provision of goods, services, facilities or accommodation customarily available to the general public,

(*b*) in the provision of commercial premises or residential accommodation, or

(*c*) in matters related to employment,

to harass an individual on a prohibited ground of discrimination.

(2) Without limiting the generality of subsection (1), sexual harassment shall, for the purposes of that subsection, be deemed to be harassment on a prohibited ground of discrimination. 1980–81–82–83, c. 143, s. 7.

15. It is not a discriminatory practice if

(*a*) any refusal, exclusion, expulsion, suspension, limitation, specification or preference in relation to any employment is established by an employer to be based on a *bona fide* occupational requirement;

(*b*) employment of an individual is refused or terminated because that individual has not reached the minimum age, or has reached the maximum age, that applies to that employment by law or under regulations, which may be made by the Governor in Council for the purposes of this paragraph;

(*c*) an individual's employment is terminated because that individual has reached the normal age of retirement for employees working in positions similar to the position of that individual;

(*d*) the terms and conditions of any pension fund or plan established by an employer provide for the compulsory vesting or locking-in of pension contributions at a fixed or determinable age in accordance with section 10 of the *Pension Benefits Standards Act;*

(*e*) an individual is discriminated against on a prohibited ground of discrimination in a manner that is prescribed by guidelines, issued by the Canadian Human Rights Commission pursuant to subsection 27(2), to be reasonable;

(*f*) an employer grants a female employee special leave or benefits in connection with pregnancy or child-birth or grants employees special leave or benefits to assist them in the care of their children; or

(*g*) in the circumstances described in section 5 or 6, an individual is denied any goods, services, facilities or accommodation or access thereto or occupancy of any commercial premises or residential accommodation or is a victim of any adverse differentiation and there is *bona fide* justification for that denial or differentiation. 1976–77, c. 33, s. 14; 1980–81–82–83, c. 143, s. 7.

16. (1) It is not a discriminatory practice for a person to adopt or carry out a special program, plan or arrangement designed to prevent disadvantages that are likely to be suffered by, or to eliminate or reduce disadvantages that are suffered by, any group of individuals when those disadvantages would be or are based on or related to the race, national or ethnic origin, colour, religion, age, sex, marital status, family status or disability of members of that group, by improving opportunities respecting goods, services, facilities, accommodation or employment in relation to that group.

(2) The Canadian Human Rights Commission may

(*a*) make general recommendations concerning desirable objectives for special programs, plans or arrangements referred to in subsection (1); and

(*b*) on application, give such advice and assistance with respect to the adoption or carrying out of a special program, plan or arrangement referred to in subsection (1) as will serve to aid in the achievement of the objectives the program, plan or arrangement was designed to achieve. 1976–77, c. 33, s. 15; 1980–81–82–83, c. 143, s. 8.

17. (1) A person who proposes to implement a plan for adapting any services, facilities, premises, equipment or operations to meet the needs of persons arising from a disability may apply to the Canadian Human Rights Commission for approval of the plan.

(2) The Commission may, by written notice to a person making an application pursuant to subsection (1), approve the plan if the Commission is satisfied that the plan is appropriate for meeting the needs of persons arising from a disability.

(3) Where any services, facilities, premises, equipment or operations are adapted in accordance with a plan approved under subsection (2), matters for which the plan provides do not constitute any basis for a complaint under Part III regarding discrimination based on any disability is respect of which the plan was approved.

(4) When the Commission decides not to grant an application made pursuant to subsection (1), it shall send a written notice of its decision to the applicant setting out the reasons for its decision. 1980–81–82–83, c. 143, s. 9.

18. (1) If the Canadian Human Rights Commission is satisfied that, by reason of any change in circumstances, a plan approved under subsection 17(2) has ceased to be appropriate for meeting the needs of persons arising from a disability, the Commission may, by written notice to the person who proposes to carry out or maintains the adaptation contemplated by the plan or any part thereof, rescind its approval of the plan to the extent required by the change in circumstances.

(2) To the extent to which approval of a plan is rescinded under subsection (1), subsection 17(3) does not apply to the plan if the discriminatory practice to which the complaint relates is subsequent to the recission of the approval.

(3) Where the Commission rescinds approval of a plan pursuant to subsection (1), it shall include in the notice referred to therein a statement of its reasons therefor. 1980–81–82–83, c. 143, s. 9.

19. (1) Before making its decision on an application or rescinding approval of a plan pursuant to section 17 or 18, the Canadian Human Rights Commission shall afford each person directly concerned with the matter an opportunity to make representations with respect thereto.

(2) For the purposes of sections 17 and 18, a plan shall not, by reason only that it does not conform to any standards prescribed pursuant to section 24, by deemed to be inappropriate for meeting the needs of persons arising from disability. 1980–81–82–83, c. 143, s. 9.

20. A provision of a pension or insurance fund or plan that preserves rights acquired prior to March, 1, 1978 or that preserves pension or other benefits accrued prior to that time does not constitute the basis for a complaint under Part III that an employer is engaging or has engaged in a discriminatory practice. 1976–77, c. 33, s. 16.

21. The establishment of separate pension funds or plans for different groups of employees does not constitute the basis for a complaint under Part III that an employer is engaging or has engaged in a discriminatory practice if the employees are not grouped in those funds or plans according to a prohibited ground of discrimination. 1976–77, c. 33, s. 17.

22. The Governor in Council may, by regulation, prescribe the provisions of any pension or insurance fund or plan, in addition to those provisions described in sections 20 and 21, that do not constitute the basis for a complaint under Part III that an employer is engaging or has engaged in a discriminatory practice. 1976–77, c. 33, s. 18.

23. The Governor in Council may make regulations respecting the terms and conditions to be included in or applicable to any contract, licence or grant made or granted by Her Majesty in right of Canada providing for

(*a*) the prohibition of discriminatory practices described in sections 5 to 14; and (*b*) the resolution, by the procedure set out in Part III, of complaints of discriminatory practices contrary to such terms and conditions. 1976–77, c. 33, s. 19; 1980–81–82–83, c. 143, s. 10.

24. (1) The Governor in Council may, for the benefit of persons having any disability, make regulations prescribing standards of accessibility to services, facilities or premises.

(2) Where standards prescribed pursuant to subsection (1) are met in providing access to any services, facilities or premises, a matter of access thereto does not constitute any basis for a complaint under Part III regarding discrimination based on any disability in respect of which the standards are prescribed.

(3) Subject to subsection (4), a copy of each regulation that the Governor in Council proposes to make pursuant to this section shall be published in the *Canada Gazette* and a reasonable opportunity shall be afforded to interested persons to make representations with respect thereto.

(4) Subsection (3) does not apply in respect of a proposed regulation that has been published pursuant to that subsection, whether or not it has been amended as a result of representations made pursuant to that subsection.

(5) Nothing shall, by virtue only of its being at variance with any standards prescribed pursuant to subsection (1), be deemed to constitute a discriminatory practice. 1980–81–82–83, c. 143, s. 11.

25. In this Act,

"conviction for which a pardon has been granted" means a conviction of an individual for an offence in respect of which a pardon has been granted by any authority under law and, if granted under the *Criminal Records Act,* not revoked;

"disability" means any previous or existing mental or physical disability and includes disfigurement and previous or existing dependence on alcohol or a drug. 1976–77, c. 33, s. 20; 1980–81–82–83, c. 143, s. 12.

Appendix IV

Ontario Human Rights Code (Abridged)

CHAPTER H.19

Human Rights Code

WHEREAS recognition of the inherent dignity and the equal and inalienable rights of all members of the human family is the foundation of freedom, justice and peace in the world and is in accord with the Universal Declaration of Human Rights as proclaimed by the United Nations;

AND WHEREAS it is public policy in Ontario to recognize the dignity and worth of every person and to provide for equal rights and opportunities without discrimination that is contrary to law, and having as its aim the creation of a climate of understanding and mutual respect for the dignity and worth of each person so that each person feels a part of the community and able to contribute fully to the development and well-being of the community and the Province;

AND WHEREAS these principles have been confirmed in Ontario by a number of enactments of the Legislature and it is desirable to revise and extend the protection of human rights in Ontario;

Therefore, Her Majesty, by and with the advice and consent of the Legislative Assembly of the Province of Ontario, enacts as follows:

PART I
FREEDOM FROM DISCRIMINATION

1. Every person has a right to equal treatment with respect to services, goods and facilities, without discrimination because of race, ancestry, place of origin, colour, ethnic origin, citizenship, creed, sex, sexual orientation, age, marital status, family status or handicap. 1981, c. 53, s. 1; 1986, c. 64, s. 18(1).

2. (1) Every person has a right to equal treatment with respect to the occupancy of accommodation, without discrimination because of race, ancestry, place of origin, colour, ethnic origin, citizenship, creed, sex, sexual orientation, age, marital status, family status, handicap or the receipt of public assistance. 1981, c. 53, s. 2(1); 1986, c. 64, s. 18(2).

(2) Every person who occupies accommodation has a right to freedom from harassment by the landlord or agent of the landlord or by an occupant of the same building because of race, ancestry, place of origin, colour, ethnic origin, citizenship, creed, age, marital status, family status, handicap or the receipt of public assistance. 1981, c. 53, s. 2(2).

3. Every person having legal capacity has a right to contract on equal terms without discrimination because of race, ancestry, place of origin, colour, ethnic origin, citizenship, creed, sex, sexual orientation, age, marital status, family status or handicap. 1981, c. 53, s. 3; 1986, c. 64, s. 18(3).

4. (1) Every sixteen or seventeen year old person who has withdrawn from parental control has a right to equal treatment with respect to occupancy of and contracting for accommodation without discrimination because the person is less than eighteen years old.

(2) A contract for accommodation entered into by a sixteen or seventeen year old person who has withdrawn from parental control is enforceable against that person as if the person were eighteen years old. 1986, c. 64, s. 18(4).

5. (1) Every person has a right to equal treatment with respect to employment without discrimination because of race, ancestry, place of origin, colour, ethnic origin, citizenship, creed, sex, sexual orientation, age, record of offences, marital status, family status or handicap. 1981, c. 53, s. 4(1); 1986, c. 64, s. 18(5).

(2) Every person who is an employee has a right to freedom from harassment in the workplace by the employer or agent of the employer or by another employee because of race, ancestry, place of origin, colour, ethnic origin, citizenship, creed, age, record of offences, marital status, family status or handicap. 1981, c. 53, s. 4(2).

6. Every person has a right to equal treatment with respect to membership in any trade union, trade or occupational association or self-governing profession without discrimination because of race, ancestry, place of origin, colour, ethnic origin, citizenship, creed, sex, sexual orientation, age, marital status, family status or handicap. 1981, c. 53, s. 5; 1986, c. 64, s. 18(6).

7. (1) Every person who occupies accommodation has a right to freedom from harassment because of sex by the landlord or agent of the landlord or by an occupant of the same building.

(2) Every person who is an employee has a right to freedom from harassment in the workplace because of sex by his or employer or agent of the employer or by another employee.

(3) Every person has a right to be free from,

(*a*) a sexual solicitation or advance made by a person in a position to confer, grant or deny a benefit or advancement to the person where the person making the solicitation or advance knows or ought reasonably to know that it is unwelcome; or

(*b*) a reprisal or a threat of reprisal for the rejection of a sexual solicitation or advance where the reprisal is made or threatened by a person in a position to confer, grant or deny a benefit or advancement to the person. 1981, c. 53, s. 6.

8. Every person has a right to claim and enforce his or her rights under this Act, to institute and participate in proceedings under this Act and to refuse to infringe a right of another person under this Act, without reprisal or threat for so doing. 1981, c. 53, s. 7.

9. No person shall infringe or do, directly or indirectly, anything that infringes a right under this Part. 1981, c. 53, s. 8.

PART II
INTERPRETATION AND APPLICATION

10. (1) In Part I and in this Part.

"age" means an age that is eighteen years or more, except in subsection 5(1) where "age" means an age that is eighteen years or more and less than sixty-five years; ("âge")

"because of handicap" means for the reason that the person has or has had, or is believed to have or have had,

(*a*) any degree of physical disability, infirmity, malformation or disfigurement that is caused by bodily injury, birth defect or illness and, without limiting the generality of the foregoing, including diabetes mellitus, epilepsy, any degree of paralysis, amputation, lack of physical coordination, blindness or visual impediment, deafness or hearing impediment, muteness or speech impediment, or physical reliance on a guide dog or on a wheelchair or other remedial appliance or device,

(*b*) a condition of mental retardation or impairment,

(*c*) a learning disability, or a dysfunction in one or more of the processes involved in understanding or using symbols or spoken language,

(*d*) a mental disorder, or

(*e*) an injury or disability for which benefits were claimed or received under the *Workers' Compensation Act;* ("à cause d'un handicap")

"equal" means subject to all requirements, qualifications and considerations that are not a prohibited ground of discrimination; ("égal")

"family status" means the status of being in a parent and child relationship; ("état familial")

"group insurance" means insurance whereby the lives or well-being or the lives and well-being of a number of persons are insured severally under a single contract between an insurer and an association or an employer or other person; ("assurance-groupe")

"harassment" means engaging in a course of vexatious comment or conduct that is known or ought reasonably to be known to be unwelcome; ("harcèlement")

"marital status" means the status of being married, single, widowed, divorced or separated and includes the status of living with a person of the opposite sex in a conjugal relationship outside marriage; ("état matrimonial") "record of offences" means a conviction for,

(*a*) an offence in respect of which a pardon has been granted under the *Criminal Records Act* (Canada) and has not been revoked, or

(*b*) an offence in respect of any provincial enactment; ("casier judiciaire")

"services" does not include a levy, fee, tax or periodic payment imposed by law; ("services")

"spouse" means the person to whom a person of the opposite sex is married or with whom the person is living in a conjugal relationship outside marriage. ("conjoint") 1981, c. 53, s. 9; 1984, c. 58, s. 39.

(2) The right to equal treatment without discrimination because of sex includes the right to equal treatment without discrimination because a woman is or may become pregnant. 1986, c. 64, s. 18(7).

Appendix V

Canadian Antidiscrimination Statutes

Canadian Human Rights Act, R.S.C. 1985, c. H-6.

Fair Practices Act, R.S.N.W.T. 1988, c. F-2.

Human Rights Act, R.S.Y. 1986 (Supp.). c. 11.

Human Rights Act, S.B.C. 1984, c. 22.

The Individual's Rights Protection Act, R.S.A. 1980, c. I-2.

The Saskatchewan Human Rights Code, S.S. 1979, c. S-24.1.

Human Rights Code, S.M. 1987–88, c. 45.

Human Rights Code, R.S.O. 1990, c. H. 19.

Charter of Human Rights and Freedoms, R.S.Q. 1977, c. C-12.

Human Rights Code, R.S.N.B. 1973, c. H-11.

Human Rights Act, R.S.N.S. 1989, c. 214.

Human Rights Act, R.S.P.E.I. 1988, c. H-12.

Human Rights Code, R.S.N. 1990, c. H-14.

Appendix VI

A. Abbreviations for Courts and Jurisdictions

Courts—Canada

A.D.	Appeal Division (or Appellate Division)
C.A.	Court of Appeal
Ch.Cham.	Chancery Chambers
Co.Ct.	County Court
Ct. of Sess.	Court of Sessions
Dist.Ct.	District Court
Div.Ct.	Division Court
Ex.	Exchequer Court of Canada
F.	Federal Court of Canada
Fam.Div.	Family Division
F.C.A.D.	Federal Court of Canada Appeal Division
F C.T.D.	Federal Court of Canada Trial Division
H.C.	High Court
Mag.Ct.	Magistrate's Court
M.T.	Master of Titles
Prov.Ct.	Provincial Court
Q.B. (or K.B.)	Queen's Bench (or King's Bench)
Q.B.D. (or K.B.D.)	Queen's Bench Division (or King's Bench Division)
S.C	Supreme Court
S.C. *in banco* (or *en banc*)	Supreme Court *in banco* or *en banc*
S.C.C.	Supreme Court of Canada
S.C.D.	Supreme Court Division
Surr.Ct	Surrogate Court
T.C.	Trial Court
T.D.	Trial Division
Ter.Ct.	Territorial Court
T.R.B.	Taxation Review Board
Wk.Ct.	Weekly Court

Courts—England

C.A.	Court of Appeal
C.C.A.	Court of Criminal Appeal
Ch.D.	Chancery Division

C.P.	Court of Common Pleas
Cr.Ca.R.	Crown Cases Reserved
H.L.	House of Lords
P.C.	Privy Council
Q.B.D. (or K.B.D.)	Queen's Bench Division (or King's Bench Division)

Jurisdictions—Canada

Alta.	Alberta
B.C.	British Columbia
Can.	Canada
Man.	Manitoba
N.B.	New Brunswick
Nfld.	Newfoundland
N.S.	Nova Scotia
Ont.	Ontario
P.E.I.	Prince Edward Island
Que.	Quebec
Sask.	Saskatchewan
N.W.T.	North West Territories
Y.	Yukon

Other Jurisdictions

Austl.	Australia
N.Y.	New York

B. Abbreviations for Canadian Report Series

Alta.L.R.	Alberta Law Reports
A.P.R.	Atlantic Provinces Reports
B.C.R.	British Columbia Reports
B.L.R.	Business Law Reports
B.R.	Rapports judiciaires de Québec, Cour du Banc de la Reine (ou du Roi)/Quebec Official Reports, Queen's (or King's) Bench, 1892–1941
[ ] B.R.	Rapports judiciaires de Québec, Cour du Banc de la Reine (ou du Roi), 1942–1966
[ ] B.R.	Recueils de jurisprudence du Québec, Cour du Banc de la Reine, 1967–1969
[ ] C.A.	Recuiels de jurisprudence du Québec, Cour d'appel, 1970 to date
C.B.R.	Canadian Bankruptcy Reports

C.B.R. (N.S.)	Canadian Bankruptcy Reports, New Series, 1960 to date
C.C.C.	Canadian Criminal Cases, 1893–1962
[ ] C.C.C.	Canadian Criminal Cases, 1963 to date
C.C.C. (2d)	Canadian Criminal Cases (Second Series), 1971 to date
C.C.L.T.	Canadian Cases on the Law of Torts
C.P.C	Carswell's Practice Cases
C.P.R.	Canadian Patent Reporter
C.R.	Criminal Reports (Canada)
C.R.N.S.	Criminal Reports, New Series, 1967 to date
C.R.R.	Canadian Rights Reporter, 1982 to date
C.S.	Rapports judiciaires de Québec, Cour supérieure/Quebec Official Reports, Superior Court, 1892–1941
[ ] C.S.	Rapports judiciaires de Québec, Cour supérieur, 1942–1966
[ ] C.S.	Recueils de jurisprudence du Québec, Cour supérieure, 1967 to date
[ ] C.T.C.	Canada Tax Cases
D.L.R.	Dominion Law Reports, 1912–1922
[ ] D.L.R.	Dominion Law Reports, 1923–1955
D.L.R. (2d)	Dominion Law Reports (Second Series), 1956–1968
D.L.R (3d)	Dominion Law Reports (Third Series), 1969 to date
E.L.R.	Eastern Law Reporter
[ ] Ex.C.R.	Exchequer Court Reports (Canada), 1923–1971
[ ] Fed.R.	Federal Court Reports (Canada), 1971 to date
F.T.R.	Federal Trial Reporter, 1986 to date
Gr.	Upper Canada Chancery Reports, by Grant
L.N.	Legal News (Quebec)
Man.R.	Manitoba Reports
M.P.R.	Maritime Provinces Reports, 1930–1968
M.V.R.	Motor Vehicle Reports
Nfld. & P.E.I.R.	Newfoundland and Prince Edward Island Reports
N.B.R.	New Brunswick Reports, 1825–1929
N.B.R. (2d)	New Brunswick Reports (Second Series), 1969 to date
Nfld.R.	Newfoundland Reports
N.R.	National Reporter
N.S.R.	Nova Scotia Reports, 1834–1929

N.S.R. (2d)	Nova Scotia Reports (Second Series), 1970 to date
O.A.R.	Ontario Appeal Reports
O.L.R.	Ontario Law Reports, 1901–1930
O.R.	Ontario Reports, 1882–1900
[ ] O.R.	Ontario Reports, 1931–1973
O.R. (2d)	Ontario Reports, 1974 to date
O.W.N.	Ontario Weekly Notes, 1909–1932
[ ] O.W.N.	Ontario Weekly Notes, 1933–1962
O.W.R.	Ontario Weekly Reporter
P.R.	Practice Reports (Ontario)
Q.L.R.	Quebec Law Reports
[ ] Que.C.A.	Quebec Official Reports (Court of Appeal), 1970 to date
Que.Q.B. or Que.K.B.	Quebec Official Reports (Queen's Bench or King's Bench), 1892–1941
[ ] Que.Q.B. or [ ] Que.K.B.	Quebec Official Reports (Queen's Bench or King's Bench), 1942–1969
Que.S.C.	Quebec Official Reports (Superior Court), 1892–1941
[ ] Que.S.C.	Quebec Official Reports (Superior Court), 1942 to date
R. de Jur.	La Revue de Jurisprudence (Quebec)
R.F.L.	Reports of Family Law
R.L.	La Revue Légale (Quebec)
Sask.R.	Saskatchewan Reports
S.C.R.	Supreme Court Reports (Canada), 1876–1922
[ ] S.C.R.	Supreme Court Reports (Canada), 1923 to date
U.C.C.P.	Upper Canada Common Pleas Reports
U.C.Q.B.	Upper Canada Queen's Bench Reports
W.L.R.	Western Law Reporter
W.W.D.	Western Weekly Digests
W.W.R.	Western Weekly Reports, 1912–1916
[ ] W.W.R.	Western Weekly Reports, 1911–1950 and 1971 to date
W.W.R. (N.S.)	Western Weekly Reports, New Series, 1951–1970

C. Abbreviations for English Report Series

Report Series Commencing Before 1865

C.B.	Common Bench
Cox C.C.	Cox's Criminal Cases
E.R.	English Reports (Reprint)
L.J.Ex.	Law Journal New Series Exchequer
L.T.	Law Times

Report Series Commencing After 1865

Law Reports First Series 1865–1875

L.R.C.P.	Law Reports Common Pleas
L.R.Q.B.	Law Reports Queen's Bench

Law Reports Second Series 1875–1890

App.Cas.	Appeal Cases
Ch.D.	Chancery Division
Ex.D.	Exchequer Division to 1880
P.D.	Probate, Divorce & Admiralty Division
Q.B.D.	Queen's Bench Division

Law Reports Third Series 1891 to Date

A.C.	Appeal Cases
Ch.	Chancery Division
F.	Family Division
P. (no longer current)	Probate, Divorce & Admiralty Division
Q.B. (or K.B.)	Queen's Bench (or King's Bench)
W.L.R.	Weekly Law Reports, 1953 to date

Other

All E.R.	All England Law Reports
Atk.	Atkyns
B. & Ald.	Barnewell & Alderson
Bl.Comm.	Blackstone's Commentaries
Ch.App.	Law Reports, Chancery Appeals to 1875
Cl. & Fin.	Clark & Finnelly
Coke Inst.	Coke's Institute
Co.Rep.	Coke's Reports
Cr.App.R.	Criminal Appeal Reports
De G. & J.	De Gex & Jones, temp. Cranworth, Clemsford & Campbell
El. & Bl.	Ellis & Blackburn
Ex.	Exchequer Reports (Welsby, Hurlstone & Gordon)
F.C.	Faculty Collections (Scotland)
I.R.	Irish Reports
Johns. & Hem.	Johnson & Hemming
L.J.P.	Law Journal Reports (Probate, Divorce and Admiralty)
L.R.	Law Reports
M. & W.	Meeson & Welsby
Mod.	Modern Reports
P. & D.	Perry & Davison
Pr.	Price

Russ. & Ry.	Russell & Ryan
Str.	Strange, J. (ed. by Nolan)
T.L.R.	Times Law Reports
Ves.Sr.	Vesey Senior (ed. by Belt)
W.L.R.	Weekly Law Reports

D. Abbreviations for Statutes

Canadian

B.N.A. Act	British North America Act, 1867
Reg.	Regulation
R.R.O.	Rules and Regulations Ontario
R.S.A.	Revised Statutes Alberta
R.S.B.C.	Revised Statutes British Columbia
R.S.C.	Revised Statutes Canada
R.S.M.	Revised Statutes Manitoba
R.S.N.B.	Revised Statutes New Brunswick
R.S.N.S.	Revised Statutes Nova Scotia
R.S.O.	Revised Statutes Ontario
R.S.P.E.I.	Revised Statutes Prince Edward Island
R.S.Q.	Revised Statutes Quebec
R.S.S.	Revised Statutes Saskatchewan
S.C.	Statutes Canada
S.N.S.	Statutes Nova Scotia
S.O.	Statutes Ontario

English

Car.	Charles
Edw.	Edward
Hen.	Henry
Vict.	Victoria
W. & M.	William & Mary

E. Miscellaneous Abbreviations

Can.BarRev.	Canadian Bar Review
C.B.A.	Canadian Bar Association
Comp.Trib.	Competition Tribunal
F.L.R.	Federal Law Reports (Australia)
Iowa L.Rev	Iowa Law Review
L.Q.R.	Law Quarterly Review
N.E.	North Eastern Reporter (U.S.A.)
N.J.C.L.	National Journal of Constitutional Law
N.Z.L.R.	New Zealand Law Reports
Queen's L.J.	Queen's Law Journal

Bibliography

The following list includes references to books, articles, and other materials found to be valuable source materials in the preparation of this dictionary. The list does not purport to cover all the materials examined or cited in the text.

(1) TEXTS

Akehurst, Michael. *A Modern Introduction to International Law*. 6th ed. London: George Allen & Unwin, 1987.

Austin, John. *The Province of Jurisprudence Determined*. 2d ed. New York: Noonday Press, 1954.

Bailey, S. J. *The Law of Wills*. 7th ed. London: Pitman Publishing, 1973.

Baker, J. H. *An Introduction to English Legal History*. 2d ed. London: Butterworth & Co., 1979.

Bissett-Johnson, Alastair, and Winifred Holland. *Matrimonial Property Law in Canada*. Agincourt: Burroughs, 1980.

Borrie, Gordon J. *Public Law*. 2d ed. London: Sweet & Maxwell, 1970.

Bouvier, John. *Bouvier's Law Dictionary*. 8th ed. by F. Rawles. St. Paul, Minn.: West Publishing Co., 1914.

Brierly, J. L. *The Law of Nations*. 6th ed Oxford: Clarendon Press, 1963.

Brown, Ray Andrews. *The Law of Personal Property*. 3d ed. Chicago: Callaghan & Co., 1975.

Casson, D. B., and I. H Dennis. *Odgers' Principles of Pleading and Practice*. 22d ed. London: Stevens & Sons, 1981.

Castel, J.-G. *Canadian Conflict of Laws*. 3d ed. Toronto: Butterworth & Co., 1994.

———. *Introduction to Conflict of Laws*. 2d ed. Toronto: Butterworth & Co., 1986.

Cheshire, G. C. and E. H. Burn. *Modern Law of Real Property*. 14th ed. London: Butterworth & Co., 1988.

Corbin, A. L. *Corbin on Contracts*. St. Paul, Minn.: West Publishing Co., 1952.

Cross, Sir Rupert, and Colin Tapper. *Cross on Evidence*. 7th ed. London: Butterworth & Co., 1990.

Curzon, L. B. *English Legal History*. 2d ed. Estover, Plymouth: MacDonald & Evans Ltd., 1979.

Davies, Christine. *Family Law in Canada*. 4th ed. Toronto: Carswell Co., 1984.

Derham, D. P., F. K. H. Maher, and P. L. Waller. *An Introduction to Law*. 6th ed. Sydney: Law Book Co., 1990.

Falconbridge, John Delatre. *The Law of Negotiable Instruments in Canada*. Toronto: Ryerson Press, 1964.

Feeney, Thomas G. *The Canadian Law of Wills: Probate*. 3d ed. Toronto: Butterworth & Co., 1987.

Fitzgerald, Patrick, and King McShane. *Looking at Law*. 2d ed. Ottawa: Bybooks, 1982.

Fleming, John G. *The Law of Torts*. 8th ed. Sydney: Law Book Co., 1992.

Fridman, G. H. L. *The Law of Agency*. 6th ed. London: Butterworth & Co., 1990.

——. *The Law of Contract in Canada.* 2d ed. Toronto: Carswell Co., 1986.

——. *Introduction to the Law of Torts.* Toronto: Butterworth & Co., 1978.

Fridman, G. H. L. *Sale of Goods in Canada.* 3d ed. Toronto: Carswell Co., 1986.

Furmston, M. P. *Cheshire, Fifoot and Furmston's Law of Contract.* 12th ed. London: Butterworth & Co., 1991.

Gall, Gerald L. *The Canadian Legal System.* 3d ed. Toronto: Carswell Co., 1990.

Gower, L. C. B., D. D. Prentice, and B. G. Pettet. *Gower's Principles of Modern Company Law.* 5th ed. London: Sweet & Maxwell, 1992.

Green, L. C. *International Law Through the Cases.* 4th ed. London: Stevens & Sons, 1978.

Greenspan, E.L. *Martin's Annual Criminal Code,* 1994. Aurora: Canada Law Book, 1993.

Grover, Warren, and Donald Ross. *Materials on Corporate Finance.* Toronto: Richard De Boo, 1975.

Guest, A. G. *Anson's Law of Contract.* 26th ed. Oxford: Clarendon Press, 1984.

Hanbury, Harold Greville. *Hanbury and Maudsley Modern Equity.* 11th ed. Ronald Harling Maudsley and Jill E. Martin. London: Stevens & Sons, 1981.

Harris, Edwin C. *Canadian Income Taxation.* 4th ed. Toronto: Butterworth & Co., 1986.

Hayton, David J. *Megarry's Manual of the Law of Real Property.* 6th ed. London: Stevens & Sons, 1982.

Hertz, Michael. *Introduction to Conflict of Laws.* Toronto: Carswell Co., 1978.

Heuston, R. F. V. *Salmond on the Law of Torts.* 14th ed. London: Sweet & Maxwell, 1965.

Heuston, R. F. V., and R. A. Buckley. *Salmond and Heuston on the Law of Torts.* 20th ed. London: Sweet & Maxwell, 1992.

Hogg, Peter W. *Constitutional Law of Canada.* 3d ed. Toronto: Carswell Co., 1992.

——. *Canada Act 1982 Annotated.* Toronto: Carswell Co., 1982.

——. *Meech Lake Constitutional Accord Annotated.* Toronto: Carswell Co., 1988.

Horsley, D., H. Sutherland, and J. M. Edmiston. *Fraser's Handbook on Canadian Company Law.* 7th ed. Toronto: Carswell Co., 1985.

Hurtig, Mel. *The Canadian Encyclopedia.* 2d ed. Edmonton: Hurtig Publishers Co., 1988.

Ivamy, E. R. Hardy. *General Principles of Insurance Law.* 5th ed. London: Butterworth & Co., 1986.

Jaeger, W. H. E. *Williston on Contracts.* 3d ed. Rochester, N.Y.: Lawyers Co-operative Publishing Co., 1978.

James, Fleming, Geoffrey C. Hazard, and John Leubsdorf. *Civil Procedure.* 4th ed. Toronto: Little, Brown & Co., 1992.

Johnston, D. L. *Canadian Securities Regulation.* Toronto: Butterworth & Co., 1977.

Keeton, W. Page, Dan B. Dobbs, Robert E. Keeton, and David G. Owen. *Prosser and Keeton on Torts.* 5th ed. St. Paul, Minn.: West Publishing Co., 1984.

Linden, Allen M. *Canadian Tort Law.* 5th ed. Toronto: Butterworth & Co., 1993.

Martin, Jill E. *Hanbury & Martin Modern Equity.* 14th ed. London: Sweet & Maxwell, 1993.

McGregor, Harvey. *McGregor on Damages.* 14th ed. London:

Sweet & Maxwell, 1980.

McNairn, Colin H. H. *Governmental and Intergovernmental Immunity in Australia and Canada.* Toronto: Univ. of Toronto Press, 1977.

Mewett, Alan W., and Morris Manning. *Criminal Law.* 2d ed. Toronto: Butterworth & Co., 1985.

Moynihan, Cornelius J. *Introduction to the Law of Real Property.* 2d ed. St. Paul, Minn.: West Publishing Co., 1988.

Mullan, David J. *Administrative Law.* 3d ed. Toronto: Carswell Co., 1979.

Oosterhoff, A.H., and W.B. Rayner. *Anger and Honsberger: Law of Real Property.* 2d ed. Aurora: Canada Law Book, 1985.

Pollock, F., and F. W. Maitland. *History of English Law.* 2d ed. London: Cambridge Univ. Press, 1903.

Pound, Roscoe. *Jurisprudence.* Vol. 1. St. Paul, Minn.: West Publishing Co., 1959.

Price, Griffith. *The Law of Maritime Liens.* London: Sweet & Maxwell, 1940.

Prosser, William L., John W. Wade, and Victor E. Schwartz. *Cases and Materials on Torts.* 7th ed. New York: Foundation Press, 1982.

Rayner, W. B., and R. H. McLaren. *Falconbridge on Mortgages.* 4th ed. Agincourt: Canada Law Book, 1977.

Reynolds, F. M. B., and B. J. Davenport. *Bowstead on Agency.* 13th ed. London: Sweet & Maxwell, 1968.

Rozovsky, Lorne E. and Fay A. Rozovsky. *Canadian Law of Consent to Treatment.* Scarborough, Ont.: Butterworth & Co., 1990.

Salhany, Roger E. *Canadian Criminal Procedure.* 6th ed. Toronto: Canada Law Book, 1994.

Seavey, W. A. *Handbook of the Law of Agency.* St. Paul, Minn.: West Publishing Co., 1964.

Shipman, Benjamin J. *Handbook of Common-Law Pleading,* 3d ed., edited by Henry Winthrop Ballantine. St. Paul, Minn.: West Publishing Co., 1923.

Sinclair, Alan M. *Introduction to Real Property Law.* 3d ed. Toronto: Butterworth & Co., 1987.

Solomon, Robert M., Bruce P. Feldthusen, and Stephen J. Mills. *Cases and Materials on the Law of Torts.* 3d ed. Toronto: Carswell Co., 1991.

Sopinka, J., and S. N. Lederman. *The Law of Evidence in Civil Cases.* Toronto: Butterworth & Co., 1974.

Story, J. *Commentaries on the Constitution of the United States.* Cambridge: Charles Folsom, Publishers to the University, 1833.

Stuart, Don. *Canadian Criminal Law.* 2d ed. Toronto: Carswell Co., 1987.

Waddams, S. M. *The Law of Contracts.* 3d ed. Toronto: Canada Law Book, 1993.

———. *Introduction to the Study of Law.* 4th ed. Toronto: Carswell Co., 1992.

Watson, Garry D., and Neil J. Williams. *Canadian Civil Procedure.* 2d ed. Toronto: Butterworth & Co., 1977.

Watson, Garry D., W.A. Bogart, Allan C. Hutchinson, and Robert J. Sharpe. *Canadian Civil Procedure.* 3d ed. Toronto: Emond Montgomery Publications Ltd., 1988.

Williston, W. B., and R. J. Rolls. *The Law of Civil Procedure.* Toronto: Butterworth & Co., 1970.

Ziegel, J. S. *Studies in Canadian Company Law.* Toronto: Butterworth & Co., 1967.

(2) ARTICLES

Arlidge, B. "Contingent Fees." *Ottawa L.R.* 6 (1974): 374.

Hertz, M. T. "Occupiers' Liability Law: A Study Paper." Halifax: Nova Scotia Law Reform Advisory Commission, 1976.

Holdsworth, W. S. "The Conventions of the Eighteenth Century Constitution." *Iowa L. Rev.* 17 (1932): 161.

McAllister, D. M. "Recent Sexual Orientation Cases." N.J.C.L. 2 (1992): 354.

Mullan, D. "The Declaratory Judgment: Its Place as an Administrative Law Remedy in Nova Scotia." *Dalhousie L.J.* 2 (1975): 91.

Robinette, J. J. "Charge to the Jury." Special Lectures of the Law Society of Upper Canada, 1959.

Slattery, B. "The Constitutional Guarantee of Aboriginal and Treaty Rights." *Queen's L.J.* 8 (1982–83): 232.

Waters, D. W. A. "The Nature of the Trust Beneficiary's Interest." *Can. Bar Rev.* 45 (1967): 219.

(3) OTHER MATERIALS

Abella, Rosalie S. *Report of the Commission on Equality in Employment.* Ottawa: Supply and Services Canada, 1984.

Forsey, E. *How Canadians Govern Themselves.* 3d ed. Ottawa: Government of Canada, Minister of Supply and Services, 1990.

———. *The Constitution and You.* Ottawa: Government of Canada, Minister of Supply and Services, 1982.

Hailsham, Lord, of St. Marylebone, ed. *Halsbury's Laws of England.* 4th ed. London: Butterworth & Co., 1973–.

Iosipescu, Michael J. *Yogis and Christie: Legal Writing and Research Manual.* 4th ed. Toronto: Butterworth & Co., 1994.

Simonds, Rt. Hon. the Viscount, ed. *Halsbury's Laws of England.* 3d ed. London: Butterworth & Co., 1952–64.

British Columbia Rules of Court and Related Enactments. Victoria: Queen's Printer, 1993.

Code of Professional Conduct. Ottawa: Canadian Bar Association, 1988.

Nova Scotia Civil Procedure Rules and Related Rules. Halifax: Queen's Printer, 1983.

Ontario Annual Practice, 1993–94. Aurora, Ont.: Canada Law Book, 1993.

Ontario Royal Commission, Inquiry into Civil Rights. McRuer Commission, 1968.

Restatement of the Law, Second: Agency 2d. St. Paul, Minn.: American Law Institute Publishers, 1958.

Restatement of the Law, Second: Contracts 2d. St. Paul, Minn.: American Law Institute Publishers, 1981.

Rosenne, Shabtai. *Documents on the International Court of Justice.* 3d ed. Dordrecht, The Netherlands: Martinus Nijhoff Publishers, 1991.

Rules of Court, New Brunswick. Fredericton: Queen's Printer, 1981.

Tang, Chin-Shih. *Guide to Legal Citation and Sources of Citation Aid.* 2d ed. Don Mills, Ont.: Richard De Boo, 1988.